Walter E. Proebster (Ed.)

Digital Memory and Storage

With 257 Fig.

Vieweg

CIP-Kurztitelaufnahme der Deutschen Bibliothek

Digital memory and storage / Walter E. Proebster
(ed.). – 1. Aufl. – Braunschweig: Vieweg, 1978.

NE: Proebster, Walter E. [Hrsg.]

ISBN-13: 978-3-528-08409-7   e-ISBN-13: 978-3-322-83629-8

DOI: 10.1007/978-3-322-83629-8

Set by Vieweg, Braunschweig

Bookbinder: W. Langelüddecke, Braunschweig
Artistic design: D. Rein, Aachen

Foreword

Digital memory and storage technologies occupy a dominant position in electronic data processing: They are intimately interwoven with almost all aspects of a data processing system, be it the control processing unit, the peripheral devices or the program and data storage. In this context, memory and storage is one of the most essential design parameters that determine performance and cost efficiency of the entire system to a very high degree.

Beyond the field of electronic data processing, digital memory and storage find ever-widening application in the areas of control and measurement techniques, in digital communication and switching, and lately, even in the area of the consumer electronic market.

This explains, why since the beginning of the computer age, digital memory and storage are finding ever increasing attention in research and development.

Of the many different memory and storage technologies investigated for application, only very few survived in the tough economic cost/performance struggle. This process still continues:

Semiconductor memories have almost completely replaced the ferrite core memories. For the "gap" in cost and performance between memory and storage — which is of growing importance for systems throughput, particularly for query and database systems — very promising proposals, such as charge coupled devices and magnetic bubble memories appear. For very high data volumes, devices with automatic storage media transport have been conceived and developed. For extremely fast memories, research on low temperature Josephson devices has made significant advances.

Two key reasons were the stimuli for calling a 3 day conference on digital memory and storage at Stuttgart in March 1977:
The importance for the systems designer, on one hand, to understand the key technologies of memory and storage as the basis for trade-off decisions in the design of system and system components, and on the other hand, the difficulty to obtain such knowledge at technical conferences, which mostly concentrate on a specific and limited field and on latest development results tailored to the specialist in a relatively narrow field.

To achieve these principal goals, the topics to be covered spanned the wide range from physical principles of the various memory and storage technologies, the cell design and operation principles to memory and storage systems architecture.

In order to cover the desired wide span of technologies and to provide the required overview, the meeting was organized jointly by the following three sections of the Nachrichtentechnische Gesellschaft (NTG), Germany:

Section 6 "Technical Informatics",
Section 2 "Passive Elements and Materials",
Section 3 "Semiconductors and Integrated Circuits",
as well as the Arbeitsgemeinschaft Magnetismus.
It should be noted that also the German Section of IEEE co-sponsored this meeting.

Soon after the conference, it became apparent that the proceedings of this conference would be of interest to a wider circle of professionals. In the pursuit of this goal, general agreement was reached with the authors to prepare an English version of the conference proceedings. I would like to acknowledge the permission of the VDE Verlag for publication of the English version.

Thanks is also due to my colleques of the program committee:
G. Arlt, H. Billing, Th. Einsele, E. Feldtkeller, W. Hilberg, H.-O. Leilich,
H. J. Schmitt, and D. Seitzer, who made significant contributions to the conception and success of this conference.

Last but not least, I thank most sincerely my collegues, in particular W. Dietrich,
H. Louis, and V. Sadagopan, for the advice and effort in the preparation and edition of this English version.

Walter E. Proebster

Böblingen, December 1977

IV

Table of Contents

VI

On the Development of Digital Memories

H. Billing

In this talk on the history of the evolution of digital memories I will make a very subjective selection. I will emphasize those memories whose inventors I have become acquainted with personally, and those developments in which I have been involved myself.

Developments during the 1940's and 1950's all aimed at providing the urgently-needed working stores for the early electronic computers. The real impetus for these developments came in 1945, when the first two vacuum tube computers came into service: Colossus in England and ENIAC in the USA.

Completion of both these computers had been rushed by the pressure of war needs. For the memory elements, compatible in speed with the switching speed of vacuum tubes, one chose what was then available, the flipflop, known since 1919 and at that time called the "Eccles-Jordan circuit" after its inventors. In the ENIAC computer, with its 18.000 vacuum tubes, a single decimal digit was stored in a ring counter of 10 flipflops, i.e. one adhered to the well known counter wheel of mechanical calculating machines. Each flipflop consisted of two vacuum tubes, and thus the memory for one single decimal digit was quite an impressive sight.

This is shown in Fig. 1 together with the proud inventors, the mathematician Cpt. H. Goldstine and the electronics expert Presper Eckert, two persons who were to play important roles in the future development of electronic computers.

The ENIAC had 200 such storage units with a total of 5600 tubes to store 20 ten-digit decimal numbers. That these two brilliant men had not struck upon more economical solutions, must be seen in the light of the great military urgency. After all, ENIAC had been built in only about two years' time and was completed shortly after the end of the war.

If, however, the ENIAC development team had included the German computer pioneer Konrad Zuse, some aspects would have been solved more elegantly. Six years earlier, Zuse had already realized the advantages of the binary number system, which alone would have saved 2/3 of all the vacuum tubes. But Zuse, on the other hand, did his work with mechanical relays. For the speeds needed by relay computers, a practicable, logically elegant "Aus mechanischen Schaltgliedern aufgebautes Speicherwerk" (Storage unit, composed of mechanical switching elements) had been submitted to the patent office as early as 1937. It stored binary numbers. To store an individual bit, a small pin could be pushed into a lefthand or righthand position with

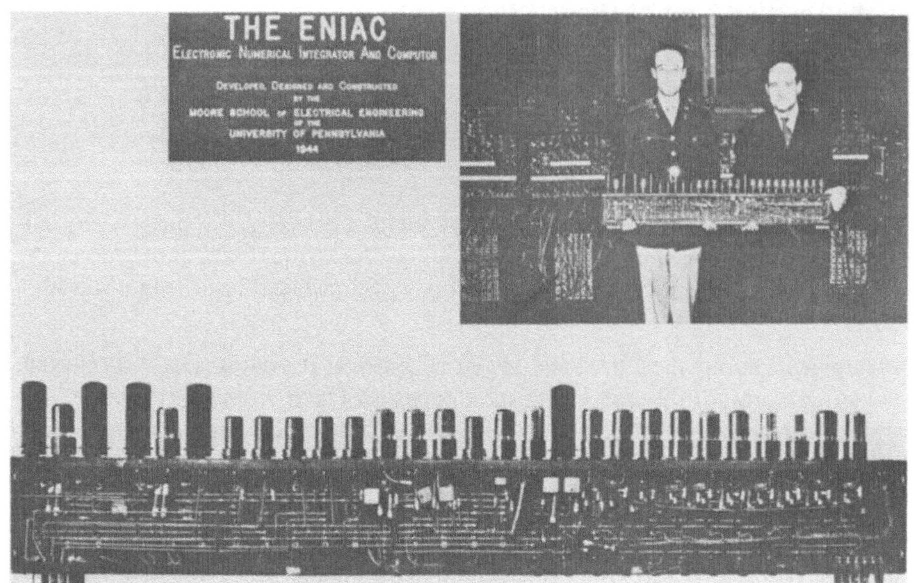

Fig. 1. Storing facility for a single decimal digit in ENIAC.

the aid of sliding metallic sheets. The pins were arranged in a matrix. With selected
sheets, a complete binary number could be written into or read out of one cell of
the matrix plane. Several matrix planes were stacked on top of each other, and they
could be selected by further switching elements. The whole setup of the pilot model
was surprisingly compact (Fig. 2). 1000 cells, of 30 bits each, would have taken
$\frac{1}{2}$ m^3 (20 cubic feet). In this memory, we already find all the logical components
which were to play such an important role in the 3-dimensional ferrite core memories.
But due to the war, Zuse's patent remained unknown and was only published
16 years later, in 1953.

But let us return to the vacuum tube computers and their memories. During and after
completion of ENIAC, in 1945/46, the concept of better electronic computers was
eagerly discussed among the ENIAC team, together with guests from England, among
them Prof. Wilkes. Cycling stores and cathode ray tubes emerged as the most promising storage media.

Let us begin with the cycling store later known as the mercury delay line. To store
the information, its individual bits are fed as acoustic pulses into one end of a liquid
column; they propagate through it at the speed of sound, and are picked up again at
the far end of the column. After amplification and pulse shaping, the string of pulses
is fed back into the input. Thus the information can be made to circulate for arbitrary
lengths of time.

2

Fig. 2. Pilot model of Zuse's electromechanical memory. One matrix plane only is completed.

For Eckert, shown in Fig. 1, the idea for such a cyclic memory was quite natural. Shockley, the co-inventor of the transistor, and, somewhat later, also Eckert, had already built similar devices in 1943, in order to record radar reflections. They needed a clock pulse with a well defined repetition period. They made a single sound pulse circulate in the liquid column. To obtain reproducible periods, a mixture of water and ethylene glycole was chosen such that its propagation speed had a vanishing temperature coefficient. (As the renowned British computer pioneer Turing remarked later, good old English gin would also have had the proper composition.)

But it was not at all clear whether this cyclic principle could also be applied to a string of many closely spaced pulses, as required in a cyclic memory. Goldstine reports of a discussion with Turing (in late 1946 or early 1947), where Turing had shown quite convincingly that it would not work, due to the poor signal to noise ratio. But Sharpless in the USA (mid 1947) and Wilkes in Great Britain (late 1947) succeeded in making it work. Both used mercury as the liquid, as it had the same acoustic impedance as the piezo quartzes used as sound transmitters. This matching resulted in a high damping of the quartzes and allowed high pulse rates.

Wilkes immediately incorporated his mercury delay lines as central core of the computer EDSAC, developed by him at Cambridge University (Fig. 3). EDSAC was

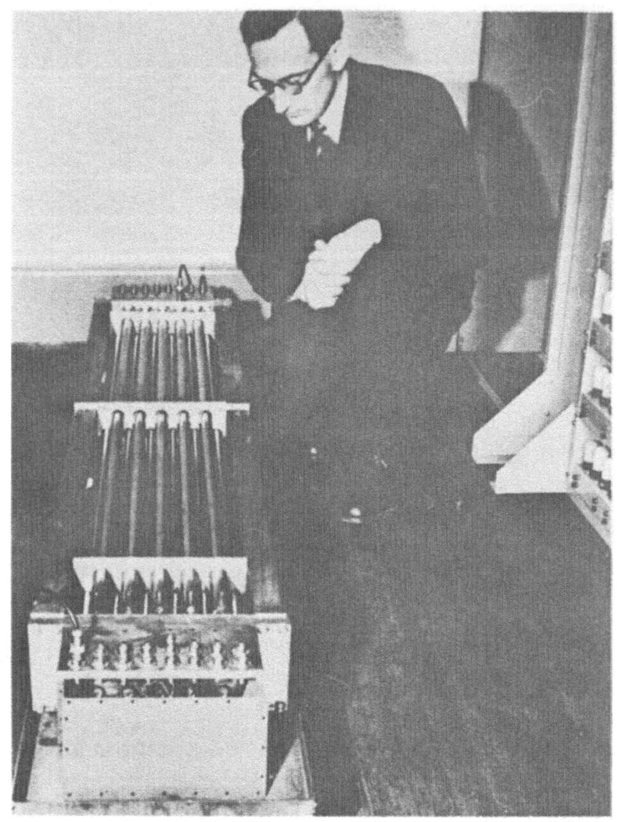

Fig. 3
Wilkes and his
mercury delay
line memory.

completed in June, 1949. Thus Eckert was beaten by more than a year, as he finished his first computer, the BINAC, in August, 1950. But it must be said in Eckert's favour that in 1946 he and his ENIAC colleague Mauchley had founded their own computer company, later to become UNIVAC; and the duties of management are known to eat up much of one's time.

It was in a somewhat cryptic manner that I first heard of the cyclic memory. In 1947, Turing, his boss Womersley, and a number of his British colleagues came to Göttingen to find out what was being done in Germany in the field of mathematical computers. Prof. Walther from Darmstadt and Zuse had been invited, and at the last moment I also gained access to this small circle of about a dozen specialists.

Womersley, seeing my eager interest, afterwards took me aside, and in a very nice and open manner gave me a private lesson on gates, flipflops, and the construction of a binary serial adder. But my question regarding a memory was answered very

mysteriously when he said, "One way to store could be the following: you write
the numbers you want to store on a letter, which you address to yourself, and put it
into the mail box; when it is delivered to you after some time, you can either put it
into the mail box again or you can read it."

During the next days, I contemplated intensely how this postal delay scheme could
be realized by physical means. As in the past I had already worked with magnetic
tapes, I came up with the idea of the magnetic drum.

In late 1947, I had a small drum running with magnetic tapes glued around its circumference, and for some time I regarded myself as the inventor of the magnetic drum
memory. But this belief turned out to be wrong. It can be assumed that at about the
same time, computer experts in the USA and in Great Britain struck upon the same
idea, which, after all, was rather obvious. In mid 1949, Thomas attached a drum to
the MARC I.

In the patent war which later ensued, I was rather glad that I had withdrawn my own
patent application in 1950. As it turned out, none of my co-inventors had any luck
with their applications, as in June 1957 a German patent application regarding a
magnetic drum memory was published, applied for on June 17, 1943.

The inventor was Dr. Dirks, who had majored in national economics, but who, as an
amateur, had also gained profound knowledge in high frequency technology. Dr. Dirks,
whom I later met several times, seems to be a very prolific inventor. According to his
patent attorney, who supplied me with some details for this talk, Dirks' inventions
number between 250 and 350. Dirks did not make his claims until a time when a
great number of magnetic drum memories were already in service, and thus caused the
commercial manufacturers considerable distress. IBM solved their part of the problem
by employing Dirks on their staff.

As I have no photograph of Dirks, I will show the title page of his patent grant,
instead (Fig. 4). His patent is — considering the date of application — very thoroughly
conceived. It not only comprised the rotating drum with magnetic heads, tracks, and
store locations on the tracks, but also an additional clock track and electronic selection circuitry for reading, clearing and writing at selected store locations. Thus it
contained everything that is essential for operation.

The actual realization of practicable drum memories was, however, done later by
others. They included such refinements as improved writing methods, floating
magnetic heads, and many other measures to increase the storage capacity.

Although Dirks had not actually contributed to the eventual development of the
magnetic drum memory — his patent having remained unknown at that time — he
must definitely be considered the inventor of this memory.

I will not elaborate on the cathode ray memory, although it had been used as working
store in such renowned computers as MARC I at Manchester and John von Neumann's

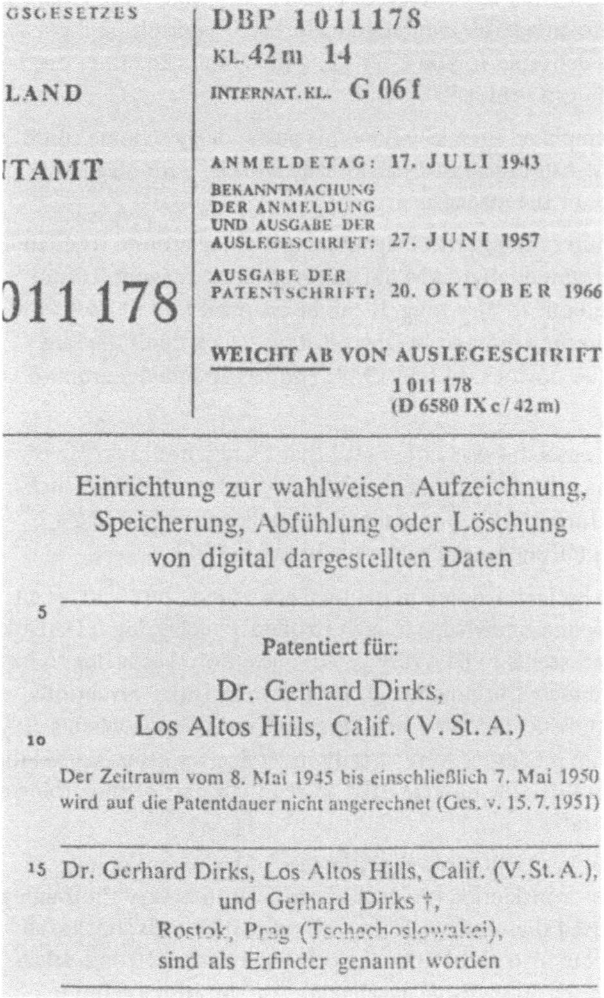

GSGESETZES

LAND

TAMT

011178

DBP 1 011 178

KL. 42 m 14

INTERNAT. KL. G 06 f

ANMELDETAG: 17. JULI 1943

BEKANNTMACHUNG
DER ANMELDUNG
UND AUSGABE DER
AUSLEGESCHRIFT: 27. JUNI 1957

AUSGABE DER
PATENTSCHRIFT: 20. OKTOBER 1966

WEICHT AB VON AUSLEGESCHRIFT
1 011 178
(D 6580 IX c / 42 m)

Einrichtung zur wahlweisen Aufzeichnung,
Speicherung, Abfühlung oder Löschung
von digital dargestellten Daten

Patentiert für:

Dr. Gerhard Dirks,
Los Altos Hills, Calif. (V. St. A.)

Der Zeitraum vom 8. Mai 1945 bis einschließlich 7. Mai 1950
wird auf die Patentdauer nicht angerechnet (Ges. v. 15. 7. 1951)

Dr. Gerhard Dirks, Los Altos Hills, Calif. (V. St. A.),
und Gerhard Dirks †,
Rostok, Prag (Tschechoslowakei),
sind als Erfinder genannt worden

Fig. 4

Dirks' patent
grant for the
magnetic drum
from 1943.

famed computer at Princeton. But I was never personally involved in the development of this memory principle. Here, the contest was between Rajchman from RCA and Williams at Manchester. Both started in 1946, with a slight head start for Rajchman. Williams chose the better approach and came in with his Williams-tube clearly ahead of Rajchman's Selectron.

The next great stride in the search for better memories came with ferrite cores. Let me begin its discussion with a personal reminiscense. At the end of July 1952, Prof. v. Weizsäcker, at that time visiting his brother-in-law Albers-Schönberg in the USA,

6

sent me some ferrite cores, developed by Albers-Schönberg. In the accompanying
letter he pointed out that these cores had a rather square shaped hysteresis loop and
might be of great interest as memory components. Their magnetization could be
switched in a few microseconds. For someone working on the problems of computer
memories, this information was sufficient to make him immediately think of a
memory element selected by two coincident currents.

How apparent the coincidence concept was for the expert can be seen from a letter
I wrote to my friend Robert Piloty around Christmas, 1952, saying, "In view of the
troublesome times it is not a golden ring that hides in the little box. At first sight it
is only a tiny ring of common iron (ferrite from the USA), but it holds a great secret.
May you succeed in discovering it. The graph at the margin – a measured hysteresis
curve – may serve you as a key". Piloty got the idea immediately and promptly asked
for some more of these rings, saying that he was interested in the storage in these
cores. Which proves that the idea was quite obvious, if only one had the cores.
Therefore I always consider it unjust that J. Forrester alone is hailed as the inventor
of the core memory.

J. Forrester was professor at MIT and had a leading part in project Whirlwind – an
extremely fast computer at that time. As early as June 1950, he had submitted a
paper to the Proceedings of the IRE, entitled "Digital Information Storage in
3 Dimensions Using Magnetic Cores", in which he explained the access method and
reported on preliminary experiments with single cores. At that time, only cores wound
from thin permalloy tapes were available. Eddy currents limited the switching speeds
to 10 msec when the cores were driven with the relatively small excess fields allowed
by the coincidence scheme. Compared to the Williams tube, such switching speeds
were completely insufficient.

In my view, Forrester's real contribution to further progress lay not so much in
proposing the general scheme, but in noting in the paper that cores of non-metallic
magnetic materials could be of great value for storing purposes. Forrester, and his
colleagues D. Brown and W. Papian of Lincoln Laboratories, started a search for such
materials. Led by a technical publication, they came across Albers-Schönberg, who
– working on ferrites – had noticed square hysteresis loops as early as 1949.

Albers-Schönberg had previously been working on ferrites in Germany at Stemag in
Porz, and had just recently come to General Ceramics in the USA. Brown made a
research contract with Albers-Schönberg, and at the start of 1952, Albers-Schönberg
supplied the first adequate ferrite cores, of which we also were to receive some
samples at the end of July.

From then on everything developed rapidly. I myself had – only 4 months later –
a small two-dimensional test matrix running with 16 rows of 10 bits each, with
5 μsec access time (published in Naturwissenschaften, Dec. 1952). In the USA, larger
ferrite core memories were included in the computer "Whirlwind" in 1953. Particular-

ly fast and extensive progress came from Rajchman (USA). By June 1952 he had a small, slow test memory with 256 tape-wound cores working. In October 1953 he produced an operational matrix of 10,000 bits, using ferrite cores developed and produced by RCA. The paper on this contains in principle everything one finds in modern text books about ferrite core memories and their access schemes. Further progress was later achieved by miniaturization and improvement of the cores, by reducing the number of access wires from 4 to 3, and by advanced technologies for testing and wiring the cores. But I will not elaborate on this.

Let me rather return to the problem of priorities. Who should win the laurels for having invented the ferrite core memory? This was not only a question of laurels, but also of good hard money. Therefore, the question was settled in court.

With respect to the fundamental coincidence scheme of core memories, Rajchman claimed at least his co-inventorship. In a publication in October, 1953, he writes, "(The coincidence scheme) was recognized independently by J. W. Forrester and the author (Rajchman), who intitiated the early efforts to develop such a memory at MIT and RCA, respectively." This is certainly true, but here the priority was decided in Forrester's favor.

Concerning the actual ferrite cores, Rajchman is somewhat vague: "The potentialities of these materials (ferrites) prompted research at General Ceramics and RCA toward obtaining sufficient loop rectangularity... Early in 1952 some materials were promising, and in the summer of that year both organizations synthesized a material for practical use."

The cores of both organizations happened to be manganese-magnesium-iron ferrites, and this made me sceptical as to the independence of the two developments.

In order to gain some insight into the true priorities, in preparing this talk I wrote to Albers-Schönberg. A dignified old man of 80 (Fig. 5), he now lives in Switzerland, blessed with full mental agility. His very nice answer came in a long letter, out of which I would like to quote some passages. Concerning the ferrite cores, he writes, "RCA did not develop the memory ferrite cores simultaneously with me, but rather RCA received early sample cores from my company and had one of their physicists analyze and duplicate them. The same also occurred with Philips, and with both companies we then got into a lawsuit about "interference". In contrast to Germany, where the date of the patent application counts, the interference suit tries to determine the true priority of invention; it takes into account that an applicant may have come in late with his patent application simply because he had worked more carefully and thoroughly.

"This principle, commendable as it is, can unfortunately be exploited in a rather questionable manner to block an earlier application. In my case, both companies followed my application with similar ones, and the patent office reacted by declaring interference.

8

"What follows is a very painstaking scrutiny of the laboratory diaries, and a sort of cross examination of the applicants by the attourneys of the opposing side. Well — I survived this procedure, and my patent was finally granted.

"But the interference suit takes a long time, in my case about 5 years. During this time one goes without any protection of one's invention ...

"However, my patent still exists to its full extent. As far as I know, it will expire in 1978. The European patents have already expired.

"You asked about the rewards from the patents. The company had quite appreciable gains from license fees, although the rather weak position of a small company against the giants has had some limiting effect. As for myself, I have not become a tremendously rich man, but I have been rewarded to such an extent that it has allowed me an adequate living after retirement." End of the letter excerpts.

This letter from Albers-Schönberg was so informative to me that I must ask your forgiveness if I perhaps have gone too far into the details. If I now had to award the laurels for contributions to the development of the ferrite core memory, I would, even though the idea at that time hung in the air, give the first prize to Forrester as the initiator and promoter at the early stages. But the second prize would undoubtedly go to Albers-Schönberg for having developed the material, because, without the ferrite core, Forrester's ideas, as many even more brilliant ideas for better memories, would have landed on the scrapyard of technology. Only the third prize would go to Rajchman for the extraordinarily fast, thorough and complete realization into a technical product.

Rajchman, who I hope will forgive me this rating, based on the total of all his work on so many different memory systems, in my view remains the most prominent figure in this field, up to the appearance of the semiconductor memories.

The semiconductor memory, however, is yet too new for a historical appraisal.

In the time inbetween, i.e. after 1953, there have been a large number of interesting and brilliant attempts to develop memories based on totally different principles. The most common goal was faster memories. Let me name here the thin magnetic films and the almost forgotten parametron.

Other efforts aimed at larger and cheaper memories. Among these are the magnetic wire memory, cryogenic and holographic memories. Undoubtedly, there is a wealth of noteworthy facts to be uncovered about the history of these memories; but only the eventual success of a technology rouses the interest in its historical development. Most of the last-mentioned memory principles have, however, not yet led to success, and probably never will.

References

[1]   *H. H. Goldstine,* The Computer from Pascal to von Neumann, Princeton, N.Y.: Princeton University Press 1972.

[2]   *B. Randell,* The Origins of Digital Computers, Selected Papers, Springer-Verlag Berlin, Heidelberg, New York 1975.

[3]   *B. Randell,* The Colossus: Conference on the History of Computers, Los Alamos Scientific Laboratory, 1976.

[4]   *K. Zuse,* Der Computer mein Lebenswerk, Verlag Moderne Industrie, München 1970.

[5]   *C. R. Eames,* A Computer Perspective, Harvard University Press, Cambridge, Ma, 1973.

[6]   *S. H. Lavington,* A History of Manchester Computers, NCC Publications, Manchester 1975.

[7]   *H. Billing,* Schnell aufrufbare magnetostatische Speicher für elektronische Rechen-maschinen, Die Naturwissenschaften **40**, 49/50 (1953).

[8]   *J. A. Rajchman,* A Myriabit Magnetic-Core Matrix Memory, Proc IRE **41**, 1407–1421 (1953).

Magnetic Data Recording

Eberhard Köster

BASF AG, Ludwigshafen, Germany

1. Introduction

In the ideal case of recording on a moving magnetic medium, a step like change in
polarity of the current in the write head leads to a likewise step transition of the
magnetization in the medium. This element of digital data storage induces in the
read head a voltage pulse in the form of a delta function, the integral of which is the
initially introduced step function. The technical implementation of heads and recording media as well as the write and read electronics lead to a gradual transition of the
magnetization and a finite width of the readback pulse. The length of the readback
pulse, mechanical limitations as well as media and electronic noise determine the
highest recording density.

It is the object of the present paper to review the principle processes of recording on
magnetic media. Many details have been omitted which are well represented in a
number of papers [1 to 17]. Write and read heads, recording media, the materials in
use and the actual write and read processes shall be discussed in separate sections.
In a final section areas are defined where improvements in both theory and practice
seem possible. International units are used throughout this paper.

2. Recording medium

Recording media in a range of 1 to 15 μm thickness generally consist of small ferrimagnetic elongated single domain particles which are coated on rigid or flexible
substrates after dispersion in an organic binder. Many interrelated boundary conditions of surface and polymer chemistry are to be observed during dispersion of the
particles in a mixture of binder, solvent and additives for a good adhesion of the
particles within the binder and to the substrate and for an uniform distribution of
the particles in a wear resistant, error free and smooth coating. Media with 0.1 to
0.5 μm thickness are predominantly in the form of thin films of CoP, CoNiP or ferrite
on rigid substrates. They are made by chemical or electrolytical deposition, by
evaporation, sputtering or by chemical transport reaction.

Since the components of the head field and of the magnetization in the recording
medium perpendicular to the plane of the medium lead to a broadened and assymetric
read back pulse, an easy direction of magnetization in the plane and a hard one

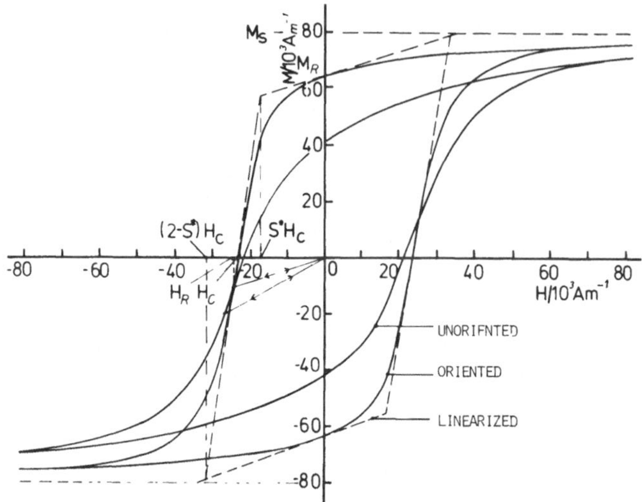

Fig. 1. Magnetization of recording media with oriented and non-oriented particles as a function of applied field strength.

perpendicular to the plane is of main importance. With extremely thin metal or ferrite media, the stray field energy already prevents the occurence of magnetization components perpendicular to the media's plane. In the case of thicker particulate media, the easy directions of the particles are aligned with a magnetic field during drying of the coating in the longitudinal direction of recording. This process leads to the additional advantage of a higher remanence and a narrower distribution of switching fields of the particles. This is exemplified in Fig. 1 which shows the hysteresis loops of oriented and unoriented particles in coatings of commercially used computer disks. It includes the usual parameters saturation magnetization, M_S, remanence, M_R, and coercivity, H_c.

It can be seen, that with an increasing degree of particle orientation, i. e. increasing squareness $S = M_R/M_s$[1]), the distribution of switching fields and the field necessary to switch half of the particles, the remanence coercivity H_R, become smaller. A representative value for the switching field distribution is $(1 - S^+)$ which is defined in Fig. 1 by the field S^+H_c [18].

The demagnetization which becomes relevant in magnetic recording takes place in the 2nd or 4th quadrant in which the hysteresis loop may well be represented by the rectangular hyperbola [19]

$$M(H) = M_R(H + H_c)(SH + H_c)^{-1} \tag{1a}$$

____

[1]) S has to be measured in saturation fields of at least 10 times the coercivity.

with the reversible subceptibility at $H = 0, M = M_R$ and on all reversible minor loops between $M(H)$ and $H = 0$

$$\chi_{rev} = (1 - S)\, M_R/H_c \,, \tag{1b}$$

the irreversible susceptibility at H_c

$$\chi_{irr} = M_R/(1 - S^+)\, H_c \tag{1c}$$

and

$$H_c/H_R = S(2 - S).$$

In many applications a linear approximation (Fig. 1) between the fields $S^+ H_c$ and $(2 - S^+)\, H_c$ with the slopes from equ. (1b) and (1c) is of sufficient accuracy.

3. Magnetic heads

3.1. Conventional ring heads

Write and read heads consist of magnetically soft cores with a narrow gap (Fig. 2) and a coil with N turns. The magnetic field, H_g, deep in the gap of length g in the magnetic circuit with the reluctance R_g and R_c of gap and core respectively is

$$H_g = \frac{R_g\,Ni}{(R_g + R_c)\,g} = \alpha\,\frac{Ni}{g} \,, \tag{2}$$

where i is the current in the coil. H_g does not exceed M_s of the core material. Using the average length of the core, l_c, its thickness, t_c, the gap height, h, and the permeability, of the core μ, one can derive by neglecting all leakage fields the efficiency of a head as

$$\alpha = \left[1 + \frac{l_c\,h}{\mu g\,t_c}\right]^{-1} \tag{3}$$

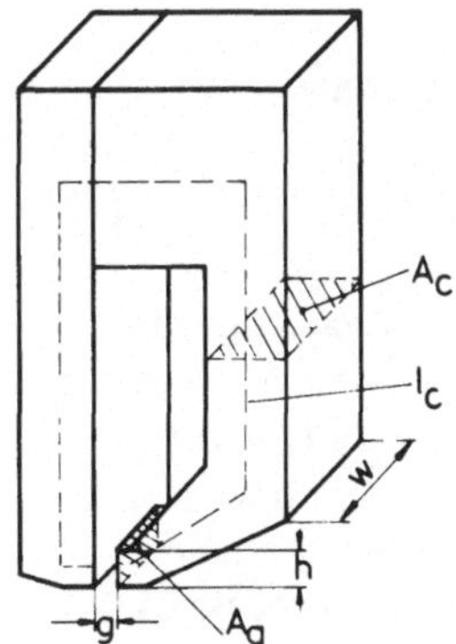

Fig. 2

Schematic view of a recording head

independently of the track width, w. An optimization of a head can be achieved by using a core material with a large μ, a thick core and a small gap height.

For writing, g must be large enough in order to avoid saturation of the core material. An approximation for the necessary minimum gap length during writing with a head to medium spacing, d, a medium thickness, δ, and the saturation magnetization, M_S, of the core material is

$$g \geqslant 2(d + \delta) \tan[\pi(2 - S^+) H_R/2 M_S]. \tag{4}$$

However, as will be shown later, for reading a short gap is of importance. For combined write-read heads a compromise according to the system requirements must be found [20]. The exact core geometry and all leakage fields must be accounted for in individual cases either analytically [21] or numerically [22].

The inductance of a head is

$$L = \mu_0 \alpha N^2 hw/g. \tag{5}$$

In order to minimize the drive voltage at high frequencies, L can only be reduced by a small gap height apart from a small N. In combined write-read heads N is limited by either the allowed drive voltage or the resonance frequency resulting from L and the capacitance of the coil and connection cable.

The stray field of the gap with the components H_x parallel to the x-coordinate in the direction of the movement of the recording medium and H_y parallel to the y-coordinate perpendicular to the plane of the medium (Fig. 3) has been calculated by *Booth* [23] and *Westmijze* [24] for an ideal head of infinite dimensions in the plane of the medium, an infinite permeability and sharp gap edges. An approximation for $y > 0.5\ g$ has been given by *Karlquist* [25, 26]:

$$H_x = \frac{H_g}{\pi} \tan^{-1}\left[\frac{4yg}{4x^2 + 4y^2 - g^2}\right] \tag{6a}$$

$$H_y = \frac{H_g}{2\pi} \ln\left[\frac{y^2 + (x + g/2)^2}{y^2 + (x - g/2)^2}\right]. \tag{6b}$$

Within this approximation the field gradient of the x-component is given by

$$\frac{dH}{dx} = -\frac{2H_g x}{\pi g y} \sin^2 \frac{\pi H_x}{H_g}. \tag{7}$$

Real magnetic heads deviate from this ideal "Karlquist head". The gap edges are rounded by imperfect machining or by saturation of the pole tips. If r is the radius of the gap edge, the gap is increased to an effective gap length $g + 2r$ $(r \leqslant 0.1\ g)$ [27, 28]. Similarly, the deviation of the gap from a straight line leads to write and read losses [29]. A permeability of the head core below 30 decreases the field gradient [30–34] and consequently leads to a degraded write-read-process. A

14

finite pole tip length results in negative field components at the edges of the pole pieces [35, 36] which improve rather than degrade the record process. The field of any head shape can be calculated using Mallinson's fundamental equations [37] together with techniques of conformal mapping and linear superposition.

3.2. Integrated and Magnetoresistive Heads

Miniaturized magnetic heads on the basis of the same techniques as used in integrated semiconductor circuits, i. e. evaporation, sputtering and photolithography, have first been proposed by *Barton* and *Stöckel* [38]. Integrated heads essentially consist of a thin conductor which is enclosed by a magnetic film with a gap. They are particularly suited for multitrack heads with extremely small track distances. They have a low inductivity and low eddy current losses. A particular problem is the low wear resistance of integrated heads [39] which further are limited in their application to short wavelengths due to their short pole tip length [37]. Further details can be found in publications by *Lazzari* and *Melnick* [40], *Valstyn* [41], *Lazzari* [42] as well as *Brock* [39].

A magnetoresistive element in the form of a thin magnetic film perpendicular to the recording medium has been proposed by *Hunt* [43] for reading of magnetically recorded data. The optimum resolution of narrowly spaced magnetization transitions can be achieved if the element is placed in the gap between the pole tips of a conventional head [15] which shields the magnetoresistive element from the leakage field of the approaching magnetization transitions. The readout voltage of the magnetoresistive head is flux sensitive, i. e. is independent of the velocity of the recording medium. The shape of the readout pulse is determined by the encompassing conventional head, i. e. by the transition length, the coating thickness, the head to medium spacing and the gap length of the conventional head [15, 44]. The main advantage of the magnetoresistive head is its up to 20 times greater readout voltage with respect to conventional heads [45]. Thus, the magnetiv flux of the recording medium can be lowered which enables a shorter transition length to be recorded. The present status of the development of these heads is outlined in papers by *Potter* [15], *Thomson* et al. [45], *Kuijk* et al. [46], *Kanai* et al. [47] as well as *Shelledy* and *Brock* [48].

4. Write, Storage and Read Cycle

4.1. Write Process

The linear recording density in saturation recording is mainly limited by the length of the transition zone between the negative and positive saturation remanence and the shift of the transition zone due to the superposition of the individual transitions which represent the recorded information. In Fig. 3, the recording medium is shown at the instant where the write field changes its polarity. The case where $(d + \delta) = 2\,g$

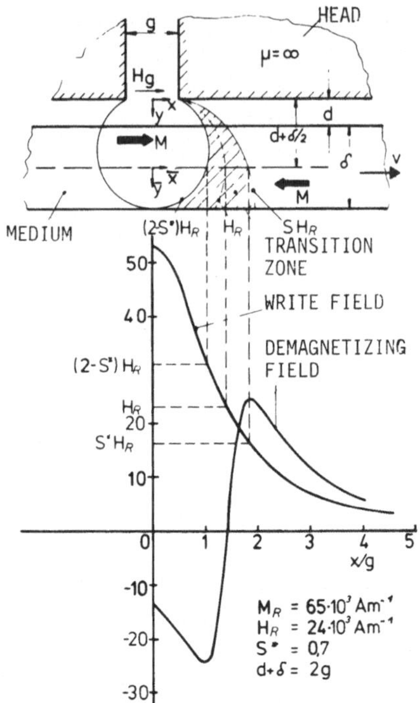

Fig. 3

Schematic representation of the write process with write field and demagnetizing field as a function of the coordinate in the direction of medium movement.

is assumed which often occurs in actual recording systems. Neglecting the y-component of write field and magnetization, the transition zone is given by the dashed area between the field contours with the lower switching field S^+H_R and the upper switching field $(2 - S^+) H_R$ of the linearised M (H)-curve. The center of the transition is at $H = H_R$ where the maximum gradient of the write field and the magnetization coincide [49]. The deep gap field is adjusted such, that the magnetization at the back surface of the medium is just being saturated. From $H = (2 - S^+) H_R$ at x = 0 and $y = d + \delta$ in equ. (5) follows

$$H_g = \pi H_R (2 - S^+)/2 \tan^{-1} [g/2 (d + \delta)]. \tag{8}$$

Any variation of d due to variations in flying height of the head in disk stores or due to asperities on the surface of magnetic tapes changes the location of the transition zone and leads to a shift of the peak of the readout voltage.

Simultaneously with the transition of the magnetization, a demagnetization field is generated by the divergence of the magnetization which is opposed to the magnetization on both sides of the zone. Using the arctan transition

$$M (x) = (2 M_R /\pi) \tan^{-1} (\bar{x}/a) \tag{9}$$

which was introduced by *Miyata* [2], the demagnetizing field can be calculated as has been done by *Potter* [9]. The transition length, a, in eq. (9) is related to the linear transition length, l, between S^+H_R and $(2 - S^+)\,H_R$ by $l = \pi a$. In Fig. 3 the write field and demagnetizing field in the plane $y = d + \delta/2$ are included as a function of x/g. The write field is reduced by the demagnetizing field on the left side of the transition and increased on the right side. Thus, the field contours S^+H_R and $(2 - S^+)\,H_R$ are being pushed further apart and the transition zone becomes broadened. Simultaneously, the demagnetizing field is lowered, whose equilibrium with the magnetization of the medium and the write field can only be found in a self consistent numerical calculation during which the write field is stepwise increased and write and demagnetizing field are at any time in equilibrium with the magnetization within the magnetic medium. *Iwasaki* and *Suzuki* [8] as well as *Suzuki* [51] calculated in this manner the vector distribution in the magnetic medium in the write field and after the transition left the write head. In their calculation, the relative head to medium movement has been neglected which becomes important in connection with the finite risetime of the write field and the interaction between the successively written transitions. All successive steps of writing on the moving medium, removing of the write field, demagnetization after entering the free space and remagnetization under the read head have been included in a one dimensional model by *Potter* and *Schmulian* [52], *Curland* and *Speliotis* [53] as well as *Chi* and *Speliotis* [54]. The one-dimensional model allows only for a longitudinal x-component of the magnetization which is assumed to be constant with respect to the y-direction. This is only legitimate in the case of very thin media, $\delta \ll a$, or in the case of partial penetration as is applied in video or instrumentation recording [11]. In saturation recording on thick media, both, the x- and y-components are of importance [55, 8]. The latter can contribute up to 20 % of the read voltage and gives rise to an asymmetry of the read pulse [9]. The results of iterative numerical calculations describe the experimental results with sufficient accuracy [56]. However, the results for only a limited number of parameters have been published which not easily allow an insight into the importance of the individual system parameters on the read pulse. Consequently, there have been early efforts to develop analytical expressions for the length, a, of the transition zone and the resulting read back pulse.

4.2. Simple Recording Theory

All theories which aim at an analytical calculation of the magnetization transition and the resulting read pulse use the one dimensional model mentioned in the previous sections, i. e. the approximation of a thin recording medium. In spite of this limitation they are very useful in the sense that they give satisfactory qualitative results for thick media. The transverse z-component of field and magnetization is zero as long as the track width is wide compared to the gap length. Further, the field rise time, t_0, is neglected. This can be done as long as the length of a single transition

$$l_0 = \pi a_0 = v\,t_0 \tag{10}$$

linearily written with a head to medium velocity v is shorter than the directly written zone of Fig. 3 — dashed area — with the average length

$$l_1 = \pi\, a_1 = (2 - S^+)\,(1 - S^+)\,(d + \delta). \tag{11}$$

In rotating disk systems with $v = 60$ m/sec, $t_0 = 40$ ns, $S^+ = 0,7$ and $(d + \delta) = 2\ \mu$m, i.e. $l_0 = 2,9\ \mu$m and $l_1 = 1,1\ \mu$m, this condition is already violated. Eq. (11) has been derived from the maximum head field gradient at $x \simeq y$ in eq. (7) with H_g from eq. (8) and the field difference $2\,(1 - S^+)\,H_R$ of the linearized magnetization curve using the approximation $(d + \delta) > g$.

Using the equilibrium condition of equal slopes of head and demagnetization field as well as the derivative of M (H), *Williams* and *Comstock* [18] as well as *Maller* and *Middleton* [57] derived an analytical expression for the transition length on the basis of eq. (9). With M (H) of eq. (1) and following *Williams* and *Comstock*, the transition length in the write field under the write head is

$$\frac{a_1}{\delta} = A + \left[A^2 + \frac{S^+ (2 - S^+)\, D\, y_0\, M_R}{\pi\, \delta\, H_c} \right]^{1/2} , \quad \delta \ll a, \tag{12}$$

with $A = S^+ (1 - S^+)\,(1/\pi Q)\,(y_0/\delta)$ and $Q = 0.866 - 0.214 \exp(- 5\, y_0/\, 3\, g)$ which increases with increasing $y_0 = (d + \delta/2)$ from 0.65 to 0.87. The factor $D = 4\, y_0 (a_1 + y_0)/(a_1 + 2\, y_0)^2$ allows for the partial shunting of the demagnetization field by the mirror image of the transition under a head with infinite permeability. After switching off of the write field and removing the transition from the write head, further demagnetization takes place which leads to a broader transition length [18]

$$\frac{a_2}{\delta} = \frac{a_1}{\delta}\, \frac{1}{2\, S^+ (2 - S^+)} + \left[\left(\frac{a_1}{\delta}\, \frac{1}{2\, S^+ (2 - S^+)} \right)^2 + \frac{(1 - S^+)\, a_1\, M_R}{2\, S^+ (2 - S^+)\, \delta H_c} \right]^{1/2} \tag{13}$$

with a_1 from eq. (12). Finally, under the read head with infinite permeability a remagnetization along the reversible minor loop between M (H) and M (0) takes place which narrows the transition length in the case of total remagnetization to

$$\frac{a_3}{\delta} = \frac{(a_2/\delta)^2}{(a_2/\delta) + 0.5\, \chi_{rev} \cdot \delta} = \frac{a_1}{\delta\, S\, (2 - S)} \tag{14}$$

with χ_{rev} from eq. (1c).

Fig. 4 shows a_2/δ and a_3/δ according to eq. (13) and (14) as a function of M_R/H_c with S^+ as parameter for $y_0/\delta = 0.5$, i.e. for $d = 0$, $D = 1$ and $Q = 2,5$ ($y_0 = g$). The same presentation is given in Fig. 5 with $y/\delta = 0.8$, i.e. $d = 0.3\,\delta$, which examplifies the pronounced increase of the transition length with increasing head to medium spacing. This fact is related to the decrease of the write field gradient of eq. (7) with increasing $(d + \delta)$ and the simultaneously increasing deep gap write field from eq. (8). The actual transition length under the read head is somewhere between a_2 and a_3 depending on the head to medium spacing and the permeability of the read head.

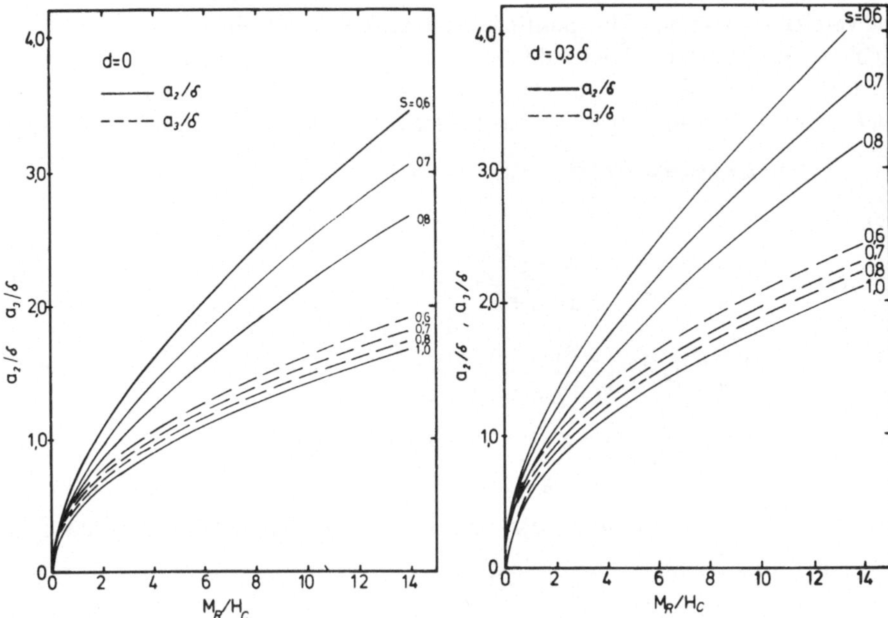

Fig. 4

Transition length in free space and under read head as a function of remanence and coercivity with direct write head to medium contact.

Fig. 5

Same as fig. 4 with distance d = 0.3 between write head and medium.

Measurements on media with M_R/H_c between 6 and 9, S^+ between 0.4 and 0.8, δ between 0.1 and 0.6 μm, d between 0.3 and 0.6 μm and g = 1 μm [58] give good agreement with the above theory although in all cases a is not much larger than δ, i.e. the assumption of thin media, $a \gg \delta$, is violated. Extensions of the shown theory to thick media have been made [59, 60] and inspite of the objections raised against theories of this kind [17], they describe very well the relative importance of remanence, coercivity, switching field distribution, medium thickness and head to medium spacing on the length of a single transition.

4.3. Read Back Process

The read back process is linear due to the low induced flux density in the read head. The read back voltage can be calculated using the principle of reziprocity [1]. From this follows that the read voltage is proportional to the product of the gradient of the magnetization in the magnetic medium, $\partial M(\bar{x} - x)), y)/\partial x$ times the reduced field function $H(x, y)/H_g$ of the read head. With $M(x)$ from eq. (9) e (x), the induced read voltage as function of the position of the medium under the read head, is essentially the product of the head field function and the Lorentzian distribution $(1 + (ax)^2)^{-1}$ as the derivative of M(x). According to *Speliotis* and *Morrision* [6] and *Potter* [9] the read voltage without the loading of the read amplifier is

$$e(x) = (2/\pi)\,\mu_0\,\alpha w\,Nv\,\{M_x\,[f(x) + f(-x)]\}$$

with

$$f(x) = \frac{d + a + \delta}{g}\,\tan^{-1}\left(\frac{x + g/2}{d + a + \delta}\right)$$

$$-\frac{d + a}{g}\,\tan^{-1}\left(\frac{x + g/2}{d + a}\right) \tag{15}$$

$$+\frac{x + g/2}{2g}\,\ln\left(\frac{(x + g/2)^2 + (d + a + \delta)^2}{(x + g/2)^2 + (d + a)^2}\right).$$

The half pulse width of the above read pulse is in the approximation $g \ll 2(y_0 + a)$

$$PW_{50} = [g^2 + 4(d + a + \delta)(d + a)]^{1/2}. \tag{16}$$

Using the example from Fig. 3 with $d + \delta/2 = 2$ g, $d = 0{,}3$ and $g = 1$ μm eq. (13) and (16) yield $a_2 = 2.4$ μm and $PW_{50} = 7.2$ μm. The example indicates that the read process is of equal importance as the write process in present day disk systems.

4.4. Superposition of single transitions

The nonlinearity of the write process is no obstacle for a linear superposition of the individual single pulses of a train of written transitions as long as an already written transition is not altered by writing the next one [61]. The lower limit for linear superposition is a transition or pulse distance, b, which is equal to the larger of the two transition lengths l_0 from eq. (10) or l_1 from eq. (11).

A reasonably good approximation of the amplitude of pulses with linear superposition relative to the amplitude of a single pulse, e_0, is an indefinitely long chain of Lorentzian distribution functions with the pulse distance, b,

$$\frac{e(x)}{e_0} = \sum_{n=-\infty}^{\infty} (-1)^n \left[1 + \left(\frac{2(x + nb)}{PW_{50}}\right)^2\right]^{-1}. \tag{17}$$

The pulse or peak shift, $\Delta b/b$, due to the superposition can be estimated from the superposition of the two pulses with $n = 0$ and $n = 1$ in eq. (17). e/e_0 at $x = 0$ in eq. (17) as well as $\Delta b/b$ are plotted as a function of b/PW_{50} in Fig. 6. The often used -6 dB packing density of transitions at $e_0/2$ is given by $1/b = 1.32/PW_{50}$. Amplitude and peak shift calculated in this way are in agreement with measurements

20

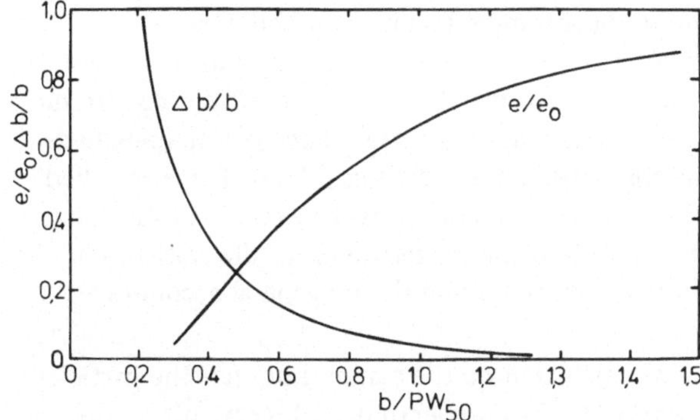

Fig. 6. Relative amplitude and peak shift as a function of the distance between magnetization transitions.

of a number of authors [59, 62–64] and own measurements on particulate media with a coating thickness up to $2 \, \mu m$.

At very short pulse distances, $e(x)$ approaches a sine wave of wavelength, $\lambda = 2\,b$ [65], whose read voltage has been calculated by *Mallinson* [66] taking into account de- and remagnetization. The results are similar to the equations by *Wallace* [67] and *Westmijze* [68] which have been frequently used for audio or video recording systems.

5. Noise Limited Recording

At very high recording densities noise considerations are of equal importance as signal amplitude and half pulse width. In the interest of brevity the consideration of electronic noise is excluded whose concepts are well known and not unique to magnetic recording systems.

In read heads made from materials with low magnetostriction, noise is generated by thermal fluctuation of the head core flux. It can be described by the complex permeability of the head. The wide band noise power between the frequencies ω_1 and ω_2 as a function of temperature is [11]

$$\text{NPS} = (2/\pi)\,kT \int_{\omega_1}^{\omega_2} R(\omega)\,d\omega \qquad (18)$$

with Boltzman's constant k and the loss resistance $R(\omega)$, which in simple cases may be calculated [71] or directly measured. In laminated permalloy or cast alfesil and sendust heads the noise is primarily due to eddy currents. In ferrite heads bloch wall relaxation processes may add to the noise of eq. (18).

21

For the magnetic medium two noise sources must be distinguished. One is due to the inherent deviation from the initially made assumption of a homogenious medium, i.e. the particulate noise. It is independent of signal and additive. Noises due to the nonuniformity of the medium, the particle packing, surface and coating thickness irregularities and track deviations are dependent on the signal level. These so called modulation noises, slight in modern recording media, must be excluded from this paper since they cannot be predicted without prior knowledge of the statistics of the particular phenomena responsible and, consequently, no general account can be given.

The particulate noise power may be calculated on the assumption that the particles are packed at random. It is proportional to the number of particles per unit volume, n, and the track width w. The signal power is in contrary proportional to n^2 and w^2 [69]. At very short pulse distances, i.e. $b < \pi\delta$, the wide band signal to noise ratio in saturation recording is [14]

$$S/N = [(2/\pi) \, nw \, b^2] \, [1/(1 + \sigma^2/v_p^2)] \, [3 \, S^2/(1 + 2 \, S)] \tag{19}$$

independent of particle moment and volume. The first term applies to identical, randomly distributed particles oriented parallel to each other. The second term allows for a distribution of particle volumes, v_p, with a standard deviation, σ, [70]. σ/v_p for usual oxide particles is slightly larger than 1; thus, this term equals approximately 0.5. The third term stands for particles with a degree of orientation less than S = 1, which amounts to 0.375 for randomly oriented particles with S = 0.5 [70]. Consequently, a narrow particle size distribution and well oriented particles are of similar importance as the number of particles per unit volume.

Neglecting the distance between recording tracks, two informative equations for noise limited recording can be derived from eq. (19) with $\sigma/v_p = 1$ and S = 0.7 [14]:

$$\text{linear density} \simeq \sqrt{w} \, \sqrt{\frac{n}{5 \, S/N}} \tag{20}$$

and

$$\text{areal density} \simeq \sqrt{1/w} \, \sqrt{\frac{n}{5 \, S/N}} \tag{21}$$

Eq. (20) and (21) indicate that in noise limited recording the areal density may be improved by rather increasing the track density, $1/w$, than the linear density. With $n = 10^{11}/mm^3$ of common particulate media and $1/w = 16/mm$ (600 tracks/inch) and a postulated S/N of 30 dB one obtaines from eq. (20) and (21) a linear density of 1100 transitions/mm (28000 transitions/inch) and an areal density of 18000 transitions/mm^2 (11×10^6 transitions/$inch^2$). These values are far beyond those usually obtained in saturation recording.

6. Materials for Recording Media

According to the previous sections, the recording medium should have a large remanence and coercivity but with a small ratio of remanence to coercivity. Here, the coercivity is limited at high values by the saturation magnetization of the write head, i. e. its maximum write field. In addition, the switching field distribution, $(1 - S^+)$, should be narrow, i. e. the squareness, S, of the hysteresis loop should be large. The particles must be as small as possible, allow a dense packing and a good degree of orientation. The demand for a stable remanence with respect to time and temperature gives a lower limit for the particle size below which they become superparamagnetic. An upper limit of particle size is given by the fact, that the particles must contain only one single domain.

Shape anisotropy of elongated particles is preferable to magnetocrystalline anisotropy as the source for the coercivity since the saturation magnetization which determines the shape anisotropy is generally far less temperature dependent than the magnetocrystalline anisotropy. Uniaxial magnetocrystalline anisotropy or uniaxial shape anisotropy are desired rather than multiaxial anisotropy since the latter does not allow the required anisotropy of easy magnetization of thick media.

The magnetic properties of the most important materials for recording media are listed in Table 1. Right on top is γ-Fe_2O_3 which in the form of elongated particles has been used until shortly exclusively for digital and analog recording. With predominant shape anisotropy and the easy directions of crystalline anisotropy parallel to the [110] axis of the shape anisotropy [72, 73], the remanence of the particles is extremely stable. At a coherent magnetization reversal of the particles, a coercivity of isotropically oriented particles up to $90 \cdot 10^3$ A/m is to be expected. For many years about $23 \cdot 10^3$ A/m have been obtained. Consequently, incoherent magnetization reversals take place due to the particle diameter between 0.5 and 1 μm which is too large for coherent reversals. In addition, the divergence of magnetization at irregularities of the particle surface leads to a further decrease of the coercivity.

The introduction of CrO_2 with its higher coercivity and a more uniform particle shape lead to new efforts to improve γ-Fe_2O_3 particles. Coercivities up to $32 \cdot 10^3$ A/m [74] with a narrower switching field distribution were obtained. This was made possible by an improved shape and smaller size of the starting product FeOOH and improved reduction and oxidation processes. Another development on the basis of a different modification of FeOOH resulted in an improved particle shape and a better orientablity of the particles up to values of S of 0.85 [75]. A thin layer of a material with high magnetocrystalline anisotropy on the surface of γ-Fe_2O_3 particles can impede the rotation of the magnetization in areas of large divergence and thus increase the coercivity towards the expected value of shape anisotropy. One indeed succeeded in forming a thin layer of cobalt ferrite on γ-Fe_2O_3 which increases the coercivity up to $43 \cdot 10^3$ A/m [76] and reduces the switching field distribution by

20 % [77]. This procedure is different to the otherwise often used doping of two valent cobalt ions into the lattice of γ-Fe$_2$O$_3$ in that it preserves the uniaxial anisotropy of the particles and their orientability.

Table 1: Saturation magnetization, magnetocrystalline anisotropy, coercivity and Curie temperature of the most important materials for recording media

Magnetic material		M_S 10^3 Am^{-1}	K_1 10^3 Jm^{-3}	$H_c^{*)}$ 10^3 Am^{-1}	θ_c °C
Particles					
γ-Fe$_2$O$_3$		360	$-$ 4,6	$<$ 32	570
γ-Fe$_2$O$_3$	1 % Co	355	25	$\simeq$ 28	$-$
	2 % Co	345	36	$\simeq$ 37	$-$
	4 % Co	310	50	$\simeq$ 78	$-$
Fe$_3$O$_4$		480	$-$ 11	$<$ 35	590
CrO$_2$		490	22	$<$ 60	127
Fe		1700	48	$>$ 80	770
Fe 30 % Co		1900	30	$>$ 80	950
Co		1430	430	$>$ 80	1100
*) Apparent sample density 1,2 gcm^{-3}					
Films					
Co-P		$\simeq$ 1100	$-$	$>$ 50	$-$
Fe$_3$O$_4$		480	$-$ 11	$<$ 45	590

In the case of the uniform doping of γ-Fe$_2$O$_3$ with two valent cobalt ions, the shape anisotropy is surpassed by the introduced crystalline anisotropy. The $\langle 100 \rangle$ easy directions of the magnetocrystalline anisotropy do not coincide with the particle axis and lead to an increased squareness of the hysteresis loop. Consequently, a strong temperature dependence of the coercivity and the squareness of the hysteresis loop [78] is observed. The particles are difficult to orient and the up to five fold magnetostriction of these oxides [79] leads to a decrease in remanence and consequently in signal at short wavelengths after mechanical stress as is encountered in recording systems. It is not to be expected that particles of this kind are going to be widely used in magnetic recording.

Fe$_3$O$_4$ as an intermediate product in the production process of γ-Fe$_2$O$_3$ with its by 20 % higher saturation magnetization and by 15 % higher coercivity is not only less expensive but also allows higher read signals at least at long transition distances. The reason for its little use in recording media is its susceptibility to oxidation which may influence the long term stability of its magnetic properties. Even more adverse are magnetic after effects which lead to difficulties with erasure in audio and video recording application. Further, the magnetocrystalline anisotropy of Fe$_3$O$_4$ is three

24

times as that of Fe_2O_3 and its easy directions do not coincide with the particle axis. This gives rise to increased print through from winding to winding of audio tapes, thus excluding Fe_3O_4 from this area of application.

In CrO_2 particles the tetragonal [001]-axis of the respective uniaxial magneto-crystalline and shape anisotropy coincide. In spite of the low Curie temperature θ_c of 125 °C and a relative contribution of the magnetocrystalline anisotropy to the coercivity of about 50 % [80], recorded information remains unaltered up to almost 100 °C [81] since H_c/M_R remains essentially constant up to 100 °C [80]. CrO_2 exhibits an extremely good needle shape with respect to γ-Fe_2O_3 and is well orientable up to squareness values of S = 0.85. CrO_2 can be produced with coercivities up to $50 \cdot 10^3$ A/m. A further increase in coercivities appears possible.

Particles consisting of iron or iron-cobalt alloy have the highest saturation magnetization which in case of coherent magnetization reversal would lead to coercivities of $380 \cdot 10^3$ A/m and in that of incoherent reversal to coercivities of up to $150 \cdot 10^3$ A/m. Over the last ten years many attempts have been made in this directions without leading to a commercial product due to the problems involved in producing the necessary morphology of the particles, their pyrophoric character and the difficulties encountered in dispersing them in the binder system. Only recently, the efforts have been increased probably due to the success of CrO_2. Metal particle tapes with coercivities above 80 kA/m have been reported which support sine wave recording of 3 μm wavelength at two times the read voltage found with CrO_2 tapes and three times that found with standard γ-Fe_2O_3 tapes [82, 83]. The interesting aspect of metal particles is that their volume can be reduced to 1/10 of that of γ-Fe_2O_3 particles without any increase in superparamagnetic particles. Consequently, at the same volume loading of the particles a considerably better signal to noise ratio can be obtained.

Thin films of CoP and CoNiP or Fe_3O_4 in a thickness range of 0.1 to 0.3 μm are used commercially on rigid rotating disks. The advantage of thin films is their low thickness and high remanence which guarantees a short transition zone at sufficiently large read voltage. Thin films are preferred objects for theoretical work in magnetic recording since they meet the simplifying assumption of a medium thickness which is small compared to the length of the transition zone and the gap length. Their production by chemical or electrolytical deposition as well as by evaporation and sputtering techniques is well understood [84, 85]. The resistance against wear of the films is increased by thin protective coatings. The main difficulties exist techno-logically in obtaining low enough error rates at the ultimate high recording densities, i. e. the small magnetization elements of 1 μm length and 30 μm width. The same holds for Fe_3O_4-films which are either produced chemically [58] or by evaporation of iron with subsequent oxidation of the iron film [86]. Their resistance to wear and chemical erosion is better than that of metal films. No commercial use of Fe_3O_4-films is known so far.

7. Materials for Magnetic Heads

According to section 3, the magnetic core must have a high permeability for a good efficiency and an extremely low coercivity in order to avoid residual fields of the head.

The most widely used materials of which none exhibits simultaneously all ideal properties are listed in table 2. All metal alloys must be used in thin lamellations in order to avoid eddy current losses and are limited to frequencies below 1 MHz. The highest recording fields can be obtained with iron cobalt alloys which need high recording currents due to their low permeability.

Ferrites with their high electrical resistivity are most suited for frequencies above 1 MHz. Particularly, the extremely dense hot pressed ferrites [87, 88] lead to a considerable progress in frequency response and wear resistance.

Mn-Zn-ferrite with its higher permeability is more suitable for write heads and Ni-Zn-Ferrite for read heads due to its better frequency characteristics.

At high frequencies, losses occur in ferrites due to after effects of the bloch wall movement. They are characterized by the real and imaginary part of the permeability, μ' and μ'', respectively which depend on the grain size, the magnetocrystalline anisotropy, the magnetostriction and the electrical resistivity which, in turn, all depend strongly on the chemical composition of the material [89]. The imaginary part of the permeability gives rise to a resistivity loss. The efficiency of a head decreases rapidly if μ'' becomes larger than μ'. At the chosen pulse frequency μ'' must always be smaller than μ'.

Table 2. Magnetic and electrical properties of some typical magnetic head materials [87, 90]

Head material	M_s $10^3\ Am^{-1}$	ρ $\mu\Omega\ cm$	μ' at 1 kHz	H_c Am^{-1}	θ_c °C
78Ni22Fe	850	16	10 000	0,6	600
4Mo79Ni17Fe	690	58	50 000	0,6	460
5Mo79Ni16Fe	605	65	90 000	0,08	
2V49Co49Fe	1900	27	800	2,5	932
"Alfenol", "Alperm" 16Al84Fe	1430	140	3 000	0,5	400
"Alfesil", "Sendust" 5,5Al10Si84,5Fe	800	80	30 000	0,6	500
11NiO 22ZnO, hot pressed 67Fe$_2$O$_3$	310	10^{10}	850	1,9	125
14MnO 16ZnO, hot pressed 70Fe$_2$O$_3$	360	10^7	10 000	0,4	110

Another important role plays the Curie temperature which in most cases is between 100 and 200 °C. When choosing a composition of the ferrite, the environmental temperature and the frictional heating must be observed since all magnetic properties vary considerably near the Curie temperature and lead to a strongly temperature dependent efficiency of the head.

Single crystals of Mn-Zn-Ferrite have been used for magnetic heads [87, 88, 91] which, however, exhibit a pronounced anisotropy of their mechanical and magnetic properties as well as their thermal expansion.

8. Areas of future Improvements

8.1. Theory

The development of recording theory tends to a greater complexity using iterative calculations in conjunction with large computers while simple forms in the case of thick media are of more immediate need. They should be applicable to distances of magnetization reversal below 2 μm where losses are already introduced during writing. Another unresolved question is the influence of the particle size at these low reversal distances.

8.2. Recording Parameters

In the previous sections exclusively saturation recording has been considered since it is being used in most of the present day recording systems. Saturation recording is necessary in the absence of an erase head in order to write over previously recorded transitions. Partial penetration recording as used in video recorders can only be applied if a seperate erase head is available. In saturation recording, the extreme nonlinearity of the over all signal channel makes amplitude and phase correction very difficult and transfers the burden of preserving a narrow read pulse on medium and head. Here, the development towards thin media with higher remanence and coercivity which appears to be limited in thickness to 1 μm for particulate media and 0.1 μm for thin films leads to transition lengths of the same order of magnitude. In the case of thin films which are coated on rigid disks and used with flying heads, the half pulse width in a system with a gap length of 0.5 μm and a flying height of 0.5 μm is approximately 1.4 μm according to the theoretical consideration of section 4. When flexible particulate media are used in contact to heads with the same gap length, the corresponding half pulse width would be 3 μm. The linear transition densities at $-$ 6 dB amplitude are then approximately 1000 transitions/mm (25000 transitions per inch) and 500 transitions/mm (13000 transitions/inch) respectively. These ultimate densities are severely questioned by the sensitivity of saturation recording to peak shift which demands extreme perfection of the medium surface and uniformity. More realistic figures may be down by 20 to 50 %.

Another type of data recording on the basis of video and instrumentation recorders [92, 93, 94] uses partial penetration and anhysteretic linearisation of the magnetization which amounts to only 20 to 30 % of the saturation remanence. With a flat frequency response up to frequencies corresponding to a transition distance of 0.5 μm and using all possiblities of amplitude and phase correction [14, 16], linear densities up to 2000 transitions per mm (50000 transitions per inch) with areal densities up to 3000 transitions/mm^2 ($2 \cdot 10^6$ transitions per inch^2) have been achieved which are noise limited in the sense of section 5.

8.3. Recording Medium

Increasing the volume fraction of magnetic particles from the present value of about 20 to 30 % up to 40 to 50 % as is the state of the art in audio recording media and respectively increasing the coercivity can improve the signal to noise ratio by 3 dB. This improvement may be full exploited in linearized, noise limited systems as mentioned in the previous section. Here, CrO_2 or γ-Fe_2O_3 particles with thin cobalt ferrite surface coating are fully sufficient. Further improvement of 10 dB in S/N is to be expected from metal particles with one thenth of the particle volume of γ-Fe_2O_3 particles. Their advantage is better utilized by narrowing the track width rather than increasing the recording density as has been shown in section 5. In all cases, the straightness of the tape edges limits the track width to lower values and must be considered in any recorder design.

Metal and oxide thin films have the before mentioned good recording characteristics but need further development with respect to surface imperfections which lead to errors in signal detection.

8.4. Magnetic Heads

The availability of very dense ferrites with small grain sizes reduces the noise of the read head to a minor problem. Gap lengths down to 0.5 μm are possible while track widths below 20 μm seem impossible due to limitation in head positioning and head wear.

Further development of integrated heads is of interest in head per track recorders. At the relatively low track densities of these recorders, thin metal and oxide films seem useful for extreme high linear data densities.

References

[1]   *A. Hoagland*, AIEE Trans. Communications **75**, 605 (1956).

[2]   *J. J. Miyata* and *R. R. Hartel*, IRE Trans. Electr. Comp. **EC-8**, 159 (1959).

[3]   *D. F. Eldridge*, IRE Trans. Audio **AU-8**, 42 (1960).

[4]   *K. Teer*, Philips Res. Repts **16**, 469 (1961).

[5]   .*G. C. Feth*, AIEE Trans. Communications **81**, 267 (1962)

[6]   *D. E. Speliotis* and *J. R. Morrison*, IBM J. Res. and Dev. **10**, 233 (1966).

[7]   *D. E. Speliotis*, IEEE Trans. Magn. **MAG-3**, 195 (1967).

[8]   *S. Iwasaki* and *T. Suzuki*, IEEE Trans. Magn. **MAG-4**, 269 (1968).

[9]   *R. I. Potter*, J. Appl. Phys. **41**, 1647 (1970).

[10]   *R. O. McCary*, IEEE Trans. Magn. **MAG-7**, 4 (1971).

[11]   *J. C. Mallinson*, AIP Conf. Proc. Magnetism Magn. Mat. **5**, 743 (1971).

[12]   *M. F. Dudson* et al., Proc. IEE, IEE Rev. **119**, 956 (1972).

[13]   *D. E. Speliotis*, Ann. New York Acad. Sci. **189**, 21 (1972).

[14]   *J. C. Mallinson*, IEEE Trans. Magn. **MAG-10**, 368 (1974).

[15]   *R. I. Potter*, IEEE Trans. Magn. **MAG-10**, 502 (1974).

[16]   *J. C. Mallinson*, IEEE Trans. Magn. **MAG-11**, 1066 (1975).

[17]   *D. L. A. Tjaden* and *E. J. Tercic*, Philips Res. Repts **30**, 120 (1975).

[18]   *M. L. Williams* and *R. L. Comstock*, AIP Conf. Proc. Magnetism Magn. Mat. **5**, 738 (1971).

[19]   *R. M. Bozorth*, Ferromagnetism, D. Van Nostrand & Co., Inc., Princeton N. J. 351 (1951).

[20]   *B. Kostyshyn*, IEEE Trans. Magn. **MAG-7**, 880 (1971).

[21]   *D. J. Sansom*, IEEE Trans. Magn. **MAG-12**, 230 (1976).

[22]   *G. F. Hughes*, IEEE Trans. Magn. **MAG-7**, 695 (1971).

[23]   *A. D. Booth*, Brit. J. Appl. Phys. **3**, 307 (1952).

[24]   *W. K. Westmijze*, Philips Res. Repts **8**, 245 (1953).

[25]   *O. Karlquist*, Trans. Roy, Inst. Techn. Stockholm Nr. 86 (1954).

[26]   *M. F. Barkouki* and *I. Stein*, IEEE Trans. Electr. Comp. **EC-12**, 92 (1963).

[27]   *S Duinker*, Philips Res. Repts **16**, 307 (1961).

[28]   *K. Steffen*, Z. Nachrichtent. Elektr. **23**, 113 (1973).

[29]   *J. C. Mallinson*, IEEE Trans. Magn. **MAG-5**, 71 (1969).

[30]   *J. P. Lazzari* and *R. H. Wade*, IEEE Trans. Magn. **MAG-7**, 700 (1971).

[31]   *W. K. Hodder* and *J. F. Monson*, IEEE Trans. Magn. **MAG-7**, 686 (1971).

[32]   *T. S. Suzuki* and *S. Iwasaki*, IEEE Trans. Magn. **MAG-8**, 536 (1972).

[33]   *C. W. Steele* and *J. C. Mallinson*, IEEE Trans. Magn. **MAG 8**, 503 (1972).

[34]   *J. Monson*, IEEE Trans. Magn. **MAG-8**, 533 (1972).

[35]   *R. I. Potter* et al. IEEE Trans. Magn. **MAG-7**, 689 (1971).

[36]   *R. I. Potter*, IEEE Trans. Magn. **MAG-11**, 80 (1975).

[37]   *J. C. Mallinson*, IEEE Trans. Magn. **MAG-10**, 773 (1974).

[38]   *J. C. Barton* and *T. Stockel*, Radio Electron. Engr. **26**, 11 (1964).

[39]   *G. W. Brock* and *F. B. Shelledy*, IEEE Trans. Magn. **MAG-11**, 1218 (1975).

[40]   *J. P. Lazzari* and *I. Melnick*, IEEE Trans. Magn. **MAG-7**, 146 (1971).

[41]   *E. P. Valstyn*, Ann. New York Acad. Sci., **189**, 191 (1972).

[42]   *J. P. Lazzari*, AIP Proc. Conf. Magnetism Magn. Mat. **18**, 980 (1973).

[43]   *R. P. Hunt*, IEEE Trans. Magn. **MAG-7**, 150 (1971).

[44] *A. V. Davies* and *B. K. Middleton*, IEEE Trans. Magn. **MAG-11**, 1689 (1975).

[45] *D. A. Thompson* et al., IEEE Trans. Magn. **MAG-11**, 1039 (1975).

[46] *K. E. Kuijk* et al., IEEE Trans. Magn. **MAG-11**, 1215 (1975).

[47] *K. Kanai* et al., IEEE Trans. Magn. **MAG-11**, 1212 (1975).

[48] *F. B. Shelledy* and *G. W. Brock*, IEEE Trans. Magn. **MAG-11**, 1206 (1975).

[49] *D. W. Chapmann*, Proc. IEEE **51**, 247 (1963).

[50] *D. J. George* et al., IEEE Trans. Magn. **MAG-7**, 240 (1971).

[51] *K. Suzuki*, IEEE Trans. Magn. **MAG-12**, 224 (1976).

[52] *R. I. Potter* and *R. J. Schmulian*, IEEE Trans. Magn. **MAG-7**, 240 (1971).

[53] *N. Curland* and *D. E. Speliotis*, IEEE Trans. Magn. **MAG-7**, 538 (1971).

[54] *C. S. Chi* and *D. E. Speliotis*, IEEE Trans. Magn. **MAG-10**, 765 (1974).

[55] *D. L. A. Tjaden*, Philips Techn. Rev. **25**, 319 (1963/64).

[56] *C. S. Chi* and *D. E. Speliotis*, IEEE Trans. Magn. **MAG-11**, 1179 (1975).

[57] *V. A. J. Maller* and *B. K. Middleton*, IERE Conf. Proc. **26**, 137 (1973).

[58] *R. L. Comstock* and *E. B. Moore*, IBM J. Res. and Dev. **18**, 556 (1974).

[59] *F. E. Talke* and *R. C. Tseng*, IBM J. Res. and Dev. **19**, 591 (1975).

[60] *B. K. Middleton* and *P. L. Wiseley*, IERE Conf. Proc. **35**, 33 (1976).

[61] *J. C. Mallisnon* and *C. W. Steele*, IEEE Trans. Magn. **MAG-5**, 886 (1969).

[62] *J. R. Morrison*, IEEE Trans. Magn. **MAG-4**, 281 (1968).

[63] *E. J. Tercic*, IEEE Trans. Magn. **MAG-9**, 335 (1973).

[64] *R L. Comstock* and *M. L. Mason*, IEEE Trans. Magn. **MAG-9**, 342 (1973).

[65] *J. C. Mallinson* and *N. Bertram*, IEEE Trans. Magn. **MAG-9**, 329 (1973).

[66] *J. C. Mallinson*, IEEE Trans. Magn. **MAG-5**, 182 (1969).

[70] *E. D. Daniel*, J. Audio Eng. Soc. **20**, 92 (1972).

[71] *P. Smaller* , IEEE Trans. Magn. **MAG-1**, 357 (1965).

[72] *G. W. van Oosterhout*, Acta Cryst. **13**, (1960).

[73] *E. Koster*, J. Appl. Phys. **41**, 3332 (1970).

[74] *Y. Yada* and *S. Miyamoto*, IEEE Trans. Magn. **MAG-9**, 185 (1973).

[75] *B. Gustard* and *M. R. Wright*, IEEE Trans. Magn. **MAG-8**, 426 (1972).

[76] *S. Umeki* et al., IEEE Trans. Magn. **MAG-10**, 655 (1974).

[77] *E. Koster* and *H. J. Becker* to be published.

[78] *E. Koster*, IEEE Trans. Magn. **MAG-8**

[79] *P. J. Flanders*, IEEE Trans. Magn. **MAG-10**, 1050 (1974).

[80] *E. Koster*, IERE Conf. Proc. **26**, 213 (1973).

[81] *D. E. Speliotis*, IEEE Trans. Magn. **MAG-4**, 553 (1968).

[82] *A. A. v. d. Giessen*, IEEE Trans. Magn. **MAG-9**, 192 (1973).

[83] *M. Kawasaki* and *S. Higuchi*, IEEE Trans. Magn. **MAG-8**, 552 (1972).

[84] *G. Bate* and *J. K. Alstad*, IEEE Trans. Magn. **MAG-5**, 821 (1969).

[85] *J. S. Judge*, Ann. New York Acad. Sci. **189**, 117 (1972).

[86] *N. Inagaki* et al., IEEE Trans. Magn. **MAG-11**, 1191 (1975).

[87] *J. Sugaya*, IEEE Trans. Magn. **MAG-4**, 295 (1968).

[88] *E. Hirota* et al., IEEE Trans. Magn. **MAG-7**, 337 (1971).

[89] *R. S. Tebble* and *D. J. Craik*, "Magnetic Materials" Wiley Interscience, London, New York, 556 (1969).

[90] *G. Bate*, AIP Conf. Proc. Magnetism Magn. Mat. **5**, 766 (1971).

[91] *M. Mizushima*, IEEE Trans. Magn. **MAG-7**, 342 (1971).

[92] *S. Damron* et al., AFIPS Fall Joint Comp. Conf. Proc. **33**, Pr II 1381 (1968).

[93] *D. Curtis* and *J. Rolfe*, 1971 Int. Telemetering Conf. Proc., 410.

[94] *P. Franson*, Electronics 141, 23 Oct. 1972.

Electromechanical Mass Storage Units – Disk Files

Peter Wentzel

Siemens AG, Data and Information Systems Division, Munich, Germany

1. Basic Information About Disk Files

1.1. Significance of the Disk File in Data Processing

Modern data processing systems process larger and larger quantities of data in times
which are becoming shorter and shorter. This applies to commercial large-capacity
computing systems as well as to process control computers and intelligent terminals.
The so-called working or main storage units which are worked on directly by the
processor are, in spite of their substantial growth in the past years, in no way capable
of accepting all necessary data. The sum of all data relevant to a system is thus filed
in the secondary storage units. Disk files and magnetic tape units are the most important secondary storage units.

The particular significance of the disk file in a data processing system is made clear
by a few of its properties.

- The total capacity of a disk file subsystem – this concept will be explained later –
  can range from a few tens of megabytes (MB) up to many gigabytes (GB), i.e.
  a maximum of almost 10^{11} bits.
- From this huge quantity, the desired data can be accessed in a few tens of milliseconds. The time which elapses from the addressing until the data is made available
  to the system is called access time.
- The information is non-volatile.
- Transfer rates in the range of a few MB/s for the data to be stored or retrieved
  are the current state of the art.

Thus, all active data, such as, private and public data sets, data bases, virtual working
storage units (paging), user programs and, last but not least, the operating system are
stored on disk files.

1.2. Principle (Fig. 1)

The storage medium of disk files consists of circular disks which have a thin magnetic
coating. One or more disks are concentrically attached to a hub or shaft and rotate
about their axis at a constant speed. The magnetic heads write and read the data to
be stored in interaction with the rapidly moving magnetic coating. In order to maintain the necessary small spacing from the coating, the heads ride on a stable air bearing of less than one micrometer thickness. All disk files record the data in a plurality
of concentric tracks. The length of such a track is proportional to the track radius,

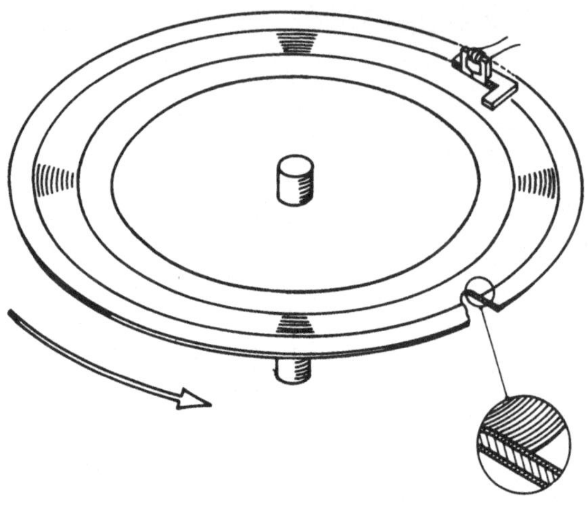

Fig. 1

Disk file principle.

i.e. the innermost track on a disk surface is also the shortest one. Since it is simpler, from the point of view of the equipment designer as well as of the user, to keep the data capacity of all tracks equal, the recording density of the track nearest to the center is the highest. This track density is the limiting factor in the track capacity. Presently 1000 tracks and more can be written onto one disk surface. There are two different possibilities to access these tracks.

1.2.1. Disk Files with Fixed Magnetic Heads (Fig. 2)

To each data track one magnetic head is assigned. This obvious method has, however, its limits in the large number of heads to be accommodated and in the enormous costs of hundreds or thousands of heads.

The large number of heads, i.e. one head per track, and the relatively small number of tracks, i.e. the head density design limitations, result in an unfavorable cost/capacity ratio in the order of presently 0.05 ¢/bit.

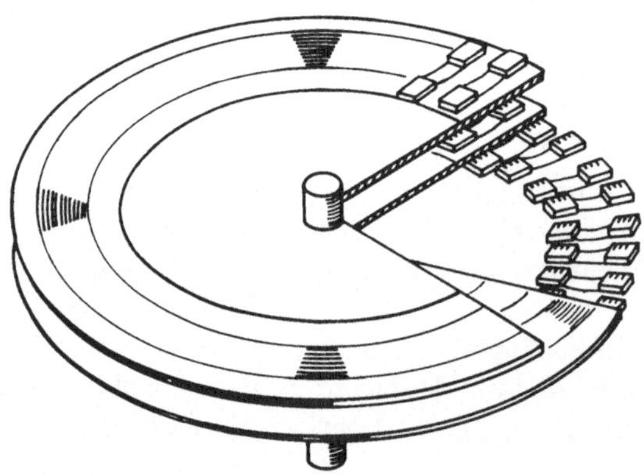

Fig. 2

Disk file with fixed magnetic heads.

For this reason, fixed head disk files are used relatively seldom in commercial systems and then only for applications where very short access times are required, such as paging.

1.2.2. Disk Files with Movable Magnetic Heads (Fig. 3)

If it is desired to overcome these limitations and if certain concessions with regard to access time are acceptable, the magnetic heads are designed to move radially and thus to serve more than one track.

Using in accurate mechanical positioning equipment, the group of heads is set to any one of many tracks (up to one thousand). After the head has been set and has come to rest after a few tens of milliseconds, data can be transferred to or from the track. In this manner, only a few magnetic heads — often only one — are required for each surface of a magnetic disk.

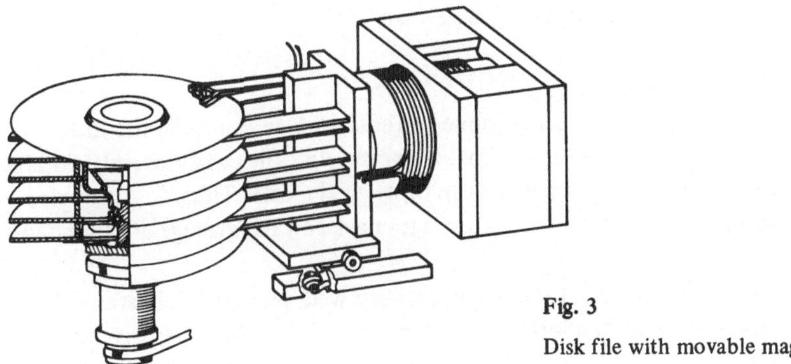

Fig. 3

Disk file with movable magnetic heads.

1.2.3. Disk Files with Interchangeable Disks

Already in the early days of disk file history, it was recognized that an additional increase in the efficiency could be achieved by exchanging the storage medium. The quantity of data processed per disk drive could be multiplied in this manner. A ratio of 2–10 disk packs per drive has become common practice. The computer center operators could easily exchange the disk pack using very precise quick-release fasteners. These disk files became more and more popular since their introduction in 1963 (IBM-1311) so that, beginning with capacities of a few megabytes, they dominated the market after a few years. Today at 300 MB, a limit may have been reached. Fig. 4 shows the extremely steep rise in disk drive capacities of roughly a factor of 2 every 2.5 years. The high capacity at favorable cost allows the specific price to drop to 0.002 ¢/bit.

Recently fixed disk files have started to compete with the exchangeable disk files again.

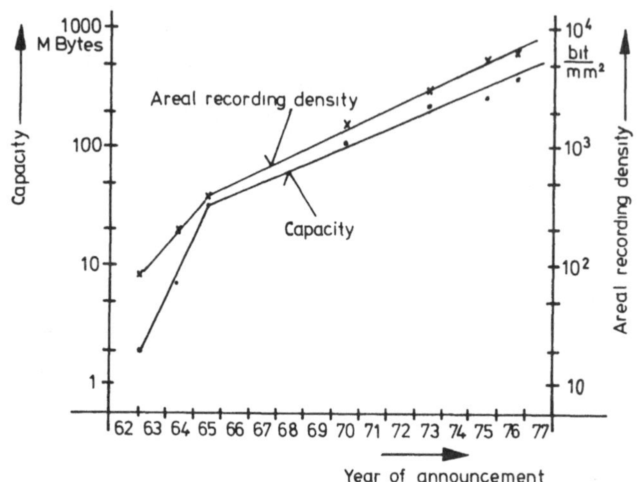

Fig. 4

Capacity per disk file drive.

There are two reasons for this:

- Changing the disk is only practical if none of the data files stored on the disk pack are used for a longer period of time. However, disk files with several 100 MB store so many data files that this is seldom or never the case. Thus, for example, with a 200 MB capacity per pack only 1.5 data packs on the average are supplied with each drive.

- This trend satisfies the needs of the engineers very well. Namely, if a data pack is brought from one drive to another, the magnetic heads at the new drive must be exactly adjusted to the data tracks which have been written in the previous device. Constant technical progress made it possible to keep pace with the tolerances which were becoming smaller and smaller with the increased track density. In this respect, there is, however, a certain limit if costs cannot be increased. In particular, improper operator handling plays an important part.

If the technical advantages provided by a non-interchangeable stack are used to further increase the recording density, disk files with total capacities up to 500 MB are obtained according to the current state of the art. In this manner, the specific price drops further to approx. 0.001 ¢/bit.

1.2.4. Data Files with Fixed and Movable Magnetic Heads

The desire for a combination of high capacity at low cost with at least partially improved access times has led to disk files which, in addition to the customary movable magnetic heads, also have a row of fixed magnetic heads. The capacity of this so-called fixed head zone of roughly 0.5 to 1.5 MB/s is less than 1 % of the total capacity. If data with especially high access frequency, e.g. certain operating system parts or index tables, are filed in the fixed head zone, an improvement in the total

36

throughput is achieved. Whether the success obtained is worth the not insignificant
additional cost is debatable.

2. Disk File Technology

As in many technologies, technological progress has concentrated on a few main
problems.

- Accurate and rapid positioning of the magnetic heads by means of an access
  mechanism.
- Construction of magnetic heads for high recording densities.
- Magnetic disks for high recording densities.
- Writing and reading of the information.

2.1. Positioning

The positioning unit has — as already mentioned — the task of locating the magnetic
heads exactly on the desired data track in the shortest possible time. A positioning
unit consists of a drive — usually a linear motor —, displacement measuring equipment for pinpointing the position of the track, and control electronics for the motor.

2.1.1. Positioning Drive

A positioning motor must satisfy a variety of requirements. It must be able to rapidly
accelerate and brake (up to 20 g) masses of the order of 1 kg. These operations should
be controllable virtually without delay. Volume, weight and power consumption are
subject to certain limitations. In the past, a large number of different designs have
been used, especially hydraulic and electrodynamic motors. In the past 5 years, the
voice coil actuator has gained wide acceptance (Fig. 5). This development was assisted
by the progress made in the area of power semiconductors since the high current and
voltages necessary for controlling the motors can now be generated reliably and at
low cost. In addition, there is now the possibility of low-inertia control and freedom
from wear.

The operation of such a voice coil actuator is in principle — as the name implies —
identical to that of the electrodynamic loudspeaker. A circular — on occasion also
rectangular — coil enters the circular gap of a powerful permanent magnet system.
The current conducting coil thus exerts the necessary acceleration and braking
forces on the carriage to which the magnetic heads are fastened. It is important to
keep the force for a given current constant independent of the coil position over a
few centimeters. This means that in addition to the current, also the magnetic flux
which permeates the coil must be constant. This can be achieved using two methods.

- As shown in Fig. 5 the coil is made so long that during motion it never leaves the
  air gap.
- Alternately, the air gap of the magnet can be constructed long enough so that a
  relatively short voice coil always moves inside the gap.

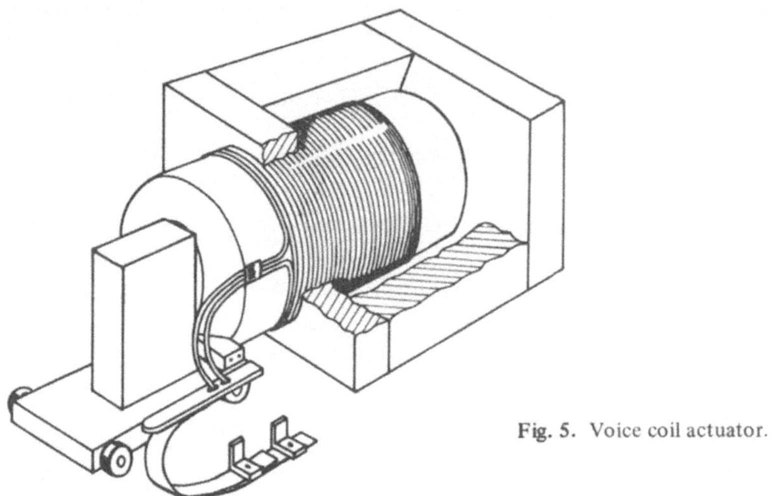

In spite of the large voice coil — it is part of the mass to be moved — and the unfavorable leakage flux relationship between the coil and the magnet the first method is used preferably. The reason for this is the relatively lower forces which can be achieved using the short voice coil. Namely, the entire magnetic flux of the air gap must permeate the central core which, due to its unavoidable saturation, limits the flux or the induction in the gap.

Surface ratios of the core to the gap of only $1:10$ to $1:5$ can be achieved. If a saturation induction of 2 Tesla is assumed for the core, hardly more than 0.4 Tesla of air gap induction can be achieved which, for example, in a 3 cm long coil with 60 turns and a diameter of 80 mm leads to a force constant of only 10 N/A. The force constant of a long voice coil with comparable dimensions and expenditure on magnetic material is greater by roughly the factor of 2.

2.1.2. Displacement Measuring Equipment

In order to be able to position successfully, a powerful drive alone is not sufficient but also precise information concerning the position of the tracks crossed by the magnetic heads during positioning is required. For practical purposes, the magnetic heads themselves are used for such a measurement.

A special magnetization pattern — a so-called servo pattern — is written onto a surface of the disk pack. One of the magnetic heads when moving radially over the magnetic coating. receives signals which alternate with the tracks (see Fig. 6).

When writing the alternating track patterns, the negative magnetization crossovers of these patterns are always at the same position, the positive crossovers between the even and odd numbered tracks, however, are offset by 1/3 of a period. If the

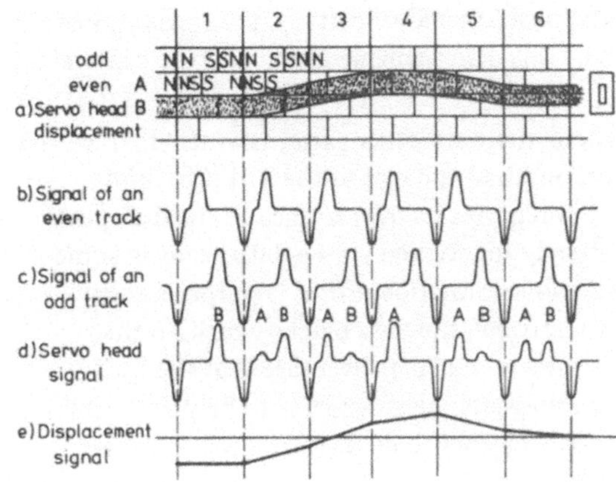

Fig. 6. Servo pattern.

magnetic head is reading an even numbered track, it provides signals as shown in b). In the case of odd numbered tracks, the pattern is as in c). Let us follow a servo-magnetic head which stays in the center between both track patterns with small fluctuations. In domain 1, it receives the signal from an odd numbered track. A pattern with an identical negative and positive (B) pulse is the result. If the head shifts upward, pulse B becomes smaller and pulse A appears, the latter becoming increasingly larger (domains 2 and 3) until pulse B disappears and A has achieved its maximum value (domain 4). If the head moves back to the center of the two tracks (domain 6), both pulses A and B are identical and are half the size of the unchanged negative synchronizing pulse. The name „Tribit Servo Pattern" (IBM 3340) is derived from these three pulses. After amplification and band limiting, these signals are fed to electronic evaluation equipment. This equipment forms the difference between A and B, using the synchronizing pulse to differentiate in time between A and B. The result in line e reproduces the motion of the magnetic head. If, for example, the carriage respectively the magnetic heads travel across a series of tracks, a voltage curve is obtained as in Fig. 7. This voltage approximates a

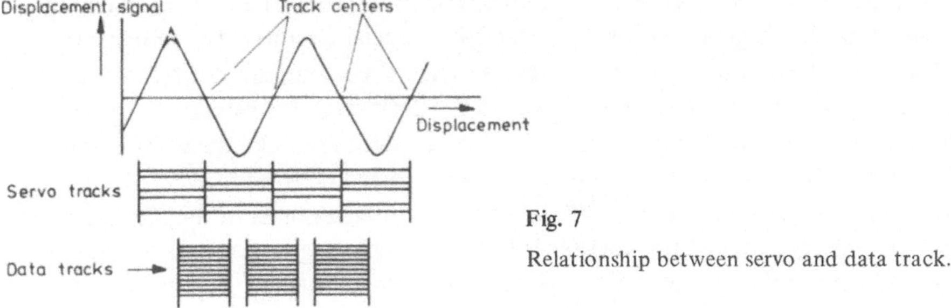

Fig. 7

Relationship between servo and data track.

triangle and provides information on the position and velocity of the carriage. For practical purposes, the zero crossovers of this displacement signal, and the centers of the data tracks, coincide.

In addition to the servo pattern shown here, there are other patterns which, by means of a more complicated set-up, avoid certain disadvantages of the Tribit pattern. While in most cases the servo information requires its own surface of the disk pack and its own servomagnetic head — as already mentioned —, the data heads in some disk files are also used for reading the servo information. For this purpose, short sections of servo information are placed between the data blocks which, in this case, are arranged in fixed sectors. This method has the advantage that the track-position information is read by the same magnetic head which is to be positioned. In principle, this results in the shortest conceivable chain of tolerances. However, general use is counteracted by two disadvantages:

- The position control information is only available at relatively seldom time intervals and for a short time period. This prevents the heads from being adjusted rapidly.
- The servo pattern which makes up only a few per cent of the track circumference is correspondingly sensitive to interference and distortion which again increases the tolerances.

2.1.3. Control Electronics (Fig. 8)

The task of moving a magnetic head from one track to another as rapidly and accurately as possible is already known to us. From the starting track, acceleration is provided with the full force which the motor can provide until the carriage has reached the maximum permissible velocity. It travels at this velocity in the direction of the desired track. At the proper time, before reaching the desired track, the carriage is braked with almost full force until the magnetic head has reached the desired track and is held there accurately. Just, how does this happen?

The present track address is compared to the wanted track address in a small arithmetic unit and the difference is determined in terms of distance and direction. The information about the required motion is now known exactly and is stored in the so-called difference register. The motor receives full power and accelerates the carriage with the magnetic heads. By means of a special circuitry, the velocity is continuously derived from the servo signals. When the maximum wanted speed is achieved — as determined by comparison of the desired/actual velocity — the power is reduced and the carriage rapidly approaches the desired track. Meanwhile, the difference register counts down with each track crossed (zero crossovers of the displacement signal) so that at any time its content corresponds to the displacement still to go. The content of this register is fed to a function generator via a D/A converter: above a certain input value, its output voltage is constant, below this value, it follows a parabolic function. A velocity curve which is parabolic over the displace-

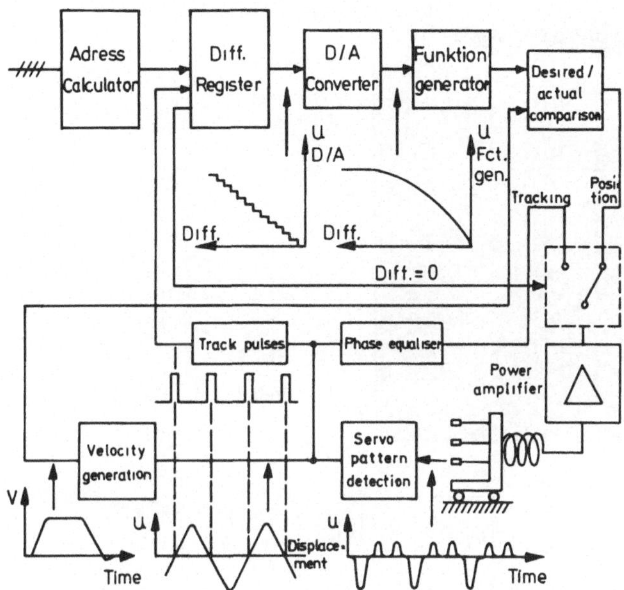

Fig. 8. Control electronics.

ment, indicates a constant deceleration force, i.e. the ideal velocity curve for braking as rapidly as possible at a specified maximum force. When the carriage reaches the transition from the straight to parabolic velocity specification, i.e. 128 tracks (SIEMENS 3470) or approx. 5 mm before the target track, the amplifier and thus the voice coil are regulated via the desired/actual value comparison so that the carriage follows the desired curve and almost comes to rest directly in front of the target track. At the same time, the difference register has counted to zero which triggers the changeover from the seek control to the tracking control. The displacement signal is now used directly for controlling purposes. In a phase equalizer, the phase-to-frequency response is set to result in an optimum transient behavior. The velocity curve of a positioning operation over 300 tracks is shown in the oscillogram below (Fig. 9). The lower, inside curve shows the velocity during positioning over only 110 tracks. Deceleration starts even before the maximum velocity is reached. The top curve shows the displacement signal as a function of time. Note the short positioning and control response times.

In addition to a favorable design of the components just described, the quality and accuracy of positioning are highly dependent on the design of the mechanical parts used. The main considerations here are .

- Lowest possible weight and highest rigidity of carriage, voice coil and magnetic heads.

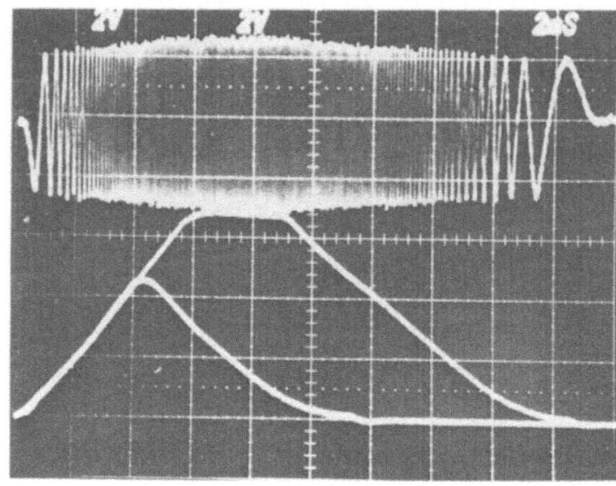

Fig. 9

Velocity oscillogram

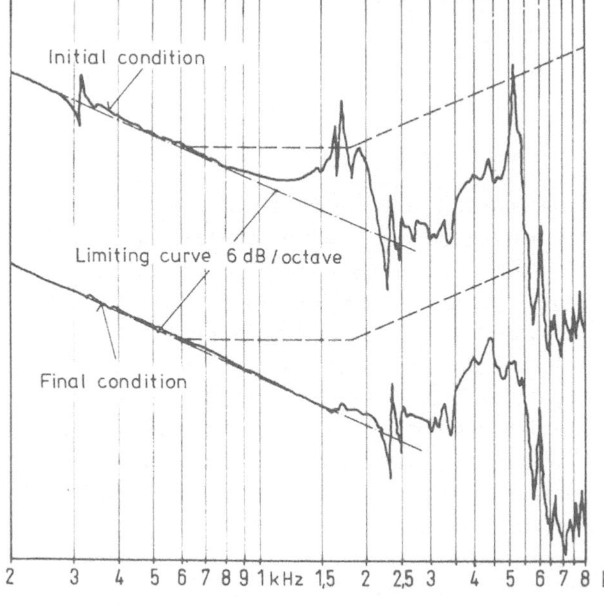

Fig. 10

Bode plot.

- The center of the motor force should coincide with the axis of inertia of the carriage in the direction of motion.
- Parts capable of vibration should either not be excited or their resonant frequencies should be so high that they do not cause interference.

The Bode plot of the open control loop (Fig. 10) gives most valuable information on the efficiency of a design.

42

The voice coil is energized by a sinusoidal constant current with sweep frequency
and the velocity of the servo head is measured as a function of the frequency. Even
if the moving mechanism was designed with care and experience, the first measurement is usually disappointing (top curve). Using vibration pick-ups, the various
sources of resonance are tracked down in months of painstaking work, damped,
relocated or the excitation is eliminated until a sufficiently smooth Bode plot is
obtained. It can be seen in the lower curve that the desired gain crossover frequency,
i.e. the frequency at which the closed loop gain is unity, in this example 600 Hz.
This means that, in this example an eccentricity of the track at a disk rotational
frequency of 50 Hz is smoothed or reduced roughly by the factor 600 : 50 = 12.
In this example, the shiffers of the carriage against a static deflection is 4 N/μm.

2.2. Magnetic Heads

The magnetic heads predominantly determine the longitudinal and transverse recording densities and thus the file capacity per unit area. While the first disk files of
20 years ago had a recording density of 4 bits/mm^2, 5000 bits/mm^2 are the current
state of the art with a longitudinal recording density of 240 bits/mm (6000 bpi) and
a transverse recording density of almost 25 tracks/mm (600 tpi). The limits of this
development cannot yet be foreseen.

Considering that the dimension of the gap of the magnetic head in the recording
direction — the gap length — is roughly 1/4 of the bit interval, gap lengths of almost
1 μm are required for the mentioned recording densities. The dimension of the gap
perpendicular to the direction of recording — the gap width — depends on the track
pitch specified by the positioner and is roughly 3/4 of the track center interval. This,
in our case, is roughly 30 μm. The spacing of the magnetic head gap from the recording layer is even smaller than the gap length; values of 0.5 μm are being reliably
achieved today.

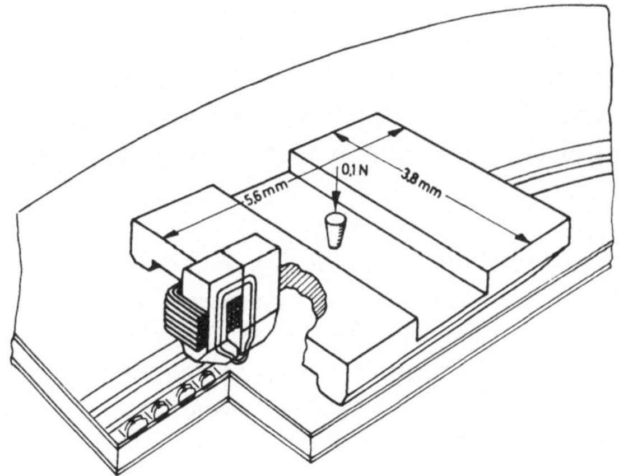

Fig. 11

Magnetic heads

The basic construction of a disk file magnetic head is shown in Fig. 11.
Essentially, it consists of two partial systems.

- Write/read magnetic system.
- Slider in which the magnetic system is installed so as to be flush with the sliding surface.

2.2.1. Write/Read Magnetic System

The magnetic system consists of a coil and a small ferrite core. In order to obtain the nonporosity and strength important for machining and operation, these ferrites are sintered at a pressure of 500 bar and at a temperature of 1100 °C. The material, which is very expensive after this procedure, receives its final shape by means of a series of grinding and polishing operations. The gap length is calibrated by means of the vacuum deposition of Cr-SiO. Both core legs are joined together at a temperature of 1200 °C by means of glass solder. Machining is highly demanding.

The hard, brittle material which is prone to chipping can only be machined using diamond tools of the finest grain — regardless of whether grinding or polishing is being performed. In addition to the mechanical values, the magnetic values are of great importance also. For reading, the magnetic conductance of the ferrite circuit should be larger than the conductance of the air gap so that the largest part of the induced magnetic flux permeates the coil. When writing, there is the danger that the pole-tips forming the gap saturate, thus, as high a saturation induction as possible is necessary. Mechanical stresses which can occur during machining and inserting of the core into the slider should only impair these magnetic values to an insignificant degree.

The difficulties of machining the brittle ferrite of the magnetic cores naturally increase considerably with higher recording densities and the smaller dimensions connected with these. For this reason, efforts are being made worldwide to produce so-called "integrated magnetic heads". Vacuum deposited or sputtered Permalloy layers form the magnetic circuit. The coil is made of copper, silver or gold layers which are insulated from one another by means of SiO_2. The ever decreasing dimensions of the magnetic circuits of disk file magnetic heads very much meet the requirements of these future structures, which are distantly related to semiconductor technology.

2.2.2. Slider

The magnetic head must, under no circumstances, touch the disk due to the high disk velocities as high as 50 m/s. On the other hand, a maximum spacing of less than 1 micrometer is indispensable for operation. This requirement is met by means of a slider into which the magnetic system is installed. The slider, which has gliding shoes in the form of a sled on the side nearest the disk, floats on the air carried along by the disk. If the slider is pressed against the disk with a defined force (e.g. 0.1 N), a stable dynamic equilibrium is established. The magnetic head must generate

relatively large restoring forces to oppose all forces which attempt to bring the head
out of its position. In this manner, positional deviations are very small. The flying
height of about 0.5 micrometer of the trailing edge of the slider which is closest to
the magnetic medium, should be accurately maintained to roughly ± 10 %; to do
this, a number of boundary conditions are to be met.

- A geometrical accuracy of roughly 100 nm of the sliding surfaces and of the
  magnetic core which is lapped so as to be flush with these surfaces.
- The magnetic disk should simulate a plane to such a degree that the vertical
  acceleration due to the rotating disk is limited to approx. 5 g.
- The surface smoothness of the sliding surface and magnetic disk must correspond
  to the best optical quality – average roughness: approx. 20 nm.
- Such minute dimensions require absolutely that all dust and other dirt be eliminated
  from this air bearing. To do so, the immediate vicinity of the disks must be supplied
  with pure air by means of so-called "absolute" filters.

After the slider and the magnetic core have been assembled and subjected to a
common lapping operation for the finish of the sliding surface, the write/read coil
is wound onto the free leg of the core. The slider is mounted onto a support arm
with pressure and gimbal springs for fixing the position of the magnetic head.

2.3. Magnetic Disks

The ferromagnetic material which carriers the information to be stored is applied in
a thin layer on both sides of circular aluminum disks which are machined with high
accuracy. These disks are fastened onto a hub. The spacing between the disks is
chosen so that the magnetic heads can move uninhibited into these spacings. A
clamping mechanism in the hub rigidly attaches the exchangeable disk pack to the
spindle. Mechanical or magnetic quickrelease fasteners provide a connection of the
shaft to the stack hub which is secure against rotation. In the following, medium
and disk will be discussed in more detail.

Ferromagnetic Material

Just as for magnetic tapes, iron oxide Fe_2O_3 embedded in organic binders is used.
The binders or lacquers, in addition to their good impact and abrasion resistance,
must exhibit outstanding surface smoothness. The lacquer-iron oxide dispersion
is applied to the carrier disks. By means of special methods (e.g. centrifuging), a
uniformly thin layer is produced (layer thickness, e.g. for a recording density of
240 bit/mm: 1.2 μm). In order to insure the troublefree sliding of the reading head
at headlayer spacing of down to 0.5 μm, the surface of the layer is smoothed to an
average surface roughness of about 20 nm by means of lapping and polishing operations. A polymeric sliding surface a few molecules thick prevents damage to the
sliding surfaces of the magnetic heads when they take-off or land on them when
the unit is turned on or off. Of the magnetic properties of the layer, predominantly

the coercivity and the remanant induction are important. The coercivity should be as large as possible in order to reduce the self-demagnetization. However, the upper limit is set by the field strength to be provided by the magnetic head to reverse the magnetic state. Values between 20 kA/m and 30 kA/m are customary. The file layer has a remanance flux density of the order of 0.1 T.

Great efforts have been under way for years to replace the oxide layers with metallic layers (e.g. nickel/cobalt) in order to achieve higher resolution or bit densities. Even at layer thicknesses of roughly 0.1 μm, these materials provide sufficient reading voltage amplitudes due to their high remanant flux densities of up to 1 T. The higher (with respect to oxide layers) resolution at a given magnetic head gap and magnetic head layer spacing is caused by the low layer thickness (low self-demagnetization) and the good rectangular shape of the hysteresis loop. Poor homogeneity of the thin file layer and the expensive manufacturing process have however prevented wide use up to now.

Carrier Disk (substrate)

These disks have been manufactured exclusively from aluminum alloys to date. In order not to affect the smoothness and uniformity of the magnetic layer, the surface must exhibit a minimum peak-to-valley height and be completely free of scratches. In order to limit axial accelerations of the magnetic head, it is to be ensured by means of appropriate machining and aging methods that the disk surfaces simulate a plane to the desired degree for a sufficiently long period. In order to keep radial deviation of the magnetic head from the written track as a function of temperature low, the thermal expansion coefficient of the disks must have a defined value matched to the drives (e.g. $24 \cdot 10^{-6}$/K).

2.4. Writing and Reading the Data (Fig. 12)

The writing and reading of data are part of the essential operations of a disk file system. The write/read electronics is used for this. It is divided into a clock channel, a writing channel and a reading channel.

The clock channel is used to generate control clock pulses which are derived from the servo signals. In this manner, the same number (e.g. 10080) of clock pulses is always generated per revolution even if the rotational speed is subject to certain fluctuations (± 2 %). The synchronizing pulses of the servo signal are used for generating the clock. They synchronize an oscillator which functions according to the principle of the phase locked loop. It generates various clock signals which are predominantly used in the unit. A clock signal with a repetition frequency of, for example, 6.45 MHz is transmitted to the control unit and synchronizes the writing clock generator there which also functions according to the principle of the phase locked loop. This generator produces the symmetrical writing clock at twice the repetition frequency.

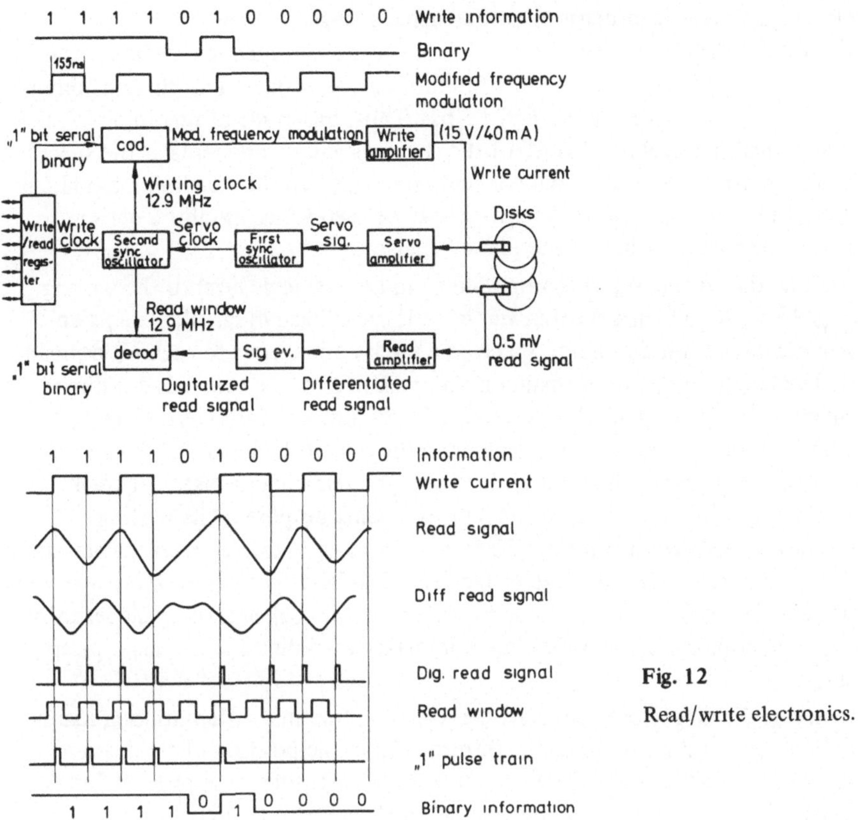

Fig. 12

Read/write electronics.

The clock channel meets the following requirements:

- The synchronization range is large. Reliable synchronization occurs up to frequency differences of $\pm 20\,\%$ and phase differences of $\pm 180°$. The guide behavior in the range of mechanical vibrations of the disks and magnetic heads ($< 1000\,$Hz) is good. Phase deviations are completely eliminated. Stationary or quasi-stationary frequency deviations of $\pm 10\,\%$ result in phase deviations of less than ± 3 ns. The inherent jitter of consecutive clock signals is less than ± 2 ns.

In the writing channel, the data available in binary form are initially coded so that they can be written. Coding in modified frequency recording is especially practical. In the case of this type of recording, a signal change (data signal change) occurs, in the case of each "1" in the center of the bit domain. If zeros occur, a signal change (clock signal change) occurs in each case at the border between two zeros. A maximum of one signal change is obtained per bit domain; continuous ones or zeros do not differ by their frequency but rather only by their phase position. In the event of a series of different information, various signal change intervals are obtained. A typical value for the duration of one bit domain is 155 ns which results in a signal frequency of 3.22 MHz in the case of continuous zeros or ones. The phase difference is, however, only 1/4 of the period (= 77.5 ns). Thus, this mode of recording requires a relatively small physical bandwidth of the channels and components at the specified bit domain duration. However, high demands are placed on the freedom from phase distortion. In the future, coding systems should be used which exhibit a better compromise between frequency and phase behavior.

After coding, the writing signal is amplified from the low logic level to the writing level (e.g. 15 V, 40 mA) and written via the write/read head in circular tracks on the magnetic disk. A bit domain in space on a track corresponds to each bit domain in time. The length of one bit domain on the track nearest the center is 4.3 mm in the tangential direction. A total of approx. 160 000 bits or 20 000 bytes can be accommodated on one track. Depending upon the size of the block, 80 % to 95 % of this physical capacity is available to the user. The remainder is used for track and block recognition, synchronization and addressing purposes. The writing currents have a rise time of typically 50 ns and fluctuate in reference to the actuation signal by a maximum of ± 2 ns. Due to the finite bandwidth of the head-layer system, the change in flux exhibits a smoother curve. Various flux change intervals result in displacements in such a manner that larger intervals are reduced and smaller intervals enlarged.

When reading, the magnetic head scans the magnetic flux in a differentiating manner. The reading signal, which contains the information in the position of the maxima and minima, is available at the head output with an amplitude of approx. 0.5 mV. This signal is amplified in the reading channel, filtered and regulated to a constant amplitude. Then, it is differentiated thus converting the extrema which carry the information into zero crossovers. The zero crossovers are scanned by means of comparators and generate one rectangular read pulse of 40 ns duration per crossover. The read pulse train contains one pulses as well as zero pulses. In order to separate them, a second synchronizable oscillator is used. It is synchronized during the reading process by the reading pulses and generates the data window signal. The data windows are periodic rectangular pulses of one half the bit time in duration (77.5 ns) which represents the period where the one pulses are expected. Pulses which occur in the window time are recognized as ones and form the one pulse train. This pulse train is converted in a simple decoding stage into binary form thus ending the tasks of the reading channel.

An essential goal of disk file development is as high a file density as possible. An increase in the file density is limited by the finite bandwidth of the head-layer system and by the lack of homogeneity in the magnetic layer. The finite bandwidth results in a deformation of the reading signals such that various reading pulses are shifted from the center to the border of the reading window. Due to the noise which

48

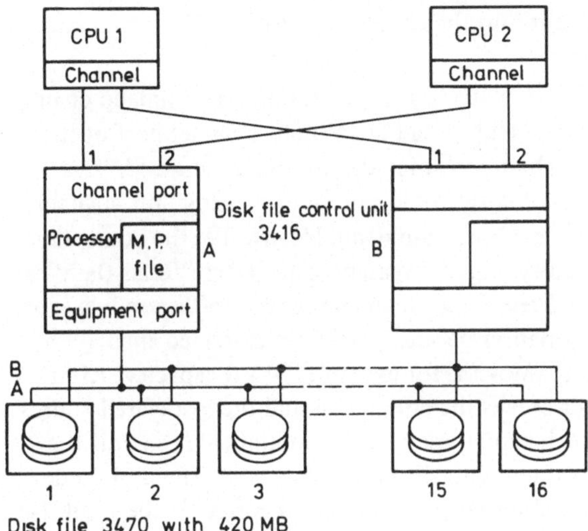

Fig. 13. Complete disk file subsystem with to controller port and two channel port. Total kapacity: 6.7 GB.

is also present, these pulses may be shifted out of the window and lost. This problem is counteracted in that the writing signal change is shifted in the opposite direction in each case. Singular deformations of individual signal points are caused by the lack of homogeneity in the magnetic layer. These also cause the associated pulses to drop out of the window. Larger spots of heterogeneity (lack of homogeneity) which cause errors during each read/write operation are eliminated in that the entire track is flagged to be inoperable or no data are placed in the points in question. However, most of these are so small that they only cause sporadic errors. These errors are eliminated by means of error correction. Each data block generates error correction bytes during writing which are written at the end of the block. Errors up to 11 bits in length can be detected and corrected during reading using these bytes. As additional measures, repeats in reading with and without radial offset of the reading head are provided.

3. Connecting Disk Files to Central Processing Units

Generally, disk files are not directly connected to the input/output port or the channel of a central processing unit. As shown in the illustration (Fig. 13), a number of devices (e.g. up to 16) are connected to a disk file control unit.

On the other side, the control unit is connected to the channel of the central processing unit. There are data processing systems with a so-called native attachment or with an integrated file port. Even in this case, a disk file control unit is present in a more or less hidden form; it is built into the central processing unit. What tasks does the control unit perform?

The software or operating system formulates a disk file call into a command chain, e.g. in a simple case "Seek", "Search" and "Read Data". The channel port of the control unit receives the command chain including the accompanying addresses, tests the completeness of all information from the central processing unit channel and returns one acknowledgement signal per command. Meanwhile, the controller checks the command chain for validity, e.g. if "Search" came after "Read Data" or if "Search" was missing, it would reject the chain and send a corresponding error message to the channel. The information necessary for this is loaded into a microprogram memory, usually a RAM with, for example, 24 kB capacity. After these formal checks, the controller breaks the commands and the associated address information down into coding which can be used by the equipment, controls the access, and monitors execution together with the equipment port. The desired device is selected by the equipment port and tested as to whether it is free. If the result is positive, the new track address is transmitted. After the position is successfully reached by the device, it sends back a signal to the control unit. This unit now transfers the number of the magnetic head and, immediately following this, the signal "Read". Read data are now transferred to the control unit. Depending upon the block numbers transferred with the command "Search", the track is searched until the start of the desired block is found. When this is done, the central processing unit is in turn notified of the data transmission which is about to occur. Byte for byte, the data is now transferred to the central processing unit during reading or to the control unit during writing. After the transmission is completed, the control unit provides the central processing unit or the operating system with status information. If, for example, by means of a defect in the magnetic layer a few bits were distorted during transmission, this situation is noted here. Then, correction information is transmitted to the central processing unit. The data which are already written into the main memory are corrected at the point specified by the control unit.

Up to now, the simplest case of a disk file subsystem has been described. The disk file drives are connected to the central processing unit via one control unit. For high requirements of data throughput and availability, the disk file drives can be connected via a second equipment interface — two-controller port — to another control unit. In turn, this uses an additional channel connection to the central processing unit. If the central processing unit has sufficient capacity, parallel and overlapping data transfers can take place from and to the equipment.

An especially interesting and advantageous operation results in the case of systems using two central processing units. The two control units are, in this case, connected to the channels of both central processing units via the so-called two channel port. Each central processing unit has access to a disk file data bank of max. 6.7 GB via

one or the other control unit. Queue problems are, to a large degree, avoided because
the free control unit in each case responds. Even in the case of the failure of one
control unit, operation can continue, albeit with a lower throughput.

4. Outlook

Of the many new competing storage principles which often enter with the claim
of being the one to put an end to the good old mechanical disk file in the near
future, only the rapidly developing semiconductor storage units have survived. They
are about to replace fixed head disk files. The considerable cost advantage which
disk files with movable magnetic heads have over semiconductor storage units (at
present, a factor of 100) will decrease with time since the development to higher
storage densities runs a somewhat more conservative course with disk files than is
the case with semiconductor storage units. However, one to two decades will pass
before a margin may be achieved by which the use of disk files nor longer appears
economical. Furthermore, the fact that the stored data are nonvolatile is a substantial feature of secondary storage units such as disk files. The fact that the data
in the case of of semiconductor primary storage units are volatile is only tolerated so
generously because, if required, the lost data can be reloaded from the disk files.

References

[1] *K. E Haughton*, An Overview of Disk Storage Systems. Proc. of the IEEE Vol. 63 No. 8,
     pp. 1148–1152.
[2] *H. Kaufmann*, Datenspeicher – Oldenbourg Verlag.
[3] *W. Berghof, H. Raith*, Neuere Ergebnisse der Magnetkopftechnologie. Siemens Forsch.-
     und Entwickl. Ber. Bd. 4 (1975), No. 5, pp. 301–304.
[4] *J. S. Heath*, Design of a Swinging Arm Actuator for a Disk File. IBM Journal of Res. a.
     Develop. July 1976, pp. 389–397.

Electromagnetic Mass Storages – Normal Tape Devices

Klaus Winkler

Siemens AG, Munich, Germany

1. Reel Devices for Half Inch Tape

Even though the magnetic tape faces strong competition from magnetic disks, it will survive for a long time as a data medium for computer files.

In many applications requiring short access times, e. g. for system and user program residency or for random access data bases, magnetic disk storage has taken the place of the magnetic tape storage. However, the magnetic tape is still the dominating technology for the storage of large data volumes in data bases and mass files, and for the sequential processing of these large data volumes, because of its unsurpassed low price and low physical volume compared to the stored data volume. In addition, standardization efforts have made tapes to become a compatible medium for data interchangeability. Because it is compact and easy to ship, it is better suited to data interchange than any other medium.

1.1. Recording Methods

In the early stages of data processing, the magnetic drum was the dominating magnetic storage device, which was mainly used as peripheral storage, but also as the main memory of the CPU. However, the first magnetic tape devices for half-inch tape were soon introduced and used as external storages, for system residence, and for filing and interchanging data. Various recording formats, codes and densities were used. As a result of standardization, some formats survived and met with commercial success. Today, there are three major recording formats associated with three different recording densities, if the old 7-track format is disregarded.

Today all common formats use 9 tracks in accordance with the 8 bit character frame and its additional check bit. Blocking, i.e. the subdivision of the data to be processed in individual blocks separated by inter block gaps (Fig. 1), is used with all formats. The access to single bytes which would be preferable in theory, is prohibited by the start and stop times and paths imposed by tape motion.

The following two major arguments can be raised against the use data blocks exceeding a certain maximum length:

- The size of the input/output areas normally provided in main memory is limited; also, the capacity of a 730 m tape would by far exceed the capacity of currently used main memories if the data were transferred in one continuous block. This is the reason why maximum block lenghts of e.g. 2048 characters are recommended in international standards.

- The likelihood of a write error due to a defect within a block increases with the block length. When such an error occurs, the whole block is backspaced and written again, if required, after erasing. If an attempt were made in an extreme case to read a 720 m long block, an enormous amount of computer time would be required and the likelihood of success would be very small.

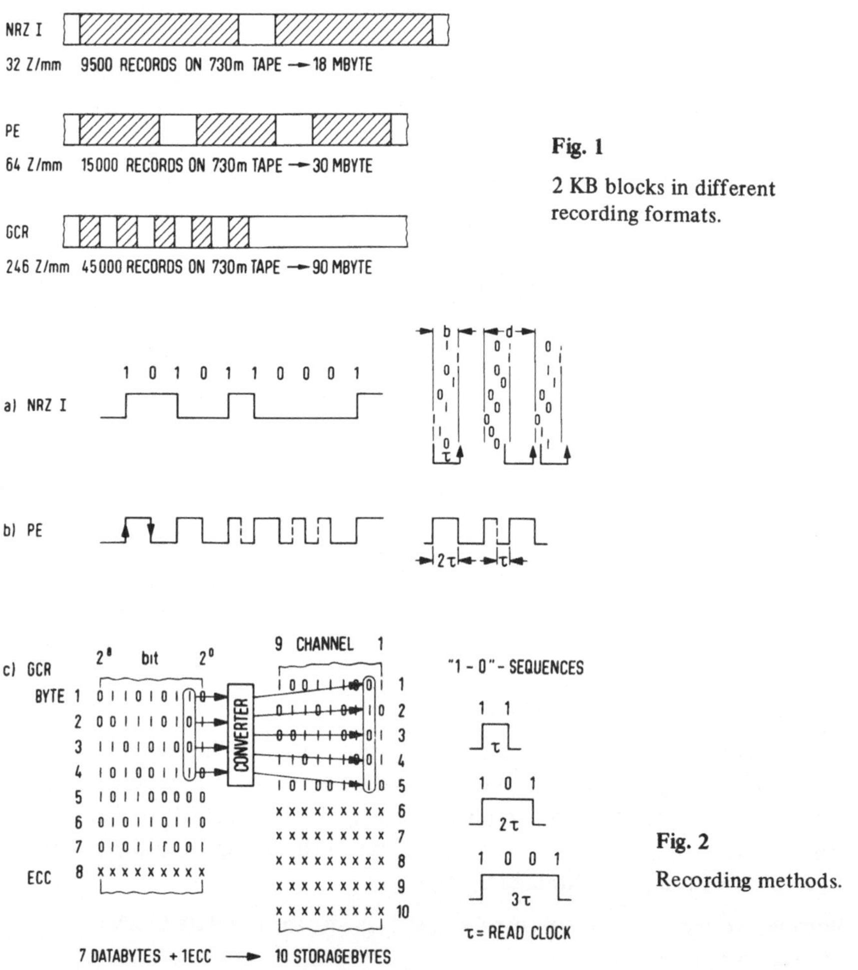

Fig. 1

2 KB blocks in different recording formats.

Fig. 2

Recording methods.

For better understanding and for the sake of completeness, the three currently used recording formats are briefly described and their respective advantages and disadvantages are discussed.

If one remembers the initial difficulties encountered in achieving the required resolution of heads and tapes, it is understandable that NRZI (non return to zero, improved) became the first recording format. It is characterized by the fact that a binary "1" is represented by a flux reversal, a binary "0" by no flux change during the respective bit time. (Fig. 2a). The advantage of this method is the relatively low flux reversal density which will, at the utmost, be equal to the bit density. The disadvantage is that zeros ("0") do not produce read signals. One solution to this problem is a separate timing track. Another solution is to derive a timing pulse train from the parallel data tracks e.g. according to the first bit method for data retrieval.

Consequently, the maximum permitted bit shift in each track due to mechanical, magnetic or electrical skew and peak-shift phenomena is limited to less than half the nominal byte width. This format is used today with a recording density of 32 characters per mm (800 bpi). At higher recording densities, the requirements on the tape drives and the data channels including the heads would become prohibitive due to peak-shift effects, particularly if unrestricted interchangeability of the magnetic tapes is desired.

For the higher density of 64 characters per mm, another method called phase encoding (PE) is used. In this method, a binary "1" is represented by a positive flux reversal and a binary "0" by a negative flux reversal, a redundant additional flux reversal being inserted between two identical bits (Fig. 2b). Data retrieval consists in separating the information from the additional flux reversals and in determining the polarity of the information flux reversals. The disadvantage of a higher flux reversal density as compared to the NRZI method (up to twice the bit density) is more than compensated by the advantage that each track is now self clocking. This advantage is used in two ways. First, the relatively slow speed variations of the tape drive can be compensated by synchronizing a phase-locked oscillator to the data frequency of each track. These oscillators control the separation of the information from the additional flux reversals. Secondly, the possibility provided by the self clocking capability to assemble the bits of a chracter in a deskewing buffer is even more important, because the character width may fluctuate over as many nominal character spaces as the buffer has byte locations, e.g. over 4 locations in practice. The advantages for error recovery will be described later.

In both methods, NRZI and PE, the blocks are separated by interblock gaps which are typically 15 mm in length. Fig. 1 shows that, for a given block length, the block/ interblock gap ratio becomes worse as the recording density increases. It is, therefore, desirable to reduce the inter-block gap length or to increase the data block length, when the recording density is increased.

When the next higher recording density was introduced, the inter-block gap was reduced to 7.5 mm. This density increase was possible by solving the associated
resolution problems by the group coded recording (GCR) method, combining the
advantages of the NRZI and PE recording methods. Here, for the first time, the more
or less one-to-one mapping of main memory data on magnetic tape was abandoned.
Instead, by appropriate coding (Fig. 2c), four input bytes are converted into five recording bytes in such a way that no more than two consecutive zeros are allowed in
each track. When such group-coded data is recorded using the NRZI method, self-
clocking for each track is obtained. The nominal recording density is 352 flux reversals per mm, which corresponds to an effective data recording density of 246 data
characters per mm when the redundancy resulting from the coding method and data
protection is subtracted (6250 bpi).

In order to facilitate the transition to a newly introduced recording method, magnetic
tape devices frequently offer two different recording densities (bimodal devices).
Most common today is PE, sometimes combined with NRZI and increasingly combined with the new GCR method.

A magnetic tape storage subsystem consists of a magnetic tape controller connecting
up to 16 magnetic tape devices, which can be accessed in turn. Subsystems comprising several magnetic tape controllers can also be designed.

The magnetic tape device consists of the mechanical tape drive with its servos and
the electronics required for operation, tape speed- and reel control and for the
head-oriented parts of the data paths.

1.2. Data Paths

The major functions of the write data paths, which are generally performed by the
magnetic tape controller, are the conversion of the data to the appropriate recording
format and the generation of the redundant error check characters.

The write amplifier is housed in the tape drive, often close to the head. It drives the
write current with the required rise-time and amplitude through the windings of the
write head, if applicable together with a pre-magnetization current.

As the data written on tape is very sensitive to remanent magnetic fields of the head,
the write head is frequently demagnetized, after a write routine has been completed,
by driving an alternative current with decreasing amplitude through its windings.

Various methods or combinations thereof (Fig. 3) are used to avoid information-
dependent peak shifts of the zero transitions of tape magnetization, i.e. of the read
signal peaks:

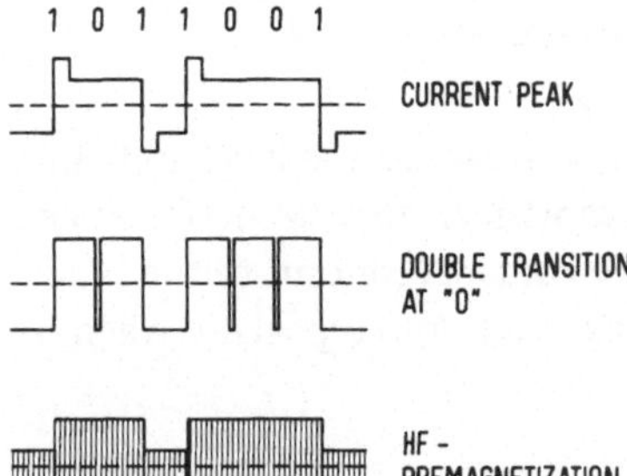

Fig. 3. Peakshift reduction.

- Every flux reversal is written with step pulse current; the initial current peak exceeds the saturation level whereas the following lower current of the pulse top stays below the saturation level.
  Optimization parameters are the current amplitudes and the peak duration.

- For a binary zero, i.e. no flux reversal, in the NRZI and GCR methods, a very short double flux reversal is written which is below the resolution limit of the head, i.e. does not produce a read signal, but reduces peak shifts in the written information.

  The optimization parameter is the time spacing of the double flux reversals.

- For linearization purposes, the data signal is superimposed on a high-frequency pre-magnetization current similar as in sound recording.

  Optimization parameters are the amplitudes of the data signal and of the pre-magnetization current.

  The objectives of the read data paths are the amplification and equalization of the read signals and data retrieval. Amplification and equalization are usually implemented in the magnetic tape device. With the GCR method, an ARA[1]) burst with 20 cm of tape motion provides automatic track-oriented amplitude adjustment by gain control. The timing (NRZI), deskewing (PE, GCR), decoding, error detection and error correction functions are generally performed in the magnetic tape controller.

  The read-write head concept has changed only little as time went by. However, magnetic head technology has been developed extraordinarily and the magnetic head still is the object of intensive research and theoretical considerations for improvement. Specific problems of high-performance heads are caused by:

- The high recording density (flux reversal spacing approx. 3 μm), the head gap geometry, and the magnetic quality of the core material (gap width, edge definition, permeability);

---

[1]) Automatic Read Amplification. See ISO/TC 97.

- The high frequencies (up to 1.25 Mb/s), the electrical quality of the core and the winding (laminations against eddy currents, winding capacitance);
- The high tape speed (approx. 5 meters per second) as it affects the head and tape lifetime (Wrap angle, improvement of the head face with an abrasion-resistant and tape-compatible coating) and the head — to — tape contact (contour of the head profile), which must be ensured under all operating conditions especially when high recording densities are used.

1.3. Error Detection Recovery and Correction

The most important characteristic of any recording method is its error detection capability which is provided by redundant check characters. In the simplest case, parity bits which provide (vertical) odd parity for each character and (longitudinal) even parity at the end of the block for each track are added.

Further check characters (CRC, ECC) also serve to correct errors.
Two error cases should be distinguished: read after write errors and read errors.

In magnetic tape devices used for data processing, the read heads are located directly behind the write heads in the direction of tape motion. During writing, the data is read back for checking purposes by the magnetic tape controller to ensure that only error-free blocks are written. When a "write" (read after write) error occurs, the error handling routine of the operating system corrects the block by backspacing the tape and attempting another write, if required after erasing to pass over possible tape faults. The severity of the checks is increased during the read after write checks.

When a read error is detected, the error recovery routines of the operating system will try repeated reading attempts, each of which is followed by a backspacing operation. There are good chances of success because reading errors are generally caused by abrasive particles caught between the head and the tape. The tape reversing operations often result in removal of the particle. Under certain restricting circumstances, it is also possible to correct data errors in the controller without the above error recovery routine. For NRZI recording, this is done by means of a cyclic redundancy check (CRC) character during reading. A necessary condition is that the error occurs in only one track. In this case, the faulty track is determined by calculating a CRC character from the data during reading and comparing it with the CRC character stored on the tape. Then, the correction can be simply made by inverting in that track, the bits of all characters with wrong parity.

In PE recording, the self-clocking characteristics allow track failures to be detected directly and to be corrected immediately during the first read pass, i.e. without backspacing, without operating system intervention, without loss of time, in short without the user noticing the operation. When the error burst is short (e.g. 6 characters or less), even the clock (phase-locked oscillator) can be phased in again, which means that serveral such errors are tolerable within one block also if they occur in different tracks but do not overlap.

In the GCR method, the data protection characters (Error correcting code, ECC; resync burst) allow even two-track errors to be corrected immediately so that similar or better error rates can be achieved compared to the other method despite the considerably higher flux reversal density.

1.4. Tape Drive

The objectives of the tape drive (Fig. 4) are to properly move the tape past the read-write head in both directions of tape motion according to the instructions, to unwind it from one reel and to wind it on the other. A good head-to-tape contact is particularly important — and difficult to achieve at high tape speeds. The tape is generally pressed against the head by the tape tension at an appropriate wrap angle. The tape path and the head profile are designed so that the tape is in contact with the head under all operating conditions. The tape is commonly driven by a single capstan with which the tape is in permanent positive contact by loop friction (e.g. 180° loop) possibly assisted by a vacuum applied through a perforated capstan surface. To support high tape speeds, particularly low-inertia dc motors with self-supporting rotor windings, hollow ceramic shafts, magnesium capstans and extremely lightweight optical tachometers were developed. The linear acceleration of the tape to reach a recording speed of 5 m/s (200 ips) within the length of the interblock gap of 7.5 mm, as in GCR, amounts to about 5000 m/s^2, which is 500 times the earth gravity

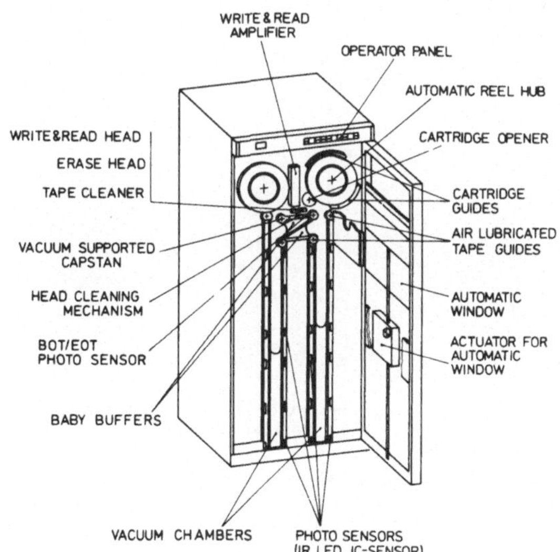

Fig. 4. Magnetic tape drive

acceleration. The dc motor speed is controlled by an electronic circuit which uses the tachometer output as the input signal. In fast tape drives for the GCR format, digital control circuits are preferred. The optical tachometer supplies digital timing pulses which serve to determine the tape speed and the distance (Fig. 5). At least for high-performance devices, the following consistent solution can then be implemented: The tape transport control operates in three different modes: acceleration is controlled in the start phase to avoid unnecessary oscillations, the speed is controlled in the motion phase, and the distance is controlled during the stop and hold phase.

The speed can be determined for example by comparing the timing pulses with a high-frequency pulse train and by applying digital control signals to the motor power amplifier via a digital to analog converter.

Distance control, which only involves tachometer pulse counting, ensures that the specified inter-block gaps will be generated during writing. Controlled stopping is particularly important so that any stopping overshoot is corrected and tape creeping particularily during extended breaks is avoided with certainty.

The two reels are each driven by servos which are controlled by a follow-up circuit. Vacuum chambers are used in high-speed devices to separate the high-intertia tape reels from the transport system and to generate the required tape tension, while in low-speed devices rocker arms are sometimes used. The amount of tape in the vacuum chambers is sensed for servo control. The designer's task is to find an acceptable

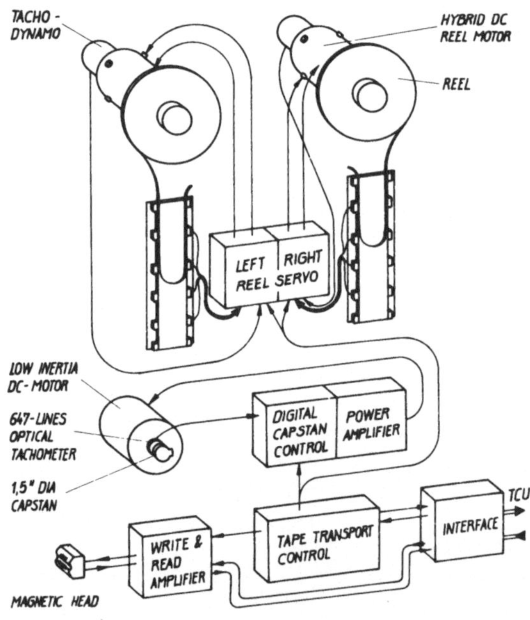

Fig. 5

Magnetic tape device electronics

compromise between the vacuum chamber length and the tape reel acceleration for a given tape speed and a known tape reel inertia. The maximum acceleration is limited by the stress at which tape "cinching" causes permanent tape damage. Tape cinching can occur in particular when the tape is subjected to unfavorable temperature cycling. It is caused by slipping of the inner layers of tape.against the outer layers of tape during acceleration due to inertia. At the interface, the tape layers are stretched and can be permanently damaged.

An optimum solution to this problem is provided by a proportional servo control because the vacuum chamber length can be used to its full length and excessive accelerations can be avoided. However, the obvious approach requires a proportional sensing of the amount of tape in the vacuum chambers, which involves considerable equipment complexity. In other approaches, the amount of tape in the vacuum chambers is sensed by discrete barriers, e.g. light barriers, and the proportional component is determined by tape driven tachometers or by tachometers mounted directly on the reel shafts. In this case, the servo is controlled by the commands applied to the tape drive (forward, stop, reserve motion), the tape speed or the reel speed, and the tape loop length. The vacuum chamber signals are used as correction signals to eliminate the unavoidable static and dynamic control errors.

2. Cartridge Devices

The tape cartridge with 3.81 mm wide magnetic tape has widely penetrated the consumer market, and is also finding increasing acceptance in the data processing market as handy medium for digital data storage. The cartridge used for data processing purposes is a hardened version (e.g. metal frame) of its otherwise consumer market equivalent.

The use of this cartridge is mainly limited to data collection. The data are transferred to half-inch tape or to a magnetic disk before processing. Lately cartridge is also being used as a large capacity storage for desk calculators.

Since the 3.81 mm tape — also its hardened version — presents some disadvantages, particularly concerning the lifetime of the tape, which requires improved tape drives and tape handling, efforts have been made to introduce other cartridge versions into the market. Possible improvements are high quality tape spools, precision guides and precision read/write heads. However, apart from the 6.3 mm tape cartridge which has also been standardized in the meantime, these efforts have been without success.

The following is a brief description of the two standardized cartridge types.

2.1. 3.81 mm Tape Cartridge (ECMA-34)

The outside appearance is known from the cassette recorders. The data cartridge is characterized by higher quality and better stability (Fig. 6).

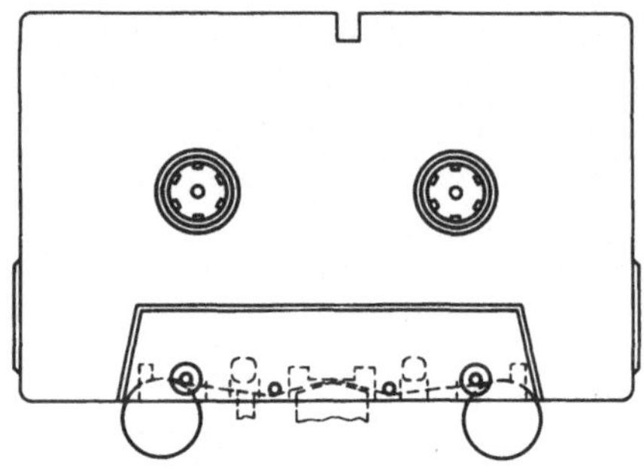

Fig. 6. 1/8″ Cartridge.

The recording format has been standardized as follows: The 3.81 mm wide, 86 m long and 19 μm thick tape is written on in two independent tracks. Unless otherwise specified, the same data is written in both tracks for data protection. The ECMA-6 code, a 7 bit code, is used; the 8th bit position is set to 0. The bits are written serially in ascending order of values at a density of 32 bits per mm using PE. The block length may range from 32 to 2065 bits and a block check character (BCC) corresponding to the longitudinal reduncancy check (LRC) of the 9 track format on half-inch tape is written at the end of each block.
8 bit preambles and postambles are used for synchronization of clock oscillators. The interblock gap has been standardized at 20.3 mm. The maximum storage capacity is thus 0.5 million characters with separate recording in two tracks.

2.2. 6.3 mm Cartridge (ECMA-46)

As can be seen from Fig. 7, the lyout of this cartridge is far more complicated than that of the 3.81 mm cartridge. In the 6.3 mm cartridge, major parts of the drive, — beginning of tape (BOT) and end of tape (EOT) sensing and the tape guides — are contained in the cartridge, so that the tape drives for these cartridges can be kept very simple. Whether this compensates for the additional cartridge cost depends on the number of cartridges used with each drive. An interesting feature of this cartridge is

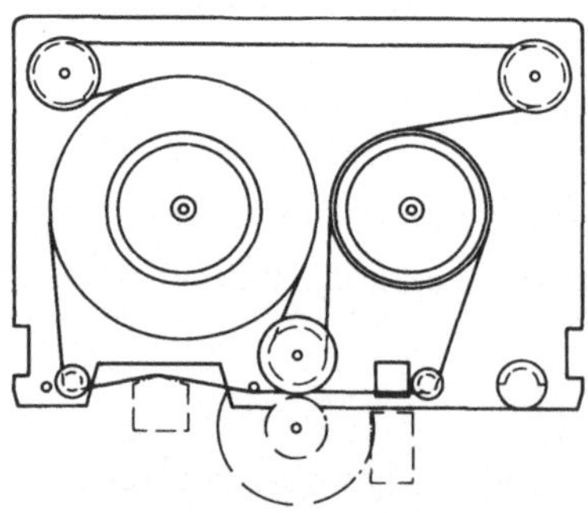

Fig. 7. 1/4″ Cartridge.

that the tape is not driven directly; instead, the two tape rolls are driven at their outer periphery by an endless elastic ribbon whose elasticity provides for the required tape tension and avoids slack. The recording format is similar to that of the 3.81 mm cartridge. The 6.3 mm wide, 91.5 m long and 31 μm thick tape is written on in four independent tracks. Bit serial recording of 8 bit characters is used with 7 or 8 bit codes at a density of 63 bits per mm. The recording method is PE. A 162 character preamble and an identical-length postamble are used for phase synchronization while a CRC character at the end of each block serves to protect the data. At a nominal inter-block gap length of 30.5 mm and a standard block length between 6 and 2048 characters, the maximum storage capacity is approx. 1.4 million characters.

3. Outlook

Developments of magnetic tape storage for data processing always aimed at strict reliability standards up to the limits of technological feasibility. Even so, the recording density could be increased from 32 chracters per mm used with NRZI – passing via 64 characters per mm for PE – to reach 264 characters per mm with the GCR method, without considerably increasing the requirements on the tape drive mechanisms. This increase is due to better recording methods and to advances in the field of electronic components. Now the GCR method introduced last opens up a number of possibilities for further development. The magnetic tape storage features which are most interesting in data processing systems are the data transfer rate and the recording density, i.e. the capacity of a reel of tape. The data transfer rate depends on the tape speed and the recording density. The tape speed cannot be increased considerably considering the short inter-block gap of the GCR format, which allows for a starting distance of only 3.6 mm. Not because there is no drive motor available to do it, but because the current tape path geometry (which is determined by the size of the read/write head, tape mark recognition facilities, cleaners, tape guides), presents a physical limit to reverse reading. It should be possible to bypass this limit by a different processing method, which would be justified by the fact that magnetic disks are normally used as an intermediary anyhow during processing. In this new method, the data would no longer be processed in blocks but in larger segments, repositioning and starting times being available for each segment. It would then be possible to dispose of nearly all of the inter-block gaps so that the storage capacity would be increased. Flying starts would be used for reading and writing.

The longitudinal recording density can surely be increased further but the GCR method also offers another solution, namely the increase of the number of tracks. While the required doubling of the number of tracks has up to now prevented the implementation of this approach, the advent of the GCR method, which abandons memory image (one-to-one) recording, allows a random number of tracks, e.g. 12 tracks, to be used.

In practice, however, neither a higher data transfer rate nor a higher recording density are urgently needed. The channel capacity of current CPU's does not require an immediate increase of the data transfer rate, and the volume reduction of the tape files could be achieved more effectively by better tape usage, even though considerable organizational difficulties would be involved. The tape volume could be reduced by using different reels or cartridge types, e.g. such as those used for mass storage. The problem presented by this solution is that the current standards for data media interchange would have to be abandoned.

As a consequence, one can expect magnetic tape storages to be used in data processing for a long time to come, the more so since there is no present need to introduce faster reel devices. Quite to the contrary, the next step will be to implement the GCR method of the high-performance devices in cost-effective, slow devices.

In the future, three different fields of application of magnetic tape devices can be seen. There are promising attempts to introduce mass storage systems providing random access to the whole data volume file (several machines with large, high-capacity tapes or a large number of small, mechanical access cartridges which are inserted and loaded into the drive automatically).

The following differentiation will consequently arise:

- Random access data processing using disks because of their short access times;

- Data interchange and sequential data processing using tape reels because of their compatibility and high data transfer rate;

- Mass storage systems with automatic access to all files.

References

Kaufmann, H., Daten-Speicher. München Wien: R. Oldenbourg 1973, 222.

Winkel, F., Technik der Magnetspeicher. Berlin: Springer 1960.

Mee, C. D., The physics of magnetic recording. Amsterdam: North-Holland Publishing Company 1964.

Hoagland, A. S., Digital magnetic recording. New York: John Wiley & Sons Inc., 1963.

DIN 66010 – DIN 66015, particularly

DIN 66014 part 2: Auf 9 Spuren mit Wechselschrift beschriebenes Magnetband, Bitdichte 32 Bits/mm.

DIN 66015: Auf 9 Spuren mit Richtungstaktschrift beschriebenes Magnetband zur Speicherung digitaler Daten, Bitdichte 63 Bits/mm.

ISO/TC97/SC11 N208, SECOND DRAFT PROPOSAL DP 5652 – INFORMATION PROCESSING – 9-TRACK' 12,7 mm (0,5 in) WIDE MAGNETIC TAPE FOR INFORMATION INTERCHANGE RECORDED AT 246 cpmm (6250 cpi) GROUP CODED RECORDING.

Tape Libraries with Automatic Reel Transport

Eckart Lennemann

IBM Deutschland GmbH, Böblingen, Germany

1. Objectives of a Tape Library

The majority of data processing systems are still tape-oriented. Large response times, low access frequencies and batch processing characterize this type of application. Cost considerations generally lead to magnetic tapes being used as data storage devices in preference to magnetic disks, even when their use prevents application of direct data access methods. Analysing the system aspect of a tape-oriented application, it is tempting to conceive a tape library with an automatic reel transport system. With such a system, all magnetic tapes with a reasonable usage factor would be stored in a suitable reel transport system equipped with a read/write station and the whole system housed in a single unit, connected to the central processor.

The objectives of such a machine offer significant advantages to the user. The job discontinuity of 'on-line' processing and 'off-line' data storage would disappear. The system throughput would be increased. The often considerable overhead for job preparation, archive administration, mounting and dismounting of the tapes would no longer be necessary, since the whole data bank would be under system control. In addition to considerable improvements in data security, several new applications would become feasible:

- large data banks with low data activity,
- implementation of documentation and text processing systems,
- the storage of 'historical' data (financial or municipal data),
- application of tape oriented processing for terminal usage.

Within the well known storage system hierarchy, the tape library belongs to the class of mass storage systems (Fig. 1).

The storage characteristics of cost, capacity and access time are highly interdependent. Low per-bit costs are achieved by a large capacity per read/write station. For a given surface bit density of the storage medium, as defined by the technology, the capacity results in library dimensions which highly influence the access time. If the access time is too long, then higher accelerations and speeds become necessary in the reel transport and read/write stations, which in turn leads to higher costs for the control and electro-mechanical components.

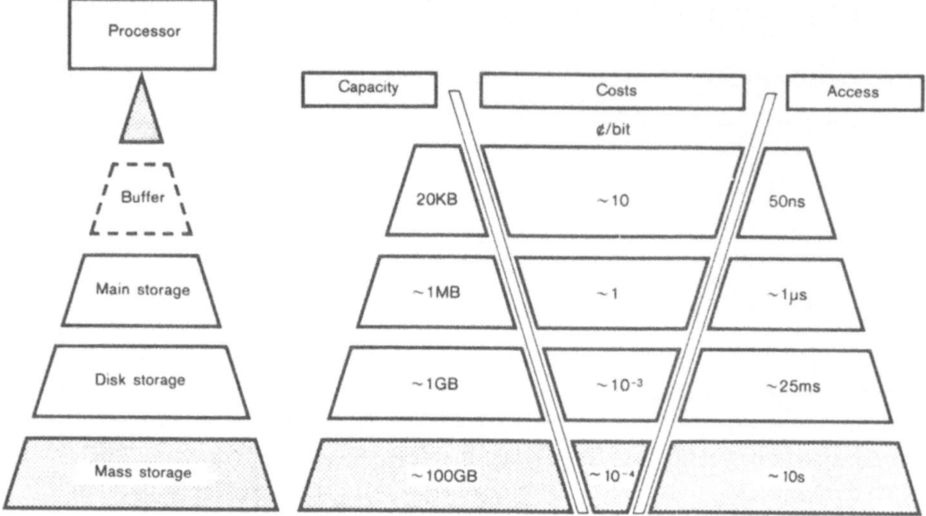

Fig. 1

The starting point for optimizing the conflicting parameters is the user's expectation of storage costs for the library equal to, or better than the system cost of older tape storage. This provides a reference point for the capacity with assumed costs for electronic control and read/write stations. The performance characteristics and the complex operational and organizational methods must then be tuned to the storage hierarchy and system architecture. In this way the access times will be optimized. The technical decision process is particularly interesting for the design, organizational structure and data flow of a tape library.

2. Design Alternatives

The design requires technological decisions in the areas:
- storage elements
- type of storage medium
- physical access method to storage medium

The main criteria for mass storage systems are minimum costs and maximum bit densities per unit volume.

Fig. 2 shows the currently available alternatives.

For storage elements, the required bit costs undoubtedly determine the choice of a homogenous surface as storage medium. The demand for reversible bit storage automatically eliminates chemical and mechanical surface storage methods [1].

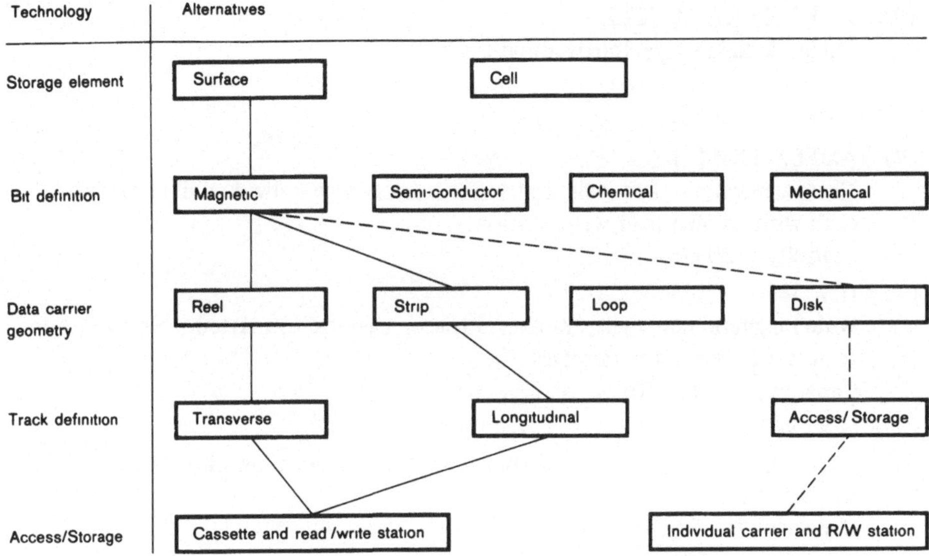

Fig. 2

Costs are also decisively in favour of the choice of magnetic surfaces. In respect of the data carrier type, both rigid surfaces (drums, disks), and flexible surfaces are available. Maximum bit/volume ratios are only achieved, however, with thin flexible media.

Track density and linear bit density determine the surface density of the carrier and hence the volume bit density of the technology. Compared for example to a standard tape with longitudinal tracks (i.e. parallel to the edges of the tape), a transverse recording method, with each track at a angle to the edge of the tape, provides an improvement in utilization of the available surface area.

Two possibilities are available for access and storage: individual volumes with one read/write station per volume, or multiple volumes with a common read/write station. An optimum compromise must be found between the electro-mechanical access time, the costs involved in additional read/write stations and the modular capacity of the data carrier.

The published information to date indicates that the following libraries are available at present:

1966 IBM 2321 DATA CELL
>   Magnetic tape strips, longitudinal tracks. Strips stored in cassettes, one read/
>   write station per library.
>   Capacity: 0.4 GB

1972 AMPEX TBM [2]
>   Narrow magnetic tape reels, transverse tracks, large individual data carriers
>   each with its own read/write station.
>   Capacity: 130 GB

1974 IBM 3850
>   Wide magnetic tape reels, transverse tracks, cassette formatted reels. Common
>   read/write station for cassettes.
>   Capacity: 45–472 GB

1975 CDC 38500 [3]
>   Wide magnetic tape reels, cassette formatted reels, common read/write station
>   for cassettes.
>   Capacity: 16–64 GB

3. Examples

Fig. 3 shows the operational principles of a magnetic strip mass storage system.

The circular cell consists of 10 individual segments. Each segment holds magnetic
strips in 20 sub-cells. The strips, which are 5.72 cm wide and 33 cm long, are extracted from the sub-cell by a mechanical claw, which then wraps the strip around a

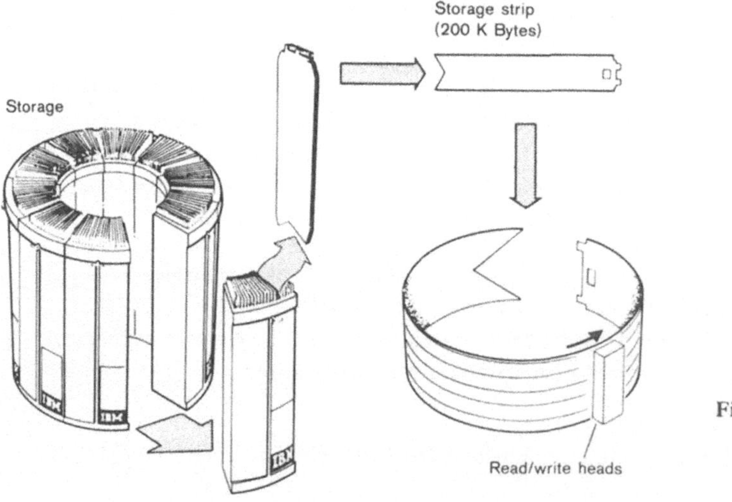

Fig. 3

drum. The drum rotates the strip past the read/write heads. The 100 tracks available on each strip are covered by 20 read/write heads which can be moved into 5 positions.

Fig. 4 shows the operational principles of a modern tape library with tape cassettes. The cassettes are stored in a honeycomb-like storage unit since a honeycomb structure provides the highest packing density for cylindrical cassettes and, therefore, shortens the access time. An electro-mechanical picker transports the cassette from the store to the read/write station, where the tape reel is removed from the cassette.

The magnetic tape has approximately the same capacity as a standard 732 m long, 1.25 cm wide (2400 ft, 1/2″) tape. The data access time within each reel is considerably shortened, compared with this standard tape, by means of the following factors:

- widening the tape from 1.25 cm to 6.9 cm,
- shortening from 732 m to 19.5 m,
- increasing the surface bit density by increasing the track density.

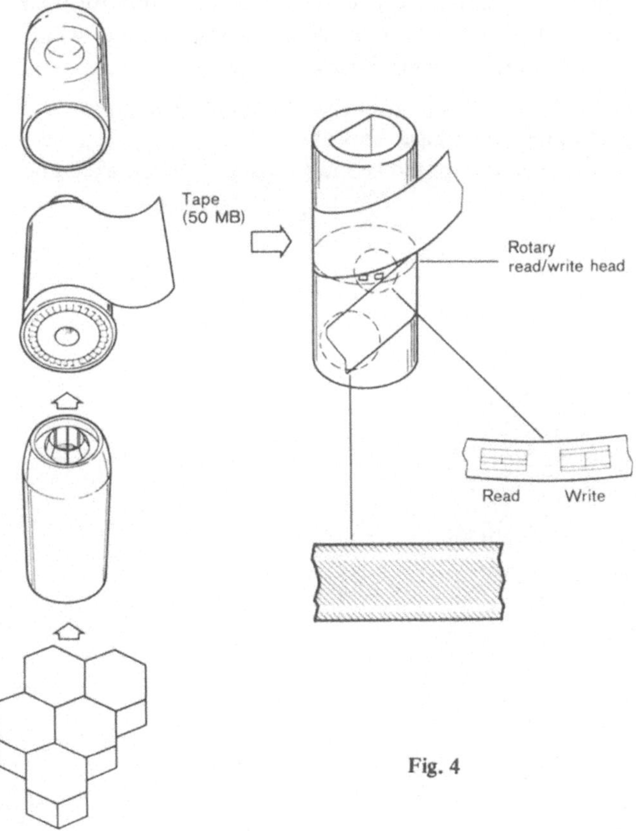

Fig. 4

The volumetric density is 0.32 MB/cm^3. One cassette has a capacity of 50 MB. Two factors determine the optimum modular capacity. A low reel capacity limits the throughput in the transport mechanism. A large reel capacity limits the throughput in the read/write station.

Theoretically, the width of the magnetic tape may be increased still further. However, practical limitations are experienced due to expansion and contraction of the tape under changing tensions, as well as tape guidance problems.

The tape is automatically wound as a helix around a cylinder and rewound onto a take-up reel on the output side. The stationary cylinder surface is interrupted in the middle by a rotating disk carrying a read and a write head. The helical winding of the tape causes the records to be written or read at an angle to the edge of the tape. Unlike standard tape read/write stations, the head moves at high speed relative to the stationary track in contrast to the track (or tape) moving past a stationary head. Normally, reading and writing operations take place with constant tape speed. Only under exceptional conditions, e.g. when the data cannot be read or written without error, a step-wise transport is necessary. Compensation for track deviation is achieved by varying the distance between steps. The principle of wide track writing and narrow track reading increases the tape guidance tolerance.

The use of a rotating head and the helical tape guidance system are vital for a relatively simple control of the super wide tape. This design allows the tape to be written with a single read/write head as opposed to multiple heads which would be

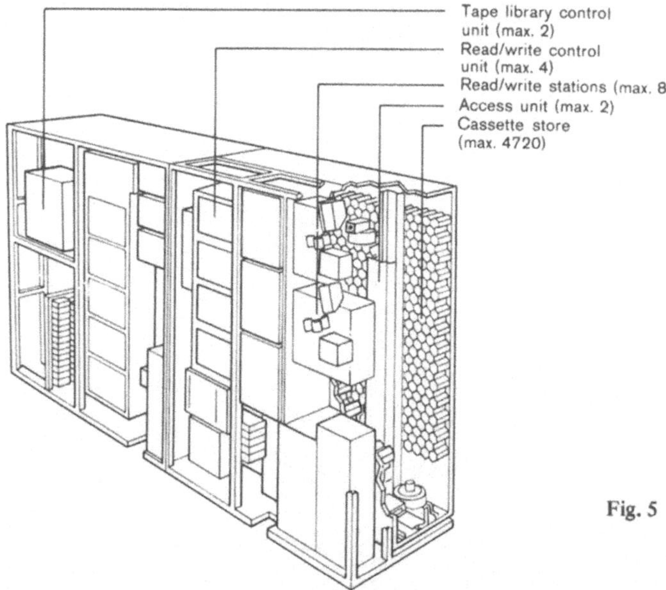

Fig. 5

needed with a longitudinal track system. An additional advantage is that high data rates can be achieved at low tape speeds and low acceleration rates, which reduces the performance requirements of the electrical drive, which in turn makes these components less expensive.

The IBM 3850 cassette library has a maximum configuration of 472 GB and is housed in two 9 m long units. This capacity is equivalent to 4720 disk drives. Each unit (see Fig. 5) has a maximum of 4720 cassettes which can be transported to any one of 8 read/write stations by 2 separate access units. The transport paths are shortened by storing the cassettes on opposite walls of the unit facing each other. With a maximum x-axis speed of 2.5 m/s, the access mechanism travels over 2500 MB per second. With the y-axis speed superimposed on the access mechanism the average access time is 7 seconds.

4. Data Organisation Concepts and Data Flow

4.1. Data Organisation Concept

The IBM 3850 tape library is organized as a "virtual disk storage" in analogy to the concept of a virtual main memory. Virtual disk storage means that the operating system of the central processor interacts with the tape library as if it would consist of a large number of disk units. The disk units however, are virtual since the data are actually stored on tape. To achieve this, a dedicated disk unit is placed in the data flow between central processor and library (see Fig. 6). The disk unit acts as a staging device for data from the cassettes before any data can be transmitted to the central processor. Disk and tape library form a subsystem with a disklike interface to the host computer. Within the subsystem, the data transfer and address translation from virtual to real takes place independently of the central processor. Management of data blocks is done by the library control unit. Active blocks are kept on the disk. Inactive blocks are returned to the corresponding cassettes if they have been changed during use. Inactive blocks, which have not been changed, are marked free for over-writing when newly requested data are staged from a cassette to the disk.

4.2. Data Flow

The data flow takes place as follows: a program in the central processor requests a specific data block. The operating system passes the request to the library via the multiplexor (MPX) channel. With the aid of a data block address table on the disk, the virtual data block address is converted into a real address which pinpoints the respective cassette location, its identifier and the location of the block on the tape. At the same time space for the block is reserved on the disk. Using the extracted information, the data block is now retrieved by the library control unit and trans-

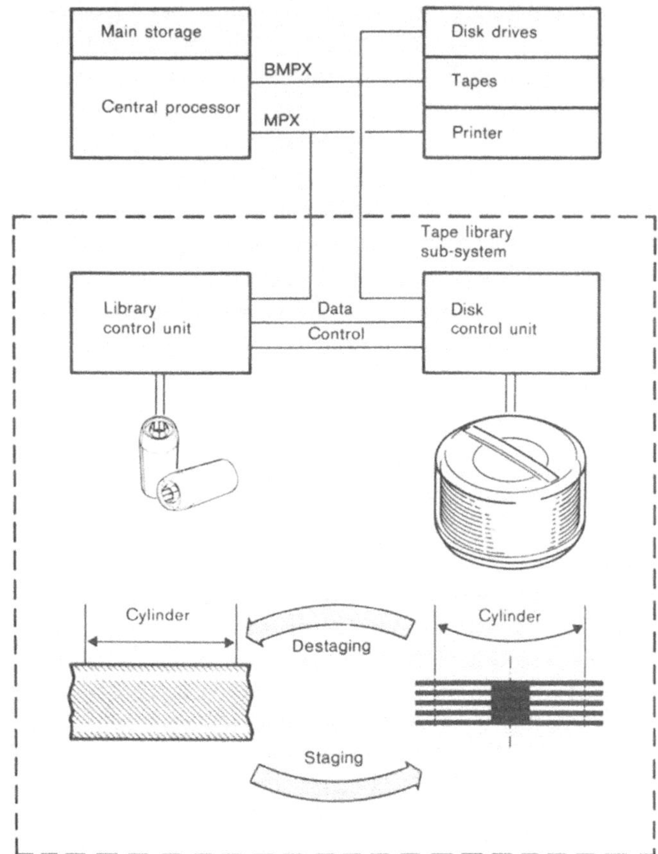

Fig. 6

ferred to the reserved space on the disk. The operating system is then advised that
the requested data block is now available and that data transfer to the main storage
may commence. Data transfer takes place via the block-multiplex (BMPX) channel
as for normal peripheral disk storage units, i.e. with the same control commands
and at the same high data rate. The data organization on the two storage media
geometries (tape, disk) has to be matched to keep the library control simple. The
data block size chosen for all data transfer operations in the subsystem is 250 KB.
The disk itself has 404 cylinders (100 MB) and is represented by two cassettes.
Each cylinder is stored on the tape in the form of 61 data tracks. 5 additional tracks
serve as spare tracks. The cylinders represent fixed areas on the tape, i.e. if the
cylinder storage capacity is not fully used, a portion of the tape will not be used. The
tape media utilization, however, is still considerably higher than the utilization of a

normal tape since the latter are usually used in the form 'one tape — one application'.
The advantage of the fixed allocation is that the required cylinder can be located
rapidly and simply by reading the edge track. The data access does not need to be
sequential.

4.3. Controls

Complex data movements are controlled by 2 subsystem processors (library, disk).
These are extensively micro-programmed and operate completely independent of
the central processor.

The library control processor performs the following functions:

* storage of cassettes and maintaining an inventory of all cassettes
* reserving disk space
* initiation of all disk processor operations
* initiation of all transport and read/write operations in the library
* control and monitoring of all data requests for up to 4 host system/370
  (Modell 145, 158, 168)
* automatic, self-initiated error correction procedures
* maintaining statistics on errors and other activities

The library control unit mainly uses tables which are stored in duplicate on two
different disk drives and which are continuously updated.

The most important function of the microprogram is the control of the data flow
between the central processor and the disk, and also the data flow between the
library and the disk. Both data flows may occur simultaneously and neither can be
interrupted. Possible contention problems are overcome by means of a 32 kilobyte
'wrap-around' storage buffer between the library and the disk. This buffer can be
simultaneously read and written which allows the microcode of the disk control
unit to give priority to the data transfer to the central processor.

5. Availability

5.1. Design

The availability of a mass storage system, in which all tape data sets for a specific
data processing installation are stored, is of enormous importance to the user.
Manufacturers publish very little information on the statistical distribution of failure
rates for the various components. The reason may be that the customer who buys
such an expensive machine does not accept the laws of statistics. To assure optimal
availability, a considerable portion of the development activity for a tape library
system is concentrated on determining and controlling the behaviour of the machine
in error situations.

The availability concept of the IBM 3850 for example contains the following
features:

- multiple redundancy in all important functions (see Fig. 7)
- multiple redundancy of data and control paths
- automatic selection of the available alternatives for modules, data paths and
  control path in case of an error
- efficient error diagnosis and correction.

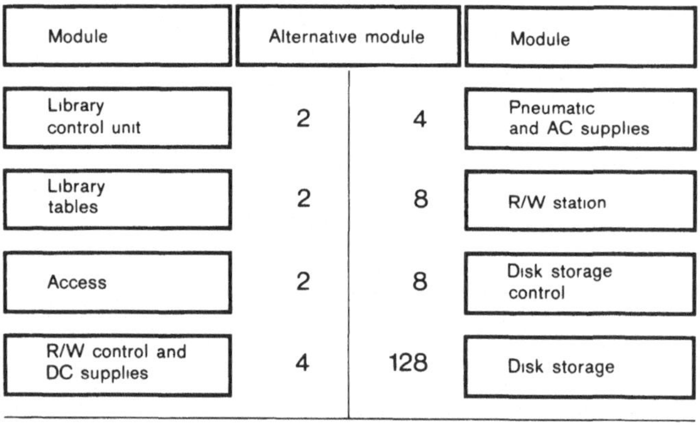

Module	Alternative module		Module
Library control unit	2	4	Pneumatic and AC supplies
Library tables	2	8	R/W station
Access	2	8	Disk storage control
R/W control and DC supplies	4	128	Disk storage

Fig. 7

5.2. Data Flow under Error Conditions

The alterations made to the data and control paths in error situations will be used as
example for the library availability despite error conditions in the hardware.

A tape library configured for maximum availability has two complete library control
units. While the main control unit is in operation, the second control is on stand-by,
with the microprogram loaded, ready for instant use if required. If the test circuits
signal an error in the main control unit, the operating system automatically addresses
the stand-by control unit and advises the system operator of the error in the main
library control unit via the operator's console. The availability of the inventory
tables is particularly critical, and for this reason the tables are stored on two separate,
independent disk drives each with its own control unit. Dependent on the type of
error which occurs, either disk control unit can control either of the disk storage
units.

The whole cassette retrieval and transport system is duplicated, complete with controls and power supplies. Should one of the systems become defective, the microprogram orders the reserve system to transport the defective transport system into
a 'garage' for repair. Each cassette may be read or written at any of the available

read/write stations. If one of the R/W stations signals an unrecoverable error to the library control unit, a new read command is issued. If this retry also fails, then the control unit looks up a configuration table which lists the available read/write stations. An alternative station is picked and the cassette is transferred.

The R/W station producing the error is then flagged as defective in the configuration tables and it is not used for subsequent operations.

Data are stored on the magnetic tape in 'extended group code'. The error correction code and the associated logic is installed in the R/W station control unit. During data transfer, 32 out of 208 bytes can be directly corrected. Since write errors which are beyond this correction capability are detected during writing by a write verify check, the data are practically error free.

The disk control units handle the error checking and correction during data transfer from disk to tape. Individual errors with a length up to 11 bits can be corrected within a data block.

Extensive duplication of modules and automatic microprogram controlled selection of data and control path alternatives considerably reduce the probability of the equipment becoming unusable due to the occurrence of individual or multiple errors. The library continues to function correctly, albeit at reduced performance in some cases, until the cause of the error is removed.

5.3. Error Diagnosis

Precise error diagnosis and rapid error correction have three prerequisites:

- The equipment must be designed in such a way that repairs to components can be made while the remainder of the machine is still operating.

- The equipment must be capable of diagnosing errors in its own components and maintaining statistics on such errors. This is of particular importance for the otherwise time consuming diagnosis of intermittent errors.

- Customer engineers must have efficient diagnostic microprograms available which enables precise, rapid error analyses to be made.

When errors are detected by the many test circuits, or when alternative equipment is activated, the library control unit is notified. Errors and machine status information are registered in an error log (Fig. 8).

The customer service engineer analyses the error log with the aid of an evaluation program and either receives a direct indication of the error and the relevant chapter in the maintenance handbook, or an indication of the area which could be causing the error, and information for subsequent location of the error. For such analyses, the unit is equipped with a maintenance console including a diskette reader which allows specific diagnostic microprograms to be loaded and executed.

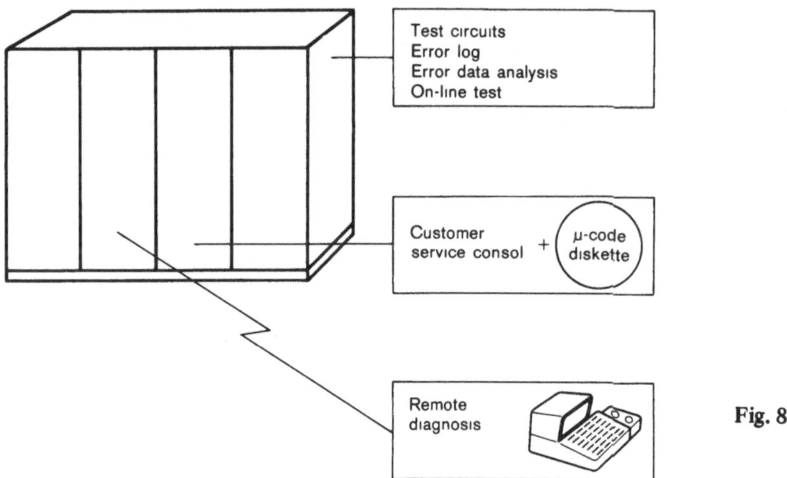

Fig. 8

Diagnostic effectiveness and therefore availability has been carried one step further by the development of a remote diagnostic terminal. The terminal is located in a major field engineering center and optionally connected with the customer installation by telephone line. Error diagnosis and analysis on a machine operating hundreds of kilometers away is certainly a novel experience for a service engineer.

Bibliography

[1] *K. McFarland* and *M. Hashiguchi,* Laser Recording Unit for High Density Permanent Digital Data Storage, PROC, AFIPS, p. 1369, 1968.

[2] *M. Wildmann,* Terabit Memory Systems: A Design History, PROC. IEEE, Vol. 63, No. 8, Aug. 1975.

[3] Datamation, p. 100, July 1975.

[4] *J. P. Harris* et al., The IBM 3850 Mass Storage System: Design Aspects, PROC. IEEE, Vol. 63, No. 8, August 1975.

[5] *R. E. Matick,* Review of Current Proposed Technologies for Mass Storage Systems, PROC. IEEE, Vol. 60, No. 3, March 1972.

[6] *W. A. Gross,* Ultra Large Storage Systems Using Flexible Media, Past, Present and Future, PROC. Spring Joint Comp. Conf., p. 957, 1972.

[7] *J. A. Rodriguez,* An Analysis of Tape Drive Technology, PROC. IEEE, Vol. 63, No. 8, p. 1163, August 1975.

Fabrication Technology and Physical Fundamentals of Components Used for Semiconductor Memories

Albrecht Moeller

Forschungsinstitut der Deutschen Bundespost beim Fernmeldetechnischen Zentralamt, Darmstadt, Germany

Introduction

In the field of digital memories, semiconductors have become more and more important besides magnetics, although they have not been able to completely replace the latter so far. They received a particular stimulus in the wake of microprocessor systems which attracted considerable interest during the last few years. Microcomputers are a main application field for the most important types of semiconductor memories as shown in Table 1. Fundamentally two groups of memories have to be distinguished, namely read-write memories (RWMs), most of them random-access memories (RAMs),

Table 1. Semiconductor Memory Types

	Memory type		Erasure	Programming	Information content if voltage supply is interrupted
RWM Read/Write Mem.	RAM	Random Access Memory	electrically	electrically	volatile
RWM Read/Write Mem.	SAM	Serial Access Memory			
	ROM	Read-Only Memory	not possible	by masks	non-volatile
	PROM	Programmable ROM		electrically	
RMM Read-Mostly Mem.	EPROM or RePROM	Erasable PROM Reprogrammable ROM	UV light	electrically	
RMM Read-Mostly Mem.	EEROM or EAROM	Electrically Erasable ROM Electrically Alterable ROM	electrically		

but also serial-access memories (SAMs), and read-only memories (ROMs), among them, besides those which can be programmed once only (ROMs and PROMs, depending on the programming operation), the reprogrammable ROMs (RePROMs). In RePROMs the operations of clearing and reprogramming may be accomplished in a number of ways. Electrically alterable ROMs (EAROMs) take an intermediate position between the ordinary ROMs and the read-write memories (in particular RAMs). Assosicative memories or content addressable memories (CAMs) — not listed in Table 1 — can be composed of ROM and RAM elements, respectively, but are addressed in a special manner.

Regardless of this subdivision into memory types, either bipolar or MOS technology is used. Bipolar memory circuits allow the highest speeds, whereas MOS memories are generally more advantageous where high capacity, high packing density and low cost are required, but nowadays the application fields of both technologies overlap in a wide range. Finally, among read-write memories, static memories must be distinguished from dynamic memories. Almost every static memory cell consists of a bistable latch or flip-flop, whereas a capacitor is the essential part of a dynamic memory element, leading to extremely high packing densities.

Practically all semiconductor memories are monolithic integrated circuits.

Before discussing individual types of memories, the basic manufacturing processes of semiconductor memories will be briefly described. All those processes amount fundamentally to the doping of semiconductor material and to the preparation and shaping of layers.

Basic technological processes

Planar technique is one of the most important bases for fabricating semiconductor circuits and, among them, semiconductor memories. This process, applied to bipolar and MOS circuits of any size starts from semiconductor wafers of best crystal quality, with adequate doping and surface pre-treatment, and comprises essentially diffusion, oxidation, and epitaxial steps. By means of photolithographic mask technology, a selective etching of the oxide can be obtained, thereby allowing selective diffusion. The photolithographic resolution attainable with visible light is between 1 and 2 μm, in the case of microprojection down to 0.6 μm. A better resolution can be obtained with radiation by shorter waves, e.g. ultraviolet light. *Electron beam lithography* [1] applies the principle of the scanning electron microscope, using electron beam sensitive materials (positive photoresists, e.g. poly-methyl methacrylate, and, recently, substances with still higher sensitivity). Resolutions as high as 0.1 μm can so be obtained. A still better resolution (50 nm) is possible with very soft X-rays (synchrotron radiation). X-ray lithography [2] requires no high vacuum, and can use the same photo resists as electron beam lithography, but masking is more difficult (gold masks).

Ion implantation [3] was introduced besides diffusion technique as another tool of selective doping — particulary for small penetration depths. The dopants which have to be ionized — mostly carrying a single positive charge — are accelerated in a strong electric field in such a way that they strike the semiconductor surface. The penetration depth is controlled by the ion energy — generally between 100 and 500 KeV — , by the crystal orientation and other parameters. The maximum of the doping concentration may be placed in a defined distance from the surface. There is little or no lateral penetration of the dopant below the mask, as distinct from diffusion technique. The effect of mass spectroscopy leads to high purity of the dopant. The process causes lattice damages, but these can be removed by annealing at relatively low temperatures. Ion implantation is self-aligning, results in reproducible data and can easily be operated automatically. It is, however, neither adequate for high doping concentrations nor for high penetration depths. It is mostly applied in MOS technology, but also for bipolar circuits.

While MOS devices within integrated circuits are in general electrically isolated from each other by their structure, in bipolar integrated circuits *isolation* is conventionally obtained by an additional diffusion step; pn-junctions in shape of a well are reverse biased during circuit operation. The transistors are produced in weakly doped epitaxial layers grown on silicon wafers with more heavily doped surface areas, such that buried layers form a part of the collector regions. This method — called *standard buried collector method* (SBC) — requires considerable chip real estate.

The *collector diffusion isolation* (CDI) [4] saves some real estate. An epitaxial layer of conduction type opposite to the type of the buried layers in grown. A ring shaped collector region assumes also the function of the isolation well. Compared with the standard buried collector method eight process steps are saved (e.g. gold doping). The increased collector capacitance, however, limits the operating speed. The thickness of the epitaxial layer has to be controlled very precisely, since thereby the thickness of the base region is determined. Similar processes are *GIMIC* (guard ring isolated monolithic integrated circuit), which uses ion implantation, and *OXIM* (oxide isolated monolith) [5, 9].

The *V-ATE process* (vertical anisotropic etch) [6] obtains the lateral isolation by v-shaped notches, which are formed, for instance, in (100)-oriented silicon surfaces, by means of an etch containing hydrazine. Contact holes are produced likewise. The isolating reverse biased junction is limited to the high-ohmic bottom area of the transistor. Thereby parasitic interactions between adjacent circuit blocks are kept low. Because of the uneven surface, the metallic interconnection requires, however, a combination of platinum, titanium, and gold.

A variation thereof, called *Polyplanar* or (nearly the same) *VIP*, v-groove isolation with polysilicon backfill [7], coats the flanks of the v-shaped grooves with an insulating layer of silica (in the case of VIP additionally with silicon nitride) and fills them up thereafter with polycrystalline silicon deposited chemically from the gaseous phase. Thereby a flat surface can be restored by mechanical means on which evaporated aluminum adheres sufficiently well.

In *anodic oxidation of silicon* [8], one connects the silicon slice to be etched selectively with the anode of an electrolytic solution (hot boric acid), and uses thermal oxide as masks. The grooves formed in the silicon have a nearly semi-circular cross-section and are filled with a porous oxide which may easily be removed or transformed into a glassy material by means of a liquid glassforming substance at 450 °C.

Isoplanar, LOCOS (local oxidation of silicon) and *Planox* (planar oxide) which are quite similar became accepted isolation methods [9]. They can be applied to bipolar as well as to MOS circuits. In bipolar circuits the circular side wall of the isolation by a reverse biased junction is replaced by a selective oxide isolation, produced with silicon nitride masking (Fig. 1). In MOS circuits, nitride as a gate dielectric provides a lowered threshold voltage (together with an oxide layer which must not be too thin). The Si_3N_4 layer is deposited from a gas mixture containing silane (SiH_4) and ammonia (NH_3); it can be etched with hot phosphoric acid of a special concentration. Oxidation always increases the total volume and causes oxide step formation which is detrimental for subsequent metallization. One of the key advantages of these processes is the selective etch of silicon preceding the thermal oxidation. This selective etch reduces oxide step formation while windows in the oxide layer are opened, even if the oxide layer is relatively thick (e.g. 2 μm). Fig. 2 shows Isoplanar, V-ATE and VIP structures. High packing densities and cutoff frequencies can be obtained by the so-called Isoplanar-II-process in which also the emitter region touches the oxide wall, by the above-mentioned OXIM technology, and by the OXIS technology (oxide isolation) [10].

The *ESFI technology* (epitaxial silicon films on insulating substrates) takes a particular position because of the complete galvanic separation of the single circuit blocks, by which, apart from avoiding the necessity of isolation potentials, parasitic interactions are minimized [11]. In this technology, a silicon layer is deposited on an insulating

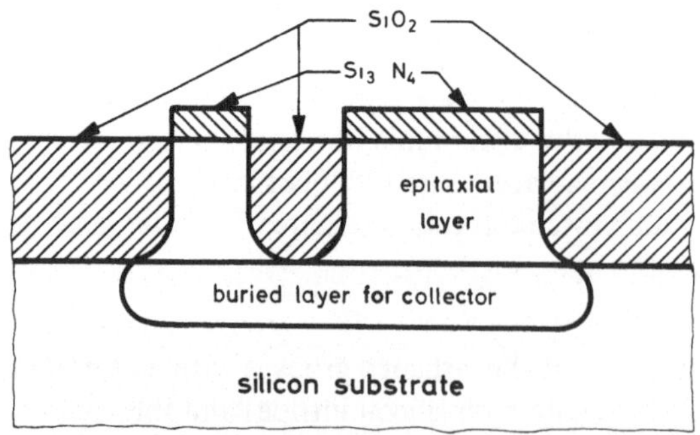

Fig. 1

Isoplanar process, isolation for a bipolar transistor.

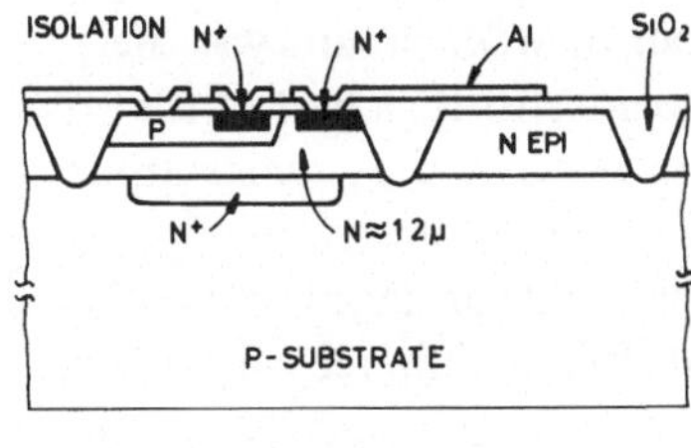

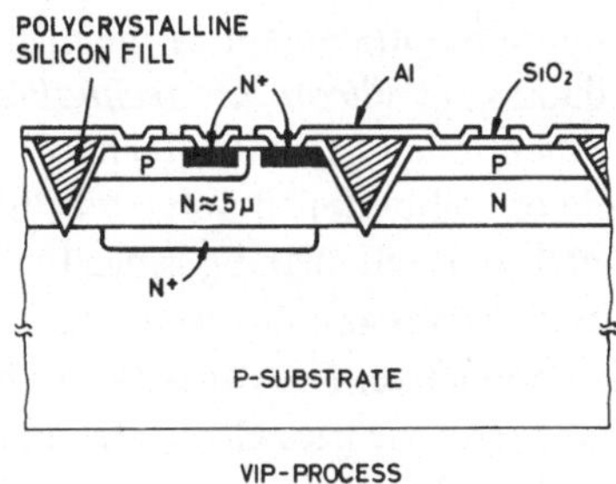

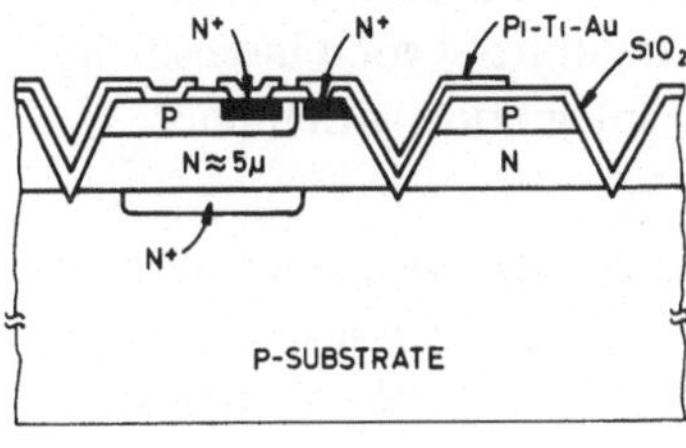

Fig. 2

Isoplanar process, vertical anisotropic etch technique, and vee-isolation with polysilicon backfill.

substrate by a heteroepitaxial process (which means as a single-crystalline layer with an orientation relation to the monocrystalline substrate which has, however, a different composition). As substrates spinel (magnesium aluminum oxide) and, mainly, corundum (colorless sapphire, aluminum oxide) are used. This last combination is — unfortunately — called SOS technology (silicon on sapphire). Silicon is pyrolytically deposited from a carrier gas containing silane at about 1000 °C on a substrate surface which has been carefully (mechanically and thermally) pre-treated. The layers (mostly thinner than 1 μm) are of poorer crystal quality than bulk silicon, especially because of the difference in thermal expansion of substrate and layer, but are quite adequate for MOS technique.

Complete electric isolation is also the aim of other technologies with rather high expenditure, e.g. beam lead technology.

In *MOS technology* both p-channel and n-channel techniques are applied ; n-channel technique has the advantage of higher speed.

Complementary MOS technology (CMOS) which uses simultaneously transistors of both channel types, permits the design of ROMs and static RAMs with a minimum power dissipation ; it is, however, a little more expensive and area consuming, due to the necessary isolations [12]. ESFI-MOS technology offers a favorable solution of this problem, and, moreover, additional possibilities [13]. As far as CMOS technology in bulk silicon is concerned the Isoplanar process is advantageous (CMOS-Isoplanar, or, again very similar, LOCMOS) [14].

An important enrichment of the manufacturing methods of MOS circuits was the introduction of *silicon gate technology* [15] which also constitutes a part of the above-mentioned LOCMOS technolgy. In silicon gate technology the gate electrode is made of highly doped polycrystalline silicon instead of metal (mostly aluminum). The method is self-aligning, since the polysilicon gate electrode arranged on the thin gate oxide serves as a diffusion mask, absorbing dopant itself and thereby becoming highly conductive. The capacitances between source and drain, respectively, on the one hand, and the gate electrode, on the other hand, are in this manner kept extremely low. The gate material (silicon) provides a low threshold voltage. After diffusion the structure is protected by an oxide layer, resulting in good insensitivity to subsequent high temperature processes and favoring integration with bipolar circuits.

The *VMOS* and *DMOS* processes are two methods which allow a very small channel length and consequently low switching times (VMOS indicates the v-shaped groove for each transistor, DMOS stands for double-diffused MOS) [16]. VMOS transistors exist in several variations, one of which is shown in Fig. 3. The channel length is defined by the thickness of a p-type layer generated by diffusion technique and can thus be made smaller than by planar technique; the channel width is, on the other hand, particularly large. The short channel of the DMOS transistor (see Fig. 4) is formed by the different penetration of two dopants of opposite type which diffuse laterally under an oxide mask. VMOS technology is especially proper to fast ROMs, both technologies are being tested for RAMs.

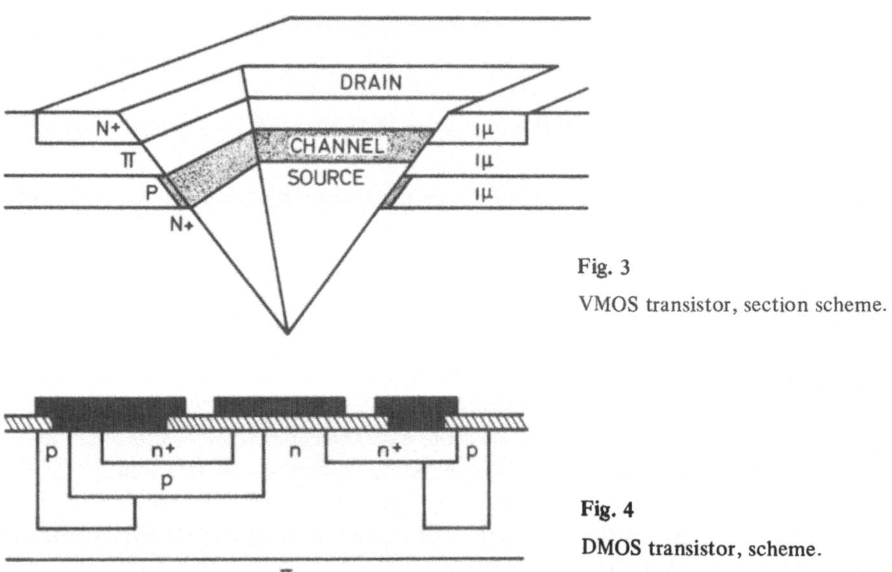

Fig. 3

VMOS transistor, section scheme.

Fig. 4

DMOS transistor, scheme.

Read-Write memory cells

Most bipolar memories are fabricated in standard TTL, Schottky TTL or ECL techniques, but lately another technique has been added, namely *integrated injection logic* ($I^2 L$) or *merged transistor logic* (MTL) [17], including numerous variations and related techniques. Originally developed for logic circuits, it is generally considered as the key to bipolar large scale integration. In this technique bistable latches for static RAMs have been developed from the beginning which are very space saving, as resistors are not required (see Fig. 5) [18]. Like in MOS circuits the packing density can be increased by the dynamic principle [19]. Fig. 6 shows a dynamic memory element built up in $I^3 L$ technique ($I^3 L$ means insulated or especially Isoplanar $I^2 L$). In this case, the n-type zone near the surface acts as the emitter of the npn-transistor, as opposed to the static $I^2 L$ RAM with its multiple collectors at the surface. In the depletion layer of the middle pn junction, charge may be stored for a short period of time.

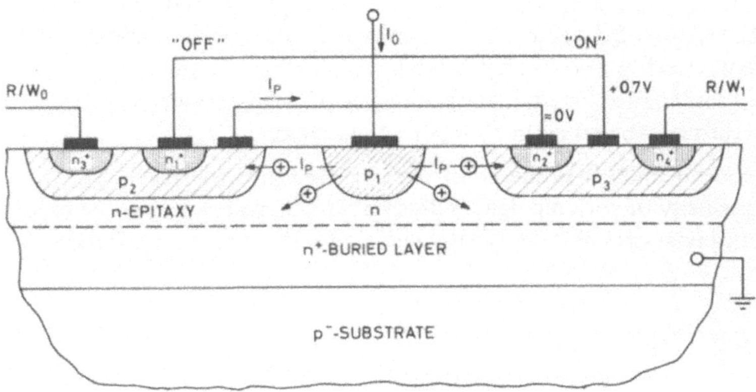

Fig. 5. Element of static RAM in $I^2 L$ (MTL) technique.

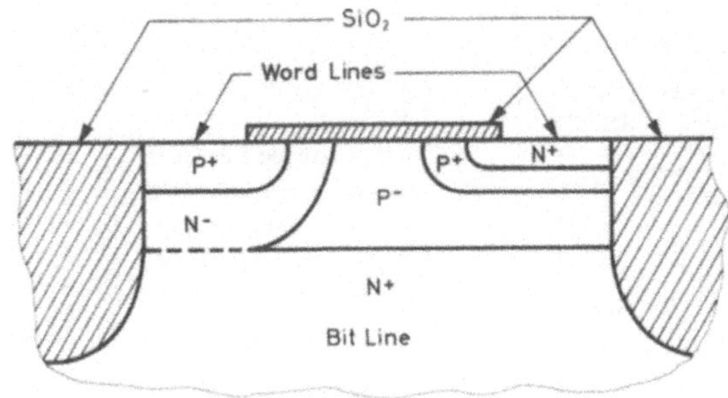

Fig. 6

Element of dynamic RAM in $I^3 L$ technique.

Memories composed of *charge transfer devices* (CTDs) are probably the most remarkable representatives of serial-access memories [20]. Charge transfer devices are subdivided in two groups, namely bucket brigade devices (BBDs) and, more important, charge coupled devices (CCDs). Both are basically shift registers for analog signals. The signals are represented in them by electric charges of different magnitude. The operation mode of a CCD is explained in Fig. 7. In essence, closely spaced MOS capacitors are biased by clocked voltage pulses in such a way that potential wells (deep depletion layers) are shifted in the semiconductor beneath the metal electrodes periodically in one direction (in most circuits near the semiconductor surface, in others in a certain distance from it). In these moving potential wells, charge-packets may be transported which are proportional in size to each analog signal sample; the charge may convert the deep depletion layer into an inversion layer. The signal charges are injected via an input electrode and led off by an output electrode. If the shift register is operated with two clock phases only, the electrodes must have an asymmetric shape (in general steps are built in, see Fig. 7b); in three and four phase CCDs the shift direction is defined by the sequence of the clock phases. The BBD differs from the CCD by regions of opposite conduction type in the semiconductor; under each electrode one such region is located, laterally displaced as shown in Fig. 8. A BBD may be considered as an alternating sequence of capacitors and MOS transistors. These in turn may be replaced by bipolar transistors.

CCD memories are dynamic memories consisting of closed shift register loops. Because of the necessity of periodic signal refresh, they can in general only be used for digital (practically always binary) signals, where not more than two different in-

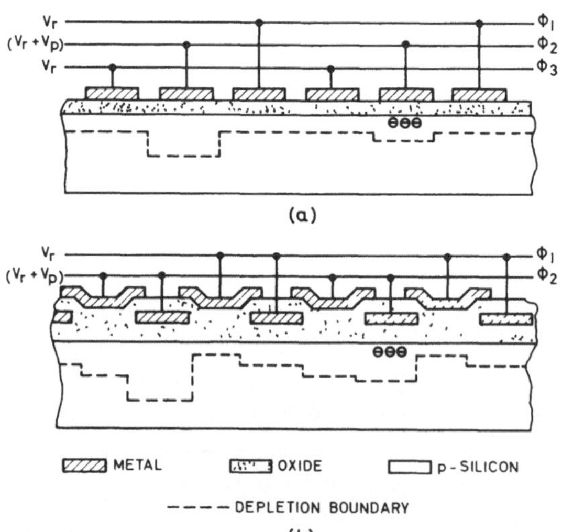

Fig. 7

Charge coupled devices, schematic cross section.
(a) Three phase structure.
(b) Two phase structure.

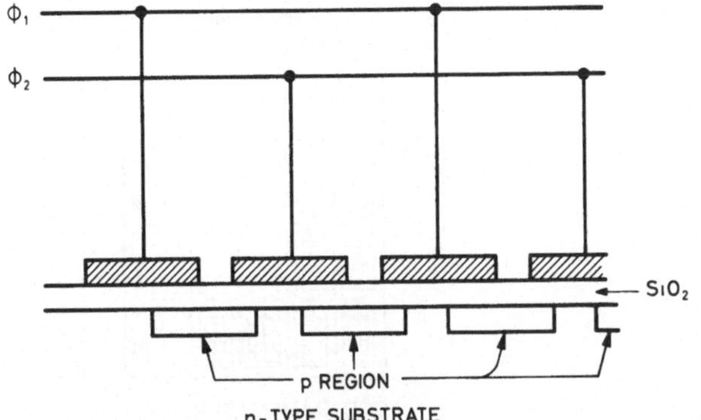

Fig. 8

Bucket brigade device, schematic cross section.

formation states must be distinguished. A subdivision of large memories into several smaller loops, possibly containing only one line each, decreases the access time. An option is possible between serpentine, loop and serial-parallel-serial organization. In this latter scheme, the bit sequence is divided into groups that are shifted relatively slowly during most of the time. In all cases there are input, output, and refresh stages within the loops.

The principle of *charge transfer* between potential wells is also applied in several *RAMs*, but these are not charge transfer devices in the normally accepted sense of the term.

Potential wells that can be generated beneath individual gate electrodes can be influenced by ion implanted regions (possibly with two impurity types, see Fig. 9), such that, in a certain sense, a simplified one-transistor cell can be made (CC RAM) [21]. Reading is destructive, as it is, at least in principle, in all one-transistor cells.

Non-destructive reading is possible in a matrix of memory elements with two electrodes each, below which a potential well is shifted back and forth. Present charge can be recognized by a potential change which may be sensed (see Fig. 10) [22].

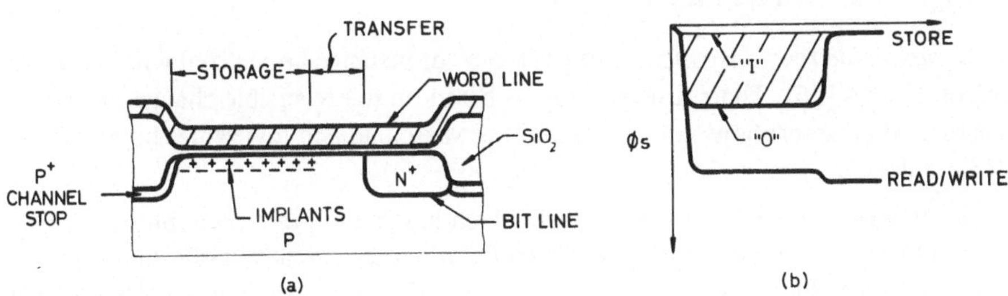

Fig. 9. CC RAM cell with implanted storage region. (a) Cross section of cell structure. (b) Surface potential for read, write, and store modes.

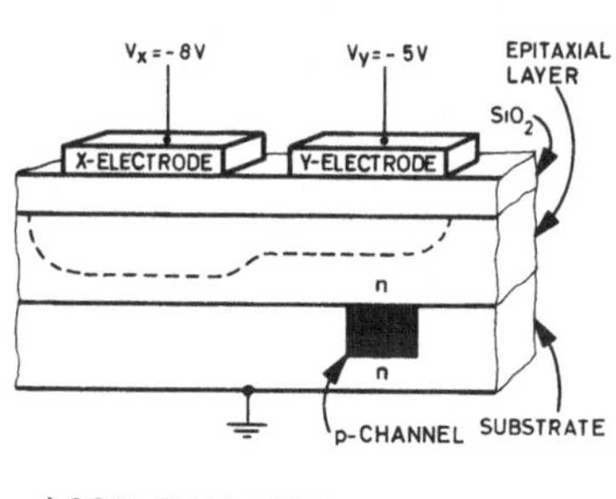

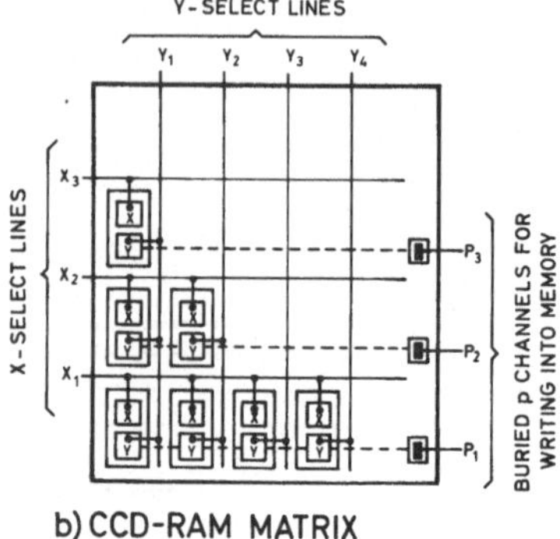

Fig. 10. RAM formed by CCD array. (a) Basic unit. (b) Array.

An intermediate type between CCD and MOS transistor memory is represented by the so-called "transistorless memory cell" of the merged charge memory (MCM) [23]. By voltage pulses of suitable height potential wells are generated beneath the crossing points of word and bit lines; according to the pulse height, the wells are filled up with low and high quantities, respectively, of minority carriers. The information can be read destructively by indirect sensing of the stored charge. One aims for the present at 64 Kbit on a 20 mm^2-chip. In the C^3 RAM (continuously charge-coupled RAM), one-transistor storage elements are connected to read-write amplifiers through an MOS transmission line [24]. This transmission line is basically formed by a long gate electrode which carries — instead of a uniform potential — a potential which rises along the gate length: each end of the gate is connected to a different voltage level. By the electric field generated in the channel below the gate electrode, the carriers are accelerated in the proper direction.

Reprogrammable memory cells

Reprogrammable read-only memories [25] can for instance be realized with amorphous semiconductors [26]. Their storage effect is based on the reversible change of the resistance of an amorphous semiconductor between high and low values by suitable voltage pulses.

The *floating gate* transistor is another cell which has found practical application. It uses a field effect transistor, the gate electrode of which (metal or polysilicon) is thoroughly embedded in insulating material. This electrode can be reversibly charged and discharged by particular effects, thereby blocking or creating a channel or facilitating its forming like in any MIS field effect transistor.

86

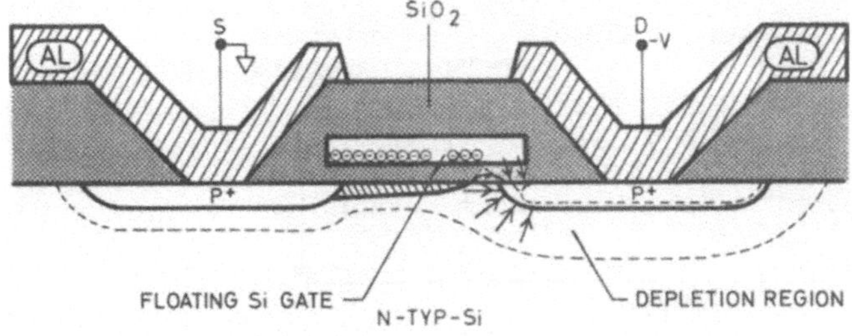

Fig. 11. FAMOS transistor, schematic cross section.

In the best known memory of this category which is called *FAMOS memory* (floating gate avalanche injection MOS) charging is accomplished by an avalanche effect that is triggered by a reverse voltage pulse between drain region and substrate (Fig. 11) [27]. The "hot electrons" (electrons rich in energy) generated thereby are able to penetrate the insulator layer. A part of them travels to the gate electrode, accumulating there and charging the electrode negatively. At the semiconductor surface an inversion layer is formed, a conductive channel connects source and drain. The information written in a memory matrix composed of such transistors is nonvolatile and may be read by checking the conductance between source and drain as often as required. In order to erase — which can only be done for the entire memory — the energy must be transferred to the electrons which is necessary to pass over the energy barrier between gate and insulating oxide. This is possible with photons of ultraviolet light and with X-rays, but it requires a relatively long time. The fabrication of FAMOS memories has reached 16 Kbit chips by now.

Numerous other storage transistors with a floating gate have been designed. Most of them have above the first gate a second one which is electrically connected in conventional manner. They are charged and discharged by avalanche brakdown, pinchoff effect, or by particularly strong electric fields, mostly aiming at electrical individual erasure of each memory element: SAMOS (stacked-gate avalanche-injection type MOS) SIMOS (stacked gate injection MOS), ATMOS (adjustable threshold MOS) and others, among them the MNMOS transistor (metal nitride metal oxide semiconductor) as an example of recent development: the floating gate is made of molybdenum, the control gate of aluminum. Moderate pulses of one polarity for writing and erasing are needed (−20 and −30 volts, respectively, 1 ms).

8 Kbit EAROMs have been made using storage transistors with two polysilicon gates each and silica as the only insulator material [28].

There is intense research and development activity on floating-gate structures. One new idea should be mentioned here: in the *DIFMOS* structure (double injection floating gate MOS) [29] separate zones exist for charging and discharging of the large

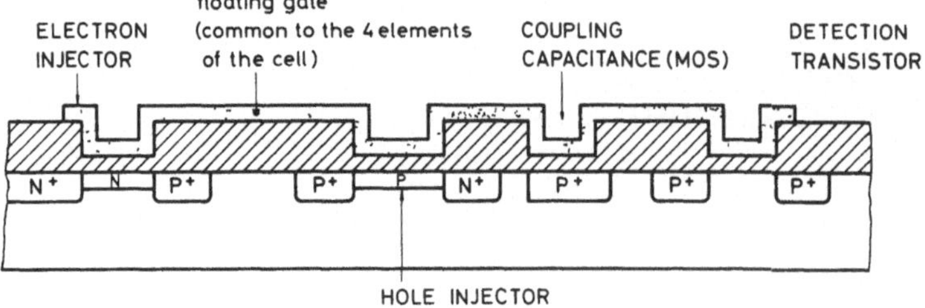

Fig. 12. DIFMOS structure, schematic cross section.

floating aluminum electrode (10^4 μm^2) by avalanche breakdown (Fig. 12). Voltage pulses of -20 volts, applied to the p^+-region of the electron injector, are sufficient to charge the gate negatively. For erase the p^+-region of the hole injector is pulsed negatively; this corresponds to a positive pulse at the n^+p-junction and generates hot holes. Simultaneously a negative voltage at the p^+-region of the coupling capacitance provides such a distribution of the field lines that hole injection is favored. Information is read in the usual way at the adjacent detector transistor.

Electrically alterable read-only memories composed of field effect transistors with a *dielectric double layer* are produced at present by several companies. Such DDC transistors (dual dielectric charge storage) have the layer sequence metal/insulator-1/insulator-2/semiconductor. Best known are the MAOS storage transistor with alumina [30] and the MNOS storage transistor with silicon nitride as the outer dielectric (i.e. adjacent to the metal) [31]. Near the interface between the two dielectrics (see Fig. 13) and in their interior, charges can reversibly be stored. To favor the transport of such charges, the insulator layer close to the semiconductor has to be extremely thin (in the order of 2 to 5 nm).

At small gate voltages the function mode of an *MNOS storage transistor* is the same as that of an MOSFET. By higher voltage pulses, however, the flat-band voltage and

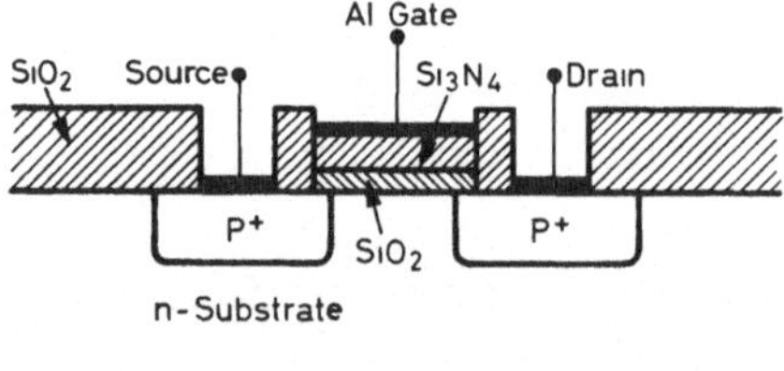

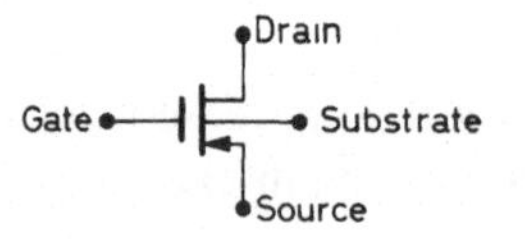

Fig. 13

MNOS storage transistor, schematic cross section.

with it the threshold voltage can reversibly be shifted by a change of the stored charge.
If the threshold voltage is plotted as a function of the height of such charging voltage
pulses (of constant duration), one obtains a hysteresis curve. The flat-band voltage
shift depends in a certain range exponentially on the voltage and logarithmically on
the duration of the charging pulses; beyond this range it approaches a saturation
value. The potential difference prevailing for the switching process drops between
the gate electrode and the silicon surface. It must be applied, according to the sign,
either at the gate electrode and the substrate (in the case of majority carrier accumulation) or at the gate electrode and the source and/or drain electrodes (in the case of
inversion). This difference is essential for the addressing possibilities of an MNOS
memory matrix.

Each memory element contains one MNOS storage transistor. For writing and erasing
the threshold voltage is switched to a high and a low value, respectively. In order to
read information, a voltage with a value between the two threshold voltages to be
distinguished is applied to the gate electrode; the conductance state of the transistor
obtained thereby corresponds to logic 0 or 1, respectively. The threshold voltage
must not be changed by the reading procedure.

As to the transport of charge from and to the traps near the oxide-nitride interface or
in the nitride, several mechanisms can occur, partly together. If the oxide layer is
more than 5 nm thick, Fowler-Nordheim emission is dominant (see Fig. 14): electrons
are injected from the semiconductor conduction band to the oxide conduction band

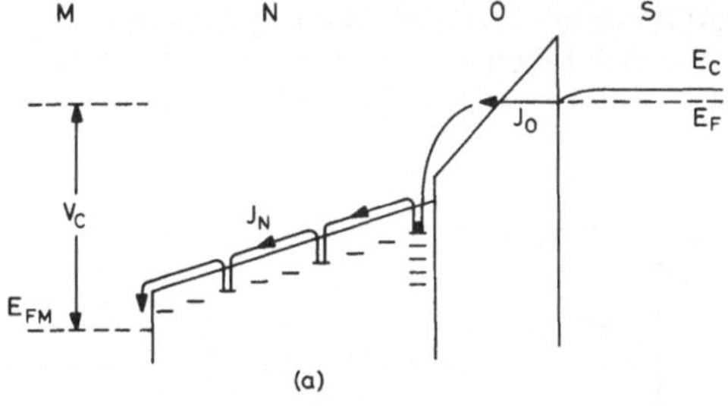

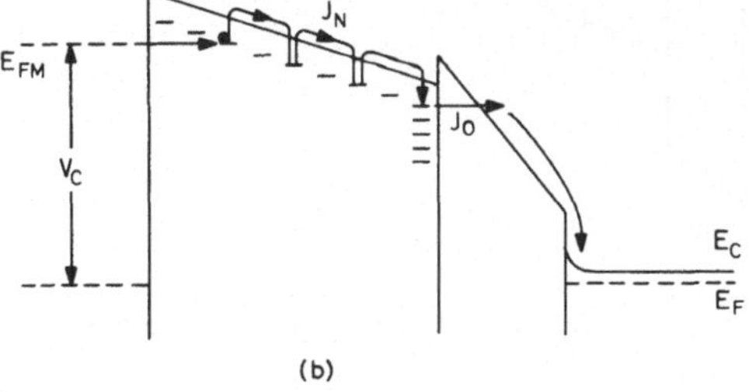

Fig. 14

Fowler-Nordheim emission:
energy band diagram of MNOS
structure under (a) positive bias
and (b) negative bias.

89

by a tunneling process, dropping into traps in the nitride; opposite bias causes the process to run in opposite direction, qualitatively in the same manner. For very thin oxide layers, a direct-tunneling model describes the charge transport best: electrons tunnel from the semiconductor valence band to the traps and from the traps to the semiconductor conduction band, respectively [32] (see Fig. 15). Also tunnel processes of electrons are considered from the silicon conduction band through the nitride conduction band to the traps (see Fig. 16) and (if the bias is opposite) of holes from the silicon valence band through the nitride valence band to the traps (where recombination occurs) [32]. Numerous other models have been designed during the last few years which describe the facts for different conditions more or less precisely.

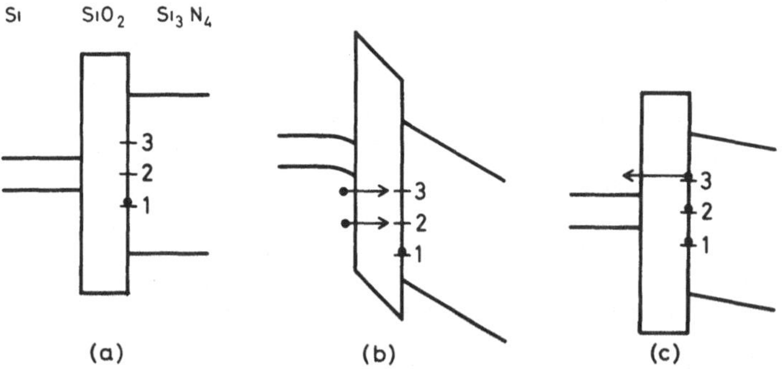

Fig. 15. Direct tunneling in MNOS structure. (a) Reference condition, assuming flat bands. (b) Charging under positive bias. (c) Return to flat-band condition (state marked "3" empties).

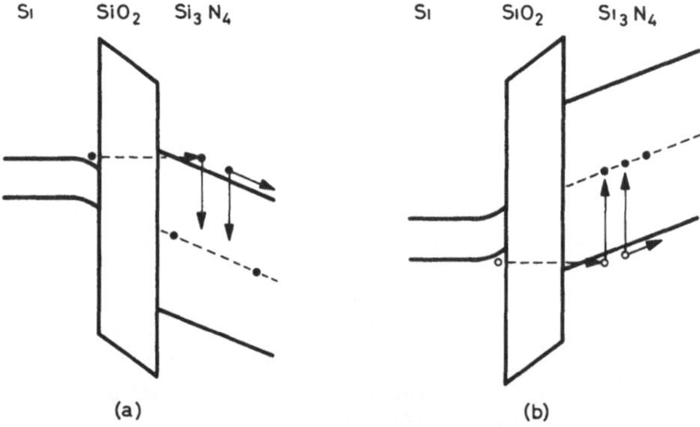

Fig. 16. Band-to-band tunneling model. (a) Charging under positive gates bias. (b) Charging under negative gate bias.

90

Special advantages result from a combination of MNOS storage technique with ESFI technology with regard to addressing possibilities [33].

Drawbacks are the limited charge retentivity, caused in particular by frequent reading cycles, and degradation of the properties as a consequence of a great number of writing cycles (insufficient endurance). Regeneration of the information after each reading may help against the influence of the reading process.
The properties of DDC memories may possibly be improved by doping the interface of the two insulating layers (W, Ir or Pt atoms), thus increasing the number of traps. Although in this case the inner insulating layer may be thicker, duration and height of the charging pulses can be decreased. A similar success was obtained even by sputterring a tungsten layer on the silica and complete removing of the metal by subsequent etching [34].

CCDs have been *combined with MNOS capacitors and transistors* in several ways [35]. Writing and reading is mainly obtained by means of a CCD shift register instead of addressing the usual matrix arrangement, thus increasing packing density. Another kind of circuit uses MNOS storage capacitors only to save information when the voltage supply is cut off. Finally, MNOS memory sites may be addressed by a standard shift register.

It is sometimes suitable to use a *programmable logic array (PLA)* instead of a (fully decoded) ROM. PLAs can be mask-programmed during production, just like a conventional ROM, but it is advantageous to apply the MNOS technique also to PLAs. Therefore an MNOS PLA using MNOS storage transistors which can be programmed or reprogrammed has been designed [36].

A storage transistor working in a similar way as those which have been described above is the *ferroelectric field effect transistor (FEFET)*. It is an IGFET with a ferroelectric in place of the gate dielectric. A reversible shift of the threshold voltage is possible by repolarizing the ferroelectric. Consequently, electric charge is not introduced from outside to be stored in an insulating layer, but it is, in a certain sense, rearranged within the device [37].

Conclusion

As compared with the existing variety, only a short review of the field of semiconductor memories was possible in this overview. Many details could not be taken into account, and numerous papers published in the field have not been cited. On the other hand semiconductor memory technology is in a continual evolution. In any case, semiconductor memories have their firm position within a foreseeable time to come.

References

[1] **Electron beam lithography**
Livesay, W. R., Sol. St. Technol. **17**, (1974), No. 6, p. 37–42; No. 7, p. 21–26
Thompson, F. L., Sol. St. Technol. **17**, (1974), No. 7, p. 27–30, 40; No. 8, p. 41–46
Funk-Techn. **31** (1976), No. 3, p. 64–69
Electronics/Dec. 23, 1976, p. 6E, 8E

[2] **X-ray lithography**
Spears, D. L., Smith, H. I., Sol. St. Technol. **15** (1972), No. 7, p. 21–26
Spears, D. L., Smith, H. I., Electron. Lett. **8** (1972), p. 102–104
Bassous, E., Feder, R., Spiller, E., Topalian, J., Sol. St. Technol. **19**, (1976), No. 9, p. 55–58.
McCoy, J. H., Sullivan, P. A., Sol. St. Technol. **19**, (1976), No. 9, p. 59–64
Spiller, E., Eastman, D. E., Feder, R., Grobman, W. D., Topalian, J., J. Appl. Phys. **47** (1976), p. 5450–5459

[3] **Ion implantation**
Eckstein, D., VALVO-Ber. XVIII (1974), No. 1/2, p. 227–234
Lee, D. H., Mayer, J. W., Proc. IEEE **62** (1974), p. 1241–1255 (numerous references)
Brown, W. L., MacRae, A. U., Bell Lab. Rec. **53** (1975), p. 388–394
Krimmel, E. F., Elektro-Anz. **28**, (1975), p. 251–253
Stone, J. L., Plunkett, J. C., Sol. St. Technol. **19** (1976), No. 6, p. 35–44
Sansbury, J., Sol. St. Technol. **19** (1976), No. 11, p. 31–37, 43.

[4] **Collector diffusion isolation**
Polke, H., Oestreich, P., Elektronik 1972, No. 1, p. 29–30
Grundy, D. L., Bruchez, J., Down, B., Electronics/July 3, 1972, p. 96–104
Bruchze, J., Microelectronitcs **5** (1974), No. 4, p. 45–54

[5] **GIMIC**
Electronic Design **6** (1973), March 15, p. 68–70

[6] **V-ATE**
Rodgers, T. J., Meindl, J. D., IEEE Trans. Electron Dev. ED-20 (1973), p. 226–232
Declercq, M. J., De Moor, J. P., Jespers, P. G., Sevrin, A. M., Electron. Lett **12** (1976), p. 150–151
Fields, St. W., Electronics/July 3, 1972, p. 65–66

[7] **Polyplanar, VIP**
Sanders, T. J., Morcom, W. R., Electronics/April 12, 1973, p. 117–120 (Polypl.),
Electronics/July 3, 1972, p. 39, 41 and p. 65–66 *(Fields, St. W.)* (VIP)

[8] **Anodic oxidation of silicon**
Cook, B., Electronics/Nov. 13, 1975, p. 109–113

[9] **General review of dielectric isolation techniques**
Bosnell, J. R., Microelectron. & Reliab. **15** (1976), p. 113–122

Isoplanar technique
Peltzer, D., Herndon, B., Electronics/March 1, 1971, p. 53–55

LOCOS
Appels, J. A., Kooi, E., Paffen, M. M., Schatorjé, J. J. H., Verkuylen, W. H. C. G., Phil. Res. Rep. **25** (1970), p. 118–132
Kooi, E., Van Lierop, J. G., Appels, J. A., J. Electrochem. Soc. **123** (1976), p. 1117–1120

Planox
Morandi, F., Bladowski, R., Int. Elektron. Rdsch. **25** (1971), p. 280–293

OXIM (Oxide Isolated Monolith)
Evans, W. J., Tretola, A. R., Payne, R. S., Olmstead, M. L., Speeney, D. V., IEEE
J. Sol. St. Circ. **SC-8** (1973), p. 373–380

Isoplanar-II-technique
Baker, W. D., Herndon, W. H., Longo, T. A., Pelzer, D. L., Electronics/March 29, 1973,
p. 65–70

[10] **OXIS**
Schwabe, U., Rathbone, R., Murrmann, H., Electrochem. Soc. Spring Meet. 1975

[11] **ESFI technology**
Schlotterer, H., J. Vac. Sci. & Technol. **13** (1976), p. 29–36
Druminski, M., Kuhl, Ch., Siemens F.- u. Entw.-Ber. **5** (1976), p. 139–145
Druminski, M., Kuhl, Ch., Preuss, E., Schwidefsky, F., Splittgerber, H., Takacs, D.,
Proc. 7th Conf. Sol. St. Dev. Tokyo 1975, p. 217–220
Ronen, R. S., Splinter, M. R., Tremain, R. E., IEEE J. Sol. St. Circ. **SC-11** (1976),
p. 431–442

[12] **CMOS memories**
Goser, K., Nachr.-techn. Z. 26. Jg. (1973), p. 9–15
Hume, S., Electronics/July 24, 1975, p. 102–106

[13] **ESFI-MOS memories**
Goser, K., Pomper, M., IEEE J. Sol. St. Circ. **SC-8** (1973), p. 324–326
Goser, K., Pomper, M., Tihanyi, J., IEEE J. Sol. St. Circ. **SC-9** (1974), p. 234–238
Pomper, M., Horninger, K. H., Tihanyi, J., Goser, K., L'Onde électr. **54** (1974), p. 187–191
Goser, K., Pomper, M., Siemens F.- u. Entw.-Ber. **4** (1975), p. 220–225

[14] CMOS-Isoplanar, LOCMOS
Brandt, B. B. M., Steinmeier, W., Strachan, A. J., Phil. Techn. Rdsch. **33** (1973), No. 11,
p. 343–347 or L'Onde électr. **54** (1974), No. 1, p. 27–30
VALVO brief (10.10.1975)

[15] **Silicon gate technology**
elektronik journal, 8. Jg., No. 12 (Dec. 1973), p. 28–34
Stein, K. U., Friedrich, H., IEEE J. Sol. St. Circ. **SC-8** (1973), p. 319–323
Wotruba, G., Siemens F.- u. Entw.-Ber. **4** (1975), p. 207–212
(the latter two papers treat memories produced in silicon gate technology)

[16] **V-MOS**
Holmes, F. E., Salama, C. A. T., Sol. St. Electronics **17** (1974), p. 791–797
Rodgers, T. J., Hiltpold, W. R., Zimmer, G., Marr, G., Trotter, J. D., ISSCC-Dig. Tech.
Pap. 1976, p. 60, 61, 232 (V-MOS-ROM)
Rodgers, T. J., Hiltpold, W. R., Zimmer, G., Marr, G., Trotter, J. D., IEEE J. Sol. St. Circ.
SC-11 (1976), No. 5, p. 614–622
Rodgers, T. J., Jenne, F. B., Frederick, B., Barnes, J. J., Hiltpold, W. R., Trotter, J. D.,
ISSCC-Dig. Techn. Pap. (1977), p. 74, 75, 239

D-MOS
Rodgers, T. J., Asai, S., Pocha, M. D., Dutton, R. W., Meindl, J. D., IEEE J. Sol. St. Circ.
SC-10 (1975), p. 322–331

Lin, H. C., Halsor, J. L., Benz, H. F., IEEE J. Sol. St. Circ. **SC-11** (1976), p. 443–452
Masuhara, T., Muller, R. S., IEEE J. Sol. St. Circ. **SC-11** (1976), p. 453–458
Yu, S. Y., Ou-Yang, P., Electron. Lett. **12** (1976), p. 605 (VDMOS)
Shimotori, K., Anami, K., Nagayama, Y., Ohkura, I., Ohmori, M., Nakano, T.,
ISSCC-Dig. Techn. Pap. (1977), p. 76, 77, 240

[17] **I^2 L = MTL**
Harth, C. M., Slob, A., Phil. Techn. Rdsch. **33** (1973/74), No. 3, p. 82–91
Berger, H. H., Wiedmann, S. K., Electronics/Sept. 4, 1975, p. 89–95; Oct. 2, 1975,
p. 99–103
Several authors, IEEE J. Sol. St. Circ. **SC-9** (1974), p. 206–227
Mulder, C., Wulms, H. E., IEEE J. Sol. St. Circ. **SC-11** (1976), p. 379–385
Armstrong, L., Altman, L., Electronics/March 18, 1976, p. 80. 82

Schottky-I^2 L
Hewlett, F. W., Jr., IEEE J. Sol. St. Circ. **SC-10** (1975), p. 343–348
Berger, H. H., Wiedmann, S. K., ISSCC-Dig. Techn. Pap. 1975, p. 172

Substrate Fed Logic (SFL)
Blatt, V., Walsh, Ph. S., Kennedy, L. W., IEEE J. Sol. St. Circ. **SC-10** (1975), p. 336–342

Current Hogging Logic (CHL)
Lehning, H., IEEE J. Sol. St. Circ. **SC-9** (1974), p. 228–233

Current Hogging Injection Logic (CHIL)
Muller, R., IEEE J. Sol. St. Circ. **SC-10** (1975), p. 348–352

Vertical Injection Logic (VIL)
Tomisawa, O., Horiba, Y., Kato, S., Murakami, K., Yasuoka, A., Nakano, T., IEEE
J. Sol. St. Circ. **SC-11** (1976), No. 5, p. 637–643

[18] **I^2 L-RAMs**
Wiedmann, S. K., Berger, H. H., Electronics/Feb. 14, 1972, p. 83–86
Wiedmann, S. K., IEEE J. Sol. St. Circ. **SC-8** (1973), p. 332–337

[19] **I^3 L-RAMs**
Sander, W. B., Early, J. M., ISSCC-Dig. Techn. Pap. 1976, p. 182–183
Sander, W. B., Shepherd, W. H., Schinelle, R. D., Electronics/August 19, 1976, p. 99–102

[20] **Charge transfer devices**
Sangster, F. L. J., Teer, K., IEEE J. Sol. St. Circ. **SC-4** (1969), p. 131–136 (BBD)
Boyle, W. S., Smith, G. E., B.S.T.J. **49** (1970), p. 587–593 (CCD)
Séquin, C. H., Tompsett, M. F., Charge Transfer Devices. Acad. Press, New York,
San Francisco, London 1975 (a comprehensive review with numerous references)
Several authors, IEEE J. Sol. St. Circ. **SC-11** (1976), p. 4–58
Ablaßmeier, U., Doering, E., Siemens F.- u. Entw.-Ber. **4** (1975), p. 226–230
Harloff, H. J., this issue, p. 147

[21] **CC-RAM**
Tasch, A. F., Frye, R. C., Fu, H.-S., IEEE Trans. Electron Dev. ED-23 (1976), p. 126–131
Tasch, A. F., Fu, H.-S., Holloway, T. C., Frye, R. E., IEEE J. Sol. St. Circ. **SC-11** (1976),
No. 5, p. 575–585

[22] **CCD-RAM**
Baker, R. T., Electronics/Nov. 13, 1975, p. 138–139

[23] **Merged Charge Memory**
Lee, H. S., Pricer, W. D., IEDM-Techn. Dig. (1976), p. 15−17 (see also Electronics/Nov. 25, 1976, p. 42−43)

[24] **C³-RAM**
Hoffmann, K., ISSCC-Dig. Techn. Pap., 1976, p. 130−131
Hoffmann, K., IEEE J. Sol. St. Circ. SC-11 (1976), No. 5, p. 591−596

[25] **Nonvolatile memories**
Chang, J. J., Proc. IEEE **64** (1976), No. 7, p. 1039−1059 (general review)
IEEE Trans. Electron Dev. **ED-24** (1977), No. 5 (special issue on nonvolatile semiconductor memory)

[26] **Amorphous Semiconductors**
Tanaka, K., Okada, Y., Sugi, M., Iizima, S., Kikuchi, M., J. Non-Cryst. Sol. (NL) **12** (1973), No. 1, p. 100−114
Van Roosbroeck, W., J. Non-Cryst. Sol. (NL) **12** (1973), No. 2, p. 232−262
Baran, N. Yu., Dovgoshei, N. I., Sov. Phys. Semicond. **9** (1975), p. 1167−1168
Weiser, K., Prog. Sol. St. Chem. (GB) **11** (1976), p. 403−445
Suntola, T., Thin Sol. Films **34**, No. 1 (May 1976), p. 9−16.
Thornburg, D. D., Thin Sol. Films **45** (1977), p. 95−105

[27] **FAMOS memories**
Frohman-Bentchkowsky, D., Sol. St. Electron. **17** (1974), p. 517−529
Card, H. C., Heasell, E. L., Sol. St. Electron. **19** (1976), p. 965−968

[28] **Other floating-gate transistor structures**
SAMOS: *Iizuka, H., Masuoka, F., Sato, T., Ishikawa, M.,* IEEE Trans. Electron Dev. **ED-23** (1976), p. 379−387
SIMOS: *Rossler, B., Muller, R. G.,* Siemens F.- u. Entwo.-Ber. **4** (1975), p. 345−351
ATMOS: *Verwey, J. F., Kramer, R. P.,* IEEE Trans Electron. Dev. **ED-21** (1974), p. 631−636
Tarui, Y., Hayashi, Y., Nagai, K., IEEE J. Sol. St. Circ. **SC-7** (1972), p. 369−375
Card, H. C., Worall, A. G., J. Appl. Phys. **44** (1973), p. 2316−2330
Kikuchi, M., Ohya, S., Kamaya, M., Koike, M., Yamamoto, H., First Europ. Sol. St. Circ. Conf. (ESSCIRC) 1975, p. 66
Rai, Y., Sasami, T., Hasegawa, Y., IEE (Japan) **111** (March 1976), p. 26−31 (MNMOS)
Muller, R. G., this issue, p. 189
Kelley, W., Millet, D. F., Electronics/Dec. 9, 1976, p. 101−104

[29] **DIFMOS**
Gosney, W. M., IEEE Trans. Electron Dev. **ED-24** (1977), No. 5, p. 594−599
El. et Microél. Ind. **228** (15-11-1976), p. 20−21

[30] **MAOS memory**
Balk, P., Stephany, F., J. Electrochem. Soc. **118** (1971), p. 1634−1638
Balk, P., Solid State Devices 1973 (3rd Europ. Sol. St. Dev. Conf.).
The Inst. of Physics London Bristol, p. 51−82
Balk, P., J. Electron. Mat. **4** (1975), p. 635−661
Gnadinger, A. P., Rosenzweig, W., J. Electrochem. Soc. **121** (1974), p. 700−705

[31] **MNOS memory**
Frohman-Bentchkowsky, D., Proc. IEEE **58** (1970), p. 1207–1219
Balk, P., see [30] (1973, 1975)
Horninger, K. H., Bull. Schweizer. Eletrotechn. Ver. **64** (1973), p. 1258–1263
Horninger, K. H., Siemens F.- u. Entw.-Ber. **4** (1975), p. 213–219
Uchida, Y., Endo, N., Saito, Sh., Konaka, M., Nojima, I., Nishi, Y., Tamaru, K., ISSCC-Dig. Techn. Pap., 1975, p. 108, 109, 220
Lodi, R. J., Wegener, H. A. R., Kosicki, B. B., Borovicka, M., Moberg, W. L., Newman, R., ISSCC-Dig. Techn. Pap., 1976, p. 62, 63, 233
Lodi, R. J., Wegener, H. A. R., Borovicka, M., Pogemiller, T. A., Eklund, M. W., IEEE J. Sol. St. Circ. **SC-11** (1976), No. 5, p. 622–630
Kirschner, N., Siemens F.- u. Entw.-Ber. **5** (1976), p. 179–182
Card, H. C., Elmasry, M. I., Sol. St. Electron. **19** (1976), p. 863–870
Raffel, J. I., Yasaitis, J. A., Proc. IEEE, Nov. 1976, p. 1629, 1630 and ISSCC-Dig. Techn. Pap. (1977), p. 192, 193, 251

[32] **Tunneling mechanisms in MNOS structures**
Gordon, N., Johnson, W. C., IEEE Trans. Electron Dev. **ED-20** (1973), p. 253–256
Ross, E. C., Wallmark, J. T., RCA Rev. **30** (1969), p. 366–381

[33] **ESFI-MNOS memories**
Horninger, K. H., IEEE J. Sol. St. Circ. **SC-9** (1974), p. 444–446

[34] **Doped DDCs**
Kahng, D., Sundburg, W. J., Boulin, D. M., Ligenza, J. R., B.S.T.J. **53** (1974), p. 1723–1739
Thornber, K. K., Kahng, D., Neppell, C. T., B.S.T.J. **53** (1974), p. 1741–1770
Kasprzak, L. A., Laibowitz, R. B., Ohring, M., Electrochem. Soc. Fall Meet. 1975 (Ext. abstr.), p. 316–317
Vitanov, P. K., Popova, L. I., Antov, B. Z., Electron. Lett. **12** (1976), p. 681

[35] **CCD combined with MNOS**
Chan, Y. T., French, B. T., Gudmundsen, R. A., Appl. Phys. Lett. **22** (1973), p. 650–652
Goser, K., Knauer, K., IEEE J. Sol. St. Circ. **SC-9** (1974), p. 148–150
White, M. H., Lampe, D. R., Fagan, J. L., Kub, F. J., Barth, D. A., IEEE J. Sol. St. Circ. **SC-10** (1975), p. 281–287
Fagan, J. L., White, M. H., Lampe, D. R., ISSCC-Dig. Techn. Pap. 1976, p. 184–185
Fagan, J. L., White, M. H., Lampe, D. R., IEEE J. Sol. St. Circ. **SC–11** (1976), No. 5, p. 631–636

[36] **PLA containing MNOS transistors**
Horninger, K. H., IEEE J. Sol. St. Circ. **SC-10** (1975), p. 331–336

[37] **Ferroelectric memory**
Wu, S. Y., IEEE Trans. Electron Dev. **ED-21** (1974), p. 499–504

LSI Semiconductor Memories

Rudolf Mitterer

Siemens AG, Integrated Circuits Division, Munich, Germany

1. Introduction

Among the read-write memory devices, low-cost dynamic MOS-RAMs for main
memories are of greatest interest. The most important development objectives for
the improvement of these memory devices are discussed. The silicon area of a
memory chip essentially determines its manufacturing costs. Advances in memory
cells — previously characterized by the numbers of transistors and lines — may in
future be measured by the reduction in the number of structural squares. Estimated
factors representing the refinement of the structures and the increase in the permissible chip size provide an indication of possible improvements and ultimate limits
for the device storage capacity and the cost per bit of dynamic MOS memory devices.

2. Read-write memory devices 1977

Semiconductor memories contribute significantly to the performance and costs of
data processing systems. Read-write memories with random access (RAMs) have taken
over the role of the magnetic core storage in this field. In main memories a dominating
position is occupied by low-cost dynamic MOS-RAMs, while bipolar RAMs are predominant in buffer memories working at high speeds (Table 1). These memory device

Table 1: Read-write memory devices 1977 (price for large quantities)

Main application	Memory type	Access time ns	Power dissipation mW	Approx. price ¢/bit
Main memories	4 K n-MOS dyn.	150–350	450	0.11
	16 K n-MOS dyn.	150–350	500–700	0.13
Small systems	4 K, 16 K dyn.	150–350	450–700	0.13
	4 K n-MOS stat.	70–550	350–500	0.17
	4 K I^2 L stat.	70–100	500	0.26
	1 K CMOS stat.	150	4	0.87
Buffers	1 K TTL stat.	40–100	500–800	0.78
	1 K ECL stat.	35–60	500–800	1.2
	4 K I^2 L, MOS stat.	70–550	500	0.26

types are also employed in small memory systems, as are static MOS-RAMs, which have the advantage over bipolar memories of low cost and power dissipation and are simpler to work with than dynamic MOS-RAMs. The particularly low power dissipation of CMOS memory devices facilitates data retention with the aid of small batteries on, for example, the printed circuit board in the event of a power supply failure.

3. Basic development objectives

Among the most important objectives in the development of dynamic MOS memory devices are:

- increasing the device capacity — reduction of the cost per bit
  by using simpler cells, finer structures and larger chips

- lengthening the refresh time
  by avoiding leakage current and crystal defects

- cutting the access time
  by using enhanced transistors and circuits

- reducing the power dissipation per bit
  by employing a lower operating voltage

- increasing the reliability per bit
  by using improved components and processes

4. Chip area and manufacturing costs

The more the chip area A of an LSI device can be shrunk through improvements in circuit design and layout, the greater is the number of chips contained on a slice and the higher is the slice yield

$$Y \approx \left(\frac{1 - e^{-DA}}{DA} \right)^2 \quad [19].$$

The defect density D decreases as control of the process increases over the period in which a device type is manufactured.

Fig. 1 gives an impression of how the manufacturing costs depend on the chip area, with no change in the complexity of the process (number of masks, structure size, for instance). The increase in the yield and the reduction in the chip area have so far made it possible to cut the costs annually by the factor 1.3. A fourfold increase in the memory device capacity was achieved approximately every 2.5 years. The introduction of a new device generation with a larger chip area and greater demands placed on the process does not, however, immediately lead to lower costs per bit. Fig. 2 illustrates the drop in price per bit for various memory devices.

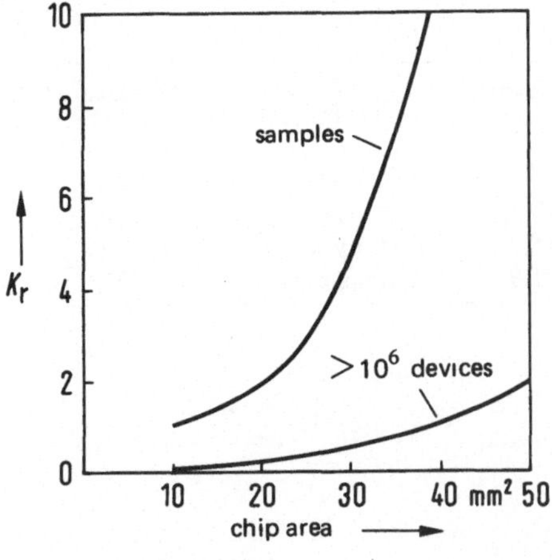

Fig. 1

Relative manufacturing cost K_r

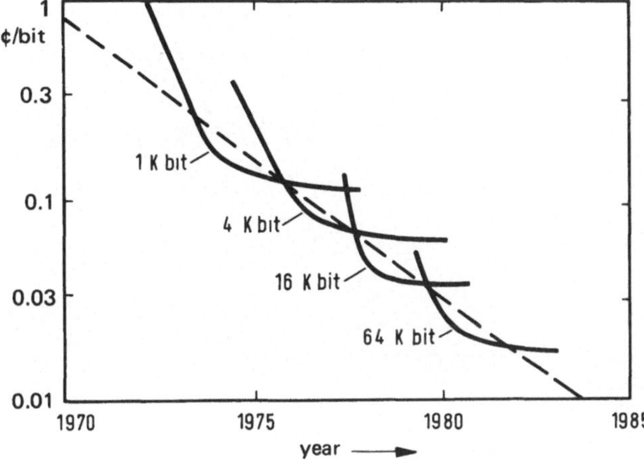

Fig. 2

Principal price development
of dynamic MOS-RAM
devices

5. Advances in MOS memories

Innovations in the circuit and process techniques have so far contributed most to a cost-effective increase in the storage capacity. The rapid development of memory cells from the static 8-transistor cell in 1968 to modern dynamic single-transistor cells [1—5] is shown in Table 2.

It was possible to systematically reduce the number of the transistors and lines (Fig. 3). Functional integration of selection transistor and storage capacitor permitted a further reduction toward the 16-K bit RAM-chip.

A transfer gate cell using this principle and fabricated by double-level silicon technique with an area of 476 μm² is shown in Fig. 4. In the case of a 16384-bit

Table 2: Advances in MOS-RAM devices

Year	Bits per chip	Technology	Chip area mm²	Cell type	Cell area µm²
1968	256	p-Al-gate	10	8-tr. stat.	23 000
1970	1024	p-Si-gate	10.2	3-tr. dyn.	3 670
1973	4096	n-Si-gate	18.6	1-tr. dyn.	1 290
1975	16384	double-level Si	21.9	1 transfer gate	455

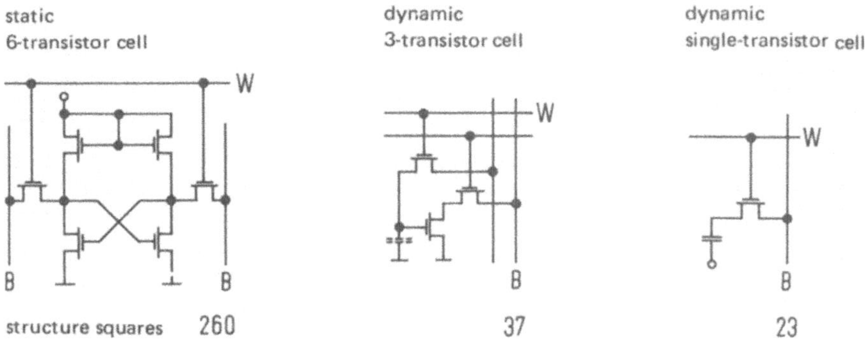

Fig. 3. Simplification of memory cells.

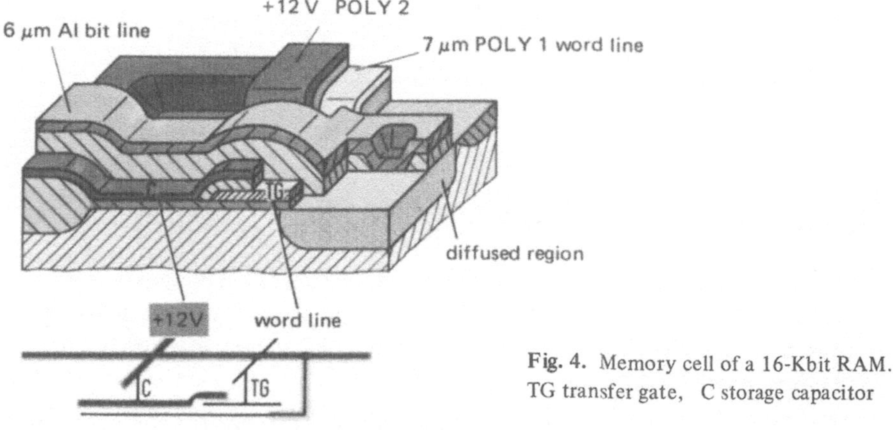

Fig. 4. Memory cell of a 16-Kbit RAM.
TG transfer gate, C storage capacitor

memory device [5] these cells take up 33 % of the chip area of 23.5 mm² (Fig. 5). A measure of the progress achieved in device design is also obtained by expressing the cell area as the number of structural squares with the width of one line.

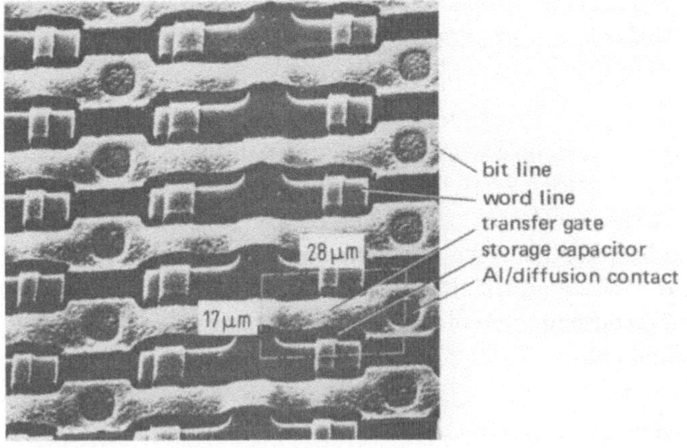

Fig. 5

Memory cells of a
16-Kbit RAM

6. Future MOS-RAM cells

A number of innovations which will permit the storage capacity of future devices to be increased are already apparent. In the CC-RAM [6] the storage capacitor and the selection transistor are combined below the word line as a common electrode. In the merged charge memory (MCM) [7] the transfer gate is used as a bit line and charge transport takes place as in CCD memories. The move from planar to vertical MOS transistors (Fig. 6) [8] also has a very promising future. In this VMOS technique storage capacitor and selection transistor can be arranged one above the other instead of next to each other to save a great amount of area [9]. In this way, a cell density equal to that of CCD memory cells is achieved.

A further method of raising the storage capacity is to store more than one bit in each cell (multi-level storage) [10]. A differentiation between, for example, two bits by

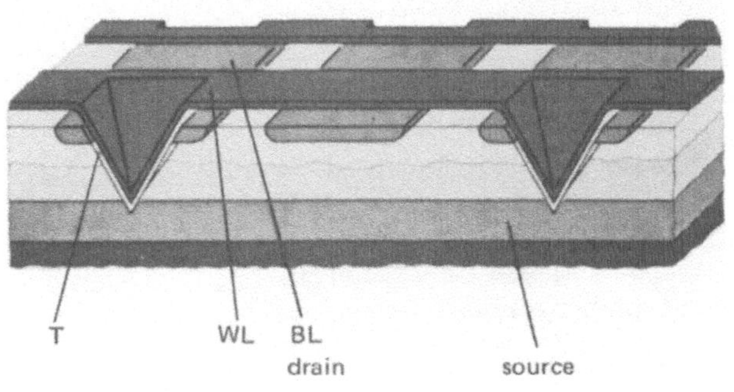

Fig. 6

Memory matrix of a
ROM in VMOS
technology.

evaluation of four different sense levels can however only be achieved with very
sensitive and stable (e.g. bipolar) sense amplifiers.

A higher storage capacity is thus obtained at the expense of sense signal amplitude,
as if the structures were scaled down. Sense principles are known which circumvent a
charge loss on the bit line, as for example with CCD cells, MOS bit lines (C^3RAM)
[11] or charge transfer sense amplifiers [12]. These methods, however, have the
disadvantage of a longer access time [13]. Through all these means it is expected that
by 1980 memory cells will be available which only take up one structural square. The
simpler the cell structure is, the more difficult it is, however, to fit the peripheral
circuits into the cell grid. The development of the peripheral circuits thus also places
very high demands on the designer.

7. Perspectives for MOS memory devices

At present, there are no prospects for further cell simplification for the period after
1980 [14]. It can however be assumed that improved processes and equipment will
permit refinement of the structures and an increase in the permissible chip size [15].
Table 3 shows the estimated factors by which the storage capacity will increase. As
the structure size decreases, disturbance-free sensing will however become more and
more difficult.

For the sense signal U_L of a single-transistor cell it follows that:

$$U_L\left(\frac{1}{\alpha}\right) \sim \frac{C_Z}{C_Z + C_{BL}} \cdot U_D\left(\frac{1}{\alpha}\right);$$

C_Z, C_{BL}: capacitance of the cell and the bit line

As the write pulse amplitude has to be decreased in proportion to the supply voltage
U_D and thus in proportion to the linear scale-down factor α [16], the sense signal is
also reduced in proportion to $1/\alpha$. By means of improved sense principles or for

Table 3: Estimated improvement factors for the annual increase in capacity

Annual improvement	until 1980	1980–2020	after 2020
Cell simplification	1.24	1	1
Square structure scale-down	1.20	1.21	1
Chip size (mm²)	1.16	1.16	1.15
Overall improvement	1.74	1.41	1.15
Fourfold increase in capacity in	2.5 years	4 years	10 years
Maximum capacity/chip	256-kbits	256-Gbits	> 256-Gbits

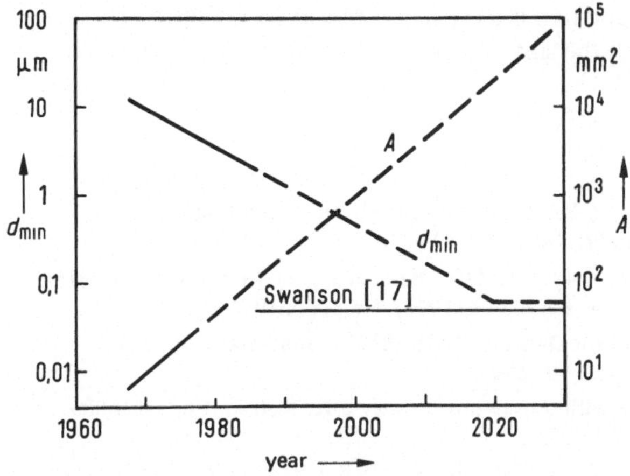

Fig. 7

Possible development of structure size d_{min} and chip area A for MOS memory devices

example by reducing the threshold voltage tolerance of adjacent transistors, the sensitivity of the sense amplifier must therefore also be increased by the factor α. A condition for this is that the ratio of the cell capacitance C_Z to the parasitic capacitance C_{BL} of the bit line remains constant. This can be achieved by keeping the number of bits per bit line constant. This measure also ensures an adequate refresh time and prevents intolerable voltage drops on the bit line.

Extrapolation can be based, for example, on a 40 mm^2, 256-Kbit memory device with a 50-mV sense signal. Assuming that the sense signal has its smallest permissible level of 1 mV at U_D = 100 mV, a fifty-fold linear reduction of structural size is permissible. For a cell which only takes up 1 structural square, the structural size can be reduced to $3\ \mu m/50 = 0.06\ \mu m$. This value is above the ultimate limits of 0.05 μm and 0.03 μm as forecast by *Swanson* and *Meindl* [17] and *Wallmark* [18]

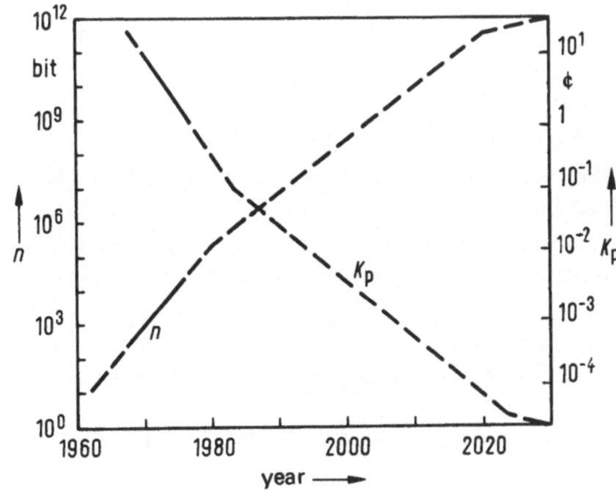

Fig. 8

Possible development of device capacity n and bit price K_p

(Fig. 8). The result of the extrapolation is a capacity limit of 256 Gbits on a 19 000 mm^2 chip. This chip with the size of an entire 6$''$ slice would enable a bit price of less than 10^{-4} ¢.

References

[1]   *R. Mitterer* and *H. Schulte,* MOS-RAM-Speicherzellen in Doppel-Polysiliziumtechnik. Elektronik-Anzeiger Vol. 9 (1977), No. 7, pp. 19–22.

[2]   *H. Heißing* and *R. W. Mitterer,* A 4096-bit MOS Memory Device with Single-Transistor Cells. Siemens Forsch. und Entw. Berichte 4 (1975), Nr. 4, pp. 197–202.

[3]   *C. N. Ahlquist* et al., A 16 384-Bit Dynamic RAM. IEEE J. Solid-State Curcuits, Vol. Sc-11, No. 5, Oct. 1976, pp. 570–574.

[4]   *C. Kuo* et al., 16-k RAM built with proven process may offer high start-up reliability. Electronics 49 (1976) 10, pp. 81–86.

[5]   *R. W. Mitterer* and *B. F. Rehn,* A 16 K MOS RAM with double-polysilicon technology. ESSCIRC-Tagung, Toulouse, 23. Sept. 1976, Tagungsband pp. 40–41.

[6]   *Al F. Tasch* et al., Charge Capacity Analysis of the Charge-Coupled RAM Cell. IEEE J. Solid-State Circuits, Vol. SC-11, No. 5, Oct. 1976, pp. 575–585.

[7]   *H. S. Lee* and *W. D. Pricer,* Merged Charge Memory (MCM) – a new Random Access Cell. IEDM Techn. Digest (1976), pp. 15–17.

[8]   *T. J. Rodgers* et al., VMOS ROM. IEEE J. Solid-State Circuits, Vol. SC-11, No. 5, Oct. 1976, pp. 614–622.

[9]   *J. Barnes* et al., VMOS EPROM and BURIED SOURCE RAM DEVICES. IEDM Techn. Digest (1976), Supplement pp. 2–3.

[10]   *R. A. Heald* and *D. A. Hodges,* Multilevel Random-Access Memory Using One Transistor Per Cell. IEEE J. Solid-State Circuits, Vol. SC-11, No. 4, Aug. 1976, pp. 519–528.

[11]   *K. Hoffmann,* MOS Transmission Line as a New Device for the Implementation of Large-Scale Integration. Siemens Forsch. und Entw. Berichte 5 (1976), Nr. 6, pp. 327–332.

[12]   *L. G. Heller* et al., High Sensitivity Charge-Transfer Sense Amplifier. IEEE J. Solid-State Circuits, Vol. SC-11, No. 5, Oct. 1976, pp. 596–601.

[13]   *K. Horninger,* Readout methods and readout circuits for dynamic charge-storage elements, this volume, p. 121

[14]   *G. E. Moore,* Progress in Digital Integrated Electronics. IEDM Techn. Digest (1975), pp. 11–13.

[15]   *K. Garbrecht* and *K.-U. Stein,* Perspectives and Limitations of Large-Scale Integration. Siemens Forsch. und Entw. Berichte 5 (1976), Nr. 6, pp. 312–318.

[16]   *G. Meusburger* and *R. Sigusch,* Scaling of n-MOS Devices: Experimental Verification of an LSI Concept. Siemens Forsch. und Entw. Berichte 5 (1976), Nr. 6, pp. 332–337.

[17]   *R. M. Swanson* and *J. D. Meindl,* Fundamental Performance Limits of MOS Integrated Circuits. 1975 IEEE Internat. Solid-State Circuits Conference, Digest of Techn. Papers, IEEE New York 1975, pp. 110–111.

[18]   *J. T. Wallmark,* Fundamental Physical Limitations in Integrated Electronic Circuits. Solid State Devices (1974), Institute of Physics, Conference Series No. 25, London 1975, pp. 133–167.

[19]   *B. T. Murphy,* Cost-Size Optima of Monolithic Integrated Circuits. Proc. IEEE, Vol. 52 (1964), pp. 1537–1545.

A High Performance Low Power 2048-Bit Memory Chip in MOSFET Technology and Its Application

Utz G. Baitinger and Rolf Remshardt

IBM Deutschland GmbH, Böblingen, Germany

1. Introduction

The models 115 and 125 of the IBM System/370, together with the memory extensions for the models 158 and 168, are the first IBM computers which use large monolithic memories in MOSFET technology for the main stores and for control stores. These memories have proven their feasibility and reliability in several thousand systems during the last three years.

The heart of these memories, which range from 64 kbytes (for the model 115) up to 8 Mbytes (for the model 168), is a 2048-bit array chip in MOSFET technology. Its nominal standby power dissipation is 20 mW; for a 200-ns cycle, the total power dissipation per chip is below 200 mW. The worst case access time on chip is 65 ns; typical values are in the range of 50 ns.

This paper presents the main features of this chip, the measures, how they were achieved, and gives a typical example of how the chip can be operated in a memory.

2. Assumptions and Design Objective

The design objective was to exploit the potential of a given MOSFET technology with respect to an optimum cost/performance ratio and a minimum power-delay product. In contrast to the prevailing p-channel technologies at that time [1], IBM had decided to take advantage of the favorable electric characteristics of an n-channel MOSFET technology. The gain in power-delay product, however, has to be paid with the need for a thin, well-controlled and clean gate dielectric.

The main features of the given MOSFET technology are the following.

1. n-channel, p-type substrate.
2. Enhancement type (achieved by substrate bias).
3. Gate-oxide thickness 700 Å.
4. Transconductance $32\ \mu A/V^2$.
5. Threshold voltage 0.3 ... 1.0 V.
6. 5-μm minimum mask dimensions.
7. Junction and gate capacitances are kept low by choice of a sufficiently high substrate bias of -3.0 V.

Furthermore, a hybrid addressing and sensing system has been assumed: the MOSFET array chip is driven by bipolar interface drivers (for the address signals), and bipolar sense amplifiers/bit drivers (for the read/write operations).

The main problems of this MOSFET chip design are related to the large spread of the threshold voltage, the deviations of bias voltages from chip to chip within a hybrid sensing system, and the variations of external signal pulses ("skews") on the memory card. The solution largely takes advantage of the on-chip tracking of device parameters. This will be discussed in detail below.

3. Array Chip Performance

In order to exploit the performance potential of the given MOSFET technology, a dc stable flip-flop type memory cell ("6-device cell") is chosen [2], [3] which avoids time consuming refresh cycles. Fig. 1 shows the addressing and sensing scheme for the memory cell. Only address signals are applied to the array chip.

1. One decoded chip select signal CS.
2. A coded word address (five signal pulses).
3. A coded bit address (five signal pulses).
4. Two decoded array select signals Y1 and Y2.

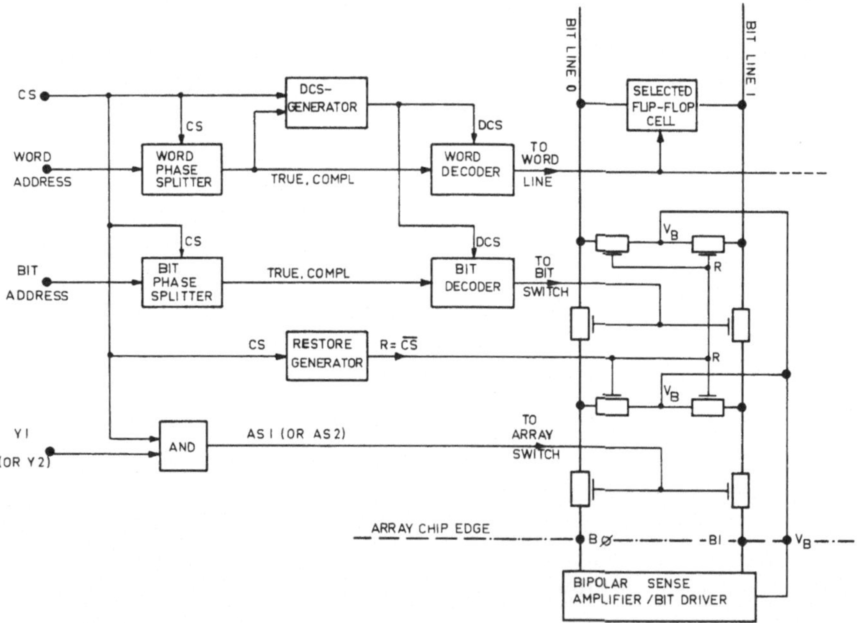

Fig. 1. Addressing and sensing scheme of the array chip. *CS*–chip select; *R*–restore pulse; *DCS*-delayed chip select; *Y1*-array select.

106

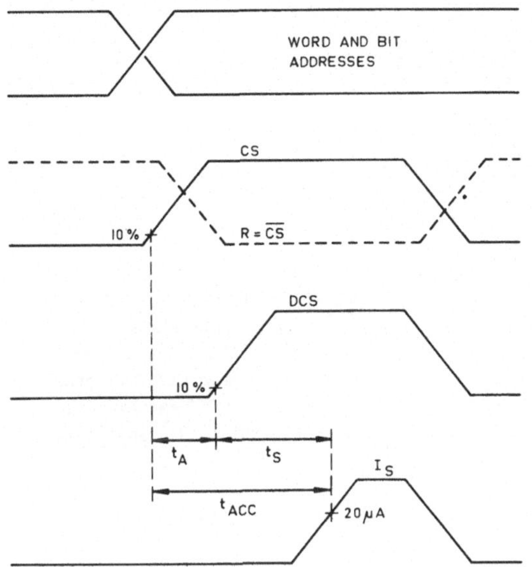

Fig. 2

Simplified timing diagram of a read operation. I_S–sense current; t_{ACC}–chip access time; t_A–addressing delay; t_S–sensing delay.

All auxiliary signals (e.g., restore pulse R, decoder clock signal DCS) are generated on-chip, thus avoiding external signals and their skews.

The chip access time t_{ACC} consists of two parts (see Fig. 2): the addressing delay t_A until DCS starts rising and the sensing delay t_S until the sense current I_S has reached 20 μA. Both are kept short by use of the tracking of device parameters.

A. Addressing Delay

The addressing mechanism is as follows (see Figs. 1 and 2). Word and bit addresses have to be valid before chip select CS becomes active. The word and the bit phase splitters, which generate trues and complements out of the address signals, are clocked by chip select CS. The decoders have to be clocked by a delayed chip select pulse DCS which is generated on-chip by the DCS generator. The required delay is equal to the sum of the phase splitter delay plus the decoder delay in order to avoid unwanted selections. Fig. 3 shows this in more detail.

Circuit NOR$'$ gets the true as well as the complement (T1 and C1) out of one phase splitter and OR's them. Thus, the phase splitter delay is already included. T1 or C1 will switch on the decoder clock signal DCS after the delay of circuit NOR$'$. Circuit NOR$''$ is very fast, but circuit NOR$'$ simulates the slow circuit NOR within the decoder and therefore the delays of both are tracking. Thus, DCS opens the AND gate to the selected wordline WL at the same instant when the NOR outputs of the decoders become valid. DCS is switched off by $\overline{CS}$, which is generated by an inverter

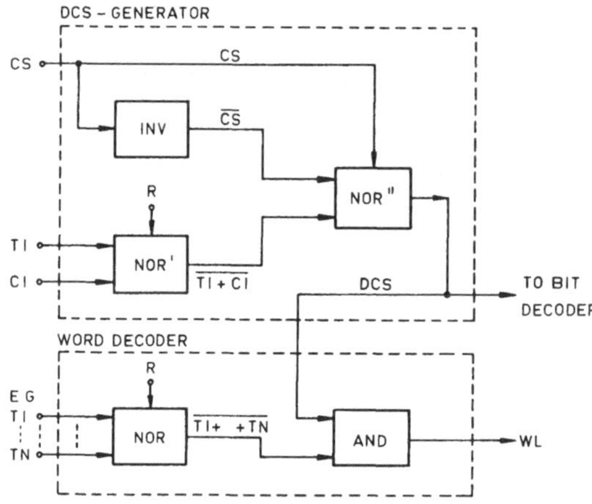

Fig. 3

Decoder and delayed chip select block diagram. *CS*–chip select; *DCS*–delayed chip select; *WL*–selected wordline; *T*1, *C*1–true/complement output of one phase splitter; *T*1 ⋯ *TN*–personalization of decoder; *R*–restore pulse.

circuit INV and fed into circuit NOR″. Circuit NOR″ is clocked by CS to avoid power dissipation during standby.

By these measures the delay of DCS tracks with the phase splitter delay and the decoder delay as required. Thus, a shorter addressing delay is reached for most of the array chips than would be the case with an externally delayed signal pulse DCS which has to wait for the worst case array chip.

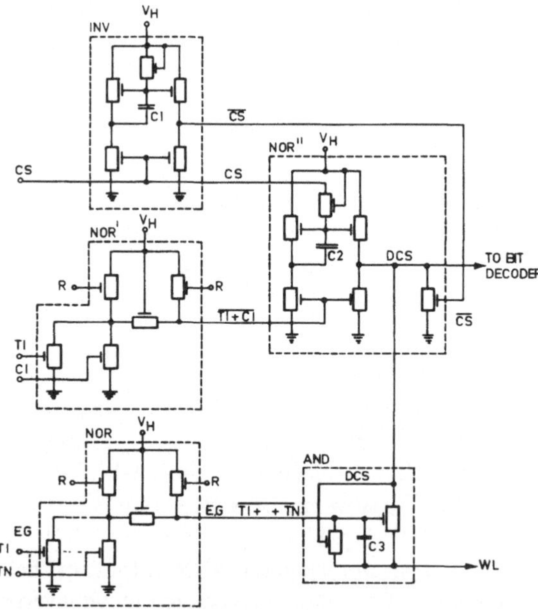

Fig. 4

Typical ac-peripheral circuits: the decoder and delayed chip select circuits.

108

Fig. 4 shows the corresponding circuits. Their concept is representative for all the on-chip peripheral circuits. The extensive use of feedback capacitors [4] can be seen (C1, C2, C3), as well as the use of fast inverter circuits where the feedback capacitor is not attached to the highly capacitive output, but to a duplication of it with low parasitic capacitance.

During standby, all the feedback and stray capacitors within the decoders are charged. This is controlled by a restore pulse R, which logically is the complement of chip select CS and which is also generated on-chip by the restore generator. This is done since discharging of unselected feedback capacitors during selection is less time consuming than charging of the selected ones.

B. Sensing Delay

The sensing mechanism is as follows (see Figs. 1 and 2). During standby, all the bit lines across the array chip, i.e., the bit line pairs between the cells and the bit switches, as well as between the bit switches and the array switches, are biased to the voltage V_B. This is also controlled by the restore pulse R. The voltage V_B is generated on the bipolar sense amplifier/bit driver chip and fed into the array chip. Both chips are mounted on different modules, but on the same memory card. The tracking of V_B results in a homogeneous bias of the bit lines not only on the array chip, but also on the modules, on the memory card, and on the sense amplifier/bit driver chip. Thus, compensating currents are avoided when the cell is sensed and the differential sense current I_S is not affected by spikes into the wrong direction. This leads to a shorter worst case sensing delay. More details about the read/write operations will be given in Section 6-B.

4. Array Chip Power Dissipation

The power dissipation of the array chip is kept low by the use of clocked on-chip peripheral circuits which dissipate only ac power (refer to Fig. 4). Thus, the total chip power dissipation is determined by the ac power of the on-chip peripheral circuits and the dc power of the memory cells.

A dc stable, flip-flop type memory cell (6-device cell) has been chosen for performance reasons. Its dc power dissipation does not contribute to the power-delay product, i.e., an increase of this dc power would not decrease the access time. Therefore, it can be kept as low as the cell stability allows it without performance impact. But both the power dissipation and the cell stability are a function of threshold voltage which suffers from a large spread. Therefore, an on-chip gate voltage driver [5] is provided for the memory cell which will be discussed below.

A. Memory Cell Stability

The circuits of the memory cell and the gate driver are shown in Fig. 5. Let us assume that cell transistor T1 is off, whereas cell transistor T2 is on. A sufficiently high gate voltage V_G is required to maintain the cell stability:

$$V_G = V_{TH2} + \Delta V_2 + V_{TH3} + \Delta V_3$$
$$= V_{TH2} + V_{TH3} + \Delta V . \tag{1}$$

$\Delta V \equiv \Delta V_2 + \Delta V_3$ is required for current flows through T2 and T3. Then T3 will compensate for the leakage current of the stray capacitance at the gate node of T2, and T2 will be kept on.

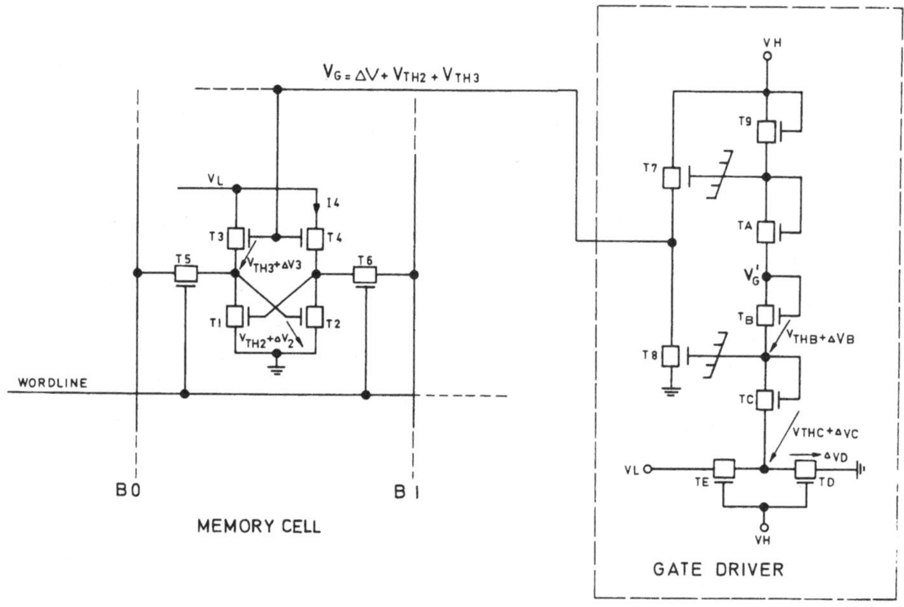

Fig. 5. DC circuits on the chip: gate voltage driver and memory cell.

The following voltage V_G' is generated by the gate voltage driver:

$$V_G' = V_{THB} + \Delta V_B + V_{THC} + \Delta V_C + \Delta V_D = V_{THB} + V_{THC} + \Delta V . \tag{2}$$

We set $\Delta V \equiv \Delta V_B + \Delta V_C + \Delta V_D = \Delta V_2 + \Delta V_3$ by appropriate dimensioning of the driver circuit.

By comparison of (1) and (2) we see that the driver circuit generates the required gate voltage even for a large threshold voltage spread if driver device TC simulates the cell device T2, and device TB simulates device T3. This is achieved by analogous layouts

110

for the corresponding devices. Then, the gate voltage for the cell's load devices T3 and T4 will track with the threshold voltage and cell stability is guaranteed. The source followers T7–T8 are required to drive the large capacitance of the load device gates at power-on.

B. DC Power per Cell

If cell device T2 is on, most of the dc power is dissipated within load device T4:

$$P_{dc} \approx I_4 V_L$$
$$\approx (V_G - V_{TH4} - V_L/2)\, V_L^2\, \gamma_m W_4/L_4$$
$$\sim (V_G - V_{TH4} - V_L/2). \qquad (3)$$

Conventionally, a constant power supply V_G would be designed according to (1) for maximum threshold voltages to guarantee cell stability. According to (3), a chip with maximum threshold voltage V_{TH4} dissipates minimum power. But the power dissipation would significantly increase for a chip with low threshold voltage.

In our case, however, V_G tracks with threshold voltage. Therefore, we get from (1) and (3):

$$P_{dc} \sim \Delta V + V_{TH2} + V_{TH3} - V_{TH4} - V_L/2$$
$$\sim \Delta V + V_{TH2} - V_L/2. \qquad (4)$$

For a chip with maximum threshold voltage the power dissipation will be equal to the minimum value in the conventional case. If the threshold voltage (i.e., V_{TH2}) assumes low values, the power dissipation will further be decreased according to (4). Thus, the chip's dc power will always be below the minimum values of a conventional design with constant external gate voltage V_G.

Furthermore, the additional power supply V_L can be kept as low as the cell stability allows it. For $V_L = 2.0$ V, the nominal dc power dissipation per cell is below 10 μW.

5. Bit Density per Chip

Since costs are directly related to the bit productivity, we have to look for a bit density on the chip which yields the maximum number of good bits per wafer.

One design point is the memory cell area, which results from the utilized memory cell (6-device cell) and the given layout ground rules with 5-μm minimum mask dimensions. The memory cell layout is shown in Fig. 6. Its area is 2.0×3.1 square mils (4000 μm^2). Another design point is the given wafer diameter of 2.25 in. The following relations apply:

    bit productivity = bits per wafer × yield
    bits per wafer   = bits per chip   × chips per wafer.

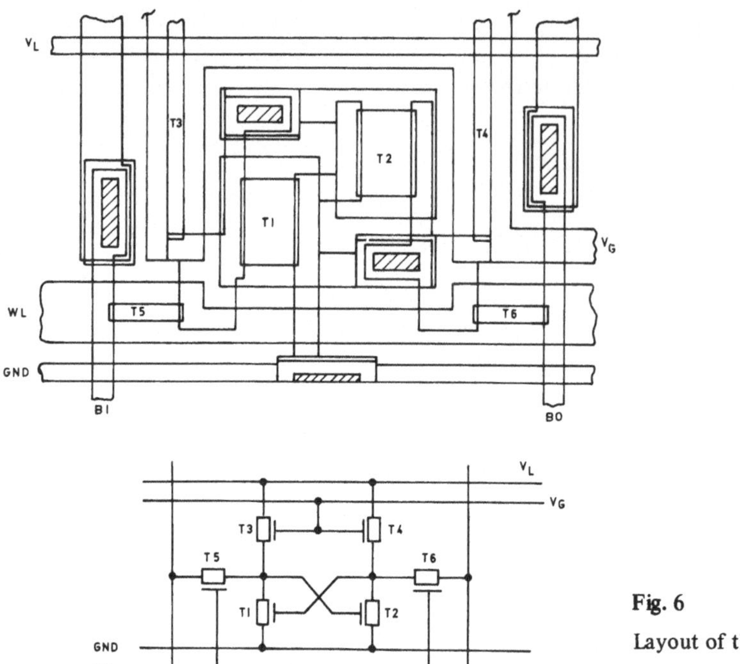

Fig. 6

Layout of the memory cell.

The bits per chip can be increased with increasing chip size. But the number of chips per wafer decreases with increasing chip area. Thus, the bits per wafer reach a maximum value for a certain chip size. The yield, however, is not only a function of the chip size, but it is also determined by the memory cell layout, since the memory matrix covers most of the array chip area. Yield has further to be investigated by considering the learning curve of the manufacturing line.

At the time of these investigations, a chip with 2 kbits offered the highest bit productivity for the estimated lifetime of this product. Today, the optimum productivity would rather be with a 4-kbit or 8-kbit chip. In 1972, however, a density of 2 kbits per chip was quite attractive in comparison to the state of the art at that time [8].

To further improve the bit productivity, especially in the early stage of production, the chip has been divided into two identical array halves of 1 kbit each. This allows a built-in half good capability if only one array half is powered. (For more details see Section 6-A.)

112

6. Chip Description

A. Chip Characteristics

The chip is organized 2048×1 bit. It consists of two 1024-bit array halves. One array half has an area of about 100×64 square mils. The total chip size including decoders, other peripheral circuits, and pads is 153×178 square mils or 3.88×4.52 mm^2 after dicing.

The chip is designed to be operated in a high performance as well as in a low or cost performance mode. Only one power supply has to be changed. The supply voltage for the peripheral circuits V_H is 9.5 V for the high performance and 8.5 V for the cost performance application. The high voltage V_H contributes to the chip performance especially in the peripheral circuitry, whereas the low voltage V_L determines the standby power dissipation of 20 mW. V_L is 2.0 V and the substrate bias voltage V_N is -3.0 V for both modes.

The total power for a selected chip is 120 mW nominal for the cost performance and 150 mW for the high performance application assuming a 200-ns cycle. The maximum power for a selected chip is 200 mW.

The access time of the chip is defined from 10 percent of the rising chip select pulse CS to the point in time when the read current I_S out of the sense amplifier has reached a threshold of 20 μA (see timing diagram, Fig. 2). The worst case access time is 75 ns for the cost performance and 65 ns for the high performance mode. Typical measured values are 60 and 50 ns, respectively.

The minimum cycle time is defined from one selection of the chip to the next possible selection. Within this time, a read or a write as well as the necessary restore operation have to be completed (see Fig. 2). The minimum cycle time is 200 ns for the cost performance and 170 ns for the high performance mode.

The chip has a built-in half good capability. Both array halves are supplied by separate power pads. Only the good half will then be powered.

The chip is very flexible with respect to timing requirements. Only the chip select pulse CS is a timed pulse. All other address and selection pulses have no specific timing conditions.

B. Block Diagram

The block diagram of the chip is shown in Fig. 7. The two array sections have 32 word lines and 32 pairs of bit lines each. Each half has its own word decoders, whereas the bit decoders are common for both parts. Each section has its own gate voltage driver, delayed chip select generator, and array decoder. The word and the bit phase splitters are common to both.

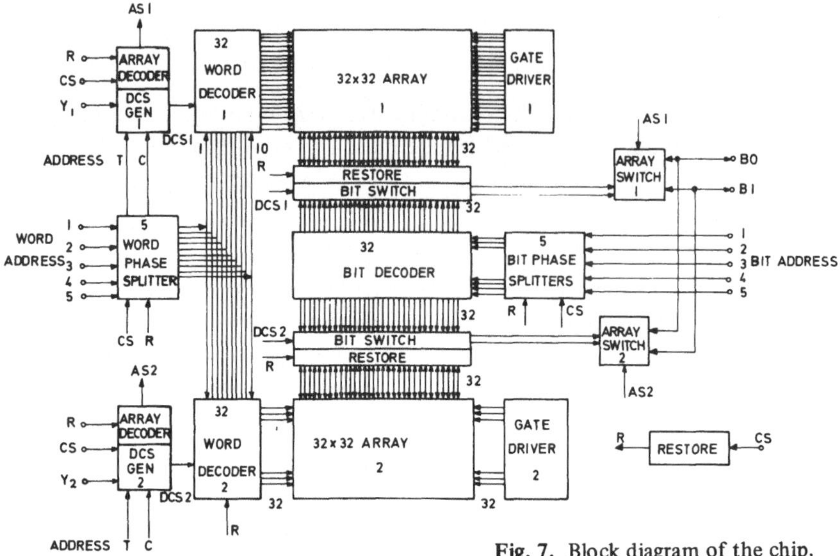

Fig. 7. Block diagram of the chip.

In order to select a cell, five word and five bit address signals have to be applied. As soon as they are valid, the CS pulse may rise and the chip is selected. CS drives the phase splitters which generate buffered and inverted address signals. The outputs of five phase splitters supply 2×32 word decoders, whereas the other five phase splitters supply the 32 bit decoders.

The CS pulse is delayed in the delayed chip select generators. The outputs of the DCS generators (DCS1 and DCS2) power the outputs of the selected bit and word decoders and drive one word line and one pair of bit-line switches in each array half. Two corresponding cells are therefore selected in each array section.

Since the chip has a one-bit organization, the array decoder has to distinguish between the two cells. It generates the internal array select pulses (AS1 and AS2) as an AND function of the already decoded address lines Y1 or Y2, respectively, and CS. AS1 and AS2 control the array switches which connect the appropriate bit-line pair to the output pads B0 and B1.

After this selection part, the chip is prepared for any read or write operation. The input/output pads B0 and B1 of the chip are connected to a bipolar sense amplifier/ bit driver on the memory card. During a read operation, the sense amplifier maintains the positive voltage V_B at both pads B0 and B1. Then, different amounts of current flow from these two pads via the bit lines into the selected cell. The current difference between the B0 and B1 line is the desired information which will be sensed by the sense amplifier.

114

During a write operation, one bit line remains positive, whereas the other one is pulled down to ground potential by the bipolar bit driver circuit. After some nanoseconds, the cell has changed its state and the lower bit line will be charged up again to standby potential by the bit driver. The restore generator and its function have already been mentioned in Section 3.

C. Chip Microphotograph

A microphotograph of the 2-kbit chip is shown in Fig. 8. The two 1-kbit array sections can be seen together with the common bit decoders in between. The word decoders are visible on the left side of each array half. The cross-shaped structures in each array are metal lines for the $V_L = 2.0\,V$ supply voltage to the memory cells, which is partly supplied by diffused lines across the array. Phase splitters and generators for auxiliary pulses and for the load device gate voltage of the memory cells are located at the chip edge between pads.

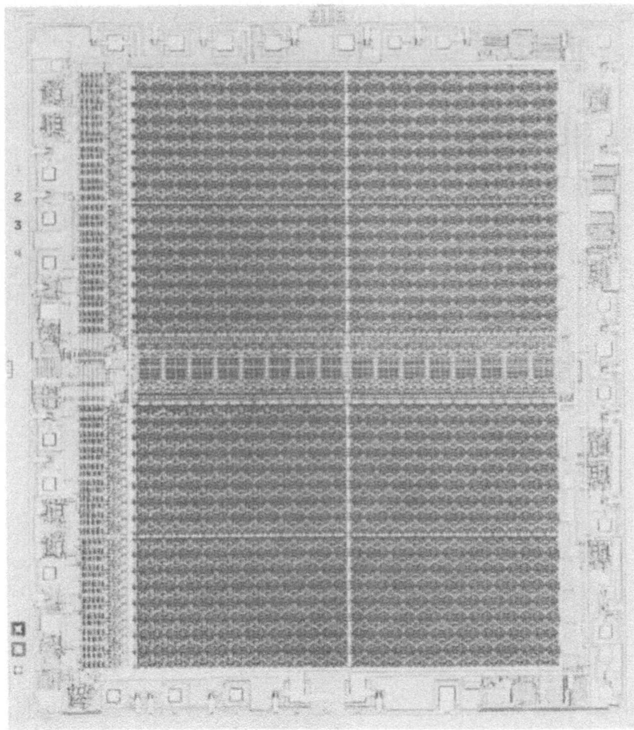

Fig. 8. Microphotograph of the chip.

7. Array Module

The first packaging level is the module. A half-inch ceramic substrate can carry two chips. An 8192-bit storage module, therefore, contains 4 chips on two stacked ceramic substrates. Fig. 9 shows a photograph of the upper and lower decks, two stacked substrates, and the encapsulated module [6].

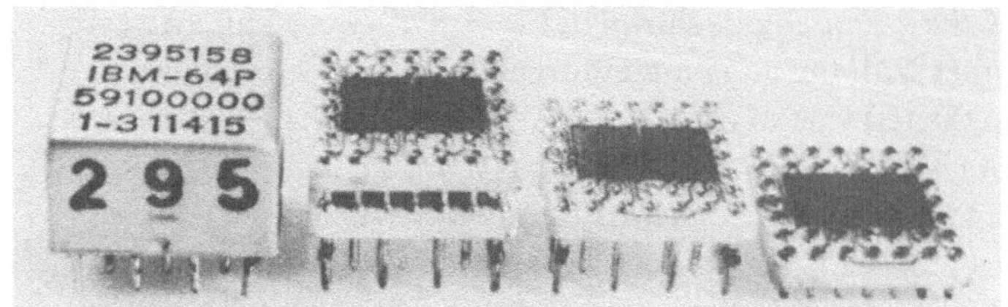

Fig. 9. Photograph of an 8K × 1 module.

One chip per module can be selected by activating one of the four CS inputs. All address lines are common for all four chips and all outputs are dotted.

Fig. 10. Photograph of a 32K × 8 memory card.

116

8. Memory Card

MOSFET memories with a high performance objective have to use the hybrid memory
card approach. MOSFET modules are used to store the information, whereas bipolar
support modules are used to drive and to sense the MOSFET storage modules.

A photograph of a 256-kbit card which actually stores 262.144 bits is shown in Fig. 10.
It carries 32 array modules (8192×1 bit each), four bipolar interface driver modules
for the address signals, four bipolar sense amplifier/bit driver modules, and four logic
modules. The organization of the 115×85 mm^2 large organic card ist $32k \times 8$ bits
[7].

The bipolar interface driver circuits are used to convert the logic levels of about half
a volt swing into about 8-V swings required by the MOSFET array modules. They
have to drive large capacitive loads within short rise times.

The bipolar sense amplifier/bit driver circuits are used to sense the low differential
read current of the MOSFET chip, detect the information, and convert it into said
logic levels of about half a volt. They are also used to write information into the
array modules.

The logic modules are necessary to generate already decoded chip address input
signals such as chip select CS and array select Y1 and Y2 out of high order address
signals.

The $32k \times 8$ bit card has a typical performance of 165 ns access/280 ns cycle time
with cost performance power supplies ($V_H = 8.5$ V, $V_L = 2.0$ V, $V_N = -3.0$ V) and
a power of 8.5 W (selected mode).

A 128-kbit high performance card ($V_H = 9.5$ V, $V_L = 2.0$ V, $V_N = -3.0$ V), which
has been built, offers a typical performance of 115 ns access/200 ns cycle and a power
dissipation below 10 W. Both card data are without error correction and detection.

9. Functional Memory Unit

Thirty-six memory cards which store approximately 1 Mbyte can be placed on one
memory board. Six boards (four memory boards and two control logic boards) are
packed into one frame of a 4-Mbyte memory which has a mechanical size of about
$1 \times 1 \times 0.3$ m^3.

It might be interesting to mention that the bit density of approximately 3×10^5 bits/
cm^3 on the chip level reduces to about 150 bits/cm^3 on the frame level (including
control logic, blowers, etc.). This shows that the present packaging technology is by
no means exploiting the density potential of the silicon chip technology.

10. Summary and Outlook

A 2048-bit read/write memory chip has been described. It uses a modified 6-device memory cell in an n-channel MOSFET technology. To exploit the potential of the given MOSFET technology with respect to the cost/performance ratio and the power-delay product, special provisions were taken.

The power was kept low by the gate driver concept as well as by clocked peripheral circuits. High performance was achieved with fast peripheral circuits, the delayed chip select concept, and a bipolar sense amplifier which also supplies the bit-line restore voltage. Circuits have been presented which successfully utilize the on-chip tracking to reduce the impact of device parameter tolerances on worst case power and performance. The high reliability of this chip has mainly been achieved by an extensive computer analysis of the on-chip circuits, together with careful layout studies. This analysis took not only the absolute values and tolerances of all important device parameters into account, but of all parasitic devices as well. These data were the result of a statistical evaluation of device measurements over a long period of time. It has been shown how the memory chip is packaged on modules, cards, and boards to build up functional memory units.

When the design was started, the goal was to come up with a chip which offered some real improvements in comparison to available products within the company and on the open market. This goal, to be better with respect to performance, power, and density, has been successfully achieved. Even if we look at the present market or at [8], which gives a comprehensive overview on available chips, one can easily see that this design is still attractive from a performance and power point of view. The density, of course, would be considerably higher if the design would have been started this year.

Acknowledgment

The MOSFET memory chip described in this paper has been designed in the IBM Laboratories, Boeblingen, West Germany. The first engineering hardware has also been processed in the Boeblingen pilotline. The success of this chip design was only possible by the close cooperation between a team of circuit and device designers in the laboratories and the pilotline engineers in the IBM Manufacturing Locations, Sindelfingen, West Germany, and Burlington, VT, USA.

References

[1] *G. Cheroff, D. L. Critchlow, R. H. Dennard*, and *L. M. Terman,* "IGFET circuit performance-n-channel versus p-channel", IEEE J. Solid State Circuits, vol. SC-4, pp. 267–271, Oct. 1969.

[2] *J. S. Schmidt,* "Integrated MOS random-access memory", Solid-State Design, pp. 21–25, 1965.

[3] *L. M. Terman,* "MOSFET memory circuits", Proc. IEEE, vol 59, no. 7, July 1971.

[4] *R. W. Polkinghorn* et al., "FET driver using capacitor feedback", U.S. Patent 3.506.851, 1970.

[5] *W. O. Haug* et al., "Halbleiter-Schaltungs-Anordnung", Offenlegungsschrift 2.232.274, Deutsches Patentamt, 1974.

[6] *C. A. Harper,* Handbook of Thick Film Hybrid Microelectronics. New York. McGraw Hill, 1974, p. 996.

[7] *W. K. Liebmann,* "Monolithic memories in IBM Systems/370-135 and 145", Czechoslovak Scientific and Technical Society, Pisek, Czechoslovakia, Apr. 1972.

[8] *R. W. Mitterer,* "A review on random access MOS memories", invited paper presented at the European Solid-State Circuits Conf., Canterbury, England, 1975.

Readout Methods and Readout Circuits for Dynamic Charge-Storage Elements

Karlheinrich Horninger

Siemens AG, Munich, Germany

1. Introduction

Progress in the field of digital semiconductor memories in the last few years has been characterized by an extremely rapid rise in the storage density, i.e. in the number of information bits per unit area of silicon. Along with the progressive technological improvements, the key to this turbulent development was the principle of dynamic charge storage. This principle involves the storage of mobile charge at the Si-SiO$_2$ interface. Depending on whether a small or large number of charges are stored, a binary "1" or "0" is present in the memory cell.

Fig. 1 comprises a micrograph of a 16-kbit memory with dynamic single-transistor cells and a row with memory cells and a sense amplifier. Prior to giving a detailed description of the readout and detection of the information stored in the memory cells, it is appropriate to briefly explain how a dynamic single-transistor cell operates. The cross-section and top view of such a memory cell are shown in Figs. 2a and 2b.

When the transfer transistor is turned on, the voltage from the bit line can de applied to the MOS storage capacitor for writing or the information represented as charge on the storage capacitor can be read out onto the bit line. It can be seen in Fig. 2b that the word and bit lines are at right angles to each other. When a word line is activated, only one storage capacitor is connected to each bit line. Thick oxide regions separate the various memory regions. Fig. 3 again shows the cross-section of the memory cell and plots the potential versus time of the storage capacitor for a binary "0" and a binary "1". In the case of a binary "0", mobile charge carriers are stored. The semiconductor is in this case in thermal equilibrium, the surface potential is approx. $2\phi_F$ [10] (for this simplified explanation the substrate bias voltage was assumed to be OV) and this state is retained. When writing a binary "1", a positive voltage is applied to the bit line and the transfer transistor is turned on. The potential at the Si-SiO$_2$ interface in the storage capacitor also assumes the value of this voltage, in other words, practically no mobile charge carriers are stored. As the conditions in the case of the binary "1" are not static, the surface potential of the storage capacitor drops to the surface potential of the binary "0" i.e. mobile charge carriers are generated. This decay of the information voltage is shown in Fig. 3b. After a certain time, the state of

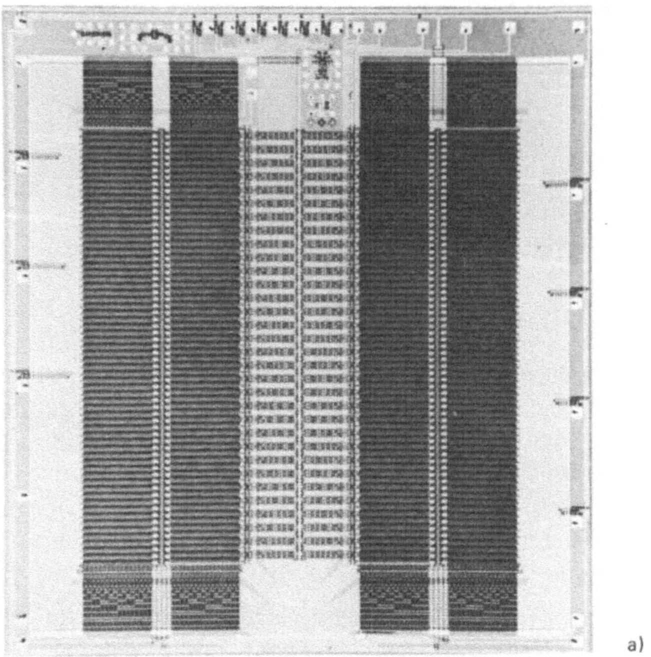

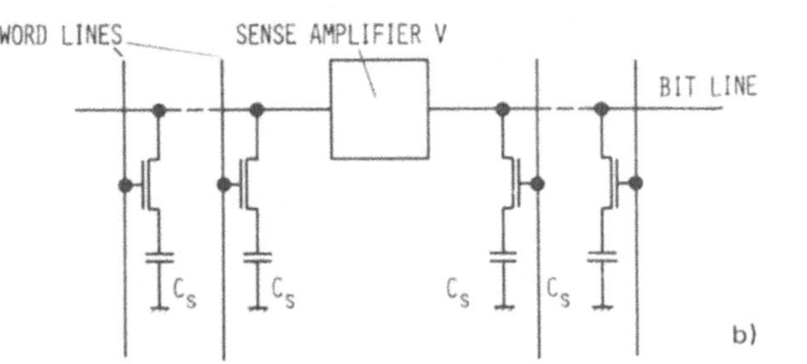

Fig. 1. Micrograph of a 16-kbit memory with single-transistor cells (a) and a row with memory cells and sense amplifier (b).

the "1" has changed to the state of the "0". In dynamic semiconductor memories, it is therefore essential to refresh the information at regular intervals. From a practical point of view, the operation of a dynamic memory with such a cell includes of course a high number of read and write processes between refresh processes.

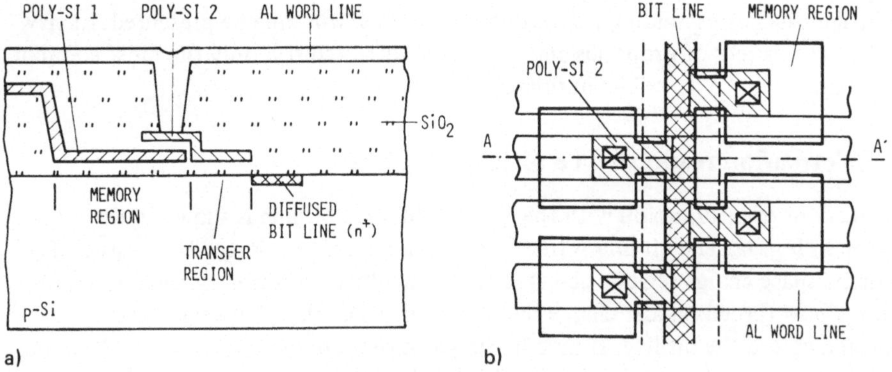

Fig. 2. Cross-section AA´ (a) and top view (b) of a dynamic single-transistor memory cell in double polysilicon technology.

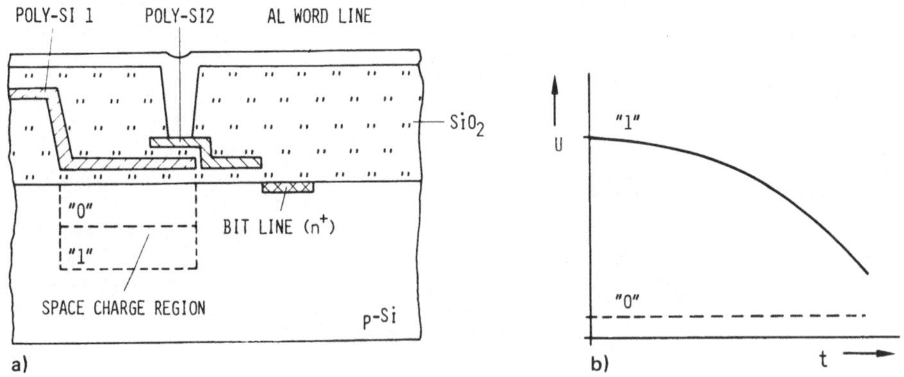

Fig. 3. Cross-section (a) and surface potential in the storage capacitor plotted against time (b) of a dynamic single-transistor cell.

A further important factor in the design of a dynamic semiconductor memory is the number of stored charges. In order to properly discriminate between the stored "1" and "0", the readout circuit should have optimum sensitivity.

As the sensitivity of the readout circuit increases, the smaller can be the charge stored for a certain output voltage and the higher is thus the packing density. The intent of the following is to describe, with the aid of simple models, the various methods of converting the stored information charge into an output signal, which can serve as input for a subsequent readout circuit and can be detected without ambiguity. The advantages and disadvantages of these methods will be discussed and compared. The readout circuits, which detect and amplify the readout signal and which are connected behind the corresponding readout configurations, will then be presented. In view of the large variety of proposals and options in this circuitry, only the most common basic circuit will be described in this paper.

2. Information readout via a diffused bit line

The readout of information with the aid of a diffused bit line is shown in the cross-section in Fig. 4a. The bit line is first biased to a reference voltage via transistor Tr1, so that a space charge region is created below the diffused region. A selection transistor is now turned on and charge redistribution takes place between the storage capacitance and the bit line. If mobile charge carriers are present (stored "0") in the storage capacitor, the potential on the bit line is reduced. This change in the potential state is reinforced with the aid of amplifier V and finally reaches the output of the memory array. It is relatively simple to calculate the change in potential on the bit line as a function of the amount of charge stored. Assuming an abrupt pn-junction and neglecting the lateral spread of the space charge region of the bit line, the change in the bit line voltage ΔU_{BL} can be expressed as

$$\Delta U_{BL} = Q_S \cdot \frac{2}{k} \cdot \sqrt{U_R + U_D} - \frac{Q_S^2}{k^2} \tag{1}$$

with

$$k = N \cdot A_B \cdot \sqrt{2e\,\epsilon_{Si}\epsilon_0 N_A}$$

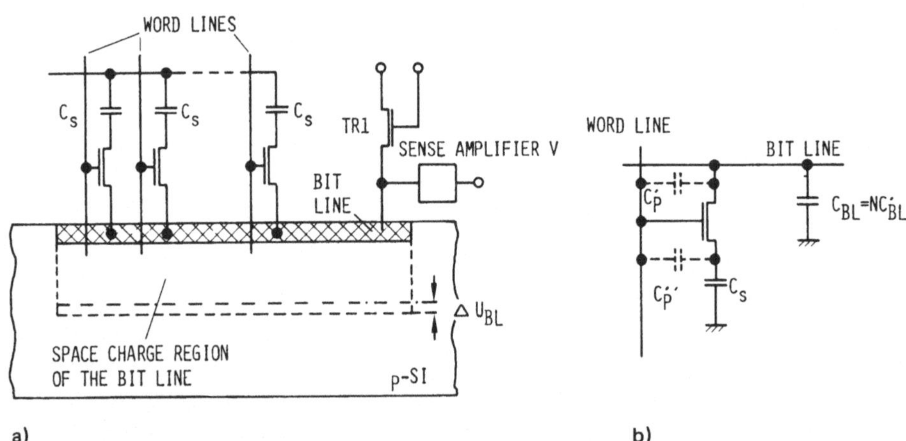

Fig. 4. Cross-section (a) and equivalent circuit diagram of a readout configuration with a diffused bit line.

In eq. (1), Q_S denotes the stored signal charge, U_R the voltage to which the bit line is biased, U_D the diffusion voltage of the bit line, N the memory cell population on a bit line, A_B the area of the bit line per cell, e the elementary charge, ϵ_{Si} and ϵ_0 the relative and absolute dielectric constants of silicon and N_A the doping of the substrate material.

It can be seen from eq. (1) that the output signal becomes smaller as the number N of memory cells per bit line increases, and becomes larger with a low doped substrate. The relationship in eq. (1) can also be demonstrated with the aid of the electrical equivalent circuit. The equivalent circuit of the configuration of Fig. 4a is shown in Fig. 4b. When the word line has been activated, charge redistribution takes place between the storage capacitance C_S and the bit line capacitance C_{BL}. Following charge redistribution, the voltage ΔU_{BL} appears on the bit line. The voltage ΔU_{BL} can be expressed as

$$\Delta U_{BL} = \frac{U_1 - U_0}{\left(1 + N\dfrac{C'_{BL}}{C_S}\right)} \tag{2}$$

In eq. (2) U_1 denotes the voltage of a stored "1", U_0 the voltage of a stored "0", C'_{BL} the bit line capacitance per memory element and N the memory cell population per bit line. Memories fabricated at the present time have a ΔU_{BL} value of the order of 100 to 500 mV. The usual method of keeping the capacitance of the bit line as small as possible is to minimize the bit line width. A typical bit line is, for example, 800 μm long and 6 μm wide [1] and thus has a relatively high resistance. This resistance causes attenuation of signals propagating along the bit line. Thus the memory cells at the far end of the bit line supply a lower voltage than those in the vicinity of the sense amplifier V. Fig. 4b also shows the parasitic capacitances $C'p$ and $C''p$ drawn as broken lines. Coupling of clock pulses over these capacitances produce erroneous signals and must be taken into account or compensated during readout.

3. Information readout via a BBD (Bucket Brigade Device) transistor

The readout method described in Section 2 has the drawback that the amplitude of the output signal is strictly dependent on the capacitances C_{BL} and C_S. A reduction in the area of the memory cell (and thus also in the storage capacitance C_S) can only be achieved by reducing the bit line capacitance C_{BL}. The capacitance C_{BL} is however determined by technological and photolithographic boundary conditions. Heller et al. [2] suggested increasing the sensitivity of the readout configuration with the aid of a BBD transistor. The cross-section of this configuration is shown in Fig. 5a.

The offset signal on the bit line is not transferred directly to the sense amplifier V in this case, but by an interposed transistor TrB. Due to its mode of operation, this transistor is generally referred to as a bucket brigade device (BBD) transistor:

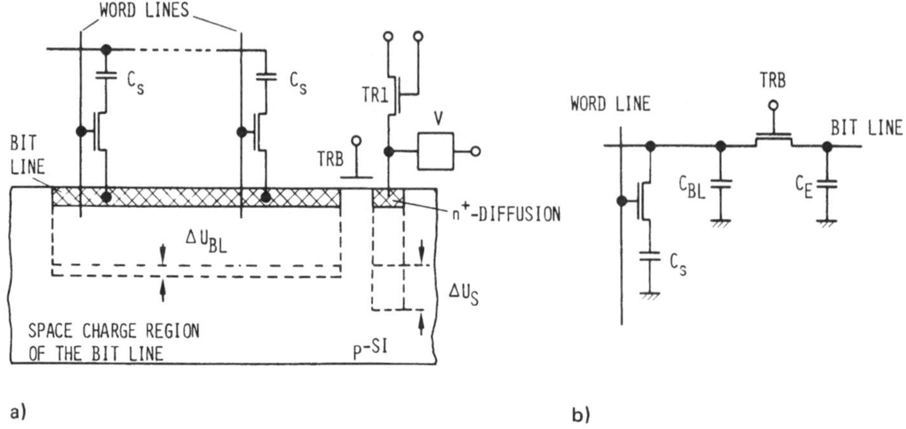

Fig. 5. Cross-section (a) and equivalent circuit diagram (b) of a readout configuration with a diffused bit line and a BBD transistor.

The drain region of the transistor TrB is first biased via transistor Tr1. As transistor TrB is operated in saturation, the bit line (= source region of transistor TrB) assumes the drain voltage minus the threshold voltage. When a word line is now activated, the source voltage dips (as per eq. (1)). Since transistor TrB is turned on, it charges up its own source region (= bit line) to the drain voltage minus the threshold voltage.

The potential change on the bit line is now observed as a larger potential change at the drain region. Fig. 5b shows the equivalent circuit diagram of this configuration. The change in output voltage ΔU_S across C_E can be expressed by the following eq. (3)

$$\Delta U_S = (U_R - U_T - U_I) \cdot \frac{C_S}{C_E} \tag{3}$$

In eq. (3) U_R is the reference level of the drain area. U_T the threshold voltage and U_I the information voltage. The capacitances C_S and C_E are shown in Fig. 5b. It can be seen, from eq. (3) that the bit line capacitance does not affect the output voltage swing, and only influences the ratio of storage capacitance to capacitance of the drain region of the BBD transistor. It is therefore possible to connect a large number of memory cells to a bit line (C_{BL} very large) and, in spite of this, to obtain a voltage swing adequate for the detection process across capacitor C_E (which can be made very small).

This readout method does however have the disadvantage that the time constant with which the drain region is recharged is a function of the W/L ratio of the transistor TrB. It is therefore necessary to make the channel width W of the transistor as large as possible and the channel length L as short as possible, so that the equilibrium con-

126

dition of eq. (3) is achieved as rapidly as possible. The maximum channel width is determined by the bit line spacing and cannot therefore be made arbitrarily large. Reducing the channel length can introduce, in addition to difficulties in the photolithographic process, further parasitic effects such as subthreshold current and punch-through effect, which then govern the lower limit of the channel length. The influence of these effects can however be kept small by means of scaling [11] or using DMOS [4] or VMOS [5] transistors. With this method, it is therefore possible to amplify very small signal swings, but more time is required for information readout than with the process described in Section 2. A way of speeding-up the readout method was described in [6]. In this case, the gate of the BBD transistor is controlled by an amplifier with a gain A, the input of which is connected to the bit line. This amplifier allows the increase of the W/L ratio of the BBD transistor, so that the effective width/length ratio of the transistor can now be expressed by

$$\frac{W}{L}' \simeq \frac{W}{L} \ (1 + A^2) \tag{3a}$$

Whereas the time needed to charge the bit line can be reduced with this method, the readout time is not reduced by the factor $(1 + A^2)$.

4. Information readout with the aid of an MOS line

With the readout configurations described in Sections 2 and 3, the stored signal charge is converted into information voltage on the bit line. It is proposed in [7] that the charge stored in the memory cell be transported to a diffusion region at the end of the line for conversion into voltage. The cross-section of such a configuration is shown in Fig. 6a. Instead of being a diffused region, the bit line is now a long polysilicon gate with high specific resistance. When a voltage is applied to the end of this line, the voltage level decreases along the line. The associated surface potential curve is also shown in Fig. 6a. The output diffusion region D is first biased to the voltage U_R. A voltage is now applied to one end of the MOS line and the word line is then activated. The signal charge reaching the space charge region is transported to the output diffusion region D with the aid of the drift field. The corresponding voltage swing is then produced in region D.

During the propagation, the charge spreads over the silicon surface. This spreading is due to a self-induced field, which is caused by the gradient of the charge and the thermal diffusion of the charge carriers. This spreading does not affect the detection process. Just as in Section 3, this is a readout process in which only the storage capacitance C_S and the capacitance C_D are of importance for the voltage swing. The output voltage is thus again given by

$$\Delta U_S = (U_1 - U_0) \cdot \frac{C_S}{C_D} \tag{4}$$

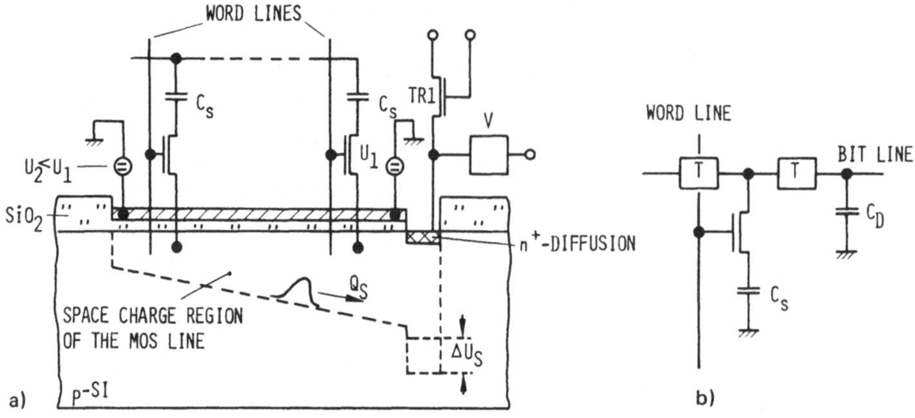

Fig. 6. Cross-section (a) and equivalent circuit diagram (b) of a readout configuration with an MOS line.

The simple equivalent circuit diagram of this configuration is shown in Fig. 6b. The MOS line is drawn as a delay element.

A disadvantage of this readout process is, that the time necessary to transport the information charge Q_S from the memory cell to the output diffusion depends on the distance between memory cell and diffusion. Different memory cells along the bit line therefore need different lengths of time for the detection process. In an example as per [7], a time of 250 ns was measured from the instant of applying the pulse to the MOS line until half the output voltage was reached. The implemented MOS line was 300 μm long and 4 μm wide. The delay time t_D is proportional to L^2 as specified in [7]. A possible way of circumventing this problem is to divide the MOS line up into sections and to clock the individual sections separately.

Although the MOS line is a very sensitive readout configuration, the time required for readout is too long for fast dynamic read-write memories.

5. Readout configuration for CCD memories

As the subject of this paper is readout methods for dynamic charge-storage elements, a description of readout methods for CCD memories should not be omitted. The readout method for CCD memories is the same as that illustrated in Fig. 4. The information charge flows into the space charge region of a diffused region and the resulting potential change is applied to an amplifier V. The problems with the sensitivity are however not so significant, as the CCD memory is of the serial type and the diffusion region is about as large as one storage electrode, in other words $C_S \approx C_{BL}$.

128

In CCD circuits, the signal is often read out via a floating gate amplifier [12]. The signal charge flows into a space charge region, which is created below a (capacitive or galvanic) biased MOS electrode and the potential change of this electrode is sensed. With the oxide thicknesses and substrate doping levels customary at present, approximately the same voltage swing per signal charge is obtained with this method as with the process described in Section 2.

Up to the present, this readout method has been mainly reserved for CCD circuits. The merged cell memory presented at the IEDM (International Electron Devices Meeting) in 1976 [13] however requires such a floating gate amplifier to read out the stored "0" and "1". A configuration of CCD circuit technology is thus employed in this case for dynamic random-access memories.

6. Readout circuit for dynamic memory elements

The previous sections have only described possible methods in which the information is read out of the cell. For a complete memory, an additional sense amplifier is always required, to amplify the signal to logic circuit levels. This amplifier was designated V in Figs. 4 to 6. While several proposals have been made for building such an amplifier, it has become general practice in almost all single-transistor memories to employ a balanced flip-flop to sense and amplify the stored information. The balanced flip-flop sense amplifier was first introduced in 1972 [8]. A large number of circuit variations, which serve to increase the sensitivity of the flip-flop, are now known. The intent of this paper is not to discuss the variety of possible circuits, but rather to describe the fundamental mode of operation with the aid of a typical circuit. The sense amplifier flip-flop [9] and the associated waveforms for readout of a "1" and a "0" are shown in Fig. 7.

In the quiescent state, the bit lines are clamped to the potential U_{ref} via the turned-on transistors Tr5 and Tr6. Before the detection process, clock CE is turned off and the bit lines are unclamped from the reference potential (transistors Tr5 and Tr6 turned off). A word line is then selected via the word decoder, in this case the word line of the right-hand memory cell, for instance. If a stored "1" was present in the cell, the right-hand flip-flop node (node 2 in Fig. 7a) is at a voltage slightly above the reference voltage U_{ref}, while if a stored "0" was present in the cell, the voltage at node 2 is slightly below U_{ref}. Clock ϕ_S and transistor Tr9 now ground the common sources of the flip-flop.

While the common sources are grounded, transistor Tr3 turns on ahead of transistor Tr4 as the voltage at node 2 (case of a stored "1") is higher than that at node 1. When the gate voltage (ϕ_L) of the load transistors Tr1 and Tr2 is now turned on, the flip-flop switches to a stable state so that the voltage $U_{DD} - U_T$ is at node 2 and the residual voltage determined by the resistance ratio of Tr1 and Tr3 is at node 1.

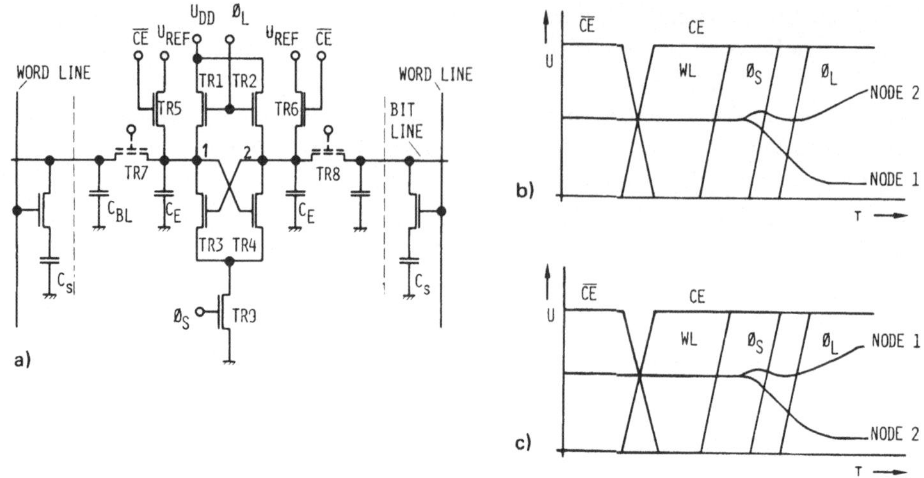

Fig. 7. Sense amplifier flip-flop (a) and waveforms for readout of a "1" (b) and a "0" (c) of a memory cell located at node 2.

The word line WL remains activated until the stable state is reached, so that following readout, the information in the storage capacitor is immediately read in again. The waveforms and the voltages at the individual flip-flop nodes are shown in Figs. 7b and 7c for the right-hand node 2 for readout of a "1" and a "0". On application of a voltage to a word line, all sense amplifier flip-flops of a column are activated and information is read out from all cells on the word line and new information is written back in again. This sense amplifier can also be made more sensitive with the aid of BBD transistors. In Fig. 7a the BBD transistors Tr7 and Tr8 are drawn as dashed lines. The relatively low readout swing on the bit line is then preamplified.

When working with such small voltage swings, it is of course necessary to take into account a number of second order factors, which can have a major effect on the operation and sensitivity of the circuit. These are, for instance, clock coupling, distribution of the threshold voltage of the transistors (resulting in a preferred state of the flip-flop), capacitances of the bit lines etc. Recent publications show that a very high sensitivity can be achieved by suitable control of the common sources of transistor Tr9 [14]. It is not however the intent of this paper to discuss these problems in detail.

7. Comparison of the various readout methods

Sections 2, 3, 4 and 5 dealt with the various readout methods. In the following, the sensitivity and the readout time for these methods will be compared. In this comparison, only the methods of Sections 2, 3 and 4 will be included.

130

To make a valid comparison, certain assumptions of the technology used must be made. For the following calculations, it is assumed that an n-channel double polysilicon technology (Fig. 2) is used with minimum line width of 2.5 μm, a gate oxide thickness of 60 nm and an operating voltage of 5 V. Fig. 8 shows the voltage swing ΔU_S and ΔU_{BL} at the input of the sense amplifier V as a function of the memory cell population N on a common bit line. The parameters are the area A_S of the memory cell and the ratio of the storage capacitance C_S to the bit line capacitance C'_{BL} per cell. It is also assumed that the area of the memory cell is only altered in the direction perpendicular to the bit line, in other words, the portion of the bit line capacitance C'_{BL} is equal for all three areas. The delay time t_D is the right-hand ordinate.

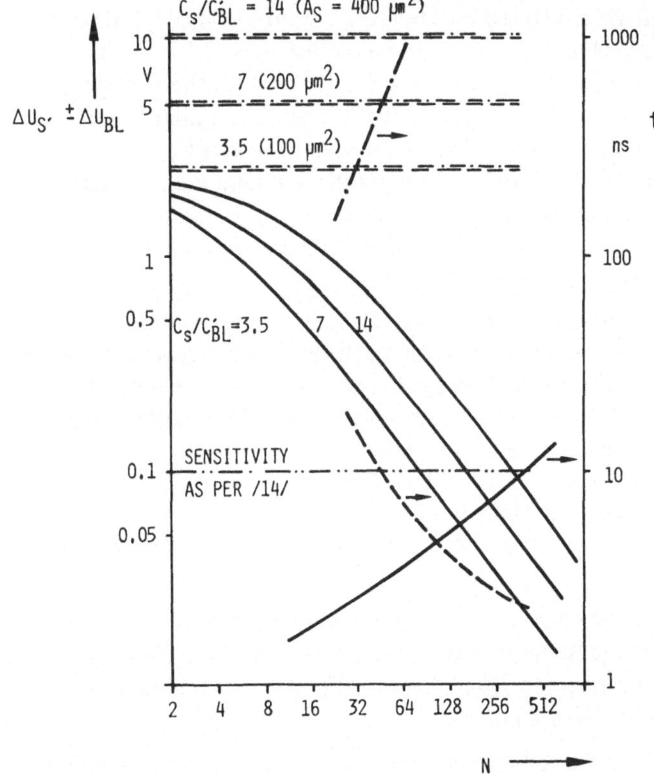

Fig. 8. Dependence of the signal voltage ΔU_S and ΔU_{BL} at the input of the amplifier V for the method described in Section 2 (unbroken curves), in Section 3 (broken curves) and for the MOS line (dash-dotted curves) on the memory cell population N on a bit line, and the dependence of the time t_D on the cell population N for the three methods. The parameters of the voltage curves are the ratio C_S/C'_{BL} and the cell area A_S.

This time was determined as follows: the diffused bit line was simulated as a distributed RC network and the delay time of this network was computed for different lengths. The time t_D was measured from the instant of activating the word line until the point at which the potential at the end of the bit line has reached 50 % of the final value. The most unfavorable case was always used, i.e. the time t_D was computed for the cell at the far end of the bit line. The time curve (unbroken line) applies for the readout method described in Section 2. A BBD transistor was then connected to the bit line simulated as an RC network and the time was computed until the same voltage swing is present across capacitor C_E as in the process described in Section 2. The times for the MOS line were obtained from the literature [7]. The time curves were computed for a C_S/C'_{BL} ratio of 7.

It is now evident from Fig. 8 that when the readout method described in Section 2 is used (conventional readout via a diffused bit line), the output signal ΔU_{BL} decreases as the cell population on a bit line increases. The theoretical lower limit of the output signal ΔU_{BL} is reached when the signal is buried in noise. With the configuration correctly dimensioned, the noise at the input FET of the sense amplifier V determines the magnitude of the signal ΔU_{BL} [15]. In realized memories however, the parameter distributions of the transistors in the amplifier V determine the highest achievable sensitivity. An estimate of the required sensitivity of the sense amplifier flip-flop was made in [16]. A sense amplifier flip-flop with a computed sensitivity of $\pm$ 100 mV is described in [14].

When a BBD transistor is located at the end of the bit line, the signal at the input of amplifier V is independent of the cell population on the bit line if one waits long enough. The lower limit for this readout method is determined by the noise during recharging of the BBD [15]. The root-mean-square value of the noise charges is proportional to the bit line capacitance. For selected cell size this boundary value is however only reached when there are more than 10^9 memory cells on the bit line. This boundary value is not shown in Fig. 8. For the broken straight lines in Fig. 8, it was assumed that the capacitance of C_E is kept constant for all three cases and is equal to $7\,C'_{BL}$.

For readout with the aid of the MOS line, there is also no reduction in the signal swing, as the total signal charge is transported — independent of the location of the memory cell — to the diffusion region. The curves for the output signal therefore also run in this case horizontal to the abscissa.

The sensitivity which can be achieved with the readout method using the MOS line must however be bought at the expense of time required for the readout operation. The time necessary to transport the charge packet from the memory cell to the diffusion region is proportional to the square of the distance L from the cell to the output diffusion ($t_D \propto L^2$ [7]). The readout time therefore increases strongly with the number of memory cells connected to the bit line. In contrast to this, the

132

dependence of read-out time on the number of cells connected to one bit line is considerably less for the readout method described in Section 2 (diffused bit line). If we now connect a BBD transistor to the bit line, the readout time will be longer than without this transistor. We would however also get a higher voltage at the input of the sense amplifier V. To make a fair comparison, we have done the following: We have first calculated the readout time for the method of Section 2 for different number of cells N on one bit line. We have then added a BBD transistor to the bit line and have calculated the time till we achieve the same voltage amplitude at the output of the BBD transistor as with the method of Section 2. So when comparing the two curves for the readout times of Section 2 and Section 3 we must remember that these values are valid for the same voltage swing at the input of amplifier V for both methods. From Fig. 8 we can see, that for practical bit line lengths (e.g. $N = 64$) the readout time is longer when using a BBD transistor.

With longer bit lines however, the voltage swing on the bit line is reduced and this small voltage swing is now reached more quickly with the aid of the BBD transistor. Above a certain cell population N, it can therefore be advantageous to use a BBD transistor. A condition is that the bit line is charged rapidly enough via the BBD transistor. Fig. 8 shows very clearly the time required for signal readout for the various methods, with a fixed sensitivity of the amplifier V.

8. Conclusions

The most important readout methods and circuits known at the present time for dynamic MOS-RAMs have been described. The commercially available 4k and 16k memories make use of the method with the diffused bit line, whereby 16 or 32 memory cells are connected to a single bit line. The sense amplifier used in practically all dynamic single-transistor memories is the balanced flip-flop (Section 6) in a number of different circuit variations.

There are a number of promising approaches for future readout methods. An advance would be the use of DMOS transistors with short channel lengths for the BBD readout method, as a means of achieving both a high sensitivity and a short access time. It may also be anticipated that the introduction of specially selected process steps will permit a further major reduction in the bit line capacitance — for instance, insulation of the bit line from the semiconductor bulk — and thus a larger voltage swing is obtained. One can safely assume that sense amplifiers will be developed which are more sensitive than the present types and are at the same time less affected by parameter distribution. Finally, it may be expected that configurations will also be found for MOS memories and dynamic bipolar memories [17] which reinforce the information in the memory cell itself. All this, together with the trend towards denser structures, shows that developments will progress in the near future to semi-

conductor memories with 256 kbit and more, integrated on a chip area of around
25 mil^2.

This work has been supported by the Federal Department of Research and Technology of the FRG. The author alone is responsible for the contents.

Literature

[1]   *R. C. Foss* and *R. Harland,* Peripheral circuits for one-transistor cell MOS RAM's, IEEE J. of Solid-State Circuits, Vol. **SC-10**, No. 5, Oct. 1975, p. 255–261.

[2]   *L. Heller* et al., High sensitivity charge-transfer sense amplifier, Proceedings of the ISSCC 75, Feb. 1975, Philadelphia.

[3]   *L. Heller, D. Spampinato* and *Y. Yao,* High sensitivity charge-transfer sense amplifier, IEEE J. of Solid-State Circuits, Vol. **SC-11**, No. 5, Oct. 1976, p. 596–601.

[4]   *T. Masuhara* and *R. S. Muller,* Complementary-DMOS Process for LSI, IEEE J. of Solid-State Circuits, Vol. **SC-11**, No. 4, Aug. 1976, p. 453–458.

[5]   *R. Rodgers* and *J. Meindl,* VMOS: High-speed TTL compatible MOS logic, IEEE J. of Solid-State Circuits, Vol. **SC-9**, No. 5, Oct. 1974, p. 239–250.

[6]   *P. Jespers* et al., An improved monolithic charge-sensing circuit for analog arrays, Proceedings of the ESSCIRC 1976, Toulouse 21.–24.9., Toulouse.

[7]   *K. Hoffmann,* The behavior of the continuously charge-coupled random-access memory (C^3 RAM), IEEE J. of Solid-State Circuits, Vol. **SC-11**, No. 5, Oct. 1976, p. 591–596.

[8]   *K. U. Stein, A. Sihling* and *E. Doering,* Storage array and sense/refresh circuit for single transistor memory cells, IEEE J. of Solid-State Circuits, Vol. **SC-7**, No. 5, Oct. 1972, p. 336–340.

[9]   *C. Kuo, N. Kitagawa, E. Ward* and *P. Drayer,* Sense amplifier design is key to one-transistor cell in 4096 bit RAM, Electronics, Sept. 1973.

[10] *A. S. Grove,* Physics and technology of semiconductor devices, John Wiley & Sons, Inc., New York 1967.

[11] *G. Meusburger* and *R. Sigusch,* Scaling of n-MOS devices: experimental verification of an LSI concept, Siemens FuE Berichte, Bd. 5 (1976), Nr. 6, p. 332–337.

[12] *D. d. Wen,* Design and operation of a floating gate amplifier, IEEE J. of Solid-State Circuits, Vol. **SC-9**, No. 6, Dec. 1974, p. 410–414.

[13] IBM stores data in no-transistor cell, Electronics, Nov. 25, 1976, p. 42–43.

[14] *R. W. Mitterer* and *B. F. Rehn,* A 16k MOS RAM in double-polysilicon-technology, Proceedings of the ESSCIRC 1976, Toulouse, p. 40–41.

[15] *C. H. Sequin* and *M. F. Tompsett,* Charge transfer devices, Academic Prrss, New York, 1975.

[16] *G. Wotruba,* A large-scale integrated memory circuit using single-transistor cells with a density of 1600 bit/mm^2 in n-silicon gate technology, Siemens FuE Berichte, Bd. 4 (1975), Nr. 4, p. 207–212.

[17] *W. B. Sander* et al., Dynamic I^{2}L random-access memory competes with MOS designs, Electronics, Aug. 19, 1976, p. 99–102.

[18] *C. N. Ahlquist* et al., A 16 384-Bit dynamic RAM, IEEE J. of Solid-State Circuits, Vol. **SC-11**, No. 5, Oct. 1976, p. 570–574.

Monolithic Memories

Wolfgang Liebmann

IBM Development Laboratory Boeblingen

1. Magnetic Core Memories – Monolithic Memories

Until a few years ago, the term "Magnetic Core Memory" was synonymous for the
main memory of a data processing system. Magnetic core memories were the predominant technology for this application, and they have been very successful as
such. In the approximately 20 years of their technological existence, their costs
have dropped several orders of magnitude, their speed has been improved by at
least one order of magnitude, and the energy consumption has been reduced by
the same factor. The introduction of powerful application and systems control
software which represent the cornerstone of modern data processing was linked
directly to the technical capabilities which the magnetic core memories offered to
the system designer and computer user. Even today in constructing a software
package, the programmer calculates how much "core" he requires for a particular
programming section. The name of a technology became the descriptive term for
an addressing space or for the physical arrangement of logical information inside a
computer memory.

In modern data processing systems, core memories have almost completely been
displaced by monolithic memories. Since the announcement of IBM Systems
/370–145 and –135, which probably have been the first data processing systems
which made large scale use of monolithic memories, hardly more than half a decade
has passed. In this relatively short time – we must consider that two to three years
can easily elapse from the point where a company makes the decision to develop
a monolithic memory product to the point of large scale production – monolithic
memories have gained in data processing an absolutely dominant position. In modern
technological development there is hardly another example where an established
technology has been replaced so rapidly by a newcomer. An exception to this
might be the silicon planar technology itself which represents the technical basis
for monolithic memories. The silicon planar technology has surpassed its competitors in all sectors of the electronic industry as vehemently as monolithic memories
have surpassed the magnetic core memories.

Monolithic memories have not brought new functions to data processing. The important forms of memory organization, memory application, algorithms for error
correction have all been developed already for use in core memories and have been

135

taken over by monolithic memories essentially unchanged. It might thus be interesting to analyse briefly why a monolithic memory is superior to a magnetic core memory, especially since such analysis might provide some insight into the possible further development and perhaps also into the technological and economical limits of monolithic memory products.

2. Advantages of Monolithic Memories

Economic reasons primarily have paved the way for the success of monolithic memories. Today, a monolithic memory bit costs far less to the user than a core bit, especially if one adds to the cost of the storage hardware also the cost for power supplies and for the peripheral logic circuits which surround the storage matrix to facilitate addressing and memory control [1]. While it is possible to project for monolithic memories a clear technical progress resulting in further cost reductions, the core memories have achieved a cost plateau which can hardly be lowered in this technology. The main limitation for further cost reductions of magnetic core memories is the fact that, despite substantial investments by some companies, they have not succeeded in automating the production of core memories to such an extent that a rapidly increasing production volume could also lead to a corresponding reduction in unit costs. The production of magnetic core memories has remained a labor intensive operation. Monolithic memories, on the other hand, can exploit the vast production capabilities of the silicon planar technology which have been established by an industry which only now passes the borderline from a laboratory operation to a highly automated production industry. Using its large capital investments and some well directed technological improvements — better photolithography, larger silicon wafers, more efficient circuit design — this industry can offer a tremendous potential for productivity improvements and subsequently for cost reduction. Generally, the primary cost reduction for monolithic memories is followed by a secondary cost reduction of all silicon planar products of an electronic components supplier, since — as one can easily verify by weighing the silicon in a data processing system which is equipped with monolithic memories — more silicon is used for memory than for logic application, and because the production of monolithic memories absorbs a considerable amount of the fixed costs of a semiconductor production facility which dominate over variable costs in a highly automated industry.

One must, nevertheless, exercise caution in extrapolating too liberally from future increase of bit densities to cost reductions; the available production capability can only be converted into cost savings if the market can absorb all these bits which can be manufactured. There are some signs that perhaps over the next decade the technological progress may still be faster than the growth of the memory market. Productivity improvement and market absorption, however, are in such a close feedback relationship that it is very difficult, at this point in time, to make very accurate projections.

The economic advantage of monolithic memories over magnetic core memories is complemented by a number of additional benefits.

Because of the relatively simple and technologically homogeneous peripheral circuits, the per bit costs of a monolithic memory are far less a function of the size of the total memory than is the case in core memories. Consequently, also small monolithic memory units can be manufactured and used economically. This fact has helped considerably the development of microprogram controlled data processing systems: It is now possible to design small read/write control memories which are engineering change insensitive since engineering changes can be implemented in software through microprogram changes. Distributed through the whole data processing system, they perform systems control functions in those places where they are actually needed. An input/output-unit for instance, equipped with its own control store, blocks the memory bus of the system only after the control code in the control store is exhausted and a new page of control code must be fetched from the main memory.

Another advantage is the large flexibility which the designer of a monolithic memory obtains through the technological homogeneity of the storage element, the peripheral circuits and often also the system logic. This design flexibility is of decisive importance. It has been the driving force that over the last few years has activated the intellectual energy which subsequently enabled the rapid progress of monolithic memories.

3. Density – Productivity – Speed

Using figure 1, some characteristics and potentials of monolithic memories will be discussed.

In figure 1, the required silicon real estate to integrate one bit on an operational monolithic memory chip is plotted as a function of the chip access time. The bit-real estate refers to the prorated storage matrix and the prorated peripheral circuits which are necessary to operate the chip. The resulting curve intends to demonstrate the general interrelationship between memory costs and memory performance. The silicon real estate for one bit has been chosen as a substitute for costs. It is left to the reader to convert this bit real estate into price or cost, depending on his assumptions on processing cost for silicon wafers, size of silicon wafers, process yield, profits, etc. Nevertheless, it is assumed that increased integration density also leads to higher throughput and thus reduced costs. The curve roughly represents the status of presently announced or described monolithic memory products, but the shown relationship is of course constantly changing due to technological progress. Instead of attempting a detailed analysis of the accuracy of every point on the curve, it is probably much more interesting to investigate how the elements of this curve will move relative to each other in the future.

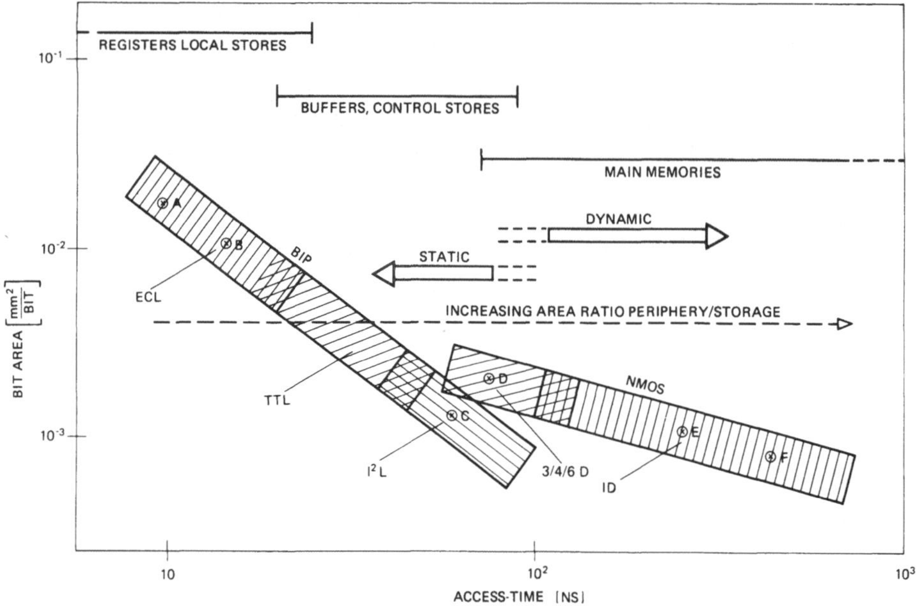

Fig. 1. Bit area requirement of monolithic memories as a function of access time.

To provide some orientation to the reader, several product points are shown within the band of the graph. "A" is a 10 nsec 256 bit chip, 5 mm² area, an extrapolation of a high performance chip described by *Glock* and *Mitterer* [2]. "B" is a 15 nsec 1K bit chip [3], "C" is a static 4K I²L chip, 55 nsec access time, "D" is a static 4K NMOS chip, 65 nsec access time, "E" is a 16K one-device dynamic memory chip, 250 nsec access time, and "F" is a 16K, 400 nsec one-device chip.

The interrelationship which is represented in Figure 1 is the technical basis for monolithic memory hierarchies in which the system designer attempts to achieve a main memory performance characteristic for the left side of the diagram combined with the costs which are characteristic for the right side of the diagram.

4. High Performance Monolithic Memories

The high performance region on the left side of the curve is the domain of the bipolar monolithic memory cells. Small register and local stores which are directly imbedded into the surrounding logic have the highest performance requirements for memory access and memory cycle. High performance is the only factor that counts, while power dissipation and costs are of secondary importance. The memory is usually accessed in a serial manner after a certain number of logical decisions

138

which are architecture dependent. All progress in the speed of logic circuitry would be useless if the performance of registers and local stores would not increase in the same manner. The same emitter coupled logic (ECL) circuits which provide the fastest logic circuits in today's data processing systems are also the basic design elements for the fastest monolithic memories.

For a very simple monolithic memory circuit, a minimum delay of 5 to 6 logic sequences is required for one access, namely two logic delays for decoding, approximately 2 logic delays to activate the addressed monolithic memory cell into a state that can supply a read signal and one to two logic delays to sense and amplify the read signal. When technological progress produces faster ECL circuits, monolithic memories will have a corresponding performance improvement. *Folberth* and *Bleher* [4] have attempted to estimate the performance limit of silicon planar circuits. They have demonstrated theoretically that the delay for one ECL stage can reach ultimately 10 psec and that silicon chips with such performance, a high LSI density and manageable power dissipation are manufacturable. The most important physical boundary which prevents further performance improvements is the size of the space charge region around a P/N junction [4]. This region ultimately determines the dimensions and thus also the capacitance of an integrated circuit. Using the ECL current delay as a base, it should therefore be possible to design fast registers and local stores with access times between 50 and 100 psec.

For very large data processing systems, there is a continuously increasing demand for higher performance. This demand will force the development of logic and storage circuits very quickly towards the limits dictated by the silicon; especially since no new fundamental technological barriers have to be surmounted once the silicon technology has moved from photo-lithography to electron beam lithography.

5. Very Dense Monolithic Memories

An analysis of the other extreme of the cost performance curve reveals the dominance of the field effect monolithic memories in this region, in particular the dynamic one-device storage cells. These storage cells consist of a single capacitor and a single transistor which, when opened, permits the flow of electric charge from the bit line into or out of the capacitor. These one-device transistor cells do not only produce the densest known random access monolithic memory chips but also can be operated over a very wide range of performances in the density-performance diagram.

The performance of a one-device monolithic memory can be increased by assuring that the read-sense circuit, which is coupled to the bit line, can detect as quickly and as reliably as possible the charge of the capacitor when the cell transistor is opened. This can be accomplished by either increasing the charge which is stored in the memory cell — which in a defined technological environment of oxide thickness and operating voltage means to enlarge the area of the cell — or by coupling very few monolithic memory cells to one particular bit line or one individual read-sense circuit in order to optimize the relationship between the cell capacitance and the parasitic bit line capacitance. With both options, the effective number of memory bits per silicon area is decreased. This means that the higher performance is obtained by trading off productivity.

The fastest one-device monolithic memories with a capacity of 16K bits per chip which have to date been described in the literature [5, 6] have an access time of approximately 200 nsec. Much of this access time, however, is consumed to generate with relatively slow on-chip FET circuitry the standard 5 volt TTL signals. If one places some of these voltage translation and driving tasks from the FET chip onto bipolar peripheral chips — for large monolithic memories this becomes a very economical option — then one-device monolithic memories using today's technologies can easily achieve access times below 100 nsec.

These one-transistor memories are dynamic memories. This means that after a certain time they lose their information through leakage currents, unless the information is periodically regenerated. During the regeneration process, the memory is not available to the processing unit.

The leakage currents in FET processes for manufacture of today's dynamic memories are so well controlled that the time intervals at which a monolithic memory cell needs to be regenerated, are comparatively long in relationship to the time required for the regeneration itself so that the availability of the monolithic memory to the processing unit is always close to 100 %.

An attempt is made here to project how the development of one-device monolithic memories might progress into the future particularily in terms of cell density and cost. Typically, today's 16K bit monolithic memory chips have a capacity per bit of approximately 0.03 pF. This capacity is integrated on an area of approximately 150 to 200 μm^2. The chips operate with oxide thicknesses of approximately 700 Å and an upper operational voltage of approximately 10 volts. In every bit position, approximately 1.5 million electrons can be stored from which the read-sense circuit can receive a signal of approximately 200 mV. *Folberth*'s and *Bleher*'s projections with respect to the minimum dimension of the space charge region for bipolar devices [4] are also valid for FET devices. In silicon, this dimension is approximately 0.03 μm. Using this dimension it is possible to calculate the size for a minimum area FET transistor, which is 2 μm^2 [4]. If the minimum area of a one-device transistor memory cell requires twice the space as a single transistor and if one assumes that 25 % of this area is available for the storage capacity, then the resulting minimum area available for the capacitor is approximately 1 μm^2. To operate a monolithic memory cell at these dimensions, however, it would be necessary to reduce the operating voltage to approximately 1 volt and correspondingly, the required thickness of the dielectric separating the field electrode and the channel to approximately 70 Å. The thin dielectric would augment the read signal by a factor of 10. Operating voltage and the area of the capacitor, however, would together decrease the signal by a factor of 1000. Thus a minimum geometry capacitor in the described environment of dielectric thickness and operating voltage could produce a sense signal of approximately 2 mV. If one considers the variations of geometry and the power supply tolerances, then it seems very difficult to construct an FET monolithic circuit which can reliably recognize and interpret this signal which is based on a mere 15000 electrons per storage node. Thus it seems very questionable whether it will be possible to drive the density of one-transistor monolithic memories to the limits which are theoretically possible for silicon. Most likely the sensitivity of the sense circuits will present an earlier barrier. If one assumes that sense signals of 20 mV can be recognized and interpreted reliably, then again using 1 Volt operating voltage and 70 Å oxide thickness, one could extrapolate a bit area of 10^{-4} mm^2. This would be the required bit area to integrate both the storage cell and its share of required peripheral circuits. This bit density would mean that it should be possible to integrate 500 000 bits on a silicon chip of today's standard dimensions. Using improved lithographic technologies and using an adapted vertical semiconductor device profile with a corresponding integrity of the dielectric it should thus be possible to improve the density of monolithic one-device memories by a factor of 20 to 30. After that, further progress will probably be extremely difficult.

Static memory cells have these difficulties to a lesser degree. Here it might be possible to drive the density of monolithic memories to the geometrical limits of the semiconductor. *Folberth* and *Bleher* [4] have shown that the material bound density of logic circuits can be 2×10^7 gates/cm^2. From this one can extrapolate that it should be possible to integrate more than 2 million bits on a silicon chip of today's dimensions.

Considering all these facts, it might be possible that further decrease of the device dimensions of semiconductor integrated circuits may cause a cross-over of the bit area requirements of dynamic and static memory cells. In the future, static memory cells might provide circuit designs with a higher bit density compared to those of dynamic memory cell designs. The best candidates to stimulate this development are monolithic memories using I^{2}L-storage cells [7]. The super-integrated I^{2}L-storage cells are in today's layout environment two to three times larger than one device NMOS-cells. The difference, nevertheless, diminishes on the operational storage chip because the static I^{2}L-chips require considerably less peripheral circuits than the dynamic one device chips. I^{2}L-circuits have a power performance product which is one to two orders of magnitude better than NMOS semiconductor circuits [8]. This provides them with a considerably better packaging density potential, in addition to a high performance capability. Already now, the I²L-memory performance is moving to a range which is characteristic for control store and cache performances.

The performance of I²L-memories is essentially determined by capacitive elements. With decreasing semiconductor device dimensions, the performance of I²L monolithic memories will increase in the same manner as was discussed earlier for bipolar circuits.

For one-device monolithic memory circuits, the performance gating process of reading a cell remains largely independent of geometry since it depends on the ratio of bit capacity to parasitic bit line capacity (transfer ratio). This ratio does not change significantly as a function of geometry. Increasing performance with decreasing device geometry will only occur for the on-chip peripheral circuits.

6. Effects on the monolithic memory storage hierarchy

To discuss the implications which may result from a cross-over between the I²L and NMOS monolithic memory cost performance curves — combined with the performance advantage intrinsic to I²L-memories — the operation of a hierarchical memory which consists of a NMOS main memory and a bipolar cache memory will be described. As an example the 8 megabyte monolithic memory of the IBM System /370—168 can be used, schematically shown in Fig. 2. To design a data processing system in which the main memory and the processor unit performance is in balance, the memory has to provide the data of the interface between memory and processor unit with the same frequency with which the processing unit requires these data. In the system 168 this is achieved with the help of a bipolar cache memory which in consecutive addresses can transfer 8 bytes of memory information to the processing unit every 80 nsec.

Ideally, this cache memory would have an indefinitely large storage capacity. For cost reasons, however, it is limited to 32K bytes and it is backed-up by an 8 megabytes FET memory.

If the required information is not located in the cache memory, it has to be fetched from the main memory. The cycle time of the main memory is 320 nsec, the data path to the cache memory is 8 bytes wide. If the storage hierarchy would only have one main memory, it would be possible to transfer 8 bytes every 320 nsec from the main memory into the cache. The cache, however, can process 8 bytes every 80 sec. To serve the cache with an optimum data rate despite the slow cycle time of the main memory, the backing store consists of 4 practically independent main memories of 2 megabytes each of which can be addressed at intervals of 80 nsec. Thus, every 80 nsec 8 bytes of data from one of the main memories can be transferred to the cache (interleaving).

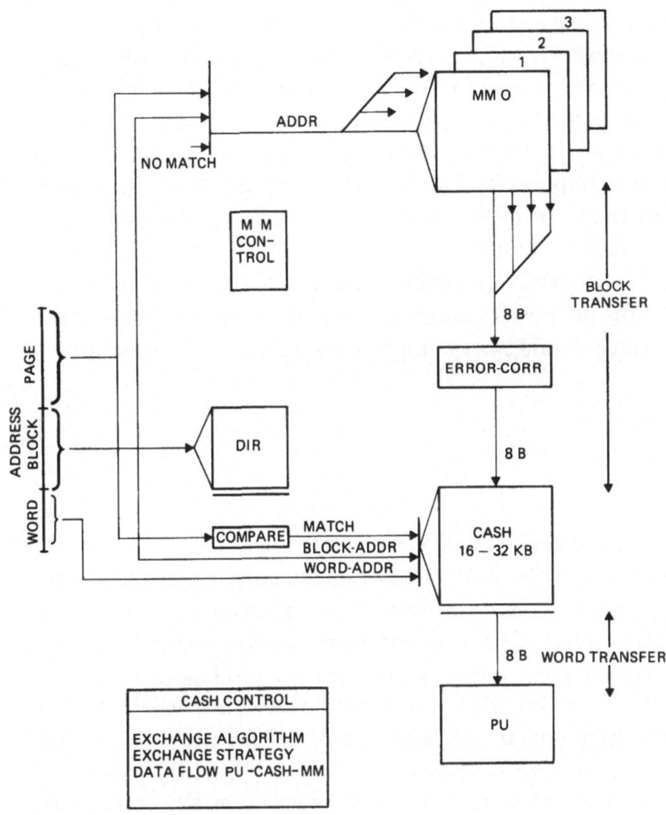

Fig. 2. 370/168 Monolithic memory.

The efficient operation of this memory hierarchy is only achieved by using a considerable amount of control logic which monitors the content of the cache, which implements the exchange algorithm between cache and main memory and which controls the addressing of the four separate main memories, as well as the branching which becomes necessary when the address sequence is not consecutive. The costs of this control logic can only be amortized if the cost difference between the cache memory and the main memory is very large. In the case of the 168 memory hierarchy, the cache is designed with a 256 bit bipolar chip, the main memory with a 2048 bit FET memory chip. The silicon area for both chips is very similar.

If it would be possible to design I^2L monolithic memories which have the performance required for a cache memory and which are in their silicon bit productivity not too different from slower main memory chips, then the investment for the

control logic will not be profitable anymore and a one-level memory will be the
more economic solution. It is believed that especially small and medium data processing systems, which are usually exposed to the most severe cost competition,
will in the future make better use of a one level monolithic memory and that, as
I^2L and one-device transistor productivity approach each other, the monolithic
memory hierarchy will lose in importance for this application. To make this projec-
ton come true, it would of course be necessary that the bit density of a semiconductor chip and the packing density of monolithic memories can be increased to such
an extent, that very large cache memories can be integrated directly with the processing unit logic, because the high performance is required directly at the processing unit and this performance should not be impaired by cables, drivers and intermediate amplification.

7. The Access Gap

Referring again to figure 1, the region which extends to the right from the one transistor monolithic memories will be discussed. This is the memory region characterized by an access time between 10^{-6} sec (one-device monolithic memories) and
10^{-3} sec (fixed head magnetic files). This region of memory performance usually
carries the name "access gap". Presently two technologies are candidates for filling
the access gap. They are the charge coupled devices (CCD) and the magnetic bubble
memories. Because of their serial operation both memory technologies have access
times which are slower than that of random access one-device monolithic memories.
It is difficult to speculate whether these memories will be economically competitive
with the one-device cells on the one side and the fixed head files on the other side.

Compared to one-device cells, the CCD's have the advantage that at the end of a
CCD chain the total memory charge — reduced slightly by losses from leakage
currents — is available for sensing through the read-sense circuit. In one-device
cell memories, only the small ratio between cell capacity and parasitic bit line
capacity (transfer ratio) is available for read-sensing. This CCD advantage combined
with simpler peripheral circuits on the memory chip provides a CCD memory chip
presently with a density advantage of two to four times compared to one-device
cell memory chips. Because of the better transfer ratio, the CCD elements have
also a better chance to surpass the bit density boundaries which exist for one-
device cells from the limits in sensitivity of the read-sense circuits, and it might be
possible to advance the CCD bit density to the limits which are determined by
the minimal dimension in the silicon physical parameters itself.

From a geometrical point of view, the minimum space requirement is identical for
a CCD cell and a one-device cell, as was demonstrated by *Hodges* [10]. Thus it can
be projected that also for CCD-cells in the ultimate design, it will not be possible

144

to integrate more than approximately 10^7 CCD-bits plus periphery per cm^2 of silicon. This would correspond to approximately 2 million bits on a semiconductor chip of today's dimensions. Ultimately, this is not more than what theoretically could also be achieved with static monolithic memories as was demonstrated earlier.

While the technologies are advancing towards these limits, CCD's, however, will use their considerable density advantage compared to competing technologies, such as I^2L. It is quite likely that in the near future we will see large data processing systems where CCD's will form one level of the storage hierarchy, probably not in addition but rather instead of one-device monolithic memories [11].

Bubble memories are more difficult to evaluate. If one uses a measure defined by the minimum dimensions achievable by the lithography processes, *Hodges* [10] has demonstrated that the area requirement of a magnetic bubble bit is considerably larger than that of a one-device monolithic memory cell. To produce magnetic bubble memories, however, one requires only very few vertical processing layers which simplifies greatly the problem of relative layer registration. Theoretically, it would be possible to define a storage matrix with only one lithography layer. The minimum dimensions achievable through lithography are thus smaller in the case of bubble memories than in the case of semiconductor memories with their many processing layers. Despite this advantage it will be very difficult to produce bubble memories as cost efficiently as semiconductor memories because they, of course, have the same handicap as was shown earlier for magnetic core memories. The transition from the magnetic environment to the peripheral circuitry for sensing and amplification requires very complex and expensive semiconductor circuits. The cost for these semiconductor circuits must be amortized over the total quantity of magnetic bubble bits. The same is true for the permanent and rotating field magnets which are required for permanent storage of the information and for the movement of the magnetic bubbles. The magnetic bubbles will most likely be competitive in very large memory units, even though they could apply their main technological advantage — i.e. the fact that in bubble memories the information is retained even if the supply voltage is turned off — in smaller memory units. A certain amount of the systems control program always must be stored in permanent storage. This is the part of the control instructions which is required to bring the system into a well defined state after power-on, namely the initial program load (IPL). Magnetic bubble memories could help in this area, if it would be possible to produce them economically in small units.

Compared to the mechanical disk storage, the bubble memories have the advantage of better reliability and insensitivity to shock. Both characteristics certainly can be of significance in special applications.

8. Summary

Because of their economic superiority, monolithic memories have displaced magnetic core memories from data processing applications.

It is possible to project the limits of development of monolithic memories in silicon planar technology. There appears still sufficient potential for future development.

In high performance monolithic memories, it is possible to envision access times between 50 and 100 psec.

A basic limitation to the bit density progress of one-device monolithic memories might be the sensitivity of read sense circuits.

Static monolithic memories, especially I^2L memories, have the potential to achieve or to surpass the productivity of one-device monolithic memories, with considerably better memory performance.

CCD monolithic memories can achieve higher bit densities more easily than one-device memories.

Magnetic bubble memories can displace both magneto-mechanical as well as semiconductor storage devices in the near future for special applications.

References

[1]   *R.J. Frankenberg,* EDN, September 5, 1968

[2]   *H. Glock, R. Mitterer,* Siemens Forschungs- und Entwicklungsberichte, 4 (1975) Nr. 4, p. 250

[3]   *R. Rathbone* et al, Digest of Technical Papers, ISSCC 1976, p. 188

[4]   *O.G. Folberth, H. Bleher* NTZ, Vol. 30, (1977) Nr. 4, p. 307

[5]   Digest of Technical Papers, ISSCC 1976 Session Memory 1

[6]   "MOSTEK", Electronic News, October 25, 1976, p. 7

[7]   *S.K. Wiedmann* "Bipolar Devices for High Density Semiconductor Memories", European Solid State Device Conference, Munich 1976

[8]   *L. Altmann,* Electronics, April 1976, p. 73

[9]   *U. G. Baitinger, R. Remshardt,* this volume, p. 105

[10] *D.A. Hodges,* Computer Design, February 1976, p. 77

[11] *P. Schneider,* National Computer Conference 1976, p. 373

Structure, Organization and Applications of CCD Memories

Hans Joachim Harloff

Siemens AG, Data Processing Systems, Munich, Germany

1. Introduction

Semiconductor memories have been used on a large scale in data processing as random
access memories (RAMs) of many types and sizes and for a large range of speeds for
a number of years now. They have nearly completely taken the place of magnetic
core memories. The availability of devices with ever larger storage capacities brings
us correspondingly nearer to the long-discussed goal of also employing semiconductor
memories in those applications which were previously reserved for smaller serial
magnetic memories, such as drums and fixed-head disks. The most likely contenders
in this respect are charge-coupled device memories (CCD memories). It is the intent
of this study to deal with the principles, characteristics and potential applications of
the CCD memories.

2. Structure and mode of operation

The principle of the charge-coupled device (CCD) was proposed by Boyle and Smith
[1] in 1969. They implemented a string of closely spaced MOS capacitors and showed
that on application of a suitable sequence of clock pulses, packets of minority carriers
are transported along the silicon surface from one capacitor to the next under the
influence of the surface potential. The presence or absence of charge at a certain
location at a certain time is interpreted as binary information.

In the meantime, a large number of practical ways of realizing this principle have
been proposed, varying with respect to the type of clock pulses, geometrical form of
the electrodes and type of charge transport. There is an abundance of circuits suitable
for writing and reading information, represented by charges, into and out of such a
shift register. As in the case of MOS transistors, the charge carriers are always introduced into the chain from a source region and collected again in a drain region. In the
following, a number of the most important CCD versions will be discussed in detail.

2.1. Surface CCDs

Fig. 1a shows in schematic form the cross-section of an n-channel surface CCD
(SCCD) in two-phase operation and the profile of the surface potential ϕ. The elec-

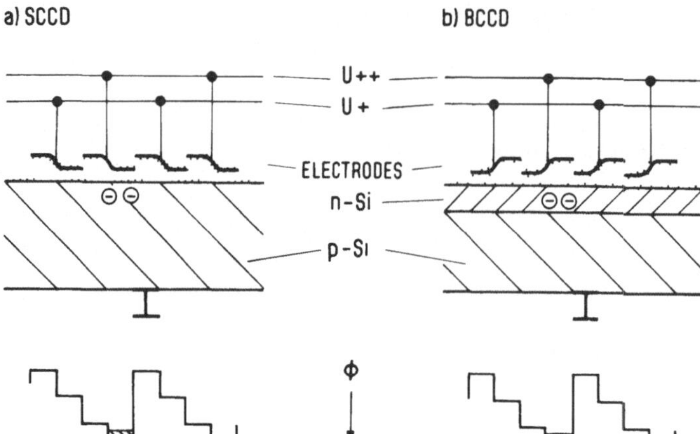

Fig. 1. Surface CCD and bulk CCD. Basic structure and profile of the potential ϕ in the charge transfer path. Two-phase clock.

trodes (gates) are arranged alternately at two levels above the silicon surface and can be connected in pairs, as shown. Two such gate pairs (i.e. four gates) constitute a memory cell. The figure depicts the instant at which the information has just been accepted by the right-hand half of a memory cell, i.e. the instant at which the charge has just flowed into the deepest surface potential well. In the next timing phase, the voltages on the clock lines are exchanged and the charge is transferred to the right. The alternating clock voltages thus provide for moving potential wells on the Si surface, which the carrier packets can follow. Disturbing potential barriers between the electrodes can be eliminated by means of suitable electrode shapes or implanted zones. Several authors have specified procedures for the computation of the horizontal and vertical potential profile as an aid to electrode design.

Charge transfer is naturally neither loss- nor noise-free. Charge is lost by incomplete transfer, diffusion, recombination and in traps. Additional charge is obtained by diffusion, generation, leakage currents and from traps. As all these effects are time-dependent, there is an upper and a lower clock frequency limit for an efficient charge transfer. These limits of course also depend on temperature. On readout, the difference between the "1" and "0" signal decreases with the length of the CCD chain, as a result of the above disturbing effects. After a certain number of electrodes — usually between 100 and 1000 — it is necessary to insert a regenerating amplifier.

Traps, the density of which depends strongly on the fabrication method, may have severe adverse effects. A very effective method of reducing their influence is to operate with a background charge or "fat-zero": a low charge adequate to keep the traps always filled is propagated through the device for the binary signal "0" as well.

148

The charge portion lost on charge transfer from one electrode to the next has been
shown to be $\epsilon = 10^{-4}$ to 10^{-3} for surface CCDs and can have an even smaller value
for background charge operation. After n transfer processes, the residual charge is

$$Q_n = Q_0 (1 - \epsilon)^n \approx Q_0 e^{-n\epsilon} .$$

If a charge transfer loss of 10 % is tolerated, $n\epsilon = - \log_e 0.9$. For $n = 1000$, i.e.
chains for 250 bits, $\epsilon \leqslant 10^{-4}$ is required. Background charge operation is therefore
practically always necessary for SCCDs, for reasons of security alone.

2.2. Bulk CCDs

In bulk or buried channel CCDs (BCCDs) or peristaltic CCDs (PCCDs) (Fig. 1b), the
potential minima which form the charge transfer channel have been shifted down
from the surface into a surface layer some micrometers in thickness of opposite conductivity. This layer is produced by epitaxy and/or ion implantation. Surface defects
now have no effect, the specific charge transfer losses are lower ($\epsilon \approx 10^{-5}$) and it is
possible to achieve, as Esser and his co-workers have shown [2], shift clock frequencies of over 100 MHz.

The lower charge transfer losses and the high speed of operation are the major
advantages of BCCDs. On the other hand, their structure is somewhat more intricate.
Their main disadvantage is, however, that the transferrable signal charge becomes
smaller, with all other conditions unchanged, as its distance from the silicon surface
increases. Efforts have been made to lessen this drawback by means of inhomogeneous doping of the n-Si layer, decreasing with the distance from the surface (profiled
peristaltic CCD [3]).

The mode of operation of the BCCD differs from that of the SCCD. The n-layer is
emptied of electrons by means of a suitable bias voltage and propagation of "0"
signals through the device. The signal charges are in that case electron packets, in
other words majority carriers. In this respect, structure and mode of operation of
the BCCD are similar to that of the MES-FET. It is therefore possible to apply the
MES-FET technology to BCCD devices. A detailed comparison of SCCD and BCCD
is given, for example, in [4].

2.3. Technology

The fabrication technology of CCD memory devices basically corresponds to that of
MOS-RAM devices. A number of variants is known, differing with respect to form and
arrangement of the electrodes, with specific technological and electrical advantages
and disadvantages. For reasons of economy, types of structure predominate which
can be manufactured with essentially the same process sequence as used for MOS-
RAMs. The present-day structures comprise two or three polysilicon gate levels and
one aluminium wiring plane.

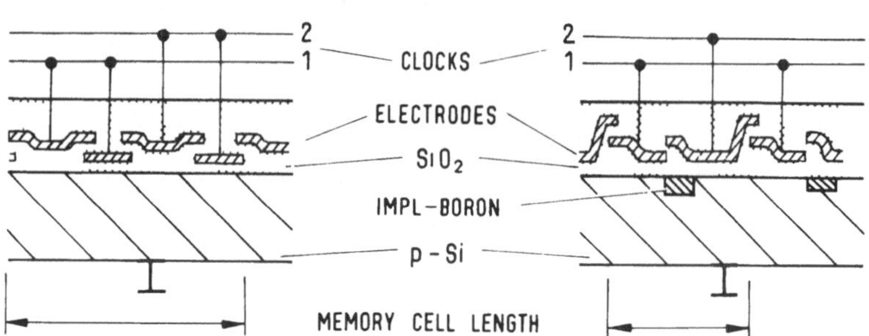

Fig. 2. CCD memory cell. Electrodes of polysilicon or polysilicon alternating with aluminium.
a) Two- or four-phase operation possible,   b) offset gate, two-phase operation.

A frequently used type is shown schematically in Fig. 2a [5]. The lower gate level
consists of polysilicon, the upper level of either polysilicon or aluminium. Two-phase
operation, as shown, or four-phase operation is possible. A memory cell includes four
gate electrodes.

A particularly high packing density is obtained with the offset gate arrangement shown
in Fig. 2b [6]. In this case, only two-phase clocking is possible. Fabrication becomes
more difficult as minimum structure width is reduced and very precise mask registration is then required.

The anticipated cost advantage of CCD memory devices over MOS-RAM devices is based
firstly on the higher storage density and secondly on a possible higher yield. As new
proposals for space-saving cell structures are still being made all the time, a general comparison of the storage densities is therefore not possible. According to recent figures
published by Terman and Heller [7], the ratio of the areas of RAM and CCD memory
cells is approximately 2:1. Furthermore, CCD devices require less peripheral circuitry
on the chip, the ratio of the cell field to the chip area is between 0.3 and 0.45 for
the RAM and 0.4 and 0.6 for the CCD memory. A 65-kbit CCD chip therefore has
about 1.5 times the area of a 16-kbit RAM chip. Advances in the geometrical storage
density of the CCD memories will be discussed in paragraph 3.

It should be possible to obtain a higher yield above all on account of the very simple
cell field with no contact holes. It is therefore anticipated that there will be cost
equality for a RAM device and a CCD memory device with a fourfold capacity.

2.4. Storage of several bits in one cell

Charge-transfer elements can of course also process analog information and are
employed in a corresponding manner in image processing and in telecommunications.

Consequently, it is possible to store more than one bit per cell by means of multi-level storage: for n bits per cell it is necessary to make a reliable distinction between 2^n amplitude steps. The economic significance of multilevel storage is obvious in view of the considerable increase in the storage density in bits/mm^2 and reduction of the manufacturing per-bit costs. No information has however as yet been published on success in the practical implementation of this method.

A number of difficulties have to be overcome. The technology must, for example, provide a way of keeping dark currents and transfer losses very low and ensure smooth transfer over the CCD chain. With regard to the circuitry, encoder and detection circuits have to be developed, which automatically match themselves to the electrical parameters subject to scatter from the production process. Noise is not the prime obstacle that has to be overcome.

On the other hand, it can be shown that CCD electrodes with those dimensions that can be implemented in production at present (structure widths of around 5 μm) are capable of transferring so much charge, that even with a division of the detection window into 8 or 16 small parts, enough charge still remains to drive one of the highly sensitive sense amplifiers customary in MOS-RAM devices. Due to the in-creasing control of the MOS-technology, the assumption is justified that devices with two-bit our four-bit cells can be manufactured in a few years. Multilevel storage is thus a promising alternative or supplementary method to increase the storage density by scaling down the structures.

3. Device organization and characteristics

CCD memory devices employ the same technology as is used for main memories. It is now possible to build relatively small serial memories. Access time, data rate and loop length can be matched to the conditions of operation within broad limits. Devices with a capacity of 65 kbits have been commercially available since the second quarter of 1977.

Two basic types of device organization have evolved. In both, the information always flows through loops, which are closed by a read-write-regenerate terminal. A loop can then be either completely linear (single loop (SL) organization), or split into many parallel chains and then reunited again (series-parallel-series (SPS) organization).

3.1. Single loop organization

In this type of organization, a device contains many individually addressable, relatively short loops. A 16-kbit device would, for example, have 64 loops with 256 bits each. The mean access time, in this case always defined as half the loop cycle time plus the delay time in the on-chip logic circuits, would be around 52 μs for a clock frequency

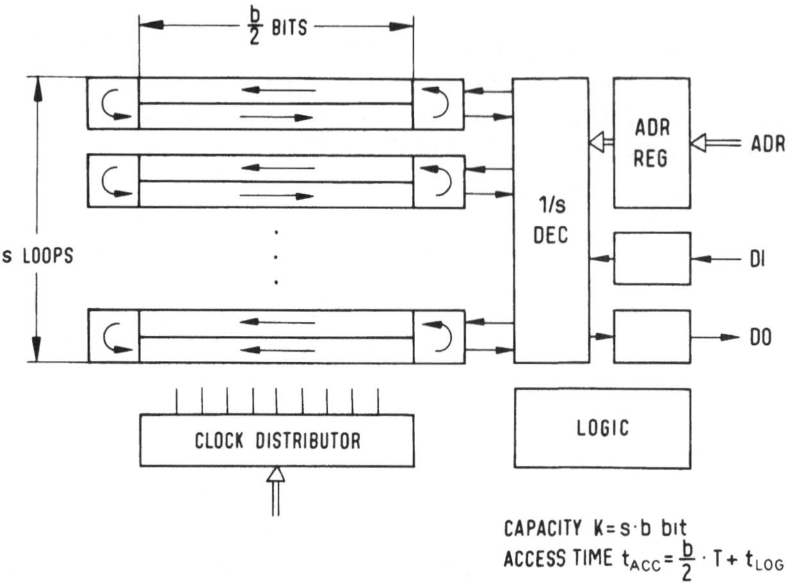

Fig. 3. Single loops or serpentine loop organization.

of 5 MHz. This historical initial type of system organization is shown in Fig. 3. The loops can have a circular or serpentine shape. The effective cell density on the chip is comparatively low.

The LARAM system organization (line addressable random access memory) shown in Fig. 4 is designed for a particularly short access time and high data rate. A 16-kbit device of this type [8] contains $g = 4$ groups each with $s = 32$ loops with $b = 128$ bits each. The device has 4 data inputs and outputs.

At a clock frequency of 4 MHz, the data rate is 16 Mbits/s and the mean access time 16 μs. There are g decoders which route the shift clock pulse in each case to only one of the s loops in each group. In the other $g(s-1)$ loops, the information meanwhile remains stationary. In this way, a considerable saving in clock pulse power, and thus in device power dissipation, is achieved. On the other hand, stationary charge disappears after a period which is heavily dependent on the dark current, as in the case of MOS-RAMs. It is therefore necessary, as in MOS-RAMs, to insert forced refresh periods during which the device is not available for normal accesses. In contrast to the original serpentine organization with shift clock pulse continually applied, the LARAM organization has the advantages of shorter access time and reduced clock pulse power at the expense of the refresh problem.

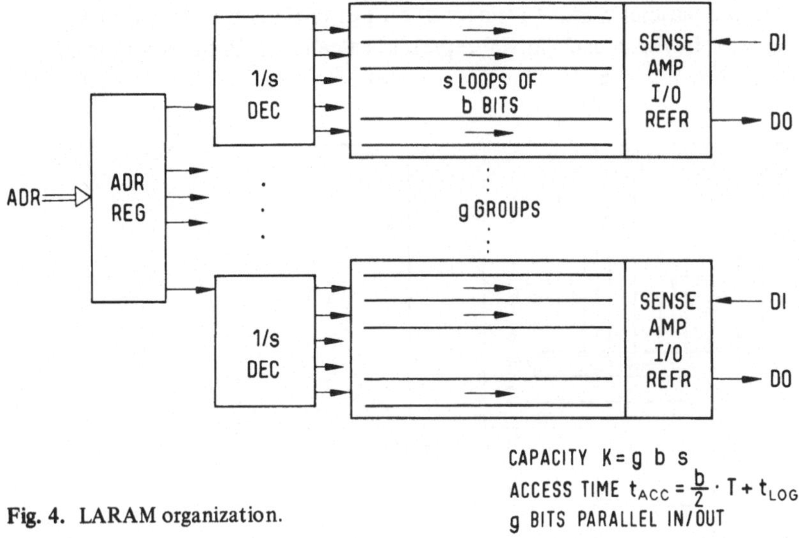

Fig. 4. LARAM organization.

3.2. Series-parallel-series organization

The SPS organization, Fig. 5, represents a breakthrough for CCD memory devices with regard to storage density and consequently to low manufacturing costs [9]. Such a device contains relatively few high-capacity loops of rectangular structure; a 65-kbit device, for example, comprises sixteen 4096-bit loops. The information enters an input chain with a length of m bits, is then transferred to m parallel chains which are clocked at an m-fold lower frequency and is finally passed to an output chain identical to the input chain. The information leaves the output chain in serial form with the original clock frequency. Each charge packet only passes through $m + n + 1$ memory cells, large loop lengths $m (n + 2)$ are therefore possible without charge transfer losses having a prohibitive effect. As the bits are shifting in the parallel chains at only 1/m of the clock frequency effective externally, the clock power dissipation remains very low.

The maximum storage density is obtained with an improvement on the SPS principle, the CSPS-EPB-CCD (condensed series-parallel-series electrode per bit CCD), shown in Fig. 6 [9, 10]. We speak of a condensed memory as the number of parallel chains is doubled. Information is first transferred simultaneously from all right-hand halfs of the serial input chain cells (cf. Fig. 2a) to the uppermost cells of every second parallel chain. Now all left-hand halfs of the input chain cells are filled with new information, which is transferred to the still empty uppermost parallel-chain cells. In-

153

formation from the parallel chains to the serial output chain is transferred in a corresponding way. In Fig. 6 each square represents a cell half, in other words an electrode pair as shown in Fig. 2a. The squares marked with a cross contain informa-

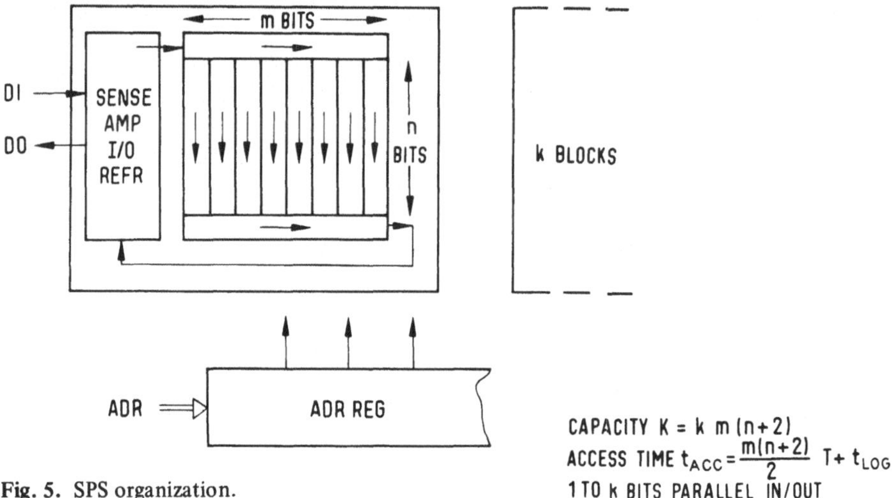

Fig. 5. SPS organization.

CAPACITY $K = k\, m\,(n+2)$
ACCESS TIME $t_{ACC} = \dfrac{m(n+2)}{2}\, T + t_{LOG}$
1 TO k BITS PARALLEL IN/OUT

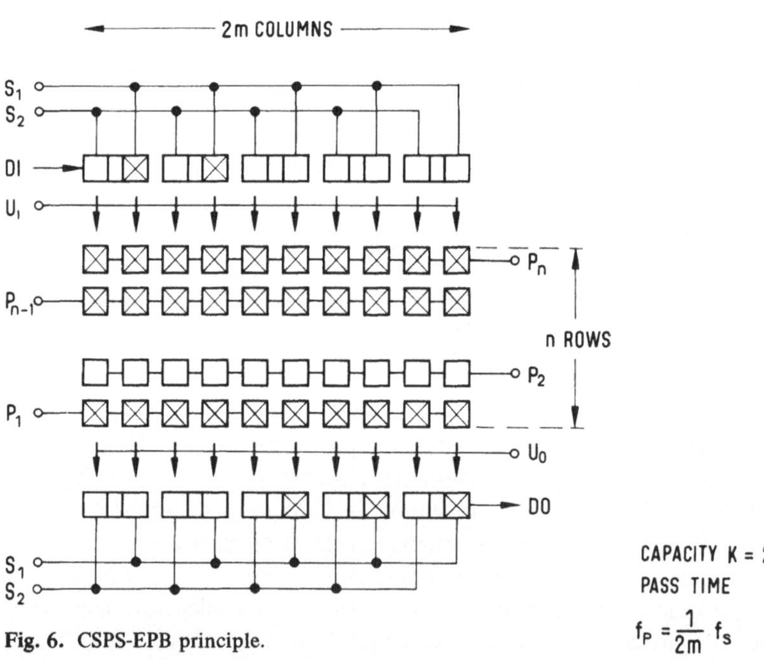

Fig. 6. CSPS-EPB principle.

CAPACITY $K = 2m\,(n-1) + m$
PASS TIME $\quad 2t_{ACC} = K \cdot T_S$
$f_P = \dfrac{1}{2m}\, f_S$

tion at a particular instant. The EPB procedure means that an empty row moves
under clock control from the bottom to the top of the parallel chain field, so that in
each chain only one bit is transferred one cell half [9]. All cell halves except the
empty row contain information. The capacity of the CSPS-EPB block (Fig. 6) is
$K = 2m(n-1) + m$ bits, the pass time of the information is $2t_{ACC} = K \cdot T_s$, where
T_s is the clock period of the input/output chains.

Using the technology shown in Fig. 2a with a structure width of 5 μm, a half-cell area
of 196 μm^2 was achieved [10], i.e. a storage density of around 5000 bits/mm^2 in the
cell field. A major problem in the implementation of such maximized storage densities
is the design of circuits for generation of the clock pulses $P_1 \ldots P_n$, U_i, U_0 (Fig. 6), which
together with the supply lines have to fit into the narrow raster of the parallel chains.

A number of the familar 16-kbit devices and all of the currently available 65-kbit devices are organized according to the SPS or CSPS-EPB principle, with blocks of 4096
bits in most cases. It is probable that this principle and possibly in addition multilevel storage present the only solution to a further increase in the device capacity.

4. CCD memories in data processing systems

Soon after the invention of CCDs, much thought was given to areas of application of
CCD memories, often in comparison with magnetic bubble memories and other
competing developments [11]. Such comparisons are however beyond the scope of
this study. Specific advantages of one particular process — speed, non-volatility of
the information, packaging technology, resistance to radiation — may in many cases
allow no freedom of choice. Availability and price/performance ratio are the factors
which usually tip the scales.

4.1. Requirements

The fundamental requirement for the introduction of new components such as CCD
memory devices is that the equipment in which they are installed is subject to an
appropriate increase in performance and/or cost reduction, without one being enhanced at the expense of the other. From the aspect of cost, CCDs must at any rate compete with MOS-RAM devices, in other words they must be markedly cheaper. The
factor by which they have to be cheaper depends on the particular application. The
frequently specified factor of 4 is certainly a useful guiding value. Advances in CCD
development must always keep pace with or even surpass those in MOS-RAM devices.

In this study, we shall ignore applications in small computers, data terminal equipment and line termination equipment etc., as little concrete information is available
on them. We shall concentrate on the memory hierarchy of medium-size and large
data processing systems. It was initially planned to use CCD memories as paging

memories in virtual main memory systems in place of drum or fixed-head disk storages.
The general line of thought then turned in the direction of multilevel main memory
systems of large capacity and multiple utilization of the buffer storage principle in
a new type of organization.

4.2. Paging memory

The memory hierarchy of a computer with virtual memory system (Fig. 7) includes a
paging memory, the capacity of which corresponds to the virtual address space. On
request, it exchanges its information in the form of pages (data blocks), of for example
4 kB, with the main memory. The operating system initiates the transfer of a page to
the main memory whenever information is required to resume execution of the program in progress, and this information is not available in the main memory (page
fault). The interrupted program may have to wait a long time for the requested page
(operating system run plus access time and page transfer time). The next program is
therefore processed in the meantime until this one too is interrupted by a page fault,
for example, and so on.

This process works well as long as the number of active programs, speed of the paging
memory and speed of the processor remain in a balanced relationship to each other.
Clearly, the enhanced speed of the processors brought about by technological advances

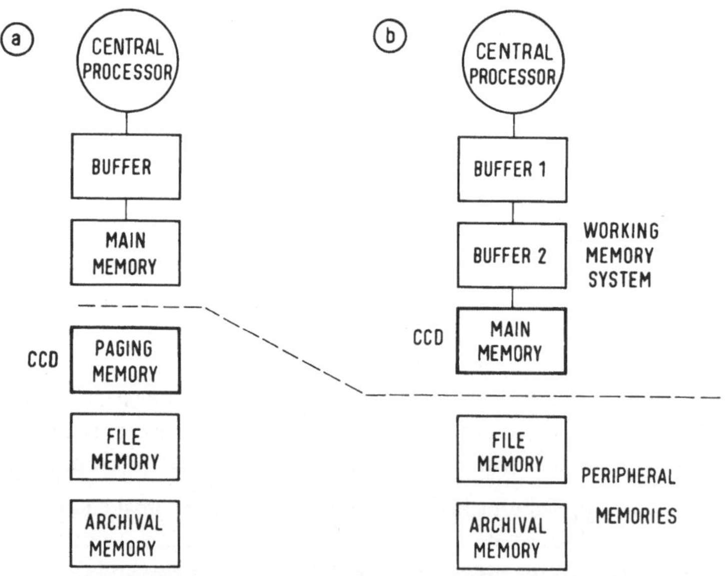

Fig. 7. Memory hierarchy. a) Two-level,   b) three-level working memory system.

(large-scale integration) will necessitate an increase in speed, or number, of the paging memories, unless losses in performance such as idle times of the processor are acceptable. A paging memory with shorter access and transfer times can definitely reduce the processing time of the programs and increase the job throughput of the computer. Processors for a higher performance (1 MIPS and more) therefore require high-speed paging memories or backing storages.

CCD memories provide this high speed, namely access times of less than 1 ms to less than 100 μs and an almost unlimited maximum data rate. It is therefore the costs which determine whether the necessary capacities (16 MB to possibly over 100 MB) can be realized [12]. Assuming that the CCD memory prices per bit are one quarter of those for MOS-RAMs, present predictions point to a CCD cost per bit of 10 to 20 mc for 1980. Even after adding a cost share for control and installation, the price should not be an obstacle to their application. Furthermore, the previously mentioned replacement of disk storages by CCD memories will not necessitate any major modifications of the system software. Maintenance and reconfiguration in the event of a fault are very simple.

4.3. Multilevel main memory system

Multilevel memory systems have been the subject of theoretical investigation for a considerable time [13]. Three-level main memories, with CCD memories having the largest capacity ([14], Fig. 7b), and with direct access to the entire capacity area of the CCD memory, offer a number of advantages over the paging memory process. In particular, the page-transfer procedure under software control would no longer be necessary and a corresponding amount of time would be saved, and the data exchange between the CCD main memory and buffer 2 would be effected under hardware control in the memories. A program would no longer have to be interrupted on account of a page fault.

A condition is of course that data transfer between CCD memory and buffer is correspondingly fast. The effective mean access time for read operations t_{eff} to the overall system, as seen from the processor, should not be too long. It is at least

$$t_{eff} = h_1 t_1 + (1 - h_1) [h_2 t_2 + (1 - h_2) t_3] \ .$$

h_1, h_2 are the hit rates in buffers 1 and 2, t_1, t_2, t_3 are the access times to buffers 1 and 2 and to the CCD memory. Assuming that $h_1 = 0.95$, $t_1 = 100$ ns and $t_2 = 800$ ns, the effective access time for a two-level system (cache, MOS main memory, $h_2 = 1$) is 135 ns. The effective access time for the three-level system should not be markedly longer, as otherwise the increase in performance may become insignificant. Assuming now that $h_2 = 0.95$ and that the access times of the CCD memory are the typical values specified in section 3 of 16 μs (LARAM), 52 μs (ES) and 500 μs (SPS), the effective access time of the three-level system is then 173 ns, 263 ns and

1.4 μs respectively. These values are heavily dependent on the hit rate h_2, which is in turn programdependent. It is quite evident that the access times are too long, above all for the low-cost SPS-CCD devices.

To solve this problem, Schneider [15] proposed the use of the working set restoration method. The working set of a reactivated program, here the set of pages which was in buffer 2 in the last processing interval, is again loaded into buffer 2 before the next processing operation, while another program is in progress. In this way, the hit rate h_2 approaches the value 1. Buffer 2 must have adequate space for at least two working sets, for resident system programs to be retained and for exchangeable system programs. Its capacity can however remain well below that of the main memory of a two-level system. Schneider has shown that the effective access time of this three-level system roughly corresponds to that of a two-level system and that, for identical capacities, the three-level system is considerably more cost-effective than the two-level system [15].

5. Outlook

The overall progress in semiconductor large-scale integration advances CCD devices just as other memory and logic devices. At present, problems connected with photo-lithographic mask technology, registration and production yield, limit storage density and chip size, i.e. the device capacity. On the basis of the successful work on electron

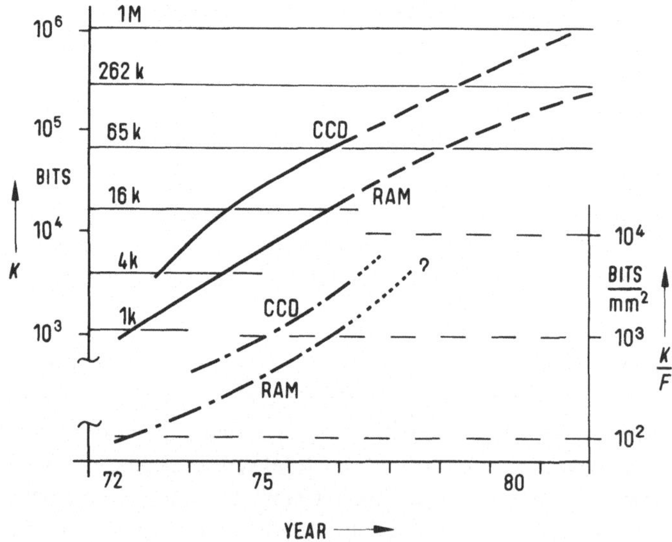

Fig. 8. Increase in the capacity K and the capacity K/F referred to the chip area F for MOS–RAMs and CCDs.

beam and X-ray lithography and on the improvement of the process technology, it can however be assumed that the exponential rise of the device capacity with time will continue on into the next decade (Fig. 8).

CCDs will be able to retain their superiority in capacity by a factor of 4 over MOS-RAM devices, above all if it becomes possible to store several bits in each memory cell (multilevel storage).

A 262-kbit device will probably permit the device price to fall below 5 mc/bit. On the basis of space requirement, reliability, costs and modularity, devices of this kind should make possible the construction of memories with a capacity of over 100 MB.

The operating speed is also still well below insurmountable barriers. Further increase in the clock frequency is at present primarily dependent on advances in the electric circuit technology. Shorter access time can also be achieved by using shorter loops, the capacity of which can, for example, be increased again by means of multilevel storage. Furthermore, the data rate can be matched to practically any requirement in the usual way by parallel read/write operations, interleaving etc.

The application examples in section 4 are intended to show that CCD memories are more than an alternative to other memory and storage types, the performance of which is no longer adequate. Future computer systems with high and very high capabilities, for example, can only be built economically if the ever widening gap between speed and capacity of the RAM semiconductor primary and mechanical secondary memories can be closed by means of suitable organization and technology. An eminently suitable solution is provided by CCD memories, on account of their wide capacity and speed range, their packaging technology and their natural compatibility with other semiconductor memories and mass memory controllers.

References

[1] *W. S. Boyle, G. E. Smith,* Charge Coupled Semiconductor Devices. Bell Syst. Tech. J. 49 (1970), pp. 587–593.

[2] *L. J. M. Esser, M. G. Collet, J. G. van Santen,* The Peristaltic Charge Coupled Device. Int. Electron Devices Meeting, Washington, 1973, Techn. Dig., pp. 17–20.

[3] *L. J. M. Esser,* The Peristaltic Charge-Coupled Device for High-Speed Charge Transfer. Int. Solid-State Circuits Conf. 1974, Dig. Tech. Papers, pp. 28, 29.

[4] *C. H. Séquin, M. F. Tompsett,* Charge Transfer Devices. Academic Prrss, Inc. New York, San Francisco, London 1975.

[5] *W. F. Kosonocky, J. E. Carnes,* Charge-Coupled Digital Circuits. IEEE J. SC-6, 1971, pp. 314–322.

[6] *R. W. Bower, T. A. Zimmermann, A. M. Mohsen,* A High Density Overlapping Gate Charge-Coupled Device Array. Int. Electron Devices Meeting, Washington, 1973. Techn. Dig., pp. 30–32.

[7] *L. M. Terman, L. G. Heller,* Overview of CCD Memory. IEEE J. **SC-11**, 1976, pp. 4–10.

[8] *K. C. Gunsagar, M. R. Guidry, G. F. Amelio,* A CCD Line Addressable Random-Access Memory (LARAM). IEEE J. **SC-10**, 1975, pp. 268–273.

[9] *D. R. Collins* et al., CCD Memory Options. Int. Solid-State Circuits Conf. 1973, Dig. Tech. Papers, pp. 136, 137, 210.

[10] *E. Gottler, O. Gruter, P. Schneider,* CCD Memory Circuits of High Bit Density. ESSCIRC 1975, Canterbury, Conf. Proc., pp. 76, 77.

[11] *W. Anacker,* Possible Uses of Charge-Transfer Devices and Magnetic-Domain Devices in Memory Hierarchies. IEEE Transact. **MAG-7**, 1971, pp. 410–415.

[12] *A. V. Pohm,* Cost/Performance Perspectives of Paging with Electronic and Electro-mechanical Backing Stores. Proc. IEEE **63**, 1975, pp. 1123–1128.

[13] *R. L. Mattson,* Evaluation of Multilevel Memories. IEEE Transact. **MAG-7**, 1971, pp. 814–819.

[14] *P. Schneider, J. Witte,* CCD Memories in a Working Memory System. Siemens Forsch.-u. Entwickl.-Ber. **4**, 1975, pp. 231–237.

[15] *P. Schneider,* Working Set Restoration – A Method to Increase the Performance of Multilevel Storage Hierarchies. AFIPS Conf. Proc. 45; 1976 National Computer Conf., pp. 373–380.

BEAMOS – Technology and Applications

Claus Schünemann

IBM Böblingen, Germany

1. Introduction

BEAMOS – Beam Accessable MOS – is the best known synonym for recent developments in the field of electronic beam memories.

The principle of storing information in a medium embedded in an electron tube and accessing it by an electron beam is not new. In the late 40 s the Williams-Tube was used as fast memory in the early data processing machines. These early developments did not result in a broad and permanent success because of the limitations of the storage medium used and because the electron-optical system allowed only poor resolution of about 1000 dots linearly at relatively high cost.

The revival of the practically forgotten electron beam memory was triggered by two factors, first general advances in the areas of vacuum and cathode technology, amplifiers, D/A-converters etc. as well as power- and high voltage supplies, second breakthroughs in the areas of the electron-optical system and the storage medium.

In order to increase the number of addressable spots, the conventional single-stage electrostatic electron-optical system with its limited resolution had been modified to a two-stage system. In principle, the first stage consists of a conventional electron-optical lens followed by a cylinder with helically arranged deflection electrodes that deflect the beam into X- and Y-directions simultaneously. The second stage is a so-called fly's eye lens system followed by a matrix of deflection electrodes [2]. To each deflection position of the first stage a lens in the second stage is assigned. Therewith, the resolution of a single-stage electron-optical system is greatly increased.

Information is stored by electrical charge in the oxide layer of a planar chip consisting of three layers: metal-silicon oxide-silicon (MOS). This medium allows non-volatile storage with respect to practical system requirements. Also, for a limited number of consecutive Reads from the same address, the read operation is non-destructive.

The combination of electronic-access, by electron beam rather than by electrical signals flowing on conductor lines, with an unstructured MOS memory chip manufactured with a fraction of the conventional semiconductor process steps and correspondingly with high yield and low cost, first created some hope for the ideal electronic bulk storage, the cost characteristic of which would even allow to replace magnetic disk files. Realistically, however, the BEAMOS-memory applications potentially should be placed somewhere between those of RAM and disk file.

The BEAMOS state of the art has been described in some publications in 1974/75 by development groups of General Electric Company [3], Micro-Bit Corporation [4, 5] and the Stanford Research Institute [6]. Storage tube capacities up to 32 million bits of current laboratory set ups were reported, with access times from less than 10 μs to 30 μs and a bit-sequential data rate of 10 Megabit per second.

These performance data, in combination with estimated bit costs place the BEAMOS technology within the storage technology spectrum in the area of the fast serial electronic devices like CCD, magnetic bubbles, etc. (Fig. 1).

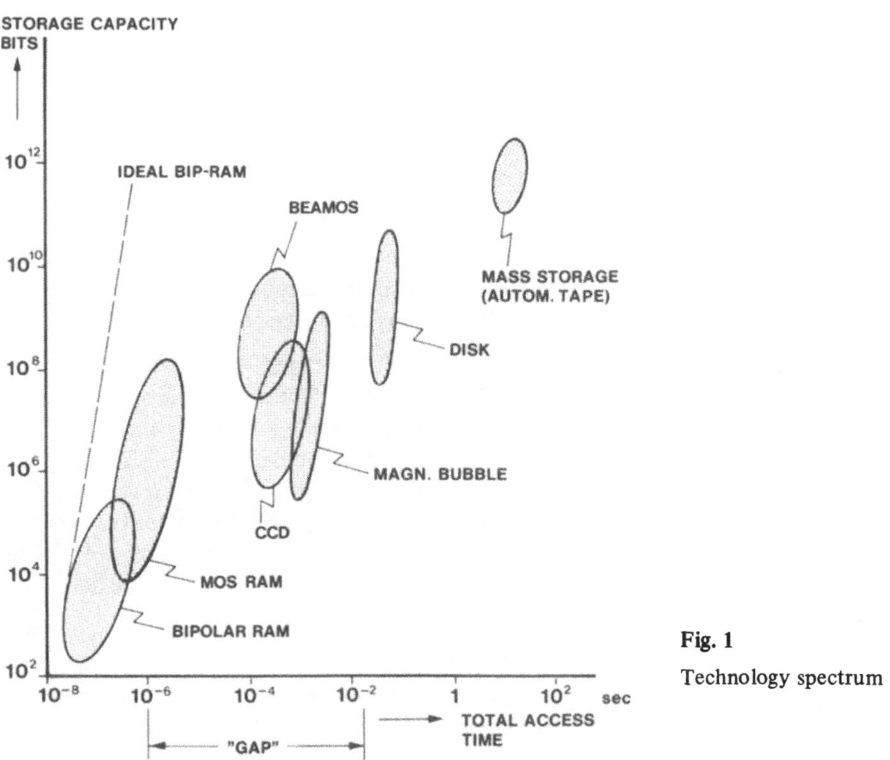

Fig. 1

Technology spectrum

In the subsequent sections, first a summary of BEAMOS technology and structure is given, followed by a discussion of potential applications as well as some further development speculation. Finally, some comparison aspects to CCD and magnetic bubble technology are presented.

2. Electron-optics

The following overview on structure and operation of the electron-optical system and storage mechanism is based on the concept described in [3]. The approaches reported in [4] and [5] are similar, while the approach [6] misses some of the attractive elements like two-stage electron-optics and unstructured storage medium. Since the scope of this paper does not allow a comprehensive discussion, the latter one is not considered.

An electron beam is generated by a conventional tungsten-cathode which at a later stage of development may be replaced by a long life dispenser-barium-cathode. The beam is focussed and modulated, i.e. switched on and off, via a conventional grid- and condensor system (Fig. 2). The roughly focussed beam is deflected to the desired position through a cascade including two electrostatic deflection stages and a fly's eye lens system with presently 18 × 18 lenses placed between the two deflection stages. Final focussing is performed within the fly's eye lens system.

The first deflection stage is a cylinder or cone subdivided basically into four sections, two of them for X- and Y-deflection each (an array of 8 electrodes also has been

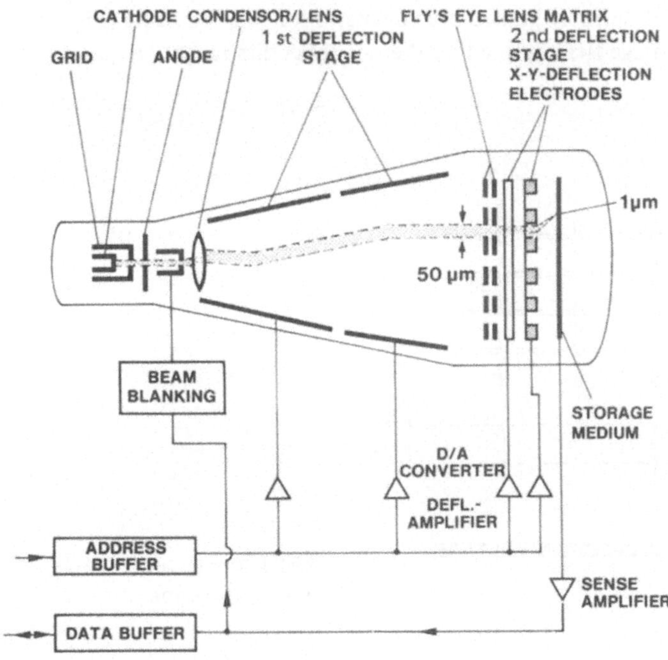

Fig. 2. BEAMOS storage-schematic.

developed [6]). The simultaneous deflection in X- and Y-direction reduces the aberrations as they occur e.g. in oscillographs due to the serial arrangement of deflection plates, thus improving focus and linearity. As an additional measure, the electrode sections are twisted around the first half of the deflection cylinder (or cone) and retwisted on the second half, rather than fixed parallel to the cylinder axis.

By the electrode twisting, aberrations in the edge zones are reduced. By twisting back into the opposite direction the spin effect is compensated.

Besides the electrode twisting and retwisting, the cylinder (or cone) of the first deflection stage is subdivided in another sense: Into a first half deflecting the beam, and a second half re-deflecting the beam (Fig. 2). The redeflection is by the same angle as the initial deflection thus resulting in a beam shift parallel to the tube axis. To each deflection position of the first stage, a lens of the fly's eye lens system is assigned. The beam hits orthogonally on one lens, is being fine focussed there, accelerated and subsequently deflected to the final x-y-position*. It is not necessary to hit exactly the center of the lens holes as long as a sufficient portion of the beam passes at all.

Basically the second deflection state is a matrix of x- and y-electrodes, crosswise arranged in two layers. The fly's eye lens system is constructed by a couple of perforated metal planes with suitably graded hole diameter for fine focussing (Fig. 2). Each lens covers one storage field defined by the x-y-deflection range. The above

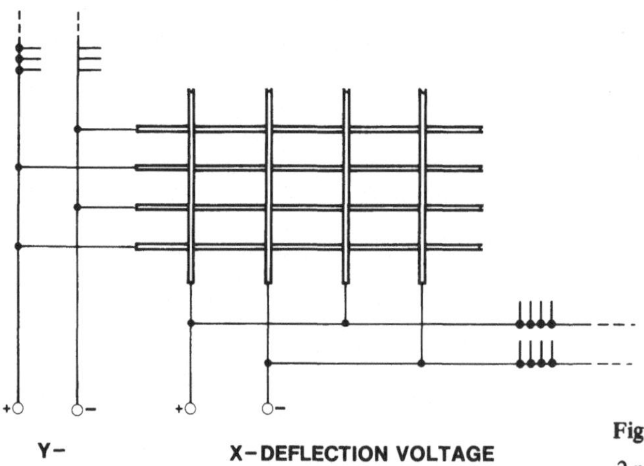

Fig. 3

2 nd deflection stage-schematic
X-Y-electrode array.

---

* The notion x-y means the fine deflection position of the second deflection stage within the pre-deflection position X−Y of the first stage.

mentioned 18 × 18 lens system thus corresponds to 19 x- and 19 y-electrodes. As Fig. 3 indicates, the x-electrodes may be connected alternatingly to the positive and negative pole of the x-deflection voltage. The same holds true for the y-electrodes.

The increase of bit resolution and deflection linearity is based on this decoupling of the first and second deflection- and focussing stage. The resolution in the first stage with a largest linear deflection of several centimeters is now no longer defined by the storage bit resolution (in the order of some μm) but by the fly's eye lens array dimension. The second stage performs the fine bit resolution, but now with a largest deflection of only 1 to 2 mm per lens.

40 % of the 10 KV-anode voltage is dropped across the first stage and 60 % across the second stage. The tube has a total length of about 40 cm.

3. Storage Mechanism

Stored bits are represented by positive charge in the oxide of the MOS-structure. The presence of a charge corresponds to the "1"-bit and the absence corresponds to the "0"-bit. The electron beam is applied for both read and write operation.

When writing a "1", the beam pervades through the aluminum layer being a few thousand Å thick and produces a positive charge in the oxide if simultaneously the metal layer has a bias of some + 40 V against the silicon (Fig. 4). The electrons in the oxide, freed by the beam, are quasi drawn off to the aluminum layer and a positive charge remains at the interface to the silicon. This charge is rather permanent, with storage times quoted from a few days to a few months. When writing a "0", − 40 V are applied to the metal layer so that the electrons freed by the beam cannot flow off but recombine with the positive charge. Actually the charge is not removed completely but there remains a rest of positive charge in the order of 10 % which howevei, does not essentially affect the bit discrimination with read operation.

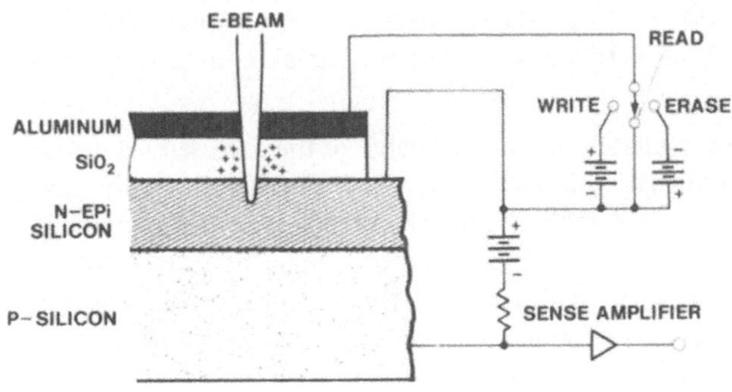

Fig. 4

Storage chip layers and operation.

In general, Read/Write is performed by starting the beam at the addressed position and scanning it, e.g. horizontally, over a certain wordlength. Thus the bit access is sequential. With write operation, and a bit pattern frequently alternating between "1" and "0"s, speed would dramatically be reduced due to the permanent switching of the metal layer voltage by ± 40 V and the corresponding charging of the electrical capacitance. Instead, a two phase-writing is performed. In the first phase, the erase phase, all charges are removed by switching the metal layer to -40 V. In the second phase, the write phase, the metal layer is on $+40$ V and the beam is switched according to the bit pattern: In case of a "1"-bit, the beam is switched on via the modulation (blanking) feature, in case of a "0"-bit it is not. If a bit change has to be performed within the data word, the whole word must be read out and stored in an external buffer during the erase/write operation.

While for the write and store function respectively only the oxide charge is relevant, with Read the oxide charge remains unaffected, ideally. The read mechanism is performed in the bulk silicon, the metal layer voltage being zero (Fig. 4). In case of an oxide charge in the bit position, a local electric field penetrating into the silicon layer is generated. The electron beam being accelerated by the same voltage as with Write pervades the metal- and oxide-layer and penetrates a few thousand Å deep into the silicon layer generating electron-hole-pairs there. With absence of the local electric field, these pairs recombine after a short time. With presence of a field, holes and electrons are accelerated in opposite directions.

With the approach described in [3], which is the basis for this discussion, the active silicon layer is realized by epitaxilly grown N-material. The P-N-junction is reverse biased. Electrons, accelerated by the local field into the direction of the oxide interface are transferred by the external voltage to the external network and can be sensed. Actually, the sense signal is a D.C. current running laterally in the epi-layer superimposed by an A.C.-pulse coupled capacitively across the oxide capacitance. For fast sensing, primarily the transient pulse is utilized.

Since a considerable portion of the beam energy (totally 10 keV) is transformed into separation of electrons/holes (with a pair-energy of 3.7 eV) there results a current gain factor of the order of 1000. That is, if the electron beam carries a current of some nA, the sense current amounts to a few μA. For this signal level, sense amplifiers can be built.

With each read operation, unfortunately the oxide charge of the accessed bit position is decreased, i.e. the stored information is partly destroyed. This effect is only slight when the read beam current is considerably smaller than the write beam current. A lower limit for the read beam current is given by the requirement of a sufficiently good signal-to-noise ratio during Read, with the specified clock frequency. The upper limit of the write beam current, on the other hand, is determined by the cathode yield and the characteristics of the electron optical system. With the present state of the art, the read beam current is about 10 times smaller than the write beam current, and the oxide charge must be refreshed, i.e. the information must be rewritten, after 10 to 20 consecutive read operations.

Besides the appearance of a certain storing volatility and the information destruction after a certain number of read operations, a more serious problem exists, the radiation damage: With the silicon medium, the structure of the silicon oxide is gradually changed by the electron beam bombardement occuring with every access (essentially with write operation). The oxide experiences a certain "fatigue" and loses its capacity to store charge permanently. With the usual electron beam current density, practical damage results after 10^8 to 10^9 erase/write-operations. With continuous access to the same address, this number is very quickly reached. However, by suitable housekeeping measures, e.g. by cyclic shifting of data blocks with the daily loading and refreshing respectively as well as by logging access accumulations and corresponding displacements, a normal life of several years should be achieved, at least when operated as backup store in a storage hierarchy. The silicon life then is in the order of the value expected for the dispenser-cathode and will not fall out of the scope of other critical BEAMOS-components' life.

4. BEAMOS Storage System

Besides the storage tube, a number of other components is required to build a storage device (Fig. 2).

In general we deal with block architecture, i.e. a complete data block (perhaps from 256 to 4 K bytes) will be transferred with each reference. The address is decoded and translated into a beam position, via a D/A-converter and deflection amplifiers for both deflection states. The silicon storage chip may be unstructured, that means the beam positioning must not be absolutely precise but must be reproducible only. To support the positioning it is, of course, conceivable to compensate tolerances and long term variations due to thermal and mechanical effects, amplifier drift, etc., by some servo control.

After the beam is set up to the addressed position, it scans over a number of bit positions, e.g. in horizontal direction, according to the data block size. In general, with Read the internal clock must first be synchronized by synchronizing bits, since the "0"-bit does not yield a sense signal for a natural synchronization. The sense signals are transformed by the sense amplifier into digital signals, may be temporarily stored in a buffer store and are then transferred to some other system component, possibly with higher speed and word parallel. During transfer, error detection and correction may be performed.

A BEAMOS storage may comprise one or several tubes operated in parallel. The latter design is especially advantageous since with parallel Read a higher data rate is achieved, and a major portion of storage components like high voltage supply, D/A-converters and amplifiers, general control and clocking, charge refreshment control, etc. may be shared by all tubes. It would be practical to handle all logical and control functions including error detection and correction by a specifically assigned micro-processor.

Only little information is available on error rate and error mechanisms, especially on spread of charge value and charge life time. A further cause of errors may be expected in the sense system area, with its very low bit-sense power in the order of 10^{-10} or 10^{-9} W and sense times within fractions of microseconds. Therefore it is difficult to estimate the error correction effort required. Experience must tell, whether a simple correction principle via Hamming-Code bits will suffice or cyclic codes with more processing requirements are needed. Those areas of the storage medium that have a high defect density or are already damaged by radiation must be permanently switch-ed off by the control processor.

The important storage performance parameters are the actual access time, the time until the first bit is accessed, and the data rate. Combined with the block size there results a block transfer time and a total access time (= access time + transfer time). With BEAMOS, the access time for consecutive operations Read or Write or Erase is determined only by the delay of beam positioning and is in the order of a few micro-seconds. In the case of switching from one operation type to another, the metal layer capacitance of the storage chip must be recharged to another voltage and the access time increases up to 30 μs typically. The bit serial data rate today is about 10 Mb/s, the data rate increases correspondingly if the tubes are operated in parallel.

5. Applications

To evaluate the BEAMOS storage, first its potential area of application is discussed. With an access time of 30 μs, an assumed block size of 1 K byte, byte-parallel tube operation and a clock frequency of 10 MBit/s the total access time amounts to 130 μs. Due to this speed, the BEAMOS store thus would excellently fit as a "Gap Filler", i.e. as intermediate level between main store and disk file in a storage hierarchy system for medium size and large computers [7]. Especially in a highly interactive mode of operation, a fast intermediate stage has a positive impact on the system's response characteristics.

There are two alternatives to incorporate the gap filler level into today's storage hierarchies. It may be accessed via channels and normal input/output commands as a replacement for fix head disks and drums or a buffer for a moveable head disk respectively, or it may be implemented as a physical extension to the main store, addressable with CPU instructions and transparent to the CPU architecture. Data transport would then be hardware controlled similar to the present hierarchy of main store − buffer store (cache). The main store, extended in this way, would then in principle cover the capacity of present virtual stores. This virtual store not only would be faster, but it would also allow a simplified system operation : accessing the BEAMOS main store extension is so fast that the current CPU process just would wait for the access and then continue, synchronously. Thus, todays frequent process (or task) switching can greatly be reduced. Process switching then occurs only with the much more infrequent disk- and tape accesses as well as with other input/output operations. Since with the usual block size, the BEAMOS transfer time is long relative to the actual access time (in contrast to the mechanical storage devices) the total access time can be tuned within wide limits by simply changing the block size.

For reasons of compatibility with existing programs, it may be desireable to access such an intermediate hierarchy level both with main store instructions and via channels with I/O commands. The programs then run not only within a fast virtual store but also have the possibility to fetch their data in the conventional way via channel commands, but now from the intermediate level rather from disk. To combine both access capabilities, the necessary two-way address decoding, possibly with dynamic assignment of the two zones, has to be incorporated into the inter-mediate level device.

Another inherent characteristic of BEAMOS favours an application within the storage hierarchy of medium size and large computers, namely its poor modularity. For cost reasons, a minimum capacity is mandatory so that the high basic component cost will be shared by a sufficiently large number of bits. As in any technology, price/performance trade offs may be considered. For instance, performance may be improved by subdividing the silicon storage chip and accordingly reduce electrical capacitances, at expense of duplicating the sense amplifiers, more complicated semi-conductor structures, etc. Vice versa the bit cost can be reduced at the expense of speed by extremely multiple usage of as many components as possible and maximiz-ing the storage capacity per tube. Bit density at the expense of speed could further be optimized via the beam accelerator voltage as parameter. A lower voltage would improve focussing and thus the bit density but would decrease the sense current yield and thus force a lower clock frequency.

6. Outlook

To estimate the tube capacity to be achieved by evolutionary development in the foreseeable future, the present state of the art is taken as a base. A present day bit area of $4 \times 4\,\mu m$, together with a bit chip size of 1 inch $\times$ 1 inch and possibly 70 %

usage results in 28×10^6 bits. This number is in conformity with todays development objective of 32×10^6 bits [3]. The storage capacity could be enlarged as well by a higher bit density as by an extension of the storage area. Thus the development must aim at improved beam focussing, better stability and control of positioning, larger deflection range, reduction of the storage chip capacitances and increased sensitivity of the sense amplifiers (higher amplification – bandwith product). If we assume, that with a mature state of development 4 to 8 times the present chip size and 2 to 4 times the present bit density can be achieved, the tube capacity would thereby be increased to 25–100 million bytes. Storage capacities predicted in literature are also within this order. If in addition, adequate parallel tube operation is performed all requirements of a "Gap Filler" function could be met.

For the discussed application as intermediate level in a storage hierarchy the access time is already minimum and thus scarcely a focal point for further development. On the other hand an improvement of the data rate, especially in one-tube-operation seems well to pay off. Short term objectives quoted in literature indicate 20 Mb/s and long-term objectives envisage 100 Mb/s and more.

Further progress which is less quantifiable but will contribute to constructive elegance and compactness, could be expected if emphasis and modern technology are aimed at: high voltage isolation by glass fibres; integrated sense amplifiers, especially if the storage medium is subdivided into areas with individual sense amplifiers, etc.

7. Comparison with CCD, Bubbles

Completing the discussion, a comparison with other potential technologies for the same application area should be included, that means at the present state of development primarily the charge coupled device (CCD) and magnetic bubble technology.

All these technologies operate sequentially with block transfer. Access time and clock frequency and thus total transfer time are similar for BEAMOS and CCD (LARAM) and are about ten times slower with bubbles. The BEAMOS technology has, moreover, the theoretical advantage that it allows to start the beam at any position and thus to approach random word access, similar to main store. With block transfer this advantage, however, scarcely counts. A further advantage of BEAMOS is the larger flexibility of the data format. While with CCD and bubbles the logical record length may have a certain relation to the length of the physical loop, the number of loops on the chip, etc.; the degree of freedom with BEAMOS is higher due to the unstructured storage medium.

With BEAMOS, for cost reasons as many bits as possible have to share the expensive base components. Therefore, and because of the variety of heterogeneous components and the complexity of control functions it seems reasonable to build a functionally and constructively integrated subsystem. Such a subsystem could also perform logical functions like search operations, access to data base, etc. In contrast, with CCD and bubbles, the access and auxiliary functions are tailored to smaller storage units and could partly be integrated with the CPU if necessary. Thus the latter technologies are more modular and offer better possibilities for smaller and compact units as well as for parallel operation.

With intensive component sharing and larger units, BEAMOS may have the chance of some cost advantage whereas the bit cost with CCD and bubbles tend to be more capacity independent. In contrast to present day semiconductor and bubble technology, the limit for bit density with BEAMOS is not determined by lithographic parameters, e.g. minimal line width, etc., but by focussing and beam deflection as well as by amplifier characteristics.

The electrical power dissipation per bit of 5 to 10 μW is similar to CCD and bubbles. Concerning nonvolatility, BEAMOS has an advantage versus CCD since with power supply interruption, switch off at night, etc. the stored information persists. The measures necessary to protect the storage material against radiation damages is a specific disadvantage of BEAMOS and possibly only to be justified with larger units.

The constructive characteristics of BEAMOS, viz. high voltage, expensive power supply, vacuum, larger volume, less monolithic structure, etc. should possibly be of minor importance in large computer systems, attractive bit cost provided. They must be traded against the advantages of BEAMOS, viz. higher speed when compared with bubbles, less volatile storage and possibly lower bit cost when compared with CCD.

References

[1] *K. Schlesinger*, "Progress in the Development of Post-Acceleration and Electrostatic Deflection", Proceedings of the IRE, May 1956, pp. 655–667.

[2] *C. Q. Lemmond*, et al., "Electron Fly's Eye Artwork Camera", IEEE Transactions of Electron Devices, Vol. ED-21, No. 9, Sept. 1974, pp. 598–603.

[3] *W. C. Hughes*, et al., "BEAMOS – A new electronic digital memory", NCC 1975, pp. 541–548.

[4] *D. E. Speliotis*, "Bridging the memory access gap", NCC 1975, pp. 501–508.

[5] *M. S. Cohen* and *J. S. Moore*, "Physics of the MOS electron-beam-memory", Journal of Applied Physics, Vol. 45, No. 12, Dec. 1974, pp. 5335–5348.

[6] *J. Kelly*, "The Development of an Experimental Electron-Beam-Addressed Memory Module", Computer, Febr. 1975, pp. 32–42.

[7] *C. Schunemann* and *W. G. Spruth*, "Technology and Structure of Storage Hierarchy", This issue. p. ... – ...

Read-Only Memories with Magnetic Components or with Integrated Semiconductor Circuits

Jürgen Scharbert

Siemens AG, Data Processing Systems, Munich, Germany

1. Introduction

For many years now read-only memories ("ROMs"), with a wide range of different designs have been performing to full satisfaction in a broad spectrum of applications. With regard to their function, they take a position midway between the electronic read-write memories and digital logic circuits as well as switching networks. They have a common form of organization as RAMs and a similar circuit configuration, evident for instance from the designations "memory matrix", "memory word", "address control" and "read control", to name but a few; linking them with the logic networks establishes the unambiguous and generally unalterable logic relationship between the signals on the input and output lines, which is determined by the information they have stored. Depending on the particular application, the predominant aspect may be in one case that of a data memory, in another case that of a logic network.

The various applications of read-only memories can be roughly classified under concepts such as "translators", "code converters", "memories for fixed constants or functions", "microprogram memories" or "hardcore memories" in, for instance, modern data processing systems with writable control memories. There is no precise dividing line between these concepts. This is for instance indicated by the required memory sizes, the typical values ranging between 10^2 and 10^4 bits for code converters and between 10^3 and 10^5 bits for memories for invariants, while microprogram memories generally have capacitances extending from 10^4 to over 10^6 bits.

The advantages of a read-only memory over a read-write memory of comparable storage medium technology, circuit technology and memory capacity are as follows: higher operating speed (i.e. shorter access and cycle times), usually higher bit density, and in most cases lower manufacturing costs per bit. What is seemingly a disadvantage – the unchangeability of the stored information – also frequently turns out to be a desirable adavantage in actual operation as no data are lost in the ROM in the event of supply voltage dropouts or operational errors.

In comparison with logic networks, read-only memories offer the advantage of high functional density and the implementation of a large variety of functions. With appropriate memory organization, practically any binary function and any code can be realized. It is also possible to change the functions by using a different data

medium or by exchanging memory devices, without the lengthy procedure of
designing new circuit boards, as it is the case with logic networks.

Earlier and present-day read-only memories are characterized, just like the corresponding read-write memories, by three different types of circuitry: the memory matrix, the
current amplifiers and read control, matched to the particular matrix, and the interface circuits depending on the requirements of the applications.

In contrast to random-access memories with bistable memory elements, read-only
memories require only coupling elements with simpler structures, the presence or
setting of which in the matrix represents, for example, the information content of
one bit of the matrix. Practically any type of coupling can be selected. Consequently, a large number of different memory principles are known and have been
implemented in many instances; examples are many components using magnetic
coupling (braided core memories, transformer memories, various memories with
inductive coupling between the lines themselves), also components using capacitive
coupling, direct coupling through resistors, charge storage in special tubes, electrooptical coupling etc. [1].

2. Modern Read-Only Memories with Magnetic Coupling

In the past, read-only memories with magnetic coupling have been of prime interest.
The main reason for this was that magnetic storage methods also dominated at that
time in read-write memories (magnetic core storages, for example). Furthermore,
in read-only memories, it is relatively simple to control the magnetic coupling
between word and sense lines of the matrix, either employing special conductor
routing or insertable magnetic materials. In accordance with the type of coupling,
it is possible to roughly classify the magnetic read-only memories as follows:

- storage devices using magnetic coupling elements, which exhibit a rectangular
  hysteresis loop
- storage devices using linear magnetic coupling between the address and sense
  lines of the memory matrix, with or without magnetic elements
- storage devices using transformer coupling.

2.1. Read-Only Memories with Coupling Elements Exhibiting a Rectangular Hysteresis Loop

Special mention should be made here of two different types using toroidal cores,
a memory medium which attained major importance for random-access memories
in the past.

In the *first type* the toroidal cores — usually made from a ferrite material — are
only used for coupling between address lines and the sense line: a bit has the value
"1" when there is coupling, otherwise it has the value "0". Depending on the
matrix version, the stored information is either contained in the wiring for the

174

address lines or for the sense lines. On account of the rectangular hysteresis loop,
coincident word selection is also possible, an advantageous way of reducing the
number of current amplifiers. Matrices have been also proposed in which one core
served as the memory medium for several bits. Particularly reliable and stable
memories can be built, as the induction swing of the switching cores is very
insensitive to operational tolerances of the current amplifiers. On the other hand,
the operating speed of these memories with cycle times of over 10 μs in some cases
is very low, as the usually large cores have switching times of between 1 and 3 μs.
The achievable sense voltage

$$U_L \approx \frac{2\Delta\phi}{S_W}\,(I - I_C)$$

$\Delta\phi$ switched magnetic flux
S_W switching coefficient
I_C coercitivity current
I read current

usually amounts to between 50 mV and 100 mV and therefore requires the use of
sophisticated sense amplifiers. With these core memories the matrix lines have to
be wired in a very lengthy manual process to set the information. In the early 60's
such memories were intended to work above all as number generators in communication systems or as particularly reliable control memories [2].

The *second type* ("permeability sensing") [3] makes use of the property of toroidal
cores with rectangular hysteresis loop, exhibiting a considerably higher permeability
in the demagnetized state than in the remanent state (Fig. 1). On applying current
pulses to the core with a field well below its coercive field strength, different inductive swings are obtained, without altering the magnetic state of the core. In most

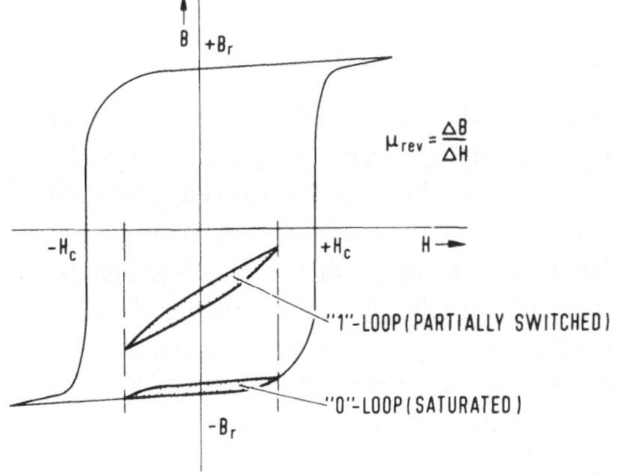

Fig. 1

Hysteresis loops of partially
switched ferrite cores for
non-destructive readout.

cases two cores per bit are used, to compensate for unavoidable noise voltages and
to make the sense voltages for the stored information easier to detect. The demands
placed on the current amplifiers and read controls are much higher than those in the
previously mentioned method. Tpyical operating parameters of a memory are:

read current amplitude $I = 100\ \text{mA}$
rise time of the read current $t_r = 10\ \text{ns}$
read voltage $U_L = 5\ \text{mV}.$

The swing of the magnetic flux during information readout is fully reversible; using
this method it is thus possible to build read-only microprogram memories in data
processing systems, which have a cycle time of 250 ns at a capacity of over $2 \cdot 10^5$ bits.
The memory matrices employ a homogeneous type of wiring. Although the write
processes for information input is complicated and time-consuming and is therefore
usually performed outside the actual memory, this method however introduces the
possibility of modifying the information in the memory without altering the hardware.

2.2. Memories with Linear Magnetic Coupling between the Matrix Lines

From the multitude of proposed and realized storage methods, only a few examples
illustrating the basic options can be given here. All methods have the following in
common:
- small coupling inductivity and an almost open magnetic flux path
- high demands placed on the address and sense circuits
- access and cycle times of the memories strongly influenced by line delays,
  parasitic capacitances and circuit delays.

Typically, the sense voltage U_L is directly proportional to the gradient of the drive
current $\dot{I}$:

$$U_L \approx L_{IK} \cdot \dot{I} \tag{2}$$

L_{IK} coupling inductivity between word line and sense line.

Example 1: Read-only memory with exchangeable ferrite rods [4]. The word and
sense line loops in orthogonal arrangement in the matrix (see Fig. 2) are coupled
via a soft-magnetic ferrite rod for a "1", for a "0" they are not coupled. There are
very simple ways of setting or modifying the stored information – manually, for
example, for individual bits or with the aid of a template for the complete matrix.
A disadvantage, however, is the large size and complexity of the setup, as the ferrite
rods are relatively long and have to be accurately positioned in the matrix holes.
This memory method was used as early as 1960 in the control memory of a data
processing system and achieved what was at that time the respectable access time
of around 200 ns for a storage capacity of over $2 \cdot 10^5$ bits.

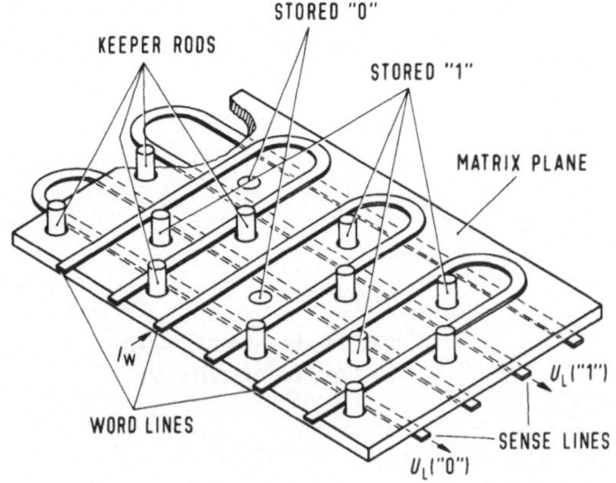

Fig. 2

Memory matrix with exchangeable ferrite rods [4].

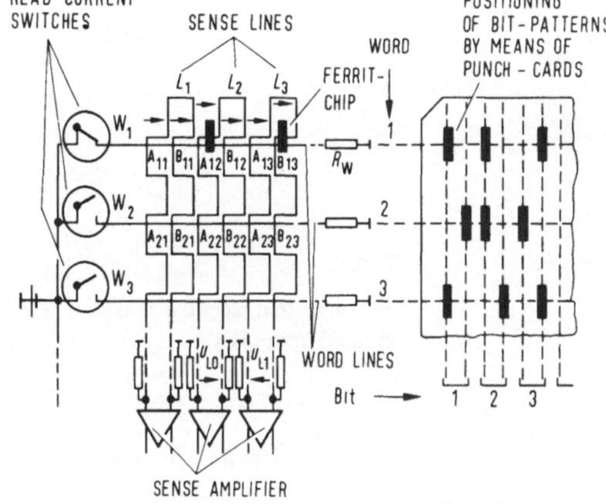

Fig. 3

Read-only memory with exchangeable ferrite chips [5].

Example 2: Read-only memory with exchangeable ferrite chips [5]. Varying from the first example, word and sense lines run parallel to each other section-by-section (Fig. 3). The stored information is defined by ferrite chips, the position of which is determined by punched cards. With this storage method, employed since 1969 in the microprogram memory of a communication system computer, an access time of 80 ns was achieved for a storage capacity of approximately $4 \cdot 10^4$ bits.

Example 3: Read-only memory with soft-magnetic spots (Fig. 4). In order to achieve an even higher operating speed, the following method [6] allows even greater miniaturization, termination of lines with their correct characteristic impedance and the avoidance of almost all parasitic coupling. In this case, the data medium in the form of foils with information-dependent etched, diagonal magnetic spots is pressed onto the conductor matrix. The direction of the spots above the word line/sense line crossing points determines the polarity of the read signals and thus the stored information.

177

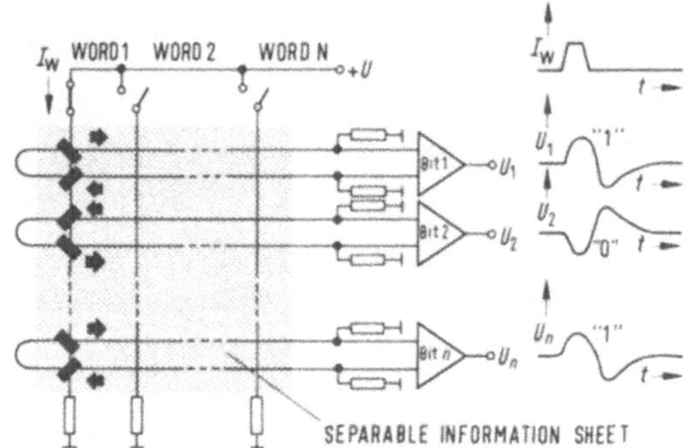

Fig. 4

Read-only memory with
soft-magnetic spots [6].

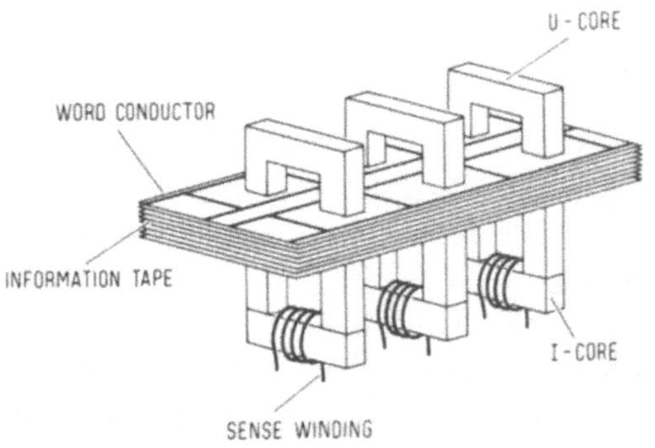

Fig. 5

Memory matrix with U-core
transformers [8].

In 1970 a microprogram memory for a data processing system with a capacity of
$2.2 \cdot 10^5$ bits realized an access time as low as 35 ns and a cycle time of less than
60 ns.

2.3. Storage Methods using Transformer Coupling

The storage principle is illustrated in Fig. 5: each U-core transformer is assigned one
bit position of all memory words. To store a "1", the transformer is driven by the
relevant word line, to store a "0" the transformer is not driven. A secondary winding of the transformer is used as the sense line. The sense signal amplitudes U_L can
be influenced within wide limits in accordance with the number of windings n of
this sense line:

$$U_L \approx n \cdot K \cdot R_L \cdot I \tag{3}$$

K   coupling factor of the transformer
R_L attenuation of the sense line
I   read current.

178

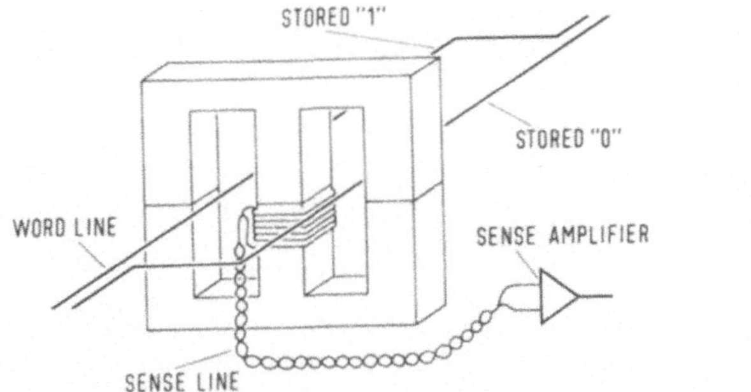

Fig. 6

Wired E-core memory.

This method can be varied by employing E-core transformers (Fig. 6). The word lines are either run through the first opening of the transformer for a "1" or through the second opening for a "0". The result is a bipolar read signal coupling in the center leg of the E-core and thus improved differentiation between the read and noise signals. A further advantage of this method is that the impedance of the word line is independent of its information-related position.

Transformer memories [7], in which the address lines take the form of wires, are very well-known. The information in the wire harness was usually fixed by means of semi-automatic or automatic wiring machines. For large storage capacities up to and over 10^5 bits, their operating speed is essentially determined by the large stray capacitances and stray inductances in the multitude of address lines. The cycle times of such memories with large capacity were therefore usually greater than 1 μs.

The most significant disadvantage of wired memories, the lengthy, complicated and error-prone fixing of the information, is avoided by transformer memories the address lines of which are provided on thin foils [8] or punched cards [9], where the information content is fixed by punching holes in these lines. In addition to simpler information input and modification, these memories exhibit usually also an improved operating speed, as stray capacitances and inductivities are substantially reduced by the layered arrangement of the address lines. Memories with a large capacity (10^5 bits) for cycle times under 500 ns have been manufactured (Fig. 7).

3. Semiconductor Read-Only Memories

3.1. The Evolution of Semiconductor Read-Only Memories [10]

Read-only memory matrices with separately wired discrete semiconductors – mainly diodes – were already in use in a number of applications in the early 60's, but the high cost of the semiconductor components and low bit density prohibited a broad area of applications.

The first *integrated diode matrices* appeared on the market in 1966. In the very first devices, the input and output lines of the semiconductor matrix were connected

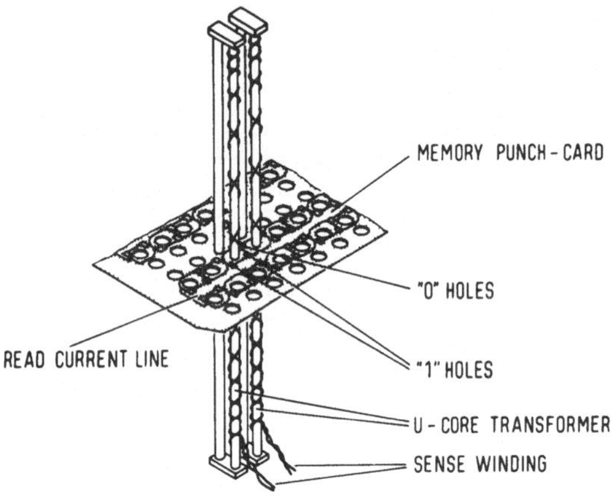

Fig. 7

Transformer ROM with memory punched cards.

directly to the device pins, the capacity was 48 or 64 bits. The information was either fixed with the aid of masks (ROMs) or could be programmed after completion of the device (PROMs) by interrupting preselected parts of the aluminium lines by means of fusion by a high current.

Shortly afterwards, *ROM devices with complete address decoding* became available — initially in MOS technology, a little later in bipolar technology — with their information fixed by means of *masks.* Their storage capacity usually ranged between 256 bits and 4096 bits, while in some cases device samples were manufactured with capacities of up to 25 600 bits (1969).

Finally, *programmable devices* with complete address decoding became available at about 1970. Nowadays, as in the case of MOS devices, the user has at his disposal a broad spectrum of bipolar devices with capacities of 256 bits to over 16 384 bits and thus has a wide choice of devices for data storage and for control applications.

3.2. Bipolar Read-Only Memories

From the point of view of circuitry, the diode is the simplest semiconductor element to use to build a ROM matrix (Fig. 8). A "1", for example, is stored at a matrix node when word line and sense line are coupled via a diode, with no coupling a "0" is stored. The static coupling between the matrix lines — as in all other semiconductor matrices — also has the advantage that noise signals are largely suppressed due to the diode characteristic.

The information in a diode matrix can be fixed in two different ways. In one case, a special information mask determines, in the course of manufacture of the memory device, whether diode coupling is realized at a matrix node or not. A special mask is therefore required for every information pattern. These ROMs are thus manufactured with full information content, ready for testing and application. In the other case, the desired information pattern for the so-called "programmable read-only memories"

180

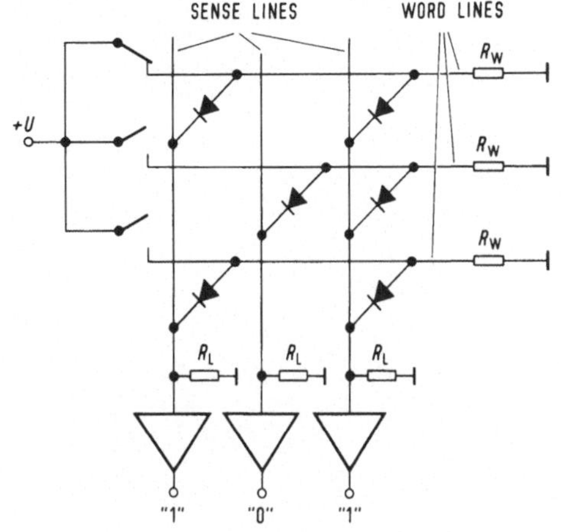

Fig. 8

ROM with diode matrix.

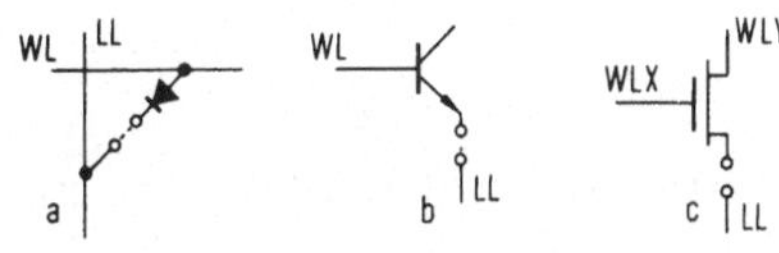

Fig. 9

Semiconductor memory cells
of various ROM devices.

(PROMs) is fixed by the user after manufacture and shipment of the device in a special programming process.

For PROMs with diode matrices, two different programming methods are known (Fig. 9d, e).

In the first type, a special resistor line is connected in series with the diode at each matrix node. To fix a "0" for example, this line can be interrupted in a defined manner with the aid of a high current.

For these resistors or "fusible links", very thin deposited films of NiCr (thickness $\sim 0.02\ \mu$m) or doped polycrystalline Si films (thickness $\sim 0.3\ \mu$m) may be used. Resistor films made of Pt, Ti, and TiW are also employed. Appropriate fuse shaping, e.g. necking, causes a high concentration of energy (i.e. local temperature increase) in the fuse when current pulses are applied during programming. Depending on how

181

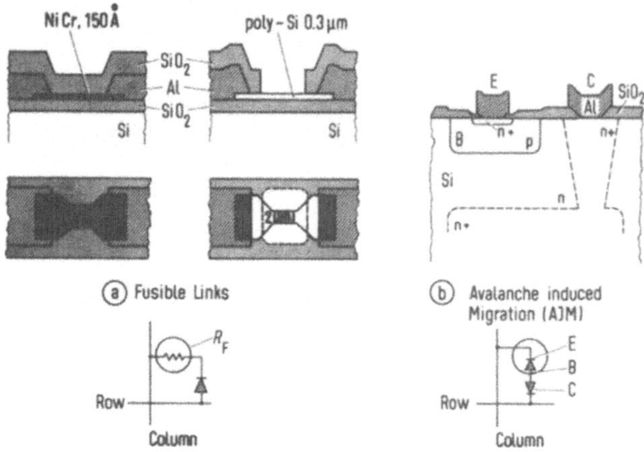

Fig. 10. Memory cells of bipolar PROM devices.

the programming process is controlled, the resistor can be interrupted by several mechanisms, for example by

- material migration at high current densities (electromigration)
- surpassing the melting or evaporation point
- chemical reaction of the film material with its surroundings.

In NiCr technology, correspondingly lower programming currents (from 15 mA) are required on account of the smaller film thickness. This technology requires however careful control of the film properties (structure, thickness, composition and sheet resistivity). If suitable conditions are provided for film fabrication and the programming process, reliable operation is assured (Fig. 10a) [11].

Polysilicon technology, on the other hand, requires significantly larger current pulses (from 50 mA) on account of the greater film thickness for comparable geometry; the fusion involves a perceptible migration of material and the reliable interruption of the relatively thick film requires additional chemical reactions (e.g. oxidation by an oxygen atmosphere in the component package) [12].

In the *second type,* another diode with inverted polarity is inserted in the diode matrix in series with each coupling diode, so that after fabrication of the device each coupling position in the matrix is at first non-conducting. In programming, those bit positions, which are to store a "1", are transformed into conducting nodes, by application of high voltage pulses. These pulses cause by means of the inverse current, the destruction of the junction of the second diode, which is thus converted into a low-resistance path (diode breakdown). This destruction results from a local rise in temperature inducing a reaction between the conductor material and the

182

silicon at the diode contact (avalance induced migration, AIM), which must be controlled such that neighboring PN junctions are not affected (Fig. 10b) [13].

At first sight, diode matrices appear very attractive also from the point of view of the technology on account of the low area and few contacts. Additional precautions however have always to be taken with PN diodes (base-emitter or base-collector diodes) to avoid undesirable parasitic elements (PNP substrate transistors or thyristors), which in turn increase the area requirements. Schottky diodes on the other hand frequently require substantially more process development in their metallization. A further disadvantage of the diode matrix as seen from its circuitry is that the overall power of all connected sense lines has to be provided by the drive circuit of the selected word line. Depending on whether a large or small number of coupling diodes are connected to a word line, access time and levels on the sense lines are affected in a corresponding manner. Moreover, the matrix peripherals need a large area in order to handle the entire programming current during the programming process.

If the coupling diodes in the memory matrix are replaced by transistors, the previously mentioned disadvantages of the diode matrix with regard to the circuitry can be almost completely eliminated, as only small drive currents have to be supplied if the programming element is inserted into the collector or emitter branch. The latter solution is often preferred because all the collectors in the matrix can then be connected to the same potential and the transistors can be integrated in a space-saving manner. Just as for the diode matrices the information is either fixed by means of masks or by the above mentioned "fusible links".

3.3. Read-Only Memories employing Integrated FET Technology

In comparison with the bipolar diode or transistor matrices, memory matrices employing FET transistors are significantly simpler to manufacture and require a smaller area on the semiconductor chip. Further differences are the larger voltage swings required to switch the FET transistors and their low operating current. FET ROM devices therefore usually have a low power dissipation, but on the other hand are only suitable for relatively low operating speeds. Cycle times between 300 ns and a few microseconds are generally being achieved. As an example, the cell for an MOS ROM matrix is shown in Fig. 9c: cell addressing via the gate or drain electrode permits the use of greatly simplified decoder circuits. The information content is fixed by means of masks.

The storage principle of *programmable FET ROMs* is essentially the same: a long-term storage of electrical charges via the source-drain channel of an MOS transistor causes a shift in its threshold voltage and thus a defined change in conductivity. Figure 9g shows the very first memory cell of this kind (FAMOS cell): a second MOS transistor with an isolated gate is connected in series with the addressing transistor. The information is fixed by avalanche operation of the addressed memory cell: high-energy electrons in the source-drain channel penetrate the barrier of the gate isolating layer and charge the gate. The charge stored at the gate cannot subsequently be discharged by applying a pulse to the cell. Its lifetime is very long: at a temperature of 125 °C discharge time coefficients of over 10 years were measured [14].

For practical purposes, charge storage is therefore nearly equivalent to mask setting as far as the fixed information content is concerned. Furthermore, it is also possible to reprogram the entire device if information has to be modified. Before reprogramming, the semiconductor chip is irradiated with shortwave UV light to activate the charge carriers of the isolated gates to the level of SiO_2 conducting band ($\Delta\epsilon \approx 3,2$ eV), and the stored charges are removed rapidly. On account of the required high excitation energy, irradiation with sunlight or artificial light does not erase information stored by the memory device.

In addition to the FAMOS memory cell, other storage principles using programmable FET matrices have in the meantime attained increasing importance (MNOS, MAS, SIMOS etc.). These storage devices will be dealt with in detail with regard to their circuit principles and technological characteristics in two further contributions to this volume [15]. Some of these principles also permit the fabrication of electrically reprogrammable ROM devices (REPROMs).

3.4. Organization of Modern Semiconductor ROMs

Simple memory devices, in which all addressing and sense lines are connected directly to the device pins, play only a minor role. The large number of pins required for medium to large storage capacities rules out any economical application.

The prevailing form of organization of semiconductor ROMs is that of the *memory module with complete address decoding*. Fig. 11 shows as an example a programmable device (ECL circuit technology) with a storage capacity of 1024 bits (256 words each of 4 bits). Word selection is controlled via 8 address lines, a common control input (CE) gates the output of the sensed data and thus permits several individual devices to be interconnected for memory expansion.

On account of the address decoding in binary steps, preference is given to certain capacity increments in these devices. The following word numbers are therefore customary: 32, 256, 512, 1024, 2048 etc. The data width is usually 4 bits or 8 bits, a very few ROM device types have data widths of 9 bits, 10 bits or even 16 bits.

An essential parameter of these ROM devices with complete address decoding is the address access time, irrespective of the type of information content fixing. FET devices have presently access times of over 500 ns, bipolar ROM and PROM devices (TTL interface) access times between 40 ns and 100 ns, depending on the storage capacity. The access time of the PROM devices with ECL interface varies between 15 ns and 25 ns.

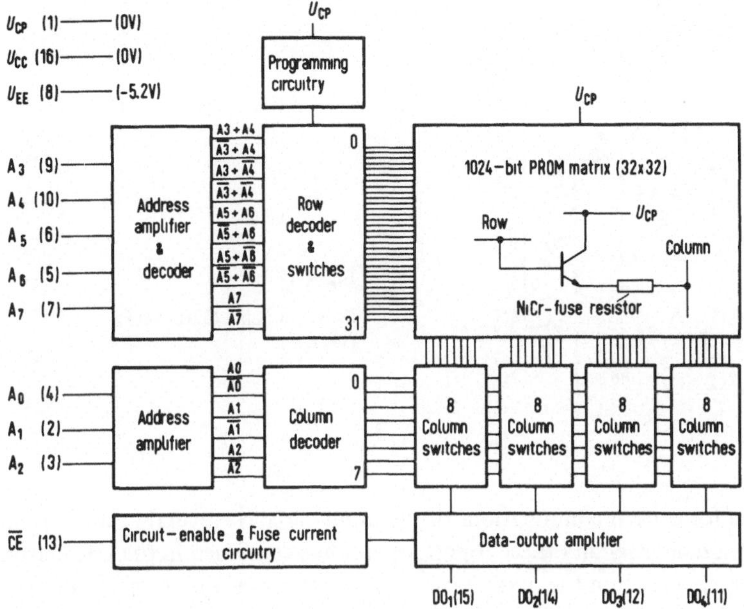

Fig. 11. Bipolar PROM device with complete address decoding.

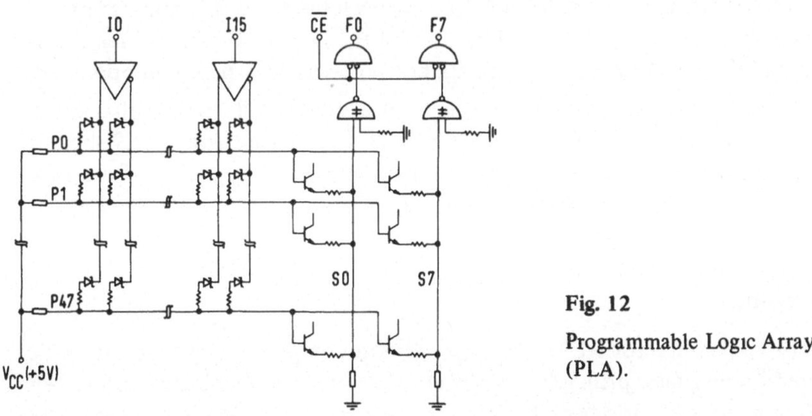

Fig. 12

Programmable Logic Array (PLA).

A further form of ROM organization is that of the *programmable logic arrays* (PLA). These devices permit the storage (OR matrix) of a basic quantity N (48 or 96) of independent functions with a data width of 8 bits (so-called "product terms"). Their addressing via a large number of input variables (usually 14 or 16) is also freely selectable (AND matrix, Fig. 12). In most cases there is a very wide variety of logic options,

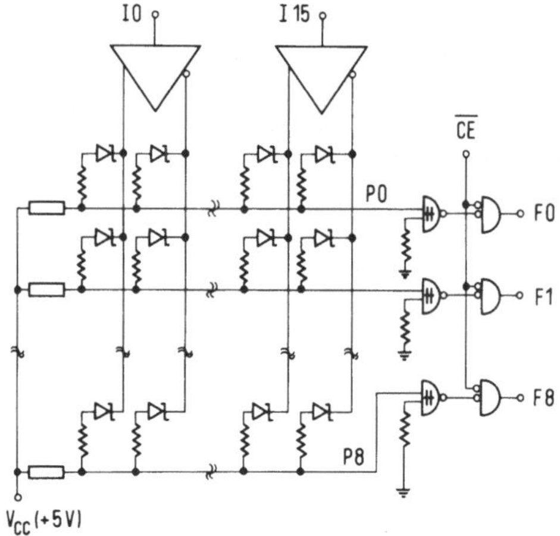

Fig. 13

Programmable Gate Array
(PGA).

particularly when for certain combinations of the input variables several product terms are addressed simultaneously and these functions are thus combined in the OR matrix [16]. PLA devices appeared on the market some years ago, originally in the form of mask programmed MOS devices. Recently developed customer-programmable bipolar devices with shorter access time (50 ns) have now enlarged the possible range of applications and give reason to anticipate more widespread use of this form of organization. No satisfactory solution has as yet been obtained to a number of questions concerning testing, above all because of the large data volumes requiring addressing and the memory terms which are not precisely measurable in operation.

A further form of organization, simpler than that of the PLA devices, is that of the *programmable gate arrays* (PGA). A typical programmable gate array has 9 separate gates, the individual addressing of which can be programmed by means of the 16 common input variables. The significance of this device organization for future logic complexes is not yet fully established (Fig. 13).

4. Conclusion

The modern semiconductor ROMs have now almost completely replaced the earlier ROMs based on magnetic principles. A broad spectrum of sophisticated and largely standardized devices in various performance categories is available to the user. New ROM devices are becoming available with larger storage capacity and/or better performance data (shorter access times, improved programmability, lower supply voltage, to name but a few). Improved semiconductor technologies and the fabrication of the devices in very large quantities permitted a drastic reduction in the manufacturing costs: for instance, the price of a bipolar 1024-bit PROM device has dropped from about $ 40 in 1972/73 to less than $ 5 in 1976.

186

The conditions under which the ROMs are used will usually govern the selection of the device type and determine whether a device with its information fixed by means of masks (ROM), a programmable device (PROM) or a reprogrammable device (REPROM) is most suitable. *ROM* devices are used to advantage when only a few information patterns but in very large quantities are required. In this case devices with special information content, which are ready for use and fully testable, are supplied by the manufacturer. Customer-programmable *PROM* or *REPROM* devices on the other hand are more suitable when very many information patterns each in low quantities are needed. The manufacturers supply standardized devices, which can be individually programmed, "personallized", without delay to obtain any desired bit pattern. User-programming is however also associated with additional problems in connection with device testing, demanding special organizational procedures (for example, between 5 % and 10 % of the bipolar PROM devices have to be rejected at present as they cannot be programmed).

While the variety of applications of semiconductor ROM devices with different forms of organization is still increasing, an upper limit for the utilization of these devices is apparently reached when the logistic problems of the stored data with regard to information fixing, testing or modifications attain greater importance than the technical or economic advantage of the ROM devices. In the latest data processing systems, for instance, attempts have thus been made to implement the microprogram memories as far as possible with read-write memories; the greater flexibility of the data is of more importance in this case than the disadvantage of the higher memory costs.

References

[1] *O. Feustel:* Elektronische Zuordner. Elektron. Rechenanl. 7 (1965), p. 9−24.

[2] *O. Feustel:* Ringkern-Zuordner. Elektron. Rechenanl. 8 (1966), p. 10−22.

[3] *H. F. Koehler* and *J. F. Covalesky:* Speed Capabilities of Ferrite Cores in NDRO Operation. IEEE Trans. **Mag-3** (1967), p. 311−315.

[4] *T. Kilburn, R. L. Grimsdale:* Digital Computer Store With Very Short Read Time. Proc. **IEEE 107B** (1960), p. 216−220.

[5] *H. Stegmeier:* Prinzip eines neuartigen, mechanisch leicht änderbaren semipermanten Speichers mit induktiver Kopplung. Entwicklungsber. Siemens-Halske-Werke **32** (1969), p. S41−S45.

[6] *Scharbert, J.:* Festwertspeicher. Entwicklungsber. Siemens-Halske-Werke **32** (1969), p. S30−S34.

[7] *J. R. Butcher:* A Prewired Storage Unit. IEEE Trans. ˹C-13 (1964), p. 106−111.
W. H. Aldrich, R. L. Alonso: The 'Braid' Transforr..er .. c:, .y. IEEE Trans. **EC-15** (1966), p. 502−508.

[8] *D. M. Taub, B. W. Kington:* The Design of Transformer (Diamond Ring) Read-Only Stores. IBM J. Res. Dev. 8 (1964), p. 443−459.

[9]   *J. Scharbert:* Änderbare Mikroprogrammspeicher hoher Geschwindigkeit. Elektron. Rechenanl. **11** (1969), p. 16–20.

[10]   *G. Rostky:* Focus on semiconductor memories. Electronic Design **19** (1971) 18, p. 50–63.

[11]   *R. S. Mo, D. M. Gilbert:* Reliability of NiCr "Fusable Links" used in PROM's. J. of the Electrochem. Society **120** (1973), p. 1001–1003.

P. Franklin, D. Burgess: Reliability aspekts of Nichrome fusable Link PROM's. Proc. of Reliability Physics **12** (1974), p. 82–86.

J L. Davidson, J. D. Gibson, S. A. Harris, T. J. Rossiter: Fusing Mechanism of Nichrome Thin Films. 14th Annual Proc. Reliability Physics (1976), p. 173–181.

[12]   *G. H. Parker, J. C. Cornet, W. S. Pinter:* Reliability considerations in the design and fabrication of Polysilicon fusible link PROM's. Proc. of Reliability Physics **12** (1974), p. 89–98.

[13]   *J. Rizzi, L. Fagan:* Electrically Alterable Integrated Circuit Read Only Memory Unit and Process of Manufacture. U.S. Patent No. 3, 742, 592 (July 3, 1973).

W. R. Brockhoff: Electrically Shorted Semiconductor Junctions utilized as Programmable Read-Only Memory Elements. 14 th Annual Proc. Reliability Physics (1976), p. 202–206.

[14]   *D. Frohman-Bentschkowsky:* A fully Decoded 2048 Bit Electrically Programmable FAMOS Read-Only Memory. IEEE J. **SC-6** (1971), p. 301–306.

[15]   *A. Moeller:* Fabrication Technology and Physical Fundamentals of Components used for Semiconductor Memories. This Volume, p. 77.

R. G. Muller: Electrically Alterable MOS-ROMs, with Particular Emphasis on the Floating Gate Type. This Volume, p. 189.

[16]   *A. Hemel:* The PLA: a "different kind" of ROM. Electronic Design **24** (1976) 1, p. 78–84.

Electrically Alterable MOS-ROMs, with Particular Emphasis on the Floating Gate Type

Rudolf G. Müller

Siemens AG, Zentrallaboratorium für Nachrichtentechnik, Munich, Germany

1. Introduction

On account of their manifold advantages digital semiconductor memories are becoming increasingly more important than magnetic memories. There is however one drawback of the customary read-write semiconductor memories with random access (RAMs), namely the volatility of the stored information: The stored information may be lost in case of disconnection or unintended interruption of the supply voltages, even if the dropout lasts only a few milliseconds. For applications in which such a loss of information cannot be tolerated, particularly if data security provided by backing storages is impossible or uneconomic, a wide variety of different nonvolatile semiconductor memories has been developed. It is the intent of this paper to discuss the latest developments in this sector, namely the EAROMs, which are memory devices programmable and erasable by purely electrical means. Nonvolatility refers not only to retention of the stored information in the absence of supply voltages, but also to data retention under such operating conditions as frequent accessing of the memory contents.

2. Overview of the Principles of Read-Only Memories

The function principle of the various types of memory is evident from the name:

ROM	read only memory
PROM	programmable ROM
EPROM	erasable PROM
EAROM	electrically alterable ROM
EEROM	electrically erasable ROM

2.1. Read Only Memories with Unalterable Information Storage

If there is no reason to expand or alter the memory contents originally stored, one can choose between two storage principles. In one case, the desired information pattern can be programmed when the memory device is manufactured. This is effected with suitably constructed masks, which for instance define the aluminium interconnections or the gate oxide thicknesses at the appropriate bit locations in one process step. In view of the relatively high mask costs, such mask-programmed memories can only be used economically if a large number of memory devices with

189

the same information pattern are required. The user is also confronted with delays, due to fabrication, mounting and test times at the manufacturing plant, until he has at his disposal the device with the desired information pattern. These two disadvantages are avoided with the second storage principle. In this case, the memory devices are manufactured and shipped to the user for programming. The desired information pattern is obtained by altering the device at appropriate locations (addresses) by for instance fusing a NiCr or polysilicon link with high current pulses (fusible link PROM). Such alterations are irreversible, it is therefore impossible to alter the data stored at some future time. The complete programmability of such a PROM cannot therefore be tested in advance. The user will have to accept the fact that between 5 and 10 % of the devices (for a 4000-bit PROM) cannot be fully programmed. As high current pulses are used for programming, only the bipolar technology is suitable for this principle.

2.2. Read Only Memories with Alterable Information Storage

The first possibility is to secure the data stored in RAMs, for example with the aid of the previously mentioned backing storages (magnetic disk or tape), or with backup batteries in conjunction with devices which consume very little power (CMOS technology) and can thus be energized by the supply voltage of the battery.

Another possibility is to integrate a nonvolatile memory in an otherwise volatile memory device. The information is only secured in the nonvolatile memory in the event of a supply voltage interruption. For example, a nonvolatile MNOS memory can be incorporated in a serial CCD memory [1].

The smallest expense is however required if the memory element is itself nonvolatile. Apart from the memories with polarizable gate insulators [2] which are not discussed in this paper, all other alterable read only memories are characterized by a common function principle: Information is stored in the form of electrical charges over the channel region of an MOS transistor, the threshold voltage of the transistor being altered in a suitable manner for the readout of the memory contents. The various techniques differ from each other with regard to where the charge is stored, how it is brought to this position during programming and how it is removed again on erasure. The nonvolatility of the memory depends on its charge storage capability. As a rule of thumb it can be said that the effort for programming and erasure increases with the length of time the information is to remain stored.

Fig. 1 shows the energy diagram of an MOS transistor in simplified form, i.e. without interface states, space charges etc. It can be seen that an energy threshold exists at the substrate/insulator interface, which amounts to 3.2 eV for the passage of electrons to the oxide conduction band and 4.6 eV for hole movement to the oxide valence band. If charge carriers are to reach the oxide over the channel region, they must either possess the above mentioned energy or the oxide must be thin enough to permit tunneling. Both options are used in alterable read only memories.

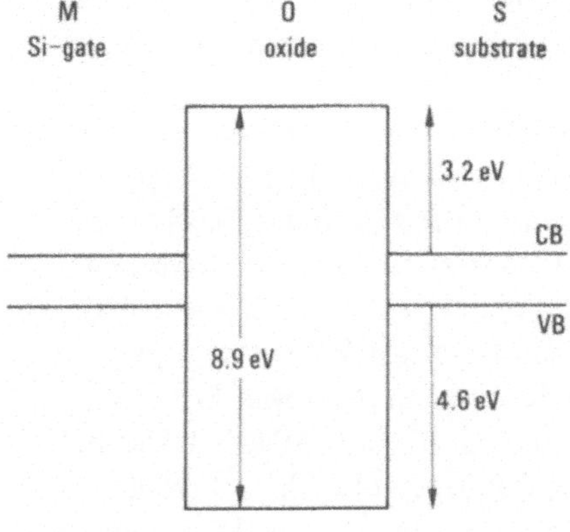

Fig. 1

Simplified energy diagram of an
MOS transistor with poly-Si-gate

3. Read Only Memory Technologies

3.1. MNOS Memory

In MNOS memories [3], discussed in detail in another part of this volume, the gate
insulator consists of a thin oxide layer above the substrate and a thicker nitride
layer between gate and oxide (Fig. 2). On applying a voltage between gate and
substrate, charge carriers tunnel from the substrate through the thin oxide (thickness < 5 nm $\rightarrow$ direct tunneling) to trap sites at the oxide/nitride interface and in
the nitride itself near the interface, and cause the threshold voltage of the MNOS

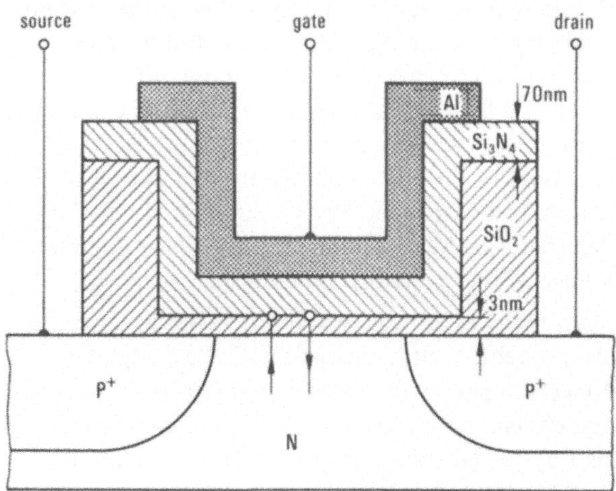

Fig. 2. MNOS memory cell. The arrows symbolize the tunneling of charge carriers through
the oxide to the traps for programming and erasure

transistor to be changed. On application of a voltage of opposite polarity, the trap
sites are discharged. To avoid unintentional charging or discharging of the traps on
information readout, when voltage is also applied to the gate, the memory cell is so
designed that considerably higher voltages are used for programming and erasure
(e.g. 28 V) than for read operations (e.g. 15 V) [4]. However, a high number of
readout operations or a long period of storage with no voltage applied lead to loss
of the stored charge. As the circuits required for address accessing also have to be
integrated on the same substrate of an LSI memory device, the requirement that
voltages with different sign be handled on one substrate calls for a more sophisticated
technology. An MNOS device with full address decoding in the slower P-channel
technology, available since the end of 1976, is the first 8192-bit MNOS device [4].
$2 \cdot 10^{11}$ readout cycles are possible. With a sense frequency of 1 MHz, it would for
example be possible with this memory device to store data for around 60 hours
without intermediate refreshing.

Fields of application of MNOS memories are both the consumer sector and above
all the military sector, on account of their high resistance to ionizing radiation.

3.2. Read Only Memories with Floating Gate

3.2.1. Mechanisms for Programming and Erasure

MOS read only memories with thick gate oxide (standard thickness 100 nm to
120 nm) between substrate and charge-storage facility (floating gate) cannot be
recharged by tunneling charges, but instead make use of charge transport via the
conduction or valence band of the oxide. For this purpose, the charge carriers must
acquire sufficient energy to surmount the energy barrier (Fig. 1). Such high-energy
charges are not in thermal equilibrium with the semiconductor lattice at the customary operating temperatures of a memory, they are therefore called "hot charges".
Programming thus comprises generation of hot charge carriers and then their
transfer to the charge-storage facility, the floating gate. This gate, which is completely
surrounded by oxide and is electrically isolated, consists of a conducting material,
usually polycrystalline silicon for reasons of process compatibility with the silicon
gate process. The injected hot charges, which are generally produced at closely confined spots in the memory cell, can therefore be distributed over the entire channel
region and cause the threshold voltage of the transistor to be shifted.

The charges are prevented from leaving the floating gate by energy thresholds to the
surrounding oxide. The theoretical probability of discharge across the energy threshold is no more than around one electron per year. However, in order to achieve
satisfactory long-term storage, high demands are placed on the insulating properties
of the oxide, which are already met by the customary method of manufacturing
the oxide for MOS devices. As a result, the read only memory with floating gate
has the excellent long-term storage capability of over 30 years without storage
duration dependence on the number of readout operations.

192

Hot charge carriers are generated in regions with high electrical field strength. The most important generation mechanisms are:

a) Avalanche breakdown of the drain- or source-to-substrate junction of an MOS transistor [5, 6]. The gate potential causes the region with the highest field strength, where the breakdown starts, to be located near the interface to the oxide (gate-assisted surface breakdown) [7]. Only a small portion of the charge carriers in the breakdown current achieve the eneigy level required to surmount the energy threshold, so that in the electron injection mode only about 0.5 % of the breakdown current is injected into the floating gate. The remaining charge carriers flow off via the substrate terminal. Despite the low injection efficiency, the programming times remain short as only the very small gate capacitance has to be charged.

b) Electrons passing through the pinched-off channel of an NMOS transistor operating in the saturation mode are heated up by the high field strength ($> 10^5$ V/cm) in the pinch-off region [8] and can be injected into the floating gate. If short channel lengths are used (3.5 μm), hot electrons are also generated from the region of drift velocity saturation [9], lower voltages than for pinch-off injection however being required.

c) An electric field causes a depletion region to be created at the surface of a suitably doped semiconductor. If band bending takes place so rapidly that the thermal generation of an inversion layer (time constant 0.1 s to 1 s in silicon) is not yet started, the breakdown field strength is reached and hot charge carriers are generated in the depletion region [10]. These charge carriers are suitable for injection into the insulator and the floating gate.

In order to erase the memory cell, the floating gate must be restored to its original uncharged condition. This can be effected in two ways: the charge injected during programming is either removed or neutralized by the injection of a complementary charge.

3.2.2. Some Examples of Floating-Gate Read Only Memories

The original proposal for a floating-gate memory device was made back in 1967 [11]. The floating gate was however built into the dielectric interface of an MNOS-like transistor, a substitute so to speak for the traps, and was charged by the tunneling method. In addition to the previously mentioned problems inherent in the MNOS principle, a further drawback of this device is that a pinhole − quite possible at the low oxide thicknesses of only a few atom layers − can cause the complete charge stored in the floating gate to leak out, whereas the charge of an MNOS transistor stored in mutually insulated traps is only lost in the immediate vicinity of the pinhole.

FAMOS

The first optically erasable read only memory with floating gate to appear on the market (1971) was the 2048-bit floating gate avalanche injection MOS (FAMOS) [5]. The memory cell consists of two transistors in P-channel technology (Fig. 3). The memory cell to be programmed is selected by voltage coincidence at the row and column lines. Hot electrons generated by the breakdown of the drain-to-substrate P-N junction charge the floating gate negatively, causing the storage transistor originally working in the enhancement mode to switch to the depletion mode. In read operations the cell is also selected by voltage coincidence at the row and column lines, but a lower amplitude is used. Depending on whether the storage transistor is turned on or off, a signal with low or high TTL level is generated at the output (logic "0" or "1"). All 2048 bits can be simultaneously erased by irradiation with ultraviolet light, which must have an adequately short wavelength to excite the charge carriers from the valence band of the degenerated P^+-polysilicon gate into the conduction band of the oxide ($E > 4.3$ eV $\hat{=} \lambda < 290$ nm). Irradiation with sunlight is therefore inadequate to cause discharge.

Investigations into long-term information retention showed that at an ambient temperature of 125 °C, 70 % of the charge would remain stored for over 100 years [12]. A charge loss of 30 % by no means involves a loss of information, all that happens is that the threshold voltage window between the unprogrammed and the programmed states is shifted to a lesser extent. The maximum value of the charge loss that does not involve information loss depends on the threshold of the detection circuit, a Schmitt trigger for instance.

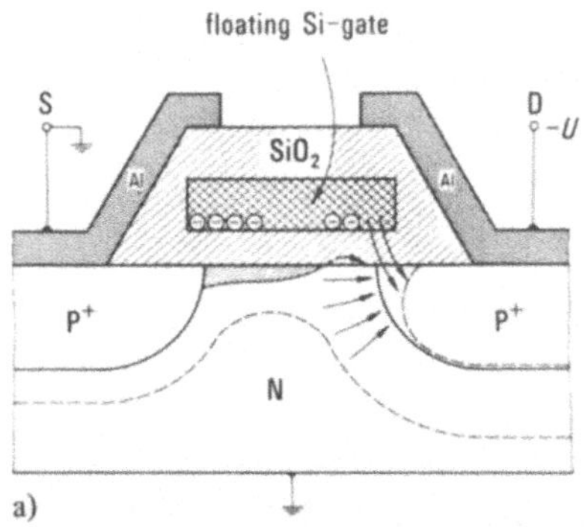

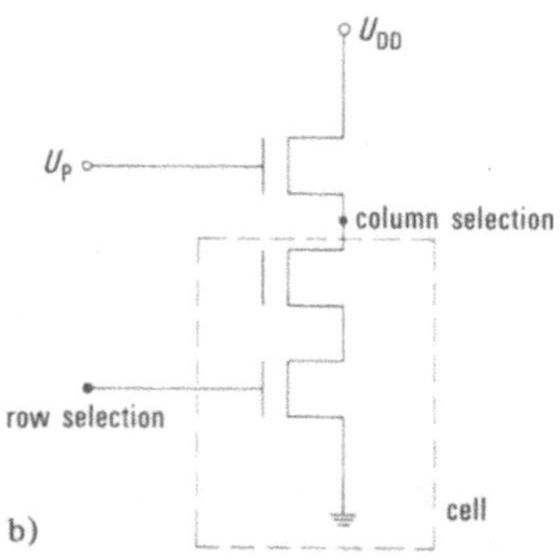

Fig. 3. FAMOS memory cell [5]

a) Cross-section of the storage transistor. Arrows indicate the direction of the electric field strength during programming by means of the gate-assisted drain-to-substrate avalanche breakdown

b) Memory cell with storage and selection transistors

A requirement of long-term reliability is however not only retention of the charged state, but also retention of the uncharged state (logic "1"). It may happen that frequent readout causes an unprogrammed cell to be gradually charged [13], as an uncharged cell can also generate a channel current by capacitive coupling into the floating gate, and this current initiates an avalanche breakdown of the drain-to-substrate junction at voltage values which are considerably below the values for the gate-assisted surface breakdown [14]. This disturbing effect must be avoided by selecting suitable sense voltages.

Although it would be desirable to fabricate the FAMOS memory in the faster N-channel technology, the simple reversal of doping and voltage sign is not possible in practice. The N-channel FAMOS memory would then work on the principle of injecting hot holes into the floating gate. This mechanism exhibits a considerably lower injection efficiency due to the higher energy barrier to be surmounted by holes on the one hand and the lower mobility and shorter free path length of hot holes on the other. Furthermore, as the trapping of carriers in the oxide is more pronounced with holes than with electrons [15], the increase in the gate-assisted surface breakdown voltage after several programming processes (walk-out [16]) is a problem. For these reasons, an N-channel FAMOS memory device would require such high programming voltages that they could not be handled by peripheral circuits in standard MOS technology.

Programming with hot electrons from the channel is therefore used for the N-channel read only memory transistor. In this way, the memory cell works in the enhancement mode in both the uncharged and in the charged condition, and it is therefore possible to build a single-transistor cell (Fig. 4b). For now selection of the cell in a matrix array a control gate is arranged above the floating gate (Fig. 4a). One version of such an N-channel memory cell erasable with UV light is the SIMOS (stacked gate injection MOS) cell [9]. With the cell in the unselected state (0 V applied to the control gate),

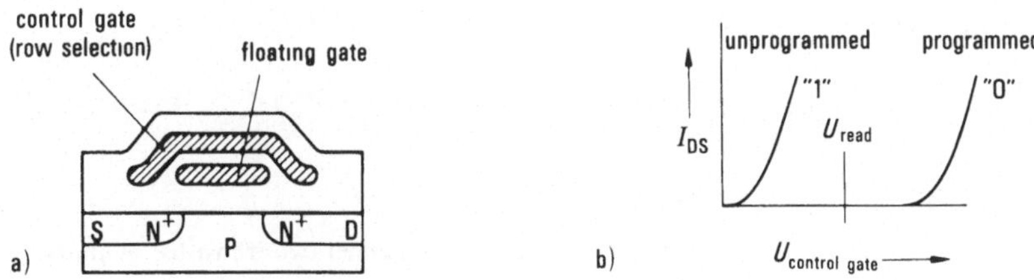

Fig. 4. UV-erasable N-channel single-transistor memory cell [17]
a) Cross-section through the stacked-gate storage transistor
b) Transfer characteristics for the programmed and unprogrammed condition. The transistor always works in the enhancement mode

current can neither flow through the cell in the charged nor in the uncharged condition. For programming, voltage is applied to the drain and gate simultaneously. As the memory cell only consists of one transistor and thus requires a low area, a memory device with high bit number can be realized. The cell shown in Fig. 4a has been on the market since 1975 in 8192-bit UV-erasable devices [17]. Judging by their imposing number of second sources, these devices rapidly found wide application as optically erasable read only memories.

NEC EAROM

For many applications it would be of considerable advantage if it were possible to alter the information in the system, i.e. without removing the device and erasing it with UV light. To this end, a number of electrically erasable read only memory principles were proposed in the last few years, of which one has so far reached the market in a device [18, 19].

The memory cell consists of two N-channel transistors (Fig. 5). Hot hole injection obtained by avalanche breakdown of the source-to-substrate N^+-P junction is used

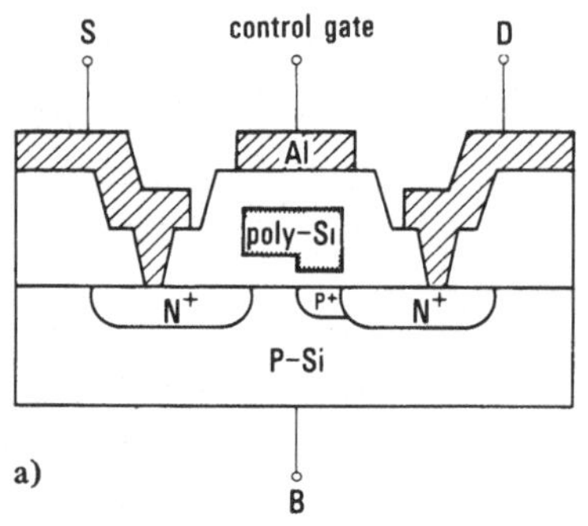

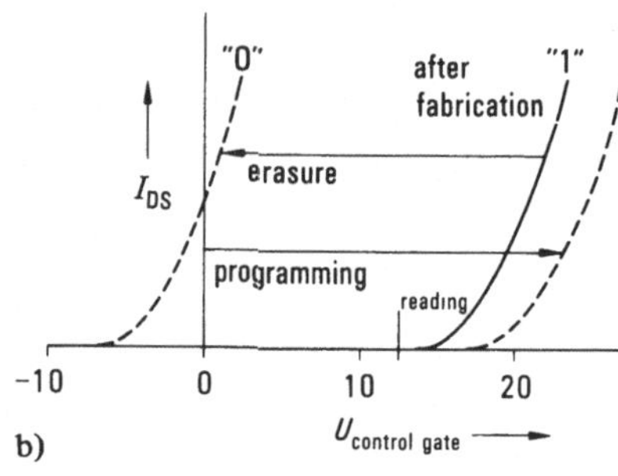

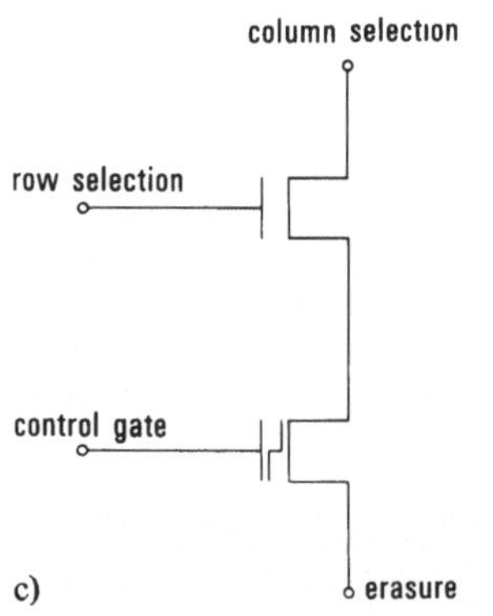

Fig. 5

Electrically erasable N-channel two-transistor memory cell [18]

a) Cross-section of the storage transistor
b) Transfer characteristics. In the erased (i.e. charged) state the transistor operates in the depletion mode
c) Memory cell, consisting of storage and selection transistors

196

for electrical erasure. The previously mentioned problems resulting from the low injection efficiency of holes are overcome by applying a negative bias voltage $(-35$ V) to the control gate during erasure, to lower the gate-assisted surface breakdown voltage and to assist the transport of holes via the oxide. For programming, an additional P^+ diffusion region was realized below the floating gate adjacent to the drain N^+ region. The hot electrons originating from the avalanche breakdown of this P^+–N^+ junction are injected into the floating gate during programming $(+25$ V at the control gate). Thinner gate oxide over the channel near the drain region improves the injection efficiency of the electrons. As the transistor works in the depletion mode after erasure (Fig. 5b), an additional selection transistor must be connected in series with each storage transistor (Fig. 5c).

A characteristic of this memory is that after manufacture, i.e. with the gate still uncharged, all memory cells must first be positively charged by means of the erasure procedure, before writing the desired information pattern by selective discharge of the relevant cells. 2048-bit memory devices are on the market, the first 8192-bit devices were available as samples at the end of 1976.

SIMOS

A further reduction in the memory area is achieved by the electrically erasable single-transistor memory cell SIMOS (stacked gate injection MOS). The structure of the cell is shown in Fig. 6. The capacitive coupling of the control gate voltage to the floating gate is increased due to an additional overlap of the two polysilicon gates outside the channel region, i.e. over the thick oxide. Programming is achieved by the injection of hot electrons from the short channel ($l_{eff} = 3.5\ \mu$m) at programming voltages which cause saturation of the drift velocity. The conditions under which

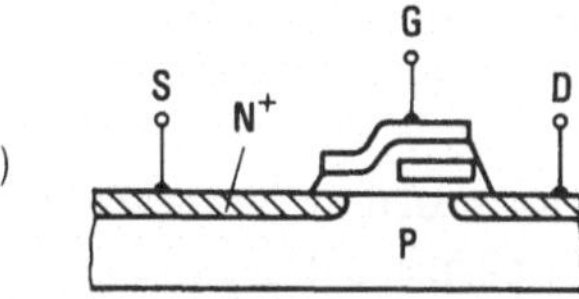

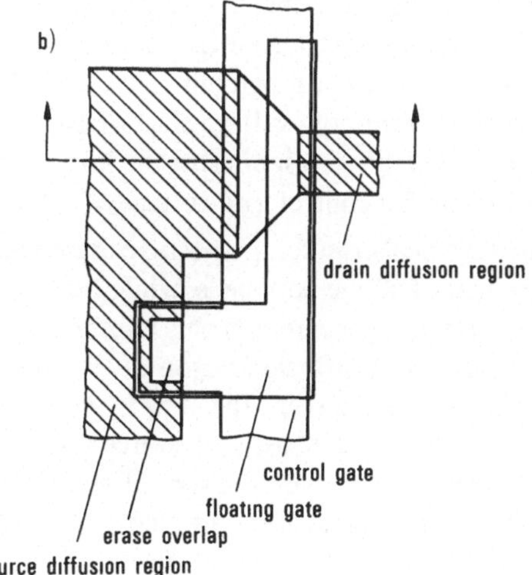

Fig. 6

Electrically erasable N-channel single-transistor memory cell SIMOS (stacked gate injection MOS)

a) Cross-section. The floating gate controls only part of the channel
b) Layout (top view). The floating gate is connected via thick oxide to the erase overlap with the source diffusion region

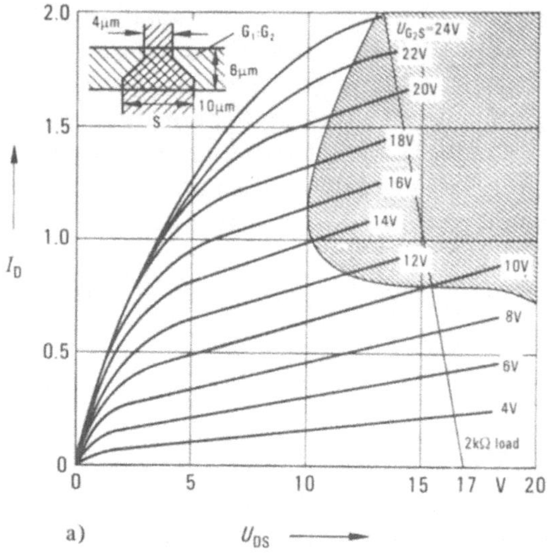

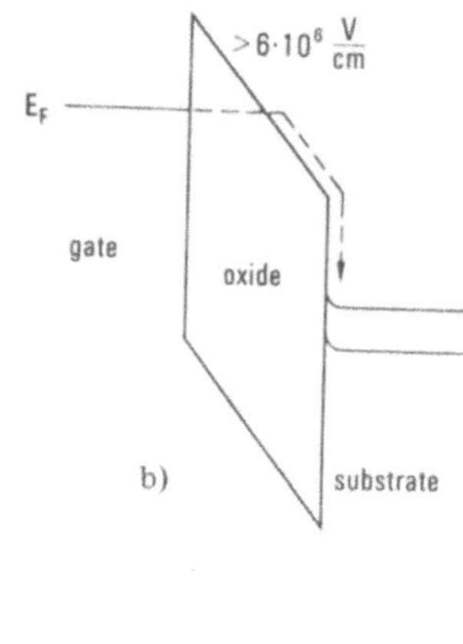

Fig. 7. Programming and erasure of the SIMOS memory cell

a) In the hatched area of the output characteristic hot electrons are injected into the floating gate from the channel (channel geometry as shown)

b) Erasure by Fowler-Nordheim emission of electrons from the floating gate to the substrate at high field strengths

hot electrons are injected into the floating gate are depicted in Fig. 7a by the hatched area of the output characteristic I_D versus U_{DS}. To operate the memory cell on an LSI memory chip low operating voltages are required. This is achieved by using on the one hand short channel lengths and on the other hand a funnel-type narrowing of the channel width near the drain (Fig. 6b), which causes the onset of velocity saturation at lower programming voltages [9]. It can be seen from Fig. 7a that a maximum threshold voltage shift of 14 V can be achieved for a load of 2 kΩ, which approximately corresponds to the lead resistance in the LSI device, a drain voltage of 17 V and a control gate voltage of 24 V.

For electrical erasure, the positive erase voltage is applied to the common source terminal of all memory cells, while the control gate is maintained at 0 V [20]. The field strength generated in this way between the negatively charged floating gate and the source diffusion region causes the gate to be discharged by Fowler-Nordheim electron emission (Fig. 7b). As a large number of memory cells are to be discharged simultaneously, gate-assisted source-to-substrate avalanche breakdown must be inhibited, as otherwise the sum of all breakdown currents to the substrate could lead to power dissipation problems. On discharge by means of Fowler-Nordheim emission, only the low erase currents flow via the oxide to the relevant cell. For

198

this reason, such thin oxide is used at the erase position ($\approx$ 50 nm) that Fowler-Nordheim emission predominates. The erase voltage is furthermore applied as a relatively slowly rising ramp, with the result that the field strength between gate and source region can only rise just so far that the field strength required for Fowler-Nordheim emission is not exceeded and the surface breakdown voltage is thus not reached or is only reached at high erase voltage values.

During erasure, the negatively charged floating gate is first discharged and then positively charged to various extents. If the threshold voltage of the cell were to be reached, the memory cell would operate in the depletion mode. An additional transistor would then be required per memory cell for selection, as in the case of the NEC EAROM, to prevent current from flowing through cells that have not been selected (0 V at control gate). As the floating gate only covers part of the channel (Fig. 6) and the rest of the channel is solely generated by the control gate, such depletion operation is reliably prevented. The connection shown in Fig. 6b between the floating gate outside the funnel-type channel and the erase overlap with the source diffusion region makes possible the erasure of the SIMOS cell on the source side.

Fig. 8 shows a photo of the SIMOS cell taken by an electron scanning microscope during manufacture, namely after the two polysilicon gates have been etched. Clearly visible are the funnel-type channel and the connection of the floating gate (only discernible as an elevation in the control gate) via the thick oxide to the erase overlap.

The SIMOS cell was used to build an 8192-bit memory with full address decoding on a substrate area of 19.7 mm^2 [21]. The complete memory device is shown in Fig. 9. For programming voltages of 26 V, the typical programming time for each of the 1024 eight-bit words is 100 ms. An erase voltage of 35 V is required for the

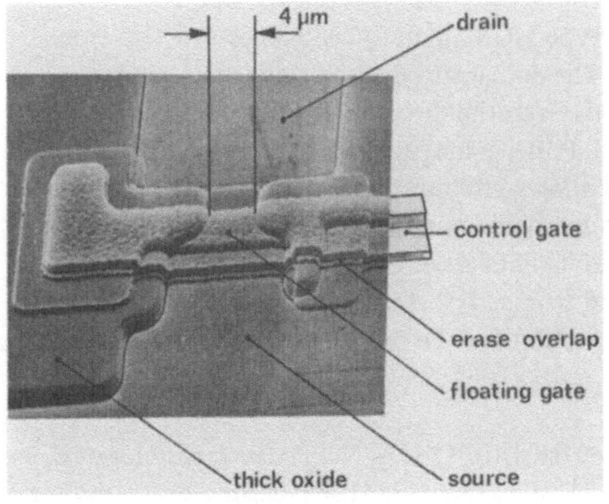

Fig. 8

Scanning electron microscope photo of a SIMOS memory cell, taken following gate etching. In subsequent process steps the cell is embedded in oxide and provided with etched aluminium interconnections

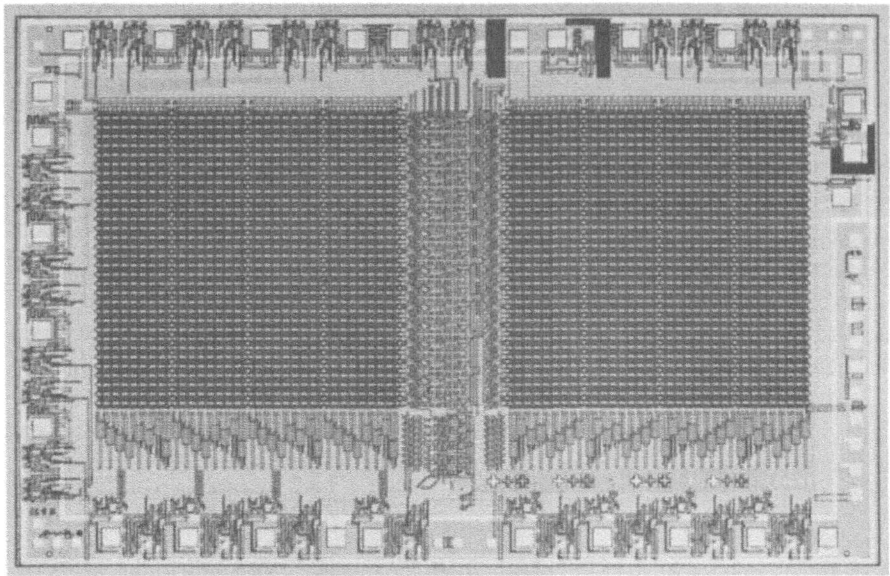

Fig. 9. Microphotograph of an 8192-bit SIMOS memory device with a total area of 19.7 mm²

joint erasure of all 8192 cells, which lasts 30 seconds. As an interesting comparison, it takes 15 to 20 minutes to erase the N-channel FAMOS memory using the recommended UV irradiation method.

To close, two further proposals for electrically erasable read only memories will be described, but they have not as yet attained commercial significance.

SAMOS

The stacked gate avalanche injection type MOS memory cell consists of two transistors in P-channel technology [22]. The actual storage transistor (Fig. 10a) is programmed by means of hot electrons from the drain-to-substrate junction breakdown, just like the P-channel FAMOS. Positive bias applied to the control gate improves the injection efficiency and allows program times of 20 μs/bit. Erasure is effected in less than 5 seconds through field emission of electrons from the floating gate to the control gate. A provisional data sheet on a 2048-bit SAMOS read only memory was however only found to specify optical erasure, according to more recent information, no plans exist at present for the production of SAMOS memories.

Atmos

The adjustable threshold MOS storage transistor [23] in N-channel technology is realized on a P epitaxial layer over an N^+ substrate (Fig. 10b). During programming,

200

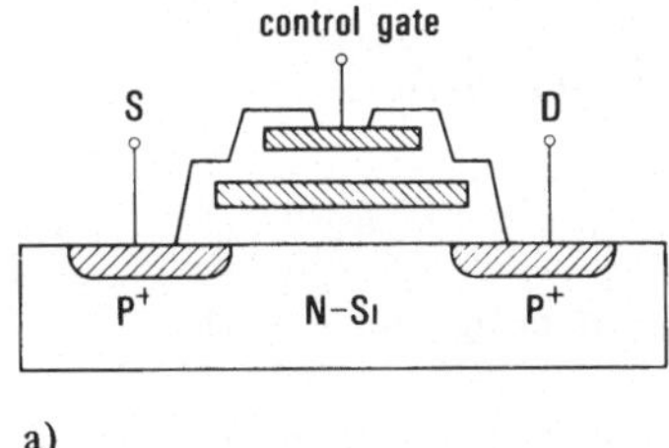

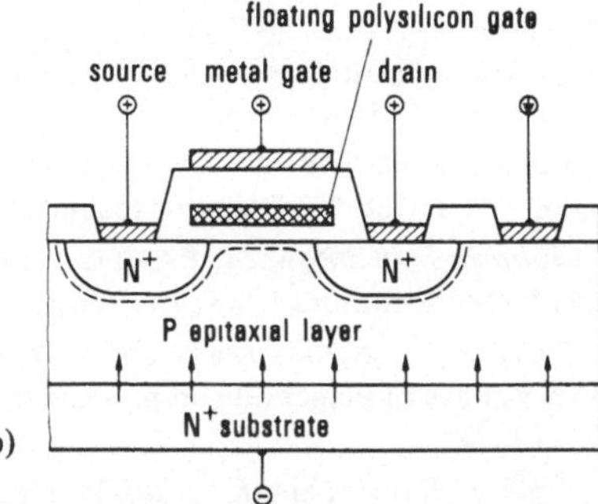

Fig. 10. a) SAMOS memory cell [22]. Programming is effected by the avalanche breakdown injection of electrons into the floating gate, erasure through field emission of electrons from the floating gate to the control gate

b) Atmos memory cell [23] in the programming mode: electrons from the N^+ substrate (arrows) are accelerated into the depletion zone at the semiconductor surface and injected into the floating gate. Erasure is effected by hole injection from a diffusion region/substrate avalanche breakdown

electrons from the forward-biased N^+–P junction diffuse to the depletion zone produced by positive voltages at gate, drain and source. There the electrons gain sufficient energy to surmount the energy barrier to the oxide and are injected into the floating gate. Fig. 10b shows the Atmos cell in the programming mode. Erasure takes place through injection of holes obtained from the avalanche breakdown of the drain- or source-to-substrate junction. If the floating gate is then positively charged, a selection transistor is required for each cell.

4. Conclusions

From the broad spectrum of different proposals for EAROMs, it was only possible within the scope of this study to discuss a few of the most important ones and to provide an outline of the physical mechanisms involved in their realization. Despite continual advances, all known proposals have the following in common: programming and erasure of an EAROM last considerably longer than writing and alteration in an MOS-RAM device. The nonvolatile RAM device will probably remain a wish, for which there is no sign of fulfillment at the moment. For the near future no alternative to the present division of duties between RAM and ROM is in sight.

References

[1] *K. Goser* and *K Knauer*, Nonvolatile CCD Memory with MNOS Storage Capacitors. IEEE J. Solid-State Circuits **SC-9**, 148 (1974).

[2] *S Y Wu*, A new ferroelectric memory device, metal-ferroelectric-semiconductor transistor, IEEE Trans. Electron Devices **ED-21**, 499 (1974).

[3]   *A. Moeller*, Fabrication technology and physical fundamentals of components used for semiconductor memories, this volume, p. 77.

[4]   General Instrument's new 8192-bit Earom relies on metal-nitride-oxide technology, Electronics, 16. Sept. 76, p. 40.

[5]   *D. Frohman-Bentchkowsky*, A Fully-Decoded 2048-Bit Electrically-Programmable MOS-ROM, ISSCC 71, Digest of technical papers, p. 80.

[6]   *D. Frohman-Bentchkowsky*, FAMOS – a new semiconductor charge storage device, Solid-State Electronics **17**, 517 (1974).

[7]   *A S. Grove, O. Leistiko jr.* and *W. W. Hooper*, Effect of Surface Fields on the Breakdown Voltage of Planar Silicon p-n-Junctions, IEEE Trans. Electron Devices **ED-4,** 157 (1967).

[8]   *Y. Tarui, Y. Hayashi* and *K. Nagai*, Electrically Reprogrammable Nonvolatile Semiconductor Memory, IEEE J. Solid-State Circuits **SC-7,** 169 (1972).

[9]   *B Rossler* and *R. G Muller*, Erasable and Electrically Reprogrammable Read-Only Memory Using the N-Channel SIMOS One-Transistor Cell, Siemens Forsch.- und Entwickl.-Ber. **4**, 345 (1975).

[10]   *A. Goetzberger* and *E. H. Nicollian*, MOS Avalanche and Tunneling Effects in Silicon Surfaces, J. Appl. Phys. **38**, 4582 (1967).

[11]   *D. Kahng* and *S M. Sze*, A Floating gate and its Application to Memory Devices, Bell Syst. Tech. J. **46**, 1283 (1967).

[12]   *D. J Fitzgerald, G. H. Parker* and *P. Spiegel*, Reliability Studies of MOS Si-Gate Arrays, 9th Ann. Proc. Rel. Phys. Symp. Las Vegas (1971).

[13]   *K. O. Jeppson* and *C. M. Svensson*, Unintentional Writing of a FAMOS Memory Device During Reading, Solid-State Electronics **19**, 455 (1976).

[14]   *R. G. Muller*, Gate-enhanced vs channel-current induced breakdown for floating gate avalanche injection, Solid-State Electronics **17**, 503 (1974).

[15]   *E. H Nicollian, A. Goetzberger* and *C N. Berglund*, Avalanche Injection Currents and Charging Phenomena in Thermal SiO_2, Appl. Phys. Lett. **15**, 174 (1969).

[16]   *H. Hara, Y. Okamoto* and *H. Ohnuma*, A New Instability in MOS Transistor Caused by Hot Electron and Hole Injection from Drain Avalanche Plasma into Gate Oxide, Jap. J. Appl. Phys. **9**, 1103 (1970).

[17]   *P J. Salsbury, W. L. Morgan, G. P Perlegos* and *R. T. Simko*, High Performance MOS EPROMs using a Stacked-Gate Cell, ISSCC 1977 Digest of techn. papers, p. 186.

[18]   *M Kikuchi, S. Ohya, M. Kamaya, M. Koike* and *H. Yamamoto*, A 2048-Bit N-Channel Fully Decoded Electrically Writeable/Eraseable Nonvolatile Read Only Memory, 1st ESSCIRC, IEE Conference Publication 130, p. 66–67, September 1975.

[19]   *M. Kikuchi*, An 8192-Bit N-Channel Fully Decoded Electrically Writeable/Eraseable PROM, IEEE Non-Volatile Semiconductor Workshop, Vail, Colorado (1976).

[20]   *B Rossler*, Electrically Erasable and Reprogrammable ROM Using the N-channel SIMOS One-Transistor Cell, IEEE Trans. Electron Devices **ED-24,** 606 (1977).

[21]   *R. G. Muller, H. Nietsch, B. Rossler* and *E. Wolter*, Electrically Alterable 8192 Bit N-channel MOS PROM, ISSCC 1977 Digest of techn. papers, p. 188.

[22]   *H Iizuka, F. Masuoka, T. Sato* and *M. Ishikawa*, Electrically Alterable Avalanche-Injection-Type MOS READ-ONLY Memory with Stacked-Gate Structure, IEEE Trans. Electron Devices **ED-23,** 379 (1976).

[23]   *J. F. Verwey* and *R. P. Kramer*, Atmos – An Electrically Reprogrammable Read-Only Memory Device, IEEE Trans. Electron Devices **ED-21,** 631 (1974).

Physical Principles of Magnetic Bubble Domain Memory Devices

Frans H. de Leeuw

Philips Research Laboratories, Eindhoven, Netherlands

1. Introduction

Magnetic bubbles are cylindrical magnetic domains that may occur in a thin plate of
a magnetic material in which the preferred (*easy*) direction of magnetization is perpendicular to the plane of the plate (Fig. 1). The magnetic bubble is separated from
its environment by the cylindrical magnetic domain wall. The magnetization in the
domain wall rotates through 180 degrees. In a bubble domain memory the presence
of a magnetic bubble at a particular place and at a particular point of time represents
a digital 'one', and its absence represents a 'zero'.

Typical materials in which the easy direction of magnetization is perpendicular to
the plane of the plate (i.e. materials possessing uniaxial anisotropy) are orthoferrites,
hexaferrites and iron garnets with *induced* uniaxial anisotropy. The value of the
uniaxial anisotropy (denoted by K_u) must be high enough for the anisotropy field
H_A ($\equiv 2 K_u/M_s$) to be greater than the saturation magnetization $4\pi M_s$. If this is not
the case, the magnetization will be in the plane of the magnetic plate, which is then
the state of lowest energy.

In a certain range of the external field (*bias field*) (Fig. 1) the isolated magnetic bubble
is in a stable state (state of lowest energy). When the field drops below a specific value
the isolated magnetic bubble is no longer stable and stripe domains arise. When the
field exceeds a critical value (collapse field) the bubbles disappear and the plate is
then uniformly magnetized in the direction of the external field.

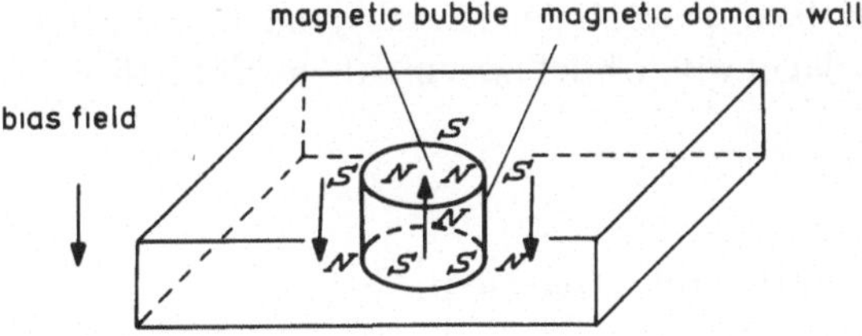

Fig. 1. The magnetic bubble is a cylindrical domain whose direction of magnetization is opposite
to that in the rest of the plate. The isolated magnetic bubble is stable only in a small region of an
external field applied perpendicular to the plane of the layer.

The diameter of the magnetic bubbles in a material determines the packing density of
the bubble memory. The maximum packing (chip) densities are of the order of 10^4
bits $\cdot$ cm^{-2} in orthoferrites and about 8×10^6 bits $\cdot$ cm^{-2} in garnets. Hexaferrites
are not used at the moment.

There are various methods that can be used to demonstrate the presence of a
magnetic bubble. The simplest for use in the laboratory is the method based on the
Faraday effect. The Faraday effect causes the electrical field vector to rotate when
polarized light is conducted through the material. The rotation depends on the direction of magnetization, and changes sign when the magnetization changes direction.
As a rule, however, the Faraday effect is not used for magnetic bubble memories,
since it requires a light source and a light detector.

The transport of magnetic bubbles is based on the principle that the bubbles are set
in motion by the application of inhomogeneous fields. The bubbles then move in the
direction in which the bias field is reduced. During the movement of a bubble the
magnetic moments in the bubble wall rotate around an axis in the plane of the plate.
A higher rotation frequency results in a higher bubble velocity. The rotation of the
moments in the wall is damped by processes in the material. These processes limit
the mobility of the wall. There is also a limit, however, to the propagation velocity.
In the simplest case the maximum velocity is roughly given by the product of a
material parameter γ, the wall thickness ($\sqrt{A/K_u}$) and the demagnetizing field in
the wall ($4\pi M_s$); see also section 2 below. This relation has to be modified for a
magnetic bubble in a thin plate, as used for a bubble domain memory device.

Magnetic bubbles were first observed by Kooy and Enz [1], who also discussed the
conditions for bubble stability. It was Bobeck who first indicated the possible
applications of magnetic bubbles [2]. Since then many laboratories have started investigating magnetic bubbles and their possible technological applications. Magnetic
bubbles are dealt with in references [3–6]. The exact mathematical treatment of the
stability of a magnetic bubble is due to Thiele [7].

Section 2 of this article looks at the magnetic bubbles themselves and considers their
static and dynamic properties. Section 3 considers the bubble domain materials.
Section 4 deals with the principle of the magnetic bubble memory and describes the
individual elements. The article concludes with a brief account of "bubble lattice
files".

2. Magnetic bubbles and their static and dynamic properties

The isolated magnetic bubble exists only in the presence of an external magnetic field
(bias field) as indicated in Fig. 1. The required magnitude of the bias field has such a
value that it can be generated with a simple permanent magnet system. We shall first

consider the stability of a magnetic bubble and its energy (Fig. 2) related to the energy of the saturated material without domains.

In the bias field the magnetic field energy of a magnetic bubble (the thickness of the magnetic plate being constant) is proportional to the surface area of the bubble (Fig. 2). The bubble's energy (demagnetizing energy) in the stray field of the bubble, however, is a complicated function of the bubble radius. A typical curve is shown in Fig. 2. The third contribution to the energy comes from the bubble wall. The specific energy (per unit surface area) of the wall is given by the equation

$$\sigma_w = 4 \sqrt{AK_u} \, , \tag{1}$$

where σ_w is the specific wall energy, A is the exchange energy density (per unit length) and K_u is the uniaxial anisotropic energy density (per unit volume). This contribution is therefore proportional to the bubble radius (Fig. 2). The sum of the three energy contributions is the total energy of the magnetic bubble. Magnetic bubbles exist when the external field is so chosen that the magnetic bubble energy has a minimum. When the field is increased, the minimum disappears at a particular value of the field H_0 (collapse field), and so the magnetic bubble disappears as well. When the field is lowered the magnetic bubble grows and stripe domains are formed (run-out field). Between run out and collapse field the magnetic bubble is stable. Thiele [7] found in his calculations that the maximum stability is reached when the diameter d of a bubble, the thickness h of the plate and a material length l ($= \sqrt{AK_u}/\pi M_s^2$) are given by the equations

$$d = 8\,l \tag{2}$$

and

$$h = 4\,l \tag{3}$$

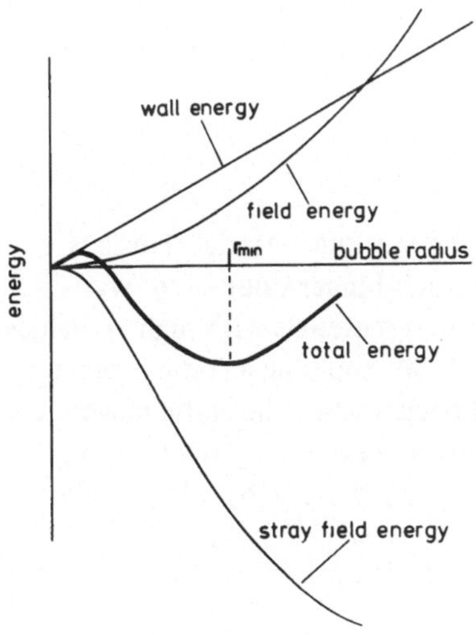

Fig. 2

The three contributions to the energy of a magnetic bubble. The radius of a magnetic bubble adjusts itself to the minimum of the total energy.

In these equations, l is only a quantity for calculation purposes. The field region in which the bubble is stable is approximately $0.1 \times 4\pi\,M_s$.

Let us now consider the constants A and K_u in eq. (1). The constant A is approximately $1 - 4 \times 10^{-7}\,\mathrm{erg\cdot cm^{-1}}$ for all materials suitable for use (iron garnets) [8]. The constant expresses the interaction between magnetic neighbours in the material. The constant K_u expresses the interaction of the magnetization and the easy direction. For magnetic bubbles to occur it is necessary to satisfy the relation

$$Q \equiv K_u/2\pi\,M_s^2 > 1 \,. \tag{4}$$

If eq. (4) is not satisfied, the magnetization is parallel to the plane of the magnetic plate. If spontaneous nucleation of domains is to be avoided, Q must be equal to approximately 4.

As already discussed, a magnetic bubble is set in motion when an inhomogeneous field (gradient field) is applied. The propagation velocity v of a magnetic bubble is given by [9, 10]:

$$\begin{aligned}
v &= (\gamma\,\sqrt{A/K_u}\,/\alpha)\cdot\{(\Delta H/2) - 4\,H_c/\pi\}, & \Delta H &> 8\,H_c/\pi\,; \\
v &= 0 & , \quad \Delta H &\leqslant 8\,H_c/\pi\,,
\end{aligned} \tag{5}$$

where γ is the gyromagnetic ratio, α the Gilbert damping constant, H_c a coercivity field and ΔH the driving field over the bubble. Low K_u values results in thick walls and hence in high bubble velocities.

It has been found that eq. (5) is no longer valid at higher fields ΔH: a saturation of the propagation velocity then occurs [11–13]. The saturation velocity v_s is $5 - 20\ \mathrm{m\cdot s^{-1}}$. A theoretical treatment of the saturation velocity has been given by Slonczewski [14]. He calculated that

$$v_s = 7.\ 1\,\gamma\,A/h\,K_u^{1/2} \,. \tag{6}$$

The saturation velocity can be increased by increasing γ in the material. This has been done by Le Craw et al. [15]. A more than 15 times higher value of γ was achieved and velocities of $300\ \mathrm{m\cdot s^{-1}}$ were measured in materials with high γ values. The velocity can also be increased (up to $300\ \mathrm{m\cdot s^{-1}}$) by applying a static magnetic field in the plane of the plate [16–18]. This effect occurs when the static magnetic field in the plane of the plate (H_1) is greater than the demagnetizing field $4\pi\,M_s$. The maximum velocity is then approximately given by $\gamma\,H_1\,\sqrt{A/K_u}$ [16]. Higher velocities have also been measured in orthorhombic materials [19] (up to $500\,\mathrm{m\cdot s^{-1}}$) and in "triple-layer" plates [20]. A survey of the dynamic properties of domain walls and magnetic bubbles has been given in [21].

206

3. Materials

The materials used in bubble domain memory devices are iron garnets substituted
with other elements [8]. The substitutions are necessary in order to adjust the
magnetization and the anisotropy. Since the magnetic plate, or layer, is produced on
a non-magnetic substrate of gadolinium gallium garnet (GGG) by liquid phase epitaxy
[8], the lattice constant of the plate a_f must be equal to the lattice constants of the
substrate a_s ($|a_f - a_s|/a_f \lesssim 0.0005$). This can also be acheived with substitutions.

The garnet structure has three types of lattice sites: dodecahedral sites, octahedral
sites and tetrahedral sites, denoted in turn by { }, [ ], and ( ). For example,
yttrium iron garnet is written as $\{Y_3\}$ $[Fe_2]$ $(Fe_3)O_{12}$. The garnets have a cubic
structure and consequently a cubic anisotropy, and not a uniaxial anisotropy, which
is needed for magnetic bubbles. However, Bobeck et al. [22] discovered that it is
possible to induce a uniaxial anisotropy in the plate by means of a crystal growth
process. The main rules that were found [8] are:

- K_u is highest when the substitutional elements used are the rare earth Samarium
  (Sm) or Europium (Eu) on dodecahedral sites;

- K_u increases when the difference between the ionic radii of the rare earths in the
  garnet increases;

- K_u becomes larger when the garnet is grown at lower temperatures.

The magnetization of the garnet can be adjusted by changing the iron content. In the
yttrium iron garnet the magnetization at room temperature is $4\pi M_s = 1800$ G.
Lowering the iron content at tetrahedral sites has the effect of reducing $4\pi M_s$ [8].
For this purpose the ions Al^{3+}, Ga^{3+}, Ge^{4+} and Si^{4+} are substituted. In order that
Ge^{4+} and Si^{4+} do not reduce the Curie Temperature as much as with Al^{3+} and Ga^{3+},
the substitution Ge^{4+} or Si^{4+} are preferably used. In this case, however, Ca^{2+} must
also be substituted (at dodecahedral sites) to keep the electrical charge equal to zero.
It is interesting to note that Blank et al. [23] have shown that the substitution of
luthetium (Lu^{3+}) can keep the temperature dependence of the collapse field equal to
that of the permanent magnet (barium ferrite) for the external field. Other 'formula-
tions' are also possible.

Table 1 shows some typical parameter values for $0.5 - 8$ μm magnetic bubble memory
materials. An example for a 5 μm (bubble diameter) material is $Y_{1.5}Sm_{0.3}Lu_{0.3}Ca_{0.9}Fe_{4.1}$
$Ge_{0.9}O_{12}$ [24] and for an 0.6 μm material $Sm_{0.85}Tm_{2.15}Fe_5O_{12}$ [25]. The properties
of these materials are listed in table 2.

Table 1. Some typical values of parameters for $8-0.5$ μm magnetic bubble materials (assuming $Q = 4$ and $A = 2 \cdot 10^{-7}$ erg cm^{-1})

d [μm]	h [μm]	l [μm]	K_u [erg cm^{-3}]	$4\pi M_S$ [G]
8	4	1	1,300	90
4	2	0.5	5,100	180
2	1	0.25	20,000	360
1	0.5	0.12	82,000	720
0.5	0.25	0.062	330,000	1400

Table 2. Some examples of magnetic bubble materials

Material	d [μm]	l [μm]	$4\pi M_S$ [G]	Q	Ref.
$Y_{1.5}Sm_{0.3}Lu_{0.3}Ca_{0.9}Fe_{4.1}Ge_{0.9}O_{12}$	5	0.54	200–240	5	[24]
$Sm_{0.85}Tm_{2.15}Fe_5O_{12}$	0.6	0.047	1378	2.52	[25]

4. The principle of the magnetic bubble memory ; individual device elements

The structure of a magnetic bubble domain memory device is given in Fig. 3 [26]. The memory is organized on the "major loop" — "minor loop" principle. In this organization the data are transferred from the minor loop to the major loop when a command is sent to the transfer gate. The device includes a bubble generator, a bubble annihilator and a sensor, together with "write" and "erase" gates.

Various methods are used to transfer magnetic bubbles in the minor and major loops. The inhomogeneous fields needed for transfer can be generated by small soft-magnetic layers (usually of Permalloy), which are vapour-deposited on the bubble plate and are magnetized by an external drive field in the plane of the layers (field access). The bubble then moves in the direction in which the bias field is lowered by the soft-magnetic structure. The pattern of the soft-magnetic layers and the direction of the external drive field then determine the path of the magnetic bubbles. In all cases a *rotating* external drive field is used to mgagnetize the soft-magnetic layers. The inhomogeneous fields can also be excited by electrical currents in a pattern of conductors (gold) vapour-deposited on the bubble plate (current access).

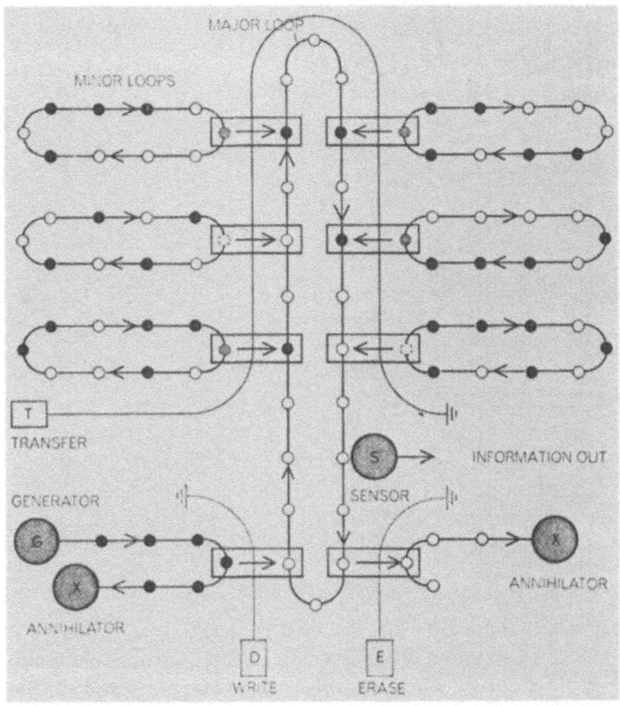

Fig. 3. Structure of a bubble domain memory device (Bobeck and Scovil [26]).

A method of rotating field drive is illustrated in Fig. 4. This is known as the "T-bar" structure [27]. The period of the T-bars must be at least eight times the radius of the magnetic bubbles in order to keep the interaction between individual bubbles negligible. The gap between the T's and I's must not be much larger than a half radius, because if the gaps are larger the attractive force of the positive poles (see Fig. 4) can no longer be experienced by the bubble. Since the attractive force becomes greater when the positive pole strength is higher the permalloy structure stabilizes the bubble even above the collapse field of the free bubbles. However, if the distance to the positive pole is made too large, the external field must be adjusted to below the collapse field of the free bubble to avoid the bubbles collapsing in the gap. The smallest gap that can be made with photolithographic methods is 1 μm. This means that 4 μm magnetic bubbles can be used in these structures.

209

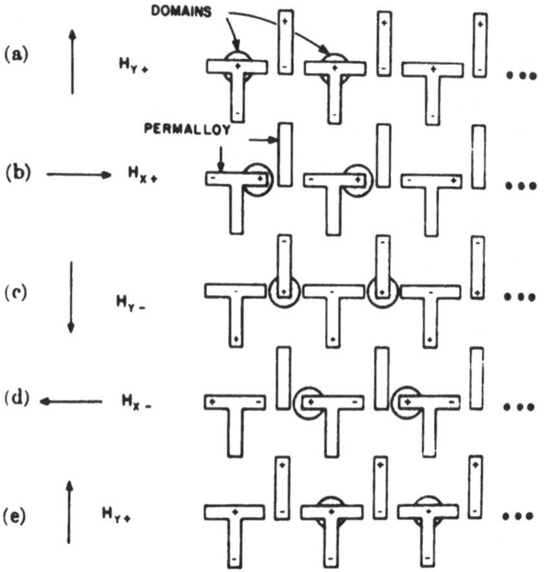

Fig. 4. Rotating field drive of magnetic bubbles in T-bars. The rotating field (drive field) is denoted by H_{y+}, H_{x+}, H_{y-} and H_{x-}. The position of the magnetic bubble domain is indicated for each direction of the drive field. At the places where a positive pole appears the external field (bias field) is lowered. (Perneski [27]).

The development of magnetic bubble memories is aimed at making the diameter of the bubble small in order to achieve a high packing density (chip density) and at the same time to widen the working range of the external field, i.e. give it a wider margin. To this end various transfer structures have been developed. Some new structures are given in Fig. 5 [28—30]. The structures are called 'half discs'. The ratio between period and gap is 8:1 and not 16:1 as with T-bars. The great advantage of this structure is that the gap is easier to pass (see Fig. 5a) than in a T-bar structure and that higher packing densities can be achieved. Fig. 6 compares the margins of various structures [30]. The structure using half discs proves to be the best.

An example of a magnetic bubble generator is given in Fig. 7 [27]. It is a *passive* generator that operates when the drive field is switched on and which generates a bubble during each field period. An *active* generator consists of a current loop. The field polarity in the loop is such that the magnetization in the material is switched over when current flows, i.e. a bubble is then generated.

210

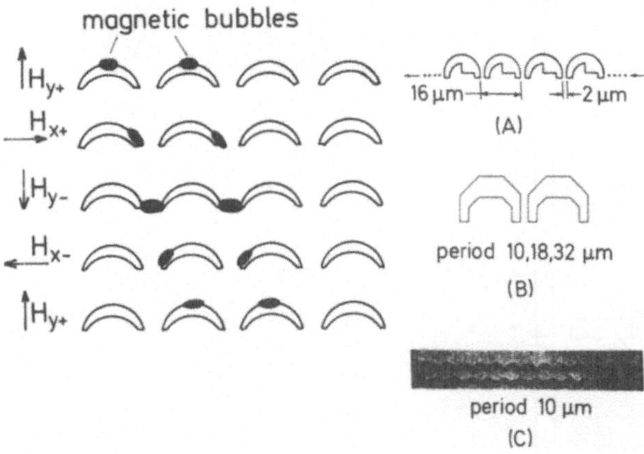

Fig. 5. Rotating field drive of magnetic bubbles with half-disc structures. The position of the magnetic bubbles is indicated for each direction of the drive field. Examples of half-disc structures: (A) (Bonyhard and Smith [28]), (B) (Gergis, George and Kobayashi [29], and (C) (Bullock, Shaikh and West Jr. [30]).

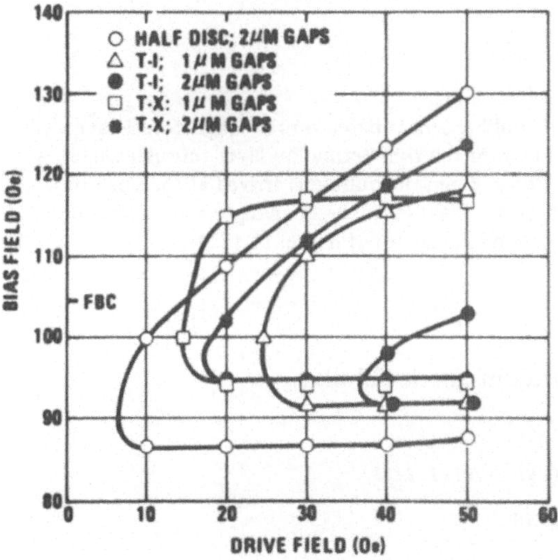

Fig. 6

Margins of the external field (bias field) as a function of the rotating field (drive field) for various transfer structures. FBC is the value of the collapse field for isolated bubbles (free bubble collapse). (Bullock, Shaikh and West Jr. [30]).

Nearly all bubble domain memory devices use the magneto-resistance effect in the sensor [31]. This effect is based on the influence of the direction of magnetization on the resistance in ferromagnetic conductors. Permalloy is usually employed. The sensor (see Fig. 8) is incorporated in the major loop as illustrated.

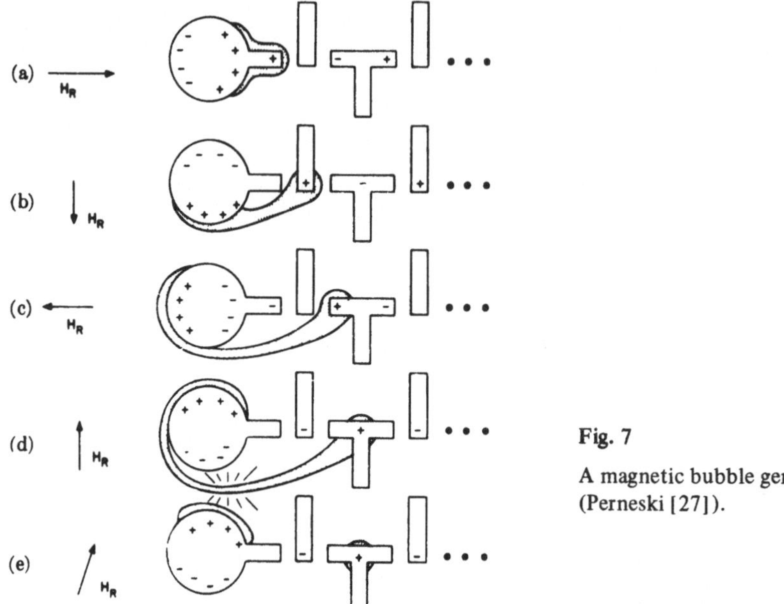

Fig. 7

A magnetic bubble generator
(Perneski [27]).

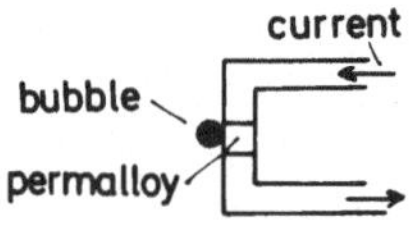

Fig. 8

A magnetic bubble sensor based on the magnetoresistance
effect. The sensor is a thin permalloy layer through which
a current flows. When the bubble is arrived at the position
of the sensor, the field in the layer changes and so too does
the resistance of the layer (Almasi et al. [31]).

Gates are provided (see Fig. 3) to transfer magnetic bubbles:

- from generator to major loop,
- from minor loop to major loop and vice versa, and
- from the major loop to the annihilator.

Use is also often made of gates for reproduction (replication). Several versions are
found. Fig. 9a represents a structure that replicates and transfers bubbles ("replicate/
transfer out" gate). The structure comprises a current circuit. The electrical currents
are shown in Fig. 9b as a function of the direction of the drive field. The structure in
Fig. 9a was incorporated in a magnetic bubble memory with separate major loops for
the read and write functions [28].

212

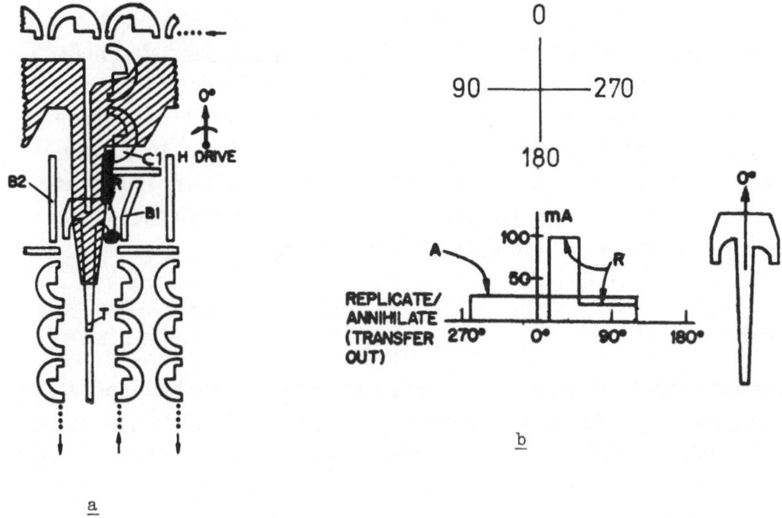

Fig. 9. Replicate/transfer out gate. The position of the magnetic bubble with the drive field in the direction 270° is denoted (●) in *a*. The transfer function can be explained as follows. When the drive field rotates to 0°, the bubble tends to move upwards, but its movement is hindered by the field of the current circuit, which has the effect of lowering the field outside the circuit. This field causes the bubble to undergo elongation (l). When the drive field rotates further towards 90°, the bubble shifts further upwards (lower edge of C1) and at 270° the bubble is in the middle of disc C1. The position 0° in the replication stage localizes the slightly elongated bubble upwards at R. A stronger current is then switched on, which divides the bubble into two parts. At the position 90° a bubble is found at each side of the current circuit, and both are jointly transferred to the 180° position. A 90° bend is illustrated at the top of fig. 9a. (Bonyhard and Smith [28]).

5. 'Bubble lattice files'

In the T-bar and half-disc structure the period is at least eight times greater than the radius of the magnetic bubbles, in order to keep the interaction between individual bubbles negligible. In a 'bubble lattice file' (BLF) [32] the magnetic bubbles are arranged in a hexagonal lattice [33] with a lattice constant which is about three times greater than the radius of the magnetic bubble. Each bubble may represent a zero or one. The smallest dimension of the elements in a BLF is about half a lattice constant. As a consequence the packing density of a BLF is about 10–20 time higher than that of a T-bar structure (assuming equal photolithographic methods). In principle the margin in the bias field is also higher in a BLF than in a T-bar structure, since the bubbles in the lattice are more stable than a free bubble.

The two types "0" and "1" of magnetic bubbles in a BLF are different in domain wall structure [34]. In what is termed the $S = 1$ magnetic bubble [34] the orientation of the magnetic moments in the wall does not change in the direction along the wall. In the S = 0 bubble, on the other hand [34], two Bloch lines are found that may be represented as rotations in the domain wall. The S = 0 and S = 1 bubbles behave different in an inhomogeneous field: the two different bubbles are seen to move in different directions, making it possible to discriminate between them. In the same field the transformation S = 0 ⟷ S = 1 can be made [34]. A uniform field in the plane of the plates is then necessary. The technology of bubble lattice files shows much promise, but is at present still in the experimental stage.

6. Conclusion

Research is currently concentrated on the materials for magnetic bubble applications, on domain propagation velocity, packing density and the technological realization of the structures. Considerable progress has been made in each area. As a result of these efforts several firms have developed 64 kbit chips, and a few have even come out with 250 kbit chips. Bubble propagation velocities result generally in bit rates of the order of 100 kHz, but bit rates up to 450 kHz have also been achieved. The prospects of a substantial further increase are good.

References

[1] *C. Kooy* and *U. Enz,* Philips Res. Repts. **15**, 7 (1960).

[2] *A. H. Bobeck,* Bell System Techn. J. **46**, 1901 (1967).

[3] *A. B. Smith,* "Bubble domain memory devices" (Artech House, Inc. Dedham, 1974).

[4] *T. H. O'Dell,* "Magnetic Bubbles" (The Macmillan Press Ltd. London, 1974).

[5] *A. H. Bobeck* and *E. Della Torre,* "Magnetic Bubbles" (North-Holland Publishing Company, Amsterdam, 1975).

[6] *H. Chang,* "Magnetic Bubble Technology: Integrated Circuit Magnetics for Digital Storage and Processings" (IEEE Press, The Institute of Electrical and Electronics Engineers, Inc. New York, 1975).

[7] *A. A. Thiele,* J. Appl. Phys. **41**, 1139 (1970).

[8] *J. W. Nielsen,* IEEE Trans. Magn. **MAG-12,** 327 (1976).

[9] *A. A. Thiele,* Bell System Techn. J. **50,** 727 (1971).

[10] *F. B. Hagedorn,* AIP Conf. Proc. **5,** 72 (1972).

[11] *B. A. Calhoun, E. A. Giess* and *L. L. Rosier,* Appl. Phys. Lett. **18,** 287 (1971).

[12] *A. P. Malozemoff* and *J. C. DeLuca,* Appl. Phys. Lett. **26,** 719 (1975).

[13] *G. P. Vella-Coleiro,* J. Appl. Phys. **47,** 3278 (1976).

[14] *J. C. Slonczewski,* J. Appl. Phys. **44,** 1759 (1973).

[15] *R. C. LeCraw, S. L. Blank* and *G. P. Vella-Coleiro,* Appl. Phys. Lett. **26,** 402 (1975).

[16] *F. H. de Leeuw*, IEEE Trans. Magn. **MAG-9**, 614 (1973).

[17] *F. H. de Leeuw* and *J. M. Robertson*, J. Appl. Phys. **46**, 3182 (1975).

[18] *J. C. DeLuca* and *A. P. Malozemoff*, AIP Conf. Proc. **34**, 151 (1976).

[19] *W. T. Stacy*, *H. Logmans* and *A. B. Voermans*, Appl. Phys. Lett. **29**, 817 (1976).

[20] *F. H. de Leeuw*, *R. van den Doel* and *J. M. Robertson*, J. Appl. Phys., Jan. (1978).

[21] *F. H. de Leeuw*, Physica **86−88B**, 1320 (1977).

[22] *A. H. Bobeck*, *E. G. Spencer*, *L. G. Van Uitert*, *S. C. Abrahams*, *R. L. Barns*, *W. H. Grodkiewicz*, *R. C. Sherwood*, *P. H. Schmidt*, *D. H. Smith* and *E. M. Walters*, Appl. Phys. Lett. **17**, 131 (1970).

[23] *S. L. Blank*, *J. W. Nielsen* and *W. A. Biolsi*, J. Electrochem. Soc. **123**, 856 (1976).

[24] *G. G. Summer* and *W. R. Cox*, AIP Conf. Proc. **34**, 157 (1976).

[25] *K. Yamaguchi*, *H. Inoue* and *K. Asama*, AIP Conf. Proc. **34**, 160 (1976).

[26] *A. H. Bobeck* and *H. E. D. Scovil*, Scientific American, **224**, June 1971.

[27] *A. J. Perneski*, IEEE Trans. Magn. **MAG-5**, 554 (1969).

[28] *P. I. Bonyhard* and *J. L. Smith*, IEEE Trans. Magn. **MAG-12**, 614 (1976).

[29] *I. S. Gergis*, *P. K. George* and *T. Kobayashi*, IEEE Trans. Magn. **MAG-12**, 651 (1976).

[30] *D. C. Bullock*, *M. S. Shaikh* and *F. G. West*, Jr. IEEE Trans. Magn. **MAG-12**, 654 (1976).

[31] *G. S. Almasi*, *G. E. Keege*, *Y. S. Lin* and *D. A. Thompson*, J. Appl. Phys. **42**, 1268 (1971).

[32] *O. Voegeli*, *B. A. Calhoun*, *L. L. Rosier* and *J. C. Slonczewski*, AIP Conf. Proc. **24**, 617 (1975).

[33] *W. F. Druyvesteyn* and *J. W. F. Dorleyn*, Philips Res. Repts. **26**, 11 (1971).

[34] *T. L. Hsu*, AIP Conf. Proc. **24**, 624 (1975).

Application of Magnetic Bubbles to Information Storage

W. Metzdorf

Siemens AG, Munich, Germany

1. Introduction

In the preceding papers a comprehensive overview was given both on the mass storage
of data in electromechanical memories of serial nature and on the random access
storage of information in large scale integrated main memories with short access
time. The magnetic bubble memory has to be classified in between these two groups
of memories. On the one hand it is a serial memory for considerable amounts of data
and on the other hand it is an integrated circuit memory with a degree of integration,
which is presently four times as large as obtained with semiconductor memories. Today the magnetic bubble memory is moving out of the research laboratories to the
development of engineering models. Several companies have installed pilot lines in
order to study fabrication and yield problems and to provide samples for various in-
house and external applications.

In the preceding paper [1] the properties of magnetic bubbles and of the magnetic
films in which they can exist were described; also the principles of bubble propagation and the organization of a memory chip are explained there. This paper is
devoted to the application of magnetic bubbles to data storage.

2. The Bubble Memory Chip

2.1. Chip Layout

The elements of bubble memories are chips cut from single crystal wafers, similar to
the chips of semiconductor memories, however, prepared from different materials,
namely garnets. The wafer diameter is $2''$ today. The bubble memory chips consists
of a number of functional elements [2–9] (Fig. 1). The largest amount of the real
estate of the chip is covered by the storage loops, which are cyclic shift registers
formed by fine Permalloy structures on the surface of the garnet storage film. The
Permalloy pattern activated by a rotating magnetic in-plane field, produces a magnetic field gradient moving along the ends of the bars. This field gradient shifts the
bubbles. In Fig. 2 three representative propagation structures are shown: T-bar,
X-bar and C-bar or half moon structures. No electrical conductors are necessary to

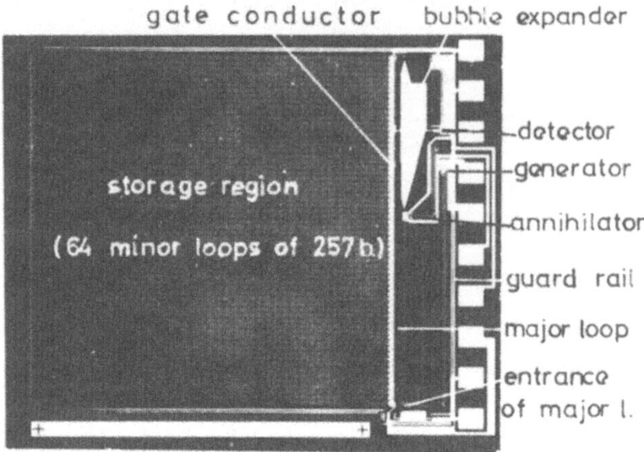

Fig. 1. Photograph of a 16 kbit bubble memory chip having X-bar propagation patterns (see Fig. 2) and major-minor loop organization (see Fig. 5 b).

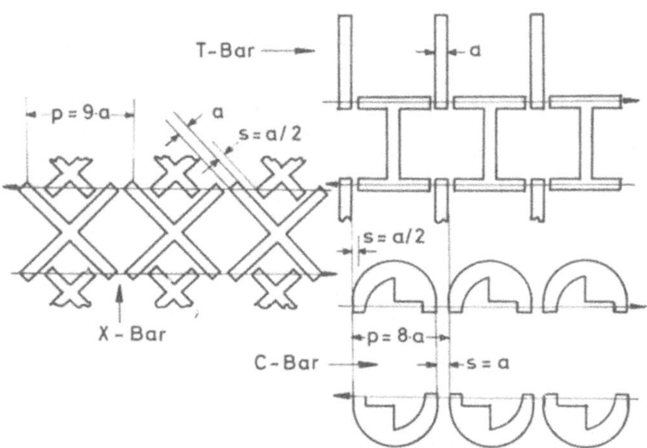

Fig. 2. Propagation patterns for bubble memories. The period of the pattern must always be at least four bubble diameters. The minimum length of a period is determined by the minimum gap width obtained with the applied technology of delineation.

shift the bubbles along their way. Most of the other functional elements, however, are controlled by current pulses and need therefore electrical conductors below their Permalloy structure. Every chip must have at least one bubble generator, one bubble annihilator and one bubble detector. Obviously the structure and the properties of

218

all functional elements have to be carefully adapted to the propagation structure. In Fig. 3 photographs of a bubble generator, a bubble annihilator and a bubble detector adapted to an X-bar propagation structure are shown.

As it is true for most of the present chips, a hair-pin-like conductor loop is used for bubble generation [3]. A short current pulse of about 200 mA is applied through this loop in a correct phase relationship to the rotating magnetic in-plane field. A bubble is nucleated at the ends of the Permalloy bars crossing the conductor by a locally confined reversal of the magnetization direction within the garnet film. This bubble is moved at once to the ends of the neighbouring Permalloy bars and so on.

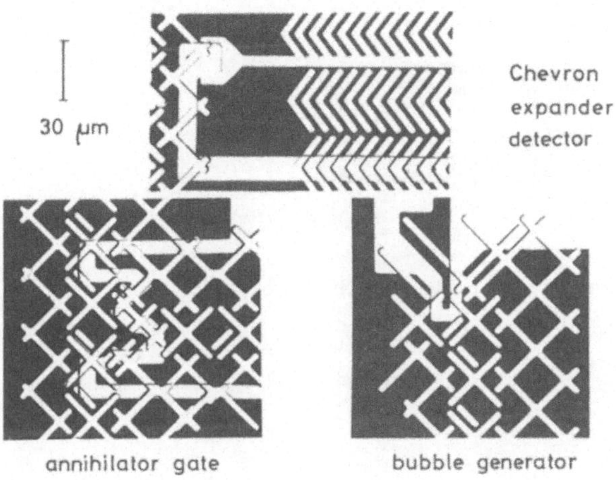

Fig. 3. Sections of the bubble memory chip of Fig. 1 showing several functional elements.

For bubble detection, the magnetoresistive effect in a small stripe of Permalloy is used [1]. Because a single bubble would generate too small a signal, the bubbles approaching the detector strip are gradually stretched in parallel to this strip by columns of so-called Chevron elements [4] (see Fig. 3 upper half) made also from Permalloy and mostly integrated into the Permalloy pattern [8]. The expansion of the bubble and thereby the magnitude of the output signal are only restricted by the amount of chip area which is necessary to perform the stretching. In Fig. 4 a sequence of "1" and "0"-signals can be seen. Obviously the magnitude and the signal-to-noise ratio are sufficient for a subsequent amplification to a 5 V logic level. As it is demonstrated in the left half of the figure, the signal amplitude may be influenced by the current sent through the magnetoresistive strip.

More complex bubble memory chips in addition contain transfer and replication elements which allow the current controlled transfer of bubbles from the storage or minor loops to one or more major loops and vice versa. A transfer element suited for X-bar propagation structures is shown in the lower left part of Fig. 4.

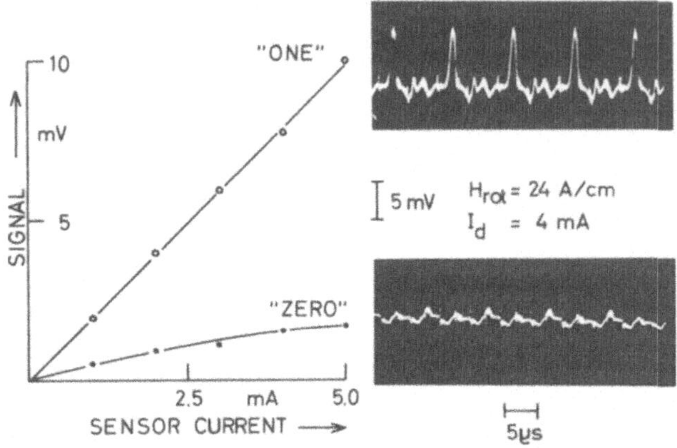

Fig. 4. 100 kHz sense signals produced by 6 μm bubbles in a chevron expander detector, 280 μm in length.

2.2. Chip Organization

The magnetic bubble memory is a shift register memory and therefore of serial nature. It is however possible to operate this memory partially in parallel. Three different kinds of organization have to be distinguished.

2.2.1. The Pure Serial Organization

In this type of bubble memory the information is stored in a single cyclic shift register (Fig. 5a). The corresponding chip structure is the most simple one, but the associated access time is rather long. Most of the samples available today have this type of organization [10–13].

2.2.2. The Major/Minor Loop Organization

In its simplest form a chip organized in this way has one major loop and a large number of minor loops, which are as long as the major loop [10–13] (Fig. 5b). For a chip capacity of N bit, the chip has $\frac{\sqrt{N}}{2}$ minor loops with $2\sqrt{N}$ bit each, if re-

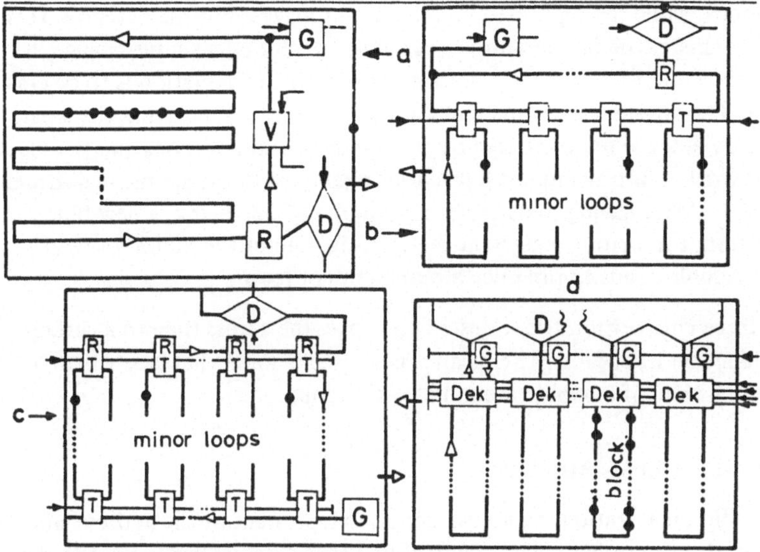

Fig. 5. Different kinds of organization of a bubble memory chip

a) Pure serial organization;
b) Simple major/minor loop organization;
c) Major/minor loop organization using replicate transfer gates and separated read and write shift registers instead of a major loop;
d) Decoder addressable chip.

G – bubble generator; V – annihilator; D – detector; R – replicate gate; T – transfer gate; R/T – replicate/transfer gate; Dek – bubble decoder. Black dots represent the position of a block of data.

dundancies and additional memory places for geometrical reasons are neglected. By a current pulse through the gate conductor, one bubble can be transferred concurrently from every minor loop to the major loop and vice versa. For geometrical reasons, only every second bit position in the major loop is occupied by a bubble after one transfer operation. Therefore, the first current pulse is often followed by a second one after one revolution period of the rotating field, in order to fill all possible bubble positions of the major loop with information. From this it may be concluded that $\sqrt{N}$ blocks of information with $\sqrt{N}$ bit each can be stored in one bubble memory chip with major/minor loop organization.

There are some modifications of this simple major/minor loop organization, the most important of which is shown in Fig. 5 c. The closed major loop is split here into two separate linear shift registers for reading and writing. Each bubble of a block of information to be read only, is replicated by a current pulse through the gate conductor and transferred into the reading loops [6, 15, 16]. Thus the information remains in the minor loops, while the replicated bubbles are propagated to the detector. It is also possible to transfer the bubbles into the reading register by a simple change in the amplitude and timing of the gate pulses, if the block of information is to be erased after reading it. The advantages of this kind of chip organization are, that the length of an information block is not restricted by the number of minor loops and the block needs not be rewritten into the minor loops after reading as in the simple major/minor loop organization. After having transferred the bubbles of one block, a new block can be transferred from the writing register at the opposite end of the minor loops after half the time a bubble needs to run once around a minor loop.

For all of the three chip organizations described above, the access time to a certain block is dependent on its address. The mean access time is somewhat larger than half of the propagation time of a bubble around a minor loop.

2.2.3. The Decoder-Addressable Chip

In this kind of chip organization the access time is independent of the address and about one order of magnitude smaller than for the other organizations [17, 18]. The decoder addressable chip (Fig. 5 d) has also parallel storage loops, but now one block is no longer distributed along all minor loops but stored in one loop. The block of interest is selected by addressing the corresponding transfer element or replicator – called decoder – which connects the storage loop to the detector or its corresponding bubble generator, respectively. All bubble generators are connected in series and produce bubbles at the same time, but only the bubbles produced by the generator associated with the selected loop can send its bubbles into this loop. The Chevron stretcher detector has as many entrances as there are memory loops.

The disadvantage of the decoder addressable chip is the complex structure of the decoders. Therefore, it is not used very much so far.

2.3. Properties of the Memory Chips

2.3.1. Maximum Shift Rate

Contrary to the charge transfer memories, the shift rate in a bubble memory may be adapted to a particular application between very low values and an upper limit f_{max}. The data rate is directly proportional to the shift rate. The maximum shift rate depends on the properties of the garnet film (wall mobility, saturation velocity), but also on the layout of the Permalloy pattern [19]. The Permalloy bars produce a non-uniform field gradient and the bubbles move therefore with different velocities at different parts of a pattern period [20]. The smallest field gradient along a period determines f_{max}. If the gradient is too high, the bubble exceeds a critical velocity above which reversible changes in its wall structure occur which in turn may be detrimental for the further propagation. Therefore, the propagation pattern should produce a field gradient as uniform as possible.

Most of the bubble memory chips which were reported in the literature are developed for a propagation frequency of 100 kbit/s. Samples of complete chips with shift rates of 300 and even 500 kbit/s were mentioned [14, 16, 21]. Researchers succeeded to propagate bubbles straight forward with a shift rate of 2 Mbit/s [22]. It may be assumed that chips allowing a propagation speed of 1 Mbit/s will be available in the next few years. Because the length of the storage loops is expected to grow with further development, this increase in shift rate is especially desirable, to reduce the corresponding increase in access time.

2.3.2. Bias Field Operating Margins

The small bias field range is a critical factor, when the practicability of bubble memories is evaluated. The theoretical limits are about $\pm 10\%$. Practically more than $\pm 4\%$ were obtained. Indeed the theoretical limt was approached very closely for single functional elements of a chip. The chip, however, consists of a number of different elements, the bias margins of which are not congruent. Undoubtedly the lowest upper bias margin and the highest lower one of any element of the chip determine the overall bias margins, which depend obviously on the careful mutual adjustment of all functional elements. The importance of the permissible bias field region results from the fact, that it determines the tolerable variations in the properties of the garnet film and the tolerable external stray fields, as well.

Principally the optimum bias field is also strongly dependent on the chip temperature. A certain temperature compensation was however possible by the development of garnet films, the mean bias field of which displays about the same temperature dependence as some Ba-ferrite permanent magnets, which are used to produce the bias field. In the literature an operating temperature range of $0°$ to $70°$ was reported and the stored information was found to be not altered in the range between $-40°$ and $+85\,°C$ [15]. Further improvements seem probable in this field.

2.3.3. Range of the Rotating Field Intensity

The bias field margins do not only depend on the overlay and the type of the garnet film, but also on the magnitude of the in-plane rotating field, which causes bubble propagation. Fig. 6 a and b show the dependence of the bias field margins on the magnitude of the rotating field for X-bar and C-bar patterns. From these figures it can be concluded, that below a certain amplitude of the rotating field no memory operation is possible at all. Furthermore the bias field range increases with increasing intensity of the rotating field, sometimes until it reaches saturation. The upper limit

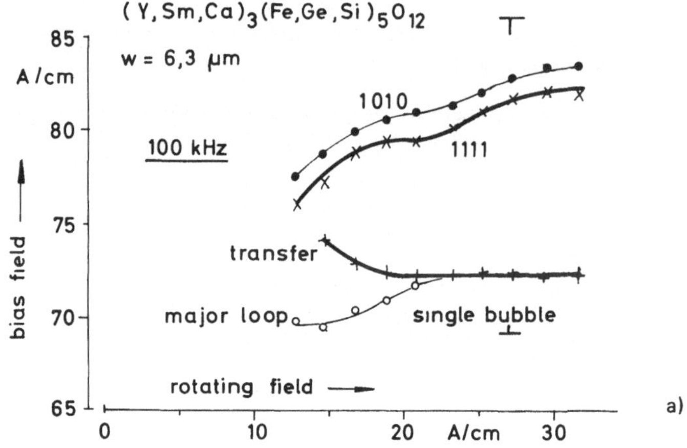

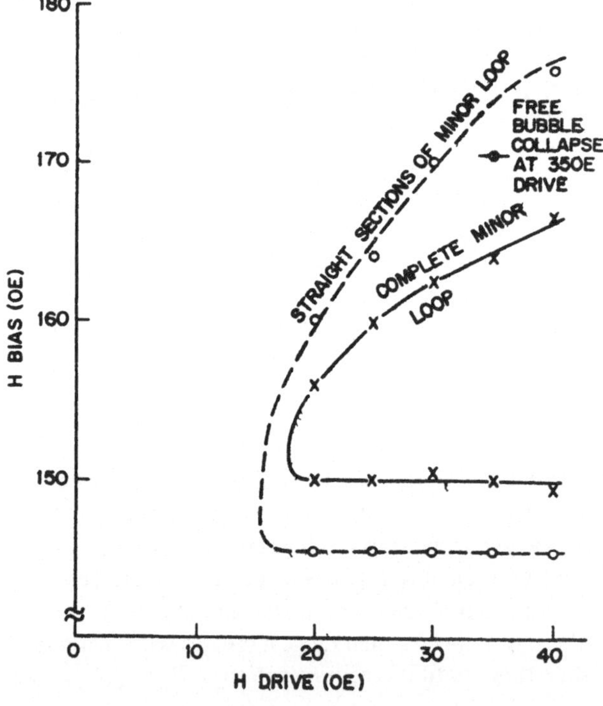

Fig. 6
Operating margins of the magnetic fields used in a bubble memory

a) Overall margins of a 16 kbit X-bar chip measured at 100 kHz shift rate using the most critical patterns of information in either case (indicated in the figure). The horizontal bars at 27 A/cm indicate the bias margins measured at the straight sections of the minor loop.

b) Margins of minor loops formed by a half moon pattern according to [6].

224

of the rotating field – not seen in the figure – is determined by the reduction in the output signal and by the nucleation of unwanted additional bubbles at the ends of the Permalloy bars. The lower margins of the rotating field are influenced by the coercivities of the garnet film, the Permalloy film and by the frequency of rotation. The lowest permissable rotating field is growing with increasing shift rate of the bubbles [5, 21]. This effect is often connected with a reduction in the tolerable bias range, especially by a reduction of the upper bias limit.

2.3.4. Reliability

High reliability, which exceeds that obtained with disk memories, is a key prerequisite for the success of bubble memories. The requirements of low bit-error rate increase with a growing degree of integration on the chip. According to the literature [25] hard errors were detected first after 10^{14} propagation steps and soft errors after 10^{12} steps. The sources of hard errors are for example statistical annihilation or nucleation of bubbles during their propagation, start/stop effects and environmental influences as, e.g., ambient temperature, external stray fields and mechanical shocks. Hard errors are reduced by a low defect density in the garnet film and in the overlay, a sufficient distance of the operation bias field from its margins and by avoiding critical bubble velocities. Measurements of the dependence of the bias field margins on the number of propagation steps allow to estimate the hard error probability.

3. Bubble Memory Modules

Contrary to semiconductor memories, bubble memories need additionally two magnetic fields namely the in-plane rotating field and the perpendicular bias field and also magnetic shielding, what is often regarded as a disadvantage. This disadvantage is the less important, the more chips are located within a field generating system, which we call the bubble memory module. The rather narrow tolerances of the bias field limits the number of chips in a module, especially in the period of introduction of that new product into the market. During this time, it is both difficult to classify chips from a high volume production into groups with narrow bias field tolerances and to keep the yield of closely tolerated chips high enough, due to a lack of fabrication experience. Probably for this reason most of the samples described today are single chip modules. The higher per-bit-costs of these single chip modules may be compensated by a high degree of integration of the corresponding electronic circuits. This way was chosen at least by one company [15].

The non-volatility of information is a main advantage of bubble memories. For this reason the bias field must be maintained, when the memory is switched off. There is an inevitable need for a permanent magnet bias field and a good magnetic shielding

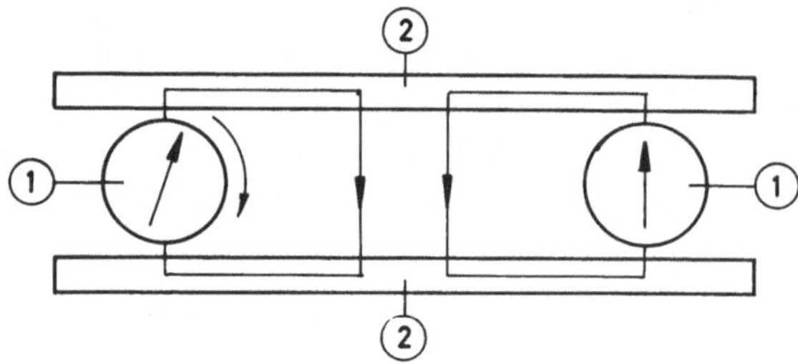

Fig. 7. Principal arrangement for the generation of an adjustable bias field 1 Permanent magnets (Ba-ferrite): 2 soft magnetic yokes.

of every module. Magnet systems of the Walker type are used mostly. An example in which the bias field can be easily vernier tuned is shown in a sketch in Fig. 7. A homogeneity of the bias field of ± 0.5 % was obtained with this arrangement.

The generation of the rotating field is much more difficult than that of the bias field. Not only optimized coil systems but also special electronic circuits for the drive field generation had to be developed. In a memory system consisting of many modules it is advantageous for energy saving reasons to have always only the coil system of the addressed module activated. After corresponding changes of the address, it must be possible to switch off the rotating field rapidly in one module and to set it up quickly in the next one. The intensity of the rotating fields used today in 100 kbit/s-modules is already rather high (e.g., 25 A/cm) and must be increased if one will use smaller bubbles and higher shift rates [27]. The rotating field consumes most of the total power needed by a bubble memory and is the main source for temperature increase in the memory module. It restricts, therefore, also the permissable ambient temperature. The rotating field is generated by a pair of flat coils, the axes of which form a right angle to each other. A sinusoidal or triangular current is sent through each coil with an exactly $90°$ phase shift between the two coils. The field vector is drawing a circle or a rhombus, respectively, in a polar diagram. Typical electrical circuits for the field generation are shown in Fig. 8 a and b. The energy necessary to build up the field and for the damping compensation is drawn from a DC-source in both cases. Resonant circuits in series to a RC-network are used in order to produce a sinusoidal current (Fig. 8 a). Large pulses to the basis of a switching transistor switch the field on and off, and a sequence of small pulses to a second transistor serves for the compensation of the coil losses. The current flowing through the switching transistor is reduced by the quality factor Q of the resonant circuit as compared to the current flowing through the coil [28]. The disadvantage of different pulses for start, stop and run and the tuning to a fixed frequency of the circuit shown in Fig. 8 a are avoided by the circuit of Fig. 8 b for the generation of a triangular shaped current. In this case the rotating field is present as long as trigger pulses are applied to the transistors. The amplitude of these

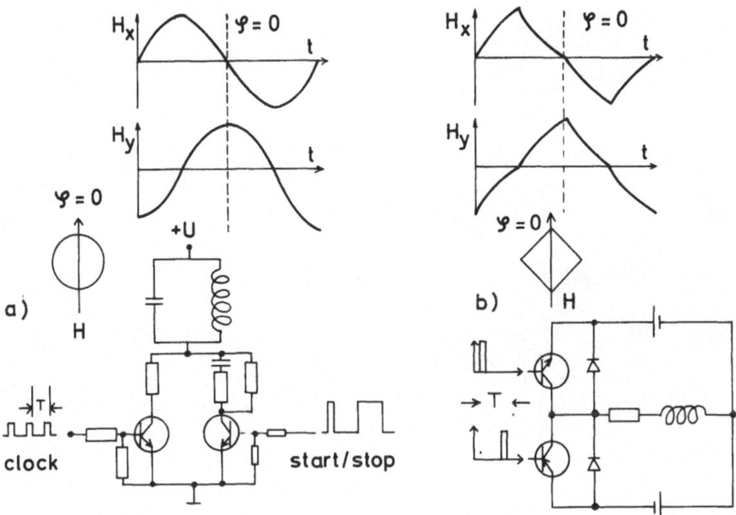

Fig. 8. Methods of rotating field generation

a) Sinusoidal current in a resonant circuit started, stopped and maintained by current pulses of different height and width [28].

b) Triangular current kept flowing by a sequence of pulses of equal width and height [29].

pulses must be of the same order of magnitude as the start/stop pulses in Fig. 8a and the switching transistors must sustain the full coil current. The coil losses are by one third less in the case of triangular shaped current. No significant differences in the operation margins were observed for both kinds of coil currents [29].

Two different arrangements of memory chips and coils are used. Either the coil system is wound around the substrate carrying the chips (Fig. 9a and [46]) or the pre-fabricated coil system is placed closely in front of a copper sheet with the memory chip in between (Fig. 9b and [30]). As a consequence of rf-mirror effects the maximum field is produced in between the coils and the copper sheet. The advantage of the second arrangement is easier assembly of the memory module. Increased attention has to be devoted to the field homogeneity, however. The necessity of magnetic fields make it impossible to house bubble memory chips in conventional dual-in-line packages and more complex constructions have to be chosen [13,15,31, 32].

An additional problem of the bubble memory module construction is to avoid un-wanted signals induced into the output leads by the rotating field, which tend to limit the shift rate. To minimize this inductive noise, the output leads must run as exactly as possible in the plane of the rotating field, the area surrounded by them must be minimized and compensation loops have to be added.

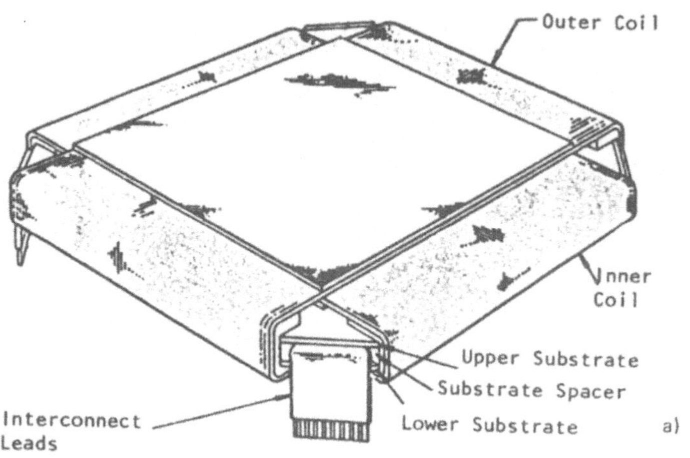

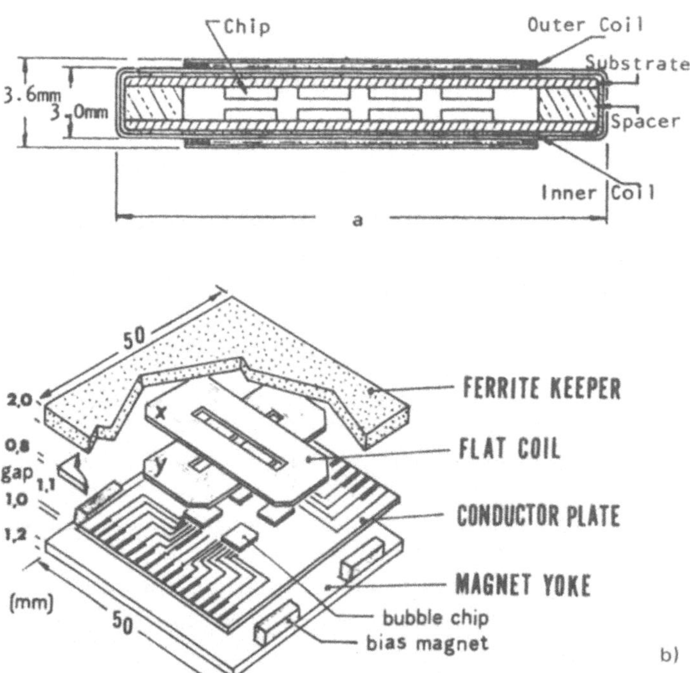

Fig. 9. Arrangement of the chips with respect to the drive field coils

a) Coils wound around the boards wearing the chips [25].

b) Chips placed in between the coils and an ample conductor plate [30].

4. Bubble Memory Systems

Generally, bubble memories are organized in such a way that as many chips are run
in parallel as a memory word has bits, e.g. 8 to 36 (Fig. 10 and [16]). The transfer
and annihilation conductors of the chips, in which a word is stored, are connected in
series. In order to assure that all bits of a word are shifted synchronously, the corresponding chips should be mounted in the same memory module [10, 12, 25]. This
could not be realized in all cases today [13, 15]

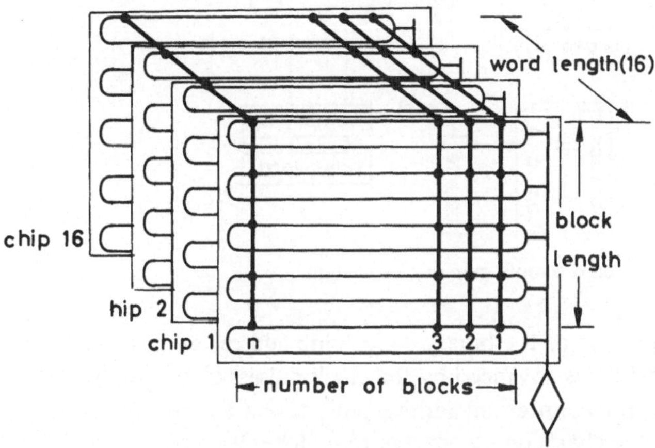

Fig. 10. Bit-parallel organization of a bubble memory module.

In view of the relatively small output signals delivered by the memory modules,
it is useful to place the signal amplifiers closely to the module. Usually they are
mounted on the same printed circuit board together with the memory module and
the drivers for the coils, the bubble generators and the magnetoresitive detectors
[13–15]. Thus one obtains a memory board. The whole memory is controlled by a
clock generator, which delivers pulses with a repetition rate corresponding to the
desired shift rate. The clock generator controls the drive field and also the memory
controller. The latter receives commands like e.g. "read", "write", "erase" and the
address from the overall system and converts them into trigger pulses for the drivers
and other components of the memory.

The principal organization of a bubble memory consisting of one memory board with
one magnetic module containing 8 chips is shown for example in Fig. 11. The chips
have major/minor loop organization. The memory board contains the drivers, the
sense amplifiers, a clock generator, a control and an address unit. In order to be able
to address the memory, a characteristic password is stored in every chip and is
shifted synchronously together with the stored information [6, 14, 15]. The address-

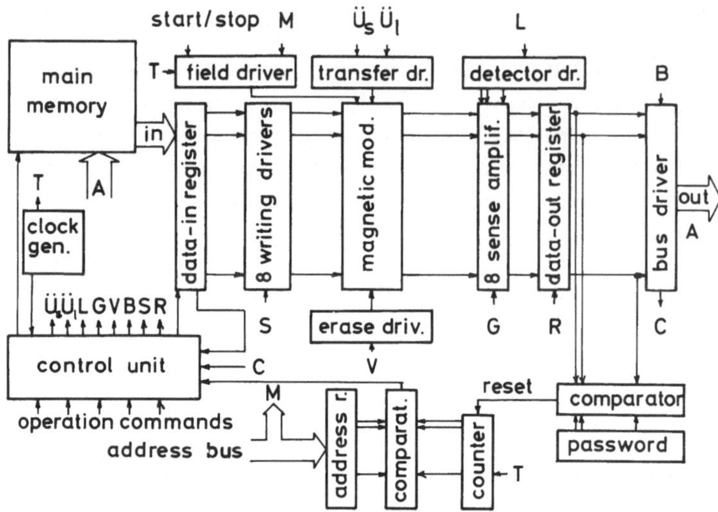

Fig. 11. Block diagram of a one-board bubble memory subsystem.

ing is performed by a comparison of the binary coded chip address with the current status of a binary counter which is advanced by the clock pulses. If the address coincides with the status of the counter, an address pulse is sent to the control unit. The counter is reset, when the characteristic password matches with the stored password.

Clock generator, control unit and the address registers may eventually be shared by more than one memory board. In this case, the address must also comprise the module address. The module address is used to start the rotating field driver as it is indicated in Fig. 11 by arrows designated by M. Thus a complete bubble memory subsystem is obtained containing a number of memory boards and a control board, as it is indicated in Fig. 12. Several subsystems or plug-ins form a large memory system, which is controlled by a master controller. A main task of this controller is error detection and correction and the control of the data transfer and distribution between the main and the bubble memory or even between the bubble memory and a larger capacity disk or tape storage system.

Often programmable read-only memories (PROMs) are used in the control unit [14, 15]. They allow to deactivate defective storage loops during memory operation. Thus chips with some defective loops may still be used, if some redundant loops are placed additionally on the chip. This leads to a distinctly higher chip yield. The reduction of fabrication costs accompanied with the increased yield by far offsets the costs for the PROM.

The Table 1 gives an overview on the bubble memory chips, modules and systems being in pilot line production as well as on those being still under development.

230

Table 1. Samples of Bubble Memories at the End of 1976

Company	capacity			word	block	clock	rate	access	redund.	under developm.	
	chip	module	system[+])	word	block	clock	rate	access	redund.	chip	system
	kbit	kByte	kByte	bit	words	kHz	kbit/s	ms	—	kbit	MByte
BELL /	68	32	32	1	var.	48	48	700	yes	262	2
WESTERN	68	32	32	4	128	360	1440	2	yes		
	92	10	40	4	144	100	50	4	yes	256	2
TEXAS I.	131	128	512	8	170	300	2400	1.5	yes	1024	12
	64	128	512	16	128	300	4800	1	no	—	12
ROCKWELL	100	100	100	8	var.	100	100	500	no		
	16	32	32	8	var.	100	100	80	no	256	—
HITACHI	64	64	256	8	128	100	800	5	un-		
						500	4000	1	known		
FUJITSU	80	32	1024	8	256	300–500	2400...4000	1	yes	256	—
PLESSEY	16	32	32	8	var.	100	800	80	no	64	—

[+]) in part yet planned

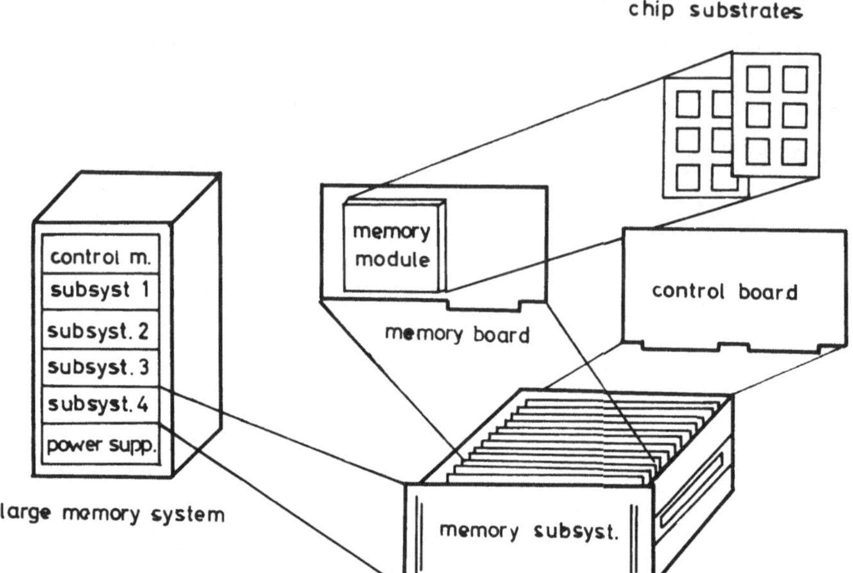

Fig. 12. Formation of a large bubble memory system from its components, i.e. subsystems, memory boards, magnetic modules and chips.

5. Research and Development Trends

The bit density of the bubble memory chips must be increased considerably above the values obtained so far (4000 bit/mm^2). Only then, bubble memories will become cheap enough to compete seriously in the marketplace. Various methods are pursued in order to reach this ambitious target.

1. Scaling down the well known propagation patterns proportionally by new methods of structure generation. This must be accompanied by a proportional reduction of the bubble diameter which seems to be not as difficult as the reduction of the feature size in the overlay. Additionally it is tried to reduce the number of critical photomask steps from now two to one and to find new patterns with fewer and less critical gaps. There are now some promising methods which have a good chance of realization. For example the X-bar structure which needs only one photomask step and the C-bar or half moon structure which has only one gap per period of double size as compared to T- and X-bar. Thus X-bar is especially suited for X-ray projection [34] and the C-bar allows a four fould packing density with a given technology of lithography.

The most promising way of future overlay design for bubble memories seems to be mask fabrication by electron beam writing and X-ray or E-beam projection [35] of

232

the mask on the wafer. Thus it should be possible to obtain reproducibly patterns
with minimum line width of 0.5 μm. This corresponds to a packing density of
16 kbit/mm^2 for the T- and X-bar patterns and even 64 kbit/mm^2 for the half moon
structures.

2. *Contiguous disk structures* are completely gapless propagation patterns [36]. The
disks have a diameter four to five times greater than the bubble diameter (Fig. 13).
Contrary to the bar patterns they are not formed by a Permalloy film, but fabricated
in the garnet film itself by ion implantation. The disks are non-implanted areas in
ion-implanted surroundings. A rotating field is used for the domain propagation.
Advantage is taken of the physical effect, that bubbles prefer sites at the boundary
between an implanted and a non-implanted region [36]. The main advantage of the
contiguous disk pattern is, that the lithographic resolution needed is equal to the
bubble diameter as compared to one quarter bubble diameter for the bar structures
and one half for the half moons. The period of the contiguous disk pattern is equal to
the disk diameter. Because the pattern period must always be at least four bubble
diameters in order to avoid mutual influence between subsequent bubbles, the
contiguous disks would allow a 16-fold packing density as compared to the T- and
X-bars for the same status of fabrication technology. It is possible also to have a
major/minor loop organization with contiguous disks, but so far no methods are
known to fabricate them by only one critical photomask step. Little has been
published on the shift rates obtained with contiguous disks.

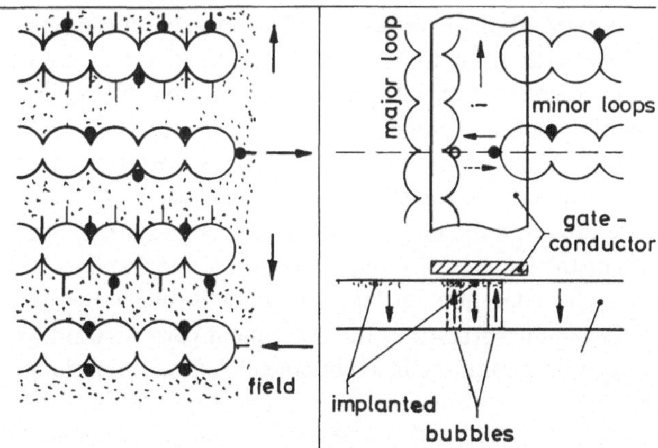

Fig. 13. Contiguous disk propagation pattern for magnetic bubbles [36].
Left side: Bubble propagation along the boundary between the implanted (dotted) area and
the non-implanted disks of a garnet film for different angular positions of the in-plane field.
Right side: Major/minor loop organization using contiguous disks.

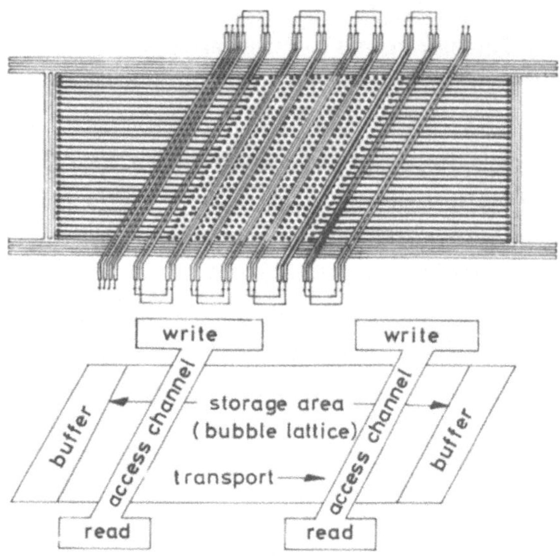

Fig. 14
Bubble lattice file [37]
Upper part: Domain pattern
crossed by meander shaped
conductors.
Lower part: Principal memory
organisation.

3. The bubble lattice file [37] (Fig. 14) is a completely new kind of bubble memory. No longer the existence or the absence of a bubble forms the status of a bit, but the kind of Bloch wall, surrounding the bubble, represents the information. The lattice arrangement of the bubbles is given by their mutual repelling interaction caused by their magnetic stray field. It allows to bring the bubbles closer together because the different types of Bloch walls do not influence the mutual interaction of adjacent bubbles. Their distance may be reduced to twice their diameter. Furthermore no rotating field is necessary to shift the bubbles. In order to process the information the whole lattice is propagated by sending current pulses through electrical conductors running in parallel to the rows of bubbles across the chip in a meander-shaped way (see Fig. 14). The width of the conductors is equal to the bubble diameter, their period many bubble diameters, because a row of bubbles, which is shifted by the field gradient produced by the conductor, pushes the subsequent rows forward by mutual interaction forces. According to the reduced bubble distance, the packing density of the bubble lattice file may be four times that obtainable with the contiguous disks and 64 times as large as that obtainable with T-bars provided the same technology of pattern generation is used.

Fortunately the different wall states give rise to different directions of bubble propagation in a field gradient. Thus they can be discriminated merely ba a proper arrangement of two detector strips.

234

A main problem of the bubble lattice file is the extraction of complete columns of bubbles from the lattice for reading purposes and their replacement by a new column (see Fig. 14 lower part).

Which of the procedures of increasing the packing density described above will succeed finally, cannot be foreseen as yet. The large number of possibilities of increasing the packing density allows the prediction that bubble memory chips of 1 Mbit capacity on about 30 mm^3 of chip area are likely to be developed soon [38]. They will contribute very much to the reduction of fabrication costs. Chips with 256 kbit have already been announced.

6. Comparison to other Storage Systems

6.1. Semiconductor Memories

It may be anticipated already today, that the bubble memory will not compete directly with the semiconductor RAM, because the bubble memory has a serial nature and its mean access time is at least three orders of magnitude longer than that of semiconductor RAMs.

A main competitor to the bubble memory in the marketplace of serial memories are the charge transfer devices, expecially the CCDs [39, 40]. These memories are semiconductor devices and as such not a new technology in contrast to bubbles. They profit from the ample technological and fabrication know-how acquired with integrated MOS circuits. Furthermore the shift rates obtainable with CCDs are about 10 times higher than those of bubbles now and will be probably also in the future. Also, in contrast to bubbles, the clock generator, the sense amplifiers and the address registers can be integrated on the chip. Thus one-chip-versions of CCD memories become economically reasonable, which gives the CCD memory a comparatively higher modularity.

On the other hand the bubble memory has impressive advantages over the CCDs. First of all, the stored information is non-volatile when the power supply is switched off. Moreover, the overlay structure of the bubble chips is simpler and therefore easier to fabricate. It leads to higher packing densities and to fewer photomask steps, namely 1 or 2 for the bubbles as compared to 7 steps for CCD [8, 21]. Higher packing density and less complex overlay fabrication make lower fabrication costs for the bubble memory possible in spite of the higher wafer costs, provided the production volume of bubble memories becomes large enough. The non-volatility gives the bubble memory significant technical advantage over the charge transfer memories in all those applications, where no other non-volatile memory is present in the background and battery operation is too expensive.

6.2. Magnetic Disk Memories

The storage medium of the bubble memory will be always much more expensive
than that used in electromechanical mass storage, e.g., tapes, disks and drums, which
also offer the advantage of non-volatility [41]. This disadvantage has to be offset by
the cost advantages resulting from the non-mechanical nature of the bubble memory.
Obviously this target is reached the better, the smaller the storage capacity is, i.e.,
the larger the share is of the disk or tape drive cost in the overall storage cost. Thus
magnetic bubbles offer the possibility to become economical even with lower capacities as it is possible with electro-mechanical storage systems.

Today there is a widerspread tendency to reduce the costs for small disk storage by
simplifying the disk drive, the disk themselves and the control electronics, however,
at the expense of a considerable loss of reliability and speed. The floppy disk and
the tape cassette are here good examples. These types of memory are already in a
widerspread use but they often generate problems by their rather large volume and
power consumption. They represent a certain anachronism to the integrated circuits
used in all other parts of a computer, which bubble memories should be able to
overcome.

Fixed head disks and drums are the fastest and also the most expensive examples of
an electromechanical storage. Their replacement has been one of the first targets of
the bubble memory development. For applications, where high speed is essential,
e.g., in electronic switching exchanges and in process control computers, bubble
memories will offer many advantages over fixed head disks, especially shorter access
time and higher reliability.

7. Applications of Bubble Memories

Today a bubble memory bit costs between 40 and 150 mc. Although these prices are
not representative for memories in mass production, system prices of 0.5 to 5 mc/bit,
extrapolated for the future, will prohibite the replacement of large disk drives by
bubble memories. Detailed calculations show that a capacity of at least 4 Mbit on
about 30 mm^2 of chip area must become possible in order to make the bubble memory
cost competitive with large disk drives. The author cannot foresee today, whether
this target can ever be reached.

The present cost situation restricts the application of bubble memories to all those
cases, where their technical advantages are indispensable for the operation of the
whole electronic equipment. The application of bubble memories will depend,
however, also on the assessment of their future availability by the equipment manufacturers. Examples of present fields of application are first of all of military nature,
but also portables, where small volume and low power consumption are indispensable.

Furthermore, the small volume of a bubble memory is a great advantage. In text editing systems, intelligent terminals, message recorders, and repertory dialers [31]. The improvement of the performance of micro- and minicomputer systems by the addition of a second, non-volatile storage level is seriously discussed at present. Here the bubble memory could find a wide field of application [10]. Probably the bubble memory must demonstrate its capability at first in the fields mentioned above. With further progress in the know-how of fabrication and the degree of integration, bubble memories will perhaps be able to replace fixed head disks and drums thereby yielding technical and cost advantages as well, especially for applications with rough environment. Pluggable bubble memory modules which can be even sent by mail over long distances [43], would increase the importance of bubble memories very much. There are also applications were bubble memory chips do not only store the information, but also perform some logic operations, e.g., the rearrangement of the stored data [44]. Content addressable memories can be realized with bubbles, too [45].

The substantial worldwide R & D-activities have created a good understanding of the physical and technological problems of bubble memories and some degree of standardization has already been obtained concerning the substrate material and the storage films. Thus the future technological development can be foreseen rather well.

References

[1]   *F. H. v. d. Leeuw,* Physical Principles of Magnetic Bubble Domain Memory Devices, this issue, p. 203.

[2]   *P. I. Bonyhard* et al., IEEE Trans. **MAG-9**, 433–436 (1973).

[3]   *T. J. Nelson, Y. S. Chen* and *J. E. Geusic,* IEEE Trans. **MAG-9**, 289–291 (1973).

[4]   *A. Lill,* J. Magnet. and Magn. **4**, 159–165 (1977).

[5]   *F. Parzefall* et al., IEEE Trans. **MAG-11**, 1160–1162 (1975).

[6]   *P. I. Bonyhard* and *J. L. Smith,* IEEE Trans. **MAG-12**, 614–617 (1976).

[7]   *I. S. Gergis, P. K. George* and *T. Kobayashi,* IEEE Trans. **MAG-12**, 651–653 (1976).

[8]   *A. H. Bobeck* et al., IEEE Trans. **MAG-9**, 474–480 (1973).

[9]   *J. L. Smith, D. F. Kish* and *P. I. Bonyhard,* IEEE Trans. **MAG-9**, 285–288 (1973).

[10]   *W. C. Mavity,* Paper F-3, given at the Int. Symp. on Industrial and Military Microprocessor Systems, San Diego, Juni 1975.

[11]   *M. Hiroshima* et al., Proc. 7th Conf. on Solid State Devices, Tokyo 1975, p. 113–117, and Electronics (16. Sept. 1976), p. 65.

[12]   *R. J. Radner* and *J. H. Wuorinen,* Paper given at the ISCC 1976.

[13]   *A. Marsh,* Paper given at the Int. Conf. on Magn. Bubbles in Eindhoven, Sept. 1976 and Electronics, p. 2E–3E (19.6.1976).

[14] *M. Takasu* et al., IEEE Trans. **MAG-12**, 633–635 (1976).

[15] *R. A. Naden, W. R. Keenan* and *D. M. Lee,* IEEE Trans. **MAG-12**, 685 (1976) and Paper A-1 given at the Int. Bubble-Conf., Eindhoven, Sept. 1976.

[16] *E. T. Brown,* Electronic **25**, 45–50 (1976).

[17] *P. I. Bonyhard, Y. S. Chen* and *J. L. Smith,* AIP Conf. Proc. 18 on the 1973 MMM-Conf. in Boston, p. 100–103.

[18] *P. K. George, T. R. Oeffinger* and *O. D. Bohning,* IEEE Trans. **MAG-12**, 411–415 (1976).

[19] *F. Parzefall* et al., IEEE Trans. **MAG-9,** 293–297 (1973).

[20] *T. Kobayashi, P. K. George* and *F. B. Humphrey,* IEEE Trans. **MAG-12**, 202–208 (1976).

[21] *W. Metzdorf* et al., Paper given at the Int. Bubble-Conf., Eindhoven, Sept. 1976, to be published in IEEE Trans. **MAG-13** (1977).

[22] *R. C. Le Craw, S. L. Blank* and *G. P. Vella-Coleiro,* Ammpl. Phys. Lett. **26**, 402–404 (1975).

[23] *J. E. Geusic* et al., AIP Conf. Proc. on the 1973 MMM-Conf. in Boston, p. 69.

[24] *I. S. Gergis, T. T. Chen* and *L. R. Tocci,* IEEE Trans. **MAG-12,** 7–14 (1976).

[25] *P. C. Michaelis* and *W. J. Richards,* IEEE Trans. **MAG-11,** 21–24 (1975).

[26] *F. B. Hagedorn, S. L. Blank* and *R. J. Pierce,* Appl. Phys. Lett. **26,** 206–209 (1975).

[27] *M. H. Kryder* et al., IEEE Trans. **MAG-10** 825–827 (1974).

[28] *F. Navratil,* IEEE Trans. **MAG-9,** 1154–1156 (1973).

[29] *K. Yamagishi* et al., IEEE Trans. **MAG-11,** 16–20 (1975).

[30] *M. Takasu* et al., IEEE Trans. **MAG-11,** 1151–1153 (1975).

[31] *A. H. Bobeck, P. I. Bonyhard* and *J. Geusic,* Proc. IEEE **63,** 1176–1195 (1975).

[32] *J. E. Geusic,* Bell Lab. Rec. **54,** 263–267 (1976).

[33] *R. A. Naden* and *F. G. West,* IEEE Trans. **MAG-10,** 852–855 (1974).

[34] *R. K. Watts* et al., Appl. Phys. Lett. **28,** 355–357 (1976).

[35] *J. P. Scott* and *T. W. Bril,* Paper C-5 given at the Int. Conf. on Magn. Bubbles Eindhoven, 1976.

[36] *G. S. Almasi* et al., AIP Conf. Proc. 24 on the 1974 MMM-Conf., Philadelphia, p. 630–632.

[37] *O. Voegeli* et al., AIP Conf. Proc. 24, wie [36], 617–619.

[38] *J. L. Archer,* Paper 11-1 given at the 1977 INTERMAG-Conf. in Los Angeles.

[39] *L. T. Terman,* IEEE Trans. **ED-23,** 72–78 (1976).

[40] *H. J. Harloff,* this issue.

[41] *C. D. Mee,* IEEE Trans. **MAG-12,** 1–6 (1976).

[42] *D. C. Bullock,* Paper C-1 given at the Int. Conf. on Magn. Bubbles in Eindhoven, Sept. 1976.

[43] N. N. Electronics, June 23, 1977, p. 79.

[44] *C. Tung, T. C. Chen* and *H. Chang,* IEEE Trans. **MAG-11,** 1163–1165 (1975).

[45] *J. L. Archer,* private Communication.

[46] *J. T. Carlo, A. D. Stephenson* and *D. J. Hayes,* IEEE Trans. MAG-12, 624–628 (1976).

Ferromagnetic Domain Memories

Hermann Deichelmann

BASF Aktiengesellschaft, Ludwigshafen, Germany

Introduction

The literature on ferromagnetic domain memories is now so voluminous that it is
safe to assume that the technical and physical fundamentals are largely known. A
review presented by the author describes the state of technology up to 1976 [1]. The
present contribution will deal with the progress that has been achieved in the meantime. Today, ferromagnetic domain memories are poised on the threshold of many
practical applications, and they must be considered as genuine alternatives to conventional storage devices.

Principle of Operation

Ferromagnetic domain memories are based on the controlled generation and transmission of magnetic domains in thin ferromagnetic layers. The actual storage
elements consist of thin, rectangular glass substrates of several centimeters length
and width, one side of which is coated with a composite layer. This layer consists of
an aluminium primer of about 30 nm thickness and an overlying 120 nm vacuum-
metallized ferromagnetic layer of a nickel-iron-cobalt alloy (Fig. 1). The composition
of this alloy is selected to ensure that its magnetostriction is as small as possible. An
example is 65 Ni/20 Co/15 Fe [2, 3].

Before the top layer is deposited by vacuum deposition, a pattern of channels is
etched in the aluminium layer (Fig. 2). The clean surface of the glass appears at the
base of each of these channels. Subsequently, the substrate is covered with the ferromagnetic layer. The channels appear as a faint relief on the final storage element [2].

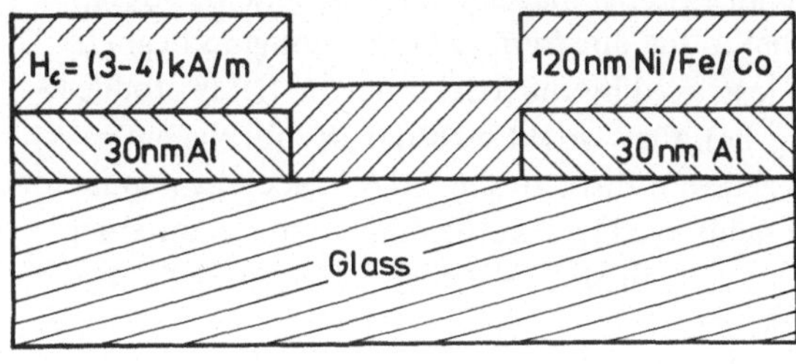

Fig. 1

Schematic Layout of Storage
Substrate.

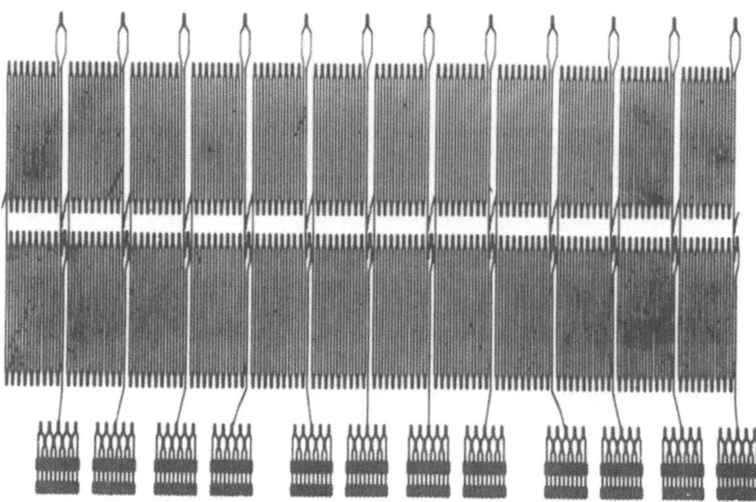

Fig. 2. Channel Pattern.

During deposition a homogeneous magnetic field is applied parallel to the surface of the glass substrates. This ensures that a preferred direction of magnetization is impressed in the magnetic layer. After this the layer is magnetically anisotropic with an anisotropy field strength of about 2000 A/m.

In the vicinity of the channels, where the magnetic layer rests on the fire-prepolished surface of the glass, the coercive force required to shift the walls is 250 to 400 A/m; whereas on the aluminium layer which is much rougher, it is 3000 to 5000 A/m.

Digital information is stored in the form of magnetic domains within the soft magnetic channels. These domains occur at the print-in points on the pattern of channels as a result of local remagnetization of the storage layer, which was uniformly magnetized at the beginning. The magnetic fields that are required for this purpose are set up by conductive loops through which current flows and which are arranged in the immediate vicinity of the input areas [4].

A stationary domain within a channel is shown in Fig. 3 (centre). Its magnetization vector M is rotated by $180°$. Now, if an external magnetic field of suitable strength, i.e., greater than H_c, is applied parallel to the direction of M, the domains begin to grow at both ends. If they were not restricted by the local magnetic fields produced by the two blocking conductors (Fig. 3c), they would subsequently fill the entire pattern of channels. Simultaneously, current flows through these blocking conductors to such an extent that the magnetic fields produced at the domain tips counteract the field of propagation and weaken it to such an extent that the resulting field strength drops below the limiting value H_c.

240

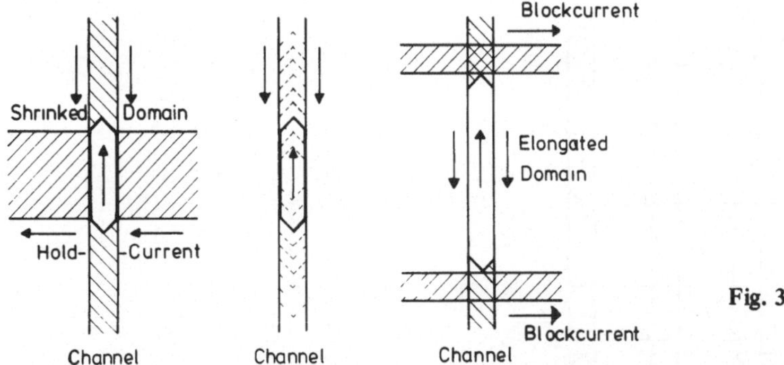

Fig. 3

If an external field stronger than H_c is applied in the opposite direction to M on a stationary domain, the domain begins to shrink at both ends. It would finally disappear completely, if it were not for the current in a "hold conductor", which simultaneously weakens the magnetic field so that the resulting field strength component is less than H_c. Thus, in this range, a residual domain is retained (Fig. 3a).

The propagation of the magnetic domains along the pattern of channels can actually be attributed to a series of controllable expansions and contractions as described above. The magnetic fields required for this purpose can be produced in various ways. An arrangement has been described [1] that requires an overall magnetic field for the expansion and contraction of the domains, a local holding field, and two local blocking fields. As an alternative, overall magnetic fields are not necessary in four-wire and two-wire systems; the only requirement is locally restricted magnetic fields [5]. The principle is shown in Figs. 4a to te.

The domains move in four different phases as is shown in Table 1.

Table 1

Conductor no.	1	2	3	4	5	6	7	8
Phase								
1	–	0	+	0	–	0	+	0
2	0	–	0	+	0	–	0	+
3	+	0	–	0	+	0	–	0
4	0	+	0	–	0	+	0	–

where

+   is the direction of current that produces a magnetic field parallel to the magnetization of the domains,

–   is the opposite direction and

0   indicates that the conductor concerned is not activated at the time in question.

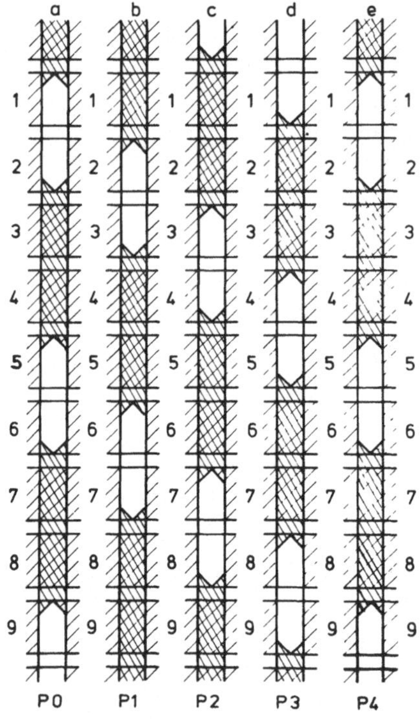

Fig. 4

Successive Domain Movement.

It can be seen from Table 1 that the current in every second conductor is in the opposite direction and that every four sets of conductor numbers form a complete cycle. Hence, in principle, four independent systems of conductors are required for operation. At first sight, no restriction need be imposed on the required current levels. However, as another condition, the positive and negative currents must always be of the same magnitude. Hence, the individual conductors in Systems 1 and 3 or 2 and 4 can be connected together in series. As a result, the original four systems can be reduced to two.

Extensive economic studies have revealed that two-wire systems are much more advantageous than systems employing an overall magnetic field. A particular advantage is that a much higher packing density can be achieved with a simpler mechanical design.

Fig. 5 shows the substrate of the spiral version. Here, the individual data channels are arranged in spirals in order to exploit the area as much as possible. The capacity of this substrate is 48 kbit, i.e., about 1600 bit/cm^2. Thus the storage density is about five times greater than that of the version described in the previous paper [1].

242

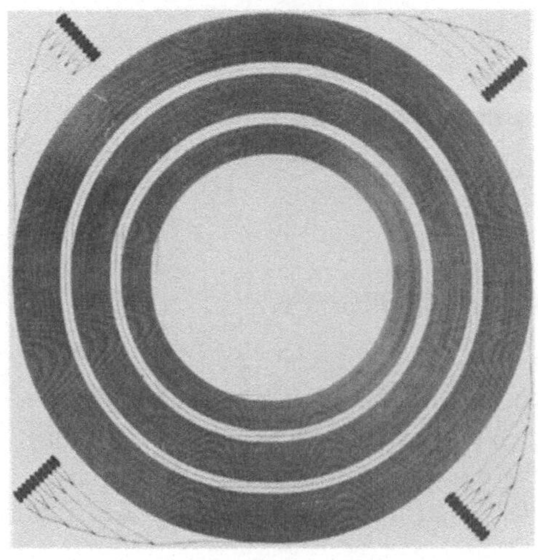

Fig. 5

Spiralversion Substrate

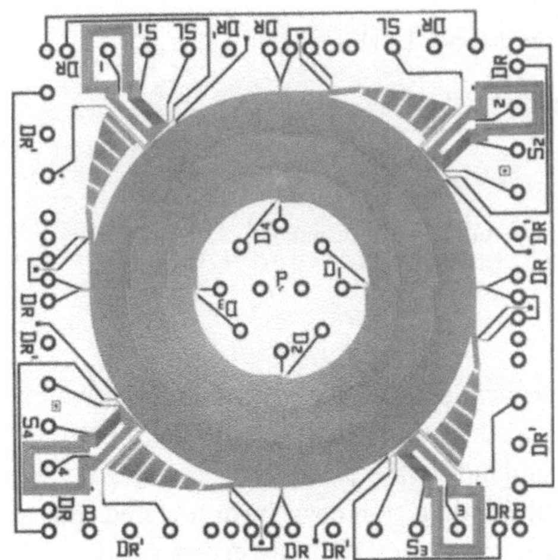

Fig. 6

One of the two control line levels is shown in Fig. 6. The other level is built up analogously. The one is at the back and the other at the front of a flexible etched circuit, and both are arranged as closely as possible and parallel to the surface of the substrate. The entire system is encapsulated and forms a module that can be electrically connected with base pins. The characteristics of the module are listed in Table 2.

Table 2. Technical Data for the Spiral Version 48 kbit

Capacity	49,152 bit
Data organization	4 shift registers à 12,288 bit
Max. frequency	100 kHz
Max. data transfer rate	400 kbit/s = 50 kbyte/s
Max. access time	123 ms
Average access time	62 ms
Power imput	ca. 8 watt
Size of module	74 × 74 × 5 mm³ (without pins)

The average access time for the spiral version, namely, 62 ms, is comparatively large. In contrast, a second version with straight channels has a much shorter access time, ranging between 35 μs and 2.8 ms. This is also a two-wire design, but the length of the shift register is only 128 bit. The technical data for this version are listed in Table 3.

Table 3

Capacity	16,384 bit
Data organization	128 shift registers à 128 bit
Max. frequency	50 kHz
Max. data transfer rate	198 kbit/s = 25 kbyte/s
Max. access time	2.8 ms
Average access time	1.4 ms
Power imput	0.7 watt
Size of module	78 × 77 × 5 mm³ (without pins)

Economic Factors

The spiral version of domain memories will be available on the market in the form of individual modules or entire systems. However, the rapid-access designs are mainly required in the form of entire storage blocks including the electronic systems for switching and driving. Detailed estimates of the production costs have revealed that in many fields of application, magnetic domain memories are more economic than other storage devices and must be considered as serious competition to them. Although magnetic domain memories are significantly more expensive than magnetic disc stores and will certainly not be able to replace them in the foreseeable future, they are still cheaper than the core and semiconductor memories known today.

Fields of Application for Magnetic Domain Memories

The most important technical properties for magnetic domain memories are listed in Table 4.

Table 4

No moving parts
Asynchronous operation
Data are nonvolatile in the event of a power failure
Short access times
Immunity to ambient conditions
Lower average power requirement, because no current is necessary for standby

From the data given in Table 4, it can be seen that magnetic domain memories are suitable for the following applications. The list does not claim to be complete:

Data processing   rapid peripheral temporary storage substitute for
                            fixed-head disc memory part for virtual storage systems
Minicomputer   substitute for fixed-head disc memory
Periphery   substitute for floppy disc memory

Data collection systems

Data concentrators

Measurement technology   buffer memories
Control systems   substitute for punched card and
for machinery   magnetic disc stores

Data Processing Techniques

It can be expected that certain types of magnetic domain memories will be available shortly.

Depending upon the kind of application, the technical data will be as follows:

Capacity: 200 kbit to 20 Mbit
Max data transfer rate: 2400 bit/s to 10 Mbit/s
Average access time: 2 ms to 100 ms

References

[1]   *H. Deichelmann,* Magnetic Domain Tip Memories, Journal of Magnetism and Magnetic Materials **4**, pp. 174–179 (1977).

[2]   *R. J. Spain* and *H. J. Jauvtis,* J. Appl. Phys. **37**, pp. 2548 (1966).

[3]   *R. Spain* and *M. Marino,* IEEE Trans. **MAG-6,** pp. 451 (1970).

[4]   *R. W. Forsberg,* EDN, pp. 18 (1969).

[5]   *K. D. Broadbent,* US Patent 2 919 432.

Application of the Josephson Effect for Digital Storage

Peter Wolf

IBM Zurich Research Laboratory, 8803 Rüschlikon, Switzerland

1. Introduction

Superconductivity is one of the most interesting phenomena of physics. There have been several early attempts to put it to use in applications, but, not only did the cooling to very low temperatures turn out to be an obstacle, but even more so, the lack of superconducting effects of practical significance. Recently, the discovery of the Josephson effect has changed the situation and increased the interest in electronic applications. The Josephson effect is already in use in highly sensitive magnetometers [1] and for precision measurements of voltages [1, 2]. Additional applications presently in the research stage are in the area of submillimeter microwaves [3] and digital circuits. Here we cover one aspect of digital circuits, namely, memory applications of the Josephson effect. The next section will deal briefly with superconductivity and the Josephson effect, then a description is given of storage principles and fabricated memory cells including a short account of drive circuits.

Several reviews have appeared on Josephson digital circuits [4–7] and two with emphasis on digital storage [8, 9].

2. The Josephson Effect

2.1. Superconductivity

Superconductivity was discovered in 1911 by Onnes. He observed that some metals completely lose their electrical resistivity if cooled below a critical temperature T_c. Today, many superconducting metals and compounds are known, examples being lead and niobium with critical temperatures of 7.2 K and 9.2 K, respectively. Only in 1957 was a satisfactory explanation of superconductivity arrived at by Bardeen, Cooper and Schrieffer, known as BCS theory, according to which, in superconductors, there exists a weak attracting interaction between conduction electrons. Below the critical temperature, the interaction causes the electrons to condense into pairs, the so-called Cooper pairs. There is coupling between these pairs and consequently, they are no longer independent of each other: all Cooper pairs have the tendency to move together in the same direction. With the Cooper pairs and their cooperative behaviour, it was possible to arrive at a satisfactory explanation of all phenomena of the superconducting state [10].

2.2. Circulating Currents and Flux Quantization

It is possible to excite circulating currents in rings of superconducting materials.
These currents persist because there is no electrical resistance in the superconducting
state. Such currents have been observed in the cooled state over years without detecting a change. This makes such rings potential elements for storage. The zero or one
of the binary system could be coded as a current circulating clockwise or counter-
clockwise, respectively.

The ring current generates a magnetic field which leads to a magnetic flux through
the ring. In agreement with theory, it has been found experimentally that the flux
cannot have arbitrary values, but has to be a multiple of the flux quantum
$\phi_0 = h/2e = 2.07 \cdot 10^{-15}\,\mathrm{Vs}$ [11, 12]. In accordance with BCS theory, due to the
Cooper pairs, twice the electron charge enters the expression for ϕ_0. Flux quantization is a macroscopic effect. For instance, in a ring with a diameter of 10 μm, one
flux quantum corresponds to a field of 0.21 A/cm, about the same as the earth's
magnetic field. Flux quantization plays an important part in the Josephson effect.
As will be shown later, it is possible to store information as single flux quanta.

2.3. The Cryotron

The cryotron was the first digital element to make use of superconductivity [13].
It consists of a superconducting electrode switched by a magnetic field from the
superconducting to the normal state. Logic and memory circuits have been realized,
but for various reasons cryotrons have found no practical use. The most important
reason is that they are not competitive with transistors with respect to speed and
power [14].

2.4. The Josephson Effect

In 1962, based on the BCS theory, Josephson made theoretical predictions about
the behavior of tunnel junctions with superconducting electrodes [15]. A short time
later this was confirmed experimentally, and after some years Matisoo showed how
the Josephson effect can be used for digital circuits [16].

The structure of a "Josephson" tunnel junction is given schematically in Fig. 1(a).
It consists of two superconducting electrodes separated by a thin insulating film with
a thickness of only some 10 atomic layers. The I–V characteristics are shown in
Fig. 1(b). The essential prediction of Josephson is that Cooper pairs can tunnel
through the junction, which makes it superconducting. In Fig. 1(b) this leads to the
vertical branch of the characteristics, where a current flows through the junction
without any voltage drop. According to Josephson, this super- or "Josephson"-current
is limited to a maximum value I_{max} which is basically proportional to the junction

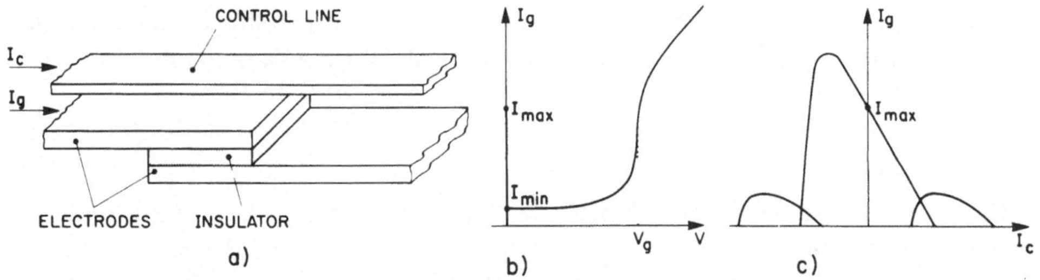

Fig. 1. Structure and characteristics of a Josephson junction. 1 (a) The junction consists of two superconducting electrodes separated by a very thin insulator. A current in the control line influences the Josephson current magnetically. 1 (b) I−V characteristics. The superconducting branch with V = 0 represents the Josephson current. 1 (c) Control characteristics. The lines drawn show the maximum Josephson current as a function of the control current I_c.

area, and which depends exponentially on the insulator thickness. If the threshold I_{max} is exceeded, then the junction leaves the superconducting state and switches into the "voltage" state which is given by the S-like branch in Fig. 1(b). This branch is characterized mainly by the tunneling of unpaired electrons. In the superconducting state the number of unpaired electrons is small, which leads to a small current only at low voltages. However, above the gap voltage V_g, which corresponds to the binding energy of the Cooper pairs, these are broken and the increased number of unpaired electrons gives rise to a steep increase in current. The gap voltage V_g is proportional to the critical temperature T_c and in the case of lead amounts to 2.5 mV. The junction switches back from the voltage state to the Josephson state if the current is decreased below a certain value I_{min}. Obviously the Josephson tunnel junction is bistable. In a certain range of currents it has two states, a superconducting state and a voltage state.

A further prediction of Josephson was that the Josephson current can be influenced by a magnetic field. As shown in Fig. 1(a), the field is generated by sending current through one or more control lines placed on top of the junction. The control characteristics for a long junction are sketched in Fig. 1(c), and it shows the threshold value I_{max} for switching from the superconducting to the voltage state as a function of the control current. As can be seen, the Josephson current can be decreased by a magnetic field. It can even be suppressed with high fields. The control characteristics consist of several lobes, the so-called vortex modes [17]. These are superconducting states, which are distinguished by the current distribution and the number of flux quanta in the junction. The main lobe contains no flux; each of the first side lobes to the left and right of the main lobe contains one flux quantum. Other lobes, omitted from the drawing, include two or more quanta of magnetic flux.

The description given here of the Josephson effect is much simplified and does little justice to the physical details. More exhaustive treatment can be found in the literature [10, 18]. However, it is important to note here that Josephson tunnel junctions are well understood experimentally and theoretically, which is a good basis for circuit design.

The fabrication of circuits with Josephson junctions is similar to that of integrated semiconductor circuits [19]. Usually, the junction electrodes and the control lines are vacuum-evaporated lead with additions of indium and gold [20]. The latter ingredients increase the thermal cycling stability. On the substrate, below the circuits there is a ground plane of niobium, which provides a well-defined wave impedance for the strip-transmission lines between the circuits. The thicker insulating layers consist mainly of evaporated SiO. The horizontal structures of the circuits are defined by a photolithographic "lift-off" process. One of the most important steps is the reproducible fabrication of the tunnel insulator. A proven process uses an rf-plasma discharge in an oxygen atmosphere, during which a thin oxide film grows on the base electrode of the tunnel junction [21]. After oxidation, the oxygen is pumped out of the bell jar, and subsequently the counter-electrode is evaporated.

The interest in Josephson junctions for digital circuits is based mainly on two properties: the high switching speed and the very small power consumption. The switching time from the Josephson state to the voltage state depends on the ratio C/I_{max} of the junction capacitance C to the maximum Josephson current I_{max}. This ratio depends approximately inversely on the density of the Josephson current. Junctions with current densities $\gtrsim 1000$ A/cm^2 switch theoretically in less than 10 ps, values which cannot be resolved with today's oscilloscopes. Measurements on such junctions gave upper limits of 30—40 ps, identical with the time resolution of the equipment [22].

Josephson junctions dissipate power in the voltage state only. The gap voltage amounts to some mV and the operating current is some mA or less, and accordingly, the consumed power is in the μW range. Therefore, the power-delay product is in the femto-[1]) Joule region. It is several orders of magnitude smaller than that of fast semiconductor circuits. Accordingly, a Josephson computer is expected to have slight or no problems with heat removal, contrary to the situation in computers with fast semiconductor circuits. In addition, Josephson memory cells can be realized which consume no power in the non-addressed state. Therefore, it seems feasible to build memory systems with extremely low power consumption.

---

[1]) femto: 10^{-15}

3. Digital Storage with the Josephson Effect

3.1. Memory Cells with Superconducting Rings (Ring Cells)

As already mentioned, circulating currents in superconducting rings are contenders for information storage. In order to be able to write and read information, Josephson junctions are included in the rings as switches. A cell design proposed by Anacker is shown in Fig. 2 [8]. For writing, there are two Josephson junctions in the storage ring, magnetically controlled by a bit line. A word line sends current through the cell. For non-destructive reading, a further Josephson junction is provided, which is influenced by the magnetic field of the circulating current. Coincident reading and writing is possible, which means that a single cell in a memory array can be addressed without influencing other cells.

Writing is illustrated in Figs. 3 (a)–(d). It is assumed that a "0" is stored as a circulating current flowing counter-clockwise through the ring and having a value of $I_w/2$ [Fig. 3(a)]. For writing a "1", the word current I_w is switched on, which splits evenly in the two halves of the ring if their inductances are equal. In the left half, circulating and word currents compensate each other, so that the full current I_w flows in the right half. Now the bit current I_b is applied in such a way that it flows parallel to the current I_w in the right Josephson junction. Under these circumstances the junction switches into the voltage state and drives the current out of the right half of the ring into the left one, as it is still superconducting [Fig. 3(c)]. After the current has left the right branch, the junction there switches back into the superconducting state. The left junction now carries a current I_w, but the bit current I_b is antiparallel to it. Accordingly, the operating point is within the left superconducting region of the asymmetric control characteristic [Fig. 1(c)] and the junction stays

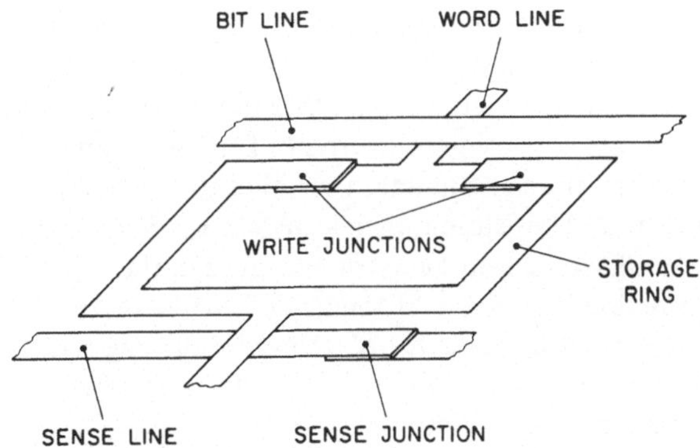

Fig. 2. Structure of a ring cell. The information is stored as a circulating current in the storage ring. Writing and non-destructive reading are accomplished by means of Josephson junctions.

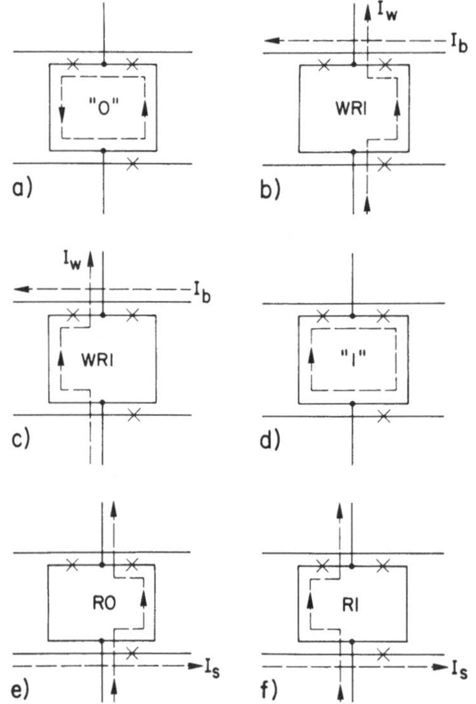

Fig. 3

Writing (a) – (d) and reading (e) and (f) of a ring cell. Both operations use coincident currents.

in the Josephson state. Finally, I_w and I_b are switched off and a clockwise circulating current remains which represents a "1". For writing a "0" the word current I_w is applied as before, but in addition a bit current I_b with reversed polarity is also applied. It is easy to show that the currents I_w and I_b can be chosen such that only fully-selected cells are written, but not the half-selected ones.

Reading is shown in Figs. 3(e) and 3(f). Again, a word current I_w is applied and in addition a current I_s through the sense junction. If a "0" is stored, then as in the case of writing, circulating and word currents superpose such that in the right branch a current I_w flows. It decreases the maximum Josephson current of the sense junction below the bias current I_s. Therefore, the sense junction switches to the voltage state, indicating that a "0" is stored. If a "1" is stored, then a current I_w flows in the left branch, the sense junction does not see a control current and stays in the superconducting state. This allows a distinction between a "0" and a "1". After switching off I_w and I_s, the original circulating current is reestablished, therefore reading is non-destructive. Obviously, in the quiescent storing state the cells need no external current and consequently have no power consumption.

Some considerations which are important in cell design [23, 24] will be dealt with briefly in the following. In general, the cell inductance is chosen large, so that the

252

stored flux $\phi = LI_w/2$ contains a large number (≈ 100) of flux quanta. Under these circumstances, flux quantization is hardly noticed; the circulating current behaves like a continuous quantity.

In the voltage state, a Josephson junction can be considered approximately as a non-linear resistor, given by the tunneling characteristics for unpaired electrons, with the junction capacitance C in parallel. This and the inductance of the ring combine to a parallel resonant circuit, which should not be too much underdamped to obtain complete current transfer from one branch of the ring into the other. This sets a lower limit to the ring inductance as well as to the cell area. The ring inductance can be decreased further by increasing the Josephson current density of the write junctions or by the introduction of damping resistors.

The so-called ac Josephson effect [10, 18] can excite cavity resonances in Josephson junctions. They are adversely felt in certain regions of the threshold characteristics, but they can be avoided by smaller margins of the drive currents. The resonance effects can be suppressed, for instance, by using very small Josephson junctions.

The cell previously described contains no ring current after cooling to the superconducting state. It has to be introduced by a special set-up cycle which requires drive-current values different from normal operation.

The first experimentally realized cell [23] had a relatively large area of about $3 \cdot 10^5 \mu m^2$, due to a minimum line width of 25 μm. Despite this, the current transfer time from one branch of the ring to the other was only about 600 ps. The energy consumed in the cell per write cycle amounted to only 2 femto Joule. After $5 \cdot 10^8$ read cycles, the circulating current in the cell still showed no change. The margins of the operating currents were between $\pm 11.5\%$ and $\pm 26\%$.

Based on the ring principle, similar cells have been realized [24—26]. The smallest of them with a minimum line width of 2 μm had an area of about 900 μm^2. The measured transfer time was about 80 ps.

3.2. Single Flux-Quantum Cells (SFQ Cells)

The flux quantum is the smallest amount of magnetic flux possible in a superconducting system. Therefore, it is tempting to use flux quantization for storage because one expects to obtain cells with minimal area and power consumption. According to Guéret, this type of storage can be accomplished with vortex modes [27, 28]. They are found in sufficiently long Josephson junctions and in ring systems with one or more Josephson junctions. As an example, the threshold characteristics of long Josephson junctions, as shown in Fig. 1 (c), are considered first. The figure shows that in certain areas the vortex modes overlap one another. Accordingly, in these overlap regions one has two superconducting states which differ by one flux quantum.

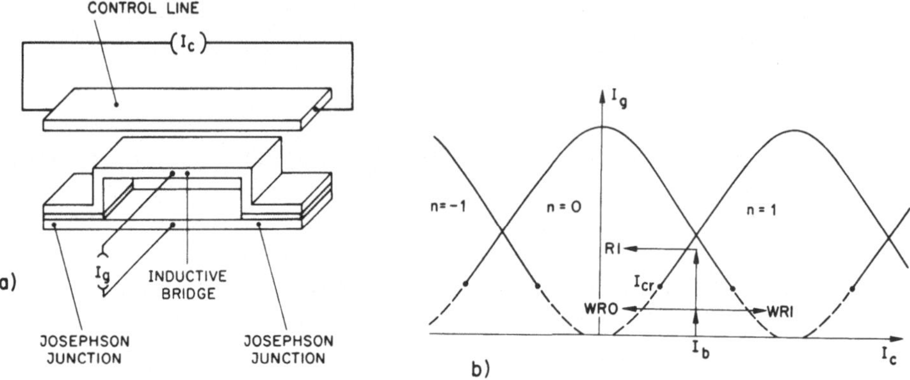

Fig. 4. Structure and characteristics of a single flux-quantum cell. 4(a) The cell consists of two Josephson junctions and an inductive bridge. The electrode separation in the bridge area is obtained by an insulator with a thickness $\approx$ 2000 Å. 4(b) Josephson threshold characteristics. It consists of several, equal superconducting branches (vortex modes), which differ by the number n of flux quanta stored in the inductive bridge. In the overlap regions either of two states is possible which is used for storing one bit of information. Writing and reading are explained in the text.

There, the junction is bistable and can exist in either one of the vortex modes. Therefore, one bit of information can be stored in this superconducting overlap region. Obviously a single Josephson junction is a memory element. In general, all superconducting systems which possess overlapping vortex modes can be considered as potential storage devices. These cells are called "single flux-quantum cells" or, for short, SFQ cells. The best suitable system found so far is the so-called interferometer [29]. As Fig. 4(a) shows, it consists of an inductive ring with two Josephson junctions. There is some similarity to the memory cell shown in Fig. 2, however, the cross-section of the ring is considerably smaller and therefore the inductance is much lower. The control line couples the magnetic field into the ring inductance and not into the junctions as in the case of Fig. 2.

The threshold characteristics of the interferometer are schematically drawn in Fig. 4(b). As can be seen, the vortex modes are all equal in size and have large overlap regions. The integer n denotes the number of flux quanta in a mode.

In the same figure, writing and reading is illustrated. Storage is only possible in the bistable overlap region. Therefore with a dc current I_b through the control line, the device is biased in the middle of an overlap area. For the moment, for writing, it is assumed that the cell is in the vortex mode n = 0. For writing a "1", currents I_g and I_c are applied in such a way that the boundary of the vortex mode n = 0 is crossed close to the I_c axis (WR1).

254

If one moves over that vortex boundary, mode n = 0 is no longer stable: one of the junctions switches briefly to the voltage state and admits one flux quantum into the inductive bridge. Now, one is in mode n = 1. After switching-off the write currents, a "1" is stored in the cell. Writing a "0" is similar; one has only to change the polarity of the write current along the I_c axis (WR0). As already mentioned, the magnetic flux in the cell changes by one flux quantum if one switches from one vortex mode to the next one. Thereby a short voltage spike with $\int V\, dt = \pm\, \phi_0$ is generated. The spike with a voltage of ≈ 1 mV and a duration of some ps can be detected with an additional Josephson junction and in this manner the content of the cell can be read [27, 28].

There is, however, another way of reading [30]. Switching from one vortex state to another takes place only if the drive current I_g is below a critical value I_{cr}. In Fig. 4 (b) this is the dotted region of the vortex boundaries. If the vortex boundary is crossed above I_{cr} (but within the overlap region), then the cell switches into the voltage state.Accordingly, a dc voltage develops over the cell which can be detected easier than a voltage spike. For reading (R1), the drive currents are applied as shown in Fig. 4(b). If the cell is in the state n = 1, then it switches to the voltage state upon crossing the vortex boundary. If it is in state n = 0, then no change occurs because the drive currents for R1 are completely within the mode n = 0. In this fashion a "0" and a "1" can be distinguished. Reading is destructive, i.e. after reading, the cell has to be brought back into the superconducting state by switching off the current I_g. Then the old or new information has to be written.

The static and dynamic properties of the cell are well understood both theoretically and experimentally [30, 31]. The overlap can be controlled by the product LI_{max} of the cell inductance L and the maximum Josephson current I_{max} per junction. Values of $L I_{max} \approx \phi_0/2$ are best suited for memory applications. The critical current I_{cr} depends only slightly on the LI_{max} product, and amounts to about $I_{max}/2$.

There are several possible addressing methods, the simplest coincident one is depicted in Fig. 5. In this case, the memory matrix consists of strings of series-connected cells in the y-direction. A drive current I_{gn} is sent through the addressed string. The control lines are in the x-direction providing the bias current I_b and the drive current $\pm I_{cn}$. For writing, first the current $\pm I_{cn}$ is applied and then the current I_{gn}. For reading, the sequence is reversed. The figure indicates independent margins of about $\pm 35\,\%$ for the drive currents. However, a fabrication spread of the maximum Josephson current I_{max} of the junction has not been included. Investigations show that this spread has to be kept quite small to obtain a reasonable operating window.

Several types of cells have been fabricated [27, 30, 31]. Figure 6 shows a Scanning Electron Microscope (SEM) photograph of two adjacent cells. Each cell has two control lines (running horizontally through the photograph) with a width of about

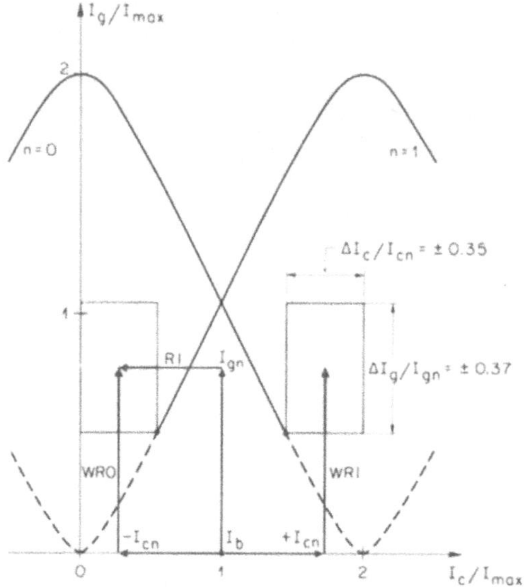

Fig. 5

One of the possible coincident addressing methods for a single flux-quantum cell. The theoretical operating window for the drive currents is also shown. Other tolerances such as those of I_b and I_{max} are not taken into account.

Fig. 6. SEM photograph of two experimental single flux-quantum cells, one in the upper and one in the lower part of the picture. The inductive bridges are in the middle of the photograph, the junctions are to the left and to the right of the bridge. Each cell has two control lines about 3 μm wide, which run horizontally through the picture. To the right there is an underpass for one of the control lines. The interferometer area without underpass is about 650 μm^2.

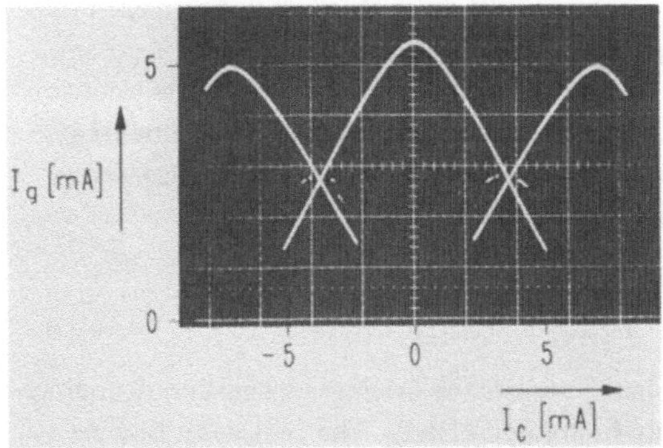

Fig. 7. Measured threshold characteristics of a cell similar to the one in Fig. 6. Only those parts of the vortex boundaries are recorded where switching from the vortex to the voltage state occurs. For storage purposes, the two overlap regions can be used which are centered at $I_c = \pm 3.7$ mA.

3 μm. One of the control lines runs over both cells, which requires an underpass visible in the right part of the picture. This arrangement allows various addressing methods to be tested. The interferometer area without underpass is about 650 μm^2. The smallest fabricated interferometer had a minimum line width of 2 μm and an area of about 150 μm^2. It was possible to read and write successfully with this small device.

Figure 7 shows the measured vortex boundaries of a cell similar to that in Fig. 6. Only those parts of the vortex boundaries are recorded where the cell switches from the vortex state to the voltage state. As can be seen, the cell currents amount to some mA. The energy stored in the cell is of the order of 10 atto Joule = 10^{-17} Joule, which, despite its small value, is several orders of magnitude larger than the thermal energy kT. Accordingly, thermal noise has little influence on the cell behaviour.

The theoretical risetime of the read voltage on switching to the voltage state is about 50 ps for junctions with a current density of 2 kA/cm^2. The measured values of about 100 ps are somewhat longer, mainly due to parasitic capacitances and inductances in the measuring equipment.

3.3. The Flux Shuttle

The cells described so far are designed for random-access applications. There are proposals for serial memories, [32], which also use flux quanta for storage. In very long Josephson junctions it is possible to generate local circulating currents which are independent of one another and are called vortices. They are a special case of vortex modes and each vortex includes one flux quantum. By proper shaping of the

electrodes one can obtain a number of energetically favorable locations, in each of
which there is either one or no vortex. With multiphase current pulses, it is possible
to shift the vortices from location to location in a similar way as one shifts electric
charges in CCD devices. A short shift-register has been investigated experimentally
[33]. Theoretically, shift times of 10 ps are predicted, the experiments, however,
have been performed so far only in the ms range.

4. Peripheral Memory Circuits

Little has been published about peripheral circuits for driving, sensing and decoding
[8, 9], therefore these circuits can only be treated briefly. The cells described previously have very short switching times, of the order of 100 ps, therefore it seems
likely that the speed of a Josephson memory depends mostly on the peripheral
circuits as is the case with memories in other technologies.

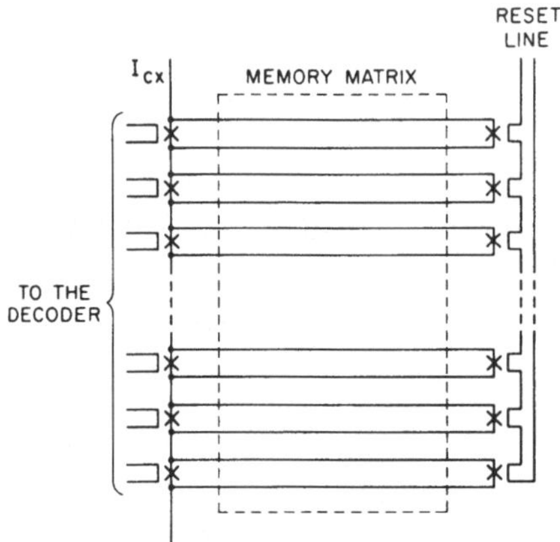

Fig. 8

Principle of a drive circuit for the control
lines. The set junctions are situated on the
left. They are controlled by a decoder and
allow setting up of a current in a selected
loop. The junctions at the right are provided
for resetting.

A possible drive circuit for the control lines of the cells is sketched in Fig. 8. The lines
are arranged in loops through the memory array, to their left and right are junctions
for setting and resetting the loop currents. On the left side, the loops are connected
in series to a dc current source with a current I_{cx}. When I_{cx} is switched on, it flows
only in the vertical string, because it has much lower inductance than the loops. If a
control current is applied to one of the set junctions on the left side, then the junction switches into the voltage state and transfers the current into the loop which is
superconducting. Upon termination of the transfer, the junction switches back into
the Josephson state. For resetting, the reset junction has to be switched by sending
a control current through the reset line. Obviously this loop system behaves like a
flip-flop [16] and is very similar to a ring cell in its mode of operation.

258

In principle, the other drive-, sense-, and decode circuits can be realized in quite a similar way with superconducting loop systems.

Proposals for peripheral circuits intended mainly for use with ring cells are described in [8] and [9]. Simple estimates can be derived for the transfer time T_{tr} of a current I_{cx} in a drive loop. It is found [8] that

$$T_{tr} \approx L\, I_{cx}/V_g \; ,$$

where L denotes the loop inductance. As a hypothetical example, a memory array with 16 kBit is considered. If it consists of SFQ cells similar to Fig. 6, then the overall length of a loop might amount to 1 cm. With a line width of 3 μm and a distance from a superconducting ground plane of 0.5 μm, the inductance L amounts to about 2 nH. If $I_{cx} \approx 2.5$ mA and $V_g \approx 2.5$ mV is assumed, then for the transfer time T_{tr} quite a small value of about 2 ns is obtained. One can estimate that the other operations on a chip, like decoding or sensing, might take place in similar times. Accordingly, it might be feasible to realize memory chips suitable for main memories with access times of perhaps 10–20 ns. Arrays with a smaller number of cells should operate faster. For a 4 kBit array with ring cells, an access time of 2.5 ns has been estimated [9]. In the quiescent state, a superconducting loop system dissipates no power. During switching of a drive loop an energy $E = 0.5\, L\, I_{cx}^2$ has to be dissipated. With the aforementioned values, $E \approx 6$ femto Joule is found, or for example with a repetition rate of 50 MHz the transient power consumption amounts to $\approx 0.3\ \mu$W. This indicates that memories with extremely small power consumption might be feasible.

5. Summary

The Josephson effect allows realization of superconducting memory cells with switching times in the 100 ps range. Cells for non-destructive reading have been realized with areas as small as 900 μm^2. Successful use of flux quantization has been made for storage leading to cells with small dimensions. The smallest device realized had an area of about 150 μm^2. The read process of these so-called single flux-quantum cells is destructive. Both types of cells are non-volatile and keep the information without external energy supply. Rough estimates for hypothetical arrays with 4 and 16 kBit indicate that access times of 2.5 and 10–20 ns might be feasible. If the peripheral circuits are realized with superconducting loop systems, then the memory chip consumes no power in the quiescent state. Transient power consumption would occur only during reading and writing.

Of course, the fabrication of such devices is a technological challenge. This is especially true for the very thin tunnel insulator which has to be made very reproducibly and without pin holes. A number of circuits realized with increasing complexity shows that encouraging progress has been made [34].

References

[1] *J. Clarke,* Proc. IEEE **61**, 8 (1973).

[2] *B. F. Field, T. F. Finnegan* and *J. Tools,* Metrologia **9**, 155 (1973).

[3] *P. L. Richards,* "SQUID and Its Applications", W. de Gruyter, Berlin, 1977.

[4] *J. Matisoo,* IEEE Trans. Magn. **MAG-5**, 848 (1969).

[5] *W. Anacker,* AFIPS Conference Proceedings **41**, 1269 (1972).

[6] *W. Anacker,* 1976 ESSDERC Proceedings, Conference Series of the Institute of Physics, London, 1977.

[7] *P. Wolf,* Bull. SEV **68**, 66 (1977).

[8] *W. Anacker,* IEEE Trans. Magn. **MAG-5**, 968 (1969).

[9] *W. Anacker,* AFIPS Conference Proceedings **44**, 529 (1975).

[10] *W. Buckel,* "Supraleitung", Physik Verlag, Weinheim, 1972.

[11] *R. Doll* and *M. Nabauer,* Phys. Rev. Lett. **7**, 43 (1961).

[12] *B. S. Deaver* and *W. M. Fairbank,* Phys. Rev. Lett. **7**, 43 (1961).

[13] *D. A. Buck,* Proc. IRE **44**, 482 (1956).

[14] *V. L. Newhouse,* "Applied Superconductivity", Academic Press, New York, 1975.

[15] *B. D. Josephson,* Phys. Lett. **1**, 251 (1962).

[16] *J. Matisoo,* Proc. IEEE **55**, 172 (1967).

[17] *C. S. Owen* and *D. J. Scalapino,* Phys. Rev. **164**, 538 (1967).

[18] *L. Solymar,* "Superconductive Tunnelling and Applications", Chapman and Hall, London, 1972.

[19] *J. H. Greiner, S. Basavaiah* and *I. Ames,* J. Vac. Sci. Technol. **11**, 81 (1974).

[20] *S. K. Lahiri,* J. Vac. Sci. Technol. **13**, 148 (1976).

[21] *J. H. Greiner,* J. Appl. Phys. **42**, 5151 (1971).

[22] *W. Jutzi, Th. O. Mohr, M. Gasser* and *H. P. Gschwind,* Electronic Lett. **8**, 589 (1972).

[23] *H. H. Zappe,* IEEE J. Solid-State Circuits **SC-10**, 12 (1975).

[24] *R. F. Broom, W. Jutzi* and *Th. O. Mohr,* IEEE Trans. Magn. **MAG-11**, 755 (1975).

[25] *W. Jutzi,* Cryogenics **16**, 81 (1976).

[26] *W. Jutzi* and *C. Schunemann,* Scientia Electrica **21**, 57 (1975).

[27] *P. Guéret,* Appl. Phys. Lett. **25**, 426 (1974).

[28] *P. Guéret,* IEEE Trans. Magn. **MAG-11**, 751 (1975).

[29] *A. H. Silver* and *J. E. Zimmerman,* Phys. Rev. **157**, 317 (1967).

[30] *H. H. Zappe,* Appl. Phys. Lett. **25**, 424 (1974).

[31] *P. Guéret, Th. O. Mohr* and *P. Wolf,* IEEE Trans Magn. **MAG-13**, 52 (1977).

[32] *T. A. Fulton, R. C. Dynes* and *P. W. Anderson,* Proc. IEEE **61**, 28 (1973).

[33] *T. A. Fulton* and *L. N. Dunkleberger,* Appl. Phys. Lett. **22**, 232 (1973).

[34] *D. J. Herrell,* IEEE J. Solid-State Circuits **SC-10**, 360 (1975).

Materials for Optical Data Stores

Eckhard Krätzig

Philips GmbH Forschungslaboratorium, Hamburg, Germany

1. Introduction

The invention of the laser revealed in the early sixties a diversity of new capabilities
for optical information storage. However, the fascinating properties of coherent light
often masked the difficulties with the introduction of optical storage techniques. By
these means, systems were proposed superior to existing stores by orders of magnitude
but with the disadvantage of non-feasibility. It had been overlooked that the limits
of optical methods in most cases are determined by material properties and not by
light properties like wavelength or light velocity. This experience initiated a period
of enhanced material studies for optical data storage.

Nevertheless, after these introductory remarks, a short description of the advantages
of light in a storage system seems to be reasonable:

- The transfer of light is very simple, no connections, as in the case of electrical
  currents, and no vacuum, as in the case of electron beams, are necessary. By means
  of acousto- or electrooptical procedures the light can be deflected very elegantly.

- Very high packing densities may be obtained: Light may be focused to a spot of
  a diameter on the order of the wavelength so that more than 10^8 bit/cm^2 can be
  obtained in a plane. The use of holographic methods and of the third dimension
  enhances the storage capacity to a theoretical limit of 10^{12} bit/cm^3.

- The parallel access brings about extremely high data rates: 10^6 pages/second with
  10^5 bit/pages can be read. Though processing of these data is not possible at the
  moment due to lack of a suitable data bus, the high data rates appear attractive
  for future applications.

To take full advantage of optical methods, appropriate storage materials are absolutely
necessary. The most important requirements for these materials are listed below:

- high optical and mechanical stability, reliability,
- simple handling: no vacuum, no low temperatures, no wet chemical development
  etc.,
- large recording sensitivity, small recording energy ($\sim \mu$J/cm^2),
- short recording time (μs),
- high optical resolution, especially in the case of holographic methods.

This list is by no means complete. But it elucidates why there exists no ideal storage medium combining all properties required.

The best-known optical storage materials are photographic emulsions, which have gained increasing importance in form of microfiche storage during the last years. In this case the extremely large storage sensitivity is quite impressing. In small spectral regions a few $\mu J/cm^2$ are sufficient for a read-out efficiency of several percent. For modern electronic data technique, however, these emulsions cannot be utilized because the storage is irreversible. Furthermore, the development and fixing processes are too slow and troublesome.

In the following chapters various materials are discussed, which can be used for recording and erasing with light though they represent no ideal solutions up to now. The storage is based on very different physical effects, partly well-known and familiar, partly discovered only during the last years.

This investigation concentrates on aspects of storage with electronic data processing. However, possible applications cover much larger domains. The materials are always interesting when the disciplines of optics and electronics come into contact. During the last years many contacts of this kind have been formed in various areas and the material problems are largely unsolved. Examples are found in the cases of the television video discs or the optical fiber communication.

2. Ferroelectrics and Photoconductors

Storage in ferroelectrics utilizes the electro-optic effect and the hysteresis of remanent electric polarization [1]. With the help of external electric fields the polarization is switched and the fields are controlled by a photoconductor (CdS, CdSe). Appropriate ferroelectrics are $Bi_4Ti_3O_{12}$- and $Gd_2(MoO_4)_3$-crystals or PLZT (Lead-Lanthan-Zirkonate-Titanate)-ceramics.

Fig. 1 shows a combined structure consisting of $Bi_4Ti_3O_{12}$ and a photoconductor between transparent electrodes. A voltage is applied to the electrodes chosen in such a way that the electric field is just too small for polarization switching. When the photoconductor is illuminated the voltage drop essentially occurs across the ferro-electric crystal and now the polarization can be realigned at that place. Read-out of the information is performed without externally applied fields. A detailed inspection of the index ellipsoid shows that the polarization properties of light, which is chosen in an appropriate way, depend on the orientation of the electrical polarization of the ferroelectric medium.

Furthermore, there exists the possibility of electrical read-out of information. In certain ceramics, illumination induces an electrical current, which contains several different contributions [2]. Nevertheless, these contributions are proportional to

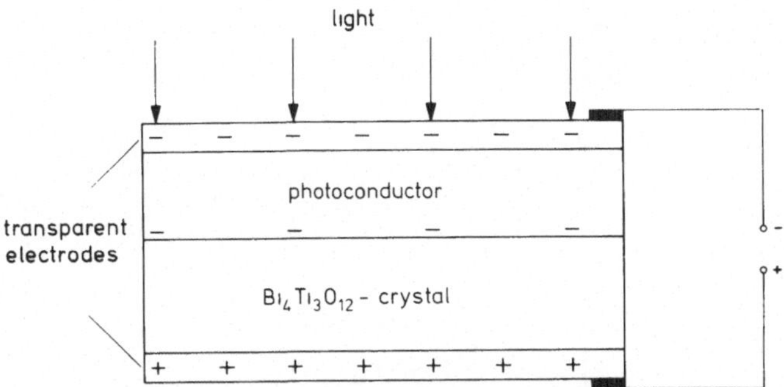

Fig. 1. Combination of ferroelectric $Bi_4Ti_3O_{12}$ and a photoconductor

the polarization of the ceramics in the illuminated region and for this reason the current can be used as a measure of polarization.

In ferroelectric $Bi_4Ti_3O_{12}$ gratings with a period of 1.3 μm have been stored. The writing energy was about 1 mJ/cm^2, the read-out efficiency 0.01 % [1]. However, these values represent by no means the limits of this material.

3. Photoconductive Electro-optic Crystals

A similar storage principle is known under the notation PROM (Pockels-Readout-Optical-Modulator). In this case materials like $B_{12}SiO_{20}$ or ZnS are used, which simultaneously show electro-optic effects and photoconductivity. Light generates free charge carriers, which are separated in an electric field. The resulting space charge fields within the storage medium influence the light during read-out via electro-optic effect.

To avoid unwanted erasure during read-out as much as possible, light of different wavelengths has been used for recording and reading. Furthermore, there is the possibility of renewed writing after read-out. — An additional difficulty is added by the short dark storage time of about one hour.

4. Thermoplastics and Photoconductors

Thermoplastics are transparent layers, which become plastic by heating. Many organic substances offer this property, among them polystyrene-methacrylate-copolymers are of special interest. For storage [4] a transparent electrode, a photo-conductor and the thermoplastic film are deposited on a glass substrate. The operation of the device is explained schematically in Fig. 2. With the help of a corona discharge, positive carriers are accumulated on the thermoplastic film, generating

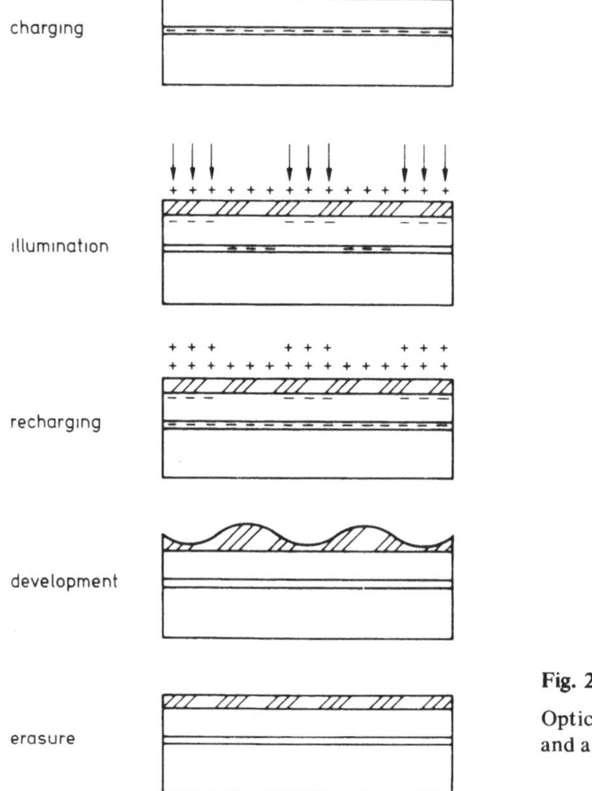

Fig. 2

Optical storage in a thermoplastic film
and a photoconductor

voltages of about 200 V. By exposure to light, electrons migrate through the photoconductor within the illuminated region. A further corona discharge causes electrostatic forces, which produce a surface relief when the thermoplastic film is heated
to about 70 °C. This relief is frozen in when the film is cooled down to room temperature. Erasure of the information is achieved by heating to higher temperatures.

In this case the large sensitivity (several $\mu J/cm^2$ for 1 % read-out efficiency), which
is determined by the photoconductor, is especially attractive. Because of the band-
pass properties, thermoplastics have been proposed for holographic storage as the
maximum read-out efficiency of 33.9 % for two-dimensional phase holograms with
interference of plain waves has been nearly attained.

Difficulties are caused by the limited number of cycles (at best several thousand
cycles have been realized), the complicated corona discharge, and the development
time, though this time has been recently reduced to 250 μs [5].

264

5. Magneto-optic Materials

5.1. Curie Point Switching

Magneto-optic materials utilize the Faraday- or the Kerr-effect for read-out of information: The light polarization rotates under the influence of magnetization, the direction of rotation depending on the position of magnetization. Writing is achieved by local heating with the help of light and simultaneous alignment of magnetization in an externally applied magnetic field.

For the first time thermomagnetic switching has been demonstrated in ferromagnetic MnBi-films [6]. The layer is heated by light above the Curie point at about 360 °C (normal phase). This leads to storage sensitivities of about 100 mJ/cm^2. Additionally, the writing energy has to be supplied in short times (several ns) to limit thermal diffusion. Furthermore, relatively high magnetic fields have to be applied because of the influence of stray fields of neighbouring regions.

5.2. Compensation Point Switching

Stray fields are avoided with the so-called compensation point writing. In this case ferrimagnetic materials with two antiparallel sublattices are utilized, e.g. $Ga_3Fe_5O_{12}$-films [7]. At a certain temperature, the compensation temperature, the moments of the two sublattices cancel each other, so that external magnetic fields have no influence. For a rise in temperature of about 40 °C (writing energy ~ 50 mJ/cm^2) the saturation magnetization can be aligned by a magnetic field of 80 Oe already. Read-out at the compensation temperature is possible, because the Faraday rotation is essentially determined by one sublattice only (Fe^{3+}-ions on octahedral sites).

Singlecrystalline garnet films have been fabricated at the Philips Forschungslaboratorium Hamburg for optical storage [8]. The ferrimagnetic layers are grown on non-ferrimagnetic $Gd_3Ga_5O_{12}$-substrates by liquid phase epitaxy. The substrates are doped with Ca and Zr to adapt the lattice constants of epitaxial layer and substrate to several 10^{-3} Å. A suitably chosen small lattice misfit generates tensions in the layer. Thus the magnetic fields necessary for switching can be reduced considerably for inhomogeneously heated layers [9]. This is very important for device applications, because the difference between homogeneous and inhomogeneous heating renders unnecessary the temperature stabilization of the layers.

The magnetic layers should meet the following requirements:
- large Faraday-rotation, i.e. large read-out efficiency,
- appropriate absorption,
- compensation temperature near room temperature,

- large slope of magnetization near compensation temperature, i.e. large writing sensitivity,
- small uniaxial anisotropy, i.e. small magnetic switching field.

These properties can be influenced by special dopants. The optimization requires 'molecular engineering', i.e. engineering in microscopic regions. The final magnetic layers can then be described roughly by the formula $(Gd,Bi,Pb)_3(Fe,Al,Ga)_5O_{12}$.

Nevertheless, the singlecrystalline garnet films have one disadvantage compared with the polycrystalline MnBi-layers. In the case of the garnet films small magnetic regions, several μm in diameter, cannot be switched without special precautions, because no appropriate pinning centers for magnetic walls are available. For this reason the layers have to be divided into small islands storing one bit each. This structuring may be done by ion etching; Figs. 3 and 4 show garnet films treated in this way.

Fig. 3. Ion etched garnet film; the dimensions of the islands are about $10 \times 10 \times 5 \ \mu m^3$

5.3. Magneto-optic Layers and Photoconductors

For many practical applications the writing sensitivity of these garnet layers is still too low. It is not very favourable, when the light only provides the heating energy. For this reason a different principle has been proposed [11]: The light acts as trigger, while the heating energy is taken from an external electric source.

266

Fig. 4. Magneto-optic contrast between oppositely magnetized islands of a garnet film

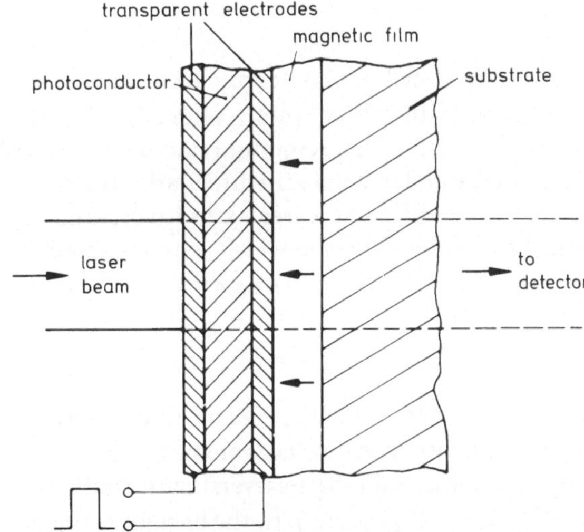

Fig. 5

Magneto-optic photoconductor
sandwich (MOPS)

This principle of a magneto-optic photoconductive sandwich (MOPS) is illustrated
in Fig. 5. A photoconductor (CdS:Cu) is deposited between transparent electrodes
$(In_2O_3:SnO_2)$ on the magnetic layer. A voltage pulse applied to the electrodes induces a current in the illuminated regions, heating the photoconductor and the
garnet film below. Switching is achieved as described above. The sensitivity was
enhanced with this configuration by two orders of magnitude (writing energy about
$500\ \mu J/cm^2$, read-out efficiency about 1 %).

6. Photochromic and Photorefractive Crystals

6.1. Three-dimensional Storage

The materials treated above utilize two dimensions for optical storage. However, holographic methods can display the whole diversity of capabilities by taking into account the third dimension. The holographic diffraction pattern is described by a three-dimensional function ('thick' holograms), spacial distances in the diffraction pattern are small compared with the thickness of the recording medium. The Bragg condition has to be taken into account additionally, and many holograms can be superimposed at the same position by rotating the crystal at an angle of only fractions of a degree. By these means the largest storage capacities at all are obtained. Holographic recording can be performed by influencing the amplitude or phase of light. For this reason materials are needed, which, under the influence of light, change the absorption (photochromic effects) or the index of refraction (photorefractive effects).

6.2. Photochromic Effects

For the first time 'thick' holograms have been stored in photochromic crystals. Appropriate effects are found in alkali halides with colour centers, in $SrTiO_3$ doped with Mo and Fe or in CaF_2 [13]. In these cases the high resolution (atomic processes) and the good linearity are attractive features. Fundamental difficulties arise from thermal bleaching, from the use of light of two different wavelengths for recording and reading and above all from the small read-out efficiency, which cannot exceed 3.7 % for 'thick' amplitude holograms with interference of plane waves.

6.3. Photorefractive Effects

Large read-out efficiencies up to 100 % can be obtained in the case of 'thick' phase holograms. For this reason light-induced refractive index changes are of special interest. Large effects of this kind have been observed [14] in several pyro- and ferroelectric crystals ($LiNbO_3$, $BaTiO_3$, $Sr_{1-x}Ba_x Nb_2 O_6$ etc.). In the beginning the effects seemed to be very undesirable ('optical damage') because the application of the materials e.g. as electro-optic modulators was strongly impaired. Very soon, however, the significance for holographic storage was recognized [15].

The photorefractive effect is illustrated in Fig. 6. Interfering light beams generate dark and bright regions in an electro-optic crystal. In the bright regions electrons are excited and migrate to different sites. In this manner space charge fields are set up which modulate the refractive index via electro-optic effect. A redistribution of the electrons, i.e. erasure of the hologram, is achieved by uniform illumination or by heating.

268

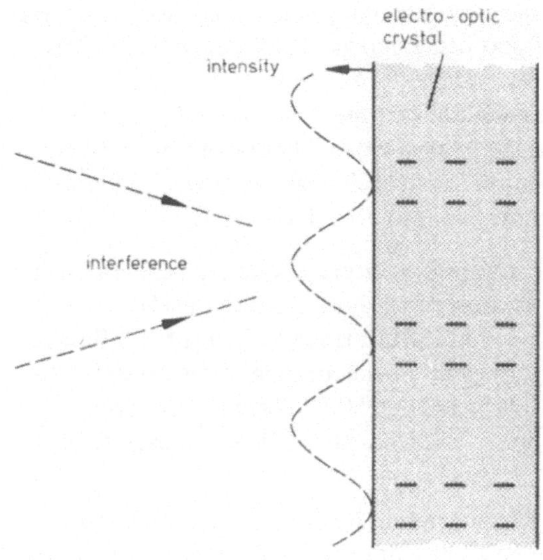

Fig. 6

Light-induced refractive index changes in ferroelectric crystals

6.4. Sensitivity and Storage Time of Photorefractive Crystals

In several crystals photorefractive effects may be easily enhanced by external electric fields. The largest writing sensitivity has been measured in the case of $K\,Ta_{0.65}Nb_{0.35}O_3$ [16]. With an electric field of 6 kV/cm a writing energy of $100\,\mu J/cm^2$ was sufficient for a read-out efficiency of 5 %. However, on account of the relatively small electric resistivity the dark storage time was limited to 10 hours only.

Large dark storage times are found in the case of $LiNbO_3$. Undoped $LiNbO_3$-crystals, however, are very insensitive for recording. Considerable improvements of storage sensitivity are possible by transition metal dopants and by reducing chemical treatments [17]. Especially large effects are obtained by Fe-impurities. In this case Fe^{2+}-ions act as donors and Fe^{3+}-ions as traps [18].

Nevertheless, these methods for enhancement of sensitivity again reduce the dark storage time. External electric fields have only small influence on the storage properties of $LiNbO_3$ for excitations with visible light, because in this case the electron transport properties are determined by a photovoltaic effect [19]. The excited electrons migrate in the direction of the polar crystal axis opposite to the direction of spontaneous polarization. The magnitude of the effect again depends on the dopants and the chemical treatments [20]. At best recording energies of about $300\,mJ/cm^2$ are necessary for a read-out efficiency of 1 % [21].

A different behaviour is found in the near UV spectral region. Spectroscopic investigations demonstrate a strong increase of photoconductivity in this region [22]. This effect yields improvements of sensitivity under external electric fields in the case of oxidized $LiNbO_3$-crystals with a large dark storage time. The sensitivity values exceed those of heavily reduced crystals, the storage time is about one year [23]. By these means the most suitable combination of relatively high sensitivity and large storage time has been obtained up to now in photorefractive crystals.

When the possibility of optical erasure is waived the storage time can be additionally increased by appropriate temperature treatments [24]. In this case the electronic charge pattern is changed into an ionic pattern, which is stable against the influence of light. Then erasure can only be performed by further heating of the crystals to temperatures above 200 °C. Utilizing this technique, 500 holograms have been stored at different angles at the same place; the read-out efficiency of each single hologram was larger than 2.5 % [24].

Further attractive aspects are offered by photorefractive effects induced by two photon processes [16]. In this case the possibility of optical reading without erasure is of particular interest. The two photon processes are a further example to show that photorefractive effects in ferroelectric crystals are not yet fully understood and that the limitations of these methods can be estimated only very vaguely.

7. Prospects

The materials and methods described above demonstrate the various possibilites for reversible optical storage of information. Of course the selection presented here is partial and incomplete.

In all cases much work has to be done to optimize the materials for practical applications. In the case of localized storage — i.e. each point in the storage plain corresponds to the binary one or zero — up to now magneto-optic garnet layers combined with photoconductors (MOPS) represent the most highly developed solution. The requirements of large sensitivity, large storage time and large reliability are satisfied to a high degree. MOPS has been tested successfully in laboratory models of optical storage systems. The manufacture, however, is relatively complicated, simplifications of the technological steps are being worked at. — Furthermore, ferroelectric $Bi_4 Ti_3 O_{12}$-layers combined with photoconductors seem to be attractive for localized storage.

Optical storage of volume phase holograms requires augmented investigations of materials with light-induced refractive index changes, in order to create a sufficient understanding of the physical processes involved and to obtain reliable estimates of the limits of these methods.

270

These topics have been intensiviely discussed with my colleagues at the Philips Forschungslaboratorium Hamburg. I am especially obliged to Dr. P. Hansen, H. Heitmann, Dr. B. Hill, Dr. U. Killat, Dr. J.-P. Krumme, Dr. H. Kurz, R. Orlowski, Dr. R. Pepperl, Dr. U. Schmidt, Dr. H. J. Schmitt and K. Witter.

References

[1]   S. A. Kenemann, G. W. Taylor, A. Miller and W. H. Fonger, Appl. Phys. Letters 17, 173 (1970).

[2]   F. Micheron, J. M. Rouchon and M. Vergnolle, Ferroelectrics 10, 15 (1976).

[3]   S. L. Hou and D. S. Oliver, Appl. Phys. Letters 18, 325 (1971).

[4]   J. C. Urbach and R. W. Meier, Appl. Optics 5, 666 (1966).

[5]   U. Killat and D. R. Terrell, Optica Acta 24, 441 (1977).

[6]   L. Mayer, J. Appl. Phys. 29, 1003 (1958).

[7]   J. T. Chang, J. F. Dillon and U. F. Gianola, J. Appl. Phys. 36, 1110 (1965).

[8]   J.-P. Krumme, G. Bartels and W. Tolksdorf, phys. stat. sol. (a) 17, 175 (1973) and J.-P. Krumme, G. Bartels, P. Hansen and J. M. Robertson, Mat. Res. Bull. 11, 337 (1976).

[9]   J.-P. Krumme, P. Hansen and K. Witter, J. Appl. Phys. 47, 3681 (1976).

[10]   J.-P. Krumme and H. Dimigen, IEEE Trans. MAG-9, 405 (1973).

[11]   J.-P. Krumme, B. Hill, J. Kruger and K. Witter, J. Appl. Phys. 46, 2733 (1975).

[12]   J.-P. Krumme, H. Heitmann, D. Mateika and K. Witter, J. Appl. Phys. 48, 366 (1977).

[13]   B. W. Faughnan, D. L. Staebler and Z. J. Kiss, Applied Solid State Science, vol. 2, R. Wolfe ed., Academic Press, Inc., New York 1971.

[14]   A. Ashkin, G. D. Boyd, J. M. Dziedzic, R. G. Smith, A. A. Ballman, H. J. Levinstein and K. Nassau, Appl. Phys. Letters 9, 72 (1966).

[15]   F. S. Chen, J. T. LaMacchia and D. B. Fraser, Appl. Phys. Letters 13, 223 (1968).

[16]   D. von der Linde, A. M. Glass and K. F. Rodgers, Appl. Phys. Letters 26, 22 (1975).

[17]   W. Phillips, J. J. Amodei and D. L. Staebler, RCA-Review 33, 94 (1972).

[18]   H. Kurz, E. Kratzig, W. Keune, H. Engelmann, U. Gonser, B. Dischler and A. Rauber, Appl. Phys. 12, 355 (1977).

[19]   A. M. Glass, D. von der Linde and T. J. Negran, Appl. Phys. Letters 24, 4 (1974).

[20]   E. Kratzig and H. Kurz, J. Electrochem. Soc. 124, 131 (1977).

[21]   H. Kurz, V. Doormann and R. Kobs, Proceedings of the International Conference on Applications of Holography and Optical Data Processing, Jerusalem, Israel 1976.

[22]   E. Kratzig and H. Kurz, Ferroelectrics 13, 295 (1976).

[23]   R. Orlowski, E. Krätzig and H. Kurz, Optics Commun. 20, 171 (1977).

[24]   D. L. Staebler, W. J. Burke, W. Phillips and J. J. Amodei, Appl. Phys. Letters 26, 182 (1975).

Optical Memory Systems

Bernhard Hill

Philips GmbH Forschungslaboratorium Hamburg, Germany

Introduction

Stimulated by the invention of the laser, a great number of ideas on optical memories appeared in the early sixties. Many of these were focussed on the so-called block-organized holographic memory which gave hope to high capacity stores with random access times in the microsecond range.

The first experimental results, however, showed that a number of complex components was needed such as light deflectors, electrooptic input- and output interfaces (page composers and detector arrays), erasable holographic storage materials etc. It turned out that these components could not be made available at short term and it took years to progress. The main problem of an erasable and fast switchable holographic storage material is unsolved even up to now.

This paper starts with a brief review on the basic principles of holographic memories and discusses their main difficulties with attention to the state of the art of the essential components.

In its nature, holographic storage works associative. Associative storage offers many advantages compared to storage systems using word- or bit adressing. To pay attention to this field, which could become important in the future, a simple associative storage method with read-out by key words is discussed in the second section.

For localized storage, (bit by bit), erasable magneto-optic storage materials are already available. On the basis of such materials, system concepts have been developed and operational "feasibility-models" are already working. The design concepts of magneto-optic stores and their essential features are summarized in section 3.

The well-known principle of a disc store is also considered for optical memories. In the last chapter, a brief outlook on optical disc-recorders using very simple storage materials for DRAW (direct-read-after write) is given.

1. Block-Organized Holographic Memories

The block-organized holographic memory handles data blocks of KBits in parallel [1–5]. Each data block is considered to be available at the input in electronic form. For the storage in a hologram, the data block is converted into a transparency image with the help of a so-called page composer (Fig. 1). In this transparency, the

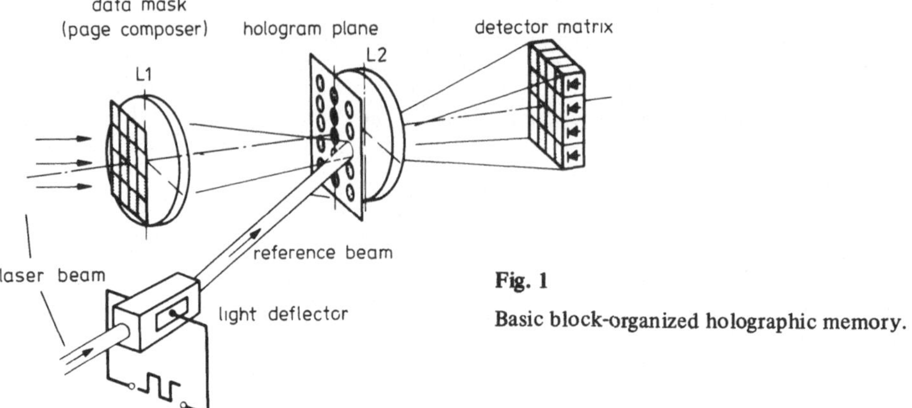

Fig. 1

Basic block-organized holographic memory.

data are represented by an array of dark and bright light spots, a bright light spot standing for a binary "1", a dark one standing for a binary "0", respectively. The data block is then stored by generating a hologram from the data transparency. Therefore, the transparency is being illuminated by a laser beam (the "object beam") and the transmitted light is superposed on a "reference-beam" at a certain angle of incidence. The superposition results in an optical interference, the intensity of which is recorded on a storage material as density or phase distribution.

For read-out of the stored information, the hologram is illuminated by the reference beam only. Then, by diffraction of light, an image of the original transparency is composed at a distance from the hologram. The reconstructed image is projected on a photo-detector-array where a photo-detector is attached to each light-spot position. The detectors measure the brightness of a reconstructed light spot and generates respective electronic output signals. For storage of further blocks of data, the storage process is repeated, every new data block being recorded in another hologram. Therefore, the storage plane is divided into a matrix of holograms that are selectively addressed by the optical beams via light deflection systems.

A simple sketch of this memory configuration with the reference beam indicated for read-out of information is shown in Fig. 1. In the more realistic systems for non-mechanical writing and reading, the selective optical addressing of holograms requires a more complex system structure with an additional number of optical components [4–6].

The size of a data block is mostly in the order of 10^4 bit for reasons of system design. Accordingly, the storage capacity of 10^8 bit, for instance, requires the arrangement of 10^4 holograms in the storage plane. The relative size of the storage plane is as large as 15×15 cm^2. The largest achievable storage capacity is, therefore, limited by the objective-lens located in the storage plane to display the data onto the detector array (see Fig. 1) [5–9]. A high quality objective-lens free of distortion

274

is difficult to realize for that large aperture. Considering a two-dimensional storage medium (photographic materials or thermoplastics, for example), the limit is hardly more than 10^8 bit. Only on the base of volume storage [41], capacities beyond 10^8 bit can be expected for the future [10]. Another difficult problem is that of system dimensions for capacities near the limit. Dimensions of more than 1 m are certainly unacceptable.

The random access time for read-out is mainly determined by the switching time of the light deflector and the response time of the detector array. Considering the fastest light deflection systems available, the overall random access time can be expected to be a few microseconds only [14, 15].

Today, realistic solutions have been found for nearly all the components of a holographic memory with the exception of the storage material. A number of laboratories have reported on operational "feasibility-models" [6, 9, 11–13]. Light deflection systems are available based on electro-optic [14, 15] or acoustooptic [16, 17] techniques. The function of an electro-optic deflection cell is, for instance, described in Fig. 2. Larger deflection systems use a number of deflection cells in

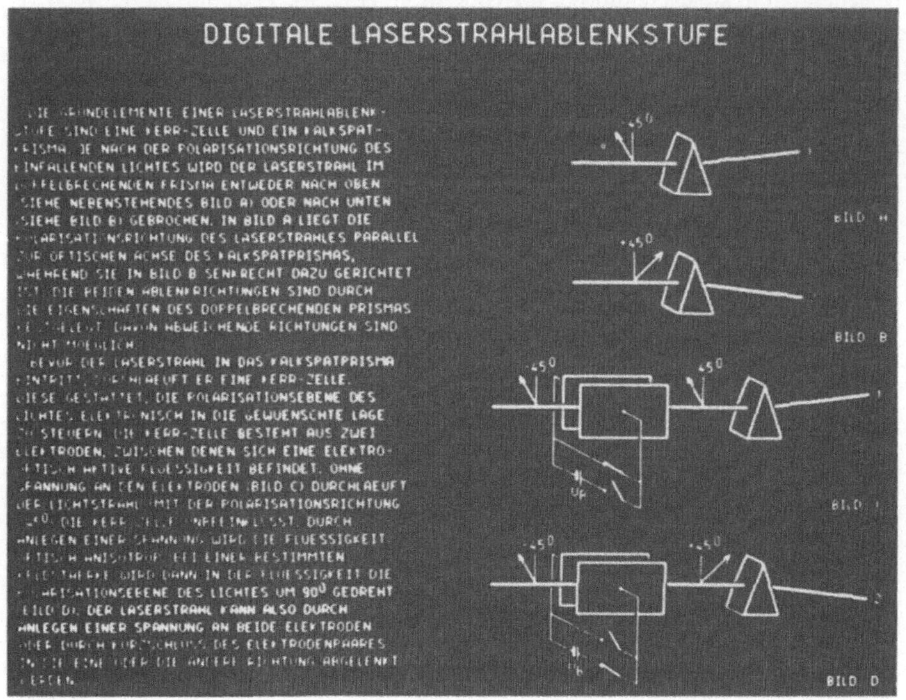

Fig. 2. Display of information by digital laser beam deflection.

series, with the deflection angle growing from stage to stage. With n stages, 2^n different positions can be addressed at random within less than 0.5 μs. The image of Fig. 2 is a self-presentation of a 20-stage electro-optic light deflection system: the image has been written point by point with the deflection system controlled from an image store.

The problem of a technology suitable for the realization of a page composer – the electronically switchable transparency – has been solved as well. Page composers have been realized using liquid-crystals [18, 19], PLZT-ceramics [20], gadolinum-molybdate [21] or CdS-crystals. The CdS-page composer, made in thin film technology, uses a thermally induced shift of a band edge for light modulation. With monochromatic laser light, the transparency of a thin CdS-plate near the band edge is high for low temperatures (ca. 10 °C) and low for high temperatures (ca. 70 °C). Electronic information to be optically presented by the page composer is therefore transformed into a "thermal image" in a thin CdS-layer (ca. 10 μm thick). Local heating is achieved by an array of transparent heating electrodes deposited on the CdS-layer. The electrodes are controlled by electronic pulses via a crossbar system. According to a thermal decay time of ca. 1.5 ms and a rise time of 20 μs, 500 images can be generated in a page composer for 16 × 18 bit (Fig. 3). The contrast between dark and bright elements is better than 100. Larger matrices with more than 1000 switching elements are being fabricated.

The third essential component, the detector array as output interface, can also be made available today with semiconductor technology [25–27].

Fig. 3a

16 × 18 bit CdS page composer with addressing by a silicon diode matrix.

Fig. 3b

CdS-page composer operated in transmission.

Nevertheless, the development of block-organized holographic storage systems has been stopped in nearly all laboratories. This is due to the still unsolved storage material problem. The erasable and fast switchable holographic storage materials has therefore become the key-component for holographic memory techniques in the future.

2. Associative Memories [28–31]

The holographic storage and retrieval process works on an associative principle. Fig. 4 shows a generalized associative storage arrangement based on two page composers P1 and P2. The page composers are used to generate two transmission images. When being illuminated by coherent light, part of the light is transmitted and focussed on to the holographic storage plane by the objective lens. Thereby, the light of the two page composers is superposed, and an interference pattern appears.

It is assumed, that the storage material stores a pattern which is approximately proportional to the irradiance of this interference.

For read out, the page composer P2 is considered to generate an image C. The light of this image is focussed on to the hologram plane and diffracted by the pattern stored in the hologram. Thus, a certain irradiance is reconstructed in the focal plane of the objective lens L2 being the output plane of the system. By mathematical treatment, one finds this irradiance to be described by the convolution integral

$$\int_{x_2', y_2'} A(x_2 - x_2', y_2 - y_2') \int_{x_2'', y_2''} \overline{B}(x_2' - x_2'', y_2' - y_2'') C(x_2'', y_2'') \, dx_2'', dy_2'' \; dx_2' \, dy_2'$$

$$= A \otimes \{\overline{B} \otimes C\},$$

where the functions $A(x_1, y_1)$, $B(x_1, y_1)$ and $C(x_1, y_1)$ describe the complex amplitudes of the irradiances in the plane of the page composers and (x_2, y_2) are the coordinates in the output plane (the conjugate complex function of B is designed by a cross bar).

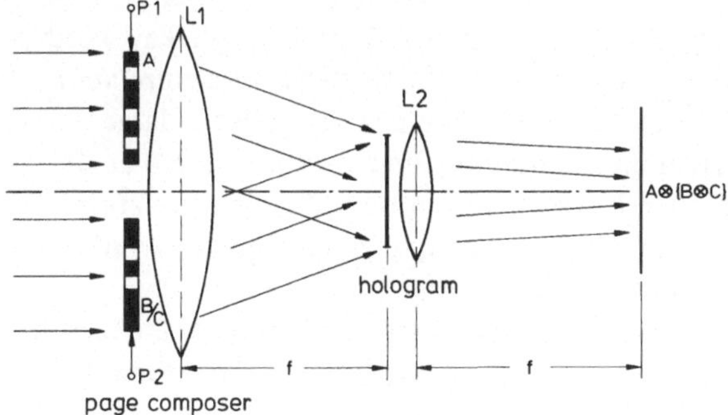

Fig. 4

Arrangement for associative optical storage.

The result implies, that the irradiance in the output plane is a convolution (a "correlation" or "association") of the function $A(x_1, y_1)$ with the convolution of the functions B and C. The function A is now considered to represent a data block, B is a reference wave and C a read-out word. Reconstruction of the original data function is then only obtained if either the convolution of B and C is a so-called delta-function or at least close to it or if B and C are simple plane waves. The last case is the basis for the block-organized holographic store as has been described in the previous section, whereas reconstruction via the delta function is typical for the associative store.

The irradiance achieved at the output, when considering a delta-function is given by

$$A \otimes \{B \otimes C\} = \int_{x_2', y_2'} A(x_2, y_2) \, \delta(x_2', y_2') \, dx_2' \, dy_2',$$

which results exactly in the data function originally stored. This ideal reconstruction is, of course, not achieved in practice. A delta function as result of the convolution of B and C can only be achieved for $B = C$. In addition, B and C must be functions unlimited in space and of random nature. In practice, the delta-function can only be approximated. It is then necessary that there is a correlation between B and C as outlined in Fig. 5a–b. Strong correlation is considered in Fig. 5a. The result of the convolution of B and C is a strong peak with only little background noise. For a reduced degree of correlation (Fig. 5b), the peak is diminished and without any correlation between B and C, only noise is achieved as sketched in Fig. 5c, which, of course, destroys the information in the output plane.

In the associative memory, the function of B is that of a reference word and C is a key word. If the key word equals the reference word for reconstruction and if both words are of a random nature, then an image of the data stored is obtained at the output superposed with background noise. Otherwise, the answer is just noise.

This basic associative storage principle discussed so far is widely verified in practice. Systems have been discussed which use a hologram with a large number of superposed data functions together with their respective reference words as well as in another case, holograms storing only one data function and scanned by a key word. Sometimes, it may also be sufficient to look only for the existence of a correlation peak without reconstructing the information itself. This can be applied in large data banks to find out where a certain information is stored or if it is stored at all. In all these systems, one severe problem is still that of noise and cross-correlation. Careful optimization of the structure of data functions, reference and key words is necessary to achieve useful reconstructions. When considering normal random objects as data functions (e.g. pictures etc.) the results are rather poor. It is necessary to use special codings and redundancy to overcome these problems. The search for optimum codings is still a matter of research.

278

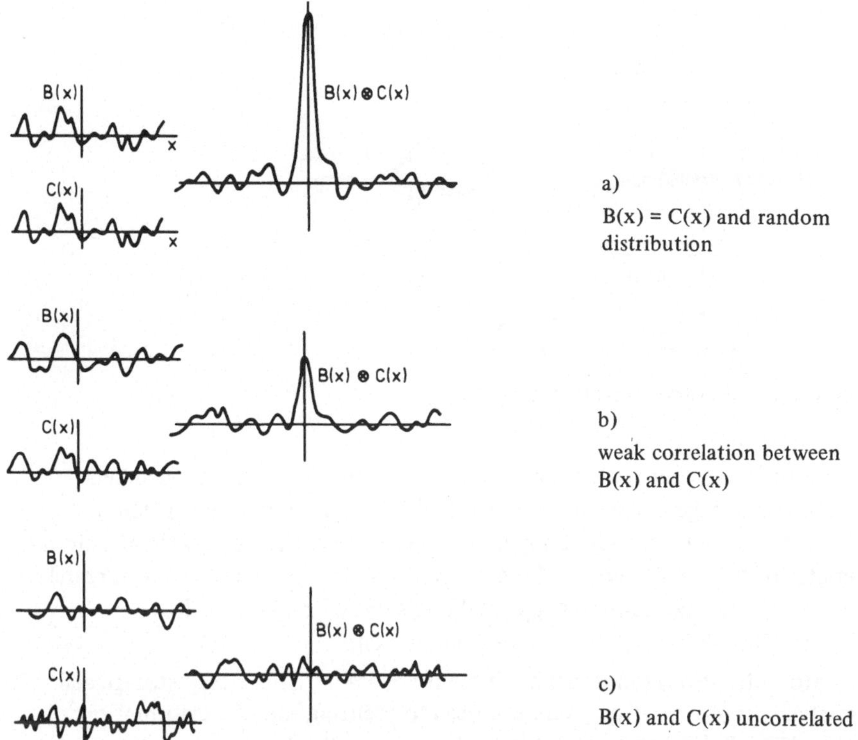

Fig. 5. Convolution (correlation) of two functions B and C.

When considering associative memories for erasable storage, the storage material is, of course, a problem as well. Therefore, read-only associative optical memories can only be considered for the near future. Nevertheless, the unconventional storage method with the possibility to read-out parts of information by key words without knowledge of the storage address as in conventional memories offers a lot of new possibilities and could, therefore, open a wide field of applications in the future, to solve data bank- or archival storage problems.

3. Magneto-Optic Point Stores

3.1. The Basic Principle of a Magneto-Optic Point Store

In a magneto-optic point store, information is stored pointwise in a thin storage layer. The storage layer deposited on a substrate is structured into individual storage cells each storing 1 bit. The cells are optically addressed by a laser beam which is

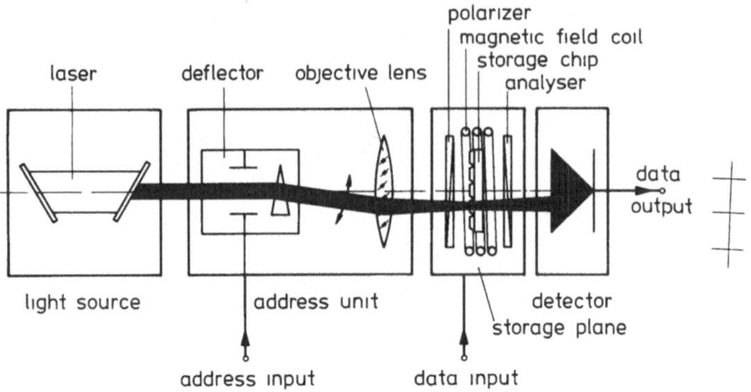

Fig. 6. Principle of the magneto-optic memory.

focussed on to the storage material by an objective lens (Fig. 6). The focussed
light spot in the storage plane can be controlled by a light deflection system in
front of the objective lens, so that any storage cell is optically adressable at random.
The diameter of the focal point is, therefore, chosen in such manner, that it equals
the diameter of a storage cell. The typical dimensions of a storage cell is
$10 \times 10\ \mu m^2$. This allows 10^6 bit to be stored in 1 cm^2.

The magneto-optic storage material has a binary characteristic. Every storage cell
can be switched into one of two stable states representing the two information
states "1" and "0". For writing of information, one cell after the other is optically
addressed and switched into the respective states by the individual action of light in
connection with one or two other global control parameters. For the magneto-optic
photoconductor sandwich MOPS [32–36, 41], the global control parameters are
an external magnetic field and an electronic pulse applied to a photoconductor
layer. Read-out of information is again performed by addressing a number of cells
sequentially, however, switching of cells is not necessary, since read-out is non-
destructive. The information state of a memory cell is made visible for an opto-
electronic detection system via the Faraday-effect and polarization optics.

The essential features of a magneto-optic memory of the type described so far are
given by the resolution of the optics, the number of addressable points of the light
deflection system, the switching speed of the deflector and the switching speed
and efficiency of the storage material. In practice, the capacity is mainly limited
by the resolution of the light deflection system. Nonmechanical digital deflectors
are able to address a point raster of 1000×1000 points today. Up to 5000×5000
points are addressable when considering servo-controlled galvanometer mirrors.
Hence, the storage capacity is limited to ca. 10^7 bit.

The random access time for mechanical systems is limited to the range of milliseconds, whereas nonmechanical deflectors offer less than a microsecond [14, 15].

280

The overall random access time of the magneto-optic store also depends on the
response time of the photodetector at the output that is a function of the laser power,
the efficiency of the storage material and the sensitivity of the detector. Typically,
the overall random access time can be in the order of microseconds, if the laser
source delivers 5 mW of output power for the case of the magneto-optic photoconductor sandwich MOPS. When considering the access time to be only 100 μs, a laser
power of 5 μW is sufficient. The data rate for read-out is approximately given by the
reciprocal value of the overall access time.

3.2. Higher capacity and data rate by beam splitting

To overcome the capacity limit given by the deflection system, beam splitting
techniques can be used. The basic principle is shown in Fig. 7. The light coming
out of the deflection system is split into a number of equispaced partial beams. The
partial beams are focussed onto a respective number of storage chips, with each
beam addressing one storage cell in each chip at a time. By switching the light deflector, the bundle of beams is deflected at once so that any storage cell on each chip can
be optically addressed.

According to the multiplication of beams, the total laser power at the input is, of
course, increased. The advantage of it is, however, an increased data rate for writing
as well as for reading. A number of rather simple beam-splitting techniques is
available [35]. The most common are specially designed optical gratings, calcite
prisms using birefringence or dielectric beam splitting layers. Two of these are
discussed in more detail in the following section.

3.3. "Feasibility-Model" of an Optical Point Store

Feasibility-models of magneto-optic point stores have already been demonstrated
in the laboratory [34, 36]. The largest system is the so-called POCOM (poly-cube
optical memory). This system is designed for 6.5 $\times$ 10^7 bit organized in words of

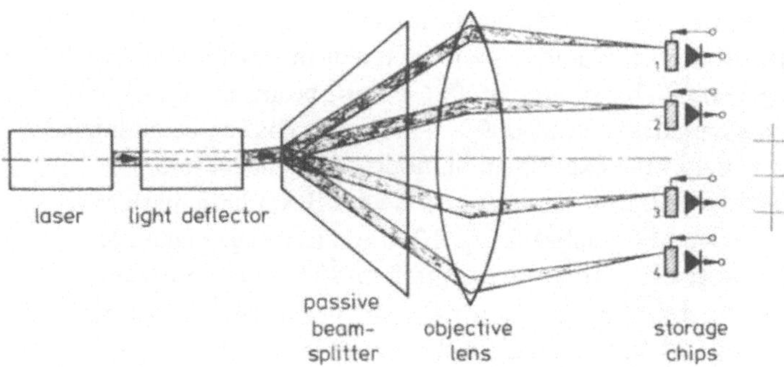

Fig. 7. Principle of a memory with addressing by beam splitting.

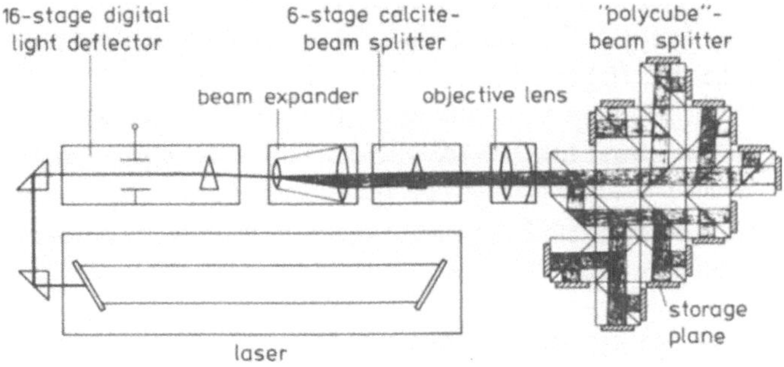

Fig. 8. A large capacity magneto-optic memory.

1024 bits due to beam splitting by the factor 1024 [35]. This store (Fig. 8) uses a
20 mW He-Ne-Laser. The light beam is deflected in one of 65 000 possible directions by a 16-stage digital light deflector. This number of points defines a basic
storage pattern (subpattern) in a storage plane. After deflection, the beam is split
into 8 × 8 partial beams by a 6-stage calcite beam splitter. The calcite beam splitter
therefore uses the effect of birefringence in a prism configuration for splitting any
incoming beam into two partial beams in a first stage. The next stage again splits
each beam into two at the output. This results in 2^6 = 64 beams at the output for
the 6 stages considered.

The finger of 8 × 8 beams is then focussed onto a storage plane by the objective
lens. The pattern of points covers the area of 3 × 3 cm^2. According to the splitting,
the storage plane is structured into 8 × 8 subpatterns, each addressed by one
partial beam. A photo taken from half of the addressable number of points in a
storage plane is shown in Fig. 9.

Between the objective lens and the straightforward storage plane another beam
splitter is installed. This consists of a multitude of cubic beam splitters with
dielectric layers arranged in the path of the beams under the angle of 45°. At each
layer, 50 % of the light is transmitted and 50 % reflected at the angle of 90° with
respect to the incoming beams. This results in 1024 output beams at 16 output
windows so that 16 storage planes with 65 000 × 64 storage cells can be addressed
in total. The storage material in the experimental model is the magneto-optic
photoconductor sandwich. Up to now, storage planes with 3 × 3 basic patterns
integrated on a substrate have been realized. Fig. 10 shows a storage plane containing about 150 000 storage cells arranged at a pitch of 20 μm. The storage
density is expected to be increased by the factor 4 in the near future, which will
result in a total capacity of 589 000 bits per substrate. In Fig. 10, the subpattern
of the slice is individually controlled electrically as may be seen from Fig. 10. The
writing time is about 50 μs. The control of the system is designed for a cycle time

282

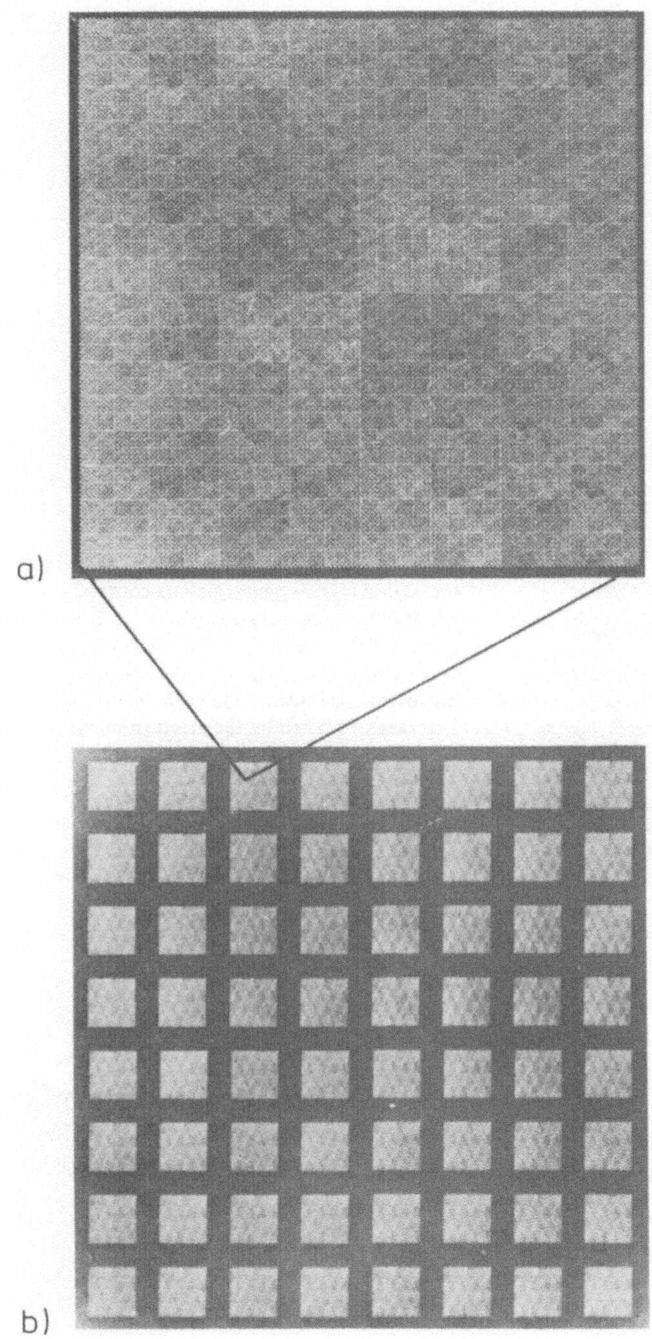

Fig. 9

a) Sub-pattern of
    addressable points
    in a memory plane

b) Splitted
    sub-pattern 8 × 8.

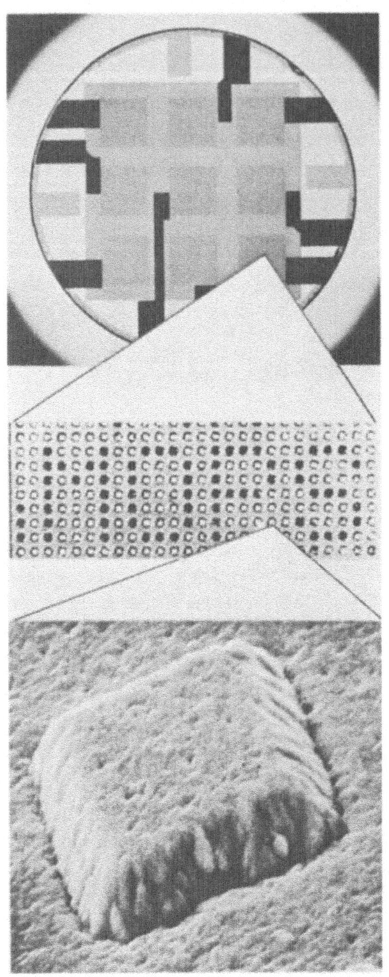

Fig. 10

Integrated MOPS-memory plane containing 150,000 storage cells arranged in 3 X 3 sub-pattern. Part of a sub-pattern with information written-in as seen in a polarization microscope is shown. Below, the photo of a storage cell taken by the electron-microscope is given.

of 100 μs if all the memory planes are installed. The storage is nondestructive and nonvolatile due to the bistable characteristic of the MOPS. More than 10^7 switching cycles have already been demonstrated without deterioration of the memory material.

The capacity of the POCOM-memory is comparable to that of a magnetic disc. The random access time, however, is smaller by the factor 100—300. In addition, read-out is word-organized in a synchronized operation mode which makes direct loading of main store possible without any buffering.

The feasibility model does not yet allow to exchange storage planes. In principle, the exchange is, however, realizable, a fact which could widen the field of application. Since the whole technology of magneto-optic memories is, however, very new, one should not expect this type of memory on the market in the near future and at a price lower than that of other technologies. Work is still pursued to improve the technology and to lower the costs.

Besides the nonmechanical version, magneto-optic memories with mechanical access are considered as well. Those memories could be very inexpensive when using simple voice coil systems for x-y-positioning of the storage plane in front of a fixed light source or an array of fixed light sources. Since the storage density is high and therefore, the steps for positioning are small compared with magnetic disc memories, the random access time achieved is quite attractive.

4. Optical Disc Memories

Extremely large storage capacities are offered by optical disc memories. The basic principle of an optical disc memory is shown in Fig. 11a. The optical disc carries, for instance, a storage layer on the lower surface. Information is recorded in this layer along a spiral or concentric track. The data along a track are mostly stored blockwise with an address number at the beginning of each block. This block can be found again when addressing at random.

The essential components of the optical addressing part are a laser, a light modulator (light switch) and an objective lens that can be positioned in radial direction. This objective lens focusses the laser beam on to the storage material. Exact focussing even for non-flat surfaces is achieved by a servo-system. A second servo-system is used for radial tracking. Both radial and vertical positioning is performed by voice-coil systems. For read-out of information, either the reflected or the transmitted light is picked up by a photodetector.

A predecessor of the optical disc memory is the so-called VLP-system (Video-Long Play) [37, 38]. This system is designed for the commercial market. It is a read-only-

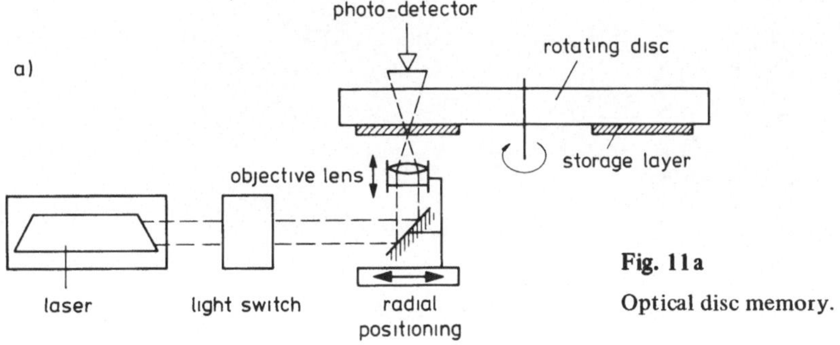

Fig. 11a

Optical disc memory.

system which allows the play-back of a television program that is pressed into a plastic disc in a similar way as is done in the well-known record.

Reliable erasable storage materials for high optical storage density are not yet available today, though, much effort is being spent to develop them. Meanwhile, however, simple materials for read-after write (DRAW) operation are used successfully. As an example of such a material, a thin metallic film (600 Å Bismuth) is shown in Fig. 11b. In this film, information is stored by burning holes with the help of the laser beam [39]. A burnt hole represents a binary "1", no hole a binary "0". With this method, an experimental storage density of 4×10^7 bit/cm^2 has been achieved. This allows the storage of 2×10^{10} bits on a disc of ca. 30 cm $\emptyset$. In experimental models, the data can be written at a rate of 2 Mbit/s with a 20 mW He-Ne-Laser and read at the same speed with reduced power.

The technical problems to realize optical DRAW-recorders for the most part have been solved today. Components for focussing and tracking are similar to those used in the VLP-system [37, 38], that is being developed by several firms and will be marketed in the near future.

In practice, of course, the introduction of DRAW-disc memories requires new software since conventional memories in data-systems are erasable. The extremely low costs that can be expected for DRAW-recorders could, however, make up for this disadvantage of non-erasability. Costs in the order of less than 10^{-4} ¢/bit for the system and 10^{-8} ¢/bit for the storage material are realistic targets. This, in addition, makes the optical disc memory an attractive competitor for microfilm storage.

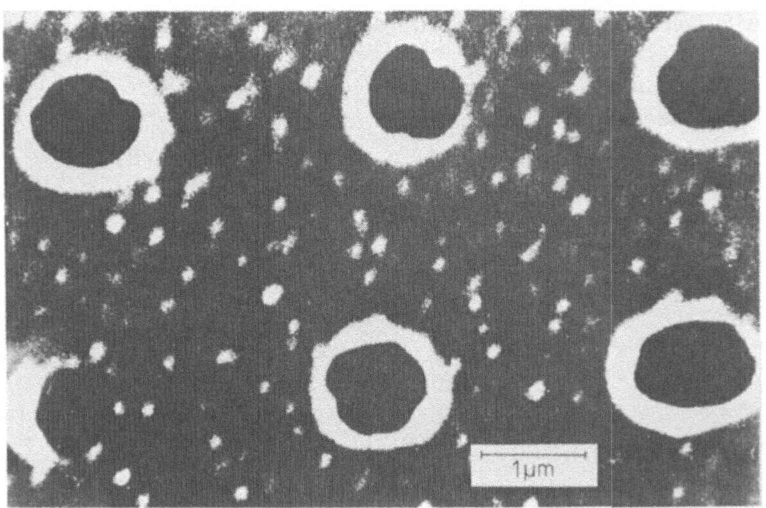

Fig. 11b. DRAW-storage by hole-burning in a Bismuth-layer.

286

Conclusions

The essential features of optical memories, the high storage density and the ability to store and address at random large amounts of information contactless without any complicated electronic addressing network seem to be attractive for the future compared with other storage technologies.

More than 15 years ago, when research on optical memories was started, most of the effort was spent on the holographic store. The capacity of this store, is, however, limited in principle. When considering nonmechanical access and thin, two-dimensional storage media, the limit may be ca. 10^8 bit. Only on the basis of volume storage, this limit could be extended in the future. In any case, the system dimensions are rather voluminous. All the essential system components required in a holographic memory such as light deflectors, page composers, detector arrays etc. have been realized in the laboratory, except one, the storage material itself. The difficulty to realize an erasable and fast switchable holographic storage material is the reason why the interest in holographic memories has dropped worldwide.

The same material problem exists for associative holographic stores. They are realizable today as read-only memories only. Optimization of such systems is still a matter of research, they seem, nevertheless, to offer new interesting solutions for archival stores in the future.

In contrast to holographic stores, a highly sensitive and erasable magneto-optic storage material is already available today for bit by bit stores. On the basis of this material, laboratory models of nonmechanical random access memories have been developed. Using light deflection techniques and beam splitting devices for optical addressing of a multitude of storage chips, capacities of the order of $10^7 - 10^8$ bit can be expected. In a certain "feasibility-model" (designed for 6×10^7 bits), random access to blocks of 1000 bits within $100-500\,\mu s$ has been realized, according to a data rate for writing and reading of $2-10$ Mbit/s. Thus, this system configuration offers the capacity of a magnetic disc memory, the random access time, however, being smaller by orders of magnitude. The information is stored erasable at will, nonvolatile and does not need any power for stand-by operation. In addition, the data are written-in and read-out in synchronism with an external clock so that buffering is not required.

Still larger storage capacities are achieved in optical disc-memories. Simple and cheap storage materials are available for direct-read after write (DRAW). In thin metallic films, information is, for instance, stored by hole burning. Though not being erasable yet, this kind of store may find its field of application in archival storage, large data banks, music and television recording. Based on low power lasers, a data rate of 2 Mbit/s has been demonstrated. Up to 2×10^{10} bit are stored on a disc of 30 cm in diameter.

Magneto-optic as well as optical DRAW-storage is, thus, fairly well developed and the design of commercial systems can be started.

References

[1] *V. A. Vitols*, Hologram Memory for Storing Digital Data, IBM Techn. Discl. Bulletin **8**, 1581 (1966).

[2] *F. M. Smits, L. E. Callaher*, Design Considerations for a Semipermanent Optical Memory, Bell Syst. Techn., J. **46**, 1267 (1967).

[3] *L. K. Anderson*, Holographic Optical Memory for Bulk Data Storage, Bell Lab. Rec. **46**, 319 (1968).

[4] *A. L. Mikaeliane, V. I. Bobrinev, S. M. Navmoy, L. Z. Sokolova*, Design Principles of Holographic Memory Devices, IEEE J. Quart. Electr. **Re-6**, 193 (1970).

[5] *B. Hill*, Some Aspects of a large capacity Holographic memory, Appl. Optics **11**, 1 (1972) 182–190.

[6] *W. C. Stewart, R. S. Mezrich, L. Cosentino, E. H. Nagle, F. S. Wendt, R. D Lohmann*, An experimental Read-Write Holographic Memory, RCA Rev. **34**, 3 (1973).

[7] *P. Graf, M. Lang*, Geometrical Aspects of Consistent Holographic Memory Design, Appl. Optics, **11**, 1382 (1972), Optik **37**, 516 (1973).

[8] *A. Vander Lugt*, Design Considerations for Holographic Memories, Aspen, Aool. Optics **12**, 1675 (1973).

[9] *B. Hill*, Holographic Memories and their Future, Advances in Holography, Vol. 3, Marcel Dekker, Inc., New York, to be published 1977.

[10] *E. Spitz, L. d'Auria, J. P. Huignard, Ch. Slezak*, Holographic Read-Write Memory Optical Organization and Capacity Enhancement by 3 D-Storage, presented at the Topical Meeting on Optical storage of Digital Data, Aspen, Col., March 19–21, 1973.

[11] *P. Waterworth*, A 1.5 × 10⁸ bit Random Access Read Only Holographic Memory, Topical Meeting on Optical Storage of Digital Data, 19–21 March 1973, Aspen Col.

[12] *H. Eschler, G. Goldmann, P. Graf, U. v. Hundelshausen, M. Lang, A. Braidt, G. Eith*, Labormuster eines Holographischen Festwertspeichers, Optik **37**, 516 (1973).

[13] *B. Hill, U. J. Schmidt, H. J. Schmitt*, Optical Memories, J. Appl. Science a. Engineering A, **1** (1975) 39.

[14] *B Hill*, Optische Speicher, Fortschritte im Systementwurf und Technologie, Bericht Datenverarbeitung in Deutschland, Herausgeber Hans Matthöfer, Umschau-Verlag 1976.

[15] *U. Schmidt, W. Thust*, Digital Light Deflection, IEEE J. Quant. Electr. **QE-5**, 351 (1969).

[16] *H. Meyer* et al., Design and Performance of a 20-stage digital light deflector, Appl. Optics, Vol. **11**, 1732 (1972).

[17] *Naoya Uchida, Nobukazu Niizchi*, Acousto-optic Deflection Materials and Techniques. Proc. IEEE, Vol. **61** (1973), 1073.

[18] *G. A. Alphonse*, Broadband Acousto-optic Deflectors, Appl. Optics, Vol. **14** (1975), 201.

[19] *J. Roberts, G. Labrunie, J. Borel*, Imageur de phase electrooptique a cristaux liquides nematiques, Prof. of the 1st European Electro-Optic Markets and Technology Conf., Geneva Sept. 1972, IPC Science and Technology Press.

[20] *G. Labrunie, R. Roberts, J. Borel*, Nematic Liquid Crystal 1024 Bits Page Composer, presented at the Topical Meeting on Optical Storage of Digital Data, Aspen, Col., March 19–21, 1973.

[21] *M. D. Drake*, PLZT-Matrix-Type Block Data Composers, Appl., Optics **12**, 347 (1974).

[22]   *Yasatsuga Takeda*, Digital Spatial Modulator, presented at the Topical Meeting on
       Optical Storage of Digital Data, Aspen, Col., March 19–21, 1973.
       *Yasutsugu Takeda, Yoshio Furukata, Akio Kumada, Sadao Nomura, Seikichi Akiyama,
       Sakichi Ashida,* Digital Spatial Modulator Made of Gadolinium Molybdate Crystal,
       presented at the „Solid State Devices", Intern. Conf. August 29–31, Tokyo.

[23]   *B. Hill, K. P. Schmidt,* A thermally controlled Page-Composer, Topical Meeting on
       Optical Storage of Digital Data, Aspen, Col., 19–21 March 1973.

[24]   *K. P. Schmidt,* A 16 × 18 bit CdS-spatial modulator (Page-Composer), to be published
       in „Special Issue of Optica Acta", 1977.

[25]   *M. Feldmann, G. L. Heiter,* Low Level Binary Light Detection in Charge Storage
       Phototransistor Arrays, The 1970 Solid State Sensor Symposium, Minneapolis, Minne
       Minnesota, June 18–19, Conf. Report Catalogue N, 70C 25 – Sensor, 10.

[26]   *G. Strull, W. F. List, E. L. Irwin, D. L. Farnsworth,* Solid-State Array Cameras, Appl.
       Optics **11**, 1032 (1972).

[27]   *O. Jantsch, U. v. Hundelshausen, I. Feigt, W. Hering,* Detektormatrix für einen holo-
       graphischen Datenspeicher, Intern. Elektr. Rundschau **10**, 211 (1973).

[28]   *M. Herrmann,* Vakuumlose Elektronische Bildaufnahmeeinheit mit 32 × 32 Bildelementen,
       Valvo-Technische Berichte, Germany, to be published Spring of 1974.

[29]   *D. Gabor,* Associative Holographic Memories, IBM J. Res. Develop., March 1969, 156.

[30]   *B. Parhami,* Associative Memories and Processors: An Overview and Selected Biblio-
       graphy, Proc. IEEE, Vol. **61** (1973), 723.

[31]   *G. R. Knight,* Holographic Associative Memory and Processor, Appl. Optics, Vol. **14**
       (1975), 1088.

[32]   *U. Wagner,* Ein holographischer Speicher mit teilassoziativem Zugriff, „Verarbeitung
       optischer Information", Tagung der DGaO/NTG 1976, 8.–12. Juni, Nürnberg.

[33]   *J.-P. Krumme, B. Hill, J. Kruger, K. Witter,* A highly sensitive reversible and nonvolatile
       hybrid photoconductive/magneto-optic storage material, J. Appl. Phys. **46**, June 1945,
       2733.

[34]   *H. Heitmann, J.-P. Krumme, K. Witter,* Magneto-optic memory materials, Optica Acta,
       Vol. **24**, 483, April 1977.

[35]   *B. Hill, J.-P. Krumme, G. Much, D. Riekmann, J. Schmidt,* Fully Operational write-read-
       write and random access optical store, J. Appl. Phys. **47**, 3697 (1976).

[36]   *B. Hill, J.-P. Krumme, G. Much, R. Peperl, J. Schmidt, K. P. Schmidt, K. Witter,
       H. Heitmann,* Polycube optical-memory: a 6.5 × 10⁷ bit read-write and random access
       optical store, Appl. Optics **14**, 2607 (1975).

[37]   *B. Hill, I. Sander, G. Much,* Magneto-optic memories, Optica Acta, Vol. **24**, 495, April
       1977.

[38]   *D. Meunic,* Television on a silver plotter, IEEE Spectr., August 1975, 34.

[39]   *K. Compaan, P. Kramer,* Das Philips VLP-System, Philips Techn. Rundschau, 7 (1973/74),
       190.

[40]   *I. Sander, R. Pepperl,* High density direct read after write (DRAW) recording, Optica
       Acta, Vol. **24**, 413, April 1977.

[41]   *E. Krätzig,* Materials for Optical Storage, this Volume.

Effects of Failures on Yield, Integration, Cost and Reliability of Large Scale Integrated Semiconductor Memories. – A Tutorial Review

Wolfgang Hilberg

Institut für Digitaltechnik, Technische Universität Darmstadt, Germany

1. Introduction

In the production of large scale integrated semiconductor circuits, and especially of semiconductor memories with high storage capacity, the deviations from the intended ideal state, i.e. the failures, are very important, as their nature and concentration determine the number of individual devices (transistors) and individual functions (storage elements) that can be combined as an integrated circuit (IC) on a single monocristalline substrate. The special dependences are characterized by the facts that with increasing integration the relation between perfect integrated circuits (i.e. without failures) and the total number of produced integrated circuits decreases, and, furthermore, that the achieved quality standard and the failure level determine the scale of integration at which the minimum cost can be achieved. Finally, the quality standard of the factory determines the reliability in a high degree, i.e. the frequency with which the integrated circuits installed in the electronic equipment fail in operation.

From the items mentioned above the importance of the achieved quality standard for the competitive firms is obvious. Knowledge of the different failure sources, influencing possibilities and their interdependencies very often decide the quality and price of the products, and thus also the fate of the producer. For this reason all producers have done much to improve yield and reliability of their products during the past few years. A few large producers have even accumulated an enormous amount of data in this area to enable them to calculate in advance very well and very precisely their progress in quality. On the other hand, nearly nothing has been published on all these important subjects. This survey, of course, cannot deal with details in this area, particularly as the internal reports of the large semiconductor producers are for the university as little accessable as for most of the auditory. However, in this paper a different way was chosen, that is to reveal the essential dependencies by highly idealized models which enable analytical treatment. It could be possible that this procedure will give here more satisfaction than the presentation of voluminous empirical data. Some of the following derivations will be new. If, in the examples chosen for illustration, numerical values should result that deviate too far from the numerical values in actual practice, those skilled in the art are hereby encouraged to publish practical data.

2. Definition of Failures

Failures and their causes have very often been classified in different ways. It therefore does not make much sense to go into details here, a rough classification will suffice. First it should be stated that our subject deals with physical failures only that also appear as errors of the circuitry. In an integrated circuit these failures can be caused by defects on the chip, defects in the connections or even by a defective encapsulation. Failures on the chip can be preferably recognized by product control, the two other types of failures can occur with considerable delay in practical application. Failures on the chip can be locally concentrated (e.g. particle defects) or have surface extension (e.g. processing defects). The localized failures can be classified in respect of their effects in functional failures (a flip-flop is permanently set to "0"), catastrophical failures (the battery voltage is shunted by a local short), and failures of tolerance (with increased temperature the logic level of a storage device is no longer within the allowed limits). In order to better understand the effects of the failures first a very simplified model will be formed as follows. We will restrict ourselves to the locally concentrated failures mainly determining the state of the art regardless of their being catastrophical failures or tolerance failures. This is quite a reasonable assumption as processing mistakes in general indicate a low quality standard or too high development goals and thus can be avoided. Defective contacts or even the encapsulation are, in contrast thereto, not so much or even not at all dependent on the scale of integration, and are therefore points of interest only with the second approximation of the effects and mechanisms of failures to be investigated.

3. Yield

The classical model is based on point defects statistically distributed over the wafer (see Fig. 1-1). The wafer is subdivided as a checker-board in n_c chips. If a single chip with n storage devices contains only one defect it is already unusable. If the wafer is divided into individual chips, only the perfect chips will be used. The relation of good chips to the total number of chips is called the yield. Coming to large production quantities, the yield equals the probability to get a good chip. The same holds true for the yield of individual storage devices. The chip yield Y_C thus results as n-times the product of the device yield Y_E.

$$Y_C = Y_E^n \tag{1a}$$

From Fig. 2 it can be seen how exceptionally large the yield Y_E of individual components (e.g. transistor or storage element) must be in order to produce a sufficiently large number of good integrated circuits. The quality standard obtained is thus to a certain degree represented by the factor Y_E.

292

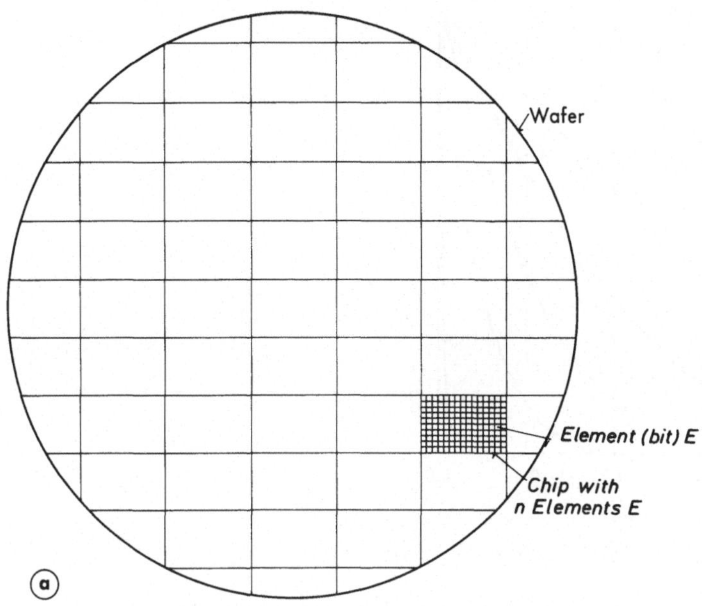

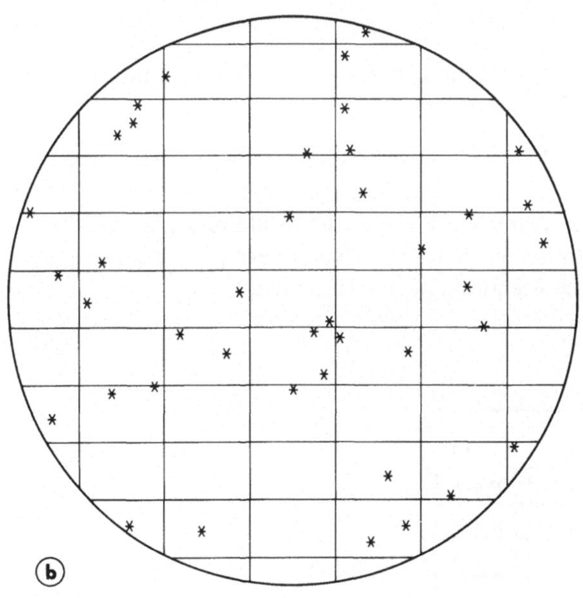

Fig. 1

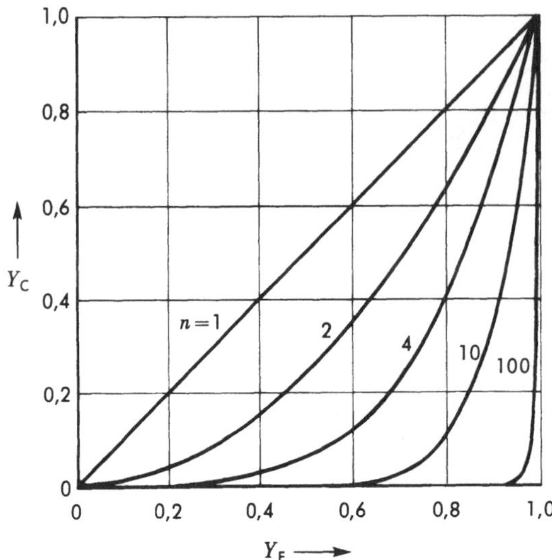

Fig. 2

If in every chip containing n elements, x elements per average fail and x is a small number — and only then we will have a practically usable yield — the eq. (1a) can still be transformed to

$$Y_C = Y_E^n = (1 - \overline{Y}_E)^n = \left(1 - \frac{x}{n}\right)^n \underset{n \to \infty}{\to} e^{-x} \tag{1b}$$

The figures in Table 1 in the bolder frames indicate for $x = 1$ that this limit is already reached very soon for not too high values of n.

In a different representation the yield can be related to the number of defects per wafer surface unit. Thus it is not related to a specific circuit with uniform components as e.g. memories but can be used in many ways. Departing from Poisson's Law, the probability can be found that with the existence of a defect density D, a surface A_C will be free from defects [1], which is equivalent to a chip yield Y_C

$$Y_C = e^{-D \cdot A_C}. \tag{2a}$$

n			Y_E		
	0,9	0,95	0,98	0,99	0,999
10	$34,9 \cdot 10^{-2}$	$59,9 \cdot 10^{-2}$	$81,7 \cdot 10^{-2}$	$90,4 \cdot 10^{-2}$	$99,0 \cdot 10^{-2}$
100	$26,6 \cdot 10^{-6}$	$59,2 \cdot 10^{-4}$	$13,3 \cdot 10^{-2}$	$36,6 \cdot 10^{-2}$	$90,5 \cdot 10^{-2}$
1000	$17,5 \cdot 10^{-47}$	$52,9 \cdot 10^{-24}$	$16,8 \cdot 10^{-10}$	$43,2 \cdot 10^{-6}$	$36,8 \cdot 10^{-2}$

Tab. 1

If it is further considered that only surface sections containing sensible circuit components can be damaged by particle defects the corresponding sensitive surface A_C' must be inserted ($A_C' < A_C$):

$$Y_C = e^{-D \cdot A_C'} . \tag{2b}$$

Assuming a certain situation with the values of Y_0 and A_0 being known, we can eliminate the density D from eq. (2a) and we obtain:

$$Y_C = Y_0^{A_C/A_0} . \tag{2c}$$

This relation, graphically shown in Fig. 3, is a calculating basis very well suited for practical purposes, as in contrast to eq. (2a), either the sensitive surface or the total surface can be inserted.

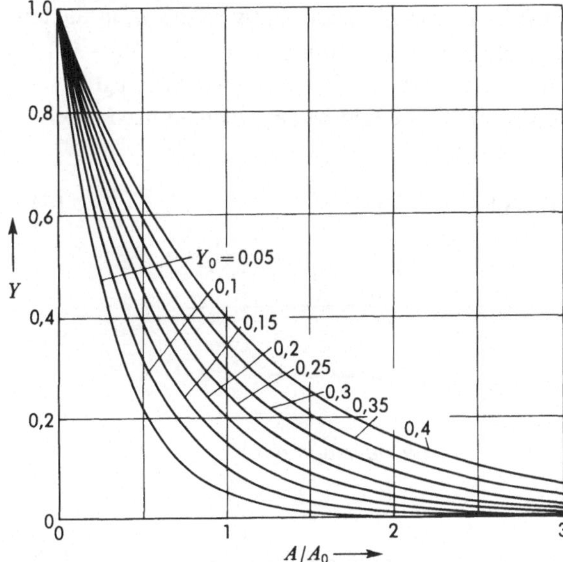

Fig. 3

Example

For producing integrated circuits a set of masks is required to structure the silicon wafer. The number of masks of the set depends on the technology and is assumed to be m. Every mask contributes a certain amount to the defect density. If there would be mask defects only, we would have to set up:

$$Y_C = Y_1 \cdot Y_2 \cdot Y_3 \ldots Y_m = e^{-A_C \sum_{i=1}^{m} D_i} = e^{-m \cdot A_C \cdot D_m} . \tag{3}$$

295

In this equation a constant defect density $D_i = D_m$ is assumed for the same masking technique. As will be noted the number of masks should be as small as possible. With a technology (MOS) with few masks e.g. $m = 4$, on an area $A = 50$ mm^2 and an average of one defect per cm^2, a yield of $Y_C \approx 0.135$ results. With a different technology (bipolar) and a higher number of masks, the same yield can be obtained only on a smaller surface. If, for example in eq. (3) the number of masks m will be doubled, then therefore the surface A_C must be divided by two. In general, it will be possible to place only a smaller number of storage elements on this smaller surface.

4. Yield Learning Curve

If a particular integrated circuit, e.g. a 1K-bit RAM, is produced by the same producer for a number of years, we find that the yield improves constantly as shown in the basic curve in Fig. 4. Beginning with a relatively low value that surely is below $Y_C = 0.1$ at the beginning of sales, the curve first rises relatively fast, and then with higher values of Y_C climbs up remarkably slower. This could be described approximately by the exponential run of two time constants:

$$Y_C = C_1 \, (1 - e^{-t/\tau_1}) + (1 - C_1)(1 - e^{-t/\tau_2}) . \tag{4}$$

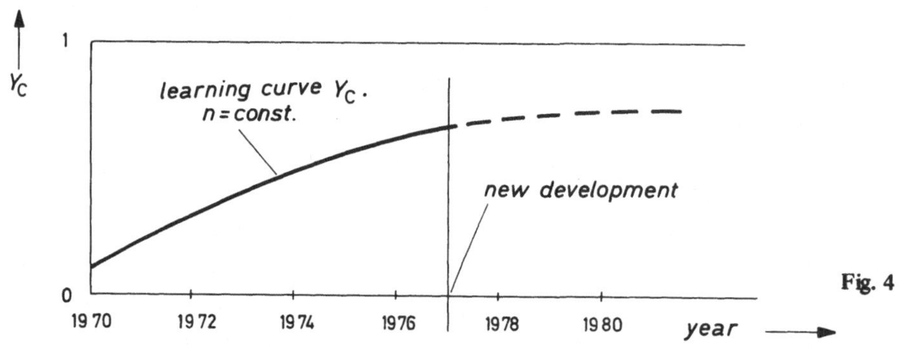

For the following we have, however, only to consider the first section of this learning curve as most producers break off the production of a particular circuit at the very moment in which the development has led to relatively high yield values. This will first make sense in context with considerations of cost.

It should be mentioned here that the slope of the learning curve of course also depends on the effort of work I, i.e. how many people endeavour for improvements and with which intensity they do it, and in which way continuous investments are made in more sophisticated equipment and installations. If for the learning curve only a single time constant is assumed and if a symbol I for the actual effort as well as I_0 for the normal effort are set up, the learning curve will take the following shape:

$$Y_C = \left(1 - e^{-\frac{t}{\tau} \cdot \frac{I}{I_0}}\right).$$ (5)

The expert will, of course, express his doubts with a statement such as: "double efforts result in half the development time", but anyway, the trend of increased efforts is in this direction. Moreover it has also proved that only companies can be leaders of the market, who invest considerable amounts in this area, and who can "learn" faster than their competitors.

5. Minimum of Cost

There is an approved theory [1, 3] for showing that well defined scales of integration have the most reasonable costs, if a certain quality standard exists. Starting from a total number n_w of wafers to be processed, containing n_c chips each and these in turn including n integrated storage elements, total costs as in eq. (6) result if the following values are given: the yield of good wafers Y_W, of good chips Y_C, and of good packaged integrated circuits Y_P: Furthermore K_W, K_C, K_P, and K_N as cost for processing a wafer (e.g. etching), a chip (e.g. testing) and mounting (e.g. contacting, packaging, final test) as well as cost for new development:

$$K_{ges} = K_W \cdot n_W + K_C \cdot n_C \cdot (n_W \cdot Y_W) + K_P (n_C \cdot Y_C)(n_W \cdot Y_W) + K_N .$$ (6)

Dividing eq. (6) by the total number n_{ges} of good storage elements

$$n_{ges} = (n \cdot Y_P) \cdot (n_C \cdot Y_C) \cdot (n_W \cdot Y_W)$$ (7)

will result in the specific price per element (price per bit) as follows:

$$\frac{K_{ges}}{n_{ges}} = \frac{K_W}{n \cdot Y_W \cdot Y_C \cdot Y_P} + \frac{K_C}{n \cdot Y_C \cdot Y_P} + \frac{K_P}{n \cdot Y_P} + \frac{K_N}{n \cdot n_C \cdot n_W \cdot Y_P \cdot Y_C \cdot Y_W}$$ (8)

As it has been shown, especially the yield Y_C depends on the scale of integration n. If Y_C is formulated according to eq. (1a), a factor of $1/n \cdot Y_E^n$ can be extracted from the first two terms in eq. (8). If this factor is plotted for different $Y_E = 1 - 1/\nu$ on n, the curve with a minimum e/n at $n = \nu$, will result as in Fig. 5. Considering the constants and the third term in eq. (8) which causes a shifting of the minimum to higher values of n, we will obtain the well known curves by Murphy as in Fig. 6.

$Y_E = 0,99$
$= 1 - \frac{1}{100}$
$Y_E = 0,999$
$= 1 - \frac{1}{1000}$
$Y_E = 0,9999$
$= 1 - \frac{1}{10000}$
$\frac{1}{n \cdot Y_E^{\,n}}$
$n \longrightarrow$

Fig. 5

$N_O = 1$
$Y_O = 0.3$
0.6
0.9
1.0
$N_O = 10$
$Y_O = 0.3$
0.6
0.9
1.0
$N_O = 100$
$Y_O = 0.3$
0.6
0.9
1.0
RELATIVE COST PER COMPONENT, R Y_{MI}/Y_{MC}
RELATIVE NUMBER OF COMPONENTS, N/N_O
RELATIVE CHIP SIZE, X/X_O

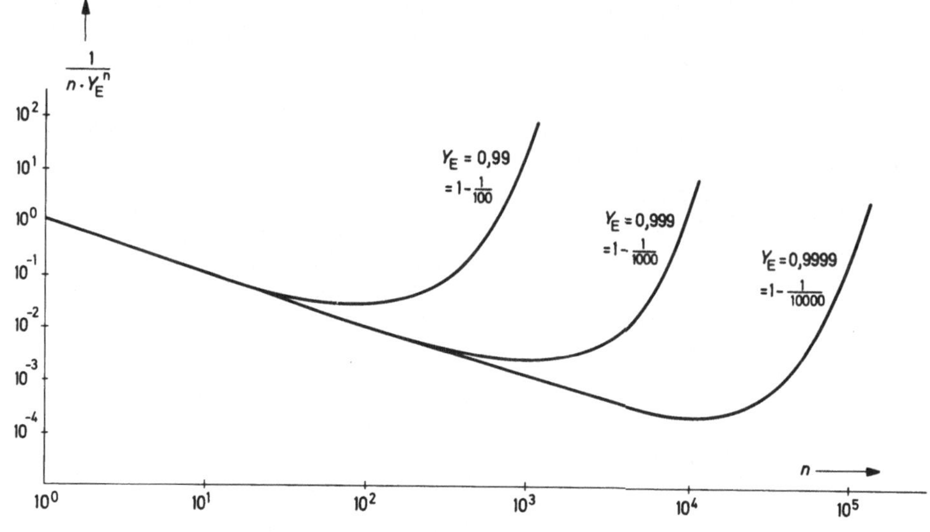

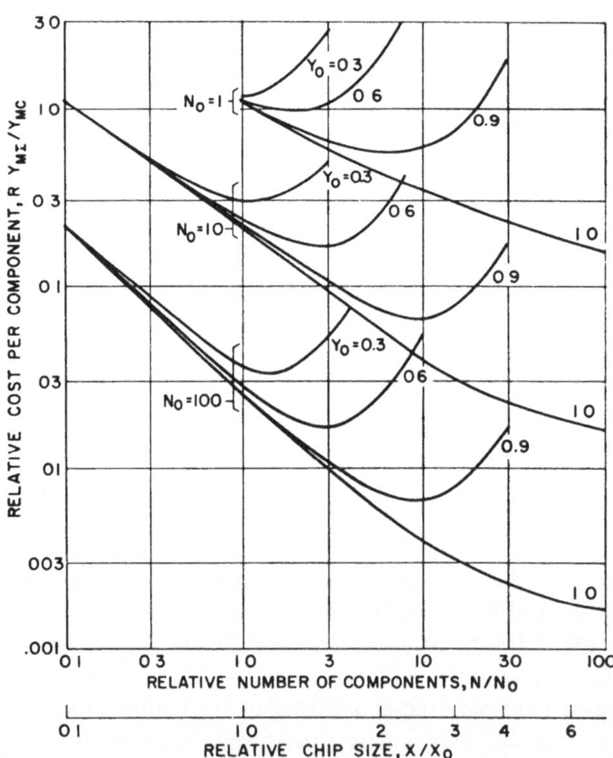

Fig. 6

6. Minimum Cost depending on Time and Effort

The cost factors K_W, K_C, K_P, and K_N can apparently be continuously reduced in the course of years. This is achieved, for example, by using better equipment, automation of production, and new procedures or even cheaper purchase of the raw materials needed in constantly increasing quantities. Starting with the assumption that in equal periods the same percentual improvements are possible, and setting up for simplification the same time dependency for every cost factor ($K = K_0 \cdot e^{-t/\tau_v}$), the common exponential factor can be extracted from the brackets in eq. (8), and this will result to:

$$\frac{K_{ges}}{n_{ges}} = \left(\frac{K_{W0}}{n \cdot Y_W \cdot Y_C \cdot Y_P} + \frac{K_{C0}}{n \cdot Y_C \cdot Y_P} + \frac{K_{P0}}{n \cdot Y_P} + \frac{K_{N0}}{n \cdot n_C \cdot n_W \cdot Y_P \cdot Y_C \cdot Y_W} \right) e^{-t/\tau_v} \tag{9}$$

It must be considered herewith that especially the yields Y will follow certain learning curves depending on time. But as Y_W and Y_P are relatively high, and even Y_W is rather independent of n, mainly the time dependency of Y_C in Fig. 4 and the approximation (5) respectively remain to be considered. This has direct consequences on the capacity values of memory chips showing the best cost relation per bit.

7. Increase of Integration Scale by Steps

In the semiconductor memory market it can be seen that within less than two years the storage capacity of integrated memories has doubled. Going into detail we find that some manufacturers put, with a certain offset in time, nearly every three years a new memory chip on the market, the capacity of which has been increased by a factor of 4, compared with its predecessor circuit. Let us first investigate the consequences that can be derived from these facts, the physical laws this rhythm is based on, and the assumption that this development will continue for some time in the future.

Each of these new developments of memory chips follows learning curves for the yield. For reasons of simplification it is assumed that all learning curves are equal and further that the exponential law (5) shall be valid in a first approximation and a normal effort shall be anticipated with $I/I_0 = 1$. Fig. 7 shows four learning curves Y_{C1}, Y_{C2}, Y_{C3}, Y_{C4}. In the first learning curve there will be, for example, at the time t_1, marking the beginning of the actual sales, a relatively small yield Y_X of about 8 %. The yield Y_{C1} increases after three years to the value of Y_y, e.g. 32 % (the values are selected in such a way that they are reasonably within the range of the first time constant). Beginning at the time t_2 with a higher integrated version $n_2 = 4 \cdot n_1$, it must be postulated that this new version is at least as favourable in cost as the previous version with n_1.

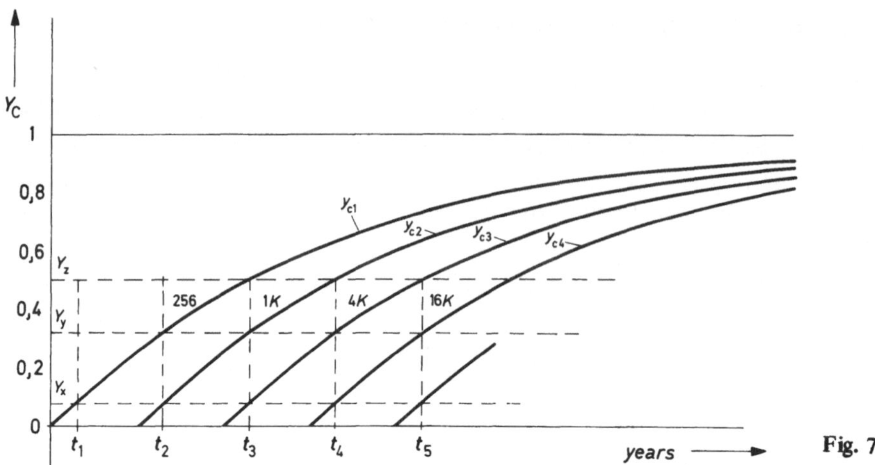

That is, if we consider first the specific costs (8), then for $n \cdot Y_C$ we will have the result

$$n_1 \cdot Y_{C1}(t_2) = n_2 \cdot Y_{C2}(t_2), \text{ resp. } n_1 \cdot Y_y = n_2 \cdot Y_x . \qquad (10a)$$

The values Y_x and Y_y can be seen in Fig. 7.

A simple calculation then shows that for the assumed values $Y_x = 8\%$, $Y_y = 32\%$, $\Delta t = 3$ years, $n_2/n_1 = M = 4$, the equality of costs is only possible for a learning curve with the time constant

$$\tau = \frac{\Delta t}{\ln \dfrac{1 - Y_x}{1 - M \cdot Y_x}} = \frac{3}{\ln \dfrac{0.92}{0.68}} = 10 \text{ years} \qquad (10b)$$

Now the question rises of the cost development after three more years, if again the production of a new version n_3 starts. For $Y_{C1}(t_3) = Y_z$ and $t_3 = t_1 + 2\,\Delta t$ the yield is obtained

$$Y_z = 1 - \frac{(1 - M \cdot Y_x)^2}{1 - Y_x} = 1 - \frac{0.68^2}{0.92} = 0.5 . \qquad (11)$$

Thus the following situation results: With $n_2 \cdot Y_y = n_3 \cdot Y_x$, the memory chips with n_2 and n_3 have the same price at the time t_3. When neglecting the two last terms in eq. (8) the relation $n_2 \cdot Y_x/n_1 \cdot Y_z = 16.8/50 = 2.56$ represents the factor by which memory chip n_1 will then be more expensive than the higher integrated memory chips. As the cost for packaging and testing, that were assumed to be constant in eq. (8), still represent a considerable portion of the total cost, the foregoing cost estimate for the memory chip n_1 is somewhat too disadvantageous.

300

What can be found concerning the development of quality standards in the course of
years? For constant values of Y_C for example Y_x, the requirement follows that
the product $D \cdot A$ also remains constant, i.e.

$$D_{t_1} \cdot A_{t_1} = D_{t_2} \cdot A_{t_2} = D_{t_3} \cdot A_{t_3} = \ldots$$

From several references [1, 4, 5] we note that A and D will follow the curves in
Figs. 8a and 9 as a function of t. Every three years approximately the chip surface
doubles and the defect density is halved according to the trend line in Fig. 9. In order
to enable a multiplication times four of the number of components when doubling the chip
surface, the surface requirements per memory element must be halved as they do
according to Fig. 8b. By improving the masking technique, the technology and the
circuit technique, this could be achieved up to now, and probably it will be achieved
even in the future according to many experts [4]. As there are furthermore physical
possibilities to reduce the linewidth that are not yet fully utilized (e.g. masking with
electron beams) there is finally no reason that the development at least in the next
10 years should not continue as up to now. If one day the linewidth could not be
further reduced, according to the simplified model the scale of integration could only
be doubled every three years. That is because the doubling of A and the division of D
by 2 will not reach physical limits within a predictable period.

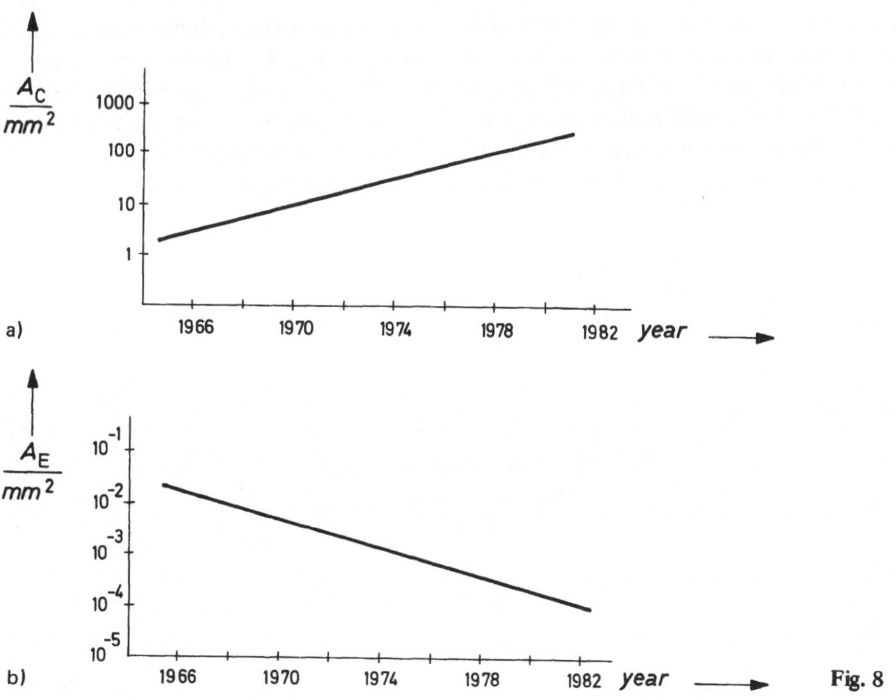

Fig. 8

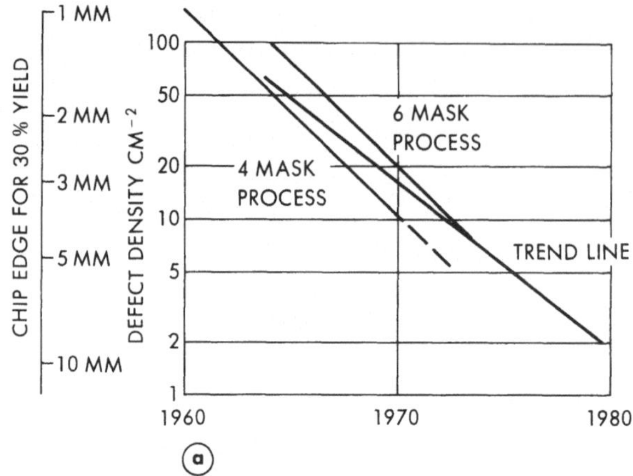

Fig. 9

Now the whole logic chain of conclusions can be inverted, of course: beginning with the time dependencies of A_C, D and A_E, the annual improvement in integration and the time constants of the learning curves can be calculated. This will approximately result in diagrams and values that were initially provided here.

A summary of cost development as a consequence of yield increase, i.e. the elimination of failure sources, can be obtained by evaluating eq. (8) and drawing an adequate curve under consideration of the learning curve Y_C in Fig. 4. Therefrom curves resembling that in Fig. 10 with vertical and horizontal asymptotes will result. The relative mutual position of the curves is fixed by the calculations made up to now but not their actual position in the diagram. The scale, therefore, has been shifted in Fig. 10 in such manner that the relations coincide approximately with the real

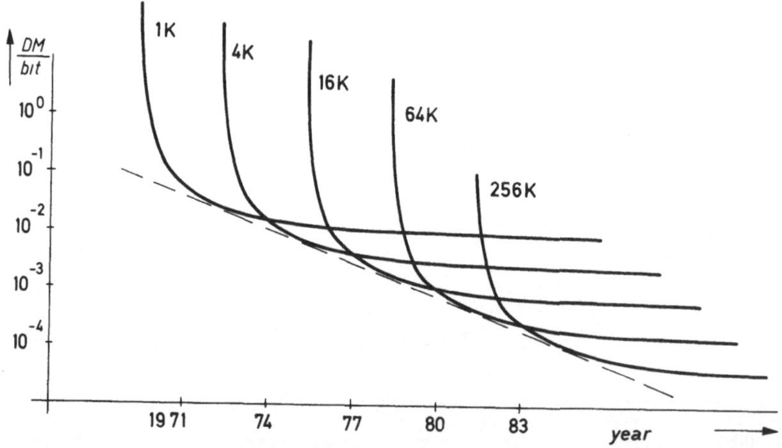

Fig. 10

302

annual numbers, with the price per bit as well as with the forecast of the experts [5].
The common tangent line to all curves has the same rise as the straight line running
through the lowest intersections of the curves. These intersections are offset to each
other in the abscissa by Δt and in the ordinate by the factor M. For the common
tangent line

$$\text{Tangent}(t) = \text{const} \cdot e^{-t/\tau_p} \tag{12a}$$

thus there results the time constant

$$\tau_p = \frac{\Delta t}{\ln M} = \frac{3}{\ln 4} = 2.16 \text{ years} . \tag{12b}$$

For the development of inexpensive memories we obtain apparently a much smaller
time constant than for the yield with the learning curves. The most favourable cost
decrease results by inserting $t = 1$ in eq. (12a) in 37 % per year. That means that in
a period of $\Delta t = 3$ years a cost reduction to a quarter of the original price occurs
and that is exactly the value that was indicated with any of the learning curves after
the first period Δt.

To further improve the model, the annual percentual improvements of production
represented by the time constant τ_v in eq. (9) can be considered. If the annual cost
reduction resulting therefrom is assumed 10 %, for example, the curve in Fig. 11
will result in specific cost continuously decreasing to the right-hand side. In actual
market conditions, however, inflation must also be taken into account, and this is
exactly the opposite of the improvements in production. As it is nearly in the same
order the curve set in Fig. 10 probably can better represent reality than the improved
curves in Fig. 11.

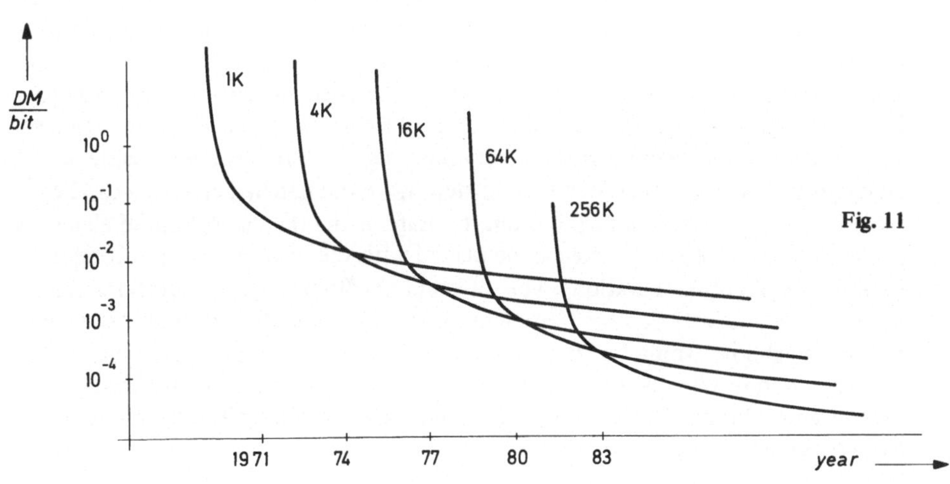

Fig. 11

Finally it should be mentioned that the derivation of the curves in Figs. 10 or 11 is based on the assumption that all the learning curves for Y_C are nearly equal. If a major manufacturer decides suddenly to invest multiples of his normal capital, these circumstances must be accounted for in eq. (5) by $I/I_0 > 1$. The learning curves can then be shortened and the periodizity in the upper diagrams will disappear.

8. The Problem of Testing

It becomes more and more evident that testing of integrated circuits means efforts that increase more than proportionally with increasing scales of integration. It is not of general knowledge that large scale integrated circuits cannot be completely tested within a reasonable time interval. The possibility that certain states in the memory will give rise to failures can never be completely excluded. This problem will be sketched briefly for better understanding. We can imagine the following tests:

1. All possible memory states are written and read once and then checked. With n memory elements there result 2^n patterns. In a 1K-bit memory chip they will amount to $2^{1024} \approx (2^{10})^{100} \approx 1000^{1000} = 10^{300}$ read/write operations for these patterns.

2. All transitions from a possible first state to a possible second state will be checked. Adding for security the transitions into identical patterns, which can technically be performed, 2^{2n} read/write operations result.

3. If all possibilities of k successively performed transitions are checked, there will result $2^{(k+1)n}$ operations. Obviously, checking all transitions will never be possible in a limited time.

4. Specific and rather long transition chains will be observed. They result from the consideration that in a single memory element, parasitic effects due to the activity of neighboured elements can be accumulated. If the change of state of the neighboured element is the reason of the parasitic neighbouring effects, then in a checkerboard pattern as is shown in Fig. 12 the double hatched elements can be fixed to L or O and then the state of the other memory elements can be changed M-times. This number M will then be selected very high, e.g. $M = 10^6$ as the parasitic increments can be very small. In a second step the single hatched elements can be fixed in the L- or O-position, and again the state of the then neighboured elements can be changed. The same game can be played with the white boxes, resulting in a total of $8 \times M$ check operations. The different neighbouring configurations can be varied without any difficulty. Many more operations would result if also the next but one neighbour would be taken into account. Much more important than their influence is, however, the mutual influence of components commonly arranged in rows and columns. Quite a series of standard checking programs have arisen from these practical considerations.

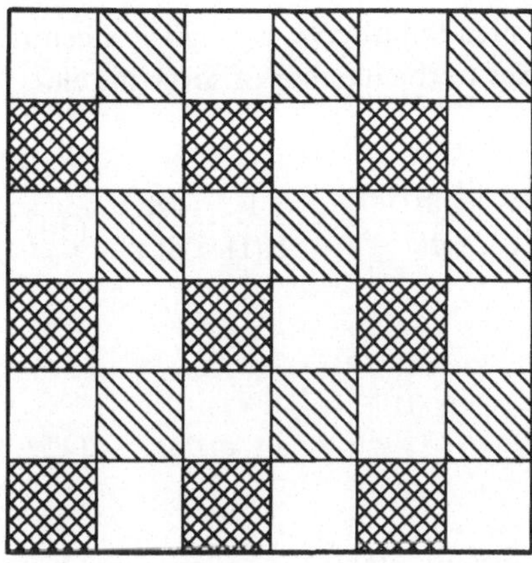

Fig. 12

5. All checking programs mentioned should finally be performed at different temperatures, voltages and other parameters.

As the conditions of production allow only the performance of relatively short
checking programs we must always take into consideration that memories in practical
usage will suddenly generate errors in a nonpredictable way under certain conditions.
This error rate will therefore be determined by the quality standard of production
as well as by the volume of checking programs.

9. Reliability, Failure Rate

Memories shall be highly reliable in usage, i.e. they shall show malfunctions theoretically not at all and in practice only after long periods of usage. Then they must be replaced unless further error correction (EC) and error detection (ED) methods
are provided. The general theory of reliability of components can be fully applied
to this finite reliability. As with large scale integrated semiconductor circuits, relations between quality of production and failure rates exist, first the general terms
should be recalled in brief for better understanding of the models still to be
developed. A large set N_0 of initially good components is observed. After some
time N_f components have failed for some reason, and N_S are still good, in other
words, they survived (f = failure, s = survival). Therefrom results the probability
$R(t)$ for a component to be still reliable at the time t

$$R(t) = \frac{N_S}{N_0} = \frac{N_S}{N_f + N_S} \,. \tag{13}$$

Often for the probability of survival $R(t)$ the term $p_s(t)$ is used. The failure
probability $F(t)$ is defined by $R(t) + F(t) = 1$. The derivative $dR/dt = -\,dF/dt$

follows. For considerations of reliability the so-called failure rate $z(t)$ plays a central part. It is defined as the ratio of increase of failures to the number of surviving elements:

$$z(t) = \frac{1}{N_S} \frac{dN_f}{dt} = \frac{1}{N_S} \frac{d(N_0 - N_S)}{dt} = -\frac{N_0}{N_S} \frac{dN_S/N_0}{dt} = -\frac{1}{R(t)} \cdot \frac{dR}{dt} . \tag{14}$$

Therefrom we obtain by integration:

$$R(t) = \exp. \left[-\int_0^t z(\tau) d\tau \right] . \tag{15}$$

If, in the simplest case, the failure rate remains constant, $z(t) = \lambda$, (in a manner analog to the radio-active decay) the exponential law of reliability will result to: $R(t) = e^{-\lambda t}$.

The third significant term is the MTTF i.e. mean time to failure t_m of the components. It is determined by the expected value of t for the failure and can be represented after partial integration as follows:

$$t_m = \int_0^\infty t \cdot \left(\frac{dF}{dt} \right) dt = \int_0^\infty \left(-t \frac{dR}{dt} \right) dt = \int_0^\infty R(\tau) d\tau . \tag{16}$$

For the constant failure rate λ there will result $t_m = 1/\lambda$ for example. With most of the technical products the failure rate as a function of time is characterized by a high infant mortality, a larger part with a nearly constant value (random) and an increase by wearout at the end (a so called bath-tub curve). For semiconductor memories it is necessary to be completely in the range of the constant failure rate during operation. In practice they will never reach the range of wearout. The failure rate of integrated circuits will be expressed as the percentage of failures per 1000 hours. It is, for example, for standard plastic IC's in the order of 0.01 percent/1000 hrs and for very high requirements in the order of 0.00019 percent/1000 hrs. The order of MTTF is given in Table 2, also compared with ferrite core memories.

Measured mean-time-to-failure

Processor W/Memory (words)	(Core) MTTF (hours)	(4K RAM) MTTF (hours)	Δ%
8,192	3847	5884	57 0
16,384	3200	4848	51 5
24,576	2721	4123	51 5
32,768	2422	3586	48.0

Tab. 2

10. Temperature Dependence of Mean Time to Failure and Failure Rate

According to Arrhenius the change of a state G as a function of time, i.e. the speed
of a chemical reaction, follows the relation

$$\frac{dG}{dt} = C \cdot e^{-\frac{E}{K \cdot T}} \quad . \tag{17}$$

Subsequently the thermal activation energy E as well as C shall be considered to be
constant (K is Boltzmann's constant) and the dependence on the absolute temperature
T shall only be investigated. If in eq. (17) the differential symbols d are replaced by
the differences Δ it follows for Δt:

$$\Delta t = \frac{\Delta G}{C} \cdot e^{\frac{E}{K \cdot T}} \quad . \tag{18}$$

If especially the state change ΔG is so large that the component becomes unusable
then apparently Δt is the time to failure. If we write eq. (18) for a definite reference
temperature T_0 with the associated time to failure Δt_0, then the elimination of
$\Delta G/C$ is possible and it follows

$$\Delta t = \Delta t_0 \cdot e^{\frac{E}{K} \left(\frac{1}{T} - \frac{1}{T_0} \right)} \quad . \tag{19}$$

If the reference temperature T_0 is chosen so high that the component is practically
unusable in this area and shows for example a time to failure of only one hour (with
silicon at nearly 250 °C), and the component is operated at lower normal temperatures T, the term including T_0 in eq. (19) can be neglected. Substituting the initially
introduced definition for the time to failure t_m for Δt the result is

$$t_m = t_{mo} \cdot e^{-\frac{E}{K \cdot T}} \quad . \tag{20}$$

Considering processes with constant failure rate according to eq. (16), then $\lambda = 1/t_m$
and eq. (20) becomes

$$\lambda = \lambda_0 \cdot e^{-\frac{E}{K \cdot T}} \quad . \tag{21}$$

That means that the time to failure decreases exponentially with rising temperature,
and the failure rate increases correspondingly. For eqs. (20) and (21) a series of diagrams can be found in literature, (see Fig. 13 as well as [22–24].

LIFE – HOURS
10⁶
10⁵
10⁴
10³
10²
10¹
10⁰
1.4eV
1.0eV
0.5eV
0.4eV
0.3eV
250
200
175
150
125
100
75
50
25
T (°C)

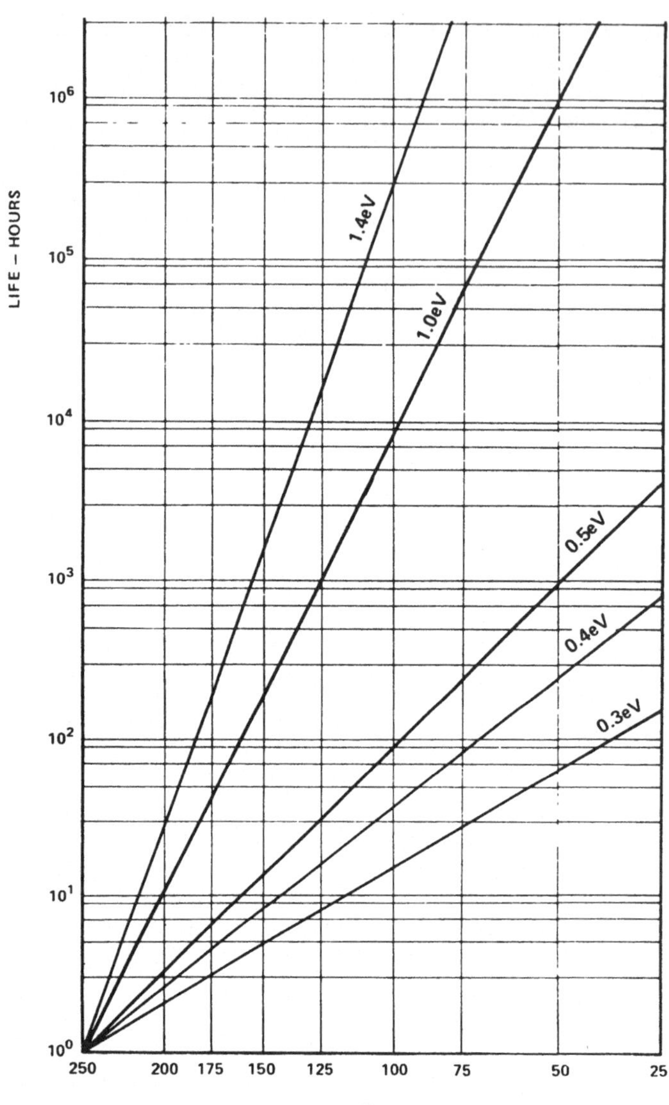

Fig. 13a

308

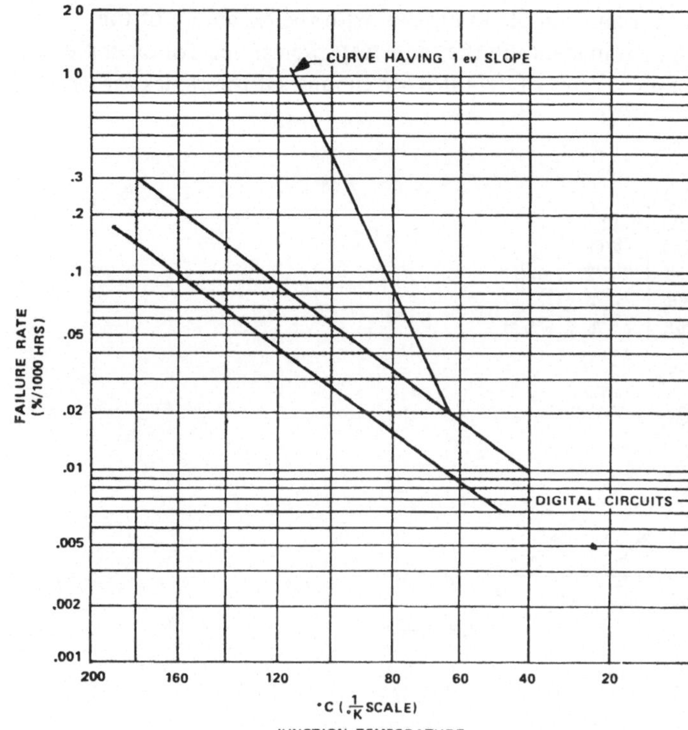

Fig. 13b

11. Reliability of Components and Systems

It must clearly be differentiated between the reliability of components and of a system, and the associated failure rates. The reliability of the system results from the product of the reliability of the components. With the usual exponential reliability function, therefore, the failure rates of the components must add up. With semiconductor memories the failure rate is predominantly related to the integrated unit, i.e. the chip and in a first approach it is relatively independent on the scale of integration. With a larger memory system comprising n_C chips and a memory capacity $C = n_C \cdot n$ the failure rate will add up as follows:

$$\lambda_{system} = n_C \cdot \lambda_C . \tag{22}$$

With the introduction of the capacity the mean time to failure (MTTF) results therefrom to:

$$t_m = \frac{1}{\lambda_{system}} = \frac{1}{n_C \cdot \lambda_C} = \frac{n}{C \cdot \lambda_C} . \tag{23}$$

This relation is illustrated for an example in Fig. 14, with the exception of the upper line [26]. From Fig. 15, made up in the same way, we can see, for example, the maximum allowable failure rates of 4K-bit RAM modules if the values for t_m and C are given.

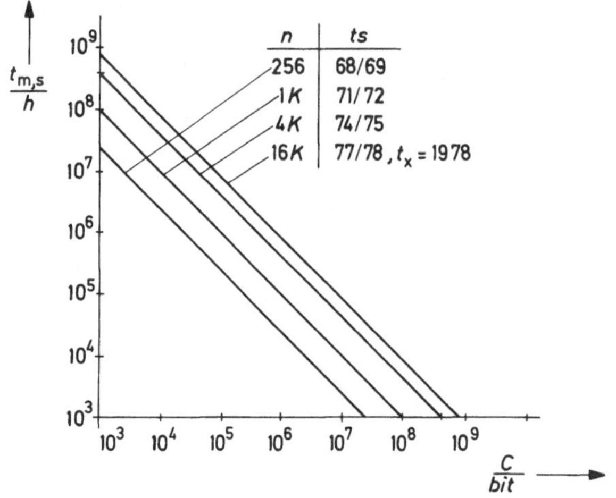

Fig. 14

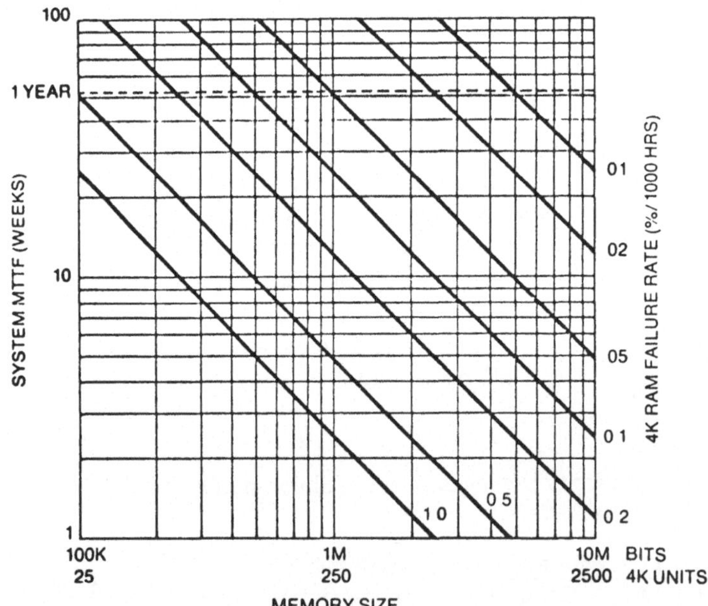

Fig. 15

310

12. Influence of Circuit Design on Reliability

A high reliability can always be achieved when a sufficient safety distance from critical
limits is maintained. That can especially be achieved by a favourable design of circuits
and layout. Consequently the electrical and thermal load of all components will be
restricted, the spaces of the conductors will be selected large enough, and the conductor width not too small, etc. As an example, here only the influence of the dissipation on the failure rate of a memory chip shall be considered. For this purpose we
return to the relation (19), however, here instead of the high reference temperature
T_0, the room temperature T_R will be used. Therefrom will result

$$\Delta t = \Delta t_R \cdot e^{\frac{E}{K}\left(\frac{1}{T} - \frac{1}{T_R}\right)} = \Delta t_R \cdot e^{-\frac{E}{K}\frac{T-T_R}{T \cdot T_R}} \approx \Delta t_R \cdot e^{-\frac{E}{K} \cdot \Delta T / T_R^2} . \quad (24)$$

In general the junction temperature ΔT is proportional to the dissipation N_V. Going back to the failure rate $\lambda = 1/\Delta t$ eq. (24) becomes with a constant factor α and
the failure rate λ_{CR} at room temperature:

$$\lambda_C = \lambda_{CR} \cdot e^{\alpha \cdot N_V} . \quad (25)$$

In the linear scale of Fig. 16 it is suggested that especially with very low room temperature the failure rate can increase imperceptible with increasing dissipation and
then after reaching a certain threshold, climb up very fast. It is the designer's job
to dimension the circuits in such a way that the failure rate is still small enough, e.g.
in the diagram on the left-hand side of the knee point.

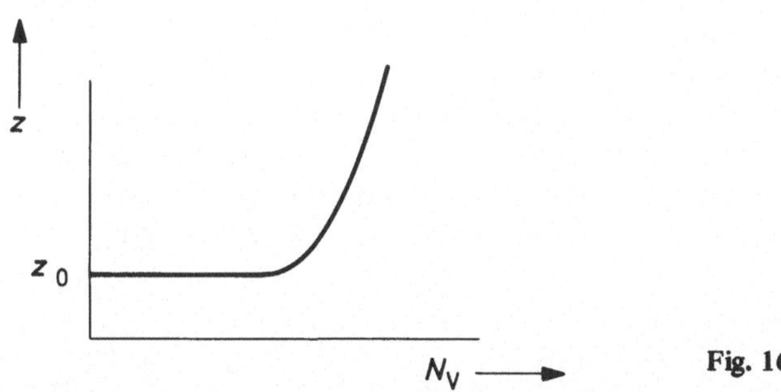

Fig. 16

13. Interrelation between Quality of Production and Failure Rate

The failure rate of integrated memory modules depends on different factors. The
dependence on time, temperature, and design has been discussed above. Of still
larger importance is checking and control of the manufacturing processes. Subsequently it shall be attempted to build up a simple and transparent new model for

the more general interrelation between the quality of production characterized by the yield, and the failure rate in operation.

In this model again single failures, statistically distributed on the wafer, shall be considered but it shall be differentiated between failures discovered at the manufacturer's, and those first realized in operation either due to incomplete testing or due to the fact that they are latent failures of production, first activated by thermal or electrical stresses. These failures arise, of course, in a time T. Also those failures shall be accounted for that arise statistically from unknown causes or that are not related to the wafer, e.g. contact defects. Now if production and operation is considered one procedure, we can utilize the means of the general theory of reliability in the following manner. All infant failures will be accounted for in the production process, and the corresponding time period is assumed to approach zero, compared with the long operating time. If the density of failures appearing at the manufacturer's is labelled D_H and the density of operating failures activated later on in a time period T is labelled D_B, the following failure rate for a chip can be set up:

$$z(t) = D_H \cdot A \cdot \frac{\delta(t)}{T} + \frac{D_B \cdot A}{T} + \lambda_p \; . \tag{26}$$

Wherein $\delta(t)$ is the Dirac pulse at the time $t = 0$ for which the definition $\int_{-\infty}^{+\infty} \delta(t/T)\, dt/T = 1$ is valid. The probability of survival results from inserting eq. (26) in (15)

$$R(t) = e^{-\int_0^t z(\tau)d\tau} = e^{-D_H \cdot A} \cdot e^{-\left(\frac{D_B \cdot A}{T} + \lambda_p\right) \cdot t} \tag{27}$$

It can be assumed with some reason that the relation of failures already appearing at the manufacturer's to the latent production failures or undiscovered failures will only little depend on the absolute value of failure density. The latent failures will probably always account for a certain percentage of total failures. Therefore with constant T the relation $T \cdot D_H / D_B$ is assumed to be constant α. Then from eq. (27) it follows by means of (2a):

$$R(t) = e^{-D_H \cdot A (1 + t/\alpha)} \cdot e^{-\lambda_p \cdot t} = Y_C^{1 + t/\alpha} \cdot e^{-\lambda_p \cdot t} = Y_C \cdot e^{-(\lambda_p - \frac{\ln Y_C}{\alpha})t} \tag{28}$$

Fig. 17 shows qualitatively the resulting probability of survival. Initially it has the value Y_C, and then according to the value of α and λ_p it decays to zero exponentially. Apparently the reliability at a later date of operation is the larger, the larger the initial value Y_C is. The constant failure rate λ_C can be calculated from eq. (28) to be:

$$\lambda_C = \lambda_p - \ln(Y_C)/\alpha \; . \tag{29}$$

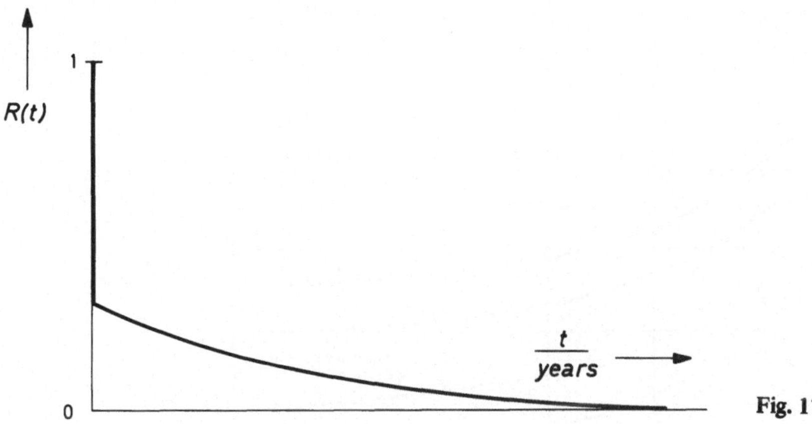

Fig. 17

It continuously decreases for increasing values of Y_C. Taking into account the improvement in yield, i.e. the learning curve of Y_C in Fig. 4, there also exist according to eq. (29) learning curves for the failure rate. That is in agreement with published diagrams of failure rate history in Figs. 18 and 19a. A more detailed discussion of this new model can be found in [26], see for instance the calculated system failure rate in Fig. 19b.

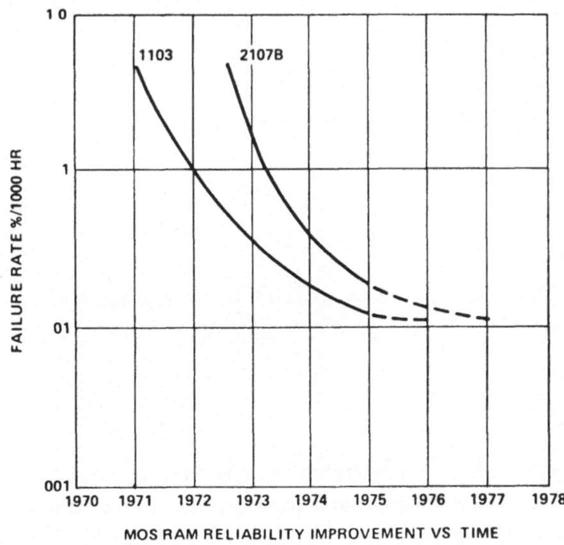

Fig. 18

313

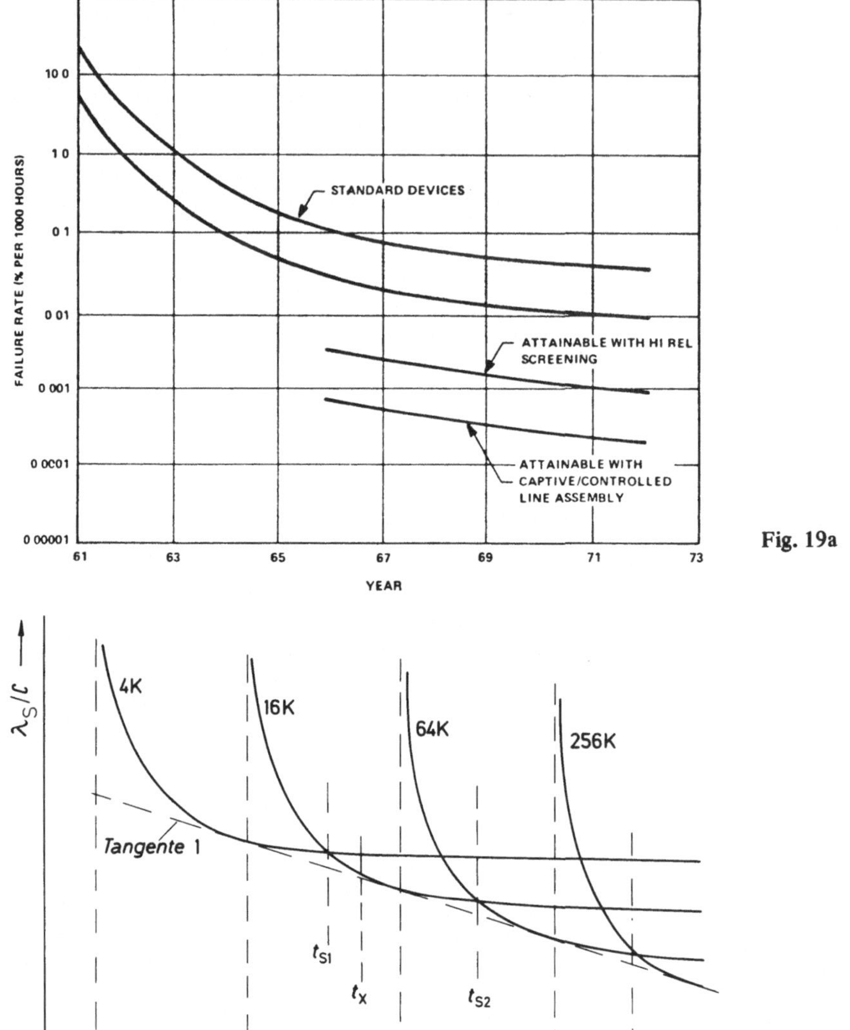

Fig. 19a

Fig. 19b

14. Lifetime and Minimum Cost

Minimum cost for the manufacturer had been investigated in sections 5 and 6. Long-term planning users are naturally interested in more, that is to say, in the total minimum cost, taking into consideration the whole operating time. Then reliability and MTTF

314

respectively play a very important part. Anybody recognices the poor business
policy, if he acquires an item very cheaply but has to discard it after a short time.
This is the more valid for circuits installed in a major unit as an expensive computer,
because here under certain circumstances the costs arising from the shut down of
the whole system must be accounted for, and moreover the testing cost for localizing
the failure and the costs for replacement of the defect circuits must be added. The
specific memory cost in eq. (9) therefore must be completed by a term containing
the time t_z up to which the memory shall function. The term must include the time
to failure $t_{m,syst}$, and a factor S for weighing the repair costs. Such a possible set up
is with possible consideration of eq. (23) as follows:

$$\frac{K_{eff}}{n_{ges}} = \frac{K_{ges}}{n_{ges}} \left(1 + S \cdot \frac{t_z}{t_{m,syst.}}\right) = \frac{K_{ges}}{n_{ges}} \left(1 + S \cdot \frac{t_z \cdot C \cdot \lambda_C}{n}\right) . \tag{30}$$

If here additionally λ_C from eq. (29) is substituted, it becomes evident that large-
scale integrated products produced with a good yield, i.e. matured products, in the
whole involve the lowest costs for the user.

15. Fault tolerant Memories

Keeping in mind that only one defective memory element is sufficient to make the
whole large-scale integrated circuit unusable, we can understand that already for
some years the challenge has been raised to use fault tolerant procedures [1, 10, 11].
It would therefore not to be understood if the memory technology would be the only
area of electrical information technique and communication technique that could do
without these procedures. It is easy to estimate the profit in yield or reliability that
can be gained, if it becomes possible to detect and correct only a single erroneous
bit per storage word. In order to enable this, a certain redundancy in memory is
necessary. This redundancy can be provided for either in the hardware or in coding.
In this context only the second at present more important possibility shall be discussed, keeping in mind that for coding and decoding always additional circuits are
required.

Two different estimates have been published. In one of them, the reliability is determined as a function of the statistically distributed single failures existing in the
memory, and in the other estimate, the reliability has been determined as a function
of time, both taking into account a correction of at best one error per word. Let us
begin with the first estimate:

If in a memory comprising W words with a length of L bit positions each, i.e. if in a
capacity $C = W \cdot L$ exactly X errors are statistically distributed, this will result in
a total of $\binom{WL}{X}$ possibilities of distribution. Under the premise that $X \leqslant W$ there are
$\binom{W}{X}$ possibilities to distribute the errors in such a way that every word contains only

a single error. As the error in every word can occur in any of the L positions, there are for every possibility of word occupation exactly L^X versions. The probability that the memory containing X errors will operate without error is determined by the relation of correctable memory patterns to the number of all possible memory patterns, and equals

$$R(X) = \frac{\binom{W}{X} \cdot L^X}{\binom{W \cdot L}{X}} \; . \tag{31}$$

This function is shown in Fig. 20 for some parameters C with the word size L = 72 depending on X. Apparently the fault tolerance has enormous effects. For practical calculations, by the way, a recursive formula to obtain R(X) from R(x−1) is used, as the factorial numbers are extremely high and the permissable ranges of computers in most cases are exceeded:

$$R(X) = P_X \cdot R(X - 1) \; . \tag{32}$$

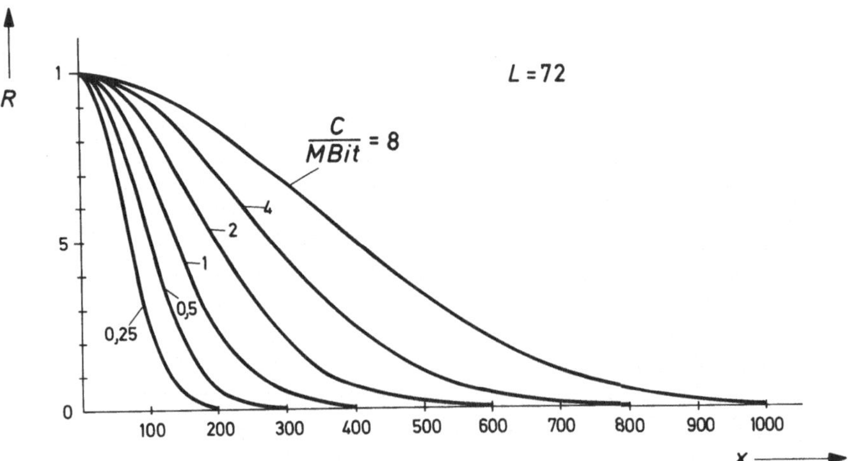

Fig. 20

Substituting eq. (31) herein, we will find the transition probability

$$P_X = 1 - \frac{(X - 1)(L - 1)}{W \cdot L - (X - 1)} = 1 - \frac{(L - 1)\,\frac{X-1}{W \cdot L}}{1 - \frac{X-1}{W \cdot L}} \; . \tag{33}$$

From eqs. (32) and (33) we finally obtain R(X) as follows:

$$R(X) = P_X \cdot P_{X-1} \cdot P_{X-2} \cdots P_2 \cdot P_1 \; . \tag{34}$$

316

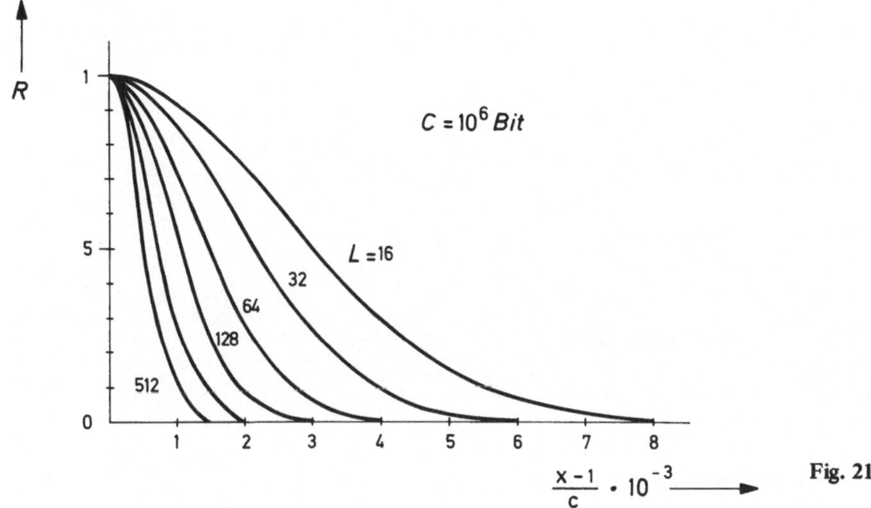

$$\frac{X-1}{C} \cdot 10^{-3} \longrightarrow$$

Fig. 21

Fig. 21 shows R(X) depending on the fault density in the memory with definite values for word size and capacity.

If X is interpreted as a failure in production, R(X) is identical with the yield, and if X is interpreted as a failure in operation, R(X) simply indicates the high reliability and the associated high mean time to failure. The result can also be applied to a mixture of both types of failures.

The calculation of the time-depending probability of survival is based on a constant failure rate λ for every memory element, see eq. (15). The probability of survival for a word consisting of L elements that may contain either no or a single error in a random location thus is

$$R_W(t) = e^{-\lambda \cdot L \cdot t} + L \cdot e^{-\lambda(L-1)t} \cdot \left(1 - e^{-\lambda t}\right). \tag{35}$$

Then the total probability is the product W times, and thus we get

$$R(t) = \left[L \cdot e^{-(L-1)\lambda t} - (L-1)e^{-L\lambda t}\right]^W. \tag{36}$$

Fig. 22 shows an example of this function as a function of time and for comparison also the situation without error correction [12].

Now the interesting question arises whether error correction should better be used to increase the yield or the reliability. Starting with the assumption that in a definite reference point without tolerating any errors, the failure density D_0 and a chip surface A_0 with acceptable yield is well under control, then $Y_{CO} = e^{-D_0 \cdot A_C}$. If it will be sufficient to reach the same value by a new development with fault

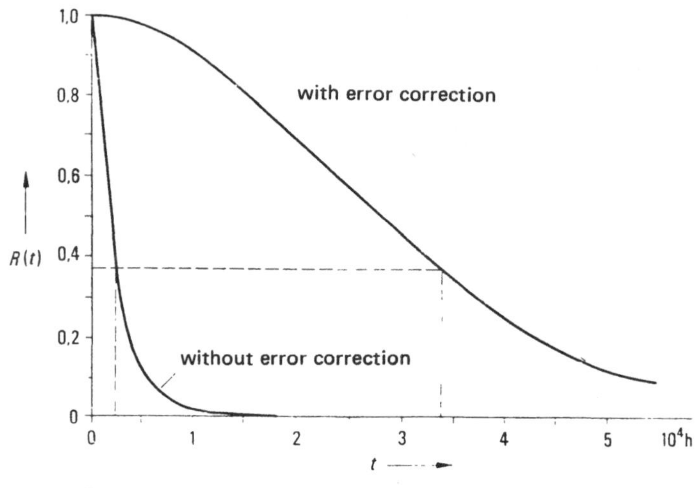

Reliability R as a function of time

Fig. 22

tolerance the permissable number of errors X can be derived from Figs. 20 or 21.
This number of errors will then be distributed over a larger area $A_{CX} = X/D_0$. The
surface required for one element is $A_E = A_C/n_0$. The scale of integration n_X to
be achieved by fault toleration thus results in

$$n_X = \frac{A_{CX}}{A_E} = \frac{X \cdot n_0}{D_0 \cdot A_C} = -\frac{X \cdot n_0}{\ln Y_{CO}} \, . \tag{37}$$

If numerical values are substituted, it appears that the increase of integration would
be remarkable. In a more detailed calculation of course, we must account for
the fact that the error correcting circuits have additional surface requirements on the
silicon wafer but this would lead too far away here.

If the error correction would only be utilized to increase the yield, it is clear that
this would at present bring nearly no advantage at all. The improvements in yield
would rapidly decrease in view of the fast improvement of conventional semiconductor circuits, and thus would no longer justify the efforts for these additional
correcting circuits, see Fig. 23. Thus we may hope that the increase of integration
by fault tolerance will play a major part if the problem of making sure the correcting circuits is investigated by somewhat greater efforts.

The advantage of fault tolerance has been shown here only by an example of the
single error correction. There are, however, other procedures with much higher performance values. Roughly they can be subdivided in procedures, in which the redundancy is increased to such an extent that more than one fault per word can be
tolerated (parallel processing), and in procedures in which successively a simple fault
tolerance is performed on different circuit levels (serial processing). The procedures

318

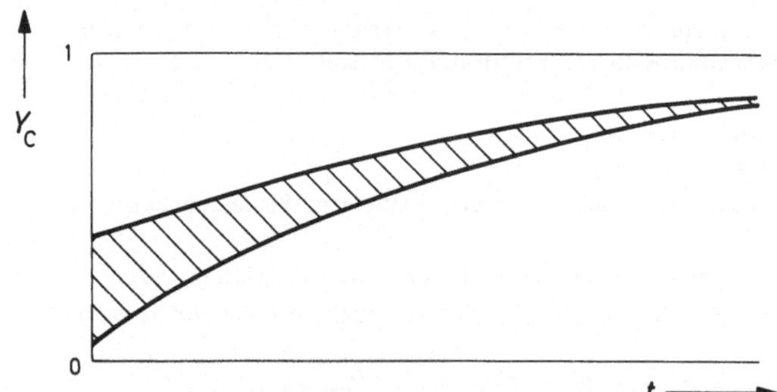

Fig. 23

mentioned first can only be implemented with a rather high effort and lead to very long read/write times, while the second mentioned procedures in general are less effective.

Conclusion

Preparing this paper discussions with Messrs. Kleedehn and Tertel (IBM), Reiner and Fischer (SEL), Hedtke, Knobloch, and Mellert (THD) were very helpfull and are thankfully acknowledged.

References

[1]   *W. Hilberg,* Elektronische digitale Speicher, Oldenbourg Verlag, München, 1975.

[2]   *W. Hilberg,* Grundlagen der Digitaltechnik II, Vorlesung TH Darmstadt SS 1976.

[3]   *B. T. Murphy,* Cost-Size Optima of Monolithic Integrated Circuits, Proc. IEEE, Dec. 1964, pp 1537–1545.

[4]   *B. Hofflinger,* Praxis der rechnerunterstützten Großintegration mit MOS-Schaltungen, Seminar Universität Dortmund, 4.–8. Okt. 1976.

[5]   *K. Garbrecht* and *K.-U. Stein,* Perspectives and Limitations of Large-Scale Integration, Siemens Forsch. u. Entwickl.-Ber. Bd. **5,** Nr. 6, 312–318 (1976).

[6]   IEEE Standard Dictionary of Electrical and Electronics Terms, IEEE Std. 100–1972.

[7]   EOQC, Glossary of Terms used in Quality Control, Fourth Edition, July 1976.

[8]   NTG-Empfehlung 3001, Zuverlassigkeit elektrischer Bauelemente. NTZ **10,** 618–626 (1967), Erlauterungen in NTZ **11,** 669–672 (1965).

[9]   NTG-Empfehlung 3002, Zuverlässigkeit von Geräten, Anlagen und Systemen. NTZ **23,** 45–56 (1970). Erläuterungen in NTZ S. 577–580 (1968).

[10] *W. Hilberg,* Zuverlassiger Betrieb von LSI-Speichern mit relativ vielen fehlerhaften Bauelementen. Elektron. Rechenanl. **11,** H. 6, 321–329 (1969).

[11] *W. Hilberg,* Einfache mathematische Modelle für die Ausbeute bei integrierten Schaltungen, insbesondere bei Halbleiterspeichern. Elektron. Rechenanlagen 14, H. 2, 67–75, H. 3, 134–142 (1972).

[12] *E. Holzler* and *H. Holzwarth,* Pulstechnik, Bd. II, Anwendungen und Systeme Abschnitt 6.5.2, Fehlerkorrektur in Speichersystemen.

[13] *W. Gorke,* Zuverlässigkeitsprobleme elektronischer Schaltungen, BI Taschenbuch 820/820a, 1969.

[14] *W. Gorke,* Fehlerdiagnose digitaler Schaltungen, Teubner Studienskripten, 1973.

[15] *E. Dombrowski,* Einführung in die Zuverlässigkeit elektronischer Geräte und Systeme. AEG-Telefunken, 1970.

[16] Reliability of Semiconductor Devices, Proc. IEEE, Febr. 1974, Vol. 62, No. 2.

[17] Technische Zuverlässigkeit, Springer 1971 (Messerschmitt-Bölkow-Blohm).

[18] *M. Weiher,* Studienarbeit DS 59, THD, 1976.

[19] *T. L. Palfi,* MOS Memory System Reliability, Semiconductor Test Symposium, Oct. 14–16, 1975, Digest of papers, pp. 37–46.

[20] *L. Levine,* Semiconductor Memory Reliability with Error Detecting and Correcting Codes, Computer, Oct. 1976, pp. 43–50.

[21] *R. J. Koppel* and *I. Maltz,* Predicting the real costs of semiconductor-memory systems, Electronics, Nov. 25, 1976, pp. 117–122.

[22] Intel Reliability Report RR-7, 1975, N-Channel Silicon Gate MOS 4K RAMs.

[23] Intel Reliability Report RR-6, 1975, Silicon Gate MOS 2K PROM.

[24] Texas Instruments Reliability Report, 4K MOS RAMs.

[25] *D. P. Fischer,* Failure Investigations on Semiconductor Integrated Circuits. Scientific Principles of Semiconductor Technology. Bad Boll, July 8–12, 1974, pp. 361–385.

[26] *W. Hilberg,* Die Auswirkung von Integrationsfortschritten und Produktionsverbesserungen auf die mittlere Lebensdauer von Halbleiterschaltungen. Frequenz 31, H10, pp. 302–311.

Reliability of Semiconductor Memories from a Practical Point of View

Dieter Fischer

Standard Elektrik Lorenz AG, (ITT), Stuttgart, Germany

1. Introduction

The application of semiconductor memories in all areas of data processing is steadily increasing. Despite continous reductions of the manufacturing costs of magnetic core memories mainly by means of improved packaging techniques, the breakthrough of large scale integrated (LSI) semiconductor memories could not be stopped [1].

Compared to magnetic core memories, semiconductor memories offer as significant advantages small volume requirements, fast access times, low power dissipation and a considerable cost reduction by the high level of circuit integration. On the other hand, it is not easy to answer the question, whether semiconductor memories offer also advantages with respect to reliability. This question is the subject of this paper where the term "semiconductor memories" refers to the basic component, and not to the entire system. Subsequent to an explanation of the major failure modes of monolithic integrated circuits, specific failure modes of LSI semiconductor memories will be discussed. This leads to considerations how to improve the reliability of semiconductor memories. Finally, some figures on failure rates will be given.

This paper deals mainly with read-write-memories, since they are of major importance.

2. Failure Modes of Integrated Semiconductor Memories

Semiconductor memories show about the same reliability behaviour as other integrated circuits of small or medium complexity as they are manufactured by the same process. Therefore, the failure modes of these circuits will be discussed first [2].

Unsatisfactory manufacturing methods sometimes result in a high thermomechanical stress which leads to cracks in the chip (Fig. 1).

Figure 2 shows a failure which occurred during cutting of the wafer into individual chips and which obviously was not detected in the course of the visual inspection during the assembly process. The properties of the unprotected junctions change with time, resulting in failures of the component.

Many failures are caused by defective electrical connections between the chip and the package leads. In Fig. 3 two connecting wires have touched whereas Fig. 4 shows a defective bond between the chip metallization and the bond wire. At high tem-

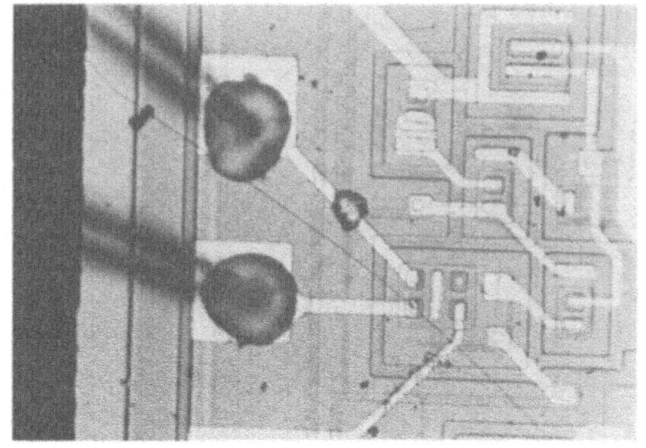

Fig. 1
Crack in semiconductor chip.

Fig. 2
Chipout.

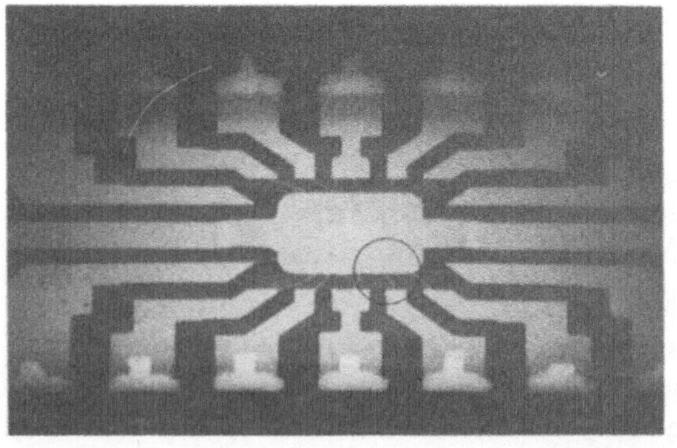

Fig. 3
Short circuit between two bondwires.

Fig. 4
Lifted ball bond.

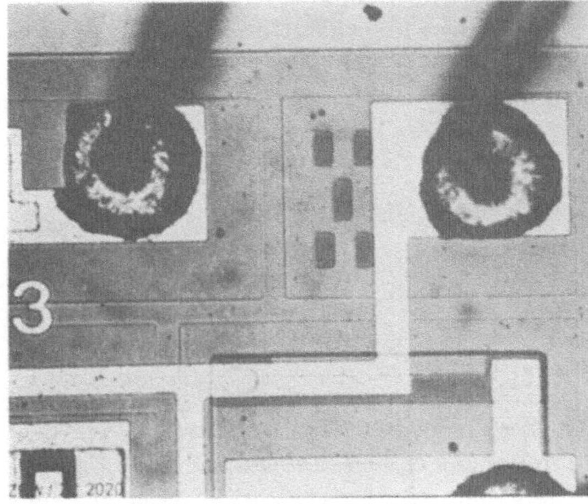

Fig. 5
Gold plague.

peratures, aluminium and gold form intermetallic compounds resulting in brittle and high ohmic contacts. The dark rings in Fig. 5 indicate the existence of such intermetallic compounds which in the literature are often termed "gold plague".

It was not easy to locate the failure shown in Fig. 6, since the small piece of wire which shorts two adjacent pins is not firmly in place. Therefore the short is not permanent, but occurs only occasionally depending upon movement and position of the component (Fig. 7).

With respect to the reliability of integrated circuits the metallic interconnections between the circuit elements on the chip are especially critical. Unfavourable etching methods for the silicon dioxide and/or unfavourable evaporation methods for the metal-

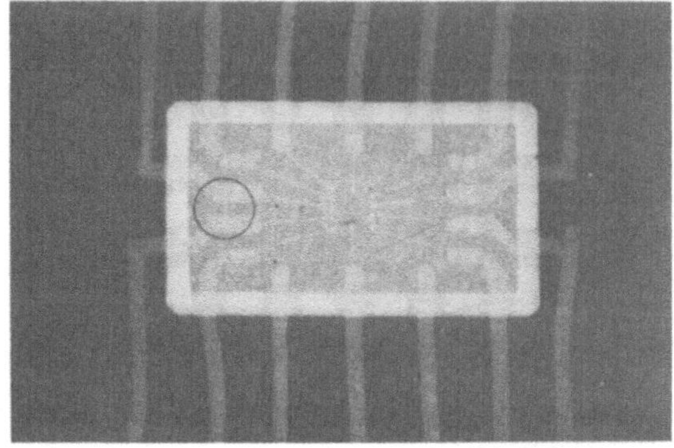

Fig. 6

Short circuit by unattached
piece of wire.

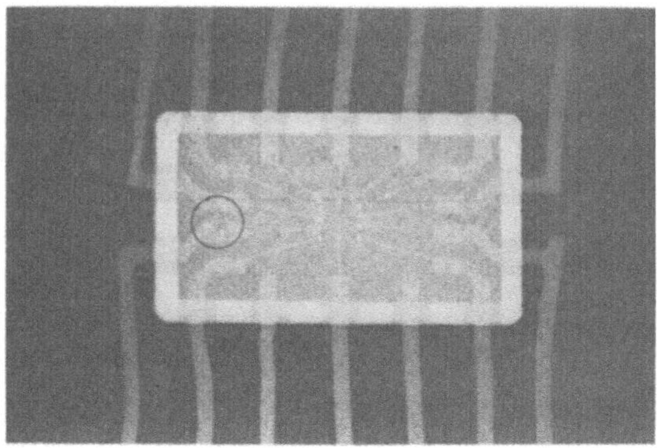

Fig. 7

Unattached piece of wire.

lization result in reduced cross sections at steep oxide steps (Fig. 8). These behave like
weak fuses which easily blow if they are stressed by temperature and current. Inproper
applications often lead to excessive currents which even break properly designed metallization lines as can be clearly seen in Fig. 9. However, there are also fast bipolar circuits
with current densities of about 2×10^5 A/cm^2 under normal operating conditions.
At these high current densities and high operating temperatures, aluminium mass
transport may occur which results in whisker growth (Fig. 10) due to accumulation
of aluminium in certain areas and in depletion of aluminium in other areas which
may cause interruptions.
Leaky packages and/or chemical contamination of the chip surface cause corrosion
which usually starts at the aluminium interconnection lines. Figure 11 shows an
obvious example of corrosion of a CMOS circuit in a plastic package. Such defects
have also been found in hermetic packages where a sufficient amount of humidity
has been sealed in. They are especially dangerous in circuits with high operating
voltages and low power dissipation.

324

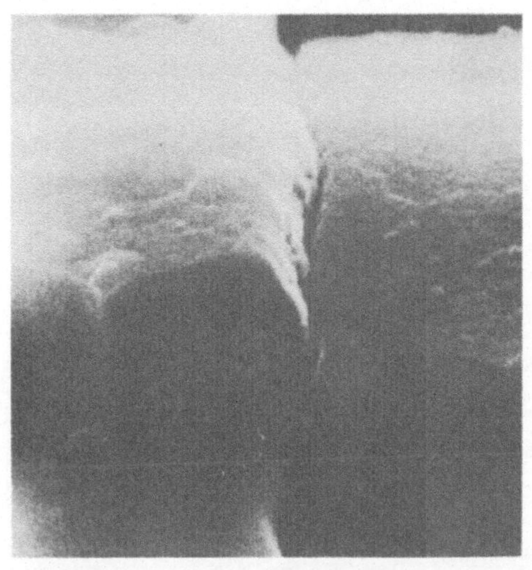

Fig. 8

Reduced cross-section of metallisation at oxide step.

Fig. 9

Failure caused by overload.

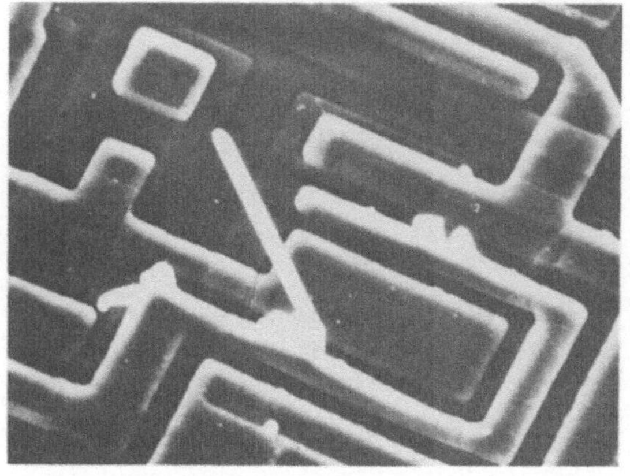

Fig. 10

Whisker growth in Schottky TTL circuits.

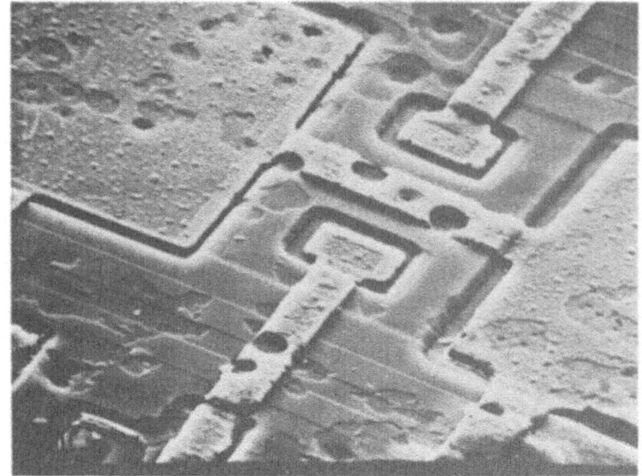

Fig. 11

Corrosion of CMOS in plastic package.

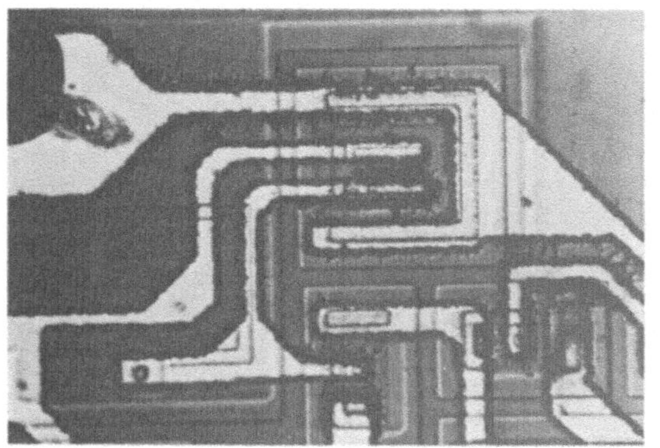

Fig. 12

Formation of Mo-whisker in Au/Mo metallisation system.

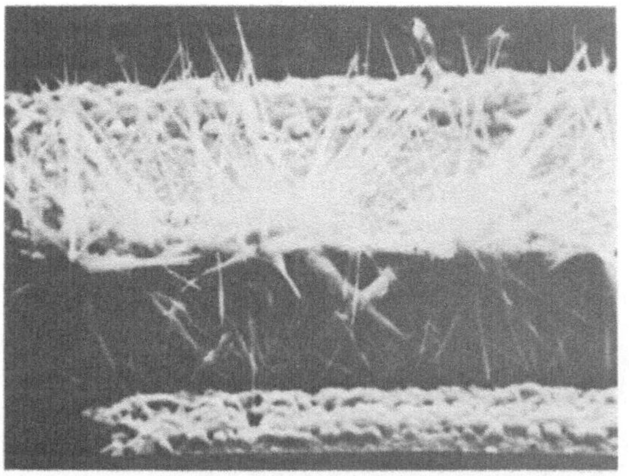

Fig. 13

Molybdenum whisker growth in Au/Mo metallisation system.

Technological changes which have been introduced in order to overcome critical effects sometimes cause undesired side-effects. The gold plague for example, can be avoided, if the metallization lines on the chip and the bonding wires are of the same material, e.g. gold. For technological reasons, a molybdenum layer has to be placed under the gold layer. In theory, this technology should yield very reliable interconnections and therefore has been applied preferably in components for HIREL (high reliability) applications such as satellites. In practice, however, molybdenum whiskers sometimes grew in a number of circuits and caused short circuits between the interconnection lines (Figs. 12 and 13). Short circuits between metal lines, between a metal line and silicon or between a metal line and polysilicon are also noticable. They are the results of manufacturing failures and appear in form of "almost shorts" which after some time of operation change into real shorts.

The gate oxide areas are critical parts in MOS circuits. If they are unprotected as can be seen in Fig. 14, contamination can penetrate and cause undesired shunts or other electrical changes.

Irreversible punch-through occurs at short voltage spikes of about 100 V since the gate oxide thickness is only about 100 nm. As the gate capacitances are in the order of a few tenths of a picofarad, even a very small amount of electrical energy easily generated by electrostatic charging can readily cause punch through defects. Fig. 15 shows such a punch through. Today almost all MOS circuits have input protection circuits in order to protect the gate oxide areas of the input transistors, which generally operate adequately. At higher discharge voltages however the protection circuits may be damaged instead of the gate oxide as can be seen in Fig. 16.

Besides the microscopic or macroscopic defects which have been described, there are also drift related changes of the electrical properties which in most cases can be traced back to contamination introduced during the manufacturing process.

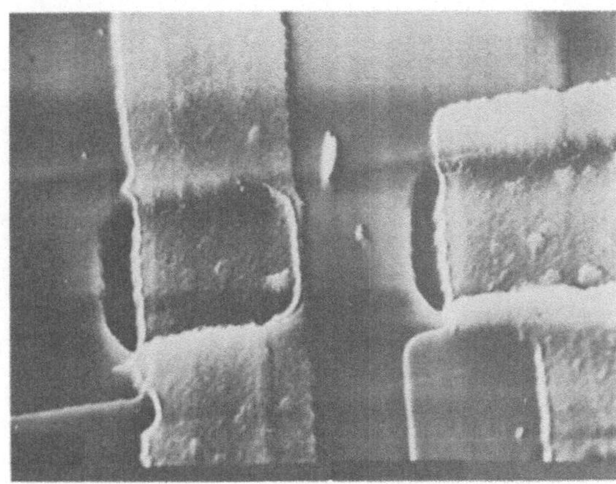

Fig. 14
Exposed gate oxide.

Fig. 15

Punch-through of thin (gate) oxide of a MOS FET switch.

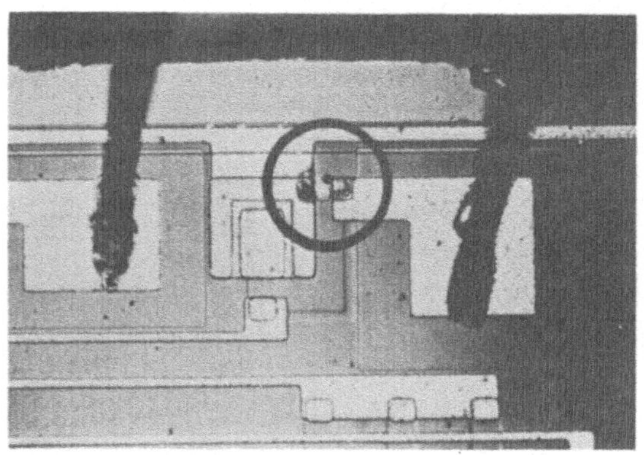

Fig. 16

Punch-through in MOS input protection device.

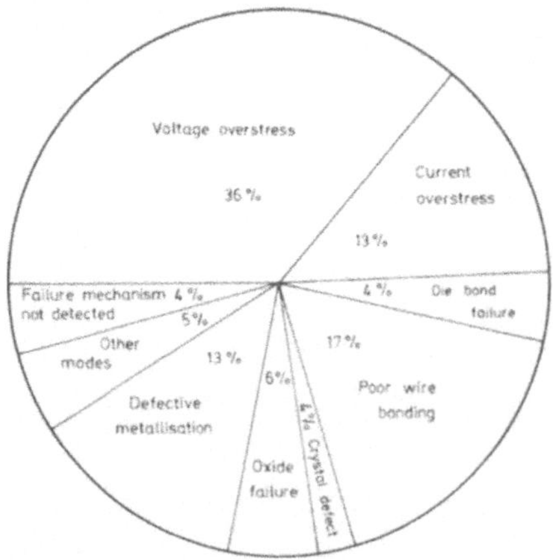

Fig. 17

Results of Failure Statistics.

328

Figure 17 shows the distribution of different failure modes which have been established during the failure analysis of more than 1000 integrated circuits. It is most obvious that more than 50 % of the defects are caused by inproper application. A relatively large portion of defects is related to the chip metallization particularly due to corrosion in CMOS circuits. Defective wire bonds also give a high contribution, while other contributions are relatively small.

3. Specific Failure Mechanisms in LSI Memories

Besides the already described failure mechanisms, additional specific failure mechanisms occur in semiconductor memories. These will be described for read-write memories and programmable read-only memories.

3.1. Gate oxide failures

Gate oxide punch-through can occur, even if the input voltages of memories are kept within the specified limits. This is due to pinholes where the thickness of the gate oxide is reduced resulting in lower breakdown voltages. Contamination with small particles before, during or after growth of the gate oxide is the major reason for this type of failure. These weak points can punch-through within the specified supply voltage ranges resulting in shorts [3]. As the ratio of gate oxide area to chip area is larger in memories than in logic circuits, this failure mechanism is more important for memories. The gate to substrate shorts cause catastrophic failures in single memory cells, single rows or single columns. In rare cases the complete circuit fails catastrophically.

3.2. Bit pattern sensitivity

Especially in dynamic memories, data loss of one or several cells may occur under specific operating conditions. It is obviously very difficult to locate such defects. There are many possible reasons for this type of defect. The reasons cannot always be completely separated and understood. Some examples are explained below:

- "Charge-pumping" for example is a failure mechanism of dynamic MOS read-write-memories which depends upon the previous history of operation. In "charge-pumping", each time the voltage of a drive line approaches the V_{ss} level, it may dump a small amount of charge into neighbouring storage cells. Over a period of time, this charge may build up incrementally to the point where it changes the data stored in a cell. This must, however, occur between two refresh cycles; once a cell has been refreshed, "charge-pumping" starts again [4].

- A specific lay-out of the dynamic 1 k bit 1103 memory had too slow address decoders. If all bits of one address are changed with respect to the preceding one, e.g. in the transition from address "0001" to address "1110", this leads to erroneous addressing. This type of error has also been observed in static memories.

- The recovery time of the sense amplifiers of several types of dynamic memories is too long resulting in error during the read operation. In these cases all cells of a column are affected which are attached to the corresponding sense amplifier.

- Very small crystal defects which are too small to block the function of an entire cell may cause another failure mechanism. Such defects can cause connections between adjacent cells which result in erroneous writing into the cell which is adjacent to the cell being addressed [4].

- Principally dynamic memories are very sensitive to excessive leakage currents which result in inadmissibly fast losses of the stored charges. In most cases this results in single bit failures.

Most of these failures do not occur permanently but are dependent on the operating conditions such as chip temperature, supply voltages, static and dynamic noise and the "bit pattern" which may be the pattern applied during the current or a preceeding cycle. Furthermore, the layout of the memory and the combination of all process parameters are of influence.

As it is very difficult to locate these failures in a memory system, it is important to screen the affected components before they enter the assembly process. In general, this can only be done by extensive functional tests. At high levels of chip complexity, the test patterns may become so extensive that the capacity of the memory of the test pattern generator used is not capable of storing all test sequences. Apart from these considerations, the programming effort would become unacceptably high. In order to overcome this problem a number of test algorithms have been developed, some of which are presented in Fig. 18 [5, 6].

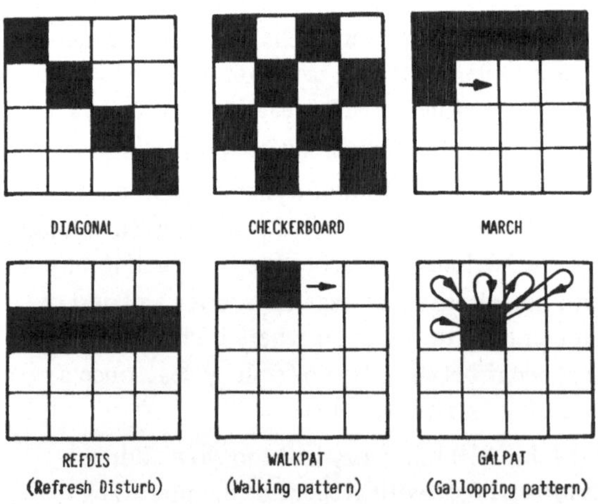

Fig. 18

Test methods for read-write memories.

3.3. Test patterns

- The "DIAGONAL TEST" starts with the memory loaded with binary "0" in every cell except those in the diagonal, where binary "1" are stored. Every cell is read in order along the columns. The memory is then reloaded with the diagonal stripe of "1" shifted one cell to the right, and is again read columnwise. This test is repeated a total of 64 times for a 4 kbit memory, each time presenting the sense amplifier with a single "1" after a long string of "0" and eventually placing a "1" in every memory cell. The test is then repeated with a diagonal stripe of "0" in a field of "1". This test mainly identifies slow recovery sense amplifiers and in addition checks the basic function of the memory.

- The "CKECKERBOARD-TEST" is very simple, the cells are alternately loaded with "1" and "0". After the read operation all "0" are replaced by "1" and vice versa. This pattern also tests the recovery times of the sense amplifiers.

- Minimal functional testing can be performed using the "MARCH" algorithm. The memory is initially loaded with "0" in all cells. The "0" is read from the first cell and a "1" is written in its place. This sequence of reading a "0" and writing a "1" is repeated for the next cell and so on, until all cells are set to "1". Read "0"-write "1" is then scanned in reverse order of addressing until all cells are set to "0". Finally the complete test is repeated with complemented data.
In testing the memory with increasing and decreasing addresses, the influence of the write operation on the adjacent cells is checked. The test will also detect decoder problems.

- More widely used, the "WALKPAT-TEST" provides a more extensive memory test. As with "MARCH", every cell in the memory is first set initially to "0". After a "1" has been written in the first cell, all cells are read to verify their proper content. The first cell is then restored to "0", the next cell is set to "1" and all cells are again read to verify their contents. The sequence is continued for every cell in the array. Its complementary pattern, walking "0" completes the test.

   In addition to proving that each cell can be set to both "0" and "1" and that any cell can be set to either state without causing any other cell to change its state, this test also verifies correct cell addressing. Furthermore, because the output amplifier remains in the same state for a long time while reading all but one cell and then switches to the other state, any tendency that the amplifier recovers too slowly is detected.

   This test however, it is inadequate to test for certain other important characteristics. For example, because addressing is only sequential, slow access time or a tendency towards multiple selection may not show up. In addition, because data output changes only once for each iteration, only a small amount of the normal switching transients take place, hiding write recovery problems and worst case noise problems.

- To test all possible address transitions with all possible data transitions, galloping "1" and "0" (GALPAT) was devised. It begins the same way as walking "1" and "0" but after the "1" has been stored in one cell and while the "0" in all other cells are being verified, the original "1" is rechecked after every "0" is verified. As with the walking tests, the sequence is repeated for every cell in the array, checking a "1" against "0" in all other cells. The test is then repeated with the complemented data pattern.

- Dynamic memories store data in the form of an electric charge on distributed capacitances. Since the charge tends to dissipate in a few milliseconds, it must be periodically refreshed — usually one full row at a time — to ensure adequate data retention. The "REFDIS" test checks the sensitivity of cells to noise signals which are created during writing into surrounding cells if the cells under test are addressed only at the end of a refresh period. For this purpose a "0" is written into all cells with the exception of one row which is set to "1". In both adjacent cells, "0" are permanently verified and restored. At the end of the refresh time the "1" is read and written into the adjacent row. This sequence is repeated until all rows are tested. The complementary pattern of a row of "0" surrounded by "1" completes the test [7].

The effectiveness of these test patterns depends to a large extent on the internal organisation of a memory. It is not always ensured for example, that the numerical sequence of cell addressing is in line with the topological sequence. If this condition is not met, a test which is tailored on a numerical sequence, will not meet its purpose.

Figure 19 gives a survey of the test patterns considered. They can be roughly classified into two groups. In simple tests, the number of test steps is proportional to the number of bits. For 4-k bit-memories with a cycle time of 540 ns, the required test times are very short and are of the order of milliseconds. The number of test steps

Test method	Test objective	Comments	No. of [1] test steps	Testing [2] time
DIAGONAL	Sense amplifiers	Min. functional tests	$2\,N$	0.003
CHECKER-BOARD	Sense amplifiers Input stages	Min. functional tests	$2\,N$	0.003
MARCH	Cells	Min. functional test	$8\,N$	0.014
REFDIS	Refresh times Cell interaction	Standard test for dynamic memories only	$6\,N^{3/2}$	0.71
WALKPAT	Sense amplifiers Addressing	Standard test Min. functional test	$2\,N^2$	15.1
GALPAT	Cells, Access time, Read write operation	Standard test Various variants like PING PONG, BUTTERFLY	$4\,N^2$	30.2

Fig. 19

Functional test patterns for RAM's.

1) For one basic pattern, N = number of bits.

2) For 4 K bit-RAM, cycle time 450 ns.

increases with the square of the number of cells. e.g. in 16 k bit-memories the test
times for these patterns will be 16 times as long as in 4 k bit-memories resulting in
test times of the order of some ten seconds. In this case the testing cost may be higher
than the manufacturing cost of the memories.

Therefore it is not economical to arbitrarily select algorithms which have proved to
be useful for one particular device, and to apply it to another one in order to detect
pattern sensitivity. Instead, it is necessary to select the patterns which are most
effective for a certain memory from a certain manufacturer after a thorough charac-
terization which also includes Schmoo-plots, i.e. operating tolerance fields. In most
cases a combination of several algorithms is most effective which have been carefully
selected after analysis of the devices which failed in the course of the characteriza-
tion tests. Since the optimum program is dependent upon design and manufacturing
processes, it is not reasonable to apply it to devices from a different manufacturer
or even to a different type of device.

3.4. Dynamic failures

Experience shows that in present commercial semiconductor memories the safety
margins of the dynamic parameters are rather low, much lower than in other comparable integrated circuits. Furthermore, in MOS circuits, the influence of temperature on speed is higher than in bipolar circuits. Especially in memories produced in
P-MOS technology the drift of the threshold voltage, which may easily increase by
0.5 V to 1 V, results in correspondingly increased switching times thus adding
another risk factor. In N-MOS technology this risk is significantly reduced.
Problems accumlate, if in addition the design of the memory system includes only
minimal safety margins or no margins at all.

3.5. PROM specific failure mechanisms

Programmable read-only memories are produced in various technologies. Figure 20
shows an unprogrammed poly-silicon fuse of a PROM which is covered by a protective layer of SiO_2. By a current pulse of approximately 30 mA, the fuse opens and is
thereby programmed. (Fig. 21).

In PROMs two specific failure mechanisms have been observed:

- Sometimes "grow back" makes a programmed fuse behave like an unprogrammed one. It has been observed only in NiCr fuses [8]. In most cases this failure is
  the result of inproper interruption of the fuse during programming. Therefore, it
  is recommended to carefully follow the programming instructions.

- During the read operation, single fuses may be blown unintentionally. The reasons
  are too small cross sections of the fuses and/or too high read currents.

Fig. 20

Bipolar PROM cell with
polysilicon fuse – unprogrammed –.

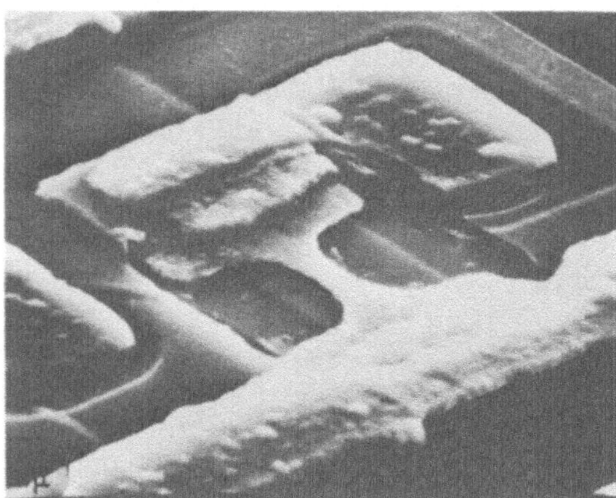

Fig. 21

Bipolar PROM cell with polysilicon fuse – programmed –.

3.6. Summary of the failure mechanisms in semiconductor memories

In Fig. 22 the failure mechanisms observed in read-write-memories are summarized.
Gate oxide failures and overload operations clearly dominate. It is noticeable, that
up to 90 % of all failures only affect single bits, whereas 5 to 10 % affect complete
rows and the complete chip fails only in about 5 % of all cases.

```
Failure mechanisms

Overload                        20 ... 30 %

Assembly                            10 %

Metallisation                       10 %

Gate-oxide                      20 ... 30 %

El. failures                        20 %


Failure distribution

Single bit failures             75 ... 90 %

Column failures                  5 ... 10 %

Complete citcuits                    5 %
```

Fig. 22

Failure mechanismus and failure
distribution in CMOS memories.

4. Measures to Improve the Reliability of Semiconductor Memories

Most users of semiconductor memories can only apply memories which are available
on the open market. Nevertheless they have a considerable influence on the reliability
of the memory devices used. Selection of the proper circuit type, testing and operating
conditions may well change the failure rate by one order of magnitude. The re-
commendations given in Fig. 23 should only be considered as a rough guide. In any
specific case only a part of the suggested measures and/or additional measures may
prove to be more useful, depending on the technology used, on the maturity of the
product design and on economic considerations.

The careful selection of the memory device type should include an analysis of the
market as well as a technical appraisal of the manufacturer and the qualification of
the circuit also with Schmoo-plots. In the course of this phase, different test algorithms will be used in order to detect test pattern sensitivity. This leads to a test program which also ensures the basic function and the specified static and dynamic

```
Careful selection of memory type and manufacturer

Thorough evaluation of the electric properties

Burn-in at increased supply voltages

Proper handling

Favourable operating conditions
```

Fig. 23

Measures to inprove the reliability
of semiconductor memories.

parameters. This program should especially reflect the requirements of the specific
system since the manufacturer cannot test all relevant conditions of all possible
systems requirements.

All received memory circuits should be acceptance tested with this program. It is
recommended to run the test at the maximum operating temperature in order to take
into account the strong temperature dependance of major memory parameters. Due
to the power dissipation of the components, the operating temperature is up to 20 °C
higher than the ambient temperature. Since the thermal time constants of the circuits
are large with respect to the testing time, the temperature of the device under test
should be adjusted accordingly. Early failures can be efficiently screened by burn-in
tests at elevated temperatures. If these tests are carried out under increased supply
voltages most of the weak gate oxide areas are screened out [9, 10] .

Proper handling especially includes avoiding of discharge of electrostatic energy as
well as of any other electrical overstress.

Favourable operating conditions give a valuable contribution to the reliability of
semiconductor memories. Low operating ambient temperatures are always advantageous since most failure mechanisms are accelerated by temperature. Sufficient safety
margins for the tolerances of dynamic parameters protect against dynamic failures,
whereas stable supply voltages and careful construction which suppresses noise,
prevent many sporadic single bit failures. Also the overall system architecture has
considerable influence on the reliability of a memory system.

5. Failure Rates of Semiconductor Memories

As for other integrated circuits a "bath tub" characteristic can be expected for the
time dependency of the failure rate of semiconductor memories (Fig. 24). The
number of early failures which is mainly caused by manufacturing failures decreases
rapidly with time, followed by a constant or slightly decreasing failure rate. Little

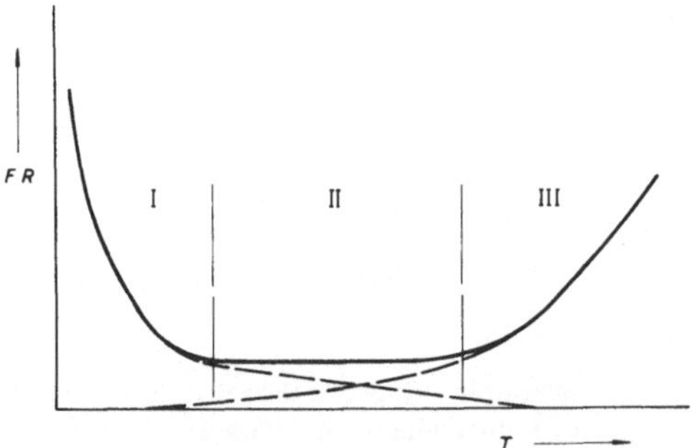

Fig. 24

Time dependence of failure rate.

information is available on the beginning and on the number of wear-out failures. In state of the art memory systems with standard components, wear-out failures are not to be expected prior to 100,000 hours of life.

Failure rate data are obtained either from life-tests or from field results.

5.1. Life test results

In order to reduce the testing cost, in mot cases relative short tests are carried out at elevated ambient temperatures. There are test results available for 4 k bit-memories which have been tested for 1000 hours at 125 °C indicating failure rates between 3000×10^{-9} h [1, 11] and $25,000 \times 10^{-9}$ [12]. However, there are problems to extrapolate these results to lower ambient temperatures. In one approach, arbitrary assumptions are made on the effective activation energy, which depending on the source, range between 0.3 eV and 1.0 eV from which the corresponding acceleration factors can be calculated. In a second approach, the acceleration factors published in MIL-STD-883 A are applied: There, an acceleration factor of 50 is specified for a temperature rise from 70 °C to 125 °C resulting in a failure rate of 4 k bit-memories at 70 °C ranging from 60 to 500×10^{-9} h. The lower value seems to be too optimistic for the present situation.

5.2. Field results

Reports on field results are very sparse for various reasons. For one, the time span of application is still very short. On the other hand, the exact collection of data requires considerable effort. Finally, such data are often considered to be confidential. On average, failure rates are given which range between 200×10^{-9} h [13] and 800×10^{-9} h [9] . In the long run, an improvement of these figures can be expected.

References

[1] *Dietrich Krause,* Zuverlässigkeitsanalyse bei Halbleiterspeichern. Wissenschaftl. Bericht AEG-Telefunken **48**, 5 (1975).

[2] *Dieter Fischer,* Failure investigations on Semiconductor Integrated Circuits, Proc. of the European Summer School, SCIENTIFIC PRINCIPLES OF SEMICONDUCTOR TECH-NOLOGY, Bad Boll, July 8–12, 1974.

[3] *T. L. Palfi,* MOS Memory System Reliability.

[4] *E. G. Cromer,* Testing Semiconductor Memories. El. Packaging and Production, February 1974.

[5]   *K. Muller,* Zur Strategie der elektrischen Funktionsprüfung an integrierten Halbleiter-speichern. Z. elektr. Information u. Energietechnik, Leipzig 5, 2 (1975).

[6]   *E R. Hnatek,* 4-Kilobit Memories Present a Challenge to Testing, Computer Design, May 1975.

[7]   *M. Marshall,* Through the Memory Cells — Further Exploration of ICs in Testingland, II, EDN, 20. Febr. 1976.

[8]   *Bill Pascoe,* Polysilicon Fuse Bipolar PROMs, Intel Reliability Report RR-8.

[9]   4 KMOS RAMs from Texas Instruments, Bulletin CR-112.

[10] *Bill Pascoe,* N-channel Silicon Gate MOS 4 K RAM, Intel Reliability Report RR 7.

[11] *S. Reddy,* NS Reliability Report RM 9.

[12] MOSTEK Reliability Report 4096-Bit Random Access Memory, January 1976.

[13] Confidential Information from a customer of memory devices.

Application of Partially Defective Semiconductor Memory Devices in Memory Systems

Hans-Jörg Penzel

Siemens AG, Data Processing Systems, Munich, Germany

Introduction

Semiconductor memory devices are currently available in a large variety of technologies and may be chosen according to the application requirements. These devices are used by an increasing number of customers for steadily expanding areas of applications. The present work is mainly concerned with applications of dynamic MOS memory devices in LSI technology which offer relatively low cost per bit combined with moderate speed. Typical applications are main memories for all types of data processing systems, terminals and peripheral devices, demonstrating at the same time the important economic significance of semiconductor memories.

An analysis of the currently required capital investment in quality assurance and reliability on device and system level is presented, followed by the formulation of strategies leading to more practical solutions than the methods now in general use, in which the essential criterion for device application is the absence of defects. A simulation model will be presented allowing the investigation of the possible applications and limits of using partially defective memory devices. Finally, the results obtained by this model will be discussed.

1. Starting Situation

The most significant trend affecting cost during the coming years is the high innovation rate on the semiconductor memory market. New devices with progressively higher levels of integration are being introduced almost regularly every two to three years. The vigorous developments in the memory field in recent years is impressively depicted in Fig. 1, which is a diagram showing the various types of printed circuit (PC) boards used to build up a memory capacity of 64 KByte. Shown on the extreme left is a magnetic core memory built in 1970. The associated PC boards for the selection circuits and sense amplifiers are seen along the edges of the matrix. Next to these is a group of 16 memory PC boards populated, for the first time, with 1-Kbit MOS memory devices. Double PC boards containing 72 4-Kbit memory devices were introduced in 1974. The most recent type, seen on the extreme right, contains 16-Kbit devices and has also a capacity of 64 KByte. This trend can be expected to continue in the coming years. It is highly probable that 64-Kbit MOS devices will already become available by 1978 and that 256-Kbit CCD memory devices will be introduced by 1980.

Fig. 1. Examples of Evolution in Memory Design

Users normally follow the prevailing trend with minimum delay by developing and selling new equipment in which the latest devices are used. Economic analyses show in fact that the increased profit which is derived from the introduction of a new generation of LSI memory devices more than offsets the capital investment involved. Finally, competition also prompts the development of equipment in which the latest devices are used.

Users derive from the application of LSI memory devices a threefold advantage:

1. The way to larger memory capacities is opened.
2. The memory systems operate with increased reliability.
3. The cost per bit of the memory devices is lower than with earlier types.

What then is the capital investment required for development and production planning in order to secure the above advantages?

When we consider the capital investment required for the introduction of a new device generation we notice that the main cost factor is the development of a new memory system. The cost of developing methods for device testing is steadily increasing as compared to the cost of system-oriented design effort and planning

340

work. More than 50 % of the capital investment in system development has to be provided for testing effort up to the acceptance test of a first prototype.

Another 10 % to 20 % of the initial capital investment in system development has to be alloted if the availability of a selected device has to be guaranteed by the qualification of an equivalent device supplied by another manufacturer. Moreover, the devices of a second manufacturer usually have been designed to somewhat different specifications and manufactured using a different production process. This of course results in devices having essentially different defect mechanisms, therefore special testing routines for device selection are mandatory.

The distribution of production cost and maintainance cost of a memory system shows the memory device related capital investment to be predominant. The purchasing cost of memory devices and the cost for subsequent system maintainance are significant. Also the cost for routine testing is substantial, however, it depends considerably on the number and scope of the test procedures. The investment currently ranges between 10 % and 20 % of the procurement cost of the device and can be expected to rise non-linearily with the increasing level of integration and the increasing importance of reliability specifications.

It cannot be assumed that investment requirements will substantially change within the near future if the described practices are maintained. Any approach towards an effective improvement of the cost situation has to be primarily directed towards a modification of the specifications for device acceptance. Many users have already taken the first step in this direction by introducing error correction circuits in memories. The advantage of incorporating such circuits is extremely important in large-capacity memory systems because the reliability is improved by some orders of magnitude by correcting single-bit errors due to inherent defect mechanisms of the memory devices. Double errors and multiple errors within a data word will lead to system failures which can only be corrected by appropriate error recovery routines within the system.

For the consistent application of this method such memories will contain after a reasonable time of operation defective memory devices wiht recognizable single-bit errors. Lateron, due to the increasing number of such errors which are still correctable, higher order composite errors ultimately appear. The result is that single-bit errors will be accompanied by further error conditions leading to double and multiple errors and consequently to system failures. Therefore, it has to be anticipated that an increasing number of error correcting routines will become necessary. Such a procedure may sometimes result in prolonging the time schedule for maintenance cost but will not reduce the total investment cost.

No appreciable improvement in operating principle is possible without first classifying the observed recoverable single-bit errors at the instant at which they appear. The appearance of the error is here taken as a signal to check the environment of the failing bit, which is usually accomplished by running diagnostic programs simultaneously with user activities. The class and scope of the failing bit are recorded for the purpose of analysis. If necessary, measures will be taken which largely prevent the subsequent appearance of double or multiple errors. These measures include the physical replacement of PC boards and the modification of the PC boards assignment to memory address areas. Any memory system can in fact be kept in operation although many thousand of its memory cells may be partially defective. The required maintainance activities are limited to an absolute minimum and can be scheduled without recognizing the actual time at which errors has been detected.

2. Future Application of Partially Defective Memory Devices

2.1. Strategies

In the preceding section, the application of originally 100 % perfect memory devices in which defects will subsequently appear during the course of their lifetime have been described. In this section, a proposal is described that assumes it would be practical to use devices which are known to be partially defective right from the beginning. Both approaches aim at a reduction in capital investment for development, production and service and/or an improvement in reliability. A further working assumption is that it will be practical to use 2-bit error correction networks in future memory systems. These main assumptions are reasonably realistic and a number of technically and economically attractive solutions are available. Supporting software aids are likewise coceivable.

In line with the importance of the investments for purchasing memory parts, first let us now consider the aspects of buying partially defective memory devices. Device manufacturers currently subject their final products to quality control tests extending from wafer testing to the electrical testing of the packaged device according to the latest published specifications. Total yields ranging between 10 % to 50 % are reached for 100 % good parts. Devices which fail the tests do so as a result of a variety of defect mechanisms. Many defects, however are confined to a single cell or a few memory cells only. In MOS memory devices, for instance, oxide and surface defects are a typical cause of such selective failures. The higher the fabrication cost of a large-capacity memory device, the more attractive appears the use of partially defective devices for manufacturers and users as well. It is conceivable that the time will come when users ask manufacturers to supply perfect devices as well as devices with single bit or multiple bit defects in a certain ratio for common use in memory systems. The partially defective devices would of course have to meet the overall electrical and reliability specifications.

Another yield-increasing and consequently cost-reducing device fabrication strategy would be to build a complete 1-bit error correction feature into each device. In that case it would be possible to use not only devices which are partially defective in the above sense, but also devices with intermittent defect mechanisms leading to data pattern errors, temperature-dependent errors, refresh errors, etc. The reliability of partially defect devices could be substantially improved by integrating an error correction feature within the device, which would require approximately some additional 10 % to 15 % of the chip area. The incorporation of a 2-bit error correction feature within the memory system would be no longer necessary.

Any memory concept allowing the use of partially defective memory devices will naturally open the way to a reduction in the cost of testing or at least prevent such cost from becoming excessive. The acceptance of certain classified defects[1] allows, for instance, a substantial simplification of the procedures required for testing devices, PC boards and modules. Even random sample testing could be conceived. The development of testing procedures could then be focused much more on reliability assurance.

All these proposals have the common objective that at final checkout the memories, before leaving the factory, have no longer to operate perfectly without error correction as in the past.

2.2. Simulation Procedure

The effect of the acceptance of partially defective devices on both fabrication yield and reliability of final assemblies will now be considered on the basis of results obtained by simulation.

Simulation Model Use of partially defective memory devices	
Simulation program phase	Simulated process steps
A	DEVICE PHASE . Device generation confined to classified defects . Device testing by manufacturer and user
B	PC BOARD PHASE . Equipment of PC boards . Selection of PC boards – yield, repairs
C	MEMORY MODULE PHASE . Assembly of equipped PC boards . Checking of defect ratios 0-th, 1-st, 2-nd and higher order – fabrication yield . Module reliability

Fig. 2. Simulation Model

---

[1] Defects leading, for instance, to single-bit errors, column or row errors and total failures.

A simulation program has been composed reflecting almost realistic conditions. The program (Fig. 2) shows three phases: a device phase (A), a PC board phase (B) and a memory module phase (C) (Fig. 2).

In phase A partially defective devices are generated. The distribution, type and percentage of these devices simulate the conditions encountered in device fabrication and quality control. The partially defective devices are classified according to predeterminable features and registered in a device master file.

It should be noted that the program also allows to study the advantage of error correction features integrated in each device.

In phase B PC boards are designed and populated according to a fixed or random distribution of 100 % perfect and partially defective devices picked out from the device master file.

A sorting program registers the perfect states as well as single, double or multiple errors by scanning the various PC board addresses. Variations in PC board format and PC board organization can be taken into account. The results are compared with the original specifications and filed. These specifications contain, for instance, the permissible number, magnitude and distribution of defects which can be taken into account in subsequent memory module production. The yield-oriented data obtained are of critical significance in evaluating the various approaches in using partially defective devices.

In phase C the memory modules are simulated. A memory module is usually an assembly of a large number of PC boards. Boards registered as usuable in the PC board file are being allocated to various assembly locations within the module. Once again either a fixed or a random distribution between perfect and partially defective PC boards may be selected. The assembled modules are then tested and the distribution of errors checked. Address areas will be located having zero, single, double or multiple errors.

Finally the effect of using partially defective devices on the reliability of the memory system can be investigated. The use of such devices will be considered under the simplified assumption that they were known to be partially defective from the beginning. The program can, of course, also be used to investigate the effect of devices with originally not detected defects. Some defects may pass undetected if, for instance, simpler test procedures are employed in memory system production.

2.3. Discussion of Results

2.3.1. Assumptions

The results obtained using this program will now be discussed. The working assumptions are:

1. The simulated devices are 16-Kbit memory devices.

2. The simulated PC boards accommodate 36 memory devices with all inputs and outputs brought out at the PC board interface, i.e. the PC board is organized in 16 384 words of 36 bit each.

3. The memory module accommodates 32 PC boards. The module interface has a data path width of 72 bit (i.e. 8 bytes).

4. Only 1-bit errors per addressed memory word are allowed for PC boards and modules.

5. For simplicity reasons, the memory devices are assumed to exhibit only hard errors. The nominal error data were based on the error statistics of 4-Kbit memory devices. The assumed error distribution of 33 : 34 : 33 for single bit errors, row and column errors and total failures is based on an analysis of long-term failures. We are aware that semiconductor device manufacturers are reporting device tests which show still larger ratios for single-bit errors due to local defects in the oxide.

The ratio of perfect devices to partially defective devices can be chosen arbitrarily and devices with certain types of defect can be rejected.

2.3.2. Assembly of PC Boards

Let us first consider the PC board yield which may be obtained in a production line if partially defective devices are to be incorporated.

Fig. 3 shows the PC board yield as a function of the percentual incorporation of partially defective devices. Two classes of errors are incorporated on a 50 : 50 basis: single-bit errors and column/row errors. This restriction is necessary because including totally defective devices will drastically reduce the PC board yield.

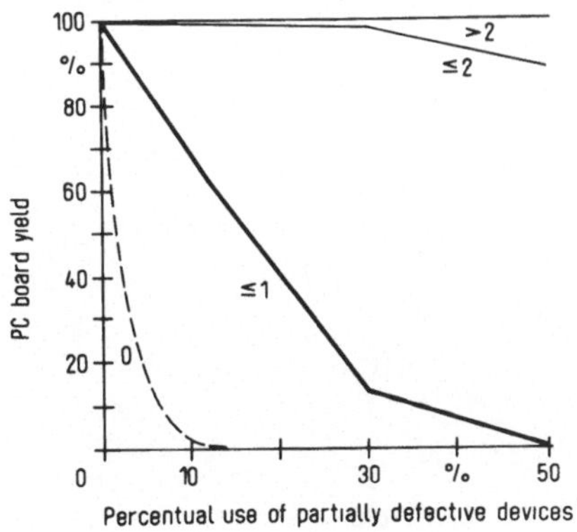

Fig. 3. PC Board Yield

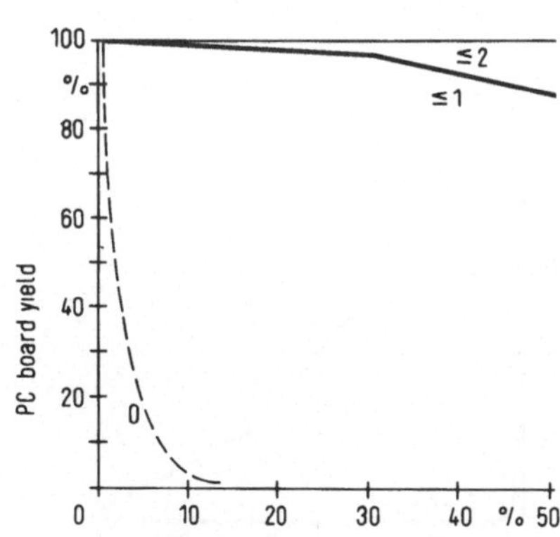

Fig. 4. PC Board Yield

The results shown in the diagram are hardly impressive. Acceptable PC board yields are obtained only if the amount of partially defective devices is very small ($<$ 1 % to 2 %). If single-bit errors are accepted and the amount of partially defective devices is 10 %, the PC board yield will be 66 %, while for a 30 % amount of partially defective devices the yield already drops to about 13 %. The majority of the PC boards have to be repaired by replacing one or more critical devices.

However, if only devices with single-bit errors are used together with perfect devices, the result is far more favorable (Fig. 4). Devices with single-bit errors can be used within wide limits. Even if up to 30 % such devices are used, the yield for PC boards with either zero errors or single-bit errors only will be beyond 95 %.

The outlined advantages for incorporating devices with single-bit errors would greatly improve the current yield data reported by the quality control departments of device manufacturers. Recently the percentage of devices with single-bit errors due to oxide defects was reported [1] to be far beyond of 50 %. Even figures of up to 90 % have been reported. Thus a substantial reduction in cost is conceivable if users could decide to accept devices with single-bit errors and manufacturers would separate such devices from other partially defective devices.

2.3.3. Assembly of Memory Modules with PC Boards

The yield data for memory modules populated with PC boards are shown in Fig. 5, the memories being assembled with a combination of perfect and partially defective PC boards. A distinction is made between two different methods of assembling memory modules. One uses only PC boards which include devices with column and row errors. A memory module populated with perfect devices and devices with only first-order defects shows a yield below 10^{-5} if the amount of partially defective

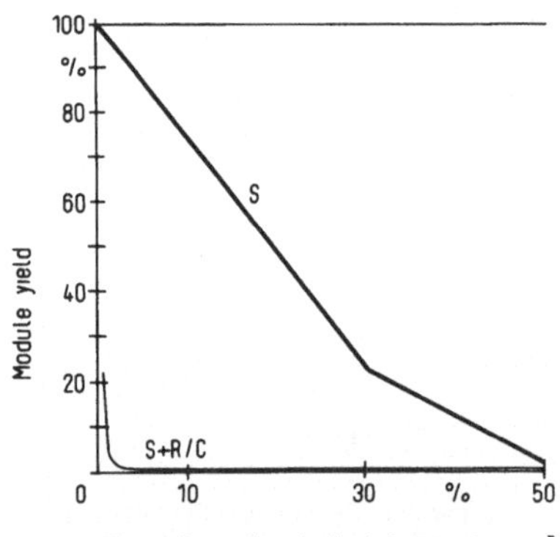

Fig. 5. Module Yield

*Use of perfect devices and devices with single-bit
and row/column errors (S+R/C)
or with single-bit errors only (S)

346

devices is only 10 %. Thus it is not practical to follow the approach of device configurations having multiple bit errors.

The second method in which PC boards populated with a combination of perfect devices and selected devices with single-bit errors are used leads, however, to useful results. If, for instance the amount of devices with single-bit errors is 10 %, approximately 75 % of all memory modules will exhibit either zero errors or only single-bit errors. If the amount of devices with single-bit errors is 30 %, the figure of 75 % will drop to 25 %. The remaining memory modules will exhibit second-order errors which can usually be reduced to single-bit errors by rearranging one or more PC boards.

2.3.4. Effect on Reliability of Memory Systems

Finally the effect of using partially defective devices on the reliability of memory systems will be investigated. The same assumptions as stated in Section 2.3.1 will be used and the following new conditions introduced:

1. Let the memory device failure rate be $1.5 \cdot 10^{-7}$/hour.
2. Let the failures occurring during the operating time of the memory be of the following distribution:

   33 % due to single-bit errors,
   34 % due to row/column errors,
   33 % due to clustered errors.

Fig. 6 shows a set of curves for the survival probability of memory systems under various starting conditions. Curve 1 (seen on the left) applies, like all the other ones, to a memory module populated with 1152 16-KB memory devices. The module is error-free at the time it is switched on and operates without error correction (0/0 %). The main reason for the small mean time between failure (MTBF) of 6000 h read off the curve is due to the fact that the very first memory defect leads a total system failure. The curve is also valid for the theoretical case of a system which

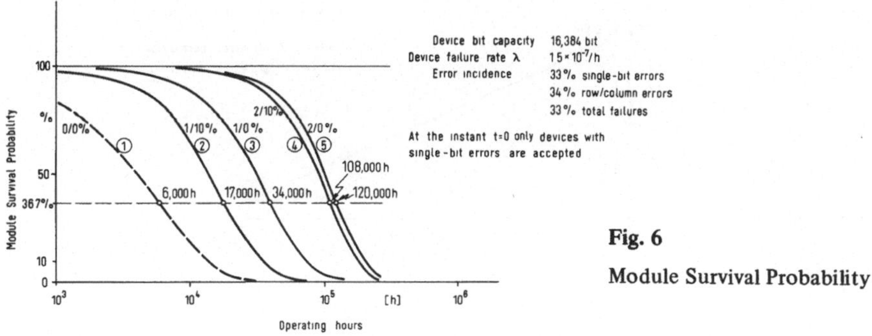

Fig. 6

Module Survival Probability

at the starting point t = 0 exhibits a single-bit error in all memory words and
operates with single-bit error correction, etc. Curve 3 holds for a starting condition
of zero errors but for a system operating with single-bit error correction.

The MTBF for memories with the described organization is accordingly improved
by a factor of 5.8. If, however, the amount of memory devices with single-bit errors
is 10 % and the amount of perfect devices is 90 % the MTBF will drop from 34 000 h
to 17 200 h, i.e. by almost a factor of 2 (curve 2). This drastical drop in reliability
is mainly due to row/column errors and clustered errors which, in conjunction with
the single-bit errors already present in the memory, form higher-order error combinations and thus contribute to system failure. Fig. 7 shows that the use of a larger amount
of partially defective memory devices will reduce the error-free interval at the start of
the operating time of the memory by only another 20 % (to 13 800 h in the case of
100 %).

Curves 4 and 5 in Fig. 6 show clearly the effectiveness of a 2-bit error correction.
Curve 5 again applies to the case of an error-free starting interval (2/0 %), the
MTBF being already about 120 000 h. For memories with single-bit error devices
this MTBF figure drops far less than in the previously described example. For 10 %
devices with single-bit errors an MTBF figure of about 108 000 h is still obtained
(curve 4), corresponding to a drop of only 10 %.

Fig. 7 shows the approximate relation between the percentage of partially defective
devices and/or errored memory words and the expected error-free starting interval
of the memory.

Since the curve approaches the MTBF limiting value of 120 000 h for 0 % defective
devices asymptotically, the figures covering the use of 30 %, 50 % and 100 % partially
defective devices may contain errors of up to + 10 %.

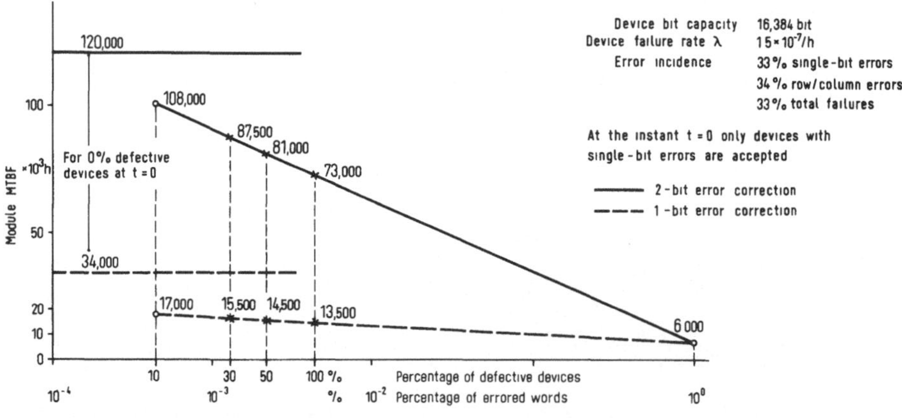

Fig. 7. Module MTBF

348

Fig. 7 again demonstrates the significance of a 2-bit error correction through which
system reliability can be increased up to a level which most users will consider to be
extremely attractive. This scheme will open the way to a wider application of
partially defective memory devices: The method described in Section 1, not to
replace memory devices which have become defective during operation unless they
cause clustered errors, can be employed with greater effectiveness.

3. Concluding Remarks

It has been demonstrated that the inclusion of classified partially defective devices
in the collective of perfect memory devices allows new approaches to the problem
of reducing capital investment in device-oriented development work as well as in
memory production and customer service. The following objectives seem to be
realistic:

1. Reduction of the cost of memory devices by another 40 % below the expected
   price trend.
2. Reduction of fabrication cost by about 25 % because somewhat looser test
   specifications can be applied and the number of test steps can be reduced.
3. Reduction in maintainance costs by about 75 %. This is not only due to the
   reduced direct repair cost but also due to the considerable reduction of necessary
   spare parts.
4. Savings in expenditure on development cost result in reduced system development time. A considerable reduction of investment devoted to the development
   of device oriented test procedures is to be expected.

The amount of savings actually achievable depends largely on the adopted approach,
which always has to take into account a large variety of user-oriented requirements.

Acknowledgements

I am indebted to Dipl.-Ing. Reinhard Schürba for analyzing the results of the
simulation.

This work has been supported under Data Processing Program of the Federal
Department of Research and Technology. The author alone is responsible for the
contents.

Reference

[1] *L. Altman* and *L. Mattera*, Several solid state technologies show surprising new paces.
     Electronics **49** (1976) 25, p. 93.

Access Methods and Associative Memories

Hans-Otto Leilich

Institut für Datenverarbeitungsanlagen, Technische Universität Braunschweig, Braunschweig, Germany

I. Access Methods and Computer Architecture

Access methods are certainly based on the access mechanisms inherent in the storage technology. It is also well-known that the types of access (serial, random-access, associative) can be viewed hierarchically in regard to their performance.

Discussing access methods beyond simple functional units like buffers, FIFO's, etc., for programmable computers, one has to take into account the requirements of the entire system. For each type of a computer, the properties of "typical programs" determine the lay-out of the memory system, e.g. block sizes or capacities of the levels in a memory hierarchy. Here we want to take an even wider view in that we regard the "program", the machine program (stored in memory) not as an invariant. The entire structure and the definition of the machine language are determined not only by the user requirements and the arithmetic units, but also they are essentially influenced by the access method. As visualized in Fig. 1, the access method is not only the link between program and store (labelled "address translator" and "decoder"), it also influences the structure of the machine code (examplified by the label "compiler").

This view of access methods therefore covers all esssential criteria of computer architecture:

> Execution time of the program and compilation
> Hardware costs for storage access mechanisms and translations
> Program production and compiler construction
> Flexibility of hard- and software in operation and their universality
> Transparency, reliability and maintenance

With some prominent examples from a wide range of computer architectures the influence of access methods shall be demonstrated. The necessary lack of details should help to convey the essential idea of this paper.

II. Serial Access

Serially accessible storage media (magnetic tapes, disks, bubbles, CCD) allow on one hand the lowest costs per bit and thereby the largest capacities, due to their minimum functional cell requirements. On the other hand, they require the appropriate structuring of programs and data, or the addition of control mechanisms.

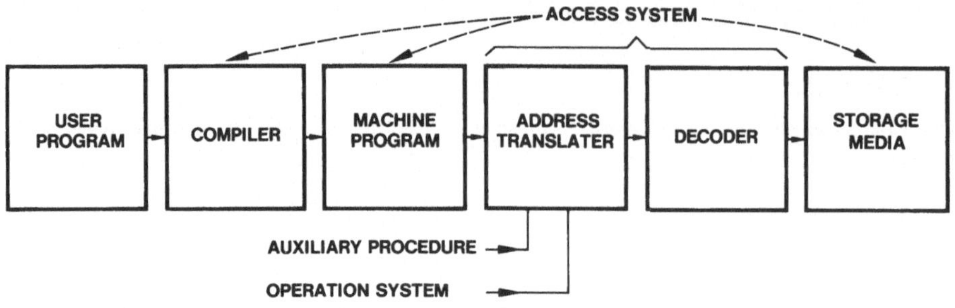

Fig. 1. Impact of access method on computer architecture.

A strictly bit or byte oriented memory (e.g. magnetic tapes) delivers, only one character per clock time, although the character rate of modern devices corresponds roughly to electronic execution rates ($r \approx 72$ KByte/s ≈ 1 bit/2 μs).

A (single-tape) Turing-machine has only one linear storage tape, reads and changes only one character and decides (with one bit information contents) whether the tape is moved one step right or left. It has been proven that all solvable problems can be computed with it, yet the programming is extemely machine oriented and lengthy, and the number of steps is extremely high.

A pure stack machine would be as clumsy unless pointer techniques were realizable, i.e. real stack machines actually use RAM's extensively. Appropriate algorithms for serial memories, e.g. tape oriented sorting procedures, use RAM's for programs and data buffers. The time required for a single non-stop sweep operation over a capacity of $C_{max} = 72$ MBytes is in the order of $T_{max} = 16$ min; one has to arrange the procedure such that an essential part of the job is performed during this time. The burden of conversion of a user oriented user task to the machine is given to the compiler function or to the programmer, in the view of Fig. 1.

A serial memory is practically not usable as a quasi-RAM, since with the data rate r the average access time for $C_{max} = r \cdot T_{max} = 72$ MBytes is $\overline{T}_1 = T_{max}/2 \approx 8$ min (Fig. 2). The access time becomes essentially smaller if a two-dimensional sequential access is possible, for instance by the movable heads of a disk store which reaches $C_t (\approx 400)$ tracks in $T_{tmax} (\approx 30$ ms$)$. Then, only an additional delay-time of maximally one revolution time $T_{cmax} (\approx 20$ ms$)$ for $C_c = 10^5$ bits per track is required. By electronical access to $Z_0 (\approx 20)$ surfaces, one accesses a capacity of $C_{max} = Z_0 \cdot C_t \cdot C_c (\approx 100$ MBytes$)$ in an average time of $\overline{T}_2 = (T_{tmax} + T_{cmax})/2$ $(\approx 25$ ms$)$. The access time is reduced by four orders of magnitude (Fig. 2).

If a continuous block of $10^4 \dots 10^5$ bits is loaded into a RAM $(\approx 10^6$ bits$)$ with electronic access $(T_A \approx 1 \mu$s$)$ and the execution is arranged such that during the

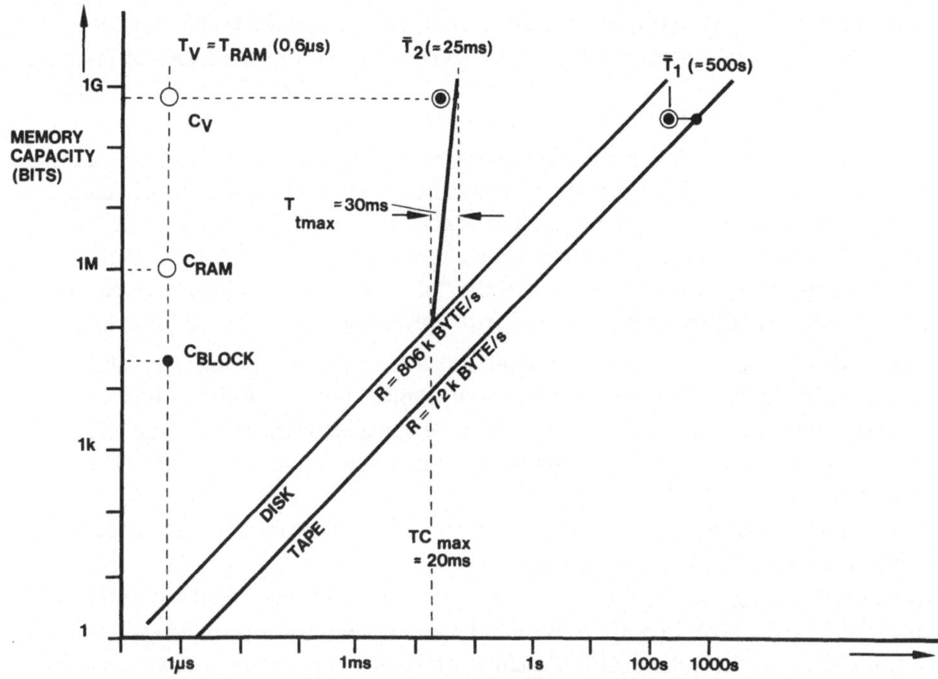

Fig. 2. Capacity-Access-Diagram for one- and two-dimensional (tape and disc) memories, RAM's and virtual memories.

transfer time the computer works with other data, one approaches a hierarchical system, which appears to the program as a random access store of $C_{max} \approx 10^9$ bits and $\bar{T}_v \approx T_A$ (≈ 1 µs). The operational procedure for this "virtual memory" should be interpreted according to Fig. 1 as "address translation". "Decoder" and "memory" consists of several and different devices [1].

The remaining access gap (of five orders of magnitude), given by the technologies, causes the well-known problems in recharging procedures. This is the reason why people search for a "gap technology" ($\bar{T}_L \approx 10^{-2} \dots 10^{-3}$ s and $C_L \approx 10^7 \dots 10^9$ bits) since decades. The present candidates (CCD and bubbles) are of serial type and two-dimensional access as well. For large systems one has "cache-memories" (≈ 100 ns and $10^4 \dots 10^5$ bits) at the fast end and for very large capacities cassette-memories with two-dimensional automated mechanical access.

III. Random-Accessible Addressable Memories

The optimum lay-out of the circuitry for address decoding for a random-access memory relies on the technology of the memory media. One uses decoding hier-

archies comprising special signal representations and energy levels. The final level
is usually part of the memory cell. In core memory times, one used various organizations (2 D, 2.5 D, 3 D), utilizing the hysteresis characteristics of the cores and the
number of cores per selection line in different ways [2].

Semiconductor Memories employ the same technology for storage, decoding and
amplification and are therefore more flexible in the manipulation of word- and
bit-oriented principles. A typical example is given in Fig. 3: a word is selected
first and one bit from it secondly, yielding a bit-oriented chip. The next level
(two-dimensionally) selects one chip from a "bit-plane". Several bit-planes form
a 3-D word-oriented memory, allowing error correction by additional bit-planes.

The motivation for this concept is the minimization of pins per chip. For VLSI
modules (16 KBits/chip and larger) one even tranfers the ($\geq$ 14 bit) address in
two steps onto the chip — the first part may be considered the micro-page name,
and the access time depends on whether the micro-page is changed or not. Theoretically, the address could be transferred serially using one pin only, similar to telephone
dialing. (Generally, it is interesting to study switching networks' sophisticated access
methods for new memory access systems).

As an example from the host of address decoding variants, the "multidimensional-
access" of the STARAN computer should be mentioned: by controlled modification
of the address of the individual RAM chips, one reads in parallel either words or bit
columns (or byte groups) from a $256 \cdot 256$ array for "horizontal" or "vertical"
processing [3].

It is well-known, that "random access" to address memories, as compared to serial
access, offers an essentially higher flexibility to the structuring of machine languages
for phrasing problem-oriented programs. Yet, for compact representation of repetitive

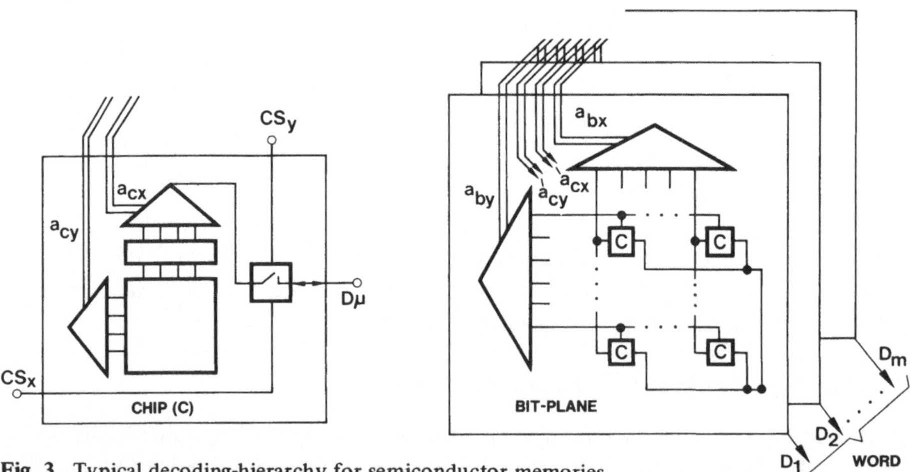

Fig. 3. Typical decoding-hierarchy for semiconductor memories.

parts (loops) and for independent referencing and placement of programs and data
in memory, John von Neumann already introduced the classical address modifications
(base address, indirect and indexed addressing). Compact addresses, to be complemented by page or segment addresses, can be considered another means to adapt machine
programs to memory.

IV. Associative Memories

We should realize that „random access" is only a limited means to solve the access
requirements of many problems, since it involves primarily storage space with a
fixed, compact, unique code label for each object in the program. It would be much
easier for problem-oriented languages, to use "names" which would not directly
correspond to the expensive address space. If, for instance, in a data base management system a new object is generated in a huge name space, say 12 letters corresponding to 100 bits, a HASH algorithm has to be applied (including a procedure for colli-
sion resolution) to compress the name to an address. Another well-known method
is the insertion of this name into an ordered list and the corresponding binary search
for retrieval.

In data base management systems (sets of) objects of the type: "Prices of all goods,
which 1974 have been sold from XY-companies from Bavaria to Hesse" have to be
accessed. The implementation based on RAMs and disks – including virtual stores –
require enormous procedures, involving data representation, inverted lists etc.; in
the view of Fig. 1 "compilation", "address translation" and memory ordering are
involved.

A hardware memory system with labels of memory objects from a huge name space
requires the recording of used names in addition to the corresponding contents and
coincidence circuitry for each object name, signalling the equivalence of stored
name and search name (Fig. 4).

The concept of the "associative memory" [4, 5, 13, 14] also allows the storage of
several names and masking those which are not used for an access (Fig. 5). Since
these names are not merely search attributes but non-compressed parts of the stored
object, one can access an object by each part (field) or any intersection, in a fully
associative store, also called "content addressable memory (CAM)" because of this
property. In general, several words (sets) are referred to by an interrogation process,
which are after marking sequentially read out by a hardware arbitration network
(Fig. 5).

By elimination of the (software-)address compression (HASH- or Search procedures)
a memory with this kind of a "decoder" has a much higher search power, i.e. the
"machine language" is more similar to the problem language. Memory management
is simplified too, since if search attribute and searched contents are a unit, the
position of this unit in memory is irrelevant, i.e. these "tuples" are stored in
arbitrary order and each word coded "empty" can accept a new entry.

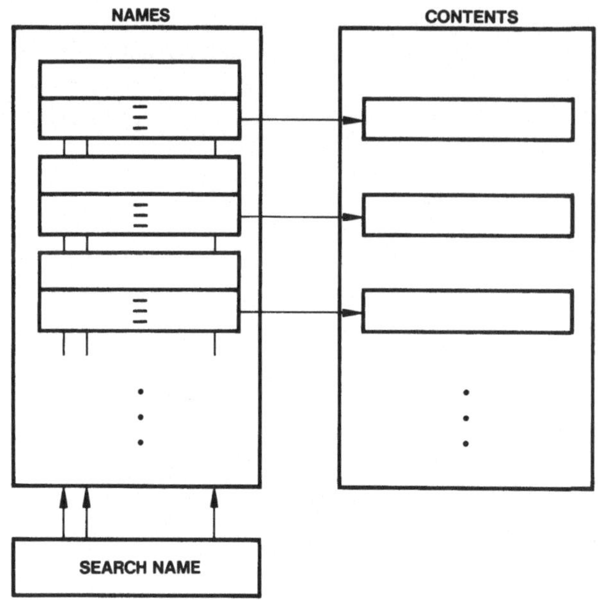

Fig. 4. Partial-associative memory with "programmable" addresses.

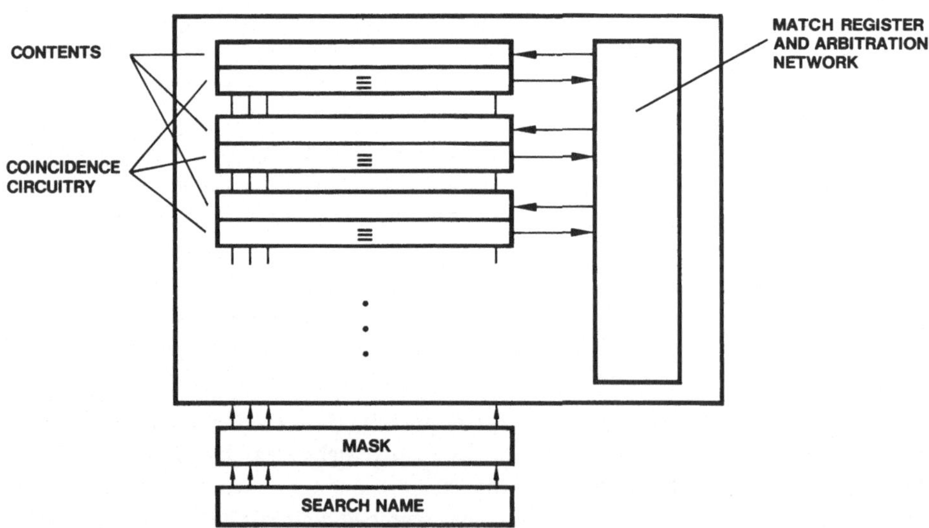

Fig. 5. (Fully) associative memory with masking.

356

The analysis and application of the logical functions of associative memories lead
to unorthodox computer architectures. Applied to the main memory of a otherwise standard processor [6–8], it leads to a new internal instruction sequence
mechanism and a corresponding machine language, which turned out to be close
to problem-oriented decision table languages.

The inherent logical properties of associative stores also allow parallel operations
on words, i.e. field operations, performed in memory. Arithmetic operations
require sequential operations by bit, but parallel by words [3].

Historically, the first realization of associative memories is the "needle file" [13].
Realistic electronic implementations were possible with integrated realizations of
the memory and coincidence circuitry (cryogenics, semiconductors, Josephson-
technology). Integrated associative memory chips are commercially available since
several years, yet merely on a low integration level (64 bits typically). A technical
reason for this is the high power requirement for each (always active) bit. There
are also pin number problems for the parallel access to many bits (of a large name
space). Partitioning a large associative array into chips requires basically a wordwise
cross connection [9]. These are some reasons why it is not easy to constitute standard
chip concepts (like with RAMs), which is the basic prerequisite for broad applications,
mass fabrication, competitive innovation, and low costs.

There is one application area for associative memories with a break-through to broad
application in recent years: "Programmable Logic Arrays (PLA)". These are read-
only partial-associative memories (ROAM) with the special feature, that single bits
of the name can be designated "don't care", i.e. irrelevant to the coincidence function. With these, one can implement combinatorial nets in minimized form; i. e.
nets with many inputs (e.g. 16) and a minimum number of terms (words) (Fig. 6)
[7, 10].

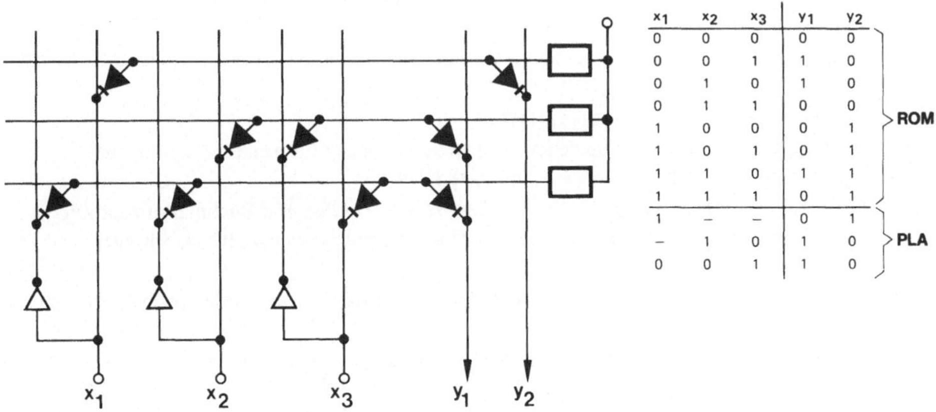

x_1	x_2	x_3	y_1	y_2	
0	0	0	0	0	
0	0	1	1	0	
0	1	0	1	0	
0	1	1	0	0	
1	0	0	0	1	ROM
1	0	1	0	1	
1	1	0	1	1	
1	1	1	0	1	
1	–	–	0	1	
–	1	0	1	0	PLA
0	0	1	1	0	

Fig. 6. Realization of combinatorial network by PLA.

357

Associative parallel read-write memories are presently used or proposed merely
for some special purposes (virtual memory management, dynamic memory and
resource management, pattern recognition).

The best-known pioneer system for associative field processing is the STARAN
computer from Goodyear [3]. It performs the word-parallel operations in a
256-bit "vertical" processing unit sequentially by bit and uses actually RAM-chips
with special "multi-dimensional" access (see section 3). The controlling program
structure is, of course, completely determined by this access method.

Content addressing systems for large data files, which presently can be stored only
in serial media, can also be implemented by word-sequential search processes.
Special peripheral hardware [11, 12] improves the efficiency of the method and
yields it competitive to conventional "navigational" systems. For example, the
"search processor" [12] investigates each record of a file (read and processed in a
real time from all surfaces of a disk concurrently) by a group of "search modules",
containing independent queries with a comparison instruction and operand per field
and a fast logical evaluation network, yielding the record match signal. In the view
of Fig. 1 these processors transform a sequential store into a problem-oriented
(virtual) associative memory. The control (query) language is an effective means
to implement relational data base management systems [15]. The search processor
is a hardware implementation of an access system, which allows a rather "high level
machine language" and eases the tasks of programming and compilation.

References

[1] *W. G. Spruth* and *C. Schunemann*, Storage Hierarchy Technology and Organization,
     this volume, p. 377.

[2] *L A. Russell, R. M. Whalen* and *H.-O. Leilich*, Ferrite Memory Systems, IEEE Trans-
     actions on Magnetics, Vol. **MAG-4,** No. 2 June 1968.

[3] *J. A. Rudolph*, A Production Implementation of an Associative Array Processor-STARAN,
     Proc. 1972 FJCC. p. 229–241.

[4] *H. Liebig*, Rechenorganisation, Springer 1976.

[5] *H.-O. Leilich*, „Assoziative Speicher" in Taschenbuch der Informatik (Herausgeber:
     Steinbuch/Weber), Bd. 1, Kap. 4.4, Springer 1974.

[6] *H.-O. Leilich, I. Karlowsky, W. Lawrenz* and *H. Ch. Zeidler*, Ein Rechnerkonzept mit
     assoziativem Arbeitsspeicher, Lecture Notes in Computer Science, Bd. 8, Springer
     1974.

[7] *W. Lawrenz*, Programmiertechnik und Ablaufsteuerung in einem assoziativen Programm-
     speicher, Diss. TU-Braunschweig 1976.

[8] *I. Karlowsky*, Ein Beitrag zur Hardwareunterstutzung der Speicher- und Namensverwal-
     tung durch Assoziativspeicher, Diss. TU-Braunschweig 1976.

[9] *W. Motsch*, Increased Chip Capacity and Extended Logical Complexity of LSI-
     Associative Memories, this volume, p. 361.

[10] *M. Flinders, P. L. Gardner, R. J. Llewelyn* and *J. F. Minshull,* Functional Memory as a General Purpose Systems Technology, Proc. 1970 IEEE, Int. Comp. Group Conf., Washington D.C., p. 314–324.

[11] *G. F. Colouris, J. M. Evans* and *R. W. Mitchell,* Towards Content-Addressing in Data Bases, The Computer Journal 1972, Vol. **15,** No. 2, p. 95–98.

[12] *H.-O. Leilich, I. Karlowsky* and *H. Ch. Zeidler,* Content Addressing in Data Bases by Special Peripheral Hardware; a Proposal called "Search Processor", Informatik-Fachberichte No. 4, Springer 1976.

[13] *A. G. Hanlon,* Content Addressable and Associative Memory Systems – A Survey, IEEE Trans. on El. Comp., Vol. EC-15, No. 4, August 1966, p. 509–521.

[14] *B. Parhami,* Associative Memories and Processors – An Overview and Selected Bibliography, Proc. IEEE, Vol. 61, No. 6, p. 722–730, June 73.

[15] *E. F. Codd,* A Relational Model of Data for Large Shared Data Banks, CACM 13 (1970), No. 6, p. 377–387.

Increased Chip Capacity and Extended Logical Complexity of LSI-Associative Memories

Walter Motsch

Department of Electrical Engineering at the Ruhr-Universitat in Bochum, Germany

1. Stagnating Development in Associative Memory Application

Associative memories have in practice by far not found the esteem and wide application they actually deserve, if they are valued by their functional features which clearly distinguish them from all other types of memories. This is the more surprizing as they have been investigated rather intensively for 20 years now [1], and that regarding their

- function and performance,
- technological implementations,
- application capabilities,
- extension to associative processors,
- impacts on future data processing concepts concerning computer structure as well as software methods.

Know-how and experience gained in this area were up to now mainly used in the military field and in a few special areas such as air traffic control and aeronautics, weather forecasting, processing of text and video information, and solving of complex mathematical problems such as matrix calculation or differential equations [2]. In addition associative memories serve to control internal executive functions in computers, especially the dynamic storage allocation when either virtual addressing of the main memory is used or a fast cache memory is provided between main memory and processor [3, 4]. It might be due to several reasons, some of which are mentioned below, that their present range of application is rather modest regarding quality as well as quantity:

a) A great number of users is not sufficiently familiar with their latent features, and thus they resort to conventional software approaches.

b) With numerous problems they have no advantage compared with the conventional random access read/write memories [5].

c) The superiority of system design using associative memories, compared against known structures, is insufficiently tested in experiments, and thus has been proven to date for a very limited area only [6].

d) The cost per bit are prohibitively high for most scientific, industrial and commercial applications.

Several partly very different storage media and technological principles were used to realize associative memories. The most important implementations base on the following items:

- superconductive devices (cryotrons),
- magnetic cores (double ring-, biax-, transfluxor cores),
- magnetic thin films,
- plated wires,
- integrated semiconductor circuits,
- holographic arrays.

Although among these, the semiconductor approach allowed up to now the smallest capacity per module, it was this technology that increasingly succeeded in the storage area compared with all other ones within the past 10 years. Apart from bulk stores it dominates already today and can undoubtedly be considered to be the technology with the best prospects.

While, however, other memory types, as RAMs and ROMs, rapidly proceeded to higher chip capacity, shorter access time, and lower cost per bit, comparatively less interest was directed to associative memories. No remarkable progress can be stated since nearly 1970. Although there is no lack of suggestions for better cell layout and chip design, only a minor part of them has ever reached the state of manufacture or even became mature for mass production. So the associative memory devices offered today contain a maximum of only 16 bits. (Some earlier units with chip capacities up to 128 bits were withdrawn by the producer.) The reason for this problem is not to be found in the more complex cell structure, because an associative memory cell requires only twice the chip area of a conventional static RAM-cell of which 4096 units can meanwhile be placed on a chip.

2. Construction Problems in LSI-Technology

2.1. Limited number of pin-connections

The essential barrier is rather the fact that IC-packages of today can be economically produced with a maximum of 64 connector pins P only. The importance of this parameter P can be seen from its functional dependence on the number of words m and the word size n implemented on the chip.

The following relationships hold for:

associative memories: $\qquad P_A = c_1 \cdot m + c_2 \cdot n + c_3$ (1)

RAMs and ROMs: $\qquad P_R = ld\,m + c_4 \cdot n + c_5$ (2)

In both cases the number of pins increases linearly with the word size. In the second case the number of pins increases only with the dual logarithm of the number of words, whereas in the first case, however, it increases linearly with the number of words. With known memory devices (Intel's 3104 or Fairchild's 93402) the following variable and constant factors are chosen, neglecting the pins for power supply: $m = n = 4$; $c_1 = 2$; $c_2 = 3$; $c_3 = 1$. Thus it results an expense of $P_A = 21$ in logical connections for only 16 bits.

It was this problem which prevented the realization of several suggestions, although they were mature regarding circuitry and extendable to a chip capacity of 512 cells [7]. Another very elegant approach [8] must be limited to 256 bits per chip for the same reason.

As an expedient in this dilemma, several times the following alternative measures were proposed:

- canceling some memory operations, e.g. writing or masking [4],
- multiple utilization of external connections,
- coding the match indication [9].

From these alternatives the first one appears to be useful in special situations only, because it limits the applications considerably. By means of the two last ones the number of pins can be successively reduced as it is discussed below.

The starting-point is the eq. (1), whereby the constant factors are taken from the device mentioned above, while the number of words and the word size shall now be variable:

$$P_{A0} = 2m + 3n + 1 \tag{3}$$

First step: Coded feed of memory address; then a chipselect signal is required, and we get:

$$P_{A1} = ld\, m + m + 3n + 2 \tag{4}$$

Second step: Combination of input- and output data on bidirectional lines; the control of the line drivers requires an additional pin:

$$P_{A2} = ld\, m + m + 2n + 3 \tag{5}$$

Third step: Time multiplexing of data and mask information on the data lines; therefore an internal mask register with associated strobe connection is needed:

$$P_{A3} = ld\, m + m + n + 4 \tag{6}$$

Fourth step: Coding the word match signals, that must be uniquely defined by means of an internal logic; it requires one more output to indicate, if one match is given at least. Thus it finally results in:

$$P_{A4} = 2 \cdot ld\, m + n + 5 \tag{7}$$

The number of the interface lines now depends as with other semiconductor memories only logarithmically on the number of words. Fig. 1 shows a comparison between the schematic pin configurations of associative memory devices derived from the eqs. (3) and (7).

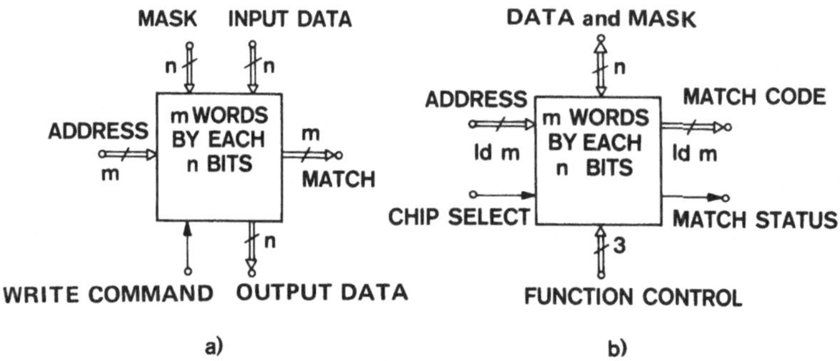

Fig. 1. Pin assignment of associative memory devices
a) With uncoded address and match indication according to eq. (3).
b) With multiple utilization and coded match indication according to eq. (7).

2.2. Handling of multiple responses

In general the result of a search operation is a match indication of some stored words. The sequential handling of these matched words is even with currently known associative memories still a problem. It is, however, facilitated by the fact that the complete match configuration is presented in a fully parallel way. With coded indications, the aggravating factor is added that the individual match informations must be transferred to the output serially, that is to say, the external match information has to be generated in several periods. For this purpose the matches must be isolated in an ordered sequence to prevent that any match is either overlooked or registered once more. The best would be the use of a priority scheme and the canceling of the already evaluated match signals [10].

2.3. Extension of capacity with coded match indication

The main difficulty accompanying the coded match indication arises with extension
of capacity in words and bits, i.e. finally in the building of memory systems. If the
total word size is increased by paralleling of q units to $q \cdot n$ bits, a word can only
be considered as selected by the reference data, if it matches in all q modules.

In the fully parallel indication mode this can be checked very simply by ANDing of
the corresponding outputs. In contrast applying the coded indication, each individual device provides the number of the internal match having the highest priority.
An utilizable total word match therefore is given only, if all q paralleled devices
generate the same match code signals. It can be stated by a compare logic checking
of all match codes for identity. An additional complication — although with similar
consequences — results from the array expanding into the bit dimension, namely if
the memory capacity shall be extended to $p \cdot m \times q \cdot n$ bits by arranging p rows
each containing q devices.

In both cases, it is important to determine as fast as possible the total word matches
of the search operation. The typical performance characteristics of associative
memories — simultaneous comparison of all stored words with the search argument
and spontaneous match marking — can only be fully utilized, if this can be done in
a successful manner. Otherwise the advantage of short search and access times of the
devices is neutralized by long evaluation periods.

3. Obtaining Higher Chip Capacities

3.1. Organization of an associative memory chip

The memory organization to be discussed in the following attempts solutions for the
above mentioned problems. The concept is based on a simple and inexpensive sequence control to be provided external to the memory chips. In this way the modular
expandability of the memory system is preserved without remarkable sacrifices in the
effective operating speed.

A memory module with a capacity of 64 words by 8 bits each has been developed
using TTL-devices. It includes the address decoding, priority control, match coding,
one data and one mask register and the control logic. The number of connecting
lines is determined according to eq. (7); for $m = 64$ and $n = 8$ then $P = 25$, when
supply connections are not included. The schematic structure is shown in Fig. 2.
The address decoder serves the selection of an externally predetermined memory
location in case of reading or writing. In a search operation the mask information
and the search arguments (content address) are sequentially loaded into the corresponding registers. The resulting match configuration appears at the output of the

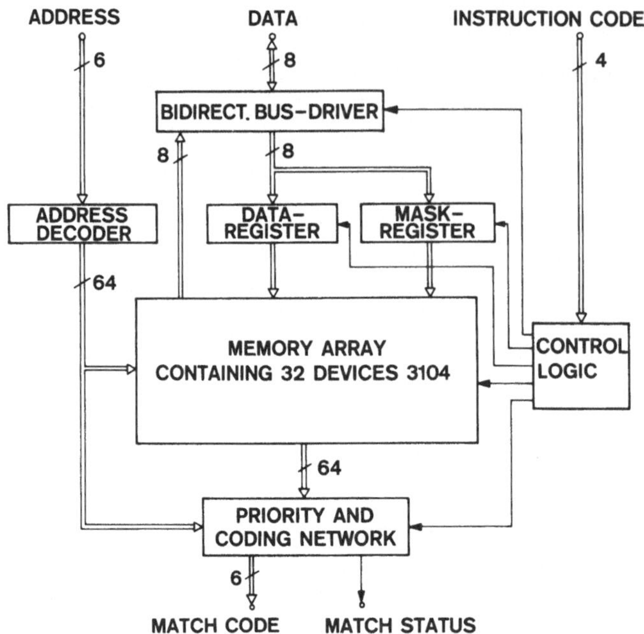

Fig. 2. Block diagram of a 64 × 8 bit memory chip with coded match indication.

memory array in a fully parallel form. The coding network indicates externally the highest priority match as a code vector. It can be directly used as local address for a subsequent reading or writing operation. Simultaneously it is fed to the coding network as a threshold value providing the exclusion from coding of all higher positions, and thus even of the evaluated match. Then again the highest order position of the remaining enabled matches will be fed to the output, coded as a binary number. This procedure will be repeated until the status signal indicates that all matches have been acquired. The control logic interprets the external instruction code and activates the desired memory function. In detail the instruction decoder generates: the control signal for the bidirectional bus driver, the strobe for the data- and mask register, the write pulse for the memory cells and the enable of the match indication.

The complete module comprises 32 memory devices of the Intel 3104 type and 65 other IC's, one third of which is implemented in medium scale integration (MSI) technology and the remainder in small scale integration (SSI) technology; it can be placed on a single 39 × 23 cm² printed card (nearly $2\frac{1}{2}$ European twinboards).

366

3.2. Searching and evaluating strategy for an associative memory system

The memory module described above is complemented by a hardware implemented control algorithm, allowing the extension of the priority controlled match evaluation, that is internal to the module, to a complete memory system, basing on the operating mode typical for associative memories: the parallel checking of all stored words for identity with a given argument and the subsequent sequential reading of the matched words.

For explaining the algorithm it is assumed that p modules in the word direction and q modules in the bit direction are connected in parallel. It is further assumed that due to a search operation an arbitrary match pattern has been formed. Now it must be determined which of the total of $p \cdot m$ data words are matched in all q sections, and then these words must be accessed. A priority that decreases with the local address from 0 to $p \cdot m - 1$ shall be assigned to the memory words. First the address 0 is used as a threshold so that all existing matches can become effective (search access). If thereupon the same code vector j $(0 \leqslant j \leqslant m - 1)$ appears at the match output of all q modules connected in parallel to a matrix row i $(0 \leqslant i \leqslant p - 1)$, then there is a total match in this position. The received binary number $i \cdot m + j$ is applied as local address and the associated word is read out (read access). If, however, such a coincidence does not exist, the maximum number of the q code vectors j_l $(1 \leqslant l \leqslant q)$ is selected, corresponding the word with the lowest priority, and is used in combination with the row number i as the new threshold value $i \cdot m + j_{max}$. From now on in all modules only those matches are considered that are still of lower order. Herein i is the binary number of the row in which the ANDing of all module status signals first provides the high level. Thus a row not containing a total match, because at least one status signal is low, can be skipped immediately.

The interplay between presetting a threshold and checking the match codes requires one machine cycle time each, i.e. with todays technology less than 1 μs. The procedure is repeated until all matches have been ascertained and the associated data words have been processed. Although it is not assured that every search access with a threshold value results in the indication of a total match, the average number of false trials, which depend exclusively on the internal match configurations, will however be very small. Thereby the time lost at the transitions between two successive evaluations (read accesses) remains short. The difference to memories using uncoded indications is only in these intervals, because even there the matched words must of course be read out sequentially.

The described procedure shall be demonstrated by an example, in which a memory array is configured with $p = 4$ modules in word direction and $q = 6$ modules in bit direction. For getting a better transparence each module shall contain only $m = 8$ words (the size n of which is unimportant), so that a total of 32 words is available.

Table 1 shows an arbitrary match pattern for the 24 modules. An "X" means a match indication of the module in row i and column l for the word no. j. It is assumed that the 2nd and 6th column of the memory array had been masked for the compare operation and therefore all their words indicate a match. The resulting total match pattern is specified in the table column preceding the last one. The last column of the table shows the effective addresses or threshold values successively applied and

Table 1. Single and total match configuration in a 4×6 memory module matrix and the associated evaluation sequence

Row No. i	Module word j	Effect. address	Column No. l						Total matches	Search access sequence
			1	2	3	4	5	6		
0	0	0	X	X	X			X		
	1	1		X	X		X	X		
	2	2	X	X				X		
	3	3	X	X	X	X	X	X	X	
	4	4		X	X	X		X		
	5	5		X		X		X		
	6	6		X		X	X	X		
	7	7		X	X		X	X		
1	0	8	X	X	X	X	X	X	X	
	1	9	X	X			X	X		
	2	10		X	X	X	X	X		
	3	11		X		X		X		
	4	12	X	X	X	X	X	X	X	
	5	13	X	X	X	X	X	X	X	
	6	14	X	X			X	X		
	7	15	X	X	X		X	X		
2	0	16		X		X		X		
	1	17	X	X		X		X		
	2	18	X	X	X			X		
	3	19	X	X	X	X		X		
	4	20		X	X			X		
	5	21	X	X	X	X		X		
	6	22	X	X		X		X		
	7	23	X	X	X			X		
3	0	24		X	X	X		X		
	1	25	X	X		X	X	X		
	2	26	X	X	X	X	X	X	X	
	3	27		X	X		X	X		
	4	28		X	X	X		X		
	5	29	X	X		X	X	X		
	6	30	X	X	X	X	X	X	X	
	7	31	X	X	X			X		

368

the skips respectively performed in the address space of the memory depending on
the match pattern. While the first two search accesses are immediately successful, i.e.
they result in a match, the third one is ineffective; starting with a threshold of 8,
the 10th data word provides the highest order code vector, presents, however, no
match as a whole. The same is valid for the words 24 and 29. A row will be left as
soon as the last match within that row has been acquired. Rows without any total
match ($i = 2$) due to a blank column are skipped without any loss of time. Nine
search accesses only are required for the external determination despite the relatively
dense match pattern; this also underlines the efficiency of the applied strategy that
can be implemented by approximately 35 TTL-circuits on a special control module.
There are no basic limitations for an extension of the memory system.

3.3. Consequences in production and application

With the present state of the art of integration, in which up to 16k bits can be
packed on a chip, the idea seems not at all to be unrealistic that even the complete
memory module comprising 64×8 bits, peripheral logic included, can be arranged
on a single chip. The module could then be encapsulated in a 28 pin IC-standard
package, if not more than three supply voltages are required.

From eq. (7) it can be derived that the chip capacity of associative memories is in this
case no longer limited by the number of pins, but — as with all other memory types —
exclusively by the chip area being economically manufactured and by the achievable
bit density. The same can be seen from the diagram in Fig. 3. Here the number of
pins P is drawn on the logarithmic scale for the number of words m per device,
with the word length n used as parameter, and separately for conditions corresponding to eqs. (3) and (7). If the pin number is limited to the commonly used maximum
$P = 40$ and three pins are reserved for power supply, one can see that with the conventional organization only 32 bits per chip (in the size 4×8 or 8×4) can be realized.
In contrast to the above case the linear curves show the extension capacity of the
presented concept.

Especially under this aspect theoretically 256×16 or even $4\,k \times 8$ bits could be
placed into a 40-pin-package. Although this seems to be highly illusory, from the
technological viewpoint, however, 1 k bit per chip could be achieved in the next
future. The actual specification of the parameters m and n is thereby only a question of expediency.

At present the cost per bit of associative memories is 300 to 700 times higher than
that for static RAMs. In bulk production of chips according to the described organization it should be possible to offer them for a price that is only 5 to 10 times higher.
Combined with the significantly more compact design of a system based on this

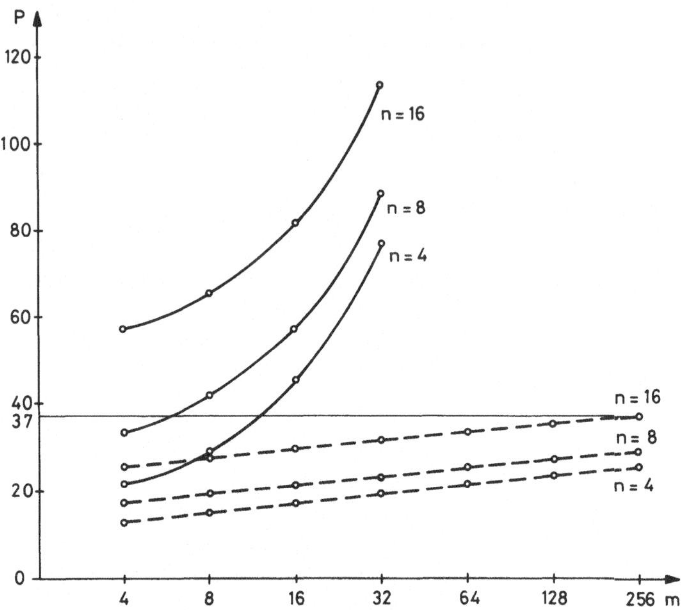

Fig. 3. Number of pins P of associative memory devices as a function of word number m and word length n on the chip according to eqs. (3) and (7).

principle, this fact would pave the way for a much more extensive application of associative memories in practice. Many new sections of industrial and commercial data processing applications would thus be opened up. Some small sized to medium sized data files e.g. could be transposed from a bulk store into the associative section of the main memory or into a special search memory. A major part of typical search operations could here be performed remarkably faster as well as with less software effort. Associative storing need not at all be restricted to the actual data, but can also include user programs. The otherwise rather expensive decision table techniques could be easily implemented by associative memories [11].

4. Additional Compare Operations in the Memory

4.1. Structure of an extended associative memory cell

With most of the associative memories, especially those implemented in semiconductor technology, the search function is restricted to the actual identity compare between the argument and the corresponding bits of the stored data. More complex and thus efficient search operations have been provided only in a few samples of memories, realized in magnetic core technology [12]. Their more intensive utilization,

370

however, was prohibited by the high cost of the logic circuits to be associated with every memory cell. Subsequently it will be shown, how the operations "greater than" and "less than" can be implemented in LSI-technology using a few additional logic circuits so that such devices allow to be economically fabricated too.

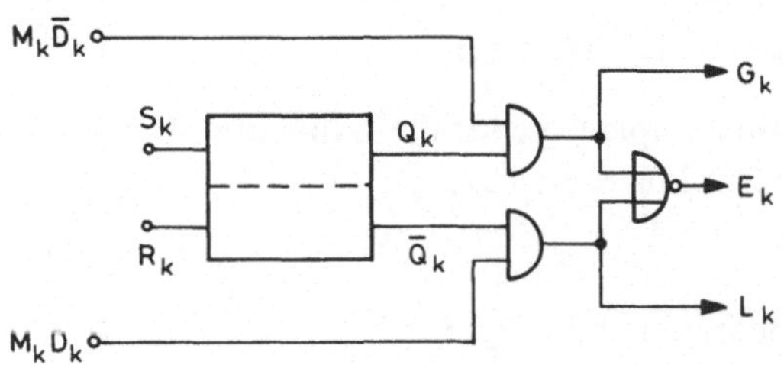

Fig. 4

Associative memory cell with matching outputs G_k (greater), E_k (equal), L_k (less) to indicate the relation of stored bit Q_k and argument bit D_k; when masking ($M_k = 0$) equality is simulated. (S_k, R_k = set and reset input signal of a cell).

Fig. 4 shows the logical structure of an associative memory cell comprising a RS-flip flop and a compare circuit. The cell is assumed to be the k-th bit of a data word. Addressing, reading and writing of the cell is of no interest in this context, but here only the mode of getting the comparison result is considered. The respective truth table is given in Table 2, in which the variables have the following meanings:

$E_k = (Q_k \equiv D_k)$ Stored bit and argument bit are identical.
$G_k = (Q_k > D_k)$ Stored bit is greater than argument bit.
$L_k = (Q_k < D_k)$ Stored bit is less than argument bit.

Table 2. Match function obtained from the comparison of memory bit and argument bit, with respect to the mask bit

M_k	D_k	Q_k	Logical function	G_k	E_k	L_k
1	0	0	$Q_k \equiv D_k$	0	1	0
1	0	1	$Q_k > D_k$	1	0	0
1	1	0	$Q_k < D_k$	0	0	1
1	1	1	$Q_k \equiv D_k$	0	1	0
0	x	x	x	0	1	0

Moreover, identity is also indicated, if the mask bit is "0". From the table combined with Fig. 4 it is readily seen that the variables G_k and L_k already exist in the circuit as parts of the identity function E_k because:

$$E_k = \overline{G_k + L_k} = \overline{G_k} \cdot \overline{L_k} \tag{8}$$

Therefore they can be used as separate outputs.

Fig. 5 shows how the relation of the stored word as a whole to the argument can be derived. The E_k-outputs and G_k-outputs of all n cells of one word are connected to give a ripple logic. By providing such a logic for each data word the corresponding word functions become available:

$$E = E_1 \cdot E_2 \cdot \ldots \cdot E_n \qquad\qquad\qquad = (Q \equiv D) \qquad\qquad (9)$$

$$G = G_1 + E_1 \cdot G_2 + \ldots + E_1 \cdot \ldots \cdot E_{n-1} \cdot G_n = (Q > D) \qquad\qquad (10)$$

In an analog way one could also build up a ripple logic for the L-function. It can, however, more simply be determined according to eq. (8):

$$L = \overline{E} \cdot \overline{G} = (Q < D) \qquad\qquad (11)$$

In this version the function has been incorporated in Fig. 5.

These considerations make clear that in an associative memory array the search operations "greater than" and "less than" can be implemented with additional three gates per cell only. This would probably increase the required cell size by less than 50 % and therefore seems reasonable with respect to the achieved performance improvement. Thereby the number of pins increases insignificantly in its constant term compared to eq. (7), as only a little longer instruction code is needed. It selects by means of the control logic one of the three matching lines per data word for the coding operation.

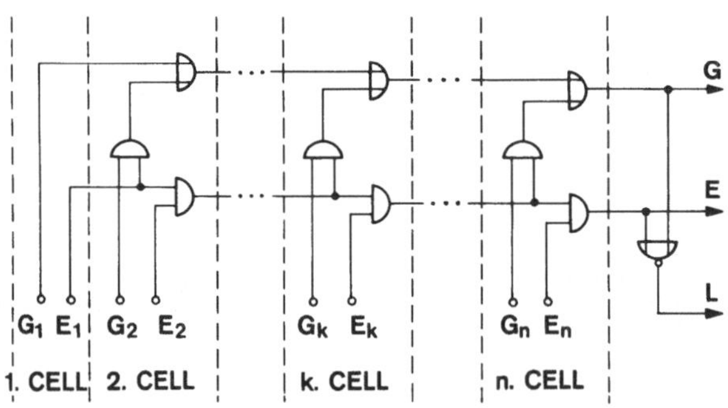

Fig. 5. Symbolic diagram of a ripple logic combining the partial results of the individual cells to a match indication for the whole word.

4.2. Execution of more complex searches

Within such a module — only slightly modified in its structure, compared with Fig. 2 — the match evaluation is performed according to the same strategy described in section 3.2. The threshold controlled coding unit signals sequentially the data

372

words that have, according to the instruction code, a numerically greater, less or equal content compared with the reference argument. The total number of words $p \cdot m$, arising from paralleling of p devices in word direction, has no affect thereupon. However, an extension of the word size by arranging of q devices in the bit direction poses a problem. An external comparison of the matching codes would be insufficient, rather the q ripple logic circuits (see Fig. 5) per word must be connected in series. For this purpose, $2\,m$ connecting lines each between two devices would be required; this is, with respect to the allowable number of pins, completely unacceptable and, moreover, would obstruct the coding mechanism.

A time conserving approach is based on the fact that for determining the relations "greater than" and "less than" the total word length has to be checked rarely. If e.g. in a memory array of $p \times q$ modules all words are to be identified having a greater binary value than the argument, the following procedure is recommended:

In the first step the devices of the first column are fetched with the compare instruction "greater than", and indicate all words that can already be identified as being greater due to their n most significant bits. In the second step, with modified instruction code, the words are determined coincident with the argument with respect to the first column. Simultaneously the second column is checked for words with a greater numerical value than the argument. The common set of the two matching results contributes those of the requested words which, due to their components $n + 1 \ldots 2n$, meets the established match condition. This procedure will be continued until the q-th column has been checked for "greater than" simultaneously applying the "equal"-operation to all other columns. As one can see, for the q segments of a whole word the same criterion is valid as for an individual segment, concerning its n bit positions. Therefore eq. (10) can directly be transferred to here, and only the subscripts of the cell numbers have to be replaced by the column numbers of the device matrix.

4.3. Combination and application capabilities

The three compare operations "equal", "greater than", and "less than" may be considered to be the base of all associative search operations. Therefrom applying suitable combinations and algorithmic support many useful logical operations can be derived, some of which are subsequently listed:

- selection of data words the contents of which are between two limits specified by the arguments;
- finding of the data containing the numerically greatest and lowest value respective to a segment defined by the mask;
- sorting of all data words or a subset of words in ascending or descending sequence of their numerical value.

The prospect is attractive in that all these and many other operations based thereupon have no longer to be performed by software methods but rather can be allocated to a special, inexpensive hardware. Not only in the traditional applications of sorting and merging programs, but also in classification and statistical evaluation of data
as well as in pattern recognition there are numerous possibilities to discharge the
processor of the relatively unintelligent sequential comparisons. It is to be expected
that standard procedures to be created will be called in future by a macroinstruction
and will then be executed autonomously by a microprogram control unit associated
to the memory. Thereby a significant step to an associative processor implemented in
LSI-technology would have already been made.

5. Conclusion

The further development of large scale integrated associative memory devices was up
to now hindered by the required large number of pins. This number can be reduced
by a design providing a coded indication of the matching results and nevertheless
maintaining all features of the modular extendability in word and bit direction. In
this way the problem of fabricating such devices is removed to the same border line
that has also been drawn for the other semiconductor memory types: the technological capabilities of chip manufacturing.

By extending the logical compare circuits of each memory cell in a relatively moderate
degree, the associative complexity can be increased by the search operations "greater
than" and "less than". Following the same principle of word parallel search and
priority controlled match evaluation numerous processing steps normally implemented by complete subroutines can be executed much more rationally. Such a displacement
of logical operations from the processor to the memory promises a considerably
higher system performance for a large class of user problems.

References

[1] *A. E. Slade* and *H. O. McMahon,* A cryotron catalog memory system. Proc. of the Eastern
     Joint Comp. Conf. 1956, 115—120.

[2] *B. Parhami,* Associative Memories and Processors: An overview and Selected Bibliography.
     Proc. of the IEEE, Vol. **61**, June 1973, 722—730.

[3] *H. S. Stone,* A logic-in-memory computer. IEEE Trans. on Computers, Vol. **C-19**, Jan.
     1970, 73—78.

[4] *H. Glock* and *K. Pfeiffer,* Assoziative Speicher. Seminar Halbleiterspeicher, Internat.
     Elektronik-Arbeitskreis e.V., München, März 1972.

[5] *L. C. Higbie,* Associative Processors: A Panacea or a Specific? Computer Design, July 1976,
     75—82.

[6]   *R. M. Lea,* Information Processing with an Associative Parallel Processor. Computer, Nov. 1975, 25–32.

[7]   *J. L. Mundy, J. F. Burgess, R. E. Joynson* and *C. Neugebauer,* Low-Cost Associative Memory. IEEE J. of Solid-State Circuits, Vol. **SC-7**, Oct. 1972, 364–369.

[8]   *R. M. Lea,* Low-Cost High-Speed Associative Memory. IEEE J. of Solid-State Circuits, Vol. **SC-10**, June 1975, 179–181.

[9]   *R. Leibbrand,* Zur Technologie des assoziativen Speichers. Techn.-Wissenschaftl. Blätter der Süddeutschen Zeitung, 189. Ausgabe vom 3. Nov. 1971.

[10] *H. O. Leilich,* Assoziative Speicher. Taschenbuch der Informatik, Band I (Hrsg. Steinbuch/Weber) 1974, Springer-Verlag, Berlin, Heidelberg, New York, 479–490.

[11] *H. O. Leilich, I. Karlowsky, W. Lawrenz* and *H. Ch. Zeidler,* Ein Rechnerkonzept mit assoziativem Arbeitsspeicher. Lecture Notes in Computer Science, Band 8, 1974, Springer-Verlag, Berlin, Heidelberg, New York.

[12] *J. A. Rudolph, L. C. Fulmer* and *W. C. Meilander,* With associative memory, speed limit is no barrier. Electronics, Vol. 43, June 22, 1970, 96–101.

Storage Hierarchy Technology and Organization

Claus Schünemann and Wilhelm G. Spruth

IBM Deutschland GmbH, Böblingen, Germany

Introduction

The storage subsystem of a data processing system comprises those components
that store programs and data. This includes the spectrum from bulk storage with
its own microprograms to the buffer stores (cache stores) and registers located in
the Central Processing Unit (Fig. 1). Present storage subsystems are almost exclusively
implemented in the form of several independent storage hierarchies with their own
address spaces. The cost of the storage subsystem can be more than 50 % of the
total system hardware cost (Fig. 2).

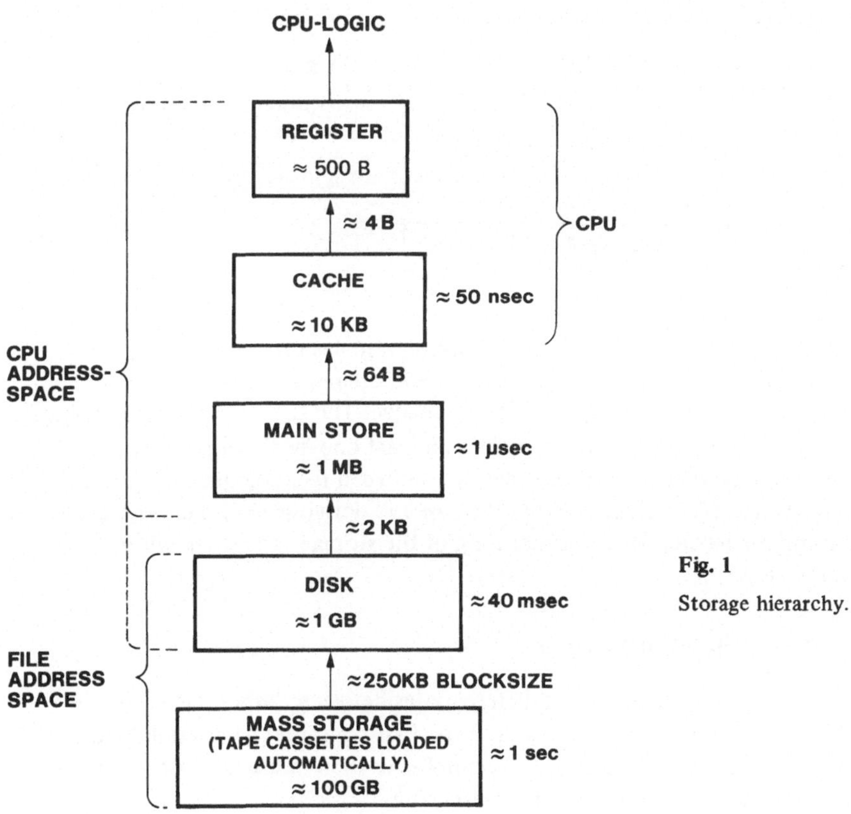

Fig. 1

Storage hierarchy.

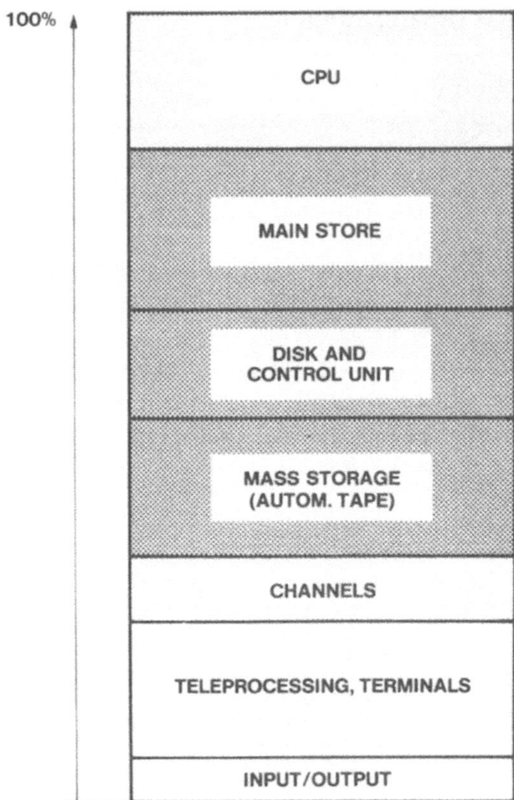

Fig. 2

Hardware cost distribution of
a large system.

As with all data processing equipment, storage hierarchies can be evaluated from
the viewpoint of architecture (transparency of addressing, automatic data communication, etc.) and from the viewpoint of performance. The first two sections of this
paper consider architecture while the fourth and last one deals with performance.
In the third section we will point out relations between technological parameters
of different storage technologies. From this, we will derive selection criteria for the
usage of components and for the structuring of the storage subsystem within a data
processing system.

1. Logical and Physical Storage

The concept of the digital computer differentiates between "input data" and
"internally stored data". Early machines of the first computer generation held
internally stored data in "main store". Technologies then in use were delay-line
memories, storage tubes, drums and magnetic core.

Independently there also was an early requirement for the storage of input and output data. Here, magnetic tape established itself as an universal technology. Conventional magnetic tape units with manual loading are typically input/output units rather than part of the storage subsystem. In contrast, disk storage and mass storage (a tape storage technology with automatic loading) belong to the storage subsystem. They are not included in the main store address space but are accessed via channels and I/O-instructions.

To improve disk storage ease-of-use, the utilization of "logical stores" with idealized access characteristics has become a widely adopted technique. Logical stores are abstractions and are implemented through a mapping onto "physical stores". Examples for logical stores are the virtual memory of the Burroughs B6700 and the IBM System 370, the index-sequential file and the logical IMS data base [1].

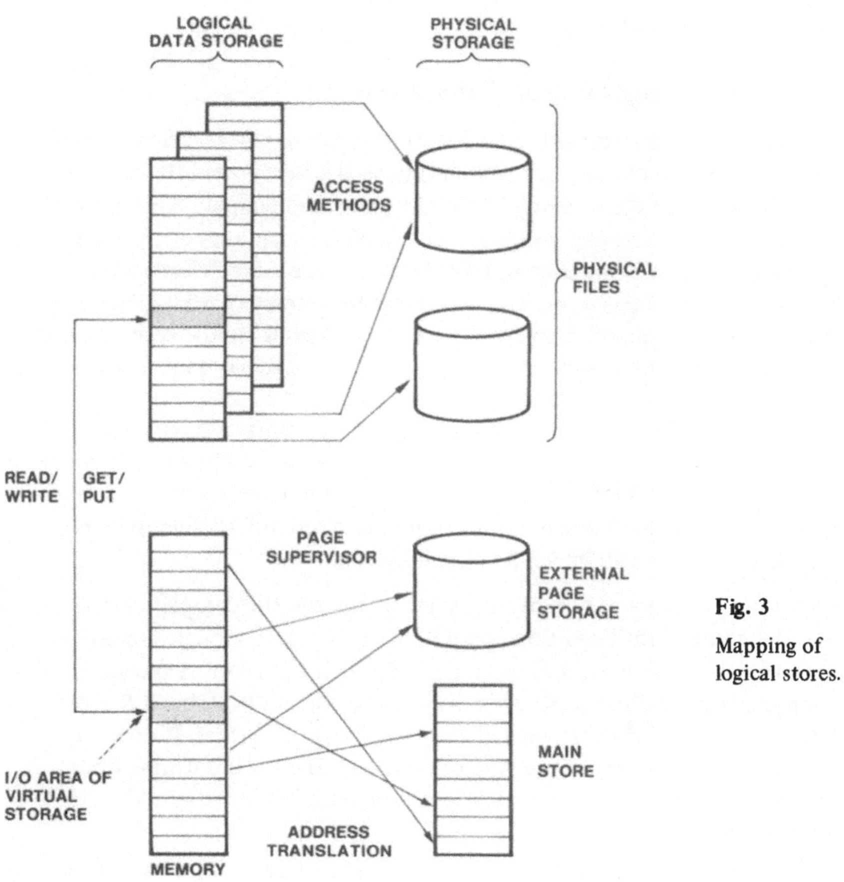

Fig. 3

Mapping of
logical stores.

The user of a data processing system as a rule utilizes multiple logical stores with
unique and independent name spaces (Fig. 3). Typically a unique logical store is
established for every data set or data base accessed by a user program. The logical
store name space is mapped into the machine architecture address space via
READ/WRITE macro instructions. With every access to a logical store, a mapping
onto the corresponding physical store is performed by both hardware and system
programs. In early machines there was a 1 : 1 relation between machine architecture,
name space and (physical) main store. Due to the limited main store capacity, only
a fraction of the name space was usable. In current machines, the (logical) virtual
storage concept permits a full utilization of the machine architecture name space.
The virtual memory maps the machine architecture name space onto both external
stores and main store with the assistance of a "direct address translation" feature
and the "page supervisor" facilities of the operating system. When accessing data
sets, data managment routines perform the mapping of the logical data set store
onto the physical external store.

2. Structure of Existing Storage Hierarchies

Parts of a logical store are frequently mapped onto separate physical stores, implemented with different technologies. Different physical stores have different access
times and are arranged in a hierarchy (Fig. 1). The storage hierarchy concept results
from the requirement to organize programs and data sets such, that elements which
have a high probability of being used in the near future are stored close to the
central processing unit. Today's implementations are limited to partial hierarchies
within a hierarchy spectrum. Examples for partial hierarchies are the combination
cache — main store [2], the virtual memory [3] and the combination disk file — tape
cassette store in the IBM 3850 mass storage system [4]. An essential feature of this
mass store is its characteristic to make data from a tape cassette available to the user
in the form of a virtual disk volume. A common architectural feature of the above
partial hierarchies is their transparency of addresses and data transfer within levels
of the hierarchy. The logical store does not show the structural characteristics of
the storage hierarchy, through which it is implemented.

A "one level store" is an extension of this concept through the complete hierarchy.
It combines the above mentioned three partial hierarchies into a single hierarchy,
and features a single name space and its transparent data transport. A precursor of
this has been implemented in the MULTICS system of the MIT. MULTICS avoids
a differentiation between virtual memory and logical data set stores. It offers a
single logical store to the user, whose segments are suitable for the storing of data
sets [5]. However, attachment of a mass store is not included in today's MULTICS
implementation.

Storage hierarchies exploit the fact that the probability of accessing a particular
address within a logical store can assume very different values. Usually, accesses are

380

clustered in certain areas of the name space and these "working sets" move only
slowly. In the cache, program loops are responsible for clustering of address references. Thereby, a fast small cache satisfies a number of CPU instruction and operand
address references for some time without reloading from virtual memory. A reloading from the slower but larger main memory must be done in the case of an access
miss. The efficiency of this procedure is expressed by the hit ratio (about 90–98 %).
This efficiency is improved through the principle of advanced loading: in the case
of an access miss not only the referenced address but an additional block of data
with consecutive addresses is loaded.

This hierarchy mechanism is the same for other levels of the storage hierarchy (e.g.
the working set phenomenon in the virtual memory).

3. Technology

The various storage technologies — in particular semiconductors and magnetic
media — may be characterized through the parameters shown in Fig. 4. The most

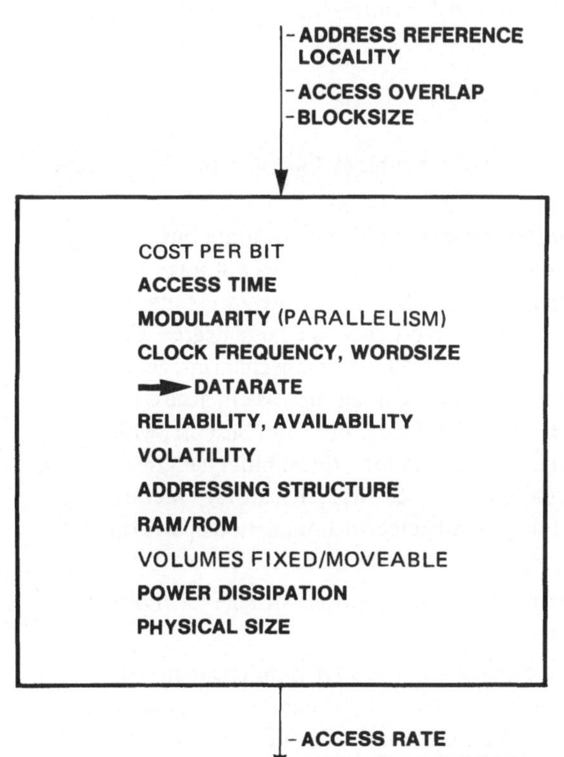

Fig. 4

Storage technology — characteristic parameter.

important ones of those will be discussed as a function of cost/bit. The cost/bit figures serve as a base reference and determine within a storage hierarchy the typical storage capacity at a particular level. It has to be remembered that a particular cost/bit value requires utilization of a certain minimum storage capacity.

Within all levels of the hierarchy, data are always transferred as blocks. Thus the "total access time" t_t can be subdivided into an "actual access time" t_A until reading the first bit, and a "block transfer time" t_B. The actual access time, in the following referred to as "access time" can, depending on technology and organization, contain the "latency time" during which the addressed position moves to the read/write station:

$$t_t = t_A + t_B.$$

The block transfer time depends on the "basic data rate" and the block length. The basic data rate is a function of clock frequency and bit width. The clock frequency ranges within approx. .3–30 MHz, with most technologies. The block length results from the operational requirements at each hierarchy level. For random access and typical block sizes we find that the block transfer time generally is small compared to the access time:

$$t_t \approx t_A.$$

The block transfer time dominates in cases of large block length as they may occur with sequential access.

There is only a weak correlation between bit cost and basic data rate but a strong dependency between bit cost and access time. In just about every storage technology the access mechanism has a large impact on cost. Sharing of the access mechanism cost by a particular storage capacity defines the bit cost to a large degree. On the other hand, if a large storage capacity shares a single access mechanism, accesses become necessarily more and more serial, resulting in an increase in access time. This results in the well-known relation between access time and bit cost, which is shown in Fig. 5. Fig. 5 shows the total access time for typical block lengths. In most cases, this time approximates the actual access time. Thus, in a storage hierarchy it is possible to transfer large blocks of data in advance without serious performance degradation.

The relation shown in Fig. 5 demonstrates a "law of surface storage technology" and suggests the following statements:

- The cost-access time relation for a given state of the art is independent of technology (lower bit cost can be achieved only at the expense of longer access time). This relation will exist also in the future and will shift evolutionarily with technological progress to lower cost and eventually to smaller access times.

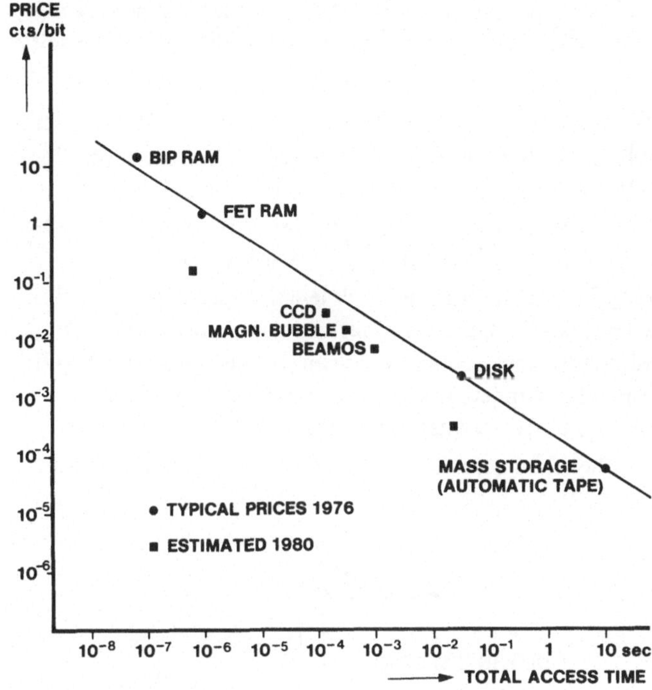

Fig. 5. Bitcost vs total access time (incl. control).

- The position of each technology in Fig. 5 is determined by its inherent capability
  to share the access mechanism. The position can be shifted for each technology
  along the shown curve. Examples are the shift register and the LARAM-approaches
  in CCDs, or magnetic disk drives with different storage capacity under each access
  arm.
- New technologies will fill existing gaps.

The shown relations will change with the introduction of three dimensional as
opposed to surface technologies, for example three dimensional holography.

The access rate $1/t_t$ [1]) results from the total access time t_t. The "effective data rate"
is defined as the access rate multiplied by the blocklength. It approaches the basic
data rate with increasing block length. The accessibility can be improved through
the use of parallel access mechanism which in turn requires a modular structure of

---

[1]) The straight-forward notion of access rate = $1/t_t$ is no longer valid in those cases where
individual components of the access mechanism work in parallel and asynchronously, thus
creating parallelism. An example is the IBM 3850 mass storage.

the storage device. A figure of merit for the accessibility of a storage technology is the "access density", $1/(t_t \cdot C)$, which is the access rate related to the storage capacity C. This figure of merit is reasonable, since we find in general that with increasing capacity the access requirements also increase.

Lower technology costs imply not only a lower access rate (law of surface technology in Fig. 5) but also less modularity. This results in a much faster decrease in access density (Fig. 6). Low cost mass storage technologies thus have extremely poor access-ability. This in turn requires organizational techniques as discussed below.

Fig. 6 plots the "access density" (with the typical block length according to Fig. 1), and the "optimum effective data rate". "Optimum" refers to an increase in block length to the maximum feasible for each access mechanism. In the case of a magnetic disk for example this is a complete cylinder. If a large physical block consists of multiple logical blocks we use the terms "sequential access" and "blocking".

It is interesting to note that, other than access rate or access density, the optimum effective data rate varies only relatively little with bit cost. This is because the trans-

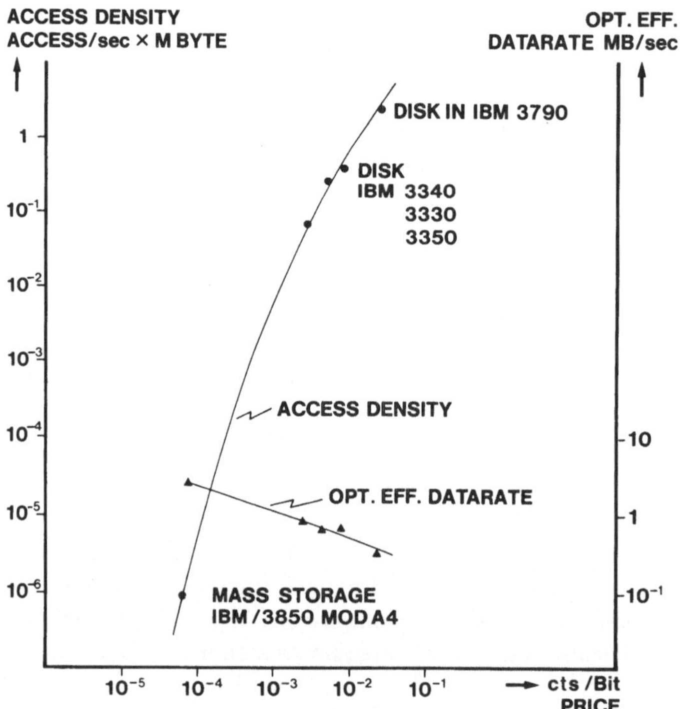

Fig. 6. Access density and optimum effective datarate.
Blocksize: disk cylinder, mass storage cassette.

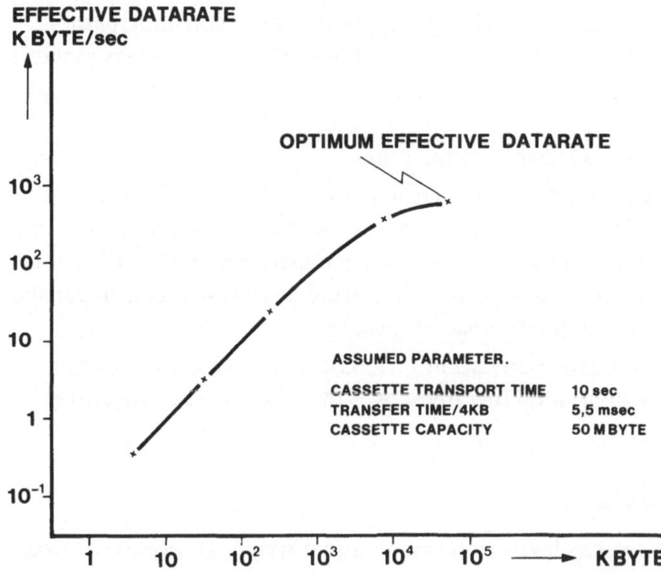

Fig. 7. Model calculation of eff. datarate vs blocksize for IBM 3850. One transportsystem and read/write station. No overlapping of transport and read/write operation.

fer time which varies little across the technology spectrum becomes large compared to the actual access time.

Of course, this mode of operation demonstrates an optimum which usually cannot be achieved. In general the effective data rate is determined by the block size that is optimum for the particular mode of operation.

In Fig. 7 a simplified model of the IBM 3850 mass storage demonstrates how the effective data rate increases as a function of the block size per cassette access [1]. This demonstrates the efficiency improvement that can be achieved by presorting of access requests and multiple utilization of cassette loadings. This presorting is

---

[1] The IBM 3850 has more read/write stations than cassette transports. In addition it is possible to position a cassette in front and behind a read/write station independent of the actual loading condition of the station. The components of the access mechanism thus operate in a decoupled and overlapping fashion. Fig. 7 neglects the overlapping parallelism potential. The total access time is assumed to be the sum of the cassette access time and block transfer time. The resulting access rate has been used to calculate the optimum effective data rate of the IBM 3850 Mod. A4 in Fig. 6. (It was multiplied by 4 according to the 4 read/write stations working in parallel.) In this case a limitation results from the 4 read/write controls due to the large block length (with optimum effective data rate). In contrast, the IBM 3850 access density in Fig. 6 is limited by the cassette transport mechanism due to the relatively small block size assumed (256 KByte).

very simple with anticipatory sequential (batch) operation. With non-anticipatory accesses, the effect can only be achieved through queue-sorting of the access requests. This is a storage-specific example of the general law that high data throughput (high effective data rate) and short response time are not compatible and that one performance parameter must be traded against the other.

The favourable situation with sequential and anticipatory access also permits direct data loading from a lower hierarchy level directly into main store without access to intermediate levels. This approach has traditionally been used, e.g. with conventional manual magnetic tapes. The more anticipatory the nature of storage access in particular application, the less hierarchy levels must be involved.

Other applications — e.g. interactive operation — do not permit prediction of the next access. Here a genuine multi-level hierarchy over the whole storage spectrum will pay off.

4. Hierarchy Performance

A storage hierarchy interconnects levels implemented in different storage technologies into a mutually supporting subsystem. Parameters used in the dimensioning of a particular level in the hierarchy are access time and access rate, block size and capacity. The efficiency of the multiple levels within the hierarchy is determined by the hit ratio at each level, as a function of block size, capacity and distribution of address references.

In the past, only very few storage technologies have been available for the implementation of a storage hierarchy. Tomorrow's technology offerings will fill the gaps in the cost/bit — access time curve.

A discussion of the performance characteristics of the complete hierarchy (e.g. effective access and data rate) at the CPU interface (see Fig. 1) is eased by reviewing the "high end", "intermediate range" and "low end" separately. At the "high end", a cache access miss requires no task switch. The CPU waits during the access time to main store, and the hierarchy efficiency is exclusively a function of the hit ratio. This hit ratio is predominantly defined by the structure and time dependence of the working set. At the "lower end" (mass store) the large access time predominantly determines the individual response time of a process or transaction. System throughput is only moderately impacted by process switching (multiprogramming) which occurs relatively infrequently. Individual response times (e.g. interactive operation) can be improved by introducing an additional hierarchy level between disk file and tape cassette storage. The "intermediate range" is the largest bottleneck in terms of system throughput and individual response time. This situation is characterized by the access gap between main store and disk file technologies. In some applications the disk accesses are anticipatory/planned and thus can be overlapped with the running process. If this is not the case, the large access time of the

disk file compared to that of main store (40 000 : 1) is bridged by task switching:
Another process in the active list receives control over the CPU. The additional
system load with heavy task switching is significant. An additional disadvantage of
heavy task switching in a multiprogramming environment is the decreasing efficiency
of the cache. Task switches require significant reloading of the cache.

Development trends for all storage technologies aim at higher bit densities and thus
an increase in the number of bits per each access mechanism. Semiconductor memories
may become faster with time, while modularity and access density of disk files will
decrease (with practically constant access times). This implies that for a given disk
file capacity fewer accesses per second will be possible, resulting in a decreased task
switching rate and reduced system throughput. With conventional means, the use of
larger main stores is the only way to solve this problem. Another difficulty is the
fact that interactive operations often require ten or more disk accesses per transaction to index tables, catalogues, etc. This results in a considerable increase in
individual response time.

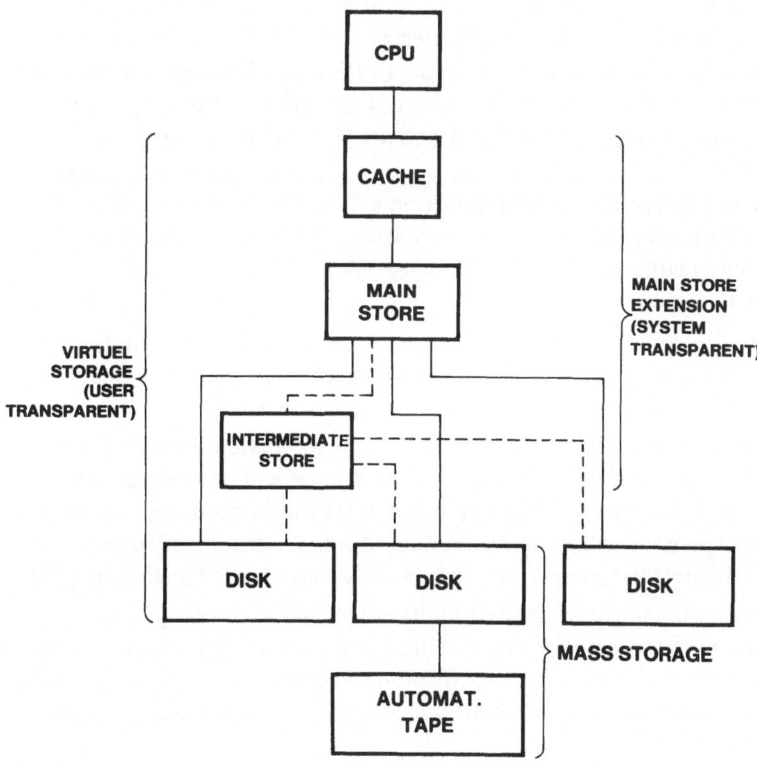

Fig. 8. Storage hierarchy with intermediate level.

The introduction of an additional hierarchy level between main store and disk store
(Fig. 8) is a way to reduce or eliminate this problem. From this results the motivation
to develop the appropriate technology. Assuming that the technology for the intermediate hierarchy level is fast enough (total access time ca. 100–500 μs), task switching is not required to bridge the access time. In this case, task switching will occur
only with accesses to the lower levels in the hierarchy which occur much less frequently. The new intermediate hierarchy level can be used as a direct extension of
main store (within the main store address space) and/or as a fast back-up store
(within the disk file address space). In both cases the architecture compatibility
with the existing operating systems can be preserved to a large extent. Fig. 8 shows
the three usages of today's disk file levels: data set store, buffer device for the mass
storage, and part of virtual memory.

Potential future technologies, especially CCDs [6], BEAMOS [7] and magnetic
bubbles [8, 9] fall into the "access gap". Charge coupled devices (CCD) are FET-
semiconductors with shift register structure. Magnetic bubbles propagate magnetic
states within a thin magnetic film and are also organized as shift registers. In the
BEAMOS store, the Beam Addressable MOS, electrical charges are stored into and
scanned from the oxide layer of a silicon chip by an electron beam within a cathode
ray tube. The sufficiently short total access time of CCDs and BEAMOS (the latter
with reduced block size if necessary) offers a potential of operation without task
switching. Magnetic bubble memories will be slower within the foreseeable future
(total access time $\sim$ 1 ms) so that their application area will be in the area of drum
and fixed head disk file replacement. At today's price/performance ratio, these
technologies are only marginally attractive as a gap filler. One can assume that
this will change with time.

Introduction of fast intermediate storage hierarchy levels without task switching
will have a significant impact on both the internal structure of data processing
systems and the organization of computer data. Examples are:

- The main store extension will perform virtual memory function. Invoking the
  page supervisor in todays "demand paging" environment will be eliminated to
  a significant extent. In general, the intermediate level will contain the requested
  data. The page supervisor will be activated only in a block paging mode, e.g.
  when loading complete programs from disk file into the extended main store [10].
- Smaller machines with single (instead of multiple) virtual memories permit
  mapping of the complete virtual memory onto the intermediate level. Accessing
  the virtual memory no longer requires activation of operating system components.
  (Loading of the virtual memory will continue to require data management routines
  as in today's systems.)
- The mapping of logical data bases onto physical data base storage devices requires
  a high CPU processing effort, in particular with the relational data base model.

388

The new technologies have a potential for flexible data structures and fast and simple serial scan operation.

It should be noted that the introduction of an additional intermediate hierarchy level, possibly implemented with heterogeneous technologies, may introduce significant compatibility problems with existing software and data. This may apply in particular to the area of data management and recovery management. Solving these problems and thus exploiting the potential of new technologies can be considered a major challenge in the area of system development.

5. Conclusion

We predict further advances in the development of storage hierarchies, in particular with the introduction of new intermediate levels above (and in the long run also below) the disk file level. This will result in an improvement in hierarchy price/performance. With non-anticipatory access, the response characteristics and access rates will be improved. With anticipatory access, the block size and thus the effective data rate of the slower levels can be increased.

References

[1] *H. Hasselmeier, W. G. Spruth* (editors), Data Base Systems, Series Lecture Notes in Computer Science, Vol. 39, Springer-Verlag 1976.

[2] *C. J. Conti* et al., Structural Aspects of the System 360, Model 85, IBM Systems Journal, 1968, p. 2–29.

[3] *H. Hasselmeier, W. G. Spruth* (editors), Rechnerstrukturen, R. Oldenbourg Verlag, 1974.

[4] *E. Lennemann,* Tape Libraries with Automatic System Transport, this issue, p. 65.

[5] *E. I. Organick,* The MULTICS System, MIT Press, Cambridge 1972.

[6] *H. J. Harloff,* Structur Organization and Application of Charge Coupled Devices, CCD, this issue, p. 147.

[7] *C. Schunemann,* BEAMOS – Technology and Application, this issue, p. 161.

[8] *F. H. de Leeuw,* Fundamentals of Magnetic Bubble Storage, this issue, p. 203.

[9] *W. Metzdorf,* Application of Magnetic Bubbles for Data Storage, this issue, p. 217.

[10] *W. G. Spruth,* Interactive Systeme, SRA Verlag, 1977.

The Performance of Small Cache Memories in Minicomputer Systems with Several Processors

Axel Lehmann and Detlef Schmid

Institut für Informatik IV, University of Karlsruhe, Karlsruhe, Germany

1. Introduction

The evolution of the last years has shown that with improving technological possibilities, concepts of cache and hierarchical memories must be taken into consideration also for minicomputer systems [2, 8, 10]. As well-known, the system performance critically depends on placing the addressed data at the time of memory access in the cache, as the memory level being next to the processor. Therefore, size and structure of the cache, as well as the organizing strategies are of decisive importance [2, 3, 4, 7, 8].

However, experiences in this connection gained up to now with large systems can only be applied to minicomputer systems under certain restrictions like, for instance, small cache sizes because different conditions are existing for these systems. Another important factor is that general qualitative statements on the cache performance are not sufficient for specific decisions of design because, for this, more comprehensive quantitative analyses are required.

This paper now presents such quantitative performance analysis. The Institut für Informatik IV at the University of Karlsruhe has performed this investigation in co-operation with the SIEMENS AG in Karlsruhe with the intention to apply in the industrial practice the methods and experiences obtained at the universities.

The investigations are based on a model which is able to simulate the execution of programs and organizational instructions in computer systems depending on the structure of the memory hierarchy and the system load [11]. In the model every processor has its own cache. So-called "synthetic" programs are used as input data which may consist of any combination of instructions and address profiles [12]. Thus, it is possible to determine principal dependencies between the access behaviour of certain program structures and a special realization of cache memories. These dependencies are especially important for the efficiency of small caches with capacities of between 32 and 2 K words which are examined in this report.

391

2. Description of the Simulation Model

The simulation program which is applied for evaluating the performance of cache
organizations is written in SIMULA $-$ 67. As shown in Fig. 1, it contains all system
components which are essential for the activities in computer systems equipped
with a virtual memory. The great number of modules and parameters in the simulation program allows to simulate execution and blocking of processes in different
system configurations.

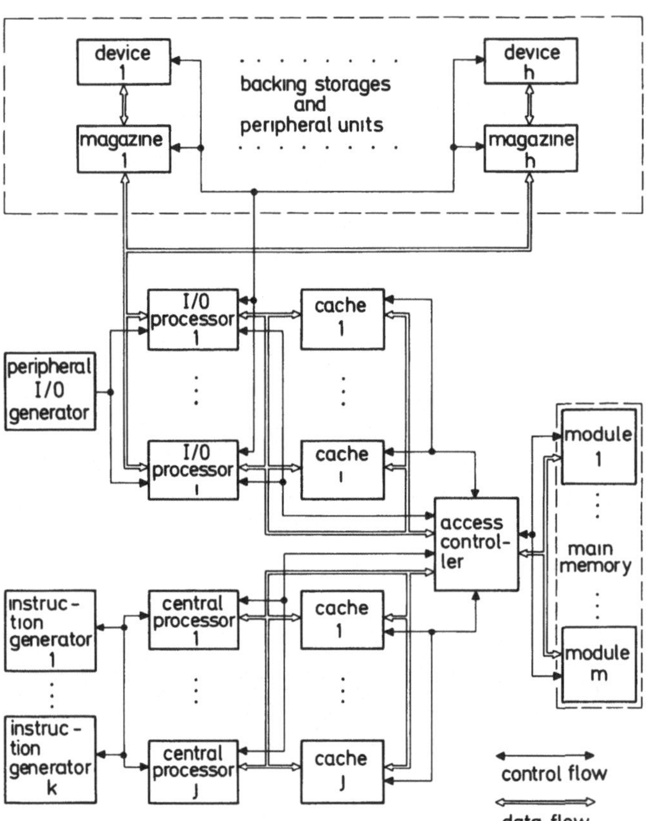

Fig. 1. System components of the simulation model.

2.1. System Components

The processing units in the simulation model, viz. central processors for execution of
operating-program, as well as user-programs, and I/O-processors for handling central
and peripheral I/O-requests, can be generated in any number by means of input para-

meters. Thus, it is possible to analyse the performance also of multiprocessor systems.
The processor registers have not been included, because only the blocking of the
processors for different instruction execution intervals are important for investigating
the memory access behaviour.

In order to be able to investigate the service times of a memory system, the different
processes running in cache and main memory or between them are exactly simulated
in the model. In addition, it is possible to simulate alternatively different technologies,
sizes and structures, as well as management strategies for these storage levels. On the
other hand, backing storages and peripheral devices are only considered by access
and transfer times which are essential for the service time behaviour of the memory
system.

For the coordination and management of memory processes, as well as for the
transformation of virtual addresses in real main memory addresses, an organization
unit is implemented in the model acting as an access controller for the main memory.

Instead of real programs, generators for instructions and peripheral I/O-requests are
being used as input into the model. According to a defined rule, they are generating a
sequence of instructions, operands and their addresses: the so-called "synthetic"
programs. These have the advantage of generating nearly any program structure by
a special selection of the input parameters for the generators.

2.2. Generation of Synthetic Programs

As the composition of instructions of the synthetic programs should be in accord
with those of real programs, the investigations were based upon the instruction set
of the central processing unit SIEMENS 340 with about 300 machine instructions.
First, these instructions were classified by associating real machine instructions of
similar characteristics to an instruction class. For simulation purposes, all instructions
included in an instruction class are represented by only one instruction type. These
instruction types are forming the so-called "reduced" instruction set. The generators
for instructions and I/O-requests are creating sequences of these instruction types
according to given distributions [12].

The criterion for mapping real machine instructions in an instruction class is the
similarity of the timing-sequence during the processing of the instructions, regardless
of their function. Since this sequence essentially depends on the number of time-
consuming memory accesses, the classification of instructions is mainly determined
by the kind and number of memory accesses during instruction processing. By this
procedure, classes are obtained which are characterized by different structures of
operands and instructions. Thus, the real instruction set could be mapped in a
reduced instruction set consisting of ten instruction types. The execution time for
these instruction types can be varied within an execution time interval which is
associated with each class (see Fig. 2).

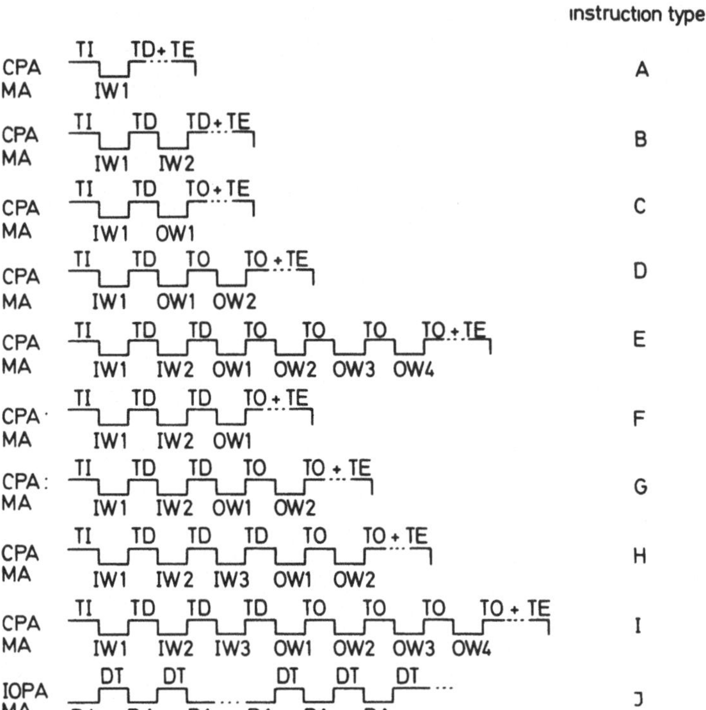

Abbreviations:

CPA	— central processor activities		OWj	— access to operand word j
IOPA	— I/O processor activities		TO	— transfer of an operand word
MA	— memory access		TE	— execution of the operation
TI	— instruction initiation		DA	— data access
IWi	— access to instruction word i		DT	— transfer of a word from/to memory
TD	— decoding			

Fig. 2. Processing of the instruction types used in the model.

All investigations are based on the assumption that the virtual address space of a
program is composed of independent areas for code, subroutines and operands.
Concerning the memory management, these areas are divided into pages of fixed
size. In addition, there is a COMMON DATA area which is common for operands
of all programs being addressed by real main memory addresses. The addresses of the
synthetic programs are created by generating jumps and loops, in addition to the
sequential addressing pattern, with defined address distances in the different program areas described above, according to given distributions. Furthermore; subroutines may be called, situated in a virtual address space which is different from
the programs code area.

394

According to a given distribution, every synthetic program is represented by a
sequence of instruction types and memory addresses which are generated by a
random number generator, a so-called instruction generator. Instead of storing the
complete sequence of instruction types and their addresses, only one instruction is
generated according to the flow chart in Fig. 3. After having executed an instruction,
the central processor reactivates the instruction generator.

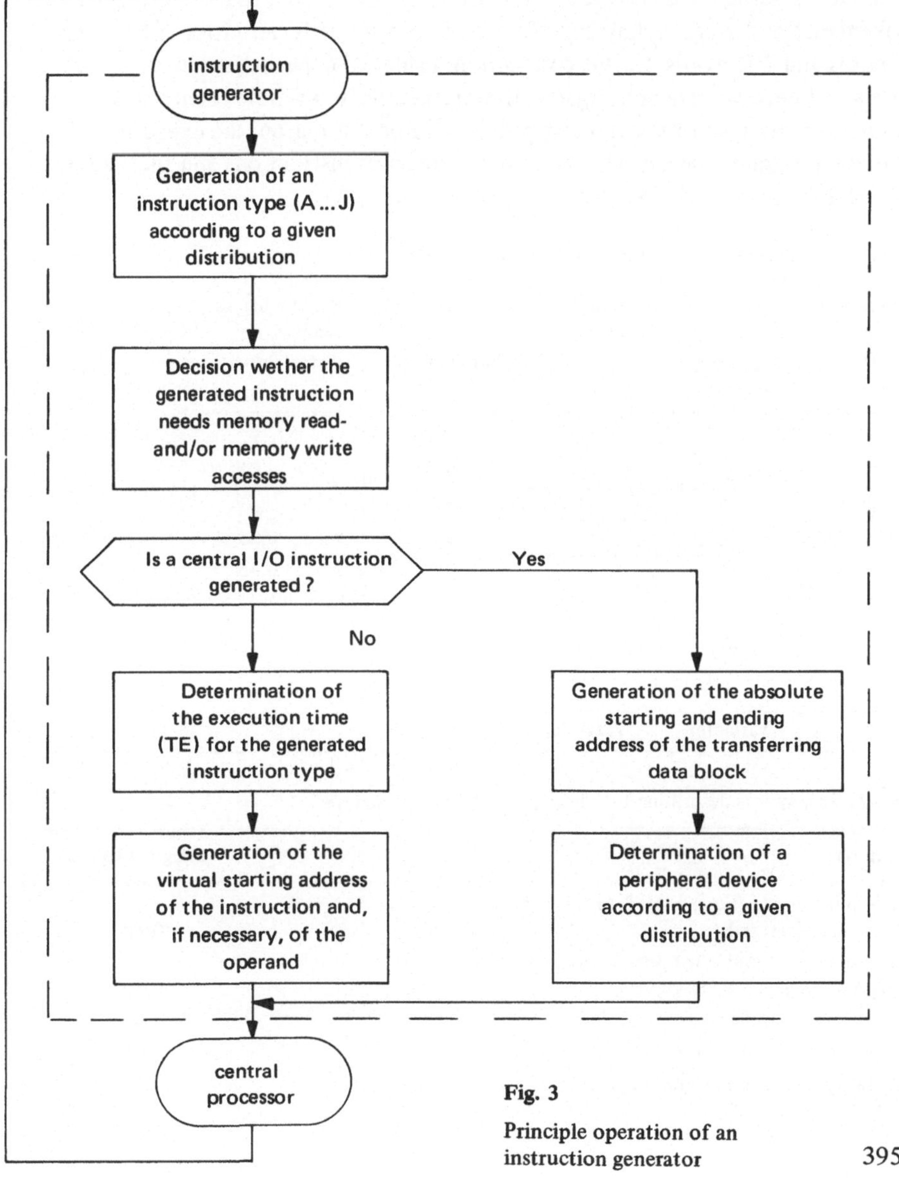

Fig. 3

Principle operation of an
instruction generator

As memory charge is essentially influenced by I/O-handling, the simulation model is equipped with a peripheral I/O-generator. This device which is operating independent of the instruction generators, produces I/O-requests of the peripheral units as block transfer instructions.

3. Characteristics and Efficiency of Small Caches for Central Processors

As described above, these investigations aimed to obtain quantitative results on the performance and access behaviour of cache memories with capacities of between 32 words and 2 K words. In this connection, principal dependencies were to be ascertained between size and organization, respectively, of these caches and the addressing behaviour of the running programs. For this reason, the execution of synthetic programs was tested. Their combination of instructions and their addressing behaviour was defined according to Tab. 1 and 2.

Table 1. Instructions of the simulated synthetic programs

| Instruction type (see Fig. 2) | Number of memory accesses during an | | Probability of appearance | Probability of read-/write operations |
	instruction fetch cycle	operand fetch cycle		
A	1	–	0,30	
B	2	–	0	
C	1	1	0,30	
D	1	2	0,05	read: 0,55
E	2	4	0	write: 0,45
F	2	1	0,30	
G	2	2	0,05	
H	3	2	0	
I	3	4	0	
J	variable	variable	0	

Table 2. Parameters describing the simulated addressing pattern

Parameter:	assigned value:
Part of jump instructions related to the total number of instructions executed:	0,10
Conditional probability for jumps forward (to higher virtual addresses):	0,60
Jump distance (address distance):	2^i, (i = 0, 1, 2, ... 9)
Probability for a subroutine call:	0,01
Probability of accesses to operands in a COMMON DATA area:	0,05

The following simulation results are based on different realizations of cache memories for central processors, however, with following common characteristics:

- Data are being transferred sequentially word by word between cache and processor.

- The transfer unit between cache and main memory is one block consisting of a defined number of words with consecutive main memory addresses. The block size depends on the width of the data paths between main memory and cache and is defined by the number of words being transferred parallel from a main memory module to a cache.

- As far as organization is concerned, the caches are divided into two separate areas of same size. The operand area (OP) is exclusively reserved for variable data, whereas all invariable parts of a program coming from the code and subroutine areas are buffered in the code area (CO) of the cache [1, 9].

- The different operations of read and write accesses are controlled by the management strategy "write through". Thus, it is guaranteed that actual data are always available in main memory because, by this strategy, writing instructions are executed at least in main memory. If the addressed data word is already available in the cache, it will be also adjusted there simultaneously. Reading accesses are principally executed in the cache only [2, 8, 10].

These investigations aimed to obtain comparable results on memory access behaviour of programs, as well as on the characteristics of differently proportioned and managed caches, regardless of any special system configuration. This is guaranteed by observing the following conditions and fixed parameter values during all simulations:

- It was assumed that all pages of the running programs are completely loaded into main memory. Thus, interrupts could be avoided which were caused by page faults and consecutive rearrangements of the cache.

- In all investigations neither central nor peripheral I/O-requests have been generated. Consequently, time delays or any interrupts due to accesses to backing storages or peripheral units did not have to be considered.

- Activities of the operating system, as well as other program interrupts have also been avoided in order not to distort the measuring results by additional transfers to the cache.

- As a measure for the access behaviour and the efficiency of alternative cache realizations, measurements of the miss ratio M_C in a cache were used:

$$M_C = \frac{\Sigma \, (\text{misses in a cache})}{\Sigma \, (\text{accesses to a cache})}$$

It should be noticed that the sum of the generated memory accesses is not equal to the number of cache accesses since a part of the writing accesses is processed only in main memory by means of the investigated strategy "write through".

3.1. Cache Size

The size of a cache is defined by the parameters

C_L: cache length (number of blocks in a cache)
C_W: cache width (number of words in a block).

The width of the data buses (D_W) per main memory module was supposed to be the same as the cache width, thus, C_W words can be transferred in parallel between a cache and a main memory module. The reserved areas for code (C_{CO}) and operands (C_{OP}) in a cache, having together a capacity of C words, are:

$$C_{CO} = C_{OP} = \frac{C}{2} = \frac{C_L}{2} \cdot C_W$$

3.1.1. Variation of the Cache Length

In Fig. 4, the access behaviour of caches with different lengths C_L but of constant block size C_W is presented as a function of the addressing profile of the executed programs. The miss ratios M_C are stated separately for code areas (index CO) and operand areas (index OP) of the caches as a function of the jump distance. The qualitatively similar shape of the measuring curves in Fig. 4 shows an advantageous cache access behaviour for programs which are processed with low jump distances. On the one hand, this is due to the management strategy to transfer not only the words demanded from the main memory to the cache but always one block (look-ahead effect). In case of sequential addressing, data words addressed afterwards are already stored in the cache very often. On the other hand, in case of returns with low address distances, it is nearly always possible to access directly words addressed before in the cache. This fact is especially characteristic for return address distances which are of the order of the capacity of a reserved cache area. A following sequential addressing affects that data being already in the cache which can be frequently accessed there directly. This fact causes a minimum of the miss ratios M_C which effects an especially advantageous access behaviour for long caches.

The following strong increase of the miss ratios M_C is due to the fact that the capacity of the cache is too small to buffer data, being already addressed, during a certain period for returns with long address distances. In this connection, a duplication of the number of blocks for both reserved cache areas does not only cause a shift of the strong increase of the miss ratios M_C but also a declination. The course of cache miss ratios then turns over to a saturation for long jump distances. There, cache efficiency is nearly exclusively depending on the look-ahead mechanism described above by loading a whole block from the main memory.

398

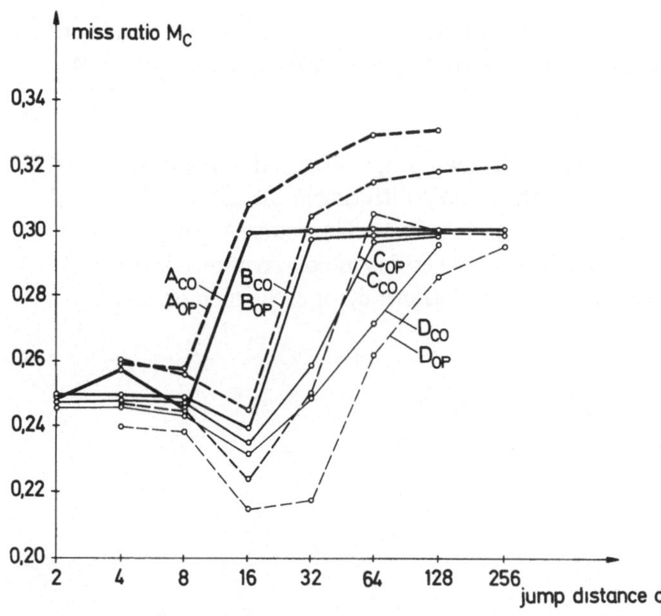

Definitions:

curve	cache length $\dfrac{C_L}{2}$ (blocks)	cache width $C_W = D_W$ (words)	cache capacity C (words)
A_{CO}, A_{OP}	4	4	32
B_{CO}, B_{OP}	8	4	64
C_{CO}, C_{OP}	16	4	128
D_{CO}, D_{OP}	32	4	256

Fig. 4. Influence of jump distance d on cache access behaviour for different cache lengths.

It is remarkable, too, that an increase of the cache length shows a different effect in the code area and the operand area, as shown in Fig. 4. The relations $A_{OP} > A_{CO}$ and $B_{OP} > B_{CO}$ are caused by the fact, that data from three different address areas sometimes are buffered in the operand area of the cache at the same time:

- data blocks from the operand areas of the programs,
- COMMON DATA, available for all programs,
- registrations of the program page tables for the determination of real main memory addresses.

However, the code area of the caches is only provided for data from the code and subroutine areas of the programs. An increase of the number of blocks for every cache therefore produces a more advantageous access behaviour, especially in the operand area of the cache.

Fig. 5 shows the cache access behaviour of two programs E and F as a function of the number of blocks in the cache. Both are only differing in the address distance d which is passed over by executing jump instructions. The course of miss ratios in the operand area and code area of the caches verifies the observations described above concerning the characteristics and the efficiency of cache memories of different length.

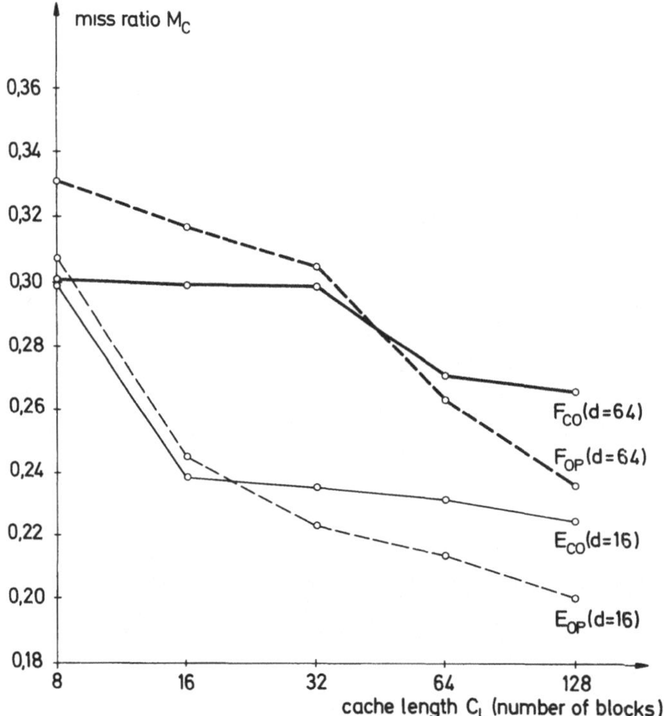

Fig. 5. Access behaviour of identical programs E, F (with different jump distances d) depending upon cache length C_L (C_W = 4 words).

3.1.2. Variation of the Cache Width

This section deals with the influence of cache width C_W and block size, respectively, on the access behaviour of small cache memories. By interpreting the results it should be considered that for all investigations, the block size was chosen identically with

400

the number of words (D_W) being transferred parallel between a main memory module and a cache.

Fig. 6 illustrates the access behaviour of two programs E and F to the code area and the operand area of a cache consisting of eight blocks each, as a function of its width C_W. The simulation shows that the miss ratio M_C is reduced by about forty per cent when the block size and the data buses between main memory and cache are increased by factor two. This effect is quantitatively nearly independent of the jump distance d. The drastic reduction of the miss ratios M_C with an increased cache width C_W is due to the loading strategy transferring relatively large data blocks from main memory into the cache. Accordingly, an increasing number of data words is already stored in the cache when they are used.

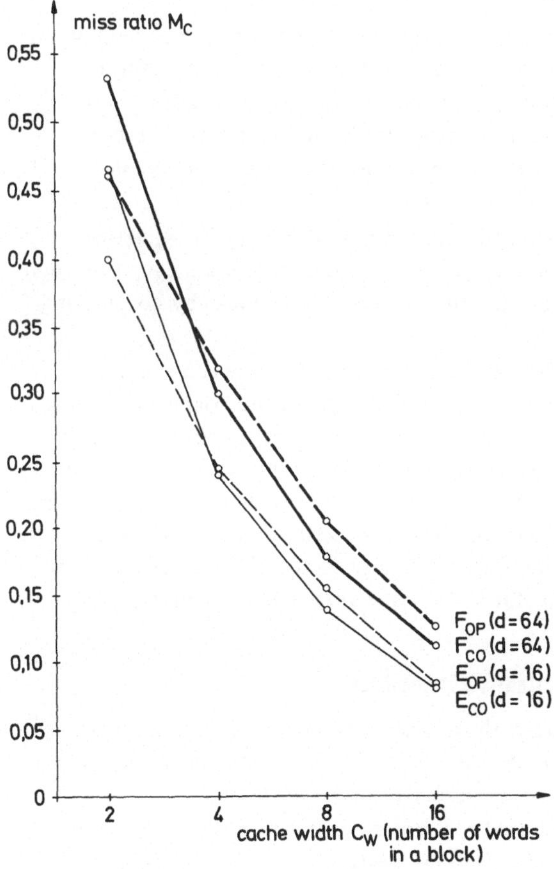

Fig. 6. Access behaviour of two programs (E, F) depending upon block size C_W (C_L = 16 blocks).

A minimal width of four words for the cache and the data buses is advantageous, especially with respect to the access behaviour to the code area of the cache. This is due to the instruction formats of the simulated synthetic programs. On the average, their execution requires more instruction words than operand words (see Tab. 1). Comparing the results of simulation, Fig. 5 and Fig. 6 clearly show to what an extent the cache efficiency can be increased by enhancing the block size in relation to an increase of the cache length.

3.2. Cache Organizations and Addressing

Possibilities of buffering data blocks at defined positions in a cache, as well as management and addressing modes are determined by organizational strategies [2, 7, 8]. The following investigations give some information on the characteristics of strategies often used in large systems.

The organization called "direct mapping" is based on a fixed mapping of data blocks into defined positions in the cache according to their location in main memory [3, 8, 10]. For this reason, main memory is divided, as far as organization is concerned, into sections the size of which is identical with the cache size. The buffer address of a data block corresponds with the block address within such a main memory section.

Using a "fully associative" organization, the data blocks can be buffered at any location in a cache [2, 3, 8]. A special cache position is selected by an algorithm such as "least recently used" which is managing the buffered data blocks by considering the access behaviour.

A "sector associative" management represents a compromise between the organizations "direct mapping" and "fully associative". The expense and cost economizing concept of firmly associated cache and main memory sections is adopted from the first mentioned organization, the latter organization offers the principle of dynamic association. According to these principles, the cache as well as the main memory are divided into sectors of same size each of them with a fixed number of successive blocks. A main memory sector can be buffered in any sector of the cache. The relative location of words in a cache sector is the same as in a main memory sector [3, 6, 8].

3.2.1. Comparison of Various Organization Principles

The following remarks are concerned with the access behaviour of a cache memory with a capacity of $16 \times 4 = 64$ words as a function of different organizations. The code area and the operand area of the cache can store 32 words each.

The simulation results in Fig. 7 show that the selection of a specific organization strategy has an insignificant influence on the miss ratios M_C in the code area of the cache. Only sectors of the size of the reserved cache areas cause an unfavourable

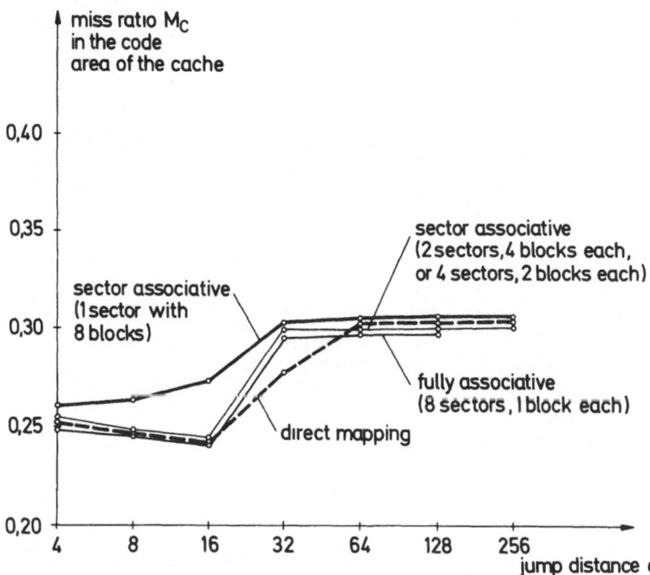

Fig. 7. Access behaviour in the code area of the cache depending on the jump distance related to different cache organizations.

cache access behaviour. This phenomenon is based on the fact described above: the data blocks from the code area of the programs, as well as parts of subroutines have to be buffered sometimes simultaneously in the code area. As a consequence, there are undesired displacements of program sectors and subroutine sectors.

This effect is very remarkable in the operand area of the cache. Its miss ratio is shown in Fig. 8 as a function of the jump distance by addressing operands. As already described in section 3.1.1., this reserved cache area stores variable data from the operand pages of the programs, COMMON DATA operands and page table entries for address translations. Because of the limited capacity of the associative memory in the access controller (see Fig. 1) sometimes accesses to page tables have to be accomplished in the cache concerning the address translation of virtual addresses. When executing jumps with long address distances, different program pages are referenced quite often. This results in an increasing number of accesses to page tables. For this reason, it is possible that sometimes data blocks from three different address areas of a program are needed nearly simultaneously. Consequently, these are competing for cache memory allocation. Hence, a reduced sector size and, as a consequence, an increased number of sectors in the cache and in main memory leads to a more favourable access behaviour for long jump distances. In this area of address distances, a cache which is organized by direct mapping has a higher miss ratio M_C than a fully associative managed cache. Because of the fixed rule of map-

403

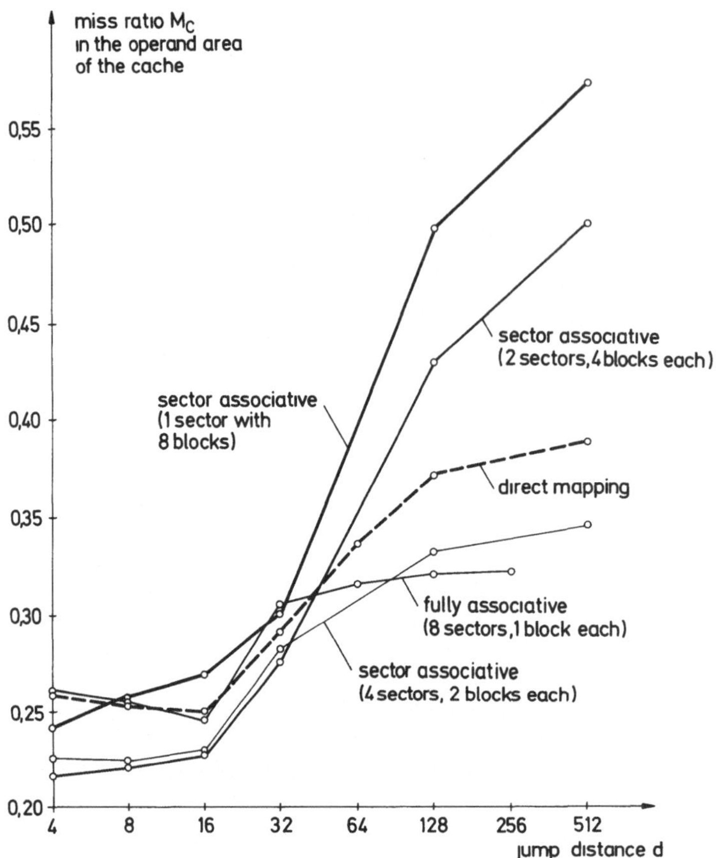

Fig. 8. Access behaviour in the operand area of the cache depending on the jump distance related to different cache organizations.

ping data from main memory into the cache often blocks from different areas of the main memory must be stored at a certain position in the cache, causing there permanent displacements.

On the other hand, the miss ratio M_C is declining in case of low jump distances nearly independent of a special cache organization. This is mainly due to the fact that page tables are accessed only relatively seldom for those running programs. In this case, at least, management of caches with two or four sectors has proved to be especially advantageous. This kind of organization allows to buffer several sectors in the cache, as well as successive data blocks within a sector. That signifies that operands from different main memory areas can be stored in the cache at the same time and it is also possible to access buffered data which have been addressed recently.

404

3.3. Example of Throughput Improvements by Using Small Caches in a Multiprocessor System

The following descriptions are dealing with different possibilities of realizing the working storage level in a multiprocessor system. The investigations demonstrate the importance of a separate small cache for every processing unit. In the following simulations, the behaviour of a computer system with three central processors was investigated as a function of the technology of the memory system, the number and size of memory modules and the corresponding structure of data paths (see Tab. 3).

Table 3. Technical data of the memory levels

memory level	capacity	technology	cycle time
main memory	256 K words	core memory	1 μs
	256 K words	MOS memory	500 ns
cache	16 × 4 words	bipolar memory	50 ns

In order to investigate a critical situation of memory charge and the resulting effect for system throughput, the processing of a mix of programs by three processing units was simulated. The processing time t_p for the execution of 30 000 instructions was measured with respect to different structures and organizations of the memory levels. The simulation results are summarized in Fig. 9.

The processing time t_p consumed in a memory system with only one core memory clearly shows how system performance can be influenced by structural arrangements. In this case, an increased number of memory modules at a constant total memory capacity is combined with an increase of the number of data paths to the main memory (see Fig. 1). This affects a reduction of access conflicts in front of the main memory and, thus, a more favourable system behaviour.

Adding a cache memory level, the processing time t_p of the program mix is reduced considerably as shown in Fig. 9 (measurements for a storage system consisting of a core memory and a cache for every processor). As described in the sections above, an essential part of memory accesses can then be directly executed in a cache. Therefore, the average memory access time is essentially reduced. Furthermore, the structural arrangement of a firm association of cache and processor guarantees that at least data words which are buffered in a cache can be accessed without a conflict. For these reasons, the average time of access and of blocking is reduced considerably.

The same fact is correct for the efficiency of a working storage system consisting of semiconductor memories. Due to the shorter cycle time of a MOS-memory compared with core memory, another essential improvement of program throughput can be obtained especially by using additionally bipolar cache memories. Which one of the

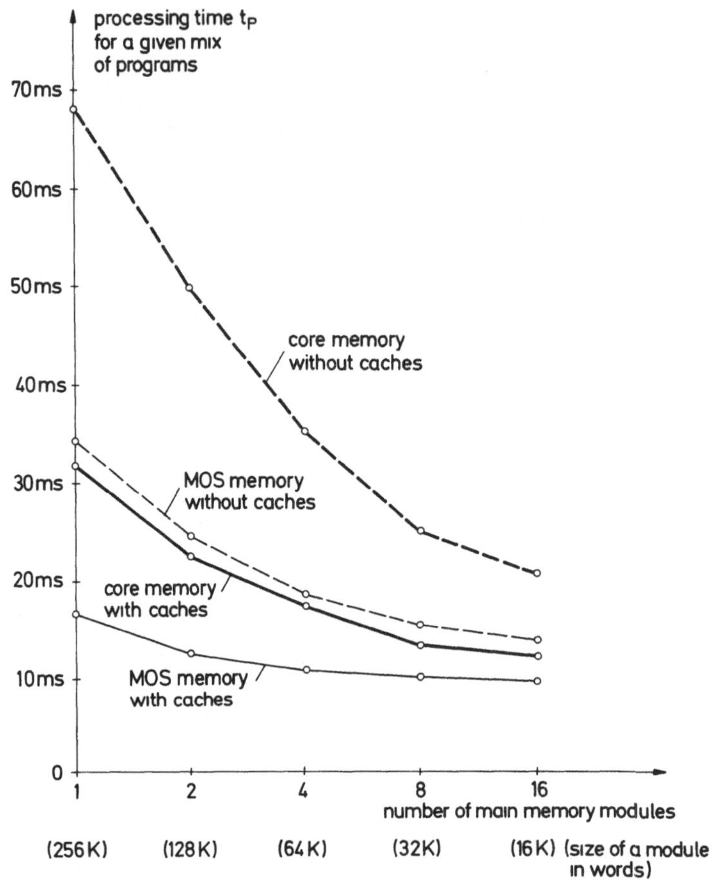

Fig. 9. Processing time for a mix of programs in a multiprocessor system depending on the structure of memory.

investigated solutions is going to be considered as the optimum does not only depend on the described time behaviour but also on technological and manufactural conditions.

4. Conclusions

The aim of these investigations was to get quantitative results permitting a useful comparison as a basis for design decisions. The investigations refer to size, as well as to organization and management of small cache memories in minicomputer systems.

The results are based on an abstracted form of a computer system. On the one hand, the abstractions are necessary to make simulation still practicable as an instrument.

406

On the other hand, they are justified with respect to the practical applicability of
the results.

The application of the results in the industrial practice proved their usefulness with
regard to design decisions.

References

[1] *A. Bachle,* Durchsatzsteigerung in Rechenanlagen bei Verwendung von kleinen Pufferspeichern. Lecture Notes in Economics and Mathematical Systems, Oct. 1972.

[2] *J. Bell, C G. Bell* and *D. Casasent,* An Investigation of alternative cache organizations.
IEEE Trans. on Comp., No. 4, April 1974.

[3] *J. Conti,* Concepts for buffer storage. Computer group news, March 1969/9.

[4] *D. H. Gibson,* Considerations in block-oriented system design. AFIPS 30, 1967.

[5] *Lee,* Study of 'Look aside' Memory. IEEE Trans. On Comp., No. 11, Nov. 1969.

[6] *J. S. Liptay,* Structural aspects of the System IBM 360 Model 85, II The cache. IBM
System Journal, Vol. 7, 1968.

[7] *R. M. Meade,* On memory system design. Cogar Coporation, Wappinger Falls, New York.

[8] *J. Niedereichholz,* Pufferspeicher-Architekturen. Elektronische Rechenanlagen 18,
1976.

[9] *O. Spaniol,* Optimale Nachladestrategien für Pufferspeicher unter Berücksichtigung der
Programmstruktur. University of Saarbrücken, Fachbereich Angewandte Mathematik
und Informatik, A 73–02, 1973.

[10] *W. D. Strecker,* Cache memories for PDP-11 family computers. IEEE, The 3rd Annual
Symp. on Comp. Architecture, Vol. 4, No. 4, Jan. 1976.

[11] *C. Stuhlmuller,* Entwurf und Programmierung eines Modells für Untersuchungen über
die Organisation und Dimensionierung von Pufferspeichern zwischen Prozessor und
Arbeitsspeicher. Thesis, Institut für Informatik IV, University of Karlsruhe, 1976.

[12] *H. Wojtkowiak,* Synthetische Programme zur Speichersimulation. Elektronische Rechenanlagen 16, 1974.

The authors thank Mr. Dipl.-Ing. J. Dittmann, SIEMENS AG, Karlsruhe, Germany, for his useful
suggestions and many stimulating discussions.

Summary of Abstracts

Magnetic Data Recording

Eberhard Koster
BASF AG, Ludwigshafen, Germany

In an outline of the basic elements of magnetic recording theory, emphasis is placed upon simple analytical forms which describe with sufficient clarity the individual steps of writing, storing and reading of digital data and indicate the relative importance of the recording parameters involved. After a review of the present status of the materials for magnetic media and heads, areas of improvements for theory and practice are discussed.

Electromechanical Mass Storage Units — Disk Files

Peter Wentzel
Siemens AG, Data and Information Systems Division, Munich, Germany

The ever increasing demand for on-line data-storage is mainly satisfied by disc drives growing in capacity by a factor of two every 2–3 years. The principles of disc storage with fixed and removable media on the one side and with fixed and movable heads on the other side are described. The short access of the movable heads to up to thousand track-positions leads to stiff mechanics with low inertia and sophisticated servo-circuits and patterns. The heads and the magnetic media are the key-components of a disc drive. Therefore, the technologies of these components and the proper design of the associated read-write circuits are of fundamental importance. The disc-controller serves as link between the host computer and a number of disc drives. It interprets and transforms the I/O-command chains of the host to the drive interface signals and organizes the data transfer between disc drive and main memory.

Electromagnetic Mass Storages — Normal Tape Devices

Klaus Winkler
Siemens AG, Munich, Germany

After a discussion of the common recording methods for 9-track $1/2''$ Computer-tape, details of a modern high performance tape drive for data processing, particularly the data path and the error detection and recovery are described. A short review of the $1/4''$ and the $1/8''$ cartridge for digital application and some prospects on magnetic tape storage is presented.

Tape Libraries with Automatic Reel Transport

Eckart Lennemann
IBM Deutschland GmbH, Böblingen, Germany

Various design alternatives for a tape library with automated reel transport are discussed. Minimum cost per bit, maximum bits per unit volume and extreme reliability requirements characterize the technical challenge of such a product. The IBM 3850 serves as an example for a mass store which brings present single tape libraries under direct system control. The machine demonstrates a basis for future large scale data base applications.

Fabrication Technology and Physical Fundamentals of Components Used for Semiconductor Memories

Albrecht Moeller
Forschungsinstitut der Deutschen Bundespost beim Fernmeldetechnischen Zentralamt,
Darmstadt, Germany

After a review of the classification of semiconductor memories, some fundamental technological
processes are dealt with: standard planar technology, ion implantation, electron beam lithography. The following approaches are discussed: standard buried collector, collector diffusion
isolation, V-ATE and VIP techniques, anodic oxidation of silicon, Isoplanar, LOCOS and
Planox processes; epitaxial silicon films on insulating substrates, silicon gate technology,
V-MOS and D-MOS. Techniques like CMOS, I^2L and CCD for memory application are reviewed.
Finally, reprogrammable read-only memories are discussed: FAMOS memory (storage
mechanism), MNOS storage transistor (charge storage, charge transfer mechanism, doping of
dielectrics), and CCDs combined with MNOS storage.

LSI Semiconductor Memories

Rudolf Mitterer
Siemens, AG, Integrated Circuits Division, Munich, Germany

After a review of present status and application of RAMs, possibilities for higher storage capacity
and lower manufacturing costs are discussed. Among these are reduction of line width, better
functional integration of storage cell elements and vertical integration (VMOS). Factors of
annual improvement in the next decades and ultimate limits for dynamic MOS-RAMs are
estimated.

A High Performance Low Power 2048-Bit Memory Chip in MOSFET Technology and its Application

Utz G. Baitinger and *Rolf Remshardt*
IBM Deutschland GmbH, Böblingen, Germany

A 2048-bit read/write memory chip is described. It uses a modified 6-device memory cell in
an n-channel MOSFET technology. To exploit the potential of the given MOSFET technology
with respect to the cost/performance ratio and the power-delay product, special provisions are
taken. The power is kept low by the gate driver concept as well as by clocked peripheral circuits.
High performance is achieved with fast peripheral circuits, the delayed chip select concept, and
a bipolar sense amplifier which also supplies the bit-line restore voltage. Circuits are presented
which successfully utilize the on-chip tracking to reduce the impact of device parameter tolerances
on worst case power and performance. It is shown how the memory chip is packaged on modules,
cards, and boards to build up functional memory units.

Readout Methods and Readout Circuits for Dynamic Charge-Storage Elements

Karlheinrich Horninger
Siemens AG, Munich, Germany

Progress in the field of digital semiconductor memories in the last few years has been characterized by an extremely rapid rise in the storage density and operation speed. Along with the
progressive technological improvements, the key to this turbulent development was the principle
of dynamic charge storage.

The intent of this paper is to describe, with the aid of simple models, the various methods of converting the stored information charge into an output signal. Four different methods will be presented:
- the diffused bit line
- the diffused bit line with a BBD transistor added to it
- the MOS bit line
- the 'floating gate' output stage

After describing the advantages and disadvantages of these methods, the operation of a cross-coupled flipflop circuit as a sense amplifier connected behind the readout configurations is presented. The readout configurations are then compared in respect to readout time and sensitivity with the help of computer simulations.

Monolithic Memories

Wolfgang Liebmann
IBM Deutschland GmbH, Böblingen, Germany

Monolithic Memories have replaced magnetic core memories for computer main- and control store applications. The causes for the superiority of monolithic memories are primarily economic in nature. Analysis of these causes also provides insight into potential future developments of monolithic memories. High performance monolithic memories will continue to be based on ECL-storage circuit designs, while FET one-device storage cells will continue to lead with respect to density and cost. As photolithographic dimensions shrink, the productivity advantage of FET dynamic memories may diminish in favour of static I^2L-memories, especially for small and intermediate data processing systems. Even though CCD-cells have no inherent density advantage over random access one-device storage cells, their superior sensing characteristics may keep them in a leading density/cost position for some time to come.

Structure, Organization and Application of CCD Memories

Hans Joachim Harloff
Siemens AG, Data Processing Systems, Munich, Germany

A wide variety of CCD memories have been proposed and implemented. They vary with respect to clock pulses, electrode geometry and charge transport. In surface CCDs, the charge packet representing information is transported right at the silicon surface. Relatively large transfer losses in surface traps can be avoided by using a "fat-zero" charge. In bulk or peristaltic CCDs, the signal charge passes through a thin surface layer. The transfer losses are much lower and the attainable shift frequency is higher, but the maximum signal charge is lower.

The fabrication of CCD components corresponds to that of MOS-RAM devices. Typical structures comprise two polysilicon gate levels and one aluminium wiring plane. A cost advantage of CCDs over MOS-RAMs is anticipated as a consequence of higher storage density and possibly better yield. Further fundamental reduction of cost per bit may be achieved if multilevel storage can be realized.

Two basic types of device organization have evolved. Single loop organization provides many individually addressable short loops and hence short mean access times. Series-parallel-series organization, complemented by electrode-per-bit storage, allows long loops, high packing density and low cost at the expense of longer access time. This latter type appears to be best suited to devices of very high capacity.

In data processing systems, CCD memories were initially and are still considered as a replacement for drum or fixed-head disk storages. Present application studies examine multilevel main memory systems and multiple utilization of the buffer principle throughout the memory hierarchy. Consideration of the progress in CCD technology indicates the superior performance of CCDs at several stages in a future hierarchy of computer memories.

BEAMOS — Technology and Applications

Claus Schunemann
IBM Deutschland GmbH, Böblingen, Germany

BEAMOS — Beam Accessable MOS — is a new and interesting version of the old electronic tube storage technology. The main component areas of BEAMOS, the electron-optical system and the bit storage and Read/Write mechanism are briefly described. Potential application of BEAMOS also in comparison with CCD and magnetic bubbles are discussed.

Read-only Memories with Magnetic Components or with Integrated Semiconductor Circuits

Jurgen Scharbert
Siemens AG, Data Processing Systems, Munich, Germany

Read-only memories (ROM) with magnetic coupling elements were of prime importance in the past. Various memory types and designs — e.g. with magnetic cores, line coupling or transformers — have been used in a large number of applications, and have proved to be reliable, fast and inexpensive in regard to comparable read-write memories.

Nowadays, ROMs with integrated semiconductors have almost completely taken the place of ROMs using magnetic principles. Memories of bipolar or FET-technology are either built as mask-programmable devices or as field-programmable devices. A broad capacity spectrum of sophisticated and largely standardized devices is available. Their prevailing organization for memory applications is that of devices with full address decoding; for logic applications, programmable logic arrays (PLA) have also been developed.

Electrically Alterable MOS-ROMs, with Particular Emphasis on the Floating Gate Type

Rudolf G. Muller
Siemens AG, Zentrallaboratorium für Nachrichtentechnik, Munich, Germany

Reprogrammable nonvolatile semiconductor memory devices are characterized by the storage of charge in traps of the gate insulator over the channel region of an MOS transistor or in an electrically insulated floating gate. A particular feature of the latter principle is good long-term storage capability. The design of various memory cells with floating gate and the mechanisms used for programming and erasure are described.

Physical Principles of Magnetic Bubble Domain Memory Devices

Frans H. de Leeuw
Philips Research Laboratories, Eindhoven, Netherlands

The principles of magnetic bubble domain memory devices are described and the stability of magnetic bubbles, the relevant magnetic parameters and the chemical composition of bubble domain materials are discussed. In the light of the underlying theory of bubble domain devices,

412

the author considers the requirements to be met by the physical properties of the materials,
the bubble propagation velocity and the possible means of increasing that velocity. The
individual elements are touched upon, such as bubble generator, annihilator, sensor and transfer
gates and a brief account is given of 'bubble lattice files'.

Application of Magnetic Bubbles to Information Storage

Werner Metzdorf
Siemens AG, Munich, Germany

Different kinds of design and organization of bubble memory chips are described as well as their
operating margins. The paper also discusses the construction and the organization of the magnetic
memory modules, the generation of the magnetic fields and the fabrication of bubble memory
boards from the magnetic modules and their associated electronic circuits. The structure of
a large bubble memory system is briefly explained. An overview is given on the future trends
of development in the field of magnetic bubble memories. Furthermore, the position of bubble
memories within the storage hierarchy and possible fields of application are discussed.

Ferromagnetic Domain Memories

Hermann Deichelmann
BASF Aktiengesellschaft, Ludwigshafen, Germany

Thin polycrystalline films of ferromagnetic alloys may be used as storage media for digital
data. A well defined switching behaviour is observed due to strong magnetic anisotropy.
Magnetic domains are moved along channel-like structures of low magnetic coercivity surrounded by highly coercive material under the influence of locally concentrated magnetic fields. The
whole assembly acts like a magnetic shift register. A special technique of domain propagation
is discussed in detail together with a description of an actually built device which features non-
volatility, asynchronous mode of operation, and insensitivity to adverse environmental conditions. Possible applications include: data collecting and concentrating systems, machine control,
fast peripheral storage devices for process control and ROM's for mini- and microprocessors.

Application of the Josephson Effect for Digital Storage

Peter Wolf
IBM Zurich Research Laboratory, Rüschlikon, Switzerland

The invention of the Josephson junction has led to a renewed interest in cryogenic digital circuits.
For digital storage, superconducting rings are suitable in which information is stored as persistent
ring currents.

One memory cell based on this principle has two Josephson junctions within its ring for writing.
The "0" or "1" is stored as a clockwise or counter-clockwise ring current respectively. A third
junction which is influenced by the magnetic field of the ring current is used for non-destructive reading. Several cells have been built with areas as small as $1000 \ \mu m^2$ and switching times
down to 100 psec.

Another cell type, the single flux-quantum (SFQ) cell makes use of the quantization of the
magnetic flux which occurs in superconducting rings. A convenient structure for SFQ cells is
the two-junction interferometer. Such cells are quite compact, however, read-out is destructive.
The smallest device realized had an area of $150 \ \mu m^2$.

At present, little information is available on drive and decode circuits. Estimates indicate that
memories with quite high speed and very low power consumption should be possible.

413

Materials for Optical Data Stores

Eckhard Kratzig
Philips GmbH Forschungslaboratorium, Hamburg, Germany

Compared with conventional technologies, optical methods offer many attractive advantages for data storage. In many cases, however, material properties restrict these advantages considerably and determine the limits of the methods.

The requirements for storage materials in optical systems are derived and interpreted. Though there exist no ideal solutions, many different media may be utilized for recording and erasure with light. Among them are ferroelectrics, thermoplastics, photoconductive electro-optic crystals and photochromic crystals. The most promising storage materials are discussed in more detail: magnetooptic garnet films combined with photoconductors for localized storage and ferro-electric crystals with light-induced refractive index changes for the storage of volume phase holograms.

Optical Memory Systems

Bernhard Hill
Philips GmbH Forschungslaboratorium, Hamburg, Germany

A variety of optical storage systems is reviewed. At first holographic techniques are described, which some years ago were considered almost exclusively for optical information storage. The main difficulties with emphasis on the state of the art of the essential components are discussed. Associative systems are also investigated.

Recently, the principle of localized storage has gained increasing importance. Erasable magneto-optic materials are now available and operational "feasibility models" on the basis of such materials are already working. The well-known principle of a disc store is also considered for optical memories.

Effects of Failures on Yield, Integration, Cost and Reliability of Large Scale Integrated Semiconductor Memories

Wolfgang Hilberg
Institut für Digitaltechnik, Technical University of Darmstadt, Germany

In this review theories are discussed at first, yield as a function of defect density and as a function of time (learning curve) and the minimum of price/bit for a given integration scale. The step by step development and production of integrated circuits of increasing integration levels is then illustrated with reference to a simplified model. This discussion is followed by a brief review of the problems of failure-free testing, and on the definitions of reliability and failure rates as a function of temperature, system integration and carefulness of circuit design. A further topic of this paper is a new proposal for an analytical formulation of the interdependence between quality in production and failure rate. The paper ends with some principle considerations on the advantage of failure tolerating methods with VLSI-memories.

Reliability of Semiconductor Memories from a Practical Point of View

Dieter Fischer
Standard Elektrik Lorenz AG, (ITT), Stuttgart, Germany

The major reasons for failures of semiconductor memories are explained. Besides the reasons generally observed in LSI circuits, problems which are specific for semiconductor memories are discussed such as pattern sensitivity and gate-oxide breakdown. Measures for improvement of reliability are discussed and failure rates observed in life tests and in system operation are presented.

Application of Partially Defective Semiconductor Memory Devices in Memory Systems

Hans-Jorg Penzel
Siemens AG, Data Processing Systems, Munich, Germany

The effort currently required for quality and reliability assurance on device and system level is analyzed in this article. Strategies are then evolved which permit also the utilization of defective memory devices. This enables the creation of less expensive and reliable systems. A simulation model is described which can be used to examine the capabilities of and the limitations on the utilization of also partially functioning memory devices. Finally, the outcome of this approach is discussed.

Access Methods and Associative Memories

Hans-Otto Leilich
Institut für Datenverarbeitungsanlagen, Technische Universität Braunschweig, Braunschweig, Germany

Access methods are viewed as means to fit the hardware access mechanisms to the task of availing data to the active data handling devices. In this context, this paper reviews the major evolutionary steps of computer architecture, starting with sequential memories for Turing machines, virtual memories, random and associative memories, reaching up to rather complex search processors for data base applications.

Increased Chip Capacity and Extended Logical Complexity of LSI-Associative Memories

Walter Motsch
Department of Electrical Engineering at the Ruhr-Universität, Bochum, Germany

While RAM-, ROM- and shift register devices in LSI-technology comprising up to 16 k bits per chip are available, the maximum chip capacity of associative memories is only 16 bits today. This disadvantage is caused by the pin limitation problem, that is the need to provide a package pin for each stored word to signal a match. As a solution to this problem, a chip organization is proposed using a coding mode of match indication. The consequences for the typical search operation and for the design of an associative memory system are discussed. By extending the circuitry, moreover, additional more complex compare operations can be implemented in hardware. Their use can simplify many user- and system routines and could be seen as the first step towards an integrated associative processor.

Storage Hierarchy Technology and Organization

Claus Schunemann and *Wilhelm G. Spruth*
IBM Deutschland GmbH, Böblingen, Germany

Storage hierarchy is the approach to improve a storage system's price/performance by suitably composing and operating a set of storage devices with different characteristics. After a review of today's storage technology spectrum including some general operation mode-performance trade offs, the different hierarchy behaviour in the virtual storage area — execution domain — and the data storage domain is discussed. Detailed discussion on the impact of a "gapfiller" technology on the hierarchy's performance and characteristic is presented.

The Performance of Small Cache Memories in Minicomputer Systems with Several Processors

Axel Lehmann and *Detlef Schmid*
Institut für Informatik IV, University of Karlsruhe, Karlsruhe, Germany

Quantitative investigations to improve minicomputer systems by small cache memories located between processors and main memory are described. After a discussion of the applied simulation model, the increased performance will be outlined, resulting from various cache organizations and cache sizes as a function of different addressing patterns of the running programs. Finally, an example is given of the throughput improvements obtained by using small cache memories in a multiprocessor system.

The investigations indicate that the performance of minicomputer systems can already be increased effectively by adding small caches of suitable organization and size.

The Authors, the Editors

Eberhard Koster
was born in 1935 in Stuttgart, Germany. He received the Dipl. Phys. and Dr. degrees in physics from the University of Stuttgart in 1961 and 1966, respectively.

In 1964 he became Research Scientist in Solid-State Physics at the University of Stuttgart. In 1966 he joined the Franklin Institute Research Laboratories, Philadelphia, Pa., as a Senior Research Scientist. His interest was concentrated on magnetization processes in single domain materials. Since 1967 he is a Member of the Technical Staff of the BASF AG in Ludwigshafen, Germany, where he is in change of the laboratory for magnetic recording materials and media.

Heinz Billing
was born in 1914 in Salzwedel, Germany. He studied physics and mathematics at the Universities of Göttingen and Munich, Germany, and received the Dr. rer. nat. degree in 1938.

After the doctoral thesis, he joined Aerodynamische Versuchsanstalt, Göttingen. He developed magnetic drum memory in 1948. Starting in 1950, he was engaged in the development and construction of electronic computers G1, G2, G3 in Göttingen and Munich. In 1949/50 he worked at the University of Sidney, Australia, and in 1956 at the Institute for Advanced Studies, Princeton, USA. Since 1961, he is a Scientific Member of Max-Planck-Institut für Physik und Astrophysik, Munich. In 1967 he became Honorary Professor at the University of Erlangen.

Peter Wentzel
was born in 1932 in Baden-Baden, Germany. From 1953 to 1957 he studied communications at the Technical University of Munich, Germany, where he received the Dipl.-Ing. degree.

Subsequently, he developed electronic controls for adjusting the velocity of rolling freight cars in shunting yards for the AEG-Telefunken Company in Konstanz, Germany. In 1960 he joined the Central Communications Laboratory of the Siemens AG, where he worked on traffic signal equipment, electronic relays, magnetic core memories, and finally on disk files. Currently, he manages the development of disk file drive and control units in the Data and Information Systems Division of Siemens AG.

Klaus Winkler
was born in 1936 in Munich, Germany. For one year, he was a trainee at Rhode & Schwarz, Munich. He studied high-frequency technique at the Technical University of Munich, where he received the Dipl.-Ing. degree.

From 1961 to 1963 he was engaged in the development of suppressed carrier modulators at LM Ericsson, Darmstadt. In 1963 he joined the Siemens AG, Munich, working on the development of tape drives for data processing, since 1968 as leader of this group.

Eckart Lennemann
was born in 1938 in Bochum, Germany. He received the Dipl.-Ing and the Ph. D. degrees in mechanical engineering from the Technical University of Aachen, Germany, and the University of Waterloo, Ontario, Canada, in 1965 and 1969, respectively.

In 1970 he joined the IBM Laboratories, Boeblingen, Germany, working on the development of direct access disk storage devices. In 1973 he became Manager of the Mechanical Analysis Department in the High Speed Printer Development group. Since 1976 he has been Manager in the System Product Assurance group, where he is responsible for attachments of input/output devices.

Albrecht Moeller
was born in 1926 in Darmstadt, Germany. He received the Dipl.-Chem. and the Dr. rer. nat degrees in physical chemistry from the Technische Hochschule Darmstadt in 1954 and 1958, respectively.

Until 1959 he was with the Technische Hochschule Darmstadt, where he was working in the field of magnetic susceptibility of alloys. Since 1959 he has been with the Research Institute of the German Post Office, Darmstadt, Germany, where he was working in the field of semiconductor technology (heteroepitaxy, MNOS structures) until 1975; he is now engaged in the research on reliability of semiconductor circuits.

Rudolf W. Mitterer
was born in 1928 in Munich, Germany, He received the Dipl.-Ing. degree from the Technische Hochschule Munich in 1954.

In the same year, he joined the Central Laboratory of the Siemens AG, Munich. He has been engaged in the development of digital measurement equipment, core memories, and disc memories. Since 1970 he has been responsible for the development of semiconductor memories, first in the computer division and since 1976 in the components group.

Utz G. Baitinger
was born 1938 in Stuttgart/Germany. He received the Dipl.-Ing. and the Dr. Ing. degrees in electronic engineering from the Technical University of Stuttgart in 1963 and 1968, respectively.

In 1963 he was employed with the Compagnie Francaise Thomson-Houston, Paris, France. From 1963 to 1968 he was employed as Scientific Assistant to Prof. Dosse, Head of the Department of Semiconductor Technologies, University of Stuttgart, where he was engaged in semiconductor physics. In 1968 he joined the Memory Circuit Development Department of the IBM Laboratories, Boeblingen, Germany, working on digital integrated-circuit designs for monolithic memory applications. From April to August 1969 he was assigned to the IBM Components Division, Poughkeepsie, NY, USA, where he worked especially on monolithic FET memories. Back in the IBM Laboratories in Boeblingen, he participated in the development of large-scale integrated monolithic memory chips, and he is presently working in the Micro-programming Department there. In addition to that he lectures on Circuit Technologies at the University of Stuttgart.

Dr. Baitinger is a member of the Nachrichtentechnische Gesellschaft (NTG).

Rolf Remshardt
was born in 1936 in Stuttgart, Germany. He received the Dipl.-Ing. and the Dr. Ing. degrees in electronic engineering from the Technical University of Stuttgart in 1964 and 1967, respectively.

From 1964 to 1967 he worked for Prof. R. Feldtkeller, Head of the Institut für Nachrichtentechnik at the University of Stuttgart. In 1967 he joined the Circuit Technology Department of the IBM Laboratories in Boeblingen, Germany. A few years later, he became Manager of the Memory Circuit Development Department. From May 1972 to December 1973 he was assigned

418

to the IBM Components Division in Burlington, VT, USA, where he worked especially on FET memories. He is presently working on bipolar logic chips with high density at the IBM Laboratories, Boeblingen.

Dr. Remshardt is a member of the Nachrichtentechnische Gesellschaft (NTG).

Karlheinrich Horninger
was born in 1944 in Graz, Austria. He received the Dipl.-Ing and the Dr. techn. degrees from the Technical University of Vienna, Austria, in 1970 and 1975, respectively.

Since 1970 he has been with the Research Laboratories of Siemens AG, Munich, Germany, working first on MNOS memories for non-volatile information storage. Then he worked on circuits in ESFI-SOS technology and on CCDs. He is currently engaged in the area of high-density MOS memories and MOS logic circuits.

Dr. Horninger is a member of the Nachrichtentechnische Gesellschaft (NTG). He received the NTG Award in 1976.

Wolfgang K. Liebmann
was born in 1933 in Berlin, Germany. He received the Dipl.-Ing. and the Dr. Ing. degrees from the Technical University of Berlin in 1956 and 1958, respectively.

Afterwards he was a "Postdoctorate Fellow" in the Department of Metallurgy of the University of Pennsylvania, and a member of technical staff, RCA Davis Sarnoff Research Center, Princeton, N. J., USA. In 1963 he joined IBM and since then was in quick changes entrusted with numerous tasks in Germany as well as in the USA, all in close context to monolithic stores. Since 1970 he was responsible for component product development in the IBM Laboratories, Boeblingen, Germany. In 1973 he became Manager of Boeblingen Component Development being responsible for the development of electronic components for logic and storage of small and medium sized IBM Data Processing systems. Since 1977 he has been Director of the Boeblingen IBM Laboratory.

Hans Joachim Harloff
was born in 1924 in Rostock, Germany. He received the Dipl. Phys. degree from the University of Kiel, Germany, in 1952.

In 1953 he joined the Siemens AG, Central Laboratory, Munich, Germany, where he started working on telephone systems and computer circuitry. Since 1957 he has been working on data storage methods including magnetic and superconducting thin films, plated wires, and semi-conductors. Currently, he is Manager of a laboratory group at the Data Processing Systems Division, working on semiconductor memory components and their application in memory hierarchy.

Mr. Harloff is member of the Deutsche Physikalische Gesellschaft and the Verband Deutscher Elektrotechniker.

Claus Schünemann
was born in 1931 in Lüneburg, Germany. He received the Dipl.-Ing. and the Dr. Ing. degrees in electrical engineering from the Technical University Darmstadt, Germany, in 1955 and 1965, respectively.

After having worked from 1955 to 1963 with the AEG company on electrical machines and electronics, he joined the IBM Development Laboratory in Boeblingen, Germany, working in the areas of computer testing, logic design, LSI memories and processors. From 1970 to 1973 he was Manager of Advanced Development Systems. From 1974 to 1975 he was assigned to the IBM Research Division working on Josephson technology. Presently, Dr. Schünemann is with the Advanced Technology staff in the Boeblingen Laboratory and primarily interested in storage and computer systems.

Jürgen Scharbert
was born in 1933 in Berlin, Germany. He studied physics at the Freie Universität, Berlin, and received the Dipl. Phys. degree in 1959.

He joined the Central Laboratory of the Siemens AG, Munich in 1959, where he first was involved in high speed memory core applications, and in the development of core memories and magnetic read-only memories. Since 1971 he is engaged in the development of semiconductor microprogram memory systems. He also works in the fields of electrical design for fast bipolar PROMs and development of test procedures for bipolar PROM and RAM devices.

Rudolf G. Müller
was born in 1940 in Munich, Germany. He received the Dipl. Phys. and the Dr. rer. nat. degrees from the Technical University, Munich, in 1965 and 1971, respectively.

From 1966 to 1972 he worked at the Technical University, Munich, on government research projects in solid-state technology and was especially involved in research work on energy direct conversion, amorphous oxides, and amorphous and polycrystalline silicon. In 1972 he joined Siemens AG, Munich, working in the Central Telecommunication Laboratories on non-volatile memory principles.

Frans H. de Leeuw
was born in 1938 in Nijmegen, The Netherlands. He received the Ph. D. degree from the Catholic University of Nijmegen in 1971.

He spent four years as a Research Assistant with the Atomic and Molecular Research group of the University of Nijmegen and was involved in research on the electric and magnetic properties of molecules by means of high resolution molecular beam spectroscopy. In 1971 he joined Philips Research Laboratories, Eindhoven, The Netherlands, where he is investigating the dynamics of wall motion in magnetic materials.

Dr. de Leeuw is a member of the Netherlands Physical Society and the European Physical Society.

Werner Metzdorf
was born in 1931 in Berlin, Germany. He studied physics and mathematics at the University of Munich, Germany, where he received the Dipl. Phys. degree in 1955.

From 1955 to 1976 he was working with the Advanced Development Department of Siemens AG, Components Division, Munich.
There he was especially engaged in the development of magnetic memory elements as e.g. ferrite cores, planar and cylindrical thin magnetic films and magnetic bubbles. From 1971 to 1976 he was the manager of the bubble project. Since 1977 he has been working with the Research Laboratory of the Siemens AG, Munich.

Mr. Metzdorf is a member of the IEEE.

Hermann Deichelmann

was born in 1938 in Lauterbach, Germany. He studied physics at the Frankfurt University, Germany, and received the Dipl. Phys. degree.

Afterwards he was engaged in development work with Pfaudler AG, Schwetzingen, Germany. There he worked on the mechanism of solids and devoted his attention to glass-like substances. In 1963 he was awarded the degree of Dr. Ing. for a thesis on this subject under Prof. Hennicke at the Technical University, Clausthal, Germany. In 1971 he joined BASF AG, Ludwigshafen, Germany, where he has been engaged in the development of new types of data storage devices.

Peter Wolf

was born in 1930 in Konstanz, Germany. He received a B. S. degree in physics from the University of Karlsruhe in 1953, a Dipl. Phys. degree from the University of Darmstadt in 1958, and the Dr. rer. nat. degree from the University of Mainz in 1963.

In 1959 he joined the IBM Research Laboratory, Rüschlikon, Switzerland, and has worked on spin dynamics in thin magnetic films, on the dynamics of spin structures in rare-earth metals, and on microwave Schottky barrier field effect transistors (MESFETs). At present, he is manager of a devices group, and since 1971 engaged in investigations on Josephson junctions.

Dr. Wolf is a member of the German Physical Society.

Eckhard Kratzig

was born in 1939 in Gleiwitz, Germany. He received the Dipl. Phys. and the Dr. phil. nat. degrees from the Johann Wolfgang Goethe-University of Frankfurt, Germany, in 1964 and 1969, respectively.

In 1969 he joined the Philips Forschungslaboratorium Hamburg, Germany, and worked on acoustic surface waves, superconducting films, and electro-optic storage materials. Since 1973 he has been Manager of the Solid State Physics group of the Philips Forschungslaboratorium Hamburg.

Bernhard Hill

was born in 1938 in Bad Kreuznach, Germany. He received the Dipl.-Ing. and the Dr. Ing. degrees in electronic engineering from the Technical University of Aachen, Germany, in 1965 and 1968, respectively.

In 1969 he joined the Philips Forschungslaboratorium Hamburg, Germany, and worked on electro-optic components and systems, as e. g. optical multiplex systems, optical stores and displays. At present, he is Manager of the Optics Research group.

Wolfgang Hilberg

was born in 1932 in Gießen, Germany. He studied communications technology at the Technical University of Darmstadt, Germany, and received the Dipl. Ing. degree in 1957.

In 1958 he commenced work in the Research Institute of Telefunken in Ulm, Germany, and participated in the development of special purpose computer and measuring units.

In 1963 he received the Dr.-Ing. degree. He remained with Telefunken until 1971 and concentrated on various research projects in the field of data processing and digital storing units, in particular in connection with the development of novel memories. He wrote numerous papers about memories, digital circuits, and problems of RF and pulse technology.

Since 1972 he has been Professor for Digital Circuits and Memories at the Technical University
of Darmstadt and has lectured on electronics and data technology.

Dr. Hilberg is a member of the Nachrichtentechnische Gesellschaft (NTG) and a Senior Member
of IEEE.

Dieter Fischer

was born in 1940 in Pforzheim, Germany. He studied electrical engineering, specializing in
communication techniques at the Technical University of Karlsruhe, Germany, and received
the Dipl.-Ing. degree in 1965.

Afterwards he joined the Central Laboratory of Standard Elektrik Lorenz AG, Stuttgart, Germany,
developing "house-keeping-systems" for satellites. After taking over the responsibility for the
Components Laboratory, the main activities were in development of multi-chip techniques, investigation and specification of integrated circuits, failure analysis of semiconductor components,
and development of customized LSI circuits.

Since winter 1970/1971 he has been a lecturer in Microelectronics at the Technical College in
Heilbronn, Germany.

Hans-Jörg Penzel

was born in 1935 in Leipzig, Germany. He received the Dipl. Ing. degree in electrical engineering
from the Technical University of Hannover, Germany, in 1962.

Afterwards he joined Siemens AG, Munich, Germany, where he has been engaged in design and
development of memory systems in different technologies. Presently, he is Manager of a laboratory
group, responsible for development of MOS and bipolar semiconductor memory systems for computer application.

Hans-Otto Leilich

was born in 1925 in Nauen, Germany. He received the Dipl.-Ing. and the Dr. Ing. degrees in
electrical engineering from the Technical University of Munich, Germany, in 1952 and 1956,
respectively.

From 1952 to 1956 he participated in the design and development of PERM (programmable
electronic computer, Munich). In 1956 he joined Telefunken in Backnang, Germany, working
on the development of the computer TR4. From 1962 to 1968 he was an advisory engineer with
IBM Development Laboratory, Poughkeepsie, N.Y., working on core and magnetic film memories.

Since 1968 he has been Professor and Director of the Institut für Datenverarbeitungsanlagen at
the Technical University of Braunschweig, Germany.

Walter Motsch

was born in 1944 in Speyer, Germany. He received the Dipl.-Ing. degree in electrical engineering from the Technische Hochschule Darmstadt, Germany, in 1971.

For two years, he was engaged in the development of semiconductor memory systems with the
Philips Electrologica Corporation in Siegen, Germany. In 1973 he joined the University of
Kaiserslautern, and since 1974 he has been employed as a Scientific Assistant with the
Ruhr-University of Bochum. Presently, he is working on computer architecture and memory
technology.

Wilhelm G. Spruth

was born in 1929 in Herne, Germany. He received the Dipl.-Ing. and the Dr.-Ing. degrees in electrical engineering from the Technical University of Aachen, Germany, in 1954 and 1957, respectively.

In 1959 he joined IBM and has been involved with the development of new computer systems and I/O devices. Presently, he is Manager of the Advanced Technology Department.
Dr. Spruth is a member of the Association for Computing Machinery and the Institute of Electrical and Electronic Engineers IEEE.

Axel Lehmann

was born in 1946 in Mannheim, Germany. He studied electrical engineering and information processing at the University of Karlsruhe, Germany, and received the Dipl.-Ing. degree in 1972.

Since 1973 he has been a candidate for a doctor's degree and an assistant of Prof. Dr. D. Schmid at the Institut für Informatik IV, University of Karlsruhe. The field of research are organization and management of memory systems, and hardware realization of operating system functions.

Detlef Schmid

was born in 1934 in Worms, Germany. He studied electrical engineering and information processing at the Universities of Mannheim and Karlsruhe, Germany, and received the Dipl.-Ing. and the Dr.-Ing. degrees in 1963 and 1968, respectively.

After research work in industry and university, he became full professor for Informatik at the University of Karlsruhe in 1972. He is leader of a research group in computer organization.

Walter E. Proebster

was born in 1928 in Mannheim, Germany. He studied electrical engineering at the Technical University of Munich, Germany, where he received the Dipl.-Ing. and the Dr.-Ing. degrees in 1951 and 1956, respectively.

From 1951 to 1956 he participated in the design and development of the computer PERM at the Technical University of Munich, Germany. In 1956 he joined the IBM Research Laboratory, Zurich, Switzerland, where he worked on computer components, amongst them thin magnetic films. From 1962 to 1964 he held the position of Director of Experimental Machines at the IBM T. J. Watson Research center at Yorktown Heights, USA and conducted research in the fields of Advances Logic, Memory and Systems. From 1964 to 1973 he directed the IBM Development Laboratory at Böblingen, Germany. His current assignment with IBM is as Director for Research and Development Coordination, Böblingen, Germany.

He is a member of the Nachrichtentechnische Gesellschaft (NTG), Germany, and of IEEE. In 1977 he was nominated as Fellow of IEEE. He lectures at the Technical University Karlsruhe, Germany on Digital Memory and Storage and Input/Output. In 1972 he became Honorary Professor at this University.